GENEALOGY AND BIOGRAPHICAL NOTES

OF

JOHN PARKER OF LEXINGTON

AND HIS DESCENDANTS.

GENEALOGY AND BIOGRAPHICAL NOTES

OF

JOHN PARKER OF LEXINGTON

AND HIS DESCENDANTS.

SHOWING HIS EARLIER ANCESTRY IN AMERICA FROM

DEA. THOMAS PARKER

OF READING, MASS.

FROM 1635 TO 1893.

BY

THEODORE PARKER,

A descendant in the ninth generation from Dea. Thomas Parker.

KALPAZ

ISBN: 978-93-5128-908-1(PB)

First Published in1893
Indian Reprint in 2017

Published by

Kalpaz Publications
C-30, Satyawati Nagar,
Delhi – 110052
E-mail: kalpaz@hotmail.com
Website: kalpazpublications.com
Ph.: +91-9212142040

Cataloging in Publication Data—DK
Courtesy: D.K. Agencies (P) Ltd. <docinfo@dkagencies.com>

Parker, Theodore, 1869-1916, **author.**
Genealogy and biographical notes of John Parker of Lexington and his descendants : showing his earlier ancestry in America from Dea. Thomas Parker of Reading, Mass., from 1635 to 1893 / by Theodore Parker.
pages cm
Reprint. Originally published: Worcester, Mass. : Press of Charles Hamilton, 1893.
ISBN 9789351289074 (HB)

1. Parker family. 2. Parker, John, 1729-1775—Family. 3. United States—Genealogy. I. Title. II. Title: John Parker of Lexington.

CS71.P24P37 2017 DDC 929.20973 23

PREFACE.

EVER feeling an interest to know more regarding my ancestors and their connection with the progress of the times in which they lived, I undertook during the summer of 1888 to prepare a small pamphlet publication showing the genealogy, if possible, of my own immediate relatives. This attempt only brought to view the necessity of a wider scope and a more complete work. Encouraged at this stage by the interest and entreaties of relatives to extend the work, and feeling the great need of preserving in printed form the historical and genealogical records, which might otherwise be lost forever in the course of time, I finally determined to procure the genealogy of the Lexington branch of the Parker family.

The compiler realizes the fact that no genealogy is complete or perfect, and the present volume doubtless has its share of errors, although accuracy has been the watchword. It is not laid in the critics' path with any idea of rhetorical excellence or fine writing; neither is such a work a pecuniary advantage, as its completion requires years of deep research, correspondence and expense, but it is given to the family with the compliments of the author for what use and service it may be to those of the living and future generations whom it does and will concern.

May it ever serve to help us cherish the memory of those devout, sturdy and industrious generations to whom we are indebted for our progress, our freedom, and our very existence.

T. P.

"CHILDREN'S CHILDREN ARE THE CROWN OF OLD MEN; AND THE GLORY OF CHILDREN ARE THEIR FATHERS."—*Proverbs*, xvii., 6.

"IF ANY ONE OF US COULD TRACE OUR ANCESTRAL STOCK BACK TWO HUNDRED YEARS WE SHOULD FIND THE PROXIMATE CAUSE OF THE DISPOSITION BORN IN US."—*Rev. Theodore Parker*.

LIST OF ILLUSTRATIONS.

THE LEXINGTON PARKER HOMESTEAD.

PARKER GENEALOGY.

THE PARKER NAME IN ENGLAND.

EVEN farther back than the commencement of English history we can trace the origin of the Parker name. It is as old as parcarius, park keeper or shepherd, and from which employment it was derived, thus extending back through the ages unbroken to the origin of the Roman language. It is a name not made from location or invented by lord or knight for himself and descendants, but is one of the names of occupation, of active out-door life, that life which made useful, independent, hearty men, who caused the name of Parker to multiply, making it one of the common names of to-day.

The Danes, Saxons and Normans had their representatives of the name; they were men of hardy and strong physique, were hunters and warriors as well as tillers of the soil, and romance made up a part of their pastime. A keeper of the king's hunting grounds must necessarily be active and enterprising. He must be a good hunter and as well informed as the civilization allowed,—a typical man of the early ages. The name is well associated with the history of England, a general usefulness, good social standing and spiritual progress have been the characteristics of this ancient family name. From its great age the name is necessarily a common one in England, ranking eleventh in the kingdom in point of numbers.

The word Parcus meant a picketed enclosure for domestic animals and also a preserve for game. Parcus and DeParco are mentioned in the Doomsday Book. They are found in Liber Feudorum and one Geoffrey Parker is noted in the reign of Edward I., who ruled from 901 to 925. He lived at Bexley on the eastern coast of England. From him there probably descended a numerous posterity. We afterward hear from Johannes le Parker, a Norman, who followed William the Conqueror (1066–1087), and was the keeper of the Royal Parks.[1] The Taxicio Ecclesiastica yields the name, and we find the following in mediæval Latinity of 1205: "Johannes le Parker tenet dimid, hidam terrae per servantium costodiendi Parcum Domini Regis et Riesam forinsicum et valet hoc annus dimidiam marcam." "John the Parker holds half a hide of land for the service (sergeantry) of keeping the King's park and pasture ground and receives this year half a mark." Fifty acres and 6*s.* 8*d.* per annum for folding the royal sheep and driving them to pasture.

James le Parker turns up in Norwich in 1261, and one Samuel Parker is noted in the reigns of Henry III. and Edward I., which would place it at about 1275. It would be difficult to ascertain from which of the foregoing Reginald le Parker was descended. He accompanied Edward I. to the Holy Land and received a royal grant of land for his efficient services. A very ancient family record which was at Park Hall, Staffordshire, but which was, many generations since, destroyed by fire, accredited Reginald le Parker as the common ancestor of the Norton Lees branch, and in turn of the Park Hall, the Earl of Macclesfield line. The reign of Edward I. embracing from 1272 to 1307, it follows that Reginald le Parker was necessarily ancestor of the Lancashire Parkers, whose descendants were the founders of the Browsholme and Norton branches. The family was early located in Lancashire and it is in this part of the kingdom where we find their records connected from generation to generation, and the mystery so characteristic of the mediæval ages here gives way for fact. William le Parker was seated in Extwistle, Lancashire, in the time of Richard II. The land which he purchased has a history also. Its first recorded owner was Adam de Preston, who conveyed in the reign of King John (at about 1200), and again in that of Henry III., the lands which he held in Extwistle to the monks of St. Mary of Kirkestall. In the reign of Richard II. John De Bardesay, Abbot of the Monastery of the Blessed Mary of Kirkestall, conveyed these lands by a deed dated 13 of that reign (1398) to William le Parker, a monk, who at the time

[1] His name was spelled many ways in English records, varying from Parker to Parchour, Parkre, Parkerre.

of Henry IV. (1399–1413) is styled "de Monk Hall in Extwistle."

He had four sons. The eldest was Lawrence Parker. He heired the estate, and from him in direct descent is preserved in Burke's Landed Gentry the male line almost complete from William le Parker to the living Parker families of Extwistle and Cuerden, which places are side by side. It comprises about twenty generations of father and son. The Lancashire branch has an interesting history, and they appear to have flourished from its earliest time. Emigration becoming necessary the sons helped settle the surrounding counties, and in turn added honor to the name. Browsholme is located just across the county line from Cuerden. The family here appear respectable and flourishing early in the sixteenth century. It is here we find at about 1470 Robert Parker, a name common among the descendants of William and who, in English records, is styled Robert Parker, Esq., in the Forest of Bolland, Yorkshire. His daughter Elizabeth heired the estate and by marriage became heir of Redmaine (also spelled Redmayn, an ancient Yorkshire family), and had an only daughter, Jennet, who was heir to both. Then Edmund Parker, younger son of Parker of Horrockford, married Jennet and thus continued the Parker name upon the Browsholme estate. He was a descendant of the Lancashire family, as is shown by this family connection and by similarities in coats of arms. They had with two daughters a son and successor, viz.:—

Robert Parker, Esq., of Browsholme, who m. Elizabeth, dau. of Edmund Chadderton of Nathurst, father of William Chadderton, Lord Bishop of Lincoln, and had issue. Robert Parker was still living in 1591.

I. Edmund, drowned at Cambridge, unm.

II. Thomas, his heir.

III. Roger, D.D., Precentor and Dean of Lincoln, and d. 29 Aug., 1629, aged 71.

IV. William, of Blisland and Warligon, in Cornwall, D.D., Archdeacon of Cornwall, living in 1620, and from him was descended in the female line John Anstis, Garter King of Arms.

The eldest surviving son, Thomas Parker of Browsholme, Bow bearer of the forest of Bolland in the Duchy of Lancaster, m. Bridget, dau. and co-heir of James Tempest of Rayne in Craven, and had by her, who d. in 1610, a numerous family of children, a son and successor.

His heir and successor, Edward Parker, Esq., of Browsholme, b. 3 Aug., 1602, m. 28 Jan., 1629, Mary Sunderland, dau. of Richard Sunderland of High Sunderland in Yorkshire. This Richard Sunderland for wife had Mary, sixth dau. of Sir Richard Saltonstall, Knight, Lord Mayor of London. This would make Mrs. Edward Parker, the niece of young Richard Saltonstall, prominent in the early settlement of America. The portrait of Edward Parker as Bow-bearer of Bolland forest is preserved. It is a fac-simile of a large rare folio etching.

Norton Lees is an attractive portion of the parish of Norton, County Derby, which adjoins Lancashire and Yorkshire. The first of the name which we find there is Adam Parker, who in the year 1352, Sept. 17, was witness to a grant of land in Norton from Sir Thomas Chaworth, knt., to John and Isabell Tynet. Thomas Parker appears in 1384, and in 1402 John Parker, both acting in similar positions. Thomas Parker of Grenehill and John Parker of Norton purchased in the year 1423 of Robert and Margaret Fletcher all of the land and tenements formerly occupied by Richard Peyne. Here their history becomes more defined and interesting. A direct descendant of the Little Norton and Park Hill lines is the Hon. E. T. Parker Vwroig of Aston Hall, Sutton Coldfield, Birmingham, Eng., who very kindly assisted in this English research, and who contributes the following: "According to the pedigree which was at Park Hall, the Norton Lees estate was granted to a Roger de Gotham, who attended Edward III. at the siege of Calais and had an augmentation of arms for his services. The above Roger had a son Thomas, who had a son Adam. This Adam had an only daughter, Elizabeth, who m. Thomas Parker of Bulwell, Co. of Nottingham." This is the first of the line that any family records mention.

In a pedigree of Moore in M. S. Gg., 3, 34, in the Cambridge University Library, England, said to be written by the hand of James Gresham of Fulham, Co. Middlesex, is the following: "Memorand. that one Booth sometimes was Bishop of Yorke [23 H. 6–1445] beeing before his promotion to that See Arch Deacon there and lay at Rotheram in the same county had two sisters. The one of them, then hee being Archdeacon, married he unto one Mr. John Parker of Bulwell in com. Nottingham esq're which Parker had by hir diverse children and was of a Cli land by the year or thereabouts . . . Memorand. that the aforesaid John Parker had a sister whose name was Elizabeth and was married to one Thomas More of Grenhill in com. Darby, grandfather to Christopher More, that is to say, son of John More son of the aforesaid Thomas More."

Thus it appears probable that the above named Thomas Parker was son of Thomas Parker, once of Grenehill, but then of Little Norton. The father Thomas was in all probability son of the Thomas of 1384, and he, possibly the son of Adam. And it is certain that the progenitor of the Parkers of Little Norton was descended from the Lancashire stock. This is shown by marked similarities in the coats of arms of the two families and by tradition.

This places the marriage of Thomas Parker and Elizabeth at about the middle of the fifteenth century, providing he was brother to the above named John. From him is traced his son and heir, Thomas Parker of Whitley and Ecclesfield. He was a "scithesmith" and a "yeoman." His will, as copied from the Journal of the Derbyshire Archæological and Natural History Society, 1510, August 20.

WILL OF THOMAS PARKER.

In the name of God, Amen, the xxth day of August the yere of o^{r} Lorde a thousande cccccth and x, I Thomas Parker, of Whitley, make and ordeyn my testament in maner and fo^{r}me folowyng. First I bequeth my soule to Almyghty God o^{r} blessed Lady seint Mary and the cōpany of hevyn, my body to be buryed w^{t}in my p̄ish chirch of Ecclesfeld. Itm I bequeth to my mortuary my best beest. Itm I bequeth to the seid chirch of Ecclesfeld for my tythes necligently forgotten vj^{s} viij^{d}. Itm I will that of all my goodes my detts be paid, and all wrongs by me doon, and trewly proved, be resonably recompensed spīally in discharge of my soule. Itm I bequeth to the making of the rode-lofte and stalles in the seid chirch, xl^s. Itm to the reparyng of Seint Mychels chapell w^tin the seid pish, iij^s. iiij^d. Itm I bequeth to Elyn Parker, my doghter, xl mrc to her mariage, if it may be born. Itm I will that Thoms Shircliff, of Ecclesfeld, John Wilkynson, of the same, and John Grubbe, of Netherhertley, or their heires imediatly aft^r my decesse surrender in to th'ands of my lorde of Sherusbury according. to his custome w^tin the lordeship of Halomeshir, all and ev such meses, landes, tents, meadowes and pastures, w^t their app^rtennes, as I have in Whitley, or in the felds of the same, purchased of William Whete, in Woodsetts, purchasid of William Houlle, holden of my seid lord as of his lordeship of Halomshir, by copy of court rolle, to the use of John Parker, my sonne, and the heires of his body laufully begotten for ev. And for defaute of such issew of his body laufully begoten, the remaynder therof to Richard Parko^r, his brod^r, and to the heires of his body laufully begotten for ev. And for defaute of such issew of his body laufully begotten, the remander therof to the right heires of me the forseid Thomas Pker for ev. Itm I will that the same Thoms Shircliff, John Wilkynson, and Robert Grubbe, their heirs or assigneis, imediatly aft^r my decesse surrende into th'ands of the prior and covent of Coventre charterhouse all such meses, lands, tents, wodds, medows, lesues and pastures, w^t their app^rtennes, as I have in Nether Hertley, late p^rchased of Thoms Barmley* holden of the seid p^ro^r and covent by copie of co^rt rolle, as of their lordeship at Ecclesfeld to the use of Richard Pker, my sonne, and heires of his body laufully begotten for ev. And for defaute of such isshew of his body laufully begotten, the remand^r therof to John Parko^r, his brod^r, and heires of his body laufully begotten for ev. And for defaute of such isshew of his body laufully begotten, the remander therof to the next heires of me the seid Thoms for ev. Itm I will that the said Thoms Shircliff, John Wilkinson, and Robert Grubbe, or their heires, immediatly aft^r they be required, surrende into the hands of the p^ro^r and Covent of the Charterhouse of Coventry, according to his custome, a mese, lands, medows, wodds, lesues and pastures, w^t their app^rtennes, as they lye in Neder Hertley, unto the use and behove of Ric. Pko^r, my sonne, and to the heires of his body laufully begotten; and for defaute of his body† laufully begotten, the remander thereoff to John Parko^r, his brod^r, in like estate, the remander thereof to the right heires of me the forseid Thoms Parko^r for ev. Also I

**Sic in reg. forsan* Barmby.

† Probably the words "such issue of" omitted; but it stands so in the copy in the Register at York.

will that immediatly after the seid surrend[r] maid unto the seid Richarde Pko[r], that the seid Richard shall make to Agnes Pko[r], my doghter, a sufficient surrende of a yerely rent of xx[s.], to be taken and paid out of all the landes, medows, wodds, lesues and pastures, w[t] their app[r]tenncs in Ned[r] hertley aforeseid, to have and holde to the same Agnes and hir assignes during hir liff at ij termes in the yere, that is to say, at the feest of Penticost and Saint Martyn, by evyn porcions, w[t] clause of distresse for noon payment of the same in the aforeseid mese, lands, wodds, medows, lesues and pastures. Itm I will that if, as God forbede, hit happen that the seid Agnes be decrepyd, or in such case that she may not stere herselff, or come to a grete necessite, then the seid Richard Parker, or his heires, shall pay yerely during the lif of the seid Agnes, ov and above the seid xx[s.], vj[s.], viij[d.], that is to say, if the seid chaunce happen, xxvj[s.], viij[d.] Itm I will that Richard Parker, my sonne, shall have the takke of my water-whels after my decesse. Also I will the seid Richard shall have a mese in Brokehouse, w[t]in the pish of Laghton, w[t] th' app[r]-tenncs. Itm I will that the seid Richard shall have an annuall rent of ix[s.] lyyng in Dennaby, in the holding of Wynter. Itm that the seid Richard shall have my right in ij closes, w[t] a medow called Horbury, w[t] a close called Longlands, and a croft callyd Ryfarecroft. Item that the seid Richard shall have at Neder Hertley a fournes, a fourmelede, a wort stoon, a kneding-trough, a mulding borde, a stepefatte, ij grete arkes, ij chayres, a mete borde, a folding borde, a chymney, ij bedds, an arke, a long chist, a saing borde, ij bedds in the new chambre, oon in the plo[r], and an awmery in the new plo[r] at Whitley. Itm that the same Richard shall have ij stythes, ij bare bales, all od[r] smythy gere, ij stoones troughed coultroughed *(sic)*. Itm I will that John Parko[r], my sonne, have at Whitley ij stones troughed called coltroughes. Itm at the whele a stythy and a pair of bellows. Itm at Whitley, a chayr, a chymney, iij mete bords in the chechyn, a kneding trough, a moldyng bord, a fournes, a wort stoon, a lede in a fo[r]me, all the bedds in the plo[r], ij yronbonde coffers, an arke, an awmery in the chambre, an arke and a bedde in the new chamber, iij close bedds in the malthouse, a stepefatt, a close bedde, and the iij close bedds to stand still for the svntes. Itm I will that out of the meses, w[t] th' app[r]tenncs in Dalton my seid feoffes shall suffer, aft[r] my decesse, the profetts yerely to be taken in fo[r]me folowyng. First xiiij[s.] vj[d.] to find a preist at Ecclesfeld to sing yerely lx messes, that is, ij tymes Seint Gregory trentall, w[t] svyce therto belonging. Itm of the seid mese yerely iiij[d.] to the vicar of the same chirche to pray for the soules of me, my ij wiffs, my fad[r] and mod[r], and all myn aunceto^{r}s and child^{r} soules, on the Sonday in the chirch. Itm for an obijt evy yere to be made for Thoms Pko^{r}, Elsabt, and Agnes, his wiffs, his fad^{r} and mod^{r} soules, out of the seid mese v^{d} yerely to be takyn and paid. Itm to the clerc for v mynnyngs yerely to be paid v$^{d.}$ of the said mese. Itm that the residew of the mese, that is ijs. iiij$^{d.}$, that my childer ther being shall have yerely j$^{d.}$, and the residew to poore folkes having most nede. Itm that seint Mychell warke if it may be shall have vj$^{s.}$ viij$^{d.}$ Itm in likecase to the p^{r}o^{r} and covent of the charterhouse, vj$^{s.}$ viij$^{d.}$ Itm I ordeyn to be ovseers of this my last will M^{r}. Herry Evinghm, esquier, to whome shalbe geven xx$^{s.}$ Thoms Evynghm, sonne of the seid Herry, to whome shalbe giffen x$^{s.}$ Sir Thoms Thorley, pson of Thorley, to whome xx$^{s.}$ Robert Pko^{r}, my sonne, Robert Gilberthorp, Willm Crofte, to evy of the seid Robert and William for rewarde vj$^{s.}$ viij$^{d.}$, and the costes of all my seid ovseers wher or whed^{r} so ev they be called to be borne at all tymes of my goodes. The residew of my goods before not bequethed, I will that my wiff shall have hir thirde parte theroff and the seconde pt to be disposed and spendyd at my buriall and afterwarde for the well of my soule. And the thirde pt therof I giff and bequethe to Richard Pker, my sonne. Itm I will that Robert Pker, my sonne, shall pay unto Agnes Pker, my wiff, yerely during hir liff, xiij$^{s.}$ iiij$^{d.}$ Itm I will that John Parker, my sonne, shall pay unto the same Agnes, his mod^{r}, evy yere during hir liff, xxvj^{s} viij$^{d.}$, in mony of hir thirde and dowery. Itm I will that Richard Pker, my sonne, shall pay unto the same Agnes, his mod^{r}, every yere during hir lif xxvj^{s} viij$^{d.}$ in mony for hir thirde and dowery, if the forseid my childer may their landes peasably enjoy w^{t}out trouble or recovy. Also I ordeyn and make Agnes Parker, my wiff, John Pkar and Richard Pker, my sonnes, myn executo^{r}s of this my psent testament.

In witnes wherof herunto I have set my seale, thes being witnesses, sir Thoms clerc, vicar of Ecclesfeld. Thoms Robt Grubbe, and Shircliff, John Wilkinson, od^{r} moo, the day and yere abovesaid.

Probatum fuit p vicariu de Sheffeld, p comissionem [1510]. Reg. Test. 8 fol. 55A.

His son Robert had a son Thomas of Little Norton, "yeoman." This Thomas had a son John Parker, also a "yeoman," and who lived in Little Norton. A deed relating to this member of the family contains the name Ryddinge, which is certainly interesting considering the connection this location (Reading) has borne with the Parkers of Massachusetts. This is its copy:

"Deed between John Bullocke of Darley, in co. Derby, Esq., and John Parker of Little Norton, co. Derby, yeoman. Being tenants in common in several closes, &c., in the parish of Norton, called the Lea Maskers, Johnsett wood field, Ryddinge, Johnsett noll, the Mawe land, the Hie field, and Howl storthe land, a piece of wood ground called Johnsett wood, and other lands in Little Norton meadow, the yard in the holding of Wm. Mawer, Norcroft, Shipley Lowage, and Lowage gate, Hie Storthe, Lyarde land, the Lea, being parcel of the land of Wm. Rawlynson, they had agreed to make a division in severalty as therein named. Witnesses, Henry Tayler, James Bullock, Robert Boothe, Willm. Simpson, James Bayte, William Rawlynson."

This John Parker had a son John, baptized 4 Sept., 1575, m. 1601, Dyonysia, dau. of Thomas Bright of Bradway, and aunt of Sir John Bright. He m. second, 2 July, 1605, Jane, dau. of James Bate of Jordenthorpe, Co. York, and by her had John, his heir, 12 Aug., 1607; Thomas, baptized 31 March, 1609; William, 23 July, 1614; Jane. Of the children of the above named family, John Parker, b. 1607, heired the estate of Norton Lees; William, b. 1614, m. Bridget Carrier, granddau. of Thomas Parker, Esq., of Browsholme, Bowbearer of the forest of Bowland. She was also niece of Edward Parker of Browsholme.

It is thus evident that our Puritan ancestor, Thomas Parker, who came from London to the New World in the year 1635, could belong to the Norton Lees branch and, through Bridget Carrier, become well acquainted with the Browsholme branch, and through Edward Parker's marriage connection with the Saltonstalls. Sir Richard Saltonstall, Jr., had been to the New World several times, had lived for years in Watertown, and had successfully transported ship-loads of pilgrims to their haven of refuge. In 1635 he was again raising a company for transportation.

William, the aforesaid, removed to Park Hall, Staffordshire, and was the ancestor of that illustrious line. He commanded a company of exparte regis and took part in many military actions, including Hopton Heath, Marston Moor, Naseby and Worcester, was taken prisoner and suffered much for his loyalty. He d. 12 May, 1703. By wife Bridget he had two daughters and three sons, the latter being: I. George Parker. Esq., of Park Hall, who heired the estate and was high sheriff. II. Thomas Parker, Esq., who studied law, removed to Leeke, was a diligent practitioner of his profession and whose son Thomas Parker by his own wonderful diligence and perseverance in study, and the use of a most retentive memory, became a most powerful lawyer and a man of invincible influence at the bar. He was known as the silver-tongued orator, instituted many reforms in English laws and was created Earl of Macclesfield, an honor which is still held by the family. III. Robert, cup-bearer to Queen Catharine.

Another illustrious line of the Parker family has been living for several centuries at North Molton, Co. Devon, near the southwest shore of England. Their history is interesting and their emigrative growth has been rapid. Some of this branch removed to Castle Lough, Ireland, and became the founders of the Parkers of this portion of the island (Tipperary Co.), where many of the name reside. They are characterized by being strongly Protestant in faith. The Irishmen in America by name of Parker are mainly descended from this line. Another earlship was attained by the early founders of the Molton Parkers, the Earl of Morley being the title which descends from father to son in like manner with the Earl of Macclesfield. Sir William Parker, standard-bearer to King Richard III. (1483), was the first of the Morley and Monteagle Parkers. Molton Parker issues emigrated to: I. Petterell Green, Co. Cumberland. II. Warwick Hall. III. Plympton, IV. Whiteway, Co. Devon. V. Homington, Co. Warwick. VI. Melford Hall, Co. Suffolk.

Extwistle and Cuerden Parker issues emigrated: I. to Browsholme, Co. York: II. Norton, Co. Derby: III. Whiteley Hall, Co. Lincoln. The Browsholme lines spread out to: I. Hareden, Co. York. Later those of Norton found their way to: I. Park Hall: II. Woodthrope, Co. York; and from the Park Hall family descended the Earl of Macclesfield, lately represented by Thomas Augustus Wolstenholme Parker (b. 1811), Shirburn Castle, Tetsworth, Carlton Club, S. W.; 94 Eaton Square, S. W. His heir is George Augustus Parker, Viscount. The Park Hall family is now represented by Thomas Hawe Parker, Esq., son and heir of the late Thomas Parker, grandson of Sir Thomas Parker, Chief Baron of the Exchequer, while the occupant of the ancient Cuerden estate, Lancashire, is Thomas Townley Townley Parker, Esq., of Cuerden Hall.

COATS OF ARMS.

THE early coats of arms of the Parkers of Extwistle were:—

Gu. a chevron between three leopards' heads, with arrow in mouth of each leopard. Crest, a buck trippant ppr. transpierced through the body with an arrow point downwards, arg.

That of the Browsholme line was very similar and the following was used by Edward Parker, son of Thomas: Vert., a chevron between three stags' heads, caboshed or. Crest, on a chapeau a stag trippant ppr. Motto, "*Non fluctu nec flatu movetur* - Parkers of Browsholme." (Unmoved by either wave or wind).

This coat of arms was granted to the Parkers of Norton Lees and used by them: Gu., a chevron between three leopards' faces, or. Crest, a leopard head affrontee erased, or, ducally gorged, gu. Supporters, two leopards regardant ppr.; each gorged with a ducal coronet; gu. Motto, "*Sepre Ande.*" (Dare to be just). The same coat of arms has descended through the Park Hall and Staffordshire lines, and is now used by Sir Thomas Parker, Earl of Macclesfield, England.

The arms of Earl of Morley: A stag's head caboshed between two flaunches ar. Crest, an arm erect vested az. slashed ar. cuff of the last, the hand grasping the attire of a stag gu. also stag, greyhound, horse's head, etc. Motto: *Fideli Certa Merces.* (The reward of the faithful is sure).

Arms of Cambridgeshire Parkers—A buck trippant betw. three phoens ar. within a burdure rugr. of the second hurtée.

Arms of Essex Co. Parkers—Or, three inescutcheons sa. charged with as many phoens ar. Crest—A lion's gamb. erased or. grasping an arrow gu. headed and feathered ar.

Park Hall (Stafford, Derby)—Chev. betw. 3 leopard faces and leopard's head guard. erased at neck or, ducally gorged.

Macclefield—Chev. betw. 3 leopard's heads, and leopard head guardant, erased at neck or, ducally gorged.

Woodthorpe (York)—Ar. a chevron pean betw. three mullets sa. on a chief az. as many buck's heads caboshed ar. Crest, a talbot's head couped ar. ears and tongue gu.

INTRODUCTORY

TO

THE AMERICAN HISTORY.

It has not yet been positively ascertained from which line of Parkers our ancestor descended. From tradition and clues we can base our own judgment. By records it is known that he was born in the year 1609.[1] What success seemed to have crowned the genealogists' efforts when the family of John Parker of Little Norton was reached, showing a son Thomas, baptized March 31, 1609! But upon searching the father's papers dated 1632, and also his will, bearing date of 1637, no mention of a son Thomas is made. That leaves us to suppose one of two things, 1st, that he died young: or, 2nd, that he went to live with his Browsholme relatives or early removed far from home. Tradition helps the case along from its statement that our ancestor was connected by marriage with the Saltonstall family. We know that the Browsholme Parkers were so connected. In this manner he could have easily become interested in the work which Sir Richard Saltonstall, Jr., was doing toward the colonization of New England. It is also traditioned that Thomas Parker was one of three brothers who came to America at an early day and settled finally in three different places, viz.: Reading, Chelmsford and Groton. In fact this tradition is so common among the Parker family in general as to make it worthy of much reflection. One of the brothers, Abraham Parker, settled in Chelmsford, and in his family there descended an heirloom, the Parker Coat of Arms, which his descendant, Dr. Wm. Thornton Parker, describes in heraldry as follows: "Gu. a chevron between three leopards' faces or. Crest, a leopard's head affrontéé erased, or, ducally gorged, gu." This seems to be the copy of the arms of the Parker family of Little Norton, and shows genealogical connection. The name in

[1] He died in Reading, Aug. 12, 1683, "aged about 74," so says his gravestone.

Norton and Little Norton was characterized with intelligence and industry. They were well known families and lived well for the times. Thus Little Norton is supplied with a majority of evidence toward claiming our ancestor. But the descendants of Abraham Parker of Chelmsford have the universal tradition that their ancestor came from Wiltshire County, England. In fact, Mr. Cutter in his history of Jaffrey, N. H. (where an illustrious family of Abraham's descendants settled), states that Abraham Parker was born in Marlborough, County Wilts, England. This might easily be so.

From Newbury, County Berks, there came to Newbury in New England, Joseph Parker,[1] brother of one Nathan Parker, who soon followed. They remained in Newbury a few years, when they removed to Andover, Joseph being one of the founders of the Church there in 1645. From Wiltshire there came Rev. Thomas Parker, a man characterized by his generous teachings of intellectual improvement and spiritual progress. He was the only son of Rev. Robert Parker, who was called "Rev." in the English *Nation* at the age of 22. The son Thomas was born in 1595, and while in England published a treatise on repentance, also several on the prophecies. Rev. Thomas Parker came to Ipswich in 1634, then in 1635 to the first settling of Newbury and taught school as well as preached. He died in Newbury unmarried, April 24, 1677. He was a finely educated man, a speaker of ability and was properly appreciated and well beloved It is said that he was born in Newbury, Eng., which is in Berkshire. He was a most prominent man of early Newbury, Mass., his good influence was widely felt and it was in his honor the town was named Newbury, which verifies the tradition that he was born in Newbury, Eng., thus in memory of his native home. Parker river in Newbury was also named in memory of him.

Doubtless Rev. Thomas, Joseph and Nathan were brothers, and descended from the family seat at Newbury, Eng. The Puritan minister had no issue, but the children of Joseph and Nathan bore the names of Joseph, Stephen, Thomas, Samuel, John; John, James, Robert and Peter. There is such a

---

[1]Joseph Parker also owned an estate in Ramsey, eight miles from Southampton, which by will he gave to his wife Mary.

striking similarity of names herein shown with the names of the five brothers who settled in Billerica, Chelmsford and Groton, and their children and of our ancestor, Dea. Thomas Parker and his children, that there seems to have been strong family connections. This method of naming in honor of relationship was in olden time more universal than at present. Our ancestor, Thomas Parker, was of the same name as the preacher of Newbury, and the name of Thomas occurs in two lists of children. Joseph of Andover was himself of the same name as one of the five brothers, furthermore, our ancestor had in 1642 a son whom he named Joseph, but who died in 1644. His next child was a son whom he also named Joseph, but who also died young. Then again, the name Nathaniel occurs among his children, as well as sons Thomas and John, and grandsons Stephen and Samuel. A Samuel is also found to be one of the sons of James, one of the five brothers. One of the five was John, and this name occurs among the children of Joseph. James and Abraham, and this James had a son James.

Abraham Parker might easily have been born in Marlborough, Eng., which is situated near Newbury, and have been connected with the Newbury line. So far as the tradition goes that Dea. Thomas was one of three brothers, he could be brother of Joseph and Nathan of Newbury and Andover, but the remainder of the tradition would not thus apply. If he was not a brother to the five he must have been related as near as cousin. The coat of arms just mentioned shows that the brother belonged to a junior branch of the Norton Lees family. There was a difference of 14 years between Rev. Thomas Parker of Newbury and our ancestor, Dea. Thomas Parker. Thus they could easily have been uncle and nephew. Further research toward this end in Newbury, Eng., may bring to light the proper records which will clear away all lingering doubts and present us with this much sought information of the past.

Mr. John L. Parker of Lynn, genealogist of the descendants of Abraham Parker, thus writes upon this subject: "Abraham Parker was born in Marlborough, Wiltshire. The exact date of his birth cannot at present be given, but it is believed to be 1612. The Parker brothers were probably young fellows who saw a chance in the New World to better themselves, and embraced the opportunity to come over and join the settlers at the mouth of the Charles river, where they first settled and where they found employment in the first building of the town. The men who settled Charlestown were of a sturdy sort, possessing the true spirit of the pioneer, and endowed with courage, independence and perseverance."

This work does not take up the descent of these Parker brothers; it has not the room to follow complete all the families descended from Dea. Thomas Parker, but takes up in full only one branch of the Dea. Thomas Parker tree. Imagine, then, the necessary research to make his genealogy complete, and what a vast amount of genealogical matter would be the collection of that relating to all of the Parker brothers. But it is hoped the completion of this genealogy will make it a less troublesome task for the succeeding historian to take up other branches of the family, and that some day the records of each branch will be preserved in suitable book form.

In the great work of reclaiming the grand, unbroken forest from its wild state; in founding this greatest of nations, and in planting for the benefit of succeeding generations the many blessings of our good government,—the public schools, the freedom of speech, worship, and all things that are right, how much are we indebted to our ancestors! Can anyone who brings these subjects into account say as many do, that this matter of genealogy is of no sense or importance? Is it not disgraceful, yes, even wicked, to so decide? Every patriotic son of America should feel proud that his ancestors took part in the American Revolution. Having once obtained full knowledge of this do we feel like parting with it? No, indeed, not for wealth! True, genealogy is an interesting study, and the deeper we go into it and contrast old times with the present the more it teaches us and the more interesting it becomes. Daniel Webster once said, "There is a moral and philosophical respect for our ancestors which elevates the character and improves the heart." It is just this spirit which prompts the genealogist and fills him with zeal to carefully gather all important matter, and in the face of financial loss in his undertaking to finish his publication. It is that worthy love for our ancestors and an effort in the writer to preserve those records and make so accessible to the family that should cause all to share a proper interest in those of their family who have gone before.

To illustrate the part in this great task which the Parker name has performed would make a most exhaustive work and many volumes. This work is confined mainly to the family in Lexington and their issue. In that town the scene is interesting. Connected with the outbreak of the war for independence will be always associated the name of Capt. John Parker, the commander of the first organized company of patriots who so nobly opposed by his guidance the advance of the British troops into our country. Near the Common there lived Jonas Parker, a martyr of that morning and who so faithfully kept his avowal that he would never run from an enemy. A grandson of the captain was the Rev. Theodore Parker, the world-renowned theologian and founder of the Parkerism faith, the most noted man which Lexington ever produced.

The Parker families of early times were universally prosperous and flourishing. In their characters we find a constant fire of devout Christian spirit, and they were in short very religious. They prayed often to the Father of us all and the Giver of all mercies. In their letters to each other they always desired the blessing of God. They all belonged to the Church and vigorously supported it. As early as 1720 there were in Reading 18 adult persons by name of Parker who were in full communion with the Church. They took no part in crime or intemperance of any kind. No evil or disgraceful act recorded against the early Reading or Lexington Parkers has been found. Up to 1834 forty-one by name of Parker had graduated from Harvard and thirty-eight from all other New England colleges. This strong New England teaching brought forth some of the most worthy men of our land; supporters of principle, well educated and thoughtful, firm minded and conscientious, while they seldom allowed their public ambition to extend but little beyond their own home.

A general view of the early genealogy of the five Parker brothers is taken up in the Appendix, together with other

Parker trees of America. There has heretofore been no printed genealogy in full of any one branch of the Parker family: the researches for this work have required the writer's spare time for five years, and everything available concerning the earliest generations has been obtained so far as known; hence may this volume be of some interest to all of the Parker name.

The following is a fac-simile extract from Horton's Copy of the London Records, from Chapter entitled:

[Regi]ster of the names of all ye Passinger wch Passed from ye Port of London for on whole yeare Endinge at Xp^{MAS} 1635.

1635—PASSINGER W^{CH} SAILED FROM Y^E PORT OF LONDON—1635.

IN the SUZAN & ELLIN EDWARD PAYNE MR for New England. Theis pties hervnder expresed have brought Certificate from the Minister & Justices of their Conformitie & that they are no Subsedy Men.*

	AGE		AGE
Husbandman John Procter with family	40	Tho: Wells	30
		Peter Cooper	28
Alice Street	28	Wm. Lambert	26
Husbandman Walter		Samuel Podd	25
Thornton	44	Jeremy Belcher	22
with family		Marie Clifford	25
John North	20	Jane Coe	30

* The term that they were "no subsedy men" implied that they were not at that time connected with the English army.

Name	Age	Name	Age
Francis Pynder with family	20	Marie Riddlesden	17
		Jo: Pellam	20
Richard Skofield	22	Matthew Hitchcock	25
Edward Weeden	22	Elizabeth Nickols	25
George Wilby	16	Thomazin Carpenter	35
Richard Hawkins	15	Ann Fowle	25
Tho: Parker	30	Edmund Gorden	18
Symon Burd	20	Tho: Sidlie	22
Jo: Mansfield	34	Margeret Leach	22
Clement Cole	30	Marie Smith	21
Jo: Jones	20	Elizabeth Swayne	16
Wm. Borrow	19	Grace Bewlie	30
Phillip Atwood	13	Ann Wells	20
Wm. Snowe	18	Dyonis Tayler	48
Edward Lumus	24	Hanna Smith	30
		Jo: Backley	15
Husbandman Richard Saltonstall with wife and child	23	Wm. Battrick	18

DEACON THOMAS PARKER.

The ships *Suzan* and *Ellen*, in which our ancestor sailed from London, March 11, 1635, were fitted out by Sir Richard Saltonstall, with whose family it is traditioned that he was connected by marriage. It is probable that one ship carried the major part of the passengers, while on the other was placed their wherewithal with which to begin life in the new land. From the articles still in preservation of those things which our ancestor brought over from England, it is evident that his outfit was large and of the best. Sir Richard Saltonstall, Jr., had already been assistant governor of Massachusetts. It was his son who accompanied the voyage and who afterward settled in Ipswich.

At this time a passage across the Atlantic was a perilous and tiresome journey of several months' duration. Would that we knew all about the circumstances which caused Thomas Parker to bid farewell to relatives and friends, to brave the dangerous ocean voyage, and to enter upon the hardships of life in a wild unsettled country. But we find that our ancestor was a devout follower of Christ. He shared the Puritan's desire for a freedom of worship. Fettered as this was at home he was obliged to share the fate or fortune of his fellow Puritans in the new country and new government of New England. In spiritual matters he took a deep interest, being one of the founders of the twelfth Congregational Church in Massachusetts.

It seems that Thomas Parker was still an unmarried man when he embarked in the *Suzan* and *Ellen*, March 31, 1635, for no Amy Parker appears at a later or earlier date upon the emigration records, and no mention of his wife is made in the list of passengers, neither is there the name of any one whose first name was Amy. It was customary in those days of faithfulness and toil for the young men to emigrate, find a proper settlement, erect a house, which was made generally of logs, and start cultivation in the thin settlement. He would then either return home and there be married, or send for his bride and marry her soon after her arrival. But the majority of the early unions came from the daughters of our sturdy Puritan ancestors who were already settled in the colony, together with those young men who had proved themselves most worthy. The peculiar arrangement of dates almost prove this the case with our ancestor. From his union with wife Amy their first child was born some time in 1636. As he sailed from London in March, 1635, and arrived at Boston or Lynn in the latter part of the same year, it seems that it required five or six months to make the voyage. His wife Amy must have been in America with him by the early part of 1636, and probably had the first records of Lynn been saved from an ancient fire we would find it recorded that Thomas Parker was married at about Christmas, 1635. Be that as it may, it is certain that she made a true and happy companion for him through life, and proved a kind, christian mother with her large family of children. He probably arrived in time to escape the greatest storm then known on the Atlantic coast. It occurred in August of 1635, and many ships and lives were lost.

A very small portion of the old records of Lynn are preserved. The part saved were jottings of public interest and called "They Lynn Annals." Therein we find the following:

"1635. Came this year, Thomas Parker, a farmer, who embarked at London, March 11, 1635."

In the Mass. Records we find the sumptuous prefix of *Mr.* to his name in the list of freemen; that was decidedly more charily pronounced in 1637 than to-day. On May 17 of that year, with scarce two years passed in America, he was made a freeman in Lynn.* This was the lawful acceptance of his allegiance to the colony, the grant of full suffrage and the right of holding public office. It was a very highly appreciated right and was very often withheld to the settler for four, five or six years. Following this in the first division of land made by

---

* It is recorded in Vol. I., page 195, of the Colonial Records.

the town in 1638, 40 acres, a high average for this division, was allotted to him. But Lynn seems to have been only a recruiting-ground for our ancestor, as at this time he removed to an inland habitation, being the first or one of the very first settlers of what is now the town of Reading. It was first known as Lynn Village. This was the abode and hunting-grounds of the Indians, whose arrow-heads are still found along the Saugus. The land was purchased from the Indians at a very early date. Mr. Parker was soon active in the establishment of a church. It was built about 1644 and stood upon the Common. He was ever active in spiritual matters and taught his large family that fear of God which he himself possessed. He was made deacon, and it seems was later honored as chief deacon, as certain documents bear the title "Thomas Parker,

In Sept., 1639, the inhabitants of Lynn petitioned the General Court for an inland plantation at the head of their bounds. The "plantation" was called Lynn Village until 1644, when it was incorporated as a town and named Reading. It is said, but has not been proven, that Dea. Thomas Parker was conspicuous in naming the town, and if he chose the name it proves his connection with the Parker family of Little Norton, Eng., who owned land by name of Ryddinge, as is spelt in the deed of 1591 of John Parker of Little Norton, and which name Dea. Parker would naturally hold in fond remembrance. Moreover, in many of the town records the name continued to be spelt *Redding* for half a century.

The location of our ancestor's home in Lynn has not been fully known. but Alonzo Lewis, the Lynn historian, is credited with placing the original homestead of Thomas Parker in the part which is now Saugus, where is now the house of Mr. Albert Parker. This is but a short distance to the north of the town hall and about 80 rods south of the very ancient iron-works which flourished at about 1630. This is a very pleasant spot. The view comprises that of the Saugus river and valley as far as Lynn itself. An allotment of 40 acres in this part of Lynn would necessarily have been a part of the land upon which is now situated Saugus Centre. This theory may be doubted, however, on the ground that the family now residing upon the place have no records or traditions pointing to such a history, and the first records of Lynn have been lost. But Mr. Lewis further added that the place has never passed out of the Parker family but has been in the family for seven generations, which would now be eight and even nine generations. If this be the case it is one of extreme rarity.

He was one of the signers of the Armitage petition, spoken of at length in the history of Lynn.

During the 256 years which have passed since the arrival of Thomas Parker in America, the goods which he brought from England have been thoroughly distributed among the ever increasing number of descendants. Among the number, however, are two ornamented jars and a hard wooden mortar still in splendid preservation. One of the jars is in possession of Mrs. Rhody Symonds of Wakefield, and the mortar is in possession of Mr. Henry Boynton of Andover. It has long been stated that the jars or vases contained tea when brought from England. They were made of earthenware and were selected from the best quality the times afforded. The ornamentation is neat and pretty. Further interest in this line ought to reveal many valuable heirlooms now unknown to the writer.

Deacon of Redding." He was selectman in 1661, and continued irregularly for five years more. He with Deacons Thomas Kendall and William Cowdrey was appointed commissioner for trying and defending "small causes." We find his signature in several places among the archives of the State attached to the petitions of the town to the General Court. In the four divisions of land made by the town, wherein all had a share, large tracts of land were added to his estate, by one of which he received over 200 acres on the north side of Ipswich river, which land he mentioned in his will. He was a gentleman of property, but had some difficulty in establishing the bounds of his large tracts of land.

The following agreement well represents the mode of division between the first settlers. Rev. Samuel Haugh, Reading's talented minister, and whose land bordered Dea. Parker's, died in 1662, which made the necessity of a definite division:

KNOW ALL MEN BY THESE PRESENTS that whereas there hath bene a division betwene the overseers of the estate of the late desesed Mr Samuel Haugh of the one side and Thomas Parker of the other side about a side and hedd line, both partis above mentioned have therfoure chosen Lieut John Smith and Johnathan Poole to run and stake the line and end the diferans between them, and gave them power to choose a thurd man to them if they saw needed have therfoure chosen Thomas Kendall to be the thurd man. ——— Who have therefore thus laid out a strait line for them both which we have run and marked according to our best understanding:—: and shown both parties together which line is to be the continuous and stated line between them. And as for the fense, the said Thomas Parker is to have one poale of the stone wall made by the afore[sd] desesed Mr. Samuel Haugh by the ould well and to have it next his own land and he is also to have that poale of stone wall that was also made by the abovesaid Mr. Haugh that now falls in his own grounds at the lower end of the lot, and in consideration whereof the said

Thomas Parker is to mark out a half of such fense as he does reservee for Mistris Brock betwene her pasture and her forest(?) at the west end of the lot and the said Thomas Parker is to sett the fense into the line between the pastures at the lower end of the lot and to give to the said M[tr] Brock four shillings for what is run in this papur.

This is our agreement in wittness whereof we have hereunto set our hands.

JOHN SMITH,
THOMAS KENDALL,
JONATHAN POOLE.

4m—3—1663.

To ascertain the location of our ancestor's home has caused much painstaking research. As a matter of ancestral respect it is our duty to know as near as possible what part of the town of Reading constituted his farm, his homestead and the scenes with which he was most familiar. The historian of Reading, Mr. Lilley Eaton, himself, seems to have been in error in regard to the original homestead. Thomas Parker's farm bordered a part of the east side of the Common and also the north and east sides of the estate of Rev. Samuel Haugh. Mr. Haugh was the second minister of Reading and his house stood where now stands the Wakefield town hall. Our ancestor being among the very first settlers secured good land in the centre of the town, where it is now thickly settled. Thus it is safe to estimate that the oldest Parker homestead was inside of a radius of 30 rods north or east of the spot where is now the Wakefield town hall. The location is a pleasant one, and the choice made by our ancestor is creditable to his judgment.

His intimate neighbors were men of sterling worth and all whom, like him, had lived first in Lynn. The most friendly and social relationship seems to have existed between them. These were the men with whom Dea. Parker's name is found almost invariably connected: Dea. Wm. Cowdrey, the most prominent citizen of the town; John Poole, the father of Reading's manufacturing industries; Nicholas Browne, a native of Inkborrow, Eng., whose land was near Dea. Parker's; Dea. Tho. Kendall and Dea. Zachary Fitch, whose son Benjamin Mr. Parker called his "well beloved and trusty friend." Each of these families intermarried with our ancestor's children, except that of Mr. Fitch. Other neighbors were John Weston, "a man deeply interested in religious matters"; Rev. Samuel Haugh, the first minister of the town, a "very pious man," and Rev. John Brock, who succeeded Mr. Haugh, and who, it is recorded, "dwelt as near Heaven as any man on earth."

His will, made Aug. 3, 1683, preceded his death only nine days. It seems that he was sick and called in his friend Wm. Cowdrey, for it was made hastily and is in Dea. Cowdrey's handwriting. Being too weak to write he made his mark to the will. The original document is on file in Middlesex Probate Records. His widow, Mrs. Amy Parker, died in Reading, Jan. 15, 1690.

WILL OF DEACON THOMAS PARKER.

The Laste will & testament of Thomas Parker of Reddinge this third of August 1683; although weake in Bodey yet of Set in Minde & Memorey

1 I give My Soule to God that gave it and My Bodey to be buried by Christian frennds In hope of A Joyfull Resurextion at the last days

2 I give unto My Dear wife Amy My house & homstead with two Akers of Medow at the Mill two Akers in the Reedy Medow And two Akers in the great Medow And three Akers in the saw Mill Medow next to the Medow of Edward Taylors, And Also the Improuvment of All my Cattell & houshold goods with the Improuvment of All the Land And Medow during her natural life

3 I give unto My son John Parker all the Land he lives upon Be it More or Less with five Akers of Medow In Bear Medow and two Akers of Medow by Jonas Eatons Medow And two Akers in Reedy Medow, And also a quarter parte of My great Devidend,* And two Akers of the wet Swamp.

4 I give unto My sonn Thomas Parker all the Land he now lives upon & five Akers of Medow in bear Medow: & the Slodge of Medow Leying near Bursham Medow

5 I give unto My sonn Nathaniel Parker all the Land he now Lives upon and the Remainder of My Medow In Bear Medow And

* "Bear" and "Reedy" Meadows are familiar terms in Wakefield at the present time. They lie along the Saugus river between the old Parker farm and the Great Pond. The "Wet Swamp" was divided among the early settlers in 1666. His "Great Devidend" was his grant of 1658, about 200 acres on the north side of Ipswich river.

the Round hole of Medow at Dustins Bridge, And tow akers of Medow in the great Medow he paying three pound within one yeare after the Death of My wife Amy: unto his Brother Thomas Parker, And I also give unto sonn Nathaniel Parker one halfe of My great Devidend and Also My Ceador Swamp, and three Akers in the Saw Mill Medow

6 Furthermore I give unto my sonn Thomas Parker two Akers of the wet swamp, And the Reste of the wet swamp I give unto my son Nathaniel Parker

7 Furthermore this is to be understod that the three Akers In the Saw Mill Medow & the two Akers in the Reedy Medow & the two Akers in the great Medow John & Nathaniel are not to have untill the Death of their Mother

8 I give unto my two Daughters Maxey & Martha fortey shillings a year to be payd them one yeare After the decease of ther mother

9 I give unto My grand children Samuel and Sarah Parker three pound apease. Samuels at twenty one years old and Sarahs at her day of Marrige provided they live with thear grandmother. Sarah while she is eighteen year old: and Samuel while he is twenty one year old provided that the over seer doo see that he hath som Trade.

Furthermore the sayd Thomas Parker shall not sell Any of his Land or Medow without the advise of his Brethren.

10 I give unto my grandchild Samuel Parker my gunn and my Reste, but is to be parte of the three pound that is to be payd him

11 I give unto my Sonn John Parker A great Bible that Boniface Burton gave to Me in Case It Com Into my hands

12 Lastly I make my Sonn Hannaniah Parker My full & sole Executor of this My laste will & testament; further More I Doo Desier my well beloved and trusty freind Benjamin Fitch and my sonn John Parker to bee the over seers of this My laste will & testament

Witnes WILLIAM COWDREY
THOMAS CLARKE

The Marke of
THOMAS + PARKER

Decon William Cowdrey subscriber to this Instrument testifieth & saith that the testator Being in perfect mind & memory maid the within and above Ritten instrument as his Last will & tesament

Taken upon oath
Before us,

WILLIAM HAZY
JNº BROWN [BROWN] } Com's for Redding.

December 18: 83: Thomas Clark appearing in court made oath as a witness to the above sd will JONATHAN REMINGTON Clerk.

An Inventory of the Estate of Thomas Parker Decon of Redding this first of October 1683.

First the house & homstead with tow Akors of Meddow at the Mill	180—00—00
More for seventy five Akors of land and Medow	96—00—00
More for housing & 29 Akors of land & Medow	103—00—00
More for 94 Akors of upland & Medow	102—00—00
More In Stock In Cattel & Swine	26—10—00
More In Land five Akors	10—00—00
More In husbandry Impliments	03—09—06
More one fetherbed & Boulster & bedsted	07—00—00
More one flock bed & bedding & bolster	02—10—00
For one bed more wth bedding thereto	03—10—00
For a Truckle bed & bedding	02—00—00
For eight paier of sheets & an od sheet	07—10—00
More for eight paier of pillow Beers	01—05—00
More for tabal Linnan	03—00—00
In puter in Brass and Iron	08—14—06
More for Chests Boxes and Chairs	02—07—00
More for Bibols and other Bokes	02—09—08
More for Barrels, Tubs, & other lumber	01—19—00
More for horse accoutrements	01—05—00
For his waring aparell, stockings & shoes	13—00—00
In Credit to the Estate	03—00—00
And no Debts	
More in wolen & linnen & coton yarn & bages	02—17—00
Arms & Amonisshon	01—15—00
The total sum is	586—01—00

This Inventory Aprized by us—

WILLIAM COWDREY—Jn° BROWNE—JERÉMIAH SWAYNE.

For the first half-century the burial-place of Reading was on the east side of the Common which was, originally, of larger area than at present. Here our ancestor was interred, but in process of time the enclosure was allowed to go uncared for and many of the old stones were broken or covered up. Finally no trace of the old burial-ground remained, but in 1834, in building a town house which stood until recently, the graves were broken into accidentally, and the stones thus recovered have been preserved. They were removed to the present cemetery where they stand in a row by the side of the Great Pond. That of Deacon Thomas Parker is a worthy memorial. It is of excellent stone, very thick and in perfect preservation, notwithstanding its age. Upon this the following inscriptions were well chisselled:—

Children:—

THOMAS PARKER, b. in Lynn, 1636; m. Deborah ———; had nine children; d. July 17, 1699. See Appendix.

HANANIAH PARKER (2), b. 1638; m. Sept. 30, 1663, Elizabeth Browne of Reading.

JOHN PARKER, b. in Reading, 1640; m. Nov. 13, 1667, Hannah Kendall; was Sergeant; had 13 children. See Appendix.

JOSEPH PARKER, b. 1642; d. 1644.

JOSEPH PARKER, b. 1645; d. 1646.

MARY PARKER, b. Dec. 12, 1647; m. Samuel Dodge of Beverly, son of Richard; she had 11 children and d. 1705. See Appendix.

MARTHA PARKER, b. March 14, 1649.

NATHANIEL PARKER, b. May 16, 1651; m. Sept. 24, 1677, Bethia Polly; removed to the West Parish, now Reading town, was Ensign; had 13 children, and was ancestor of illustrious and very numerous descendants. See Appendix.

SARAH PARKER, b. Sept. 30, 1653; d. Oct. 26, 1656.
JONATHAN PARKER, b. May 18, 1656; served in the Indian wars; d. June 10, 1680.*
SARAH PARKER, b. May 23, 1658.

---

* The military spirit was very strong among our ancestors when fighting was the final cause of training. They always, from the time of landing, kept a musket for the frontier, against Pequod, King Philip, French and Ojibways; they never shrunk from pain nor fainted at the inevitable blood-lettings of discomposed times, and always made a solemn business of military drill, as old family almanacs and account books attest, in which the phrases of field manœuvres and words of command alternate with the price of hay and lumber and the settlement of a neighbor's bill. Jonathan had passed through perils of the field in King Philip's War; perhaps he was one of the 150 volunteers under Turner, or one of Lathrop's picked company. This was in 1675–6, but he was spared to die at home. The following seems to have been written by his nephew John Parker, son of Hananiah, and who was in 1680, at the age of 16. A discolored sheet, which has long been treasured and preserved, bearing the date of 1680, is a most tender and God-fearing document:—

"THE DEYING WORDS OF JONATHAN PARKER."

"There was heard to say that he desiered that if it wear the will of God, that this cup might pass from him, but if not he did desier to submit, allso he desiered that God would soport his parents and make them wiling to submit, if he must dey, that God would be Pleased to make his pasedg easy into glory & if that he did dey he hoopt to go to a heavenly Father. Lord let my prayers com before Thee as ensence and lifting of his hands as erning sackerifice he did entreate his father and mother to forgive him all his ofencis telling of them that he would entreate them to submit to the will of God in parting with them saying that he had cometted his case to God: and if it may make most for Gods glory and youer comfort I desier to live, if not I am wiling to dey: he was ott whither or which; was wiling to doo what might make most for God.

"My afflictions wer great yet the love of God was greater: for he would live to sinne, that he did believe that God would provide for his parents so that they should never want: he begd of his mother to be wiling to part with him and his mother sayed that she would have something when he was gone; and [he] said that he hopt he was going to Jesus Christ——Beeing asked if he were not afraid of death, he sayed noe, for Christ had taken away the sting of death—the sathon had thrust at him to make him fall but sayed he had no foothould and had not yet prevailed & he hopt that he never should for he was a coward. Then his mother sayd that it was a great merci that God did coop him in the sins of the wars and brought him home to dey by his Parents. I had but a litol grace then but I had so much that I didn't fear Evil or Death— There was notice taken of him that he prayed for he had nothing els to doo: —he did desier to be remembered to his two Sisters and tell them that if they do see him no more they should not see him sinne—XhonX"

In the lower corner is written in the same hand:—

"Diference betwene kings of thrones then John Parker; his exampl to you youths."

Of the 11 children of Dea. Thomas Parker we pass on now to the second son*—

Lt. Hananiah Parker, b. in Lynn(?),† 1638, son of Dea. Thomas and Amy. He m. Sept. 30, 1663, Elizabeth Browne, who seems to have had a twin brother Joseph, and born in Reading, Dec. 10, 1647, dau. of Nicholas and Elizabeth.‡ The father, Nicholas, was a native of Inkberrow, Worcestershire, England, the son of Edward Browne. He was a man of property. He lived in Lynn ten years, during which time he was her representative to the General Court from that town. Hananiah Parker settled on land which bordered his father's farm.§ The assessors' list of 1667 credits him with a house and farm. He was made a freeman Oct. 15, 1679. He belonged to Reading's military company, of which he was chosen ensign in 1680, and lieutenant in 1684. It is evident that his Puritan townsmen had confidence in his

---

* See Appendix for the history of the remaining children of Dea. Thomas Parker.

† It is uncertain whether he was born in Lynn, as the earliest records of both Lynn and Reading are lost.

‡ Savage says she was a dau. of Jonathan Brown of Reading. His authority is most excellent, but other records makes it more probable that she was dau. of Nicholas. Savage describes this Jonathan Brown as "a man of substance."

§ This it seems was situated about a half-mile east of Dea. Thomas Parker's, on the main road from Lynn to Lowell, now Lowell Street in Wakefield, and upon which place Hananiah's descendants, through his son Ebenezer, occupied and lived for five generations in the Parker name. The last one of these was Thomas Parker, a namesake of the original ancestor, and a deacon also. He is remembered by some of the old residents of Wakefield, formerly Reading. From Thomas it passed into the hands of his niece, Mrs. Obed Symonds, lately deceased. Since sold by her it has passed through many hands, and the large house was destroyed by fire in 1880, while owned by a Mrs. Rogers. Now only a cellar-hole and well remain, which is noticeable a short distance to the east of Samuel Parker's on the north side of the road. This place is credited by Lilley Eaton, historian of Reading, as the original homestead, that of Dea. Thomas Parker. This is incorrect, however, as is proved by close examination of the will of Lt. Hananiah Parker. Hananiah's three brothers settled as follows: Thomas, Jr., succeeded upon his father's homestead in the centre of the town; Sergt. John settled on Cowdrey's Hill; and Ensign Nathaniel removed to the West Parish, now the centre of modern Reading. This explains to us why Dea. Thomas Parker in his will, 1683, forbade his son Thomas to sell any of his land or meadow without the consent of his brethren.

ability and character at an early date, for in 1679 he with two others were given charge of building a new Meeting-house. He was then chosen by the General Court one of the Committee to "rectifie and settle the highway between Woburn and Reading." Consider the energy and industry of our ancestor when we say that in addition to the great work of changing the primeval forest to a fertile farm he performed the duties of selectman, town clerk and representative, each for a long period. The military affairs required much of his time, if not active service at certain periods. Trainings were frequent and an absence cost a heavy fine. Every Sunday found him at church, to which he and wife connected themselves very soon after marriage. The Church records mention his name with respect. As a representative of Reading to the General Court at Boston he served seven years. He was a typical Puritan yeoman, the father of a rugged, honorable family of children. He gave thought to the education of the young. In 1707 Lt. Hananiah Parker and Capt. John Browne were appointed committee "to provide a Scool Master for the towne school." They reported that John Webb of Braintree "be chosen to teach reading, writing, casting accounts and the Latin and Greek tongues" for the three months next ensuing. His wife Elizabeth died Feb. 27, 1697.

He married 2nd, Dec. 12, 1700, Mrs. Mary (Bursham) Bright, dau. of William Bursham and widow of Dea. John Bright of Watertown. She survived him. He died March 10, 1724, aged 86. She d. Jan. 4, 1736, aged 87. Thus she was 11 years younger than he. Hananiah Parker had no children from his second marriage.

WILL OF HANANIAH PARKER.

In the Name of God Amen the 20th of May 1703 I Hananiah Parker of Reading in the county of Middlesex in the province of the Massachusetts Bay in New England Yeoman being aged and weak in body but of perfect mind and memory (thanks be unto God therefor) calling to mind my own mortality as knowing that it is appointed for all men once to dye do make and ordain this my Last Will and Testament that is to say principally and first of all I Give and recommend my Soul into the hands of God that gave it and my body to the Earth from whence t'was taken to be decently buried in a Christian manner by my Executour heafter named hopeing that at the Resurrection of the Just I shall receive the Same again by the mighty power of God. And as touching Such Worldly Estate as it hath pleased God to endow me with—all I do bequeath and dispose of the same as here followeth

I Will that all my Just Debts and funeral charges be duly discharged in convenient time after my decease by my Exec^{rs} hereafter named

I Give unto Mary my well beloved Wife the use of the west End of my house from the top to the bottom with the back Lean to and Cellar with the use of the Buttery and also a sufficient garden Spott to be kept well fenced and in good manner for her use as she shall see cause to improve it for planting of roots beans squashes and also the keeping of one Cow Summer and Winter during her life or so long as she shall remain my Widow, also an horse to Ride on when she shall have occasion, also the going of one or two swine summer and winter if she see cause and [also] a liberty keep fowls. And I do give to my said wife firewood sufficient to be brought ready cut for her use and laid conveniently near her door by my Executour also I do give to her so many apples as she shall need to lay in for Winter: also one Barrel of Cyder to be placed in her Cellar annually by my Executour so long as she shall live and remain my widow—My Will is that her garden and part of housing be kept in good Repair for her and all taxes lawfully set thereon and demanded to be paid by my s^{d} Executour—Moreover I do give and bequeath unto my s^{d} Wife all such Provisions as I shall leave at my decease as also such woolen and Linen Cloth that shall remain not made up into garments—also I give to her fifty shilling to be paid her annually for so long as she shall remain my Widow by my Executour hereinafter named

I do give and bequeath to my son John Parker and to his heirs and assigns forever that house and land that was his Grandfather Parker's which is that housing and Lands that he now occupieth and liveth upon; as also that three acres of Meadow which I bought of Edwd Taylor and those Dividends which did of right belong to the land abovesaid.

Moreover I give to my said son John that three acres of meadow which was his Grandfather Brown's Gift to his Mother; also I give unto him five pounds in passable money to be paid unto him by my Execu^{r} afternamed within two years after my Decease

I give and bequeath unto my son Samuel Parker & to his heirs and assigns all that Tenement that he now dwelleth on the which I bought of Edward Taylor, all which I gave to my s^{d} son Samuel Parker by a Deed of Gift formerly and do now confirm the same to him by this my Last Will and Testament which is the whole I intend him as his Part and Portion of my Estate

I give and bequeath unto my daughter Mary Poole over & above what she hath already had, one brass pan, and my best feather bed with all the appurtenances thereunto belonging; and also I will and bequeath to her that six acres of meadow called Reedy meadow or else thirty pounds in passable money to her by me Executour within three years after mine and my wife's decease—

I Give and bequeath to each of my Grandchildren five shillings to be paid unto them out of my Estate by my Executour when they shall come to full age—

I do give and bequeath unto my son Ebenezer Parker all my housing and Lands where I now dwell together with that three acres of meadow called the Wiggwam meadow together also with all the Rest of my Estate whatsoever or wheresoever it may be found that is not herein willed or otherwise before this legally conveyed: moreover I do herein Nominate and Appoint, Constitute and ordain my s^{d} son Ebenezer Parker to be sole Executour of this my last will and Testament and to see it fulfilled in every part according to my true Intent therein: and if my said Executour fail or refuse to pay to my wife Mary according to this my Will, Then my Will is that my brother Nathaniel Parker shall have full power to make Sale of any part of my lands for payment of the Same—

And I do hereby utterly revoke, make Null and void all and every other former Will or Wills by me heretofore made and do own allow, Ratifie and Confirm This to be my Will and my last Will and Testament—

In Witness whereof I have hereunto set my hand and Seal the day and year first above written.

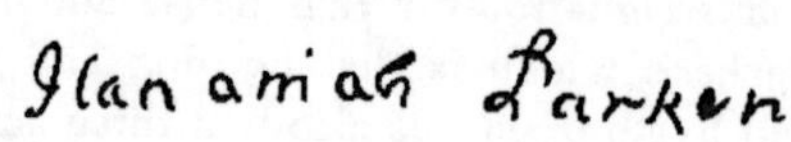

Their children were:

3. JOHN PARKER, b. Aug. 3, 1664; m. Deliverance Dodge of Beverly.

SAMUEL PARKER, b. Oct. 24, 1666; m. Martha Brown of Cambridge. See Appendix.

ELIZABETH PARKER, b. June, 1668; m. Nov. 17, 1685, Samuel Cowdrey, son of Nathaniel Cowdrey of Reading. See Appendix.

Mary Parker, m. Samuel Poole of Boston.
Sarah Parker, b. Feb. 20, 1672; d. Oct. 2, 1673.
Hananiah Parker, b. Nov. 2, 1674; d. Jan. 3, 1677.
Ebenezer Parker, b. Feb. 13, 1676; m. Rebecca Newhall of Reading. See Appendix.
Hananiah Parker, b. April 30, and d. Aug. 7, 1681.

Of the above children only one is taken up in full in this genealogy, that is the eldest, John Parker, who removed to Lexington, and was the ancestor of all the Lexington Parkers. This volume was originally designed for the posterity of John Parker only, but much relating to other branches has been added as an Appendix. In the Appendix can be found a brief history of the other children of Lt. Hananiah Parker.

3. **John Parker** *(Hananiah,[2] Thomas[1])*, son of Lt. Hananiah and Elizabeth (Browne) Parker, was b. in Reading, Aug. 3, 1664. His life covered the period of the early growth of the colonies, the hardships, wars and rugged life of the times. A preserved record, now at Lexington, is in his own handwriting and reads: "John Parker and his wife Deliverance were Married the 2: of October 1689." She was Deliverance Dodge of Beverly, dau. of John and Sarah, and b. 10 or 15 March, 1661.* They settled soon after marriage on a part of the original Dea. Thomas Parker place in the centre of the town, which farm adjoined that of Lt. Hananiah Parker. Three of John Parker's deeds made at this period are preserved at Lexington. In 1699 he purchased of John Poole land on the north end of the Great Pond, "Lake Quanapowit." In 1705 he added 21 acres to his estate by a purchase of Mr. Francis Smith "for a valuable sum of money." This land lay upon the bounds of Lynn and Reading. He sold to his cousin "Nathaniel Parker of Redding Jr. Cooper," 11

*The grandfather, Richard Dodge, must have been well known by Dea. Thomas Parker. He was in Salem in 1638, removed to Beverly, where he was one of the founders of the Beverly Church. He had son John, b. in England, who by wife Edith had children Deliverance, 1661, John, 1662, Josiah, 1665, Sarah. 1667, Ebenezer, 1670, Mary, 1672, and Andrew, 1676. This accounts for the introduction of the names Andrew, Josiah and others into the Parker family,—from the brotherly affection which the wife Deliverance Parker cherished.

acres, "which land was laid out to Dea. Thomas Parker of Redding and now in possession of John Parker." We observe by the deed that it was "in the fourth year of the Reign of our Soveraign Lady Queen Anne."

John Parker was constable of Reading.* The following is a copy of one of his preserved receipts. In these olden times the constable was a prominent factor, holding the same position of power as the deputy sheriff of to-day, except that his powers were confined to his own town. The people were very careful whom they chose for this honorable position, and the fact that John Parker was constable of Reading is a strong voucher for his integrity, force of character and popularity:

"CHARLES TOWNE, y[e] 11 May, 1693.

"Then Recd. of Mr. John Parker, Constable of Reading, the sums of Fifty Nine pounds Twelve shillings in full of s[d] Townes Last Assessments. I say Received

by me HUMP[e] PARSONS."

It must have been a hard blow to the family to learn of the death of the son Hananiah, who, a promising lad of 18, was in the Annapolis expedition of 1710, and died of the prevailing

* Before removing to Lexington he sold his homestead estate to his neighbor and friend, Jonathan Poole. The record is at Lexington in the form of a simple agreement, as follows:—

"This draft of bargaine made this twentieth day of May Ano. Dom. 1712 betwene John Parker of Reding in the County of Midd[x]. in New England. Joyner on the one part and Jonathan Poole of y[e] same towne yeoman on the other part witnesseth that y[e] s[d] John Parker hath sold and doth promas to make alination of to s[d] Poole all his whomsted with building on it consisting of 23 acres more or less of upland and medo land bound west by y[e] land of Capt. Herbert decesed, northardly by Thomas Weston, southardly by s[d] Capt. Herbert decesed and e s[d] Jonathan Poole, estardly by Timothy Willard, s[d] Poole and also 3 acres of medo joining to y[e] south side of s[d] Jonathan Pooles and called y[e] cranbery meddo.—And the s[d] Jonathan Poole doth ablidg himself to pay for s[d] Land two hundred and ninety five pounds in mony or bills of credit of this province."

This record is very valuable in more than one way. It shows to us where John Parker lived in Reading, which proves the location of the first Parker homestead, that of Dea. Thomas Parker—see Hananiah Parker's will. Capt. Herbert lived on the spot where now stands the Wakefield Town Hall, where Rev. Samuel Haugh and Rev. John Brock preceded him. Jonathan Poole's house was where is now the Wakefield Rattan Factory. Thus we find the true location of our Reading ancestors, and from the above record we know into whose hands the homestead passed.

sickness 1711. But with the remaining three sons, Andrew, Josiah and John, Jr., the parents removed to Lexington (then called Cambridge Farms) in the spring of 1712. He settled upon the same homestead still occupied by his descendants. The history of the town of Lexington makes mention of him by saying :—

"John Parker was chosen fence viewer in 1714 and tythingman in 1715 and '21. He must have been a man of dignity of character, for in seating the meeting-house, 1731, where they had reference to age, honor and property, they placed him in the second seat below with Ensign John Mason, Thomas Mead and other highly respectable citizens."

The following is the copy of a precept used by John Parker and is still preserved among the old family papers at Lexington :—

"To the Constable of Redding which was in the yeare 1692. Whearas James Ribboe and Samuel Merrow do refuse or neglect to pay their proportion of the Rate Committed unto you which was made the 25 Novem: 1692 which was the first part of the thirty thousand pounds. Therefore, this is in the Majestys names to require you to make Distrese upon the goods of James Ribboe for his refusing or neglecting to pay his proportion of the above s[d] Rate which is twenty shillings, and of the goods of Samuell Merrow for his refusing or neglecting to pay his proportion of the above s[d] Rate, which is ten shillings, which goods are to be apprized as the law directs and to be Sould, and to return the overplus to the owner if there any be, and if goods cannot be found to pay the above s[d] sums, then you are to seize the body of James Ribboe, and the body of Samuell Merrow, and commit them to the County Goal there so to be kept without bail or mainprize until payment shall be made with all due charges

Witnesseth our hands and seals in Redding
this first of March, 1693/4

John Browne
John Bacheller } selectmen"

The ancient deeds of purchase, still preserved at the Lexington homestead, show that "John Parker, Sen[r], Joiner, of Redding, purchased in Cambridge Farms" one small mansion house and sixty acres of land, bounded southerly on Watertown line, elsewhere by Daniel White, John Stone and Thomas

Cutler, and of Thomas Cutler he bought "a certain messuage or Tenement lying and being scituate in Cambridge, In the Farms, containing one mansion house, barn and about one hundred and ninety acres of land." These aggregated 250 acres, and the total cost was four hundred and sixty pounds.*

Mrs. Deliverance Parker died in Lexington March 10, 1718. The records concerning his second marriage have not been found, but we know her name was Sarah. All the children were by the first wife.

John Parker was a joiner. He built a shop in which he made from wood necessary farm implements, furniture and useful things. This trade he taught his sons, and they in turn from generation to generation. The Parkers in Lexington were all skilful woodworkers.

John Parker made the following agreements with his sons in place of a will:

"Know all men by these presents, that we John Parker and Andrew Parker Do fully & freely Consent and agree that Josiah & John Parker Jr. or their heirs or assigns shall have full Right and Lawfull authority to Take, Emproove & Enjoy for Ever all y[e] Moovable Estate Belonging to John Parker my Hon[ord] father of what kind or nature soever it may be and we likewise promise that we will not either directly or indirectly keep or Conseal any thing or things that shall or may at any time appear to be y[e] s[d] John Parkers movable Estate upon Penalty of Paying all Damages that may arise by our withholding any of y[e] Goods of y[e] nature above s[d].

"Except all such movables as are needed for house keeping which at y[e] Decease of our Hon[ord]: Parents: John Parker & Sarah his wife are to be Equally Divided Betwen Andrew: Josiah & John Parker or their heirs.

"as Witness our Hands and Seals this fourth Day of January 1739-40

DAVID MEAD	JOHN PARKER
JABEZ KENDALL	ANDREW PARKER."

JOHN PARKER'S POWER OF ATTORNEY TO HIS SONS.

"Know all men by these Presents that I John Parker of Lexington In the County of Middlesex in his Majesties Province of y[e] Massachusetts Bay in New England Joyner Have assigned, ordained & made & in my stead and place have put & Constituted my dutifull Sons Josiah Parker of said Lexington yeoman & John Parker of Framingham in the County & Province afores[d] yeoman to be my true & Lawfull attorneys for me & in my name & to my use, to all, sue, fee, levey, require, recover, & receive of all & every person or persons whatsoever, all & every such debts, rents & sums of money as are now due unto me or which at any day or days, time or times hereafter shall

---

* In 1728, however, John Parker sold a farm of one mansion house, one barn, two outhouses and 100 acres of land to Mr. Joseph Brooks of Weston. Amount paid, 600 pounds. It bordered the Watertown line and was in part the land formerly bought from the Cutlers.

John Parker died Jan. 22, 1741, aged 78. The record of the death of Mrs. Sarah Parker has not been found. All the children were born in Reading, although their record of birth is found upon the town records of both Reading and Lexington.

Their children were:

SARAH PARKER, b. July 5, and d. July 9, 1690.
HANANIAH PARKER, b. Oct. 10, 1691; d. 1711, on service of Queen Anne's War, while in the Annapolis, N. S., Expedition. See his letter, page 40.
4. ANDREW PARKER, b. Feb. 14, 1693; m. Sarah Whitney of Lexington.
5. JOSIAH PARKER, b. April 11, 1694; m. Anna Stone of Lexington.
MARY PARKER, b. Dec. 4, 1695; d. 1709, aged 14.
JOHN PARKER, b. and d. 1696.
EDIE PARKER, b. Aug. 19, 1697; d. 1709, aged 12.
6. JOHN PARKER, b. Nov. 8, 1703; m. Experience Clayes of Framingham.

The following letter, well written, is among the family papers at Lexington. Hananiah was but eighteen when he wrote this letter. It shows his sturdy bringing up, and we can well imagine the parents anxiously awaiting the return of

---

be due owing, belonging or appertaining unto me by any manner of ways or means whatsoever: Giving and Granting unto my said attorneys, by the tenner of these presents, my full & whole power, strength & authority in & about the premises & upon the receipt of any such debts rents & sums of money afore S[d] acquittances, or other discharges for me & in my name to make, seal & deliver, and all & every other act & acts, thing & things, dencè & dencès in the Law whatsoever, needful & necessary to be done, in or about the premises, for the recovery of any such debts, rents & sums of money goods or chattels, for me and in my name, to do execute & perform as fully, largely, and amply in every respect, to all Intents, Constructions & Purposes as I myself might or could do if I were personally present ratifying allowing and holding firm & stable all & whatsoever my said attorneys shall lawfully do, or cause to be done in or about the execution of the same by virtue of these presents thereby Revoking all former powers by me given to any person or persons whatsoever. In Wittness whereof I have hereunto sett my hand & seal the sixth day of August Anno Domini 1740

"Signed Sealed & Delivered
In Presence of
JAMES CLAYES*
JOHN JONES"

John Parker

---

*John Parker of Framingham had married Experience Clayes, niece of James Clayes of Framingham, whose signature appears on the deed.

their strong and promising son, and with him to remove to Lexington. But their hopes were never realized, for he died of the prevailing sickness sometime in 1711, having been kept in garrison after the capitulation.

"From ANNAPOLIS ROYAL March ye 8th 1710.

"Ever Honored father and mother after my Deuty Remembered to you and to my Grandfather and Grandmother: and my Love to all my brothers and all my friends—Hoping theas few lines of my Love Will find you in as Good health as I am at this present Writting, Blessed be God for it. And this is to let you understand that I Recived youer Second Letter, and that is a verey sickly time with us and we have Lost above Three Scor men that belong to New England and thear is above fifty men sick. Barnabas Cook is sick; Daniel Dove is sick; William Hopkins is sick; Benjamin Johnson is amost well of his wounds but he has had a verey bad sweling upon his thigh above his wounds but we hope he will doe well.

Sr Charles* has lost 11 men out of his Redgement. Coronal Whiting has lost 16 or 17 and he has 24 men sick. One man Dyed out of our company: he belonged to Wobone, his name was Robert Pierce.

Johnathan Eaton is verey sick. But we hope to see you in a little time, they that are living, but if we stay hear much Longer their will but few of us see New England, but Sr Charles saies he will carrey us home as soon as ye govenur coms: we hope to see you in a month or six weaks If we Live—for Sir Charles is a wearey of this place and amost Discouraged and wants to get hom as much as we do.

Out of all New England men thair is but 40 men fit for Deuty, and thair is hardly men Enough to berrey ye dead and look after ye sick for we berrey 2 or 3 men Everey Night: for we berrey them in Night becaus ye french Should not know how many men we loos and we berrey them out of ye buring place down by ye water side below ye fort and spread ye ground leavel over them that they might not be seen. I have had a verey Easey time this winter for I have been freed from Deuty to Look after Benjamin Johnson and I have had my health as well as ever I had in my life for which I have caus to be thankfull.

I would not have you be Discouraged nor Discontented nor think ye time Long for I hope to see you Quick, for as soon as the Govenur coms hear Sr Charles sayes he will carrey us home. We hear that thair is men a coming from New York to Releave us.

* Four regiments were raised in New England, two of which were commanded by Sir Charles Hobby and Colonel Tailer of Massachusetts.

But No mor at Present for I have No News to send you.

So I Remain Youer Deutyfull Son

HANANIAH PARKER.

But I desier youer prayers for me that I may be kept from sin & sicknes beeing in a dangerous place for them both: for thair is nothing but wickedness carried on hear, cursing and swearing in everey mans mouth."

4. **Andrew Parker** (*John,*[3] *Hananiah,*[2] *Thomas*[1]), son of John and Deliverance (Dodge) Parker, was b. in Reading, Feb. 14, 1693; was at the age of 19 when he removed with his parents and brothers to Lexington in 1712. He was favored with a sound and vigorous training in his youth. He was well bestowed physically for the mammoth task of the early pioneer, and he entered into the work heartily. He married in Lexington at the age of 27, Aug. 2, 1720, Sarah, bap. April 22, 1703, dau. of Isaiah and Sarah Whitney of Lexington.* She was third in order in a family of seven children. Nov. 4, 1724, they made their peace with the Church, when three of their children were bap. They were admitted to the Church in 1728.

He was a husbandman and woodworker, thus succeeding his father in the occupation which soon became well known as a characteristic talent of the Lexington Parkers. He was energetic and industrious. He was a man of strong physique,

*The grandfather, Eleazer Whitney, was settled at Cambridge Farms in 1693, where he d. in 1697. The Whitneys, however, did not long remain in Lexington.

"Although the Whitney name has become common in almost every town in the country, most of this family are descended from John and Elinor Whitney of Watertown. The children of this ancestor, though eight in number, were all sons, six of whom had families of their own. Five of the children were b. in England before he, John Whitney, aged 30, embarked from London, in April, 1635, for N. E. in the ships *Elizabeth and Ann*, Roger Cooper master. His early admission as a freeman, his early elections as a selectman by the town, and constable of Watertown by the court, show that he occupied a respectable social position."—*Watertown Genealogies.*

Our Eleazer Whitney, father of Isaiah, was doubtless the one given in Watertown Genealogies as son of Thomas Whitney of Watertown, and b. April 7, 1662, twin brother of Elnathan (as recorded on page 643). This Thomas was son of John and Elinor Whitney and was b. in England 1629, and m. in Watertown, Mary Kedall (or Kettle), dau. of John of Watertown. Therefore Sarah Whitney's ancestry ran thus: Sarah,[5] Isaiah,[4] Eleazer,[3] Thomas,[2] John.[1]

as tradition claims that he was of very large size and powerfully built. He was a kind father and was attentive to the physical and spiritual needs of his large family.

Andrew Parker was chosen fence viewer of the town at "the meeting of ye freeholders and other inhabitants orderly convened on ye 9th of March 1725," as the Lexington records attest. Soon after this he was honored with the rank of constable. He thus rendered his town the same public service which his father had served in Reading. It was a position of much higher dignity and social standing then than now. His wife Sarah died Dec. 18, 1774, aged 70. She was the mother of 12 children. He survived her.

Andrew Parker lived in the reigns of five English sovereigns, was seven years of age when the year 1700 came, and yet lived to see the first armed expedition of British soldiers against the colonists put to rout at Concord and Lexington, June 17, 1775, and this accomplished partly by his own family. As he on occasion gathered his children, his ever increasing grandchildren and inquisitive great-grandchildren at the old homestead around that open fireplace filled with blazing logs, what a story he must have oft related concerning the hard struggle for existence, but final development of the colonies together with that of their own allied families! He must have remembered events before 1700, knew all about Queen Anne's War against the French and Indians, 1702 to 1713, and the capture of Port Royal, N. S., from the French, in which war his brother Hananiah served and died. It was in his time that the devout colonists were obliged to carry their guns to Church and into the fields when at work, and have them ever ready to fight off the prowling savage. He could tell all about the Georges, the Louisburg expedition of 1744–48, and the last great French and Indian war of 1754 to '63. At the time of his death, which occurred April 8, 1776, his great-grandchildren numbered over a score. He thus died at the age of 83.

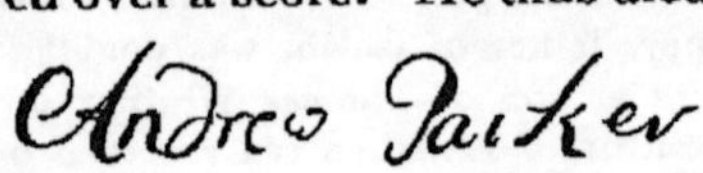

Their children were:

7. SARAH PARKER, b. Feb. 9, 1721; m. June 21, 1739, Jabez Kendall of Woburn.

8. JONAS PARKER, b. Feb. 6, 1722; m. 1745, Lucy Monroe of Lexington.

9. AMOS PARKER, b. July 27, 1723; m. 1745, Anna Curwen Stone of Lexington.

ELIZABETH PARKER, bap. Aug. 22, 1725; d. young.

10. THOMAS PARKER, bap. Dec. 24, 1727; m. March 8, 1750, Jane Parrot, then of Chelmsford.

ABIGAIL PARKER, bap. July 27, 1729.

11. LUCY PARKER, bap. April 4, 1731; m. May 24, 1750, Joshua Mead of Lexington.

ELIZABETH PARKER, bap. June 22, 1735.

12. ANDREW PARKER, bap. April 16, 1738; m. Nov. 29, 1759, Abigail Jennison of Weston.

13. KEZIAH PARKER, bap. June 1, 1740; m. June 1, 1759, Joseph Wyman of Lunenburg.

EBENEZER PARKER, bap. Feb. 28, 1742; probably d. 1743.

MARY PARKER, bap. Oct. 21, 1744.

By a deed from father to son, dated 30th April, 1728, it is evident the Lexington estate was then located as the following plan shows:

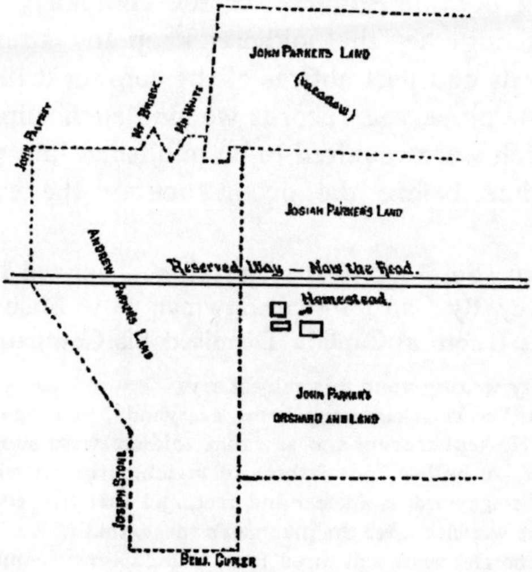

5. Lt. Josiah Parker (*John*,[3] *Hananiah*,[2] *Thomas*[1]), b. in Reading, April 11, 1694, son of John and Deliverance (Dodge) Parker. He seems to have inherited the sturdy qualities and industry of his father, the assessor, constable,

joiner and farmer of Reading. He was 18 when his parents and three brothers removed with him from his native town to Lexington in 1712. He worked with his brothers upon the new farm, also in his father's shop, where the latter taught his sons in making all kinds of wooden implements, wagons and furniture. He was of use to his father in many ways, notably in surveying and proving the bounds of his estate, and in the same manner to his neighbors and townsmen, who needed such service. When he had been but two years in Lexington he was one of the three chosen by "ye freeholders" of the town to "estimate and fix the boundary line" between Lexington and her mother town, Cambridge.

He of course belonged to the military company, in the days when soldiers were scarce and the Indians and French sometimes too common for the comfort of the English settlers. Hananiah Parker, his brother, of much promise, had already perished in the Port Royal Expedition. Loving memories of him doubtless inspired the three remaining brothers to more active training and in anticipation of coming troubles. Josiah Parker soon became "clark" of the company. His duties were to call together the soldiers, keep the attendance and "fine" records and post notices of the coming drill day.*

Among the preserved records we find such slips as the following, which were required to be published in a public place a certain time before the occurrence of the event named therein:

"LEXINGTON Sep^tm^: ye 16th: 1729: Was Appointed & Observed as a training Day By Capt: Joseph Bowman & ye Major Part of his Company: & Before s^d^ Captain Dismised his Company he ordered

*An authority writing upon this subject says:

"The 'clarke' of each company knew everybody, and was an important functionary. He kept account and saw that soldiers were supplied with one pound powder, 20 bullets, one fathom of match, priming wire, worm and scourers, muskets, sword, bandeleer and rest, and that live coals were ready at all times; he watched after the pikeman's spear, that it was bright, that his headpiece and corslet were well cared for. Should a man come to his notice who was without a musket, he would take him to the surveyor-general, where arms could be procured with a ticket, which the surveyor would turn over to the town treasurer, who would pay for the purchases and charge them to the man, and make him work it out. Every man must be ready at the alarm and should any fail to respond it was his duty to so report and the excuse for the same, which, if not deemed important, the delinquent was heavily fined."

& Appointed tuesday ye twenty first Day of Octo^br^: Next Insuing to Be Observed & attended as a training Day in s^d^ town & also Published & Declared ye Same at ye head of his Company.

"Attest JOSIAH PARKER Clark of ye Company above s^d^."

He m. in Lexington, Dec. 8, 1718, Anna Stone, one of the four daughters of John and Rachel (Shepherd) Stone of Lexington. She was b. in Lexington, Nov. 27, 1694. Her father was a corporal; was the son of Dea. Samuel and grandson of Dea. Gregory Stone of Cambridge, who came from England in 1635 and was the ancestor of a large issue of his name in America.*

With which to begin his married life his father, John Parker, Esq., gave him "towards his portion" 55 acres of land. The deed of gift also reads: "for diverse causes and considerations me hereunto moving, and more especially for the good affection I bear my well beloved son Josiah Parker of Lexington."

They were admitted to the church Aug. 13, 1719. His first service as assessor of the town of Lexington originated from the choice of "ye freeholders in meeting assembled," March 6, 1726, they granting him besides the honor and work of his position a yearly salary of 2 pounds, 8 shillings, 4 pence! Chas. Hudson, Esq., in his History of the Town of Lexington, says:

> "Lt. Parker was one of the most popular men in town for many years. He filled almost every town office. He filled the office of town clerk four years. He was an assessor 19 years from 1726 to 1755, with occasional intermissions, and selectman seven years."

He discharged the duties of these offices with ability. He was an excellent penman and good grammarian, and his accurately and neatly kept records are of great historical value. At his old homestead, descended five generations down, are still in perfect preservation some of Lt. Parker's interesting papers and in fact some town records besides. "Josiah Parker's Book, 1738," is worth perusing. Take for

* Dea. Samuel Stone was the fourth child of Dea. Gregory. He m. June 7, 1655, Sarah Stearns of Watertown, dau. of Isaac, an original proprietor of Watertown. They had eight children, the fourth of whom was John Stone as before named.—*Watertown Genealogies.*

instance this specimen, showing the terms used in manual by all the fighting men of Lexington, somewhat out of date at present, but showing the process necessary to wield the flint-lock gun:

"Joyne your right hand to your F.* Present your F. Rest your F. Cock your F. Present—Fire. Recover your F. Half cock your F. Handle your primer. Prime. Shut your pan. Cast about to charge. Handel your carthrige. Open your carthrige. Charge with carthrige. Draw your rammers. Shorten your rammers. Put them in the barrels. Ram down your carthridge. With-draw your rammers. Shorten your rammers. Return your rammers. Cast off your F. Your right hand under the Lock. Poise your F. Shoulder your F. Rest your F. Ground your F. Take up your F. Rest your F. Club your F. Rest your F. Secure your F. Shoulder your F."

May ye first, 1744.

Then settled ye Dignity of Officers in Colonel Phipps Ridgement.

Captains.	Lieutenants.
Saml. Green.	John Tainter.
Benj. Reed.	Saml. Hendly.
Saml. Livermore.	Josiah Parker.
Capt. Hayes.	John Beal.
Capt. Codman.	Thom. Symms.
Capt. Fuller.	Wm. Hide.
Capt. Kendrick.	Jos. Bryant.
Capt. Brooks.	Robert Mordock.
Capt. Dana.	Benj. Blany.
	Stephen Hall.

This was the year previous to the Louisburg Expedition of 1745. It is very probable that he and his company saw service in this war, and perhaps accompanied his son John, who went all through this expedition. And here is a note made by the painstaking captain, ambitious of perfecting his company drill:

"Reare half files, double the depth of your right flank. Left half files of left flank face to the left about. Front half files of left flank face to the left. Reare half files of right flank face to the right—march 10 paces—the whole face to the right—march 10 paces—face to the right."

*In the corner of the page is written: "N. B.—that F. stands for firelock."

Such matter as this lies mixed with charges made for mechanical labor and farm produce, for all the family knew how to wield a good many kinds of tools:

"1752. To a harrow and axeltreeing your cart—to mending your Cyder-mill—to a chees mill—to making 3 keelers and a churn—to making a coffin—to 6 pair of Bed Screws at £7-10s a pair old tenor—to a beetel and how handle and sithe snath—to my oxen to Cambridge and 3 Cartouch Boxes.—to my oxen to plough in your Rie."

Lt. Josiah Parker must have possessed a strong constitution, physically as well as mentally, which enabled him to victoriously combat as he did the many obstructions in the road of progress of his day. In addition to his varied abilities, he was a successful farmer and the honored father of a large and noble family of children. He d. in Lexington, Oct. 9, 1756, aged 62. His widow Anna, who survived him four years, made her will May 1, 1760. She d. Sept. 8 of the same year. She bequeathed a part of her estate to each surviving child, mentioning "My Beloved Sons Josiah, John, Thaddeus & Joseph Parker," and "My Beloved Daughters Anna Smith and Deliverance Monroe," and made her sons John and Joseph Parker executors.

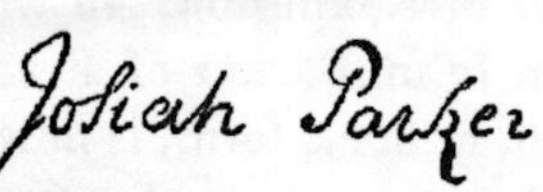

Their children were:

14. ANNA PARKER, b. Sept. 9, 1719; m. Benjamin Smith of Lexington.

15. DELIVERANCE PARKER, b. May 28, 1721; m. Marrett Monroe of Lexington.

MARY PARKER, b. July 3, 1723; was living March 2, 1738, when she placed her signature on her uncle John Parker's bond. But as no family records exist which give any further mention of her it is practically certain that she died in early life.

16. JOSIAH PARKER, b. April 11, 1725; m. Mary Monroe, then of Weston.

LOIS PARKER, b. Aug. 20, 1727; d. July, 1735.

17. JOHN PARKER, b. July 13, 1729; m. Lydia Moore of Lexington.

18. THADDEUS PARKER, b. Sept. 2, 1731; m. Mary Reed of Lexington.

19. JOSEPH PARKER, b. Nov. 28, 1733; m. Eunice Hobbs of Weston.

6. John Parker *(John,[3] Hananiah,[2] Thomas[1])*, son and last child of John and Deliverance (Dodge) Parker, b. in Reading, Nov. 8, 1703, removed in 1712 with family to Lexington; removed about 1730 to Shrewsbury; m. in Shrewsbury, Feb. 18, 1731, Experience Clayes of Framingham, dau. of Peter and Mary (Preston) Clayes. Her parents came from Salem. She was b. in Framingham, Nov. 19, 1702. John and Experience Parker were admitted to the Church in Shrewsbury 1732.

"The only surviving brother of Mrs. Parker, Peter Clayes, d. in 1736, and her father desired them to return to Framingham and take the home place (the Col. David Brewer place, now James Fenton's), and Jan. 6, 1737, gave them a deed of the same, conditioned that said John and Experience should support said Clayes and wife during their lives and give them christian burial. The estate comprised the home lot of 8½ acres and buildings and 55 acres lying on both sides of the road from Caleb Bridges to the meeting-house. Peter Clayes d. 1739, and John Parker sold part of the home lot and buildings to James and John Clayes and built where is now the house of the late Dr. Peter Parker."—*Temple.*

The ancestral line of John Parker is clearly proved by two weather-stained sheets at the homestead in Lexington of Mr. John Parker, "joiner of Lexington," in which he makes mention "My dutiful son John Parker of Framingham, yeoman." A treatise on religion, in book form, is now in preservation and contains on the inside cover sheet these words: "From John Parker of Lexington to John Parker of Framingham."*

He and his wife Experience were admitted to the Church in Framingham 1738; he was selectman; was a member of the Framingham company of alarm soldiers, commanded by Capt. Henry Eames: was an overseer of the workhouse and of the poor; d. in Framingham, Feb. 23, 1783. His wife Experience d. Oct. 13, 1780. He was unfortunate with his family, as it seems only two out of seven children survived. His will is preserved among the Cambridge Probate records. In it he mentions son Peter Parker and dau. Submit Bent.

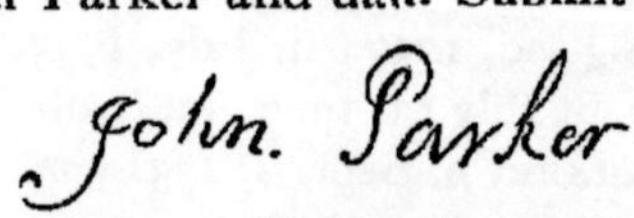

*"Mrs. Fay of Framingham has a Bible which once belonged to John Parker of Lexington. It bears his name and the date 1709."—*Barry's History of Framingham.*

Their children were:

JOHN PARKER, b. in Shrewsbury, Jan. 28, 1732.
EXPERIENCE PARKER, b. in Shrewsbury, Oct. 8, 1733.
HANANIAH PARKER, bap. in Shrewsbury, Sept. 21, 1735.
ABIGAIL PARKER, b. in Shrewsbury, Dec. 1, 1736.
20. PETER PARKER, b. in Framingham, Oct. 3, 1738; m. Ruth Eaton of Framingham.
21. SUBMIT PARKER, b. in Framingham, Dec. 3, 1742; m. Thomas Bent, Jr., of Framingham.
NATHAN PARKER, bap. in Framingham, March 2, 1746.

7. **Sarah Parker** (*Andrew*,[4] *John*,[3] *Hananiah*,[2] *Thomas*[1]), dau. of Andrew and Sarah (Whitney) Parker, b. Feb. 9, 1721, m. June 21, 1739, Jabez Kendall of Woburn, b. Nov. 26, 1717, son of Jabez and Rebecca Kendall of that town, but who later removed to Framingham.

The first ancestors of this family in America were Francis and Mary (Tidd) Kendall, to whom 19 births are recorded on the Woburn records. Their son Thomas had son Jabez, who with wife Rebecca were the parents of the above Jabez. Thomas, son of Thomas, removed to Lexington, and his family, living there at this time, doubtless introduced the Parker family to the Kendalls of Woburn. Thomas Kendall later removed to Framingham, whither John Parker, Jr., had settled. She was 17 years the elder of her brother Andrew Parker, who lived in Barre, and in whose pocket diary we find these words: "Sister Kendall Departed this life the 12 of March 1774." He does not tell us, however, where she had resided. She thus died at the age of 53. Few records have been found regarding this branch of the Kendall family.

8. Jonas Parker (*Andrew*,[4] *John*,[3] *Hananiah*,[2] *Thomas*[1]), son of Andrew and Sarah (Whitney) Parker, b. Feb. 6, 1722, m. in the summer of 1743 Lucy Monroe of Lexington. At the Lexington homestead there is a large record book containing a portion of the old town records in Lt. Josiah Parker's handwriting. It is therein entered: "Jonas Parker and Lucy Monroe, both of Lex. were published June 30, 1745." This is all that has been found concerning his marriage. Being one of this worthy Monroe family, it may be taken for granted

4

that she was a lady of ability and independence, and that she probably assisted him at a later period in his remarkable devotion to the American cause. They made their peace with the Church Sept. 15, 1745, which must have shortly followed their marriage. They removed to Holden, where he purchased a farm and saw-mill, but returned to Lexington after a few years. It is very fitting to state and very creditable to the physical standing of the Parker family, that Jonas is credited by tradition as being the strongest wrestler in the town. He was a woodworker and farmer.

Jonas Parker was a typical Lexington minute-man. He was tall, well built and possessed great strength. In the celebrated painting, "The Battle of Lexington," which hangs in the Lexington town hall, he appears as the central figure. As he there stands in an erect position awaiting the British charge, the look of determination is well depicted on his handsome face.

He lived in the centre, next house to that historic residence where lived Rev. Jonas Clark, the patriot minister, and which was the destination of the ride of Paul Revere. Mr. Parker had evidently imbibed a double portion of the Doctor's lofty spirit. When war with England was imminent he was often heard to say that be the consequences what they might and let others do what they pleased, he would never run from the enemy. He was as good as his word,—better. On the morning of the 17th of June, 1775, having loaded his musket, he placed his hat containing powder, wadding and bullets between his feet in readiness for his second charge. As the first fire from the British was harmless the Americans did not reply. At the second volley he was wounded, and sunk upon his knees; in this condition he discharged his gun. The company of patriots dispersing, his nephew, Ebenezer, who later removed to Princeton, approached Jonas that he might assist his uncle in retreating, but whom he saw was fulfilling his pledge. He insisted that he better retreat with him and thus save his life. But Jonas very forcibly replied that he would never run from the "redcoats." Thus badly wounded, but striving to reload his gun, he was the next moment transfixed by a bayonet upon the spot where he first stood and fell.

Too much pluck had caused his death, but what an example he set for his fellow-citizens!

"History, Roman history," said Edward Everett, "does not furnish an example of bravery that outshines that of Jonas Parker." It was his most sacred wish that America should be free and like brave Arnold of Wilkenried, history will never forget him. The names of the eight martyrs for American Independence are cut deep in the granite monument which stands upon the green; and still deeper in the admiration of the American people. He thus died at the age of 53. April 20, 1835, the remains of these eight soldiers were removed from their former resting-place in the grave-yard and deposited in a vault prepared for the purpose near the base of the monument.

Their children were:

LUCY PARKER, b. in Holden, Oct. 9, 1745. She was both deaf and dumb. After the decease of her father, she chose Joshua Mead of Waltham guardian, but soon afterwards her uncle, Thomas Parker, Esq., of Princeton, took her into his family and provided her a home. She lived in Princeton until her death, which occurred Sept. 16, 1813, aged 68. She was buried at the head of the row in the family burying-ground.

JONAS PARKER, b. in Holden, March 29, 1747; d. young.

SARAH PARKER, b. in Holden, Aug. 29, 1748; bap. Sept. 4, 1748; m. Jan. 4, 1768, Ebenezer Morse of Newton; residence unknown. They had one son, Ebenezer Morse, Jr., of Randolph, Vt.—*Morse Memorials*.

NATHAN PARKER, m., had dau. Abigail, and it seems he d. soon after, as in the settlement of Mr. Jonas Parker's estate we find these words: "Abigail, only dau. of Nathan, the eldest son," for whom Simon Blanchard became guardian. It is not known what became of her, but she probably removed to Billerica, and may have been the Abigail Parker who m. in Woburn, Sept. 23, 1795, Wm. Barnes of Woburn.

22. EUNICE PARKER, m. June 9, 1772, Asa Morse of Newton.

23. JONAS PARKER, b. July 10, 1753; m. Aug. 15, 1776, Martha Hosley of Billerica.

24. PHILEMON PARKER, b. 1755; m. Suzan Stone, and removed to Princeton and later to Vermont.

PRUDENCE PARKER, bap. April 27, 1757; was living in 1778, but no more is known of her.

ELIZABETH PARKER, b. 1758; bap. March 18, 1759; chose, 1778, Joseph Farmer of Billerica as her guardian.

POLLY PARKER, b. Jan. 4, 1761; chose, 1778, Dr. Joseph Fisk of Lexington as her guardian.

Owing to the premature death of Mr. Parker, the family, largely of girls as it was, were taken into different families, and probably some removed from town, making it extremely difficult to follow them. May future research bring to light the history and descendants of these missing connections.

9. Amos Parker *(Andrew,[4] John,[3] Hananiah,[2] Thomas[1])*, second son of Andrew and Sarah (Whitney) Parker, b. in Lexington, July 24, 1723, was the first of the family to bear the name Amos, which has since been common among all the descendents of Andrew Parker. From the town records of marriage intentions kept by Josiah Parker, we find that "Amos Parker and Anna Stone were Posted December y[e] 16, 1744." This shortly preceded their marriage, for they made their peace with the church Jan. 27, 1745. A romance is connected with Anna, which is thus preserved for us by her grandson, Amos A. Parker, Esq., who is still living:

"Before the Revolution an Englishman came to Boston and engaged in trade. He belonged to an aristocratic family in England and was successful in business. In time he married a widow with three children. Two children, a boy and a girl, were born unto them. When these two children, who were named Christopher and Anna,* were eight or ten years of age, the Englishman, whose name was Curwen, fell heir to a large estate in England by the death of an elder brother. Thereupon he sold out in Boston, took the three children of his wife, and left the two children of his own and returned to England. Why he abandoned any of the children, or took those of his wife, does not appear. What became of the boy Christopher I know not, but the girl Anna has a history.

"A man in Lexington by the name of Isaac Stone, a well-to-do farmer, took much of his produce to market at Boston, especially milk. In his rounds he saw this girl Anna, and as she was a bright, intelligent girl about 13 years old, and he having no children, informally adopted her as his daughter. She then was called Anna Stone. She soon became a favorite in the family. In process of

* Born Oct. 21, 1726.

time my grandfather, Amos Parker, married her, and after three children were born unto them, came to Shrewsbury. This was about 1750. She died in 1799. I remember seeing her once at my father's. She was then rather under size, but a brisk, bright, intelligent woman. She talked with me much and I long remembered what she said. This visit was when she was a widow and not long before her death. I remember when my father went to her funeral at Shrewsbury and quite a number of things he brought home with him.

"It is said that Curwen had no children in England, and why he left his own children and heirs and took those of his wife who were not his heirs is a mystery. It would seem he did not wish to have any heirs in England; and how a mother could consent to abandon any of her children when abundantly able to support them, for they were all hers, is a problem difficult to solve. Perhaps our family are heirs to a large estate in England, but I shall not trouble myself about it. These facts I learn by tradition in our family, and also by a diary kept by my uncle Frederick, which has lately fallen into my hands, and which is now before me. In it I find these words:

"'Widow Kent, born in Boston, married an Englishman who died leaving her 3 children—after which by Mr. Curwen she had Christopher and Anna, then left these 2 children and went with the 3 to England to heir a large estate—Curwen of high extraction.'

"This extract is under the date of January, 1791."

He was aged 12 and she 10 when adopted by them. She was a charming girl, naturally attractive, and modest and graceful in her manner. She and Amos became well acquainted at school, and as her home was not far from his he learned to appreciate her worth. She had a most charming voice, and would sing to the great delight of the family and friends. But when urged to sing in the choir it was to no avail, as she felt it would make jealousy in the end, and she closely guarded against it when at Church. The Stones had no children of their own and so at first they opposed the marriage, as in this arrangement their rainbow of sunshine, that she was, would be gone from them. But as Anna insisted they joined Mr. John Parker and gave them a grand wedding for the time.

They removed from Lexington in 1745, in which year "Amos Parker of Lexington, joiner," bought of "William Nichols of Holden, tanner, a tract in Holden of 65 acres with the buildings thereon." Thus he and brother Jonas were together again for a few years. It seems that they remained here until 1750, when he purchased an estate in Shrewsbury of Mr. Isaac Stone of Lexington. This deed dated 20 of Decem. 1750, granted Mr. Parker a farm of 100 acres, in part the same place later owned by Dr. Amos Parker. The amount paid was £206. To the deed are also attached the signatures of John Hancock* and Benjamin Muzzy, Jr., both of Lexington. Again, by a deed dated "in the twenty-second year of our Reign of George ye Second," he purchased seven acres of Nahum Ward of Shrewsbury. They were admitted to the Church at Shrewsbury in 1753. His brother, Andrew Parker, Jr., although living at different times in Lexington, Weston and Barre, visited frequently, and we find his signature attached to his brother's deeds. In addition to rearing his large family he accumulated a goodly estate, very creditable to his characteristic industry and prudence. At his decease his personal estate alone was appraised at £129.

He was a man of mind, very energetic and of strong physique. Very conscientious, with a strong firm mind of his own, and a moral, unimpeachable character, he well represented the type of the Parker family of Lexington at and before his time. He gave his children a careful and sturdy bringing up and they followed in his paths. While at work he allowed no talk except such as pertained to the work itself, for he said "Work and play cannot go together,—one spoils

Although there is not a Parker resident of Shrewsbury at the present time, there were others of the family who settled in the town much earlier than Amos. His uncle, John Parker, was settled in 1730; later removed to Framingham. He was followed by a distant relative, Stephen Parker, a native of Reading, who in 1735 bought the Robins farm of 71 acres, which adjoined the land of John Parker. Stephen remained in Shrewsbury, and of his children, Nehemiah Parker graduated at Harvard University, and in 1770 accepted a call as pastor from the first settlers of Hubbardston. Stephen and Amos Parker were aware of their relationship and were also intimate friends. Amos in 1770 purchased of Edward Parsons of Berwick, Me., 295 acres of land in Hubbardston, and two years later he, with Mr. Nathan How of Shrewsbury, purchased Great Farm, No. 1, in Hubbardston, which made him an exceedingly large landholder there. He thus provided farms for his sons.

* He must have been Rev. John Hancock, the second minister of Lexington, a minister of high ability and influence, and the grandfather of Gov. John Hancock, of Revolutionary fame.

the other. There is time enough for each." Thus, when not engaged, the boys joined all the more hearty in their sports, much to the satisfaction of Mr. Parker.

Amos Parker was a home man, quiet and undemonstrative. She, however, was not only an angel in her family, industrious, careful and attentive, but was a blessing to her neighbors and the town. She was here and there, assisting, helping or comforting all who were needy or afflicted. She was reverenced by every person in Shrewsbury, and when her funeral occurred in December, on a warm Indian Summer's day, the church held only a part of the great assemblage. A multitude escorted the body from the homestead to the church.

Shortly before her death she travelled horseback from Shrewsbury to Fitzwilliam, 60 miles, when at the age of 72! She stopped one night with her son Amos Parker in Hubbardston. Her grandson, of Fitzwilliam, who is now living, remembers her, and well recalls her visit. What a grand satisfaction it must have been to her to take into her lap the children of her many children and sing to them the sweet songs of her childhood! Her grandson also states that she had then the best voice he ever heard, and remembers some of the stories which she told him.

The family homestead in Shrewsbury, situated in a very excellent locality for scenery and health, may partially account for his large family of strong and rugged children, whose descendants are so numerous. The selection of this locality throws credit upon the Shrewsbury ancestor, Mr. Amos Parker of Lexington. It was a large farm of fertile land, situated just north of the town centre. A view of 30 miles is distinctly seen and seven distinct towns meet the eye, Marlborough, Northborough, Southborough, Westborough, Hopkinton, Framingham and Shrewsbury. Amos Parker was also a "joiner," a trade which he learned of his father in Lexington. A part of the front side of his original Shrewsbury home, built in 1750, is still well preserved. It includes the front door, the large antique latch and door cap, and is doing service as the front part of the continuous row of sheds which runs from house to barn. The house was rich in old-fashioned furniture, much of which still exists, scattered among his descendants. Around the open fireplace we can well imagine the times past at this homestead where halted many who, emigrating westward, sought the advice and knowledge of Mr. Parker. Here his brothers Thomas and Andrew often visited, before and after making their final settlements in Princeton and Barre. The farm is now smaller than formerly, houses having been erected on the east part. The appearance of the buildings is as they were when the estate was owned by Mr. Hollis Parker. The place is now carried on by Mr. Samuel Allen.

The following is taken from an interesting letter written by his youngest son, Rev. Frederick Parker, at Canterbury, N. H., 1798, regarding the family. It also related to the death of his brother Isaac Parker.

"At Portland, Bro. Isaac (with Br. Hollis, who accompanied him) walking with me feelingly observed the cause of gratitude for the prosperity of our family—he recounted to my fixed attention from what small beginnings the estate arose, the difficulties of dry years—a broken leg—and Sir I. Stone—but notwithstanding both our parents live with their 9 children—the brothers especially all provided for well to live, men of a pretty good share of sense and sound constitutions and 'no very mean one he said among them all,' that a *whole* family should make out so well and be so creditable and prosperous he thought rather singular. I know not why I write these things, unless because I intend to write not a short letter and 'tis much easiest to write upon those things which fancy is most busy in conjuring up to view.—Well do I remember the scene when I first knew sorrow, viz: at the death of our honored Father—to Isaac's lot it fell to be sitting by him, wiping from his brows the damp of death when he died—that night I slept or rather talked with him for late it was before we closed our eyes—He believed, he said, that our honoured Father was a man of *real Religion*, and one reason he particularly mentioned his often having overheard him in secret prayer; a hearty strong man in his day; went forward in his work and said 'Come boys' or at other times 'Follow me.' In a work infinitely more important we must sooner or later all 'follow' him to that land of spirits from which there is no return."

Out of ten children nine grew to maturity, the oldest and youngest being daughters, while all of the seven sons were in the Revolutionary War, more or less, except the youngest. He was the common ancestor of very numerous descendants, and these have won worthy laurels for themselves and their ancestors. He d. Dec. 23, 1790, at the age of 68 years. The widow Anna d. Nov. 18, 1799, at the age of 73.

Their children were:

25. Anna Parker, b. in Holden, Oct. 6, 1746; m. Dea. Jonas Stone of Shrewsbury.

26. Amos Parker, b. in Holden, Sept. 26, 1748; m. Lucy Robinson of Barre.

27. ISAAC PARKER, b. July 15, 1750; m. Margery Maynard of Westborough.

28. HOLLIS PARKER, b. Oct. 2, 1752: m. Louisa Bragg of Royalston.

29. ELISHA PARKER, b. Dec. 31, 1754; m. Sally Baker of Westborough.

30. EPHRAIM PARKER, b. Oct. 4, 1757; m. Abigail Baker of Royalston.

31. NAHUM PARKER, b. March 4, 1760; m. Mary Deeth of Gerry (now Phillipston).

32. FREDERICK PARKER, b. March 4, 1762; m. Susan Foster of Canterbury, N. H.

BETSEY PARKER, b. March 18. 1764. When but a child of towards three years of age, she one day went into the field wherein her father, Amos, was mowing. She stepped towards him, and speaking, picked some wild flowers, saying "Pretty flowers," and then went into the house and died. This occurred Aug. 20, 1766. This was a sad blow to the family, who loved their daughter dearly. and it also touched a tender chord in Mr. Parker's nature. Ever afterward in mowing and coming to this spot, he would stop, lean on his scythe, and with downcast countenance shed a tear, then turn around and leave that corner of the field to grow as it would. He held too sacred a feeling for those flowers to ever disturb them.

BETSEY PARKER, b. March 23, 1769; m. Amos Whitney of Worcester. They were farmers and lived northwest of the village. They had no issue.

10. **Thomas Parker** *(Andrew,[4] John,[3] Hananiah,[2] Thomas[1])*, third son of Andrew and Sarah (Whitney) Parker, was baptized in Lexington, Dec. 24. 1727; m. in Lexington, by Rev. Ebenezer Bridge, March 8, 1750, Jane Parrot, then of Chelmsford, b. 1729. Toward the opening of the Revolutionary War many records are found regarding him. He took an active interest in his country's welfare, being, like all his name in Lexington, firmly patriotic to the American cause. He lived upon a part of his father's homestead in the south part of the town, neighbor to Capt. John Parker, his cousin. He was quartermaster of the Lexington military Co. 1774.*

In the years 1776 and 1777 when the duties imposed upon the town officers were arduous and responsible, in conse-

*This is proven by the assessors' sheets of the highway tax rate of 1774, Capt. John Parker being then assessor.

quence of the peculiar situation of affairs, Mr. Parker was chosen each year selectman. What the town regarded as an important movement was the Lexington Declaration of Independence, which they drew up at this time. Thomas Parker was one of the 26 signers of this document, thus placing himself in open defiance against English rule, and pledging his assistance and future prospects to the Colonies. These patriots fully realized their responsibility in this act, knowing the fate which would await them in case King George should ever be able to punish his Colonial children. It seems that he was not with Capt. Parker's company at the Lexington fight. Tradition says he was ill at this time and was confined to the house. The British wantonly ransacked houses on and near their line of march. Two "redcoats" broke open the entrance to Mr. Parker's house and demanded of Jane, his wife, to be shown through the rooms. He had but one son and he, Corp. Ebenezer Parker, was doing service with his company. Thomas Parker was a tall and very large, broad shouldered man; he had great vitality and strength, and although sick was not helpless. He was of a strong family. Jonas Parker, who had been murdered by the British the morning of that day, was the strongest wrestler in the town. Amos Parker, the eldest brother, who was settled in Shrewsbury, is said to have been a remarkably strong man in his day. Mr. Parker's family was equal to the emergency. Apparently complying with the soldier's demands, she presently brought them into her husband's room. It seems that the daughter had meanwhile brought her father strong cord and he had quickly prepared himself. He seized them both and with ropes bound them tight. The tradition also says that he turned them over to the Colonial authorities. He was 48 years of age at this time.

The Parkers of these early times were industrious and prudent. By his characteristic foresight he dealt successfully in real estate and accumulated a respectable property. He sold his land in Lexington to his cousins there, also bought timber land in Shrewsbury, and new land in Hubbardston, formerly owned by his brother Amos. In 1777 he made the purchase of the estate in Princeton,* whereupon he with his son settled and made it their home. The grantor was Elisha Hedge, then of Marlborough.

"For and in consideration of the sum of Thirteen Hundred and Thirty pounds [over $6,000], well and truly paid by Thomas Parker of Lexington, gentleman, one certain tract or parsal of Land situate and being in Princeton containing Four Hundred Acres, together with the Road passing through the Same, it being the Black Grove farm, so called, and it being all the land which the sd Mr. Hedge ownes in Princeton."

No buildings are mentioned in the deed. He located the home upon the beautiful spot so familiar to the family as the old homestead. Here Mr. Parker's descendants are still living. This place was then, as now, a charming locality. It is an elevated region overlooking water close at hand and the West Sterling valley toward the east, while at the west Mount Wachusett stands noble and distinct, and picturesque Princeton centre lies nearly in the same direction. He soon added a few more hundred acres to the estate, a part of which he later sold out to his friends, thus regulating who his neighbors should be. Other Lexington families settled in Princeton in this way. The beautiful rich valley here, miles in extent, is a rich farming district. It was originally a part of the "Black Grove" farm; it now contains many valuable farms, and as many more dwellings. Thomas Parker's estate extended from Sterling line to Rutland line, and also more than a mile to the north of the homestead.

The small red house which was first erected upon the place, was after a number of years partially superseded by a large

*It is said that previous to his selection of the Princeton estate he thought very favorably of buying a large tract at "Valley Village," now West Boylston, including the valuable water-power there. A century's development has highly prospered this locality, and we may be apt to judge that his financial prospects at least would have been better had he selected this site. But this was not all-sufficient in Mr. Parker's esteem. He was a farmer, not a manufacturer, and the water-power at Princeton could run a saw-mill. He must attend constantly to his spiritual needs, and the Church at Princeton was favorable. Again, the land in Boylston was less in area and more in price, while the fact of its adjacent location to Worcester was of no weight then, as railroads were not thought of and Worcester was no more populous than the average town.

brick house adjoining the red one. This was used as a tavern by Thomas Parker and later by his son Ebenezer, while the original house continued duty as kitchen only. He purchased land in Rindge, N. H., in 1790, which he rented from year to year.

Thomas Parker was 50 years of age when he came to Princeton. Upon settling he purchased the meeting-house pew which was long used by his descendants. The deed, under date of 1788, shows that he, "Thomas Parker of Princeton, Gentleman," bought of John Bradley and wife of Holden, the one undivided half of a pew in the meeting-house in Princeton, situated in the southwest part of the body seat. He d. July 3, 1799. His widow Jane d. Aug. 17, 1814, aged 85. They were both interred in the pleasant family grave-yard at the homestead. His children were all b. in Lexington.

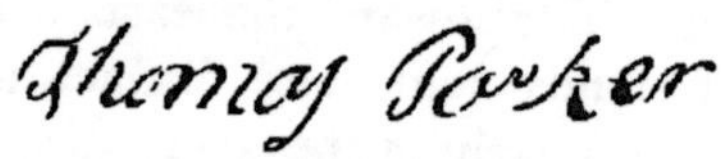

Their children were:

33. EBENEZER PARKER, b. Aug. 13, 1750; m. Dorcas Monroe of Lexington.

WILLIAM PARKER, bap. Dec. 29, 1751; d. young.

They buried two infant children, probably b. between William and Mary.

34. MARY PARKER, bap. July 13, 1760; m. Jonas Smith of Waltham.

11. Lucy Parker *(Andrew,[4] John,[3] Hananiah,[2] Thomas[1])*, dau. of Andrew and Sarah (Whitney) Parker, baptized in Lexington, April 4. 1731; m. March 24, 1750. Joshua Mead, b. Nov. 9, 1715, son of David and Hannah (Smith) Mead of Lexington. This David was b. in Cambridge, 1678, son of David and Hannah (Warren) Mead, and m. in Watertown, Hannah Smith, in which town he lived before coming to Lexington. They were admitted to the Church Dec. 8, 1751. Though Joshua Mead united with the Church in Lexington, and a part of his children were baptized there, he resided within the limits of Waltham. His uncle was Hopestill Mead, whose dau. Abigail, bap. Aug. 30, 1713; m. Oct. 23. 1729. Nathaniel Jennison of Weston, and whose dau. Abigail m. Andrew Parker of Lexington. Joshua Mead d. in Waltham, March 31, 1794.

Their children were:

1. LUCY MEAD, bap. Jan. 19, 1752; d. Dec., 1752.
2. MARY MEAD, b. May 1, 1753; m. Dec. 3, 1772, Abraham Whitney.
3. MOSES MEAD, b. Dec. 2, 1754; m. May 22, 1777, Lizzy Viles, last of the 13 children of John and Suzanna (Bemis) Viles of Waltham. He was in the Revolutionary war. Children:
   - I. MOSES, b. March 7, 1778.
   - II. DAVID, b. Oct. 23, 1779.
   - III. SUZANNA. b. March 22, 1781.
   - IV. ELIZABETH, b. Feb. 20, 1783; d. Sept. 28. 1800.
   - V. JACOB. b. Jan. 20, 1785; d. Jan. 9, 1786.
   - VI. ABNER, b. March 19, 1787.
   - VII. NATHAN, b. March 29, 1789.
   - VIII. SOPHIA, b. Feb. 20, 1792.
   - IX. WATSON, b. March 14, 1794.
   - X. CLARISSA, b. Aug. 27, 1796; d. Oct. 3, 1800.
4. LYDIA MEAD, b. May 17, 1756; m. June 1, 1775, Joseph Adams of Newton.
5. ELIJAH MEAD, b. Sept. 30, 1758; m. Abigail ——. Children:
   - I. POLLY, b. Sept. 25, 1779.
   - II. BETSEY, b. July 30, 1781.
   - III. ISAAC, b. May 7, 1783.
   - IV. SAMUEL, b. May 14, 1785.
   - V. LYDIA, b. June 20, 1787.
   - And perhaps NABBY, bap. July 1, 1787.
6. JACOB MEAD, b. Oct. 30, 1760; d. Sept. 14, 1816. By wife Polly had:
   - I. JACOB, drowned Jan. 9, 1796.
   - II. JACOB, b. Aug. 10, 1797; d. Sept., 1800.
   - III. Child, d. April 5, 1799. aged 4 weeks.
   - IV. JACOB, b. May 3, 1802.
   - V. GEORGE MURDOCK, b. Aug. 22, 1804.
   - VI. JOHN, b. April 17, 1807.
   - VII. CHARLES, b. April 4, 1810.
   - VIII. MARY, b. Oct. 3, 1812; d. 1813.
   - IX. JESSE, b. Sept. 20, 1815.

12. Dea. Andrew Parker, Jr. *(Andrew,[4] John,[3] Hananiah,[2] Thomas[1])*, youngest surviving son of Andrew and Sarah (Whitney) Parker, was b. in Lexington, April 11, 1738; bap. April 16, 1738. His diary is in preservation at Worcester. In it he inscribed these words:

"I, Andrew Parker, was born in the year 1738, in April, the eleventh day thereof—my wife born in April 22 day, 1737, one year older than I, lacking eleven days.

"I moved from Lexington to Weston about ye middle of April, 1763. then Last Week in August I came to work at Rutland District & Prepared to move my family. I went down & brought up my family the last week in November.

"I took possession of my house at Rutl^d^ District ye 8 day of December 1763.

"I Andrew Parker was given in marriage in ye year 1759 on the 29 day of November."

His wife was Abigail Jennison of Weston, dau. of Nathaniel. She was twin sister of Sarah. Her mother was Abigail Mead. See Mead family, page 61. Her father, Nathaniel Jennison, was b. April 5, 1709, son of Samuel and Mary (Stearns) Jennison of Watertown, the fifth of their family of 11 children. He, Samuel, was son of Ensign Samuel, and the latter was son of Robert Jennison, one of the earliest proprietors of Watertown, and who was the common ancestor of the name. The intention of marriage of Andrew Parker, Jr., of Lexington, and Abigail Jennison of Weston, was entered upon the records of Weston April 8, 1759. They made their peace with the Church in Lexington, April 20, 1760, and were dismissed to the Church of Rutland, May 10, 1765. "Rutland District," then a part of Rutland, was what is now the town of Barre, it being incorporated as a separate town in 1774. We find that her brother had previously removed to the district, as on Aug. 4, 1763, Nathaniel Jennison, then of Rutland District, sold to "Andrew Parker of Weston," 63 acres of land in said district, bounded at length upon the west "from an upper to ye lower fording of Moose Brook, and is a part of Great Farm No. XXVIII." He later, in 1777, purchased of Ichabod Robinson 56½ acres of new land "lying at the Northwest of the Meeting House Lot."

Favorable mention is made of Andrew Parker in Mr. Edwin Woods's Historical Discourse of Barre, in which he says:

"There soon came to be associated with the town Dea. John Mason, Nathan Sparhawk, Asa Hapgood and Dea. Andrew Parker. The last named came from Lexington, and possessed many of the traits exhibited by his blood relation of Revolutionary fame, Capt. John Parker, and also the late distinguished reformer and preacher, Theodore Parker. Under the management of these men the district advanced rapidly in population and prosperity. Forests were felled, roads were opened, streams were spanned with bridges, saw-mills turned out lumber, houses went up, harvests ripened and on every hand were signs of thrift which made all hearts glad. In the important convention at Cambridge, 1777, for the purpose of framing a constitution of government, Barre was represented by those clear sighted and trusted men, always foremost when any grave and public service was to be rendered, John Mason, Esq., Lieut. Andrew Parker and Lieut. Asa Hapgood."

Subsequently Mr. Parker served upon an amendment committee. He was one of the five chosen Committee of Correspondence for Barre during the year previous to the outbreak of the Revolution. A full account of his public service would be too tedious. But his able assistance was given at the time it was most needed; it was when our ancestors, with cool heads and stout hearts, dared to be their own masters, and unitedly risked all in the common cause. Then they laid the foundations of government of this now greatest of nations, and "built better than they knew." He was selectman 1783, 1787, town clerk 1787, moderator of town meetings 15 times, on committee to remonstrate against loan by bills of credit, Dec. 10, 1777; on committee to enlarge common and draw plan of new meeting-house, May 9, 1785; on Shays rebellion grievance committee, Jan. 6, 1787: on school district committee, Jan. 25, 1790.

He was very intimate with his brothers, Thomas Parker who lived in Princeton and Amos Parker of Shrewsbury. He visited often and his name is found attached as witness to his brothers' most valuable papers. In his pocket diary, already referred to, is a reference to a transaction with his brother in Lexington, he probably little thinking that his odd statement would be preserved for centuries—

"Oct. ye 25, 1768. I bought two heifers of brother Jonas for which I was to give four pounds eight shillings, and broke my shins a coming home with them."

Our ancestors for many generations have possessed a good knowledge of that important trade in their day, woodworking. A woodworker was called a joiner. All farm implements and most of the common machinery were then made of wood. Thus a very extensive and thorough knowledge was required to rank well in this art. In Barre Dea. Parker continued this vocation during his spare time. He made wagons and all farm implements, house furniture and was expert in making spinning wheels. Probably most of the spinning wheels used in Barre—that indispensable machine—were made by Dea. Parker. One of his make has been preserved by the family. It was made at an early date, perhaps in Lexington, and he gave it to his dau. Abigail in her outfit for marriage. It remained at the Allen homestead after Mrs. Allen's decease, passing into the possession of the dau., Mrs. Elizabeth Carter. It is in perfect preservation, although it was used by mother and dau. for over 80 years, and its age necessarily exceeds 100 years. It is fondly cherished as a souvenir of Dea. Andrew Parker, as it properly deserves to be.

Dea. Andrew Parker was a devout man. It is said that before he removed from Lexington he was an officer in the Church there. When in Barre, for several years he and his family were obliged to go to Rutland, ten miles, in order to attend church. This he traversed, probably horseback, until sufficient families had settled in Rutland District to build a church. Dea. Parker helped build the first church in Barre. He was made its deacon. He was a conscientious man and entertained views of his own accordingly. In one instance he warned the minister, it is said, that he would not pay him anything for preaching doctrine in which he did not believe. In his diary he made notes of many of the first sermons preached in Rutland District (now Barre), and in its midst is a treatise on religion of great length. His homestead was in the northwestern part of the town. As his farm extended south from Petersham line to the "lower fordway of Moose Brook," it seems that his house must have been situated on the road from Barre to Petersham, a short distance south of the junction of this brook and the Petersham road.

One-sixth of the population of the town of Barre served in the Revolutionary war. In 1774 Dea. Andrew Parker was chosen lieutenant of the first company of militia. He must have seen some service, although no records are known to exist. He was one of the committee who, previous to the Revolution, officiated for the town in changing its name from Hutchinson to Barre. The name of Hutchinson, the Tory, was very disgusting to the patriots of this town of liberty.

"The committee who had the petition in charge was made up from the best minds in town—men commanding respect for their attainments and force of character."—*History of Worcester County.*

It seems that his wife Abigail d. soon after 1766, thus living but a few years in Barre. He m. (2) Mary ———. By Mary he had son Artemas Parker, born 20 years after the birth of his previous child. Andrew Parker died in May, 1791. The widow Mary m. again, this time to Aaron Chamberlain of Chelmsford, who was a gentleman of education and means. They lived in Chelmsford until 1816, when they removed to Swanton, Vt. Mr. Chamberlain was deceased before Nov. 4, 1822. She may have spent the remainder of her days with her son Artemas.

"This inventory, apprized at the present true value in Lawful money all the Estate whereof Dea^{n} Andrew Parker late of Barre, Deceased, died seized and possessed of that has been shown to us by Mr Abel Loring Ad^{r} of s^{d} Estate viz:"

Among the items were the following:

"The Farm with the Buildings thereon	£270-00-0
One Pew in the meeting-house	8-02-0
One horse stable at the meeting-house	3-00-00
One old horse £2-8, one mare & Colt £12.	14-08-00
Four Cows and a Calf	15-15-00
One three year old heifer	3-15-00
Two heifers two year old—Two Yearling heifers and two Calfs	8-02-00
Nineteen Sheep and Lambs and three Swine	9-06-03
Three suits of clothes, one gown, cap, shirts, stocks, stockins, mits, two pears boots	6-07-03

One pear Shoe Buckels 2s. 6d. One pear Knee Do. & Shock buckels 5/ 7-06-00

One pear Spectacles 9-00

Four beds, bedding, bedsteads, furniture, coverleds, blankets, etc. 15-09-01

One Timepiece £1-16. One Desk and Bookcase 20/ and one Case of Draws 15/ 3-11-00

Old chests and tables 1-02-00

One Candle stand, three armed chairs, and twenty seven small Do. 3-02-10

18 Puter Plaits 15/ old Puter Dishes 5/3 four Platers and eight Plaits 13/8 1-13-11

Two Brass Kettles £1-10 old Brass ware 3/ handirons 14/ fier Peals & tongs 7/ Crains & hooks 8/ tosting & Grediron 4/6 Case knives & forks 3/ Candlesticks 2/ Snufers /6 Stilerds 1/ Two pear of bellowses 4/ Two Seves 1/6 two brushes and brooms 2/4 2-13-08

Glass Bottles, tea Canester, warming pan, teapot, cups, saucers, brown Earthen ware, five silver tea spoons, plates and small vials 30-13-00

One honed Razor and Box 1/10 Gun and Bagnut 12/ and Sword 1/6 Two woolen wheels 8/6 one Lamb and tackler £2 One flaxcomb 24/ 3-12-06

One Cradle and Scales 3/8 two Cheese tubs, one churn and six pails 12/10 16-06

Thirteen Barrels of Cyder £3-18. twenty one barrels 36/ three meat tubs 4/6 and four meal chests 10/ 6-08-06

A Lining wheel, 30wt of wool 40/ and six baskets 6/ 2-13-00

One womans saddle 30/ one mans Do. 12/ Pillion 6/ Saddle bag 12/ Bridles and Sirsingle 12/ and three mealbags 4/ 3-16-00

Three old Bibles with a number of other Books £2-36/ 3-16-00

Timber on hand £3-4-6. The one half of a Cyder mill £2-5-0. 5-09-06

Meet in the tub £2-10-0 Grain on hand 12/4. Malt 7/6. 3-09-10

seven wheels partly made 27/ four Sets of Irons for Linen wheels 8/ and three Sets of Screwcutters with the other Shop tools £11-12-0 13-07-00

Carts & wheels 30/ two plows 25/ ox yoke 5/ horse 3-00-00

tackler 19/6 Sled 2/ Sickels 2/ Iron forks 5/ Raks 1-08-06

3/10 Grass Cythes and tackler 10/2 Grindston 6/ 1-00-02

and Crosscut Saw 4/6. 4-06"

Other items accompany the inventory, among them being a score of notes receivable, making a sum total of £468-13s.-1d.-3far., a very respectable estate for his time. It was appraised by Isaac Toby, Joel Bent and Timothy Hastings.

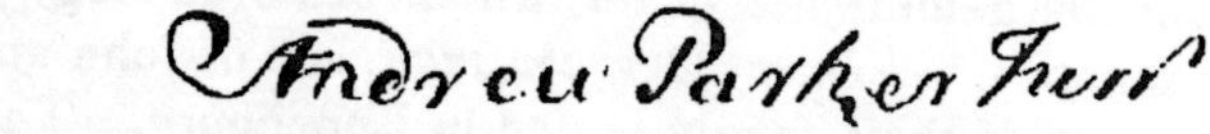

From a family record is copied the following:

"The Division of the Estate of Dea. Andrew Parker of Barre. 1st—The widows thirds to Mrs. Mary Parker. The remainder to be divided into five parts—

One Part to Capt. Smith.
One Part to Mrs. Tobey.
One Part to Capt. Nathan Allen.
One Part to Sally Mayhew.
One Part to Artemas Parker."

The first two children were born in Lexington, remainder in Barre. The following is copied from the deacon's diary *verbatim:*

"My Daughter Rhoda, born on ye 19 day of June 1760, about eleven oclock forenoon.

"My Daughter Abigail, born on the 29 day of January 1762, about 12 oclock daytime.

"My Daughther Sally, born ye 17 day of March 1765, at one oclock afternoon.

"My Daughter Bettey, born the 13 day of January, 1766, about 4 oclock afternoon."

ARTEMAS PARKER, by his 2nd wife Mary, b. Aug. 5, 1786, thus 20 years junior to his last sister.

His five children all lived to maturity and married.

35. RHODA PARKER, m. Capt. Joseph Smith of Barre.
36. ABIGAIL PARKER, m. Nathan Allen of Barre.
37. SALLY PARKER, m. Jonathan Mayhew of Phillipston.
38. BETTEY PARKER, m. Paul Tobey.
39. ARTEMAS PARKER, m. ——— Spaulding.

13. Keziah Parker *(Andrew,[4] John,[3] Hananiah,[2] Thomas[1])*, dau. of Andrew and Sarah (Whitney) Parker, bap. in Lexington, June 1, 1740; m. June 21, 1759, Joseph Wyman of Lunenburg. Her intention of marriage is recorded upon the records of Lunenburg with date "May ye 4th Anno Domini 1759," to Silas Wyman, brother of Joseph, but she m. in June, Joseph Wyman. She removed to Lunenburg, where her husband was an active man. He was a farmer, and she lived in Lunenburg until her death, which occurred Aug. 7, 1776. He was b. in Woburn, Oct. 27, 1734, son of John and Rebecca, who with their family settled in Lunenburg. This John[4] was son of John[3] and Rebecca of Woburn, who was son of John[2] and grandson of John[1], a Lieut. and tanner in Woburn, the originator of the line in America. Joseph Wyman m. 2nd Sarah Allen.

Their children were:

DAVID WYMAN, b. at Lunenburg, April 29, 1762.
JOSEPH WYMAN, b. at Lunenburg, April 3, 1764.
OLIVER WYMAN, b. at Lunenburg, March 26, 1766.
THOMAS WYMAN, b. at Lunenburg, Sept. 27, 1768.
SARAH WYMAN, b. at Lunenburg, Feb. 27, 1771.
JOHN WYMAN, b. at Lunenburg, Oct. 14, 1760.
ELIZABETH WYMAN, b. at Lunenburg, Nov. 10, 1773.

14. Anna Parker (*Josiah*,[4] *John*,[3] *Hananiah*,[2] *Thomas*[1]), b. in Lexington, Sept. 9, 1719, dau. of Josiah and Anna (Stone) Parker, m. in Lexington, Nov. 6, 1737, Benjamin Smith, Jr., b. in Lexington, July 20, 1714, son of Benjamin and Martha (Comee) Smith.* Benjamin, Jr., was the road surveyor. She d. a widow in Waltham, June 10, 1768. Benjamin, Sr., was for a long time very popular with the townsmen, being often elected to public office. He was 12 years on the board of selectmen. He was the son of Thomas and this Thomas was the son of Thomas who was born in England and came to this country in 1635 with his father John. The original ancestry is found to be the same as that of Jonas Smith of Waltham, who m. 1775, Mary Parker of Lexington and settled in Princeton.

---

*The Smith family was at the outset so common in all settlements as to make it a difficult task for the genealogist, but through continued research much has been effected in this line. The best authority, and to whom we are the most indebted for the work, is the compiler of the *Watertown Genealogies*. The writer is indebted to *Hudson's History of Lexington* for much regarding the issues of the Smith and Monroe families which now follow.

Their children were:

1. SOLOMON SMITH, b. Oct. 27, 1738; d. April 16, 1741.

2. BENJAMIN SMITH, b. March 7, 1741; m. Mary Lee. They were admitted to the Church in Lexington, June 24, 1768. They had the following children b. in Lexington:

   I. ANNA SMITH, b. April 2, 1770; m. Abijah Wyman of Burlington.

   II. BENJAMIN SMITH, b. Sept. 1, 1774. He went to Townsend. There he m. a Turner. He was killed by the upsetting of a cart.

   III. DAVID SMITH, b. Sept. 29, 1776. He went to Ashby and m. a Foster.

3. ANNA SMITH, b. March 31, 1743; m. William Monroe, b. in Lexington, Oct. 28, 1742, son of William and Sarah (Mason) Monroe. She was a lady of great worth, which was well reciprocated by her husband. Her choice was one of the most esteemed and prominent men of hardy Lexington—Col. William Monroe. Six children were born unto them, after which she d. Jan. 2, 1781, aged 38. William Monroe was orderly sergeant of Capt. Parker's Co. in 1775; it was under him that the guard was posted at Mr. Clarke's house on the evening of the 18th of April, 1775; and he paraded the men on the common the next morning in the very face of British troops. The services which he performed in the opening of the Revolution were followed up by other services in the progress of the war. He was a lieutenant in the Northern army at the taking of Burgoyne in 1777. He was a prominent citizen and filled important town offices. He was selectman nine years and represented the town two years. He was a colonel in the militia and marched towards Springfield during Shays' rebellion, but the dispersement of the insurgents enabled him to return home in a short time. Col. Monroe kept the public house long known as the Monroe Tavern. This is an important relic of the many historical preservations of Lexington. The house was built before 1700 and looks well to-day. Here the British regaled themselves, and committed many outrages on the 19th of April; here they shot down in cold blood John Raymond, who was about leaving the house; here Gen. Washington dined in 1789, when he visited the first battle-field of the Revolution, and here the house is well preserved to-day and still occupied by descendants of the Monroe family, who cordially show the old portion of the tavern to all

interested in its history.* An excellent steel portrait of Col. William Monroe is given in Hudson's History of Lexington. He d. Oct. 30, 1827, aged 85. The Monroes of Lexington did all they could to help the struggling colonies and gained a well-earned renown. Col. William was brother to Capt. Edmund Monroe of Col. Bigelow's regiment, and he served all through the war until the battle of Monmouth, where he was killed. They were sons of William and Sarah (Mason) Monroe. The latter William was son of Ensign William Monroe, son of William Monroe from Scotland. the ancestor of all the Monroes of Lexington. Their children were:

i. William Monroe, b. May 28, 1768; m. Susan B. Grinnell of New Bedford. He was killed at Richmond, Va., by the upsetting of a stage in 1814.

ii. Anna Monroe, b. May 9, 1771; m. Sept. 20, 1798, Rev. William Muzzy of Sullivan. N. H. She d. in Lexington, 1850, aged 70. He was graduated at Harvard College 1793, and was ordained at Sullivan, N. H., Feb. 7, 1798. He left in 1828 and returned to Lexington with his family, where he d. April 16, 1835. They had five children b. in Sullivan, two of whom d. in 1814 of the spotted fever. Their children were:

1. William Muzzy, b. June 30, 1804; lived in Philadelphia.
2. Emily Muzzy, b. Nov., 1800; d. unm.
3. Abby Ann Muzzy, b. June 15, 1806; m. Dea. William Brigham and resided in Lexington. Their only child was Laura Muzzy Brigham, b. July 20, 1836.

iii. Sarah Monroe, b. Oct. 21, 1773; m. Jonathan Wheelock of Concord. She d. aged about 77.

iv. Lucinda Monroe, b. April 9, 1776; d. unm. June 2, 1863, aged 87.

v. Jonas Monroe, b. June 11, 1778; m. March 17, 1814, Abigail C. Smith, dau. of Joseph and Lucy (Stone) Smith, descendant of the ancient Smith line of Lexington. Jonas Monroe was a lieutenant in the United

*At the old Monroe Tavern there were exhibited on Nov. 5, 1889, the 100th anniversary of Washington's visit to Lexington, many articles of historic interest. Among the articles shown was the wedding furniture of William and Anna Monroe, to wit: Round mahogany table, two arm chairs, looking glass, hat tree, britannia teapot, spinning-wheel, rush-bottomed chair, pewter candlestick, copper sauce pan, block used during Revolution for stamping fabrics, iron fire-dogs, warming-pan, "loggerheads" for making flip, lemon squeezer for making punch.

States Dragoons in 1807, resigned his commission, and on the breaking out of the War of 1812 was commissioned as lieutenant of infantry and was engaged for a short time in the recruiting service. He kept the "Monroe Tavern," and was extensively and favorably known to the travelling public. He was drowned at Somerville, while bathing, July 2, 1860, aged 82. His widow d. April 4, 1861, aged 68. Their children were:

1. William Henry Monroe, b. March 2, 1815. He is doing business in Philadelphia.
2. Harriet Monroe, b. Nov. 25, 1816. She is unm.
3. Abby Smith Monroe, b. Aug. 28, 1819; d. Dec. 21, 1822.
4. James S. Monroe, b. June 6, 1824; m. Alice B. Phinney. He resided in Lexington and had three sons.

VI. EDMUND MONROE, b. Oct. 29, 1780; m. (1) Harriett Downes, (2) Lydia Downes, (3) Sophia Sewall. He was a broker in Boston. He d. April 17, 1865.

4. MARTHA SMITH, b. April 19, 1745; m. May 27, 1771, Ebenezer Monroe, b. Nov. 15, 1744, son of Robert and Anna (Stone) Monroe. The father, Robert, was a soldier in the French War; was the standard bearer at the taking of Louisburg in 1758, and was also in the service in 1762. He was ensign in Capt. Parker's Co., and fell, one of the first victims of British oppression, April 19, 1775, right in his native town, after having served England so faithfully and well. Ebenezer Monroe was enrolled with Parker's patriots, and was in the battle of Lexington in 1775, and was also in the campaign of the Jerseys in 1776. He d. Aug. 22, 1826, aged 82; she d. Oct. 13, 1834, aged 86. Their children were:

I. PATTY MONROE, b. Feb. 19, 1772; m. Dec. 25, 1804, Isaac Pierce of Waltham.

II. EBENEZER MONROE, b. Feb. 2, 1777; d. June 6, 1798, aged 21.

III. ESTHER MONROE, b. Oct., 1783; m. Jan. 19, 1806, David Tuttle, b. in Winchendon, Dec. 2, 1782, son of Jedediah, a Revolutionary veteran. She d. in Lexington, Oct. 14, 1809, aged 26, and left no issue.

IV. JOHN MONROE, b. April 28, 1785; m. Dec. 11, 1811, Charlotte Bacon of Woburn. He d. Feb. 17, 1865, aged 79. Their children were:

1. John Harrison Monroe, b. June 3, 1813, who lived at Fall River.
2. Charles Henry Monroe, b. Aug. 10, 1814; d. at Buffalo, N. Y., July 17, 1850.

3. Harriet Monroe, b. April 29, 1816; d. Feb. 2, 1835.
4. Ebenezer Monroe, b. Dec. 3, 1817; m. Margaret M. Wilson; d. Jan. 5, 1868, aged 50, and had children: Julia Maria and Robert.
5. Jonas Monroe, b. Sept. 10, 1819; d. Aug. 15, 1843.
6. Lavina Monroe, b. Oct. 16, 1821; m. April 4, 1839, Galen Allen; resided at Lexington; he was selectman; she d. April 22, 1865, and their children were: Harriett A., Annette A., John G., Lavinia M., Jonas M.
7. Oliver Monroe, b. April 10, 1825; d. May 4, 1857.
8. Charlotte Monroe, b. March 28, 1827; m. George Mulliken; she d. Dec. 8, 1861; she had five children, viz.: Charlotte M., d.; George F., d.; Charles Henry; Clarence M.; Harriett M., d.

5. ESTHER SMITH, b. April 1, 1751.

6. ESTHER SMITH, b. Dec. 26, 1753; m. Simeon Snow of Holden, and d. Jan. 14, 1780.

7. DAVID SMITH, b. Aug. 15, 1756. He was a member of Capt. Parker's Co.

8. THOMAS SMITH, b. July 24, 1760; m. Oct. 3, 1782, Sarah Taylor of Charlestown, b. March 12, 1760; he d. Aug. 11, 1807. Their children were:

I. SARAH SMITH, b. Oct. 17, 1783; m. John Underwood, second cousins, as their great-great-grandfather was Lt. Josiah Parker. See Underwood, page 76. Their children were:

1. Mary Underwood, d. 1814.
2. Napoleon Underwood.
3. Abigail Underwood, m. Nov. 22, 1836, John Fillebrown of West Cambridge.
4. Mary Underwood, bap. May 21, 1815.
5. Sarah Underwood, b. Sept. 4, 1817; d. young.
6. Joseph Underwood, bap. Jan. 24, 1819.
7. Sarah Underwood, bap. July 9, 1820; m. Feb. 9, 1843, John A. Tufts of Cambridge.
8. Nathan Underwood, bap. Aug. 17, 1823.

II. ABIGAIL SMITH, b. March 30, 1785; m. Sept. 27, 1809, David Tuttle. They probably removed from town.

III. THOMAS SMITH, b. June 12, 1788; d. Aug. 12, 1809, unm.

IV. WILLIAM TAYLOR SMITH, b. Aug. 3, 1789; m. May 27, 1812, Cynthia Child of Gardner; no issue. They were both living 1868.

V. CHARLES SMITH, b. July 27, 1791; m. Hannah Hammond.

VI. PATTY SMITH, b. Aug. 10, 1793; m. Sept. 27, 1810, David Tuttle, her cousin Esther's widower, as his second wife; she d. Dec. 15, 1816, aged 32, and he m. again. Their children were:

1. Esther Tuttle, b. Aug. 3, 1812; m. 1833, Caleb S. Tuttle, and settled in Alton, Ill.
2. Abigail Tuttle, b. Aug. 2, 1814; m. Dec. 29, 1835, Jonathan S. Parker of Lexington.

VII. JONAS LEONARD SMITH, b. June 11, 1795; d. March 16, 1801.

VIII. LARKIN SMITH, b. Oct. 15, 1797; m. Lucy S. Smith, dau. of Jonas.

IX. EBENEZER R. SMITH, b. Dec. 3, 1799; m. Almira Reed; she d. 1860, aged 56. Their children were:

1. Sarah E. Smith, b. Oct. 27, 1829; m. April 23, 1851, Edmund Reed of Burlington.
2. Eustis R. Smith, b. March 6, 1832; d. Dec. 10, 1832.
3. Almira J. Smith, b. Oct. 1, 1833; d. Nov. 22, 1834.
4. Almira J. Smith, b. Oct. 24, 1835.
5. Eustis Reed Smith, b. June 30, 1839.
6. Octavia Smith, b. July 16, 1841.

X. JONAS LEONARD SMITH, b. April 10, 1803; m. Sarah Cowley of Watertown. They had a child who d. young. He d. Dec. 10, 1845.

15. Deliverance Parker (*Josiah,[4] John,[3] Hananiah,[2] Thomas[1]*), b. in Lexington, May 28, 1721, dau. of Lt. Josiah and Anna (Stone) Parker; m. in Lexington, April 7, 1737, Marrett Monroe, b. in Lexington, Dec. 6, 1713, son of Lt. John of Lexington and last in a family of ten children. This John was however the eldest of the ancestor William Monroe's family of 12 children. John Monroe and others had 900 acres of land granted to them in 1735 for services rendered in the Indian fight at Lamprey River, June 6, 1690. Marrett Monroe was selectman. They resided near the common, in the house now occupied by the family of John Hudson. He and wife Deliverance became parents of a large and sturdy family of the Monroe name. His will, dated Feb. 18, 1789, and proved May 1, 1798, mentions wife Deliverance, sons Josiah, Nathan and Thaddeus, and daughters Rachel, Mary Underwood, Bethia, Deliverance Winship, Elizabeth Buckman and a child of dau. Ann Nurse, deceased.

Their children were:

1. RACHEL MONROE, b. Nov. 29, 1737; d. unm. in Boston, where she lived.
2. JOSIAH MONROE, b. June 29, 1742; d. June 12, 1743.
3. JOSIAH MONROE, b. Feb. 12, 1745; m. Nov. 15, 1768, Suzan Fitch of Bedford. He was in the French War in 1762. He also served three months in the Jerseys in 1776. He then entered the Continental line and served two and a half years. After the close of the war he drew land in what was afterward Ohio. He settled in Marietta in that State, where he was for a time postmaster. He had at least one child b. in Lexington, viz., Suzanna, bap. Nov. 10, 1771. They had another dau. and a son b. in Bedford before he moved to Ohio.
4. NATHAN MONROE, b. Aug. 9, 1747; m. Oct. 3, 1769, Elizabeth Harrington, b. Sept. 17, 1750, dau. of Henry and Sarah (Laughton) Harrington of Lexington. He was a member of Col. Parker's minute-men and took part in the battle of Lexington 1775. He succeeded to his father's homestead, residing on Monument Street, where Mr. John Hudson now resides. His house received several balls, which were taken out subsequently when the house was repaired. She d. Dec. 24, 1812. Their children were:

    i. DOLLY MONROE, b. Nov. 18, 1769; m. Jan. 28, 1788, Elijah Pierce, b. Jan. 1, 1765, son of Ephraim of Waltham. They resided in Woburn, where he d. aged 54.

    ii. ARETHUSA MONROE, b. March 10, 1773; m. June 20, 1793, Capt. William Fox of Woburn. They resided on the West Side in Woburn, neighbors to her Parker relatives. They had nine children:

    1. William Fox, b. Jan. 22, 1794.
    2. Celenda Fox, b. Nov. 11, 1795.
    3. Samuel Fox, b. June 11, 1799.
    4. Elizabeth Fox, b. June 14, 1801.
    5. Warren Fox, b. Jan. 16, 1804; m. in Woburn, May 17, 1827, Eliza Richardson Parker.
    6. Dorcas Fox, b. May 11, 1806.
    7. Thomas Fox, b. May 14, 1808.
    8. Martha Fox, b. April 22, 1810.
    9. John Fox, b. July 29, 1812.

    iii. BETSEY MONROE, b. April 5, 1776; m. March 20, 1798, Munson Johnson, who came from Woburn to Lexington in 1795. It is said he was son of Francis Johnson of Woburn. They had two children b. in Lexington, viz., Charlotte Johnson and Adelia Johnson.

IV. JOHN MONROE, b. June 15, 1778; m. —— Macy of Nantucket, where they settled.

V. NATHAN MONROE, b. Oct. 23, 1780; removed to Concord; m. Susanna Loring, b. in Lexington, June 30, 1784, dau. of Joseph Loring, a Revolutionary veteran who saw very hard service. They lived in Concord, where he d. Their children were:

1. Elbridge Monroe, b. in Lexington, July 28, 1804.
2. Nathan Monroe, b. in Concord, July 28, 1808.
3. Jonas Clarke Monroe, b. in Lincoln, Sept. 22, 1812.
4. James Monroe, b. in Concord, Feb. 27, 1817.

VI. JONATHAN MONROE, b. May 26, 1783; m. Feb. 13, 1812, Rhoda Johnson, dau. of Frederick and Rhoda (Reed) Johnson. She d. July 19, 1865, aged 72. He d. Dec. 4, 1867, aged 85. Their children were:

1. William Monroe, b. Dec. 17, 1812; m. Dec., 1846, Elvira Merriam of Concord, dau. of Joseph Merriam. They reside in Southbridge.
2. Elizabeth Monroe, b. March 21, 1814; m. June 7, 1839, Francis Johnson of Woburn, now Winchester, b. April 18, 1813, son of Maj. Francis and Mehetable (Parker) Johnson. They were fourth cousins, as it so happened that the great-great grandfather of each was Lt. Josiah Parker of Lexington. (See page 43.) Their child was:
   1. Elizabeth Johnson, b. in Winchester, Sept. 19, 1841; resides at Lexington.
3. Josiah Monroe, b. Oct. 21, 1818; m. Oct. 10, 1847, Adeline Dodge of Boston. They reside in Roxbury.
4. Faustina Monroe, b. Feb. 1, 1821; m. June 12, 1859, Frederick Stimpson.

VII. POLLY MONROE, b. March 11, 1785; m. June 13, 1811, Thomas Hunnewell of Charlestown.

VIII. DORCAS MONROE, b. March 31, 1788; m. Nov. 29, 1810, Leonard Brown, b. Jan. 3, 1788, son of James of Lexington. They lived in Lexington. Their children were:

1. Elizabeth Brown, b. June 15, 1811; d. March 2, 1820.
2. Mary Brown, b. May 9, 1814; d. March 3, 1820.
3. Leonard Brown, b. March 19, 1818; d. Sept. 4, 1819.
4. Leonard Brown, b. Feb. 24, 1821; m. Sarah Ann Goodnow of Stow, and resides in Lowell.
5. Elizabeth Brown, b. March 8, 1823; m. Elias V. Blodgett.
6. Mary Brown, b. July 30, 1825; m. George Patch of Littleton.
7. Hiram Brown, b. July 20, 1827; m. Cynthia Farrar of Waltham; resides in Arlington.
8. Nathan Brown, b. Feb 8, 1830; m. March 7, 1852, Hannah E. Fiske.

IX. THADDEUS MONROE, b. Sept. 14, 1790; settled in Quincy, Ill.

X. HARRIS MONROE, b. May 29, 1793; d. in Dedham, 1829.

5. MARY MONROE, b. March 3, 1749; m. March 21, 1771, Joseph Underwood, b. in Lexington, April 30, 1749, son of Joseph. He seems to have been a worthy member of the Underwood family. He was among that brave band who stood up with Capt. Parker, April 19, 1775; he also marched with the detachment to Cambridge, May 10, and also June 17, 1775. They were admitted to the Church, March 22, 1772. He d. Feb. 27, 1829, aged 80. She d. July 10, 1802. They had nine children; many of them d. young, and among the remainder were:

JOSEPH UNDERWOOD, bap. July 5, 1772; m. March 2, 1800, Eusebia Harrington; was selectman, and d. without issue, Sept. 6, 1845.

POLLY UNDERWOOD, bap. Dec. 7, 1777; m. March 26, 1798, Jonas Smith, son of Joseph, and one of a family of 13. Their children were:

1. Mary Monroe Smith, m. John C. Brackett of Woburn.
2. Lucy Stone Smith, m. Larkin Smith.
3. Sophronia Smith, m. Orin Knapp of Somerville.

JOHN UNDERWOOD, bap. March 26, 1780; m. Sarah Smith, dau. of Thomas and Sarah (Taylor) Smith of Lexington, b. Oct. 17, 1783; they were admitted to the Church July 5, 1812; he d. Aug. 8, 1855, aged 76; she d. Jan. 25, 1848, aged 64. Their dau. Mary d. young. (See John Underwood, page 72.)

6. BETHIAH MONROE, b. Jan. 22, 1753; lived at Bellows Falls, Vt.; d. unm. aged 93.

7. DELIVERANCE MONROE, b. July 22, 1755; m. John Winship, b. in Lexington, May 12, 1754, son of Samuel, and one of 11 children; he d. in West Cambridge, April, 1825, and his widow Deliverance Monroe Winship administered upon his estate. He was a soldier in Capt. Parker's Co. 1775; he also served in the first campaign of eight and 12 months in New York. They had seven children:

I. JOHN WINSHIP, b. Dec. 28, 1779.
II. STEPHEN WINSHIP, b. July 15, 1782.
III. CHARLES WINSHIP, b. June 30, 1784.
IV. SALLY WINSHIP, b. July 23, 1786.
V. POLLY WINSHIP, b. April 26, 1788.

vi. HENRY WINSHIP. b. June 28, 1790.

vii. NAGUS WINSHIP, b. Aug. 4, 1793.

8. ANNA MONROE, b. June 23. 1758; m. Josiah Nurse of Framingham.* I am, however, unable to follow them in the Framingham records.

9. THADDEUS MONROE, b. Oct. 26. 1760; traded in South Carolina, where he d. unm.

10. JOHN MONROE, b. and d. April 3, 1763.

11. ELIZABETH MONROE, b. Oct. 4, 1765; m. July 1, 1787, Jacob Buckman of Woburn, where they finally settled. They were the parents of Hon. Bowen Buckman of Woburn. Their children were:

i. BOWEN BUCKMAN, b. in Lexington. April 19, 1788; m. and lived in Woburn, a prominent and distinguished man, and had children Eliza, Maria, and Julia Ann.

ii. DENNIS BUCKMAN, b. in Lexington, May 13, 1794; m. and lived in Woburn. Children: Elizabeth, Joseph, Lora, Otis, Lavinia, and Ruth.

iii. WILLIS BUCKMAN, twin of Dennis, b. in Lexington, May 13. 1794; m. and lived in Woburn. Children: Bowen, Alvah, Austin, and Minot J.

iv. IRA BUCKMAN, b. in Woburn, Nov. 19, 1802; m. and lived in Woburn and whose children were: Harrison, Harriett, Zachariah Symmes, and William M.

v. WILLIAM MORTON BUCKMAN, b. in Woburn. July 13, 1806; m. and lived in Woburn. Children: Catharine and Catharine B. M. Many of these families or their descendants still live in Woburn.

16. **Josiah Parker, Jr.** (*Josiah,*[4] *John,*[3] *Hananiah,*[2] *Thomas*[1]). b. in Lexington, April 11. 1725, son of Lt. Josiah and Anna (Stone) Parker, inherited from his ancestors a vigorous constitution, strong intellect and good morals, which he in turn transmitted to his children after settling for life in Woburn.

It seems, also, that he inherited his father's military spirit, for in later years he became a lieutenant in Woburn. He was probably connected with the Lexington military company while yet a lad, as was then the custom, and as his father was (1744) lieutenant in Col. Phipps' Mass. Reg. The plan on

* From *History of Lexington*.

page 43 shows where his father, one of the foremost men in Lexington, lived and carried on his farm, and where his "well beloved son" lived until the age of 23, when he married in Weston, Oct. 27, 1748, Mary Monroe, then of Weston. She was b. in Lincoln, March 18, 1729, being one of a family of 11 children, and sister to Martha Monroe, who m. Isaac Stone of Lexington. Her father, Benjamin Monroe, whose wife was Mary Merriam, was youngest child of a family of 14, the father being William Monroe, the Scotch emigrant ancestor of the name, who settled in Lexington near the Woburn line. Mary Monroe must have been a lady of much worth, coming from this flourishing and sturdy Monroe family.

The year following his marriage he purchased, May 29, 1749, of John Burt's heirs, then of Boston, an estate in Woburn of 200 acres of rich farming land for the sum of £2,000. It was in the west part of the town and but a few miles from his home in Lexington. It was in this part of Woburn where the Kendalls resided; where Jabez Kendall lived until his marriage to Sarah Parker of Lexington. The farm was bordered by Samuel Kendall on the north and on the west by Samuel Wyman. Later, in 1771, Josiah Parker bought much more land, bounded, as the deed reads, north by the highway to Lexington, and east by the highway to Charlestown. This was in the southwest part of the town and was adjacent to a part of his other land. It is said that his house, the homestead site, stood between Cambridge and Lexington Streets.

Mr. and Mrs. Parker were connected with the Church in Woburn. It may be that he saw service in the French and Indian wars, or perhaps accompanied his brother, Capt. John Parker of Lexington, in the memorable Louisburg expedition of 1745, or in the French and Indian war; but one thing is certain, that he was honored with the title of Lieut.

Characteristic of his family he was "joiner" as well as a farmer. He had his "shop," which he mentions in his will, wherein he made wagons, furniture and all farm implements. In his will, which is preserved in Middlesex Probate Records, he mentions Mary, my dearly beloved wife, Mary, my well beloved dau., my eldest son Josiah Parker, my dau. Lydia, son Edmund, dau. Martha, and sons Nathan and Benjamin.

He d. in Woburn, April 18, 1774, at the early age of 49. All of his family were b. in Woburn.

Their children were:

40. Mary Parker, b. Dec. 25, 1749; m. (probably) John Gilmore.

41. Josiah Parker, b. Nov. 25, 1751; m. Hannah Gardner of Charlestown.

42. Lydia Parker, b. Dec. 10, 1753; m. Jesse Wright, then of Woburn.

43. Benjamin Parker, b. Jan. 30, 1756; m. Mehetable Tidd of Woburn.

Nathan Parker, b. April 1, 1758; d. young.

Anna Parker, b. Feb. 12, 1760; probably d. young.

44. Edmund Parker, b. March 17, 1762; m. (1) Lydia Johnson, (2) Mrs. Elizabeth Reed, both of Woburn.

Martha Parker, b. July 29, 1764.

Ruth Parker, b. Oct. 1, 1766. She probably d. young, as she was not mentioned in her father's will.

45. Nathan Parker, b. Feb. 21, 1769; m. Polly Richardson of Woburn.

Betty Parker, b. July 23, 1771.

In Woburn Death Records is recorded the death of a John Parker, May 30, 1790. His identity is not plain. Perhaps he belonged to the Reading families.

17. Capt. John Parker *(Josiah,[4] John,[3] Hananiah,[2] Thomas[1])*, son of Lieut. Josiah and Anna (Stone) Parker, was b. in Lexington, July 13, 1729. He passed his boyhood upon his father's farm amid the hardships and warfare of the early times.

He was early connected with the military company of the town, and was trained by his father, Lieut. Josiah Parker. Unfortunately the period of his services in the French and Indian wars cannot be ascertained, as all the rolls of the Lexington men have not been preserved. Some of the Lexington men were attached to the famous corps known as "Rogers's Rangers," to which Capt. Edmund Monroe at one time belonged, and quite likely John Parker as well. This company is thus described by the historian of Lexington:

"This was the corps in which Stark served his military apprenticeship;—a corps whose name was expressive of the life they led—*ranging* through the wilderness, seeking their wary savage foe by day or by night in silent glens or secret ambush;—a corps whose winter quarters were in tedious marchings amid drifted snows, frozen lakes and ice clad hills,—relying sometimes upon snow shoes and sometimes on skates for locomotion, and carrying their only arsenal and commissariat in their packs. In such a corps were some of the hardy sons of Lexington trained—they, knowing that their lives were in their own hands and that their escape from the tomahawk and scalping knife, the tortures of the faggot or ignominious slavery, depended entirely upon their own severe trials, perpetual watchings and determined courage."

John Parker was at the capture of Louisburg in 1758, and was at the taking of Quebec in 1759. He was made a sergeant in this war. The war of the Revolution which followed, and the great armies in the service of the late Rebellion have thrown the French and Indian War in a great measure into the shade. Few people at the present time realize the toils, the sufferings and the sacrifices made by the colony at that time to sustain the cause and strengthen the arm of the mother country, which was shortly after raised to crush the patriotic colonists. From 1755 to 1763 Massachusetts performed an amount of military service almost unparalleled. Minot, the historian, says that in the year 1757 one-third of the effective men in the colony were in some way or other in the field. The patriotic devotion of the colony, and the zeal with which the brave soldiers served Great Britain should have excited her gratitude and induced her to respect their rights.

John Parker m. in Lexington, May 25, 1755, Lydia Moore, b. in Lexington, Jan. 18, 1731, third dau. of Thomas and Mary Moore of Lexington, who lived, if tradition be correct, in a house, many years since in ruins, not far west of the present poor farm. They were admitted to the Church Oct. 31, 1756. After the settlement of his father's estate the other sons in course of time removed from town and he bought out their shares. Mr. Parker was a successful farmer and collected a respectable estate. He was a skilful "joiner" as well as a good mechanic. He became assessor, constable and collector of his town. Royal assessments known as "the stamp act," involving consequences of great importance, were levied often upon the colonial towns. The collector received the document and was obliged to collect its quota or go to jail.

As John Parker was assessor this duty fell upon him, and at Lexington is preserved one of the papers, which best explains the condition of affairs at this time. The citizens could not anticipate their coming, which was irregular, or the amount which might be stated in them.

John Parker was a stout, large framed man, of medium height, somewhat like his illustrious grandson, Theodore Parker, in personal appearance, but had a much longer face. He was fond of learning and reading, as from Parson Clark's diary we learn he was one of those who often borrowed his valued books, treasures at that time.

The Church and town were one, consequently the minister was the most influential man in the town. The ardent patriot, Parson Jonas Clark, plainly exposed the doctrine for which Massachusetts rose in arms. He levied high treason in the house of God, and upon his fellow-citizens, and finally upon the whole country — his influence was inestimable. The Parkers for several generations used to love to go to Church, they were the best of hearers of the Word, and faithful doers too, but they had their own thoughts and resolved as well as listened.

Probably the name of Capt. John Parker would have no place in history had not the events and circumstances of the times brought the British to Lexington. But do not the results well show that no better man could have been chosen to represent the colonists in their first defence? He was equal to the emergency, and may we ever honor his name.

The whole country was equally alive and it needed only a spark to kindle the fire of liberty, and any village might have been the scene of the first resistance. The Lexington company of minute-men, formed about 1774, comprised the principal men of the town. John Parker was at that time 45 years of age. He must have been a man of admitted character and one who commanded the confidence of the people. When in 1774 and '75 the town made an effort to organize a company of minute-men, we have a record over his signature in this language, showing his military leadership, and seems the first note of preparation to the bloody drama so soon to be enacted:

"LEXINGTON, March 14, 1775.

"Agreeable to the vote of the town I have received by the hands of the Selectmen the drums—there were two—provided by the town for the use of Military Company in this town until the further order of the town.

JOHN PARKER."

There were in town at that period Lieut. Edmund Monroe and Ens. Robert Monroe, both of whom had held commissions in the French War, besides 25 or 30 more who had seen service on the "tented field," and the fact that Parker was selected to command that company and that these officers and soldiers were willing to volunteer and serve under him, shows that he was a man of more than ordinary ability and one to be trusted in any emergency.

Capt. Parker shouldered his gun on the evening of the 18th of April, left his home and seven young children, proceeded to the village and there awaited the arrival of messengers from Boston. He placed a guard composed of Sergt. Monroe and eight men around Rev. John Clark's house, where the hunted patriots, John Hancock and Samuel Adams, were that night stopping. Paul Revere arrived in Lexington at midnight. He immediately gave the alarm at the parson's house. At two in the morning Capt. Parker caused the alarm to be sounded from the belfry on Lexington green and by the beating of drums. The minute-men hastened from their firesides, and all finally assembled upon the common. The night being cool the company was soon dismissed with orders to assemble again at the beat of the drum. The greater portion retired to Buckman's tavern near the place of parade. At half-past four Parker called the roll of his company, forming the line near the meeting-house. He then commanded—

"Every man of you who is equipped follow me, and those of you who are not go into the meeting-house and furnish himself from the magazine and immediately join the company."

Afterward came the order to load the guns. As the British approached and the little band of 60 stood before 600 disciplined troops, a few of them naturally for a moment faltered, Capt. Parker sternly replied, "The first man who offers to run shall be shot down." When the British halted and

BATTLE OF LEXINGTON.

Pitcairn cried out "Disperse, ye villians, ye rebels," etc., our Captain showed his cool and prudent judgment in evading the mighty disaster which aggression on the part of his troops would have been, by firmly ordering, "Don't fire unless fired upon. but if they want a war let it begin here." He was always gentlemanly. As he stood before the British host no profane sentence sullied his lips, sorely tempted though he may have been in the peril and excitement of that hour. What a contrast did the language of the American commander present to that of Maj. Pitcairn, when, with oaths, he discharged his pistol and ordered his men to fire. They overshot and no one was injured, but at their second discharge nearly one-fourth of the little company were killed or wounded. The little band then returned the fire with some effect and the war was begun! The British charged upon them, upon which perilous state of affairs Capt. Parker ordered his men, "Disperse and take care of yourselves." With a cheer the British resumed their march, having first bayoneted Jonas Parker, who was determined to face the British. He was Capt. Parker's cousin and the first man bayoneted in our American Revolution. (See page 50.) Far better would it have been for Major Pitcairn and his command to have reflected from the brave resistance shown by Jonas Parker of the probable reception awaiting them. Far better for his men if he had then and there wheeled around and marched back to Boston. How heartily the example offered by Parker, together with the fate of the other victims, was told from mouth to mouth, and how the minute-men responded by their presence that day!

Capt. Parker had not only trained his company but had formed an "Alarm List," as was the custom, to which the boys and old men belonged. He trained all who could carry a musket, and during the day many of them got in chance shots at the enemy, and some of the boys carried water in wooden bowls to the men. Besides Capt. Parker and his cousin Jonas Parker, there was the latter's nephew, Corporal Ebenezer Parker, and the Captain's brother, Thaddeus Parker, who were in the fight that day. It is shown in another part how Ebenezer's father, Thomas Parker, defended his family and property from British insult, although he was still confined to his house. In the forenoon Capt. Parker gathered the remainder of his company and marched toward Concord to intercept the British at the best advantage. In Lincoln, as they saw the enemy returning, he led the men into an open field, and they fired once more upon the enemy. Troops from Woburn, Acton, Reading and other towns had arrived. From Woburn were Captain Parker's nephews, Edmund and Josiah Parker. From Reading came 17 who bore the name of Parker, who, under command of Capt. Brooks, kept up a hot fire upon the enemy's column during the remainder of the day.

In the following May John Parker led a part of his company, 45 men, to Cambridge, upon order of the Provincial Congress, and they served from the sixth to the tenth. Again on the day of the battle of Bunker Hill he was with 69 men at Cambridge ready for action. He was not in perfect health on the day of the battle of Lexington. At Bunker Hill he was too ill to be allowed to enter the turmoil of the battle, so he discontentedly commanded troops who guarded the "Neck" that day. He was never well afterwards and an epidemic dysentery in September found him an easy prey. He died at an early age for his long-lived family, aged 46, Sept. 17, 1775. He who was so brave and true at the beginning of the struggle saw not the end nor the glory.

His direct descendant, Elizabeth Parker of Lexington, writes of him:

"I think one can say of John Parker, although perhaps a man plain and simple like his name, he must have been a man of some mental and much executive ability, a man of strong will, bold, earnest and daring—wise, prudent and determined. A man sure of his convictions and true to his convictions. Jonathan Harrington, the last survivor of the battle, said that 'He looked as though he could face anything,' and most bravely did he face the responsibilities and dangers of that trying time."*

It has been eloquently said of him:

"But Parker commanded more than that little company who stood on yonder green; he led the embattled host that partook of his

*Extract from an article entitled Capt. John Parker, written for and preserved by the Lexington Historical Society in its publications.

and their spirit henceforth. When he rallied his men in the afternoon of that signal day he prefigured our noble army, which again and again, with thinned ranks and amid fallen comrades, returned to the dread fields of that long and bloody struggle." *

At the Lexington homestead is preserved Capt. Parker's affidavit of the actions of the 19th of April, very valuable to history as his official account of the direct cause of the Revolutionary War. It is here copied in full.

"LEXINGTON, April 23, 1775.

"I, John Parker of lawful age, and commander of the militia in Lexington, do testify and declare that on the 19th inst. in the morning about one of the Clock, being informed that there were a number of Regular officers riding up & down the road, taking and insulting people, and also was informed that the Regular troops were on their march from Boston, in order to take the Province Store at Concord, immediately ordered our militia to meet on the common in Said Lexington, to consult what to do, and concluded not to be discovered nor to meddle or make with said Regular Troops, (if they should approach) unless they should insult or molest us; and upon their sudden approach I immediately ordered our militia to disperse and not to fire; immediately said Troops made their appearance and Rushed furiously to & fired upon and Killed Eight of our party without Receiving any provocation therefor from us.

John Parker

"Midd^{ex} ss April ye 23^{d} 1775.

"The Above named John Parker appeared and made Solemn Oath to the truth of the within deposition by him subscribed before us.

JOHN CUMING
JON^{a}: HASTINGS } Justices of Peace."
DUNCAN INGRAHAM

In the Massachusetts Senate Chamber there hangs two muskets, priceless relics, appropriate memorials to the State of Capt. Parker, the gift of his grandson, Rev. Theodore Parker. On one, Capt. Parker's own light fowling-piece, which he carried at Quebec and Lexington, is inscribed:

*A. B. Muzzy, April 19, 1871, a descendant of Isaac Muzzy, who was killed in the battle of Lexington.

"THIS FIREARM WAS USED BY
CAPT. JOHN PARKER
IN THE BATTLE OF LEXINGTON,
APRIL 19,
1775."

And on the other, which he took from a grenadier in Cambridge on the 17th of June:

"THE FIRST FIRE ARM
CAPTURED IN THE
WAR OF INDEPENDENCE."

These invaluable mementos were received by the State with appropriate ceremonies, and are conspicuously suspended for public view in the Senate Chamber of the State House. May they ever be prized with reverence, and "Tell to our sons how our fathers have died."

In the year 1884 the town appropriated the sum of $1,500 to mark spots of historic interest in Lexington, and among others the grave where his remains were supposed to rest received a substantial and fitting monument bearing this inscription:

"TO THE MEMORY OF CAPT. JOHN PARKER,
COMMANDER OF THE MINUTE-MEN, APRIL 19TH, 1775.
BORN JULY 13TH, 1729, DIED SEPTEMBER 17TH, 1775.
THE TOWN ERECTS THIS MEMORIAL.
1884."

Their children were:

LYDIA PARKER, b. Nov. 8, 1756.

46. ANNA PARKER, b. Jan. 11, 1759; m. March 16, 1781, Ephraim Pierce of Waltham.

47. JOHN PARKER, b. Dec. 7, 1761; m. Feb. 17, 1785. Hannah Stearns of Lexington.

48. ISAAC PARKER, b. May 11, 1763; m. in Charleston, S. C.

49. RUTH PARKER, b. Dec. 7, 1765; m. Nov. 14, 1787, David Bent; removed to Nova Scotia.

50. REBECCA PARKER, b. June 28. 1768; m. Peter Clarke of Watertown.

51. ROBERT PARKER, b. April 15, 1771; m. Oct. 22, 1794, Elizabeth Simonds of Lexington.

18. Thaddeus Parker (*Josiah*,[4] *John*,[3] *Hananiah*,[2] *Thomas*[1]), son of Josiah and Anna (Stone) Parker, b. in Lexington, Sept. 2, 1731; m. May 27, 1759, Mary Reed, b. July 17, 1751, dau. of William and Abigail (Stone) Reed. He sold in 1761 to his brother, John Parker of Lexington,

The accompanying engraving shows the appearance of the homestead as it was at this time. It is the house which stood upon the place when the estate passed into the ownership of John Parker of Reading in 1712. It also shows the old belfry building which, previous to the nineteenth century, stood on the common, on the site of the present monument, and from which in 1775 went forth those peals of alarm which called the patriots to arms on the morning of the 19th of April. Although the old house has been replaced by another the belfry still stands at the Parker homestead.

THE PARKER HOMESTEAD.

In this ancient house several generations of large families were born. Here was also born the Rev. Theodore Parker, who in early life drew the picture which is here shown. He wrote in regard to it as follows: "It faced as near the south as the rude science of the owner or builder could make it, and so was a perpetual sun dial. It had but one chimney, that a huge one in the centre of the building. The large bricks, made half a mile off, were laid in clay as far as the ridge pole, while the part of the chimney above the roof was pointed with mortar. Limestone was not found within many miles, and the want of it was a serious inconvenience in building. The house, like all the others in that neighborhood, was two stories high in front and only one in the rear. The rooms were few but large and airy, the windows not numerous, of various size, but all small; originally all the latches, except afterwards captain, a part of his share of his father's, Lieut. Josiah Parker, estate for £175. He lived in Lexington, probably at or near the centre of the town. He was like his brothers, and doubtless his ancestors, a strong, large boned, muscular man. His career in Lexington stands out brightly in two ways, first as a citizen, and second as a patriot. It is a lamentable fact that of his large family there is not a living descendant of this worthy man.

Thaddeus Parker was one of the selectmen in the years preceding the Revolution, a period when the most important duties of the town were devolved upon that board, and when only men of true character and firm patriotism were chosen. His name appears as assessor of the town of Lexington during

---

that of the 'fore-door,' were of wood with wooden thumb pieces, but these had nearly all passed away before my recollection. The house, as it stood in my day, had been built at different times, the eastern end being considerably younger than the western, and not furnished with the massive oak beams which everywhere stuck out in the older part. A New England farmer of 'comfortable estate' would hesitate a good deal before setting up his household in such a cheerless shelter; but three generations of stout and longlived men were born and grew up there, and if the fourth be more puny and sink quicker to the grave, it is from no fault of the old house, but from the consumption which such spongy meadows in New England seldom fail to produce in the course of time; even children, who have removed to healthier situations, carry with them the fatal poison in their blood, and transmit it to their sons and daughters."

A history of the old belfry is found in Mr. C. A. Staples's "*Sketch of the History of Lexington Common*," published by the Lexington Historical Society, from which I copy the following: "At a town meeting held in June, 1761, Isaac Stone, as the record says: 'came into y[e] meeting and gave y[e] town a bell to be for y[e] towns use forever; which bell was there und weighed 463 lbs. —and y[e] moderator in y[e] name of y[e] meeting gave him thanks.'

"Accordingly the town set to work building a belfry for the bell, and the building was finally settled upon the common. This was the famous bell which rung the alarm on the morning of the 19th of April, 1775, whose tongue is still preserved among the precious relics at the Cary Library, Lexington. But when the new meeting-house was built in 1794 the belfry was sold to John Parker, the father of Theodore Parker, and carried away to the Parker homestead, where it long did duty as a wheelwright shop and where it is still standing. Soon we trust, under the auspices of the Lexington Historical Society, it will come creeping back, to find its final resting-place near the spot of its birth. It should be placed on some height overlooking the village and restored to its original form, a bell procured of the exact size of Dea. Isaac Stone's gift, the old tongue put in it, and on every anniversary of the 19th of April it should be rung to let people know how the summons sounded which called the minute-men to the common on that eventful morning."

the years 1770, '71, '73 and '77. At a time of deep despondency, the closing months of 1776, when the patriot army was a mere handful of ragged, disheartened men, he enlisted from Lexington for a campaign in the Jerseys, there to join Gen. Washington. This was during the retreat through New Jersey, the battle of Trenton, when Washington crossed the Delaware and turned the tables of his country's history, followed by the battles of Princeton, Brandywine and Germantown, and it is probable that in all of these Mr. Parker assisted. He was in the service at least eight months. He d. in Lexington, Feb. 10, 1789. From the note-book of his nephew John Parker we read:

"LEXINGTON, February 12, 1789.

"Was intered Mr. Thaddeus Parker, Esq. aged 58, who died of a motification in his bowels, it being the 6th person that died in one house since the 4th day of September in the year 1787, whereof Mr. Joseph Parker, brother of Thaddeus, was the first, who died of a consumption, Polly Parker followed after and Bettey and Thaddeus Parker, junr. and Sally Parker all of a consumption, and all children of Thaddeus Parker."

Mary, widow of Mr. Parker, survived him many years. She d. in Lexington, Oct. 9, 1811, aged 73.

Their children were:

MARY PARKER, b. Sept. 26, 1760; d. June 3, 1787, aged nearly 27.

SARAH PARKER, b. Aug. 24, 1762; d. Feb. 2, 1789, aged 26.

BETTY PARKER, b. Aug. 28, 1764; d. Aug. 27, 1788, aged 24.

THADDEUS PARKER, b. July 10, 1767; d. June 14, 1789, aged nearly 22.

JOSIAH PARKER, b. Sept. 19, 1770. The estate of Thaddeus Parker was appraised in 1789 at £726. 12s. 15d. Josiah was then the sole heir to his father's property; but he was not living, however, 1842, when Jonathan S. Parker of Lexington attested that Josiah Parker was then deceased, that he had never married and thus had left no issue. Therefore the Thaddeus branch of the Parker family became extinct.

19. Joseph Parker (*Josiah,*[4] *John,*[3] *Hananiah,*[2] *Thomas*[1]), son of Lieut. Josiah and Anna (Stone) Parker, was b. in Lexington, Nov. 28, 1733, the last child in the family of eight. He m. July 5, 1759, Eunice Hobbs of Weston, b.

in Weston, April 22, 1741, the fourth in a family of eleven children, dau. of Ebenezer and Eunice (Garfield)* Hobbs. After the birth of their first child, in 1760, they settled in Lincoln, where the births of the remainder of their children are recorded. He must have owned property, however, in Lexington, as by a deed bearing date of April 13, 1763, to him from his cousin Thomas Parker, Esq., we read, "Joseph Parker of Lexington, Husbandman." He probably lived in Weston during the latter period of his life, for his family were finally connected with that town. He seems to have been a quiet farmer, and not particularly prominent in town affairs. Although the town records of Lincoln do not show his name on the muster-rolls of her Revolutionary soldiers, yet almost every male citizen there was a participant and it is not at all probable that he staid away from danger and duty.

She d. in Lincoln, Jan. 3, 1784. He d. in Lexington, as we are informed by his nephew, Sept. 4, 1787, at the house of his brother, Thaddeus Parker, Esq.

Their children were:

52. SUSANNA PARKER, b. Dec. 31, 1760; probably m. —— Gregory.†

53. LEVI PARKER, b. April 16, 1762; m. Mary Lyon of Hubbardston.

54. LOIS PARKER, b. Nov. 17, 1763; m. John Coburn of Weston.

AARON PARKER, b. Dec. 5, 1765; killed by the Indians, 1791.‡

55. JOSEPH PARKER, JR., b. Oct. 4, 1767; m. Polly Fisk of Weston.

JONATHAN PARKER, b. Oct. 17, 1769. Inheriting a military spirit, he was in the St. Clair expedition against the Indians. In this he perished as did his brother Aaron.

---

* She, Eunice Garfield, was one of the twelve children of Lt. Thomas Garfield, a sturdy and prosperous citizen of Watertown. Among the brothers and sisters of Eunice were Isaac, Samuel, Anna, and Elisha, thus showing the origin of these names in Levi Parker's children and grandchildren.

† Uriah Grigory of Weston belonged to the minute-men of that town; but we know not the given name of Susanna Parker's husband.

‡ Aaron Parker shared the military spirit of his family. His brother Levi, nearly four years his senior, was just old enough to participate in the last part of the Revolution. The time soon came when Aaron was able to lend his hand for his country against the Indians, who, encouraged by British officers, barred all western emigration and who were, 1790, scalping inhabitants and

ELISHA PARKER, b. Dec. 7, 1772; d. in 1773.

56. ELISHA PARKER, b. Sept. 10, 1775; m. Jerusha Wentworth of Weston. } Twins.

57. REBECCA PARKER, b. Sept. 10, 1775; m. Elisha Rand of Weston. }

20. Peter Parker *(John,[4] John,[3] Hananiah,[2] Thomas[1])*, son of John and Experience (Clayes) Parker, b. in Framingham, Oct. 3, 1738, succeeded upon his father's homestead; m. Dec. 8, 1761, Ruth Eaton, b. in Framingham, Feb. 16, 1744, dau. of Noah and Hannah (Vinton) Eaton. He was also a cordwainer; with wife was admitted to the Church in 1763. He was a leading citizen of his town; was one of the Committee of Correspondence in the stirring times of the Revolutionary war; was one of the committee to provide for the families of the soldiers who enlisted into the Continental army, and which committee was continued with full powers from year to year; assisted in Church affairs; selectman 1777, '79, '80, '81, '82; town treasurer 1783, '86. During and following the war the prices on goods were very fluctuating, and the town chose a committee of ten men, Peter Parker being one, to state the prices of labor, country produce, manufactures, innholders' charges, etc.; was on a committee of fifteen to examine the new Constitution, May, 1780; was constable and collector, and was a member of the Framingham company of alarm soldiers, under Capt. Emmes, in the French and Indian war, 1757.

---

burning the towns along the frontier. With his brother Jonathan, who it seems also inherited a love for liberty, he joined the national troops in Pennsylvania in the Indian troubles of 1790. Their success was varied. Finally, under Gen. St. Clair, they were among the force of 2,000 men who proceeded westward and at last arrived at the southeastern head-waters of the Wabash, at about where the division of Ohio and Indiana now is. They had encamped for their first night on this wooded plain, and were preparing breakfast, Nov. 4, 1791, when the Indians rushed furiously upon them. A stout resistance did not prevent a bad defeat and retreat, the loss to the 2,000 being 800 killed and missing. This was known as St. Clair's defeat by the Indians, and in this Aaron and Jonathan Parker are said to have perished. This ended St. Clair's career, and in 1793, Gen. Anthony Wayne having assumed command, sent a strong detachment to the scene of the defeat who buried the bleaching bones of 600 men and built Fort Recovery. Aaron Parker was aged 26 and Jonathan aged 22 at the time of St. Clair's defeat.

"An incident occurred in 1777 which made a lasting impression on the public mind. While Mr. Wheaton was supplying the pulpit he negotiated for the purchase of a horse, and arranged with Mr. John Clayes, who lived at Salem End, where is now the L. O. Emerson house, to examine and try the animal. June 3, a little before noon, some of the neighbors came together to witness the trial. Besides Mr. Clayes there were present Abraham Rice, Peter Parker, Simon Pratt and his son Ephraim. Mr. Parker mounted the horse and had ridden to a considerable distance away, when a small cloud suddenly came up from the northwest. On his return, the company, who had been in the house during his absence, came out towards the road. A few drops of rain were at this moment falling. As Mr. Parker rode up Mr. Clayes stepped outside the gate, leaving the others leaning against the fence within, and just as he took the horse by the bridle the lightning struck the party and prostrated them all on the ground. Mr. Clayes, Mr. Rice and the horse were instantly killed. Mr. Parker lay as if dead, but gradually recovered consciousness, though a long time elapsed before he fully regained his health. The boy who was standing a short distance from the rest recovered immediately. Mr. Pratt came to slowly and suffered from the stroke for a long time. The horse was struck in the head and marks of the lightning were visible down both forelegs. The party all wore woolen clothes and were all singed in body and dress. There was but this single flash of lightning from the cloud and only a few drops of rain."—*Temple.*

The wife, Ruth (Eaton) Parker, d. March 20, 1800. Peter Parker d. Nov. 5, 1803, aged 65.

Their children were:

58. John Parker, b. Nov. 16, 1762; m. Deborah Lamb of Framingham.

59. Nathan Parker, b. Oct. 23, 1764; m. Catherine Murdock of Newton.

60. Abigail Parker, b. Dec. 15, 1766; m. Lovell Howe of Marlborough.

61. Ruth Parker, b. Jan. 8, 1769; m. Joseph Bigelow, Jr., of Holliston.

62. Experience Parker, b. Feb. 19, 1771; m. Dea. Luther Haven of Framingham.

63. Patty Parker, b. April 15, 1773; m. Eleazer Bullard of Holliston.

64. Sally Parker, b. May 25, 1775; m. William Eames of Holliston.

PETER PARKER, b. March 16, 1777; d. Dec. 17, 1784.

65. JOSIAH PARKER, b. April 26, 1779; m. Olive Stone of Framingham.

66. ARTEMAS PARKER, b. Dec. 20, 1781; m. Almy Clark of Framingham.

ANNE PARKER, b. April 25, 1784; d. Jan. 8, 1785.

PETER PARKER, b. July 10, 1787; d. May 7, 1788.

21. Submit Parker *(John,[4] John,[3] Hananiah,[2] Thomas[1])*, dau. of John and Experience (Clayes) Parker, b. in Framingham, Dec. 3, 1742; m. Thomas Bent, Jr., b. July 4, 1738. He was the fourth generation in descent from the emigrant ancestor, John Bent, who came from Penton, Eng., in the ship *Confidence*, in 1638, and settled in Sudbury. He, Thomas, bought June 14, 1764, of Elias Whitney 60 acres (the Joel Coolidge place), which he sold 1786 to Jos. Bixby. He bought June 13, 1766, of James Glover, 31 acres, the old Dr. Timothy Merriam place, which he sold 1785. He built the old Dr. Merriam house; was taxed 1787; probably d. that year.

The children recorded in Framingham were:

ALVAN BENT, b. June 3, 1769; m. Olive Rice.

POLLY BENT, b. April 5, 1771.

BETSEY BENT, bap. July 18, 1779.

22. Eunice Parker *(Jonas,[5] Andrew,[4] John,[3] Hananiah,[2] Thomas[1])*, dau. of Jonas and Lucy (Monroe) Parker, m. June 9, 1772, Asa Morse of Newton, b. Dec. 30, 1748; d. 1815. Was a descendant of the fifth generation from Samuel Morse, who came to America 1635, and settled at Dedham 1637.

They lived at Newton for many years. He m. as 2nd wife Parthena Wetherbee and resided at Sturbridge. The children may not all have been by Eunice Parker.

Their children were:

PARKER L. MORSE, who m. and had Emeline. She m. Jedediah Bottom of Southbridge.

LUCY MORSE.

POLLY MORSE.

WILLARD MORSE.

ISA MORSE, lived in Southbridge. He is now deceased and left no issue.

MOSES MORSE.

23. Jonas Parker *(Jonas,[5] Andrew,[4] John,[3] Hananiah,[2] Thomas[1])*, son of Jonas and Lucy (Monroe) Parker, was b. in Lexington, July 10, 1753; m. Aug. 15, 1776, Martha Hasley of Billerica. He was a wheelwright, following the trade of his ancestors. He succeeded to his father's estate, and with Martha, his wife, was admitted to the Church Feb. 28, 1779. Just well started in life, however, he d. July 14, 1783, and his widow administered on his estate.

Their children were:

PATTY PARKER, bap. May 16, 1779. } Twins.
BETTY PARKER, bap. May 16, 1779. }
JOHN H. PARKER, bap. Nov. 26, 1780.
JONAS PARKER, b. March 2, 1783.

It is probable that these children removed from town with the mother soon after 1783, as no records are found of them after that date. May the descendants of these children, if any there be, let it be known who they are and where they may be found.

24. Philemon Parker *(Jonas,[5] Andrew,[4] John,[3] Hananiah,[2] Thomas[1])*, son of Jonas and Lucy (Monroe) Parker, was b. in Lexington in 1755. After the decease of his father he removed to Princeton, where his uncle Thomas Parker, Esq., and son Ebenezer Parker had already settled. He purchased of Thomas Parker in 1787 a part of the "Black Grove Farm" for £600. He lived at the spot where is now a cellar-hole, not far from the Keyes place in East Princeton. He purchased a grist-mill and mill privilege of Ebenezer Parker in 1800. He owned a kit of boot maker's tools and was familiar with the trade. He lived later for a time in Sturbridge, then in Richmond, N. H., and in Peru, Vt., after which he settled in Chester, Vt., where he lived a few years. His wife was probably Susan Stone, by whom all the children were born. She d. April 17, 1812, aged 52. He then went to live in Richmond, N. H., where he built the large two-story house for Elisha Perry.* He was a good carpenter. They lived together in the house until 1822, the former working at his trade, the latter cultivating the farm. He m. 2nd in 1814, Rhoda Bump Boyce of Richmond, N. H. She was the dau. of Jacob Bump,† one of the earliest settlers of Richmond. Her first husband was Jacob Boyce, who was killed by the kick of a horse. He returned to Chester, Vt., and there he d. Feb. 7, 1829, aged 74 years.

The children were:

SULLIVAN PARKER, b. probably 1783; d. April 26, 1827.

JONAS PARKER, b. July 1, 1785; d. Dec. 29, 1810. } Twins.

67. SALLY PARKER, b. July 1, 1785; m. Samuel Burt of Newton. } Twins.

68. NANCY PARKER, b. Sept. 28, 1786; m. Timothy Wyman of Chester, Vt. (?)

ANNA PARKER, b. probably 1787; d. "Feb. 14, 1811, aged 19."‡

NATHAN PARKER, b. 1788; d. "Dec. 19, 1810, aged 22."

SUSANNAH PARKER, b. probably 1789; d. "Jan. 14, 1811, aged 21."

LUCINDA PARKER, b. probably 1793; m. John Jacobs; d. "Feb. 12, 1815, aged 21."

69. LUTHER PARKER, b. April 7, 1796; m. Dolly Byam of Templeton. } Twins.

70. CALVIN PARKER, b. April 7, 1796; m. Seba Cutler. } Twins.

71. JOHN PARKER, b. in Princeton, June 11, 1798.

25. Anna Parker (*Amos,[5] Andrew,[4] John,[3] Hananiah,[2] Thomas[1]*), dau. of Amos and Anna C. (Stone) Parker, was b. in Holden, Oct. 6, 1746: m. Feb. 28, 1788, Dea. Jonas Stone of Shrewsbury as his second wife. He was an ardent friend of his country in her Revolutionary struggle; represented the town in General Court, when held at Watertown,

*Hon. Amos A. Parker of Fitzwilliam, N. H., writes: "I knew Elisha Perry very well, his farm adjoined Fitzwilliam line, and he did his store business here. I have been to his house,—a large two-story house of some sixteen rooms. He had a good large farm and was a good farmer and a man of property."

†Jacob Bump came to Richmond from Smithfield, R. I., Sept. 29, 1760. He d. Dec. 17, 1829, aged 92. He had ten children, of whom Rhoda was the sixth.

‡The record of Anna, Nathan, Susannah, and Lucinda Parker is found in Philemon Parker's family Bible.

May 19, 1775, and rendered long and important services in town and parish affairs. He d. March 22, 1809, aged 83; his widow then, Jan. 18, 1810, m. Dea. Ebenezer Reed, then of Shrewsbury, but afterwards of Worcester. She left no issue.

26. Amos Parker *(Amos,[5] Andrew,[4] John,[3] Hananiah,[2] Thomas[1])*, son of Amos and Anna C. (Stone) Parker, was b. in Holden, Sept. 26, 1748; m. in Barre, by the Rev. Joseph Dana, Dec. 25, 1771, Lucy R. Robinson of Barre. Her father, Dennison Robinson, was an intimate friend of Andrew Parker, Jr., lived near him in Rutland District and sold him land there in 1777. It seems that his family was brought into notice of the Shrewsbury Parkers through Andrew Parker. Great farm, No. 1, of Hubbardston, lay in the west corner of the town, and contained 481 acres of new timber land,* the Burnshirt river and the valuable water supply which now feeds the Williamsville Mills. Upon the marriage of his son, Amos Parker, Sr., made him a possessor of part of his Hubbardston estate, and they removed there immediately following. The next year he bought 93 acres more of his father. The remainder of the land was sold partly to "Mr. Dennison Robinson of Rutland," who took 98 acres, and to his brother, "Thomas Parker, together with John Chandler, both of Lexington, Gentlemen."

Dennison Robinson m. at Rochester, Mass., Oct. 12, 1752, Martha, dau. of Elijah Perry of Sandwich. They removed to Rutland District (Barre) in 1754, and their dau. Lucy R. was there b. March 1, 1755. Her grandfather was James Robinson, whose wife was Patience, dau. of Samuel Ruggles

*At an early day the Willard family purchased a tract 12 miles square of the Indians. They named the N. W., E., and N. E. divisions Rutland, the E. wing Princeton, and the W. wing Oakham. They first offered "Rutland" for common settlement, and made two divisions, viz.: the N. W. district which was named Hubbardston, and the N. E. district Barre. The land was then divided into great and small farms. The name of the town which has bounded Great Farm No. 1, on the north has been changed five times. It was first "Narragansett No. 6," and which name we find mentioned in an early deed of the place; later it was called "Gerry," afterwards changed to Phillipston, then the Burnshirt river was made to divide Templeton, a part of original Phillipston, and present Phillipston the remainder.

7

of Roxbury. James was son of Thomas, and this Thomas was son of Thomas Robinson.

Amos Parker, Jr., was joined soon by his brother Isaac Parker, who lived on the same Great Farm with Amos for four years and then removed to Westborough. Their cousin Levi Parker was their neighbor as well.

Amos Parker was thus a first settler and one of the builders of the town of Hubbardston. He was a very worthy citizen, esteemed and loved by all. He was, it is needless to say, a man of much and varied ability, and a successful farmer. He extended his possessions into "Gerry," besides owning "a mill spot in Templeton adjoining with mill and buildings thereon." He d. 1801, at the early age of 53; she d. 1845, aged 90.

The dates of birth of the children of Amos and Lucy (Robinson) Parker have not all been ascertained, but their names and order of birth were as follows:

72. LUCINDA PARKER, m. Nathaniel Bangs.
73. JOSEPH PARKER, b. 1772(?); m. Relief Earl.
74. SYLVESTER PARKER, b. May 31, 1774; m. Alice Davis.
75. PATTY PARKER, m. ——— Felton, and had a son Horatio.
A child, b. and d.
76. DANA R. PARKER, b. Nov. 4, 1781; m. Sarah Williams.
77. AMORY PARKER, b. Dec. 8, 1783; m. Lydia Parker.
78. LUCY PARKER, m. Jan. 12, 1812, Silas Richardson.
AMOS PARKER, b. ———; d. in boyhood.

27. Isaac Parker *(Amos,[5] Andrew,[4] John,[3] Hananiah,[2] Thomas[1])*, son of Amos and Anna C. (Stone) Parker, was b. in Shrewsbury, July 15, 1750; m. May 16, 1770, Margery Maynard of Westborough, b. Dec. 30, 1749. He was probably named in memory of Isaac Stone of Lexington, who in 1768 showed his good will by a deed of gift of five acres of land in Shrewsbury to Isaac Parker, with the following testimonial:

"for and in consideration of the affectson which I have towards Isaac Parker of Shr. in Co. of Worc. Minor, and second son of Amos Parker of s[d] Shr. and in Con. of being called Isaac and for divers other Good Causes & Cons me heruntο moving."

He served in the Revolutionary war. His services have not been ascertained, but it is known that he was honored with the title of Lieut. as is recorded upon the Westborough records. After marriage he removed to Hubbardston, where his brother Amos had already settled, and remained three years. In 1773 he bought a farm in the west part of Princeton; was miller and farmer. Then in 1777 he bought 80 acres in Westborough of David Maynard, and there settled for life. He dealt with Joseph Baker, later of Bakersfield, Vt., and bought largely in Westborough. He was an energetic farmer: had also saw-mills and dams. He lived one mile southwest of the village, adjoining the old Maynard homestead.

His death occurred Jan. 16, 1798. This death was the first out of the seven sons. Judge Nahum Parker of Fitzwilliam, N. H., informed his brother, Rev. Frederick Parker of Canterbury, N. H., of the sad event. The latter replied in a loving manner by letter dated Feb. 20, 1798, as follows:

"Exactly as you anticipated I received & opened your letter, looked first to the name of the signer, finding that it came from my well beloved B^r^. N—— pleased myself with the expectation of news, &c., in the usual entertaining way, but soon I found it to contain *news indeed*—Am Sorry to hear of Betsey's illness. B^r^. Hollis, for former deaths and present sickness in his family has my sympathy—But how was I astonished beyond all measure to learn of the calamitous tidings from Westborough—Alas poor Isaac! who showed me his mill and presented me with a neat box filled with maple sugar the first year he lived at Princeton when I was but a child & first went so far from home.—Who visited me at Cambridge, and lent me money to help me out of college—came from Westboro to Casco Bay more than 150 miles to see me and was always good to me; at whose house both you and I have often been treated with good cheer but what was more with right true brotherly love.

"Even he has paid his debt to nature and well may all of us be sorrowful that now we shall 'see his face no more.' Many have been his kindnesses to me and the recollection of which is both pleasing and painful. It seems now as I never had thanked him enough and certain it is I never knew before how much I loved him."

Widow Margery Maynard Parker d. April 20 or 30, 1801.

Their children were:

79. JOEL PARKER, b. in Hubbardston, Sept. 16, 1770; m. Hannah Bond, native of Marlborough.

80. GARDINER PARKER, b. in Hubbardston, March 4, 1772; m. Asenath Sherman.

81. OTIS PARKER, b. in Princeton, April 1, 1774; m. (1) Polly Ann Nourse of Westborough, (2) ——— Kendall.

82. JABEZ MAYNARD PARKER, b. in Princeton, Aug. 9, 1776; m. Nancy Patterson of Framingham.

LUCY PARKER, b. in Westborough, Aug. 27, 1778; d. Oct. 5, 1795.

ANNA PARKER, b. in Westborough, May 25, 1781; d. Nov. 7, 1795.

83. SOPHIA PARKER, b. in Westborough, Dec. 30, 1783; m. Stephen Green.

84. DAVID PARKER, b. in Westborough, May 1, 1785; m. Betsey Eager of Northborough.

85. LEWIS PARKER, b. in Westborough, March 1, 1787; m. Elizabeth Seaver of Sterling.

28. **Hollis Parker** *(Amos,[5] Andrew,[4] John,[3] Hananiah,[2] Thomas[1])*, son of Amos and Anna C. (Stone) Parker, was b. in Shrewsbury, Oct. 2, 1752. He served in the Revolutionary war. He m. 1775, Louisa Bragg of Royalston, who was b. in Northborough, June 27, 1754. They settled in Hubbardston, where in 1774 his father, of Shrewsbury, transferred 95 acres of his "Great Farm No. one" in Hubbardston to him. This was in the western corner of the town. He lived in the near neighborhood of his brother Amos Parker, Esq., of Hubbardston. He later, with his brother Isaac Parker, removed to the eastern corner of the town, where they lived as neighbors upon the same "Great Farm." It was here where their distant cousin, Levi Parker, native of Lincoln, lived, who was also a Revolutionary veteran. This "Great Farm" was afterward set off to Princeton, in which town Hollis Parker lived a few years. He returned to Shrewsbury in 1791, when he succeeded to his father's homestead and bought off all his kindred's shares, and lived thereon until his death, the place passing in his declining years into the possession of his son, Dr. Amos Parker, and by this name, "The Dr. Parker place," the old Shrewsbury Parker homestead is known to this day. He kept the appearance of the estate pretty much the same as in his father's time, as he himself told his nephew, A. A. Parker of Fitzwilliam, N. H., who is

still living (1892). He loved his relatives: he appreciated their society and worth. He once travelled from Shrewsbury to Bakersfield, Vt., over 150 miles, to visit his brother and family. At another time we find him in Portland, Me., with his brothers Frederick and Isaac, at about the year 1780. He is remembered by his nephew as a man of strong physique, possessing much intellectual power and fond of learning. He was a man of noble nature, but was unfortunate in his marriage.

Their children were:

MARY JENNISON PARKER, d. in infancy.

A son, d. in infancy.

86. AMOS PARKER, b. in Hubbardston, Oct. 17, 1777; m. Elizabeth Whitney of Bolton.

87. MARY JENNISON PARKER, b. in Hubbardston, July 31, 1780; m. (1) Josiah Harrington, (2) Asahel Allen.

SILAS PARKER, d. young.

FREDERICK PARKER, d. young.

88. SILANCE PARKER, b. Oct. 17, 1786; m. James Hall of Shrewsbury.

SILAS PARKER, b. Oct. 17, 1788; d. 1836, unm.

ANNA PARKER, b. Dec. 23, 1790.
BETSEY PARKER, b. Dec. 23, 1790. } Twins.

HOLLIS PARKER, b. in Shrewsbury, March 23, 1793; m. Nov. 13, 1817, Pamelia Ann Pease, dau. of Levi Pease, Jr. They removed from town. They may have had issue, but I have no record of them.

HENRY PARKER, b. in Shrewsbury, May 10, 1795; m. 1815, Sarah Fuller of Phillipston. She d. in Shrewsbury, May 4, 1819, aged 23. Of his issue or history little is known.

29. Maj. Elisha Parker *(Amos,⁵ Andrew,⁴ John,³ Hananiah,² Thomas¹)*, son of Amos and Anna C. (Stone) Parker, b. 1754; served in the Revolutionary war; m. Sally, dau. of Esq. Joseph Baker and wife Martha Death of Westborough. He was a man of energy and enterprise, and dealt largely in land. In Templeton, Westminster, Winchendon, Sterling and Phillipston he bought and sold much original land. He first settled in Templeton, where, until about 1788, he was quite active in the early settlement of the town. He then removed to Gerry, of which town he was an early and influential settler. This is now Phillipston. He lived in the house and upon the farm now occupied by J. Damon Parker of that town. From this place he again entered the U. S. service, enlisting as a private but returning as Major.

The father-in-law, Esq. Baker, was one of the early pioneers of Vermont. He removed through the settled part of the State, pushed on beyond new towns into the virgin forests to the northern part, where he founded and was the first settler of the thriving town of Bakersfield. It was one year before his wife and daughter saw the face of a woman, then Stephen Maynard, their son-in-law, and wife came. They were followed in 1800 by Maj. Elisha Parker and family, and later by his nephews. In this way Bakersfield was settled for the most part by Mr. Baker's descendants. Maj. Parker settled in the south part of the town. He was a worthy citizen and a kind father.

He was a fine singer, as quite a number of the family were. And when he and his brother Nahum lived at Gerry, and they two were in the singers' seats, no matter who else sang or did not sing, the audience had very fine singing. Nahum's voice was for the bass, and Elisha sang the air or leading part and had great compass of voice, which was bold, sonorous and powerful. He could sound the highest notes with perfect ease and no one could wish to hear a sweeter voice. Had he turned his attention to music he might have been one of the celebrities of the country.

He d. Nov. 9, 1818. His widow, Mrs. Sally (Baker) Parker, survived him and went to live with her son, Jonas Parker, until her death, which occurred Jan. 7, 1838.

Elisha Parker's commission is still preserved:

"By His Excellency INCREASE SUMNER, Esq., Governor and Commander in Chief of the Commonwealth of Massachusetts.

"Increase Sumner to Elisha Parker, Esquire. Greeting:

"You being appointed Major of the fifth Regiment in the Second Brigade Seventh Division of the Militia of this Commonwealth, By Virtue of the Power vested in me I do by these Presents (reposing special Trust and Confidence in your Ability, Courage, and good Conduct) Commission you accordingly:—You are, therefore, carefully and diligently to discharge the Duty of Major in Leading,

Ordering, and Exercising said Regiment in Arms, both inferior Officers and Soldiers; and to keep them in good Order and Discipline: and they are hereby commanded to obey you as their Major. And you are yourself to observe and follow such orders and Instructions, as you shall from Time to Time receive from me, or your superior Officers.

"Given under my Hand, and the Seal of the Said Commonwealth the fourth Day of September in the year of our Lord 1797, and in the Twenty Second Year of the Independence of the United States of America.

"John Avery, Sec'y."

His eldest dau., Sally E. Parker, thus wrote to her uncle Nahum Parker, Esq., of Fitzwilliam, N. H., under date of Nov. 14, 1818:

"My Dear Uncle Nahum:

"Gladly would I save you the trouble of reading a letter of my composing, but it must not be so—I must write, tho it wrings my heart. Death has come boldly and resolutely into our windows and taken my Dear Father and laid him low, even in the grave. Yes, Dear Uncle, your *Brother* Elisha and *my* Father, lies shrowded in the tomb!! He died on Monday morn, about five oclock, aged almost sixty four. O Hard we find it to part with our Father—There was everything done for him that could be done; my Mother waited on him by night and by day, and now she bears up her trouble with Christian fortitude. We have always been to my Father for advice, and now when we want his advice the most we can not have it. Uncle, if you lived here what a benefit you would be to us. We all join with Mother in sending love to you and Aunt, and all your children. Dear Uncle, may we all be prepared to meet Death, whenever it comes. Adieu.

"Sally E. Parker."

Their children were:

Sally E. Parker, b. Jan. 10, 1780; d. unm. at her brother Elijah's home at Cambria, N. Y. She was a school-teacher, a very accomplished and remarkable lady.

89. Betsey Parker, b. March 25, 1782; m. Gardner Paige, native of Hardwick.

90. Lydia Parker, b. March 8, 1784; m. Amory Parker (cousin), native of Hubbardston.

91. Elisha Parker, b. Nov. 23, 1787; m. Eunice Dean of Barnard, Vt. } Twins.
92. Elijah Parker, b. Nov. 23, 1787; m. Rhody Butler of Fairfield, Vt. } Twins.
93. Patty Parker, b. May 3, 1790; m. Elijah Barnes.
Francis D. Parker, b. May 13, 1792; d. Feb. 9, 1793.
Francis Dana Parker, b. July 18, 1794. He removed from town but where he settled is not known.
Augusta Parker, b. May 29, 1796; d. April 3, 1809.
94. James Sullivan Parker, b. Aug. 1, 1798.
95. Jonas Parker, b. Sept. 15, 1800; m. Lima Freeman, native of Barnard, Vt.
Frederick Parker, b. Aug. 10, 1802; d. Dec. 4, 1804.
Frederick Parker, b. April 11, 1805; d. May 7, 1809.

30. Ephraim Parker *(Amos,[5] Andrew,[4] John,[3] Hananiah,[2] Thomas[1])*, the fifth son of Amos and Anna (Stone) Parker, was b. in Shrewsbury, Oct. 4, 1757; d. Dec. 1, 1810, aged 53 years.

[The following sketch was written by Hon. Amos A. Parker of Fitzwilliam, N. H., who still survives, aged 100 years, to tell us the true story of the olden time:]

Ephraim Parker was a Revolutionary soldier, but the time of service cannot be ascertained. There were seven brothers and all but the youngest went into the army. The latter, Frederick Parker, was too young to be a soldier, but he was also a firm patriot and wrote encouraging letters to his brothers while in actual service; some of them are now before me.

Ephraim Parker, after the Revolution, went to Royalston and resided there a few years, then removed to Fitzwilliam, N. H., in 1786, and settled on two lots of land in the west part of the town and bordering on Richmond town line. After he had cleared land and erected a comfortable house he m. Abigail Baker of Royalston. She was a cousin of Abel Baker, one of the earliest settlers of the town of Fitzwilliam, and her residence was near that of her cousin; so they were neighbors during life.

Ephraim Parker was a good and successful farmer. He owned some 200 acres of good land, which he so well cultivated that in time it became one of the best farms in town.

He had two large barns, sheds, corn-barns, etc., all in their season well filled of the products of the farm, such as hay, grain and vegetables. He had much to sell besides supplying his own family. He was a man of good judgment, honest and exact in all his dealings, and might have filled many of the offices of the town, but he would not take any, though often urged to do so. And the only office he was ever known to take was that of highway surveyor in his own district. On being asked the reason of his declining all office, he said he *preferred* his farm, others *preferred* office, and so his course of life was gratifying to himself, and to his fellow-citizens also, and therefore was a wise course to take.

He lived on a farm bordering on the Richmond town line on the west, and my father, Nahum Parker, lived on a lot bordering on the Rindge town line on the east, so they were as far apart as they could be and live in the same town. Six miles of the town was between them, but as the roads were at the time it was one mile further, but notwithstanding the seven miles the families frequently visited, generally on horseback.

Both brothers were constant attendants at meeting on Sunday, and at noon, in some secluded place, they met and had an hour's interesting conference. If anything happened so that my father did not attend meeting I had to take his place at the noon conference. But it was no irksome task, for he was a man of mind, solid good sense, a great reader and interesting in conversation. Although pleasant "in manner," he was always sedate. I never heard him laugh or crack a joke or make a pun.

Strangely enough (although not a solitary case), as he became rich he felt *poor*, and as he became richer and richer he felt poorer and poorer, until he really imagined he should come to want. He was on the alert, looked after his affairs with much zeal, urged economy at his table and in all things, indoors and out. My father tried every way to convince him that he was *really* far above want, that it was not possible he should end life in a poor-house, that he had an abundance of property, and no probability of any loss, but *all*, *all* in vain. No one could convince him of the *true* state of his affairs, though he "rose from the dead."

This, finally increased as time wore on, so much so he could not sleep nights in any good, quiet, healthy sleep. and some nights none at all. At last, he became an excited monomaniac, and on the first day of December, 1810, after a sleepless night, he rose at daybreak, went to his corn-barn and with the reins of a harness strangled himself! Thus lived and thus died Ephraim Parker,—an honest man, good citizen, kind husband and true friend, and in the full vigor of health, wealth and at the early age of 53.

My uncle, Hollis Parker, came from Shrewsbury to attend the funeral. I went with them, the Rev. Mr. Sabin officiated, and it was an impressive scene, better imagined than described. At the grave-yard, after the body was place in the grave, Mr. Sabin came forth and made a short address—more fervent and pathetic than I ever heard him before or since. He began "In the midst of life we are in death," and closed with "Let this event be another instance of the frail nature of man."

He had but one child, a daughter, named Abigail, after her mother.

96. ABIGAIL PARKER, b. March 5, 1796; m. March 31, 1812, Joshua Worcester of Jaffrey, N. H.

The widow of Ephraim Parker m. for a second husband, March 24, 1814, Jonas Fay of Mason, N. H. She d. Feb. 13, 1840, aged 82.

31. Hon. Nahum Parker *(Amos,[5] Andrew,[4] John,[3] Hananiah,[2] Thomas[1])*, son of Amos and Anna Curwen (Stone) Parker. This sketch is a son's memory of his honored father. It was written in April, 1889, by Hon. Amos A. Parker in the 98th year of his age.

Nahum Parker, the sixth son of Amos Parker of Shrewsbury, was b. at Shrewsbury, March 4, 1760. He was a Revolutionary soldier and went to the war at the early age of 16 years; was in the Continental army; was at the surrender of Burgoyne at Saratoga in 1777.

After the war he m. and settled in Gerry, now Phillipston, August 11, 1783. He moved to Shrewsbury in 1784, and to Fitzwilliam, N. H., in March, 1786. *The History of Fitzwilliam* truthfully says:

Hon. Nahum Parker.

"The fidelity and ability of Mr. Parker were at once recognized by the people of Fitzwilliam, and he was soon called to fill offices of trust. The proprietors of the township elected him their clerk and treasurer, and he held these offices till the closing up of the business of the proprietors in 1815. Though not admitted as a lawyer, he was well acquainted with the forms and merits of civil proceedings, and brought to all his public duties a well trained mind, a habit of exactness in all legal proceedings, and accounting for all the funds in his possession. To all these qualifications for public service he added an almost faultless penmanship, so, from the date of his election as clerk of the proprietors, their record books became easy of comprehension.

"In 1790 Mr. Parker was chosen one of the selectmen of Fitzwilliam, and held the office for four successive years. Beginning with 1792 he was chosen moderator of town meetings, and served

Nahum Parker at the age of 15 years, with five of his brothers, was a soldier in the Continental army and was present and took part in the battles that resulted in the capture of Burgoyne's forces near Saratoga, N. Y., in 1777. After the surrender he was discharged and came home on foot, walking with his luggage from Saratoga, N. Y., to Shrewsbury. At Fitzwilliam the family still has in its possession, and will with pleasure show to those interested in such things, a relic which Nahum Parker brought off from the field of battle after the surrender of Burgoyne's army. It is a bottle of dark glass with a very short neck, holding about a quart. This was doubtless lost in the fight by some British soldier or Hessian trooper.

in that capacity more than twenty years. In 1792 he was chosen to represent the town in the Legislature and served in that capacity annually until 1804—a period of ten years. In 1806 he was again chosen Representative and served the town in that capacity for twelve years. He was also Councillor, member of the State Senate, of which he was chosen President, and for some twenty years was a Judge of the Court of Common Pleas. In 1806 he was chosen by the Legislature a Senator in the United States Senate. He died November 12th, 1839, aged 80 years. His disease was paralysis of the brain.

"He was a Revolutionary pensioner, and during the Revolutionary war he kept a diary and sent that to the Secretary of War with his oath, declaring he was the identical person who kept it, and asked what further testimony was needed to obtain a pension. The answer was '*none*,' and immediately he received his pension certificate. John C. Calhoun was then Secretary of War."

Nahum Parker never had the benefit of a public school. He attended a private school a few weeks, and his mother did all she could to instruct him, but she was not an educated woman and had but little time to devote to any one of so large a family of children. But with little *instruction* he at last became well *educated*. He had learned to *read* well before he went to the Revolutionary war, and there began the practice of writing by keeping a journal of events, and in after-life, when selectman of Fitzwilliam, he kept a journal of all his transactions. At length, he became a very perfect penman. On a page it looked elegant and faultless. He was a deep thinker and a great reader. After settling in Fitzwilliam he took the *Columbian Informer*, printed at Keene, and when that was merged in the *New Hampshire Sentinel* took that to the day of his death. He also took a newspaper printed at Worcester, as that would give him news of his friends settled in and around his native town of Shrewsbury. Books of instruction he bought as fast as he was able, but no novels. He also accumulated quite a law library. In short, he became a well posted citizen and a good lawyer, so that in all the various offices he held he was well able to discharge all their duties with ability and credit.

He was given much employment as a draftsman by his fellow-townsmen in drawing up deeds, agreements and all contracts, however difficult to make. When he was chosen selectman in 1790, the town's affairs were in a confused state and it took him four years to bring order out of chaos.

In 1795 he was chosen moderator of the annual town meeting, and he was such an efficient officer that he preformed that duty for more than twenty years, as has been stated. Although courteous, he had a sedate, positive manner and a strong, commanding voice, and when he called for order, order came. Few men could accurately dispatch business like him. Solemn, sedate and silent was his walk, yet he appeared to be in deep thought. He was seldom known to crack a joke or laugh at one, and yet his deportment was always such as to indicate a kind heart and true benevolence. His charities were many, yet private, for his motto was "Not to let his right hand know what his left hand was doing."

One fine trait in Nahum Parker's life was, he was not an office seeker. His motto was that "Offices were for the public and not for the individual." In proof of this two letters are now extant, one from Gov. Langdon and the other from Gov. Plummer, both urging him to accept the office of Judge, when they severally sent him his commissions. What a contrast now! Men are now running mad for office and will compass heaven and earth to obtain it, and those the least fit for office are ahead in the race.

He was also a man of strict morals and pure in speech. No one ever heard him use profane, vulgar or obscene language. He was a keen observer of passing events and a deep thinker. On the road, nothing worth seeing escaped his notice, and when he had passed over a long distance he could give another man correct directions over the entire route.

At work in the field, he did not permit story-telling or talk, except in regard to the work in hand. At home, he was never talkative, but generally absorbed in deep thought or reading a book and oblivious to all surrounding movements. And yet, at times he would hold forth on some important subject and sift it to the bottom. It was marvellous to hear him take hold of a subject with such an irresistible grasp, and so fully and clearly explain it. Sometimes, he would enter into particulars and give his children solid advice, teach them *how* to behave, *how* to act and *how* to learn. He would observe that a person might learn something all the days of his life did he note passing events. The besetting sin of the people was lack of *attention*. Few people were good listeners, interested in the subject before them, and could give no particular account of what they had heard. Few people could tell much about a sermon, or discourse immediately after delivery, and because they had not paid attention when it was delivered. In fine, he was a safe example to follow, in word, thought and deed. Sometimes hard to follow, but I am glad I did.

When in the full vigor of life his business was great and extensive, for he not only superintended the cultivation of a large farm, keeping one of the best stocks of cattle, but in settling estates, acting as referee and in making deeds, contracts, etc., far and near. No townsman was equal to him in laying handsome stone wall, and this he continued to do until all the cultivated part of his farm was walled in.

In wakeful hours, he spent no idle time. He was never known to go to a party, take tea or dine in his own neighborhood or in the village. But he had his strong friendships and pleasant companions, among whom was Dr. Phillip Monroe of Surry, N. H., some 20 miles away. The Doctor was a man of mind, well educated, social, pleasant and good company. When they met, they became so much interested that they took no note of time, and midnight came before they were aware, and still they must have a few last words.

Among the stated visitors was Judge Abel Parker of Jaffrey, N. H., eight miles distant. They were distant relatives. It was settled that each with his wife should visit the other, alternately, twice a year. The men had been acquainted with each other many years before their wives met, and when they did meet, a practical joke was played upon them. But this was planed and engineered by Judge Abel, Judge Nahum simply looked on and enjoyed it. It was in this wise, Judge Abel in coming over on their first visit to Fitzwilliam told his wife that the lady she was about to visit was *very deaf* and she must halloo quite loud to make her hear. So when they arrived and passed into the house Judge Abel said in a loud voice,

"Mrs. Parker, shall I make you acquainted with my wife?" His voice was so loud she thought his own wife was deaf. The reply was in a loud voice, "Pretty well, I thank you." The first speaker said, "You need not talk so loud for *I am not deaf* if *you* are." "But I ain't *deaf*." "Then neither of us are." They stared at each other a moment, and then looked around and saw their two husbands in a broad grin; the joke was manifest, and all four had a jolly time over it. The acquaintance of the wives, so facetiously begun, ripened into a strong friendship and ended only with life.

In regard to the religious belief of Judge Parker little need be said, for one thing is clear, he honestly *practised* religion, whatever might have been his belief; and it is well said that an honest man is the noblest work of God. No doubt he had clear and well defined views of the Christian religion and was not "tossed about by every wind of doctrine." He and his wife were members of the Congregational Church in Shrewsbury. They transferred their connection with that Church to the Church in Fitzwilliam when they came here in 1786. The Covenant of the Church was adopted in 1771. To this they agreed and became regular members in full communion. The First Brigham Covenant answered the purpose for which it was made for more than half a century, until 1825, when new light was said to be discovered. The creeds of the several Congregational Churches in the County of Cheshire were not all alike, and some of them not up to the strict standard of Calvinism. Accordingly, the Monadnock Association of Ministers, in solemn conclave at Keene, adopted a new creed for all the Churches in the county, with instructions to discard the old and adopt the new.

The New Lights had a large majority and were determined to exercise that power, but lacked a plausible pretence. After quite a number of Church meetings and various forms had been considered, at last one short undefined resolution was adopted. In substance this: *Resolved*, That A. B., etc., be and hereby are excommunicated from this Church *for error in doctrine*. Judge Parker and wife, with nine others, were included in the resolution. He was present at the time, and in a quiet, dignified, firm voice said, "I thank God that the new Church of Fitzwilliam don't hold the keys of Heaven or hell," and departed to return no more. From this time the town was divided and the contest sharp and severe. Judge Parker spoke of it with unending regret and it no doubt shortened his days.

As it has been said, the Judge was not a talkative man. Some one of his neighbors would occasionally call upon him to have a social chat. He would receive them pleasantly and then quietly sit and hear all the gossip of the neighborhood in silence. The neighbor would do all the talking and he all the hearing. When asked why he did not say something himself, he would answer that his neighbor would not have comprehended anything more than mere gossip, and as he liked to talk and he had rather listen, both were gratified.

The wife, Mary Deeth, was a dau. of John and Jerusha Deeth of Hopkinton. She is remembered as an efficient woman and a good housewife. She d. June 4, 1837, aged 77.

Their children were:

97. Hannah Parker, b. in Shrewsbury, Dec. 26, 1784; m. Luna Foster of Fitzwilliam, N. H.

98. Austin Parker, b. in Fitzwilliam, N. H., Jan. 24, 1787; m. Susan Martin of Gardner.

Maria Parker, b. in Fitzwilliam, July 26, 1789; m. Dr. Samuel Lane, Jr., at her father's house in Fitzwilliam, June 1, 1814, and settled in Swanzey, N. H. Their infant child was b. March 25 and d. March 27, 1815; after great distress she herself d. April 1, 1815, aged 25 years. He survived her but a few months. He was a skilful physician and had a large practice.

99. Amos Andrew Parker, b. in Fitzwilliam, Oct. 8, 1791; m. (1) Miranda W. Sanders of Medfield, (2) Mary McClary of Epsom, N. H., (3) Julia E. Smith of Glastonbury, Ct.

100. Ephraim Parker, b. in Fitzwilliam, Aug. 18, 1793; m. Lucy Stone of Fitzwilliam.

101. Nahum Parker, b. in Fitzwilliam, March 16, 1797; m. ——— Bean of Nottingham, N. H.

Selina Parker, b. in Fitzwilliam, July 5, 1799; m. John Damon of Fitzwilliam.

102. Elmon Parker, b. in Fitzwilliam, Jan. 20, 1802; m. Abigail M. Gray of Belfast, Me.

Sidney Parker, b. in Fitzwilliam, July 3, 1804; d. April 26, 1815, aged ten years.

32. Rev. Frederick Parker *(Amos,[5] Andrew,[4] John,[3] Hananiah,[2] Thomas[1])*, the youngest son of Amos and Anna (Stone) Parker of Shrewsbury, was b. in Shrewsbury, May 4, 1762; graduated at Harvard University in 1784, and licensed to preach in June, 1787; m. Nov. 25, 1793, Susanna Foster, dau. of Dea. Asa Foster and Hannah Simonds of Canterbury, N. H. She was a niece of the Hon. Abiel Foster, a member of Congress when the United States Government was at Philadelphia.

He was ordained in the pastoral office of the Congregational Church in Canterbury by a unanimous vote of the Church and town, Jan. 5, 1791, and suddenly died there April 21, 1802, in the fortieth year of his age.

In 1795 he came to visit my father at Fitzwilliam. I was but a small boy then, but I remember his personal appearance very well. He came on horseback and was dressed in the usual style of the ministers of that day, cocked up hat, small-clothes, knee buckles and fair top boots. He talked pleasantly to us boys, preached on Sunday for Rev. Priest Brigham, and left after a few days' visit. That was the only time I ever saw him, but he corresponded with my father till the day of his death in 1802. Many letters of his to my father, as well as a diary, are in my possession at the present time.

I find by his diary that he began preaching in June, 1787, and for four years he preached at various places before he was ordained at Canterbury in 1791. He made a list of the various places he preached, and the number of times in each place, which is now before me. It appears that he preached at the following places, to wit: Falmouth, Casco Bay, now Portland, Black Point, Kennebunk, Biddeford, Me.; Charleston, Hampton Falls, Plaistow, N. H.; Westminster, Princetown, Grafton, Andover, Haverhill, Amesbury, Newbury, Methuen, Hopkinton, Shrewsbury, Hardwick, Braintree, Greenage Lock, East Hampton, Chesterfield and Middlefield.

On hearing that a vacancy had occurred in Canterbury, N. H., by the resignation of the Rev. Abial Foster, he went there to preach as a candidate. In due time, he had a call to settle, cordial and unanimous. He was thereupon ordained January 5, 1791, and as he died April 21, 1802, he was the pastor for a few months more than 11 years. He was then not quite 40 years old, but in the full vigor of life and usefulness. But at midnight, in his bed, without warning, he suddenly started for eternity, and left many relatives and friends in tears!

As a preacher, he was fervent and interesting. No one could sleep within the sound of his voice when he was in the pulpit. It is said that his sermons were unequal; sometimes dry and uninteresting; yet at times he would truly "be in the spirit of the Lord's day," his face would glow with emotion, and he would burst forth with such a flow of eloquence that would seemingly wake the dead and leave the audience drenched in tears.

I had in my possession perhaps 500 sermons of his writing, and spent much time in trying to read any one of them in vain. He wrote in cipher, hieroglyphics, marks, lines and dots. No one could read them but himself, and, therefore, I have put them all into the fire. But after preaching awhile he did not write his sermons as a rule, but only on some particular occasion. Some of his most powerful sermons were delivered without notes.

After he graduated he spent some of his time in teaching school and in *that* was very successful. In one of his letters to my father he says:

> "I am tolerably happy, have got the best school-house I ever saw. I have kept in it 5 weeks. supported good government and order, have not corrected one scholar—and have the satisfaction to see the scholars make daily progress in learning—and to have the approbation of the inhabitants beyond my expectations. The methods of discipline are various—some of them perhaps droll, but all tended to the *reformation* of the boys. I have never but once appeared to have been angry in school; and this is *one* valuable method, among many others, to make a school love and obey. I have 60 to 70 scholars, some girls."

A *model* teacher and a *model* neighborhood, surely.

He seems to have been very much attached to his kindred, father, mother, brothers and sisters. Although it is apparent from his writings that he had a preference, it seems he sadly lamented the death of his father in 1790. He attended upon him in his last sickness, and noted what was done and said.

I give an extract from his diary under date of December 20, 1790, in the evening:

"Father, we think you are dying.

"What makes you think so?

"Because you grow weaker and don't speak so plainly as you did.

"Are you willing to die?

"In some measure.

"Do you hope to be happy hereafter?

"He squeezed my hand.

"Do you know me?

"Yes, I know you all.

"You have prayed for us and we thank you, and we all pray for you.

"I have prayed for you with all my ability and used my best endeavors."

Dec. 21. He said "Anna." His oldest daughter.

23. At ten oclock in the evening he died—breathing his last, and a mortal paleness came over his face. Aged 67 yrs. 4 m. 16 days.

Dec. 24. Friday—Uncle Thomas expected here.

25. Isaac here—Saturday.

26. Sunday, at night came Amos, Hollis, Ephraim, Nahum.

27. Isaac and Elisha; and uncles Andrew and Thomas.

"Attended funeral in sleighs reaching this side causeway to Mr. Goddard's—and committed the remains of our departed friend to the cold prison of the grave." More than a mile.

Mrs. Susan (Foster) Parker survived her husband 44 years. About the first half of it was at the homestead at Canterbury, but owing to the early death of her youngest and very promising son, Cyrus Parker, she removed to Lowell, and the other half was spent in keeping a boarding-house for the factory girls in that city. She, with her only dau. Harriet, managed it with great success. Everything was done in such a neat and tidy manner, and the girls were treated more like relatives and friends than boarders, that their house was eagerly sought for and always full. The daughter was well educated, of fine personal appearance, of great intelligence and ladylike in all her movements. She had great conversational powers, and no one could chat with her, even for a short time, without feeling interested, highly entertained, and pronounce her at once very good company. Although she lived almost half a century, and would have made a first-rate housekeeper and a model wife, she never married, and for two reasons, first, she did not like to part with her widowed mother, and second, the fear of not finding a suitable companion. Any one who visited them would at once see that an unusual affection existed between mother and daughter, and that they were intimate companions as well as relatives.

Aunt Susan Parker came to visit my father at Fitzwilliam on horseback in 1807. They were intellectual, enjoyed books and had many. Many an interesting chat we had, and in time I was able in some good measure to appreciate their real worth.

After the death of Harriet at Lowell, the mother went back to Canterbury and lived with her father's family until her death, Feb. 24, 1846, aged 70 years.

The children were all b. in Canterbury, N. H.:

HARRIET PARKER, b. Aug. 21, 1794; d. at Lowell, 1842, aged 48.

HOLLIS PARKER, b. Aug. 15, 1796, and while a boy went to live with his aunt Elizabeth at Worcester, who was the wife of Amos Whitney. He stayed there until he was 21, when he in April, 1818, bought a farm of 45 acres in the south part of Holden. His cousin, Amos A., who knew him well, says: "He was a very promising young man, of perfect habits and much intellectual power." He kept a diary from which is copied the following: It describes his attempt to find a school to teach in his journey west in 1817. It well illustrates the effect of modern inventions regarding travel. He required two days and two nights for his trip to Albany, and the use of many horses. Now, by the tourist's power alone, this journey is easily made in less time with the "noiseless steed."

"March 27, 1817, started from Worcester in the stage for Albany about 3 o'clock P. M.; Ariv'd in Leicester at ½ past 5 and at Spencer at ½ past 6 & at Brookfield at ½ past 8.

"March 28, started from Brookfield and Ariv'd at Northampton not till 4 o'clock P. M.; started from N. H. about ½ past 11 in the stage. After we left Northampton about 10 miles we were forced to take sleighing in consideration of their being so much snow on the mountain that it was impassable in any other way. We arrived at Pittsfield on the 29th at 4 o'clock; started again at 6, changed sleigh for carriage at Lebanon, in which we arrived at Albany about 2 o'clock, stopping on the E. side of the River.

"* * * I have had the chance of 6 schools but no more than ten dollars per month. Not until this afternoon did I ever realize the blessings of a good home. On this first of April how different do things appear to what they usually have. I almost envy the birds their happiness, for they are pouring forth their notes of gratitude while I can scarce keep from despair.—The weather is most delightful but I would rather be following the plow than in such business that I am now. Knowing that I can do better than ten dollars per month at home, I presume that unless 'Bhos' has had better luck than myself, one week more will find us both in Worcester.

"B is to start tomorrow on foot and myself on Monday next to start in the stage until I overtake him, then he will take the stage and I shall walk the remainder of the way back to Albany, and then I think we shall not turn back until we get as far as Worcester."

Honest boy! We can easily sympathize with him in this his first experience with the outside world.

In Holden he was a farmer eight years. For several years before his death he was partially blind, so he could not see near objects but could discern time three miles distant on the town clock. He d. at Holden, Jan. 2, 1827, aged 31 years, and unmarried.

SUSANNA FOSTER PARKER, b. Jan. 23, 1799; d. Dec. 6, 1799, perishing by her clothes taking fire. She lived but a few hours after the accident in great distress. A very promising child and the idol of her parents. Her death in that awful manner so sadly afflicted them that they gave way to their grief and refused to be comforted.

CYRUS PARKER, b. Dec. 4, 1800; graduated at Dartmouth College in 1824; then went to Georgia as a teacher in a planter's family, and d. there Sept. 22, 1825, aged nearly 25 years.

None of these children married and this branch of the Parker family became extinct.

33. Dea. Ebenezer Parker (*Thomas,*[5] *Andrew,*[4] *John,*[3] *Hananiah,*[2] *Thomas*[1]), son of Thomas and Jane (Parrott) Parker, b. in Lexington, Aug. 13, 1750, and bap. Aug. 19, 1750. He m. in Lexington, Dec. 3, 1772, Dorcas, b. in Lexington, Nov. 14, 1750, dau. of William and Tabitha (Hobbs-Jones) Monroe. Her mother's original name was Hobbs, dau. of Josiah Hobbs who settled in Weston. She m. (1) —— Jones, and (2) William Monroe, as above stated. Dorcas was the tenth of a family of 11 children. Mr. Monroe was a blacksmith, and son of Lieut. John Monroe of Lexington, who with others had 900 acres of land granted to them in 1735 for services in the Indian fight at Lamprey River, June 6, 1690, besides filling nearly every public office of the town. The Monroe family of Lexington, with whom the Parkers intermarried more frequently than with any other, have always been one of the foremost families of the town. They were always remarkable for bravery, coolness, strength of body and of mind, and were always active and prominent in military affairs. Their genealogy is easily traced to 1300, in connection with the history of Scotland.

Ebenezer Parker was an active member of Capt. John Parker's company of minute-men, having the duty of corporal. At the time of the fight he showed much coolness in remaining upon the field while the company were dispersing, in an attempt to dissuade his uncle Jonas Parker from his vow, that under no circumstances would he run from the British. The enemy were approaching and surrounding them, and as he was unable to change his uncle's determination he had to leave him to the enemy and flee for his own life. This must have been very disheartening for young Ebenezer, who would have been glad to have carried his uncle bodily from the field. In addition to participating in the affairs of the morning he joined in the march to Concord, the return and the lively work which ensued during the enemy's retreat. He was with his company when they marched to Cambridge, May 6, 1775, remaining there some time to prevent any further excursions of the British into the country. Again, at the time of the battle of Bunker Hill a detachment of 60 was made up, and with Capt. John Parker he proceeded to Cambridge, where they were ordered to guard the "Neck," at Charlestown, much against their wishes, as they preferred to be in the thickest of the fight.

He removed from Lexington with his father to Princeton in 1777. He and his wife were dismissed from the Church in Lexington to the Church in Princeton, Nov. 9, 1788. His father in the year 1795 transferred his estate to Ebenezer, as follows:

"I Thomas Parker of Princeton in Co. of W. and Com. of Mass. Gentleman, for and in consideration of the love and affection which

DEA. EBENEZER PARKER.

I bear to Ebenezer Parker, being my only son do give by these presents unto him the s[d] Ebenezer Parker a certain tract or Messuage of land lying and being in Princeton afores[d] containing about 300 acres."

He mentioned also the "Pond and Saw Mill Dam," also "the Grist Mill and Saw Mill and all the privileges of the stream." Two hundred acres had already been set off from the large "Black Grove Farm": 100 to Philemon Parker, his cousin, and 100 to Mrs. Jonas Smith, Thomas Parker's only daughter, and her family. But in 1794 Ebenezer bought out Mr. Smith, and soon increased his estate to 600 acres, besides owning farms in Stamford, Vt., Rindge and Fitzwilliam, N. H., and in Barre, Mass.

He was actively associated with Church and town affairs. He was a deacon of the Church, and was familiarly known as Deacon Parker. When he came to Princeton he with Jonas Smith were signers of the Princeton Declaration of Independence, probably drawn up about 1775. He was made assessor of the town in 1782, in which capacity he served almost continuously for 20 years. Beginning with 1786 he was selectman almost constantly until 1805. He was a true, generous friend and a very valuable citizen. All matters, whether political, theological or intellectual, pertaining to the benefit of his townsmen, received his active and influential support. During 1796, '97 and 1800, he was elected representative from the district of Princeton, Rutland and Oakham. He was administrator of estates and guardian. His tavern business was considerable, as he kept as many as ten ridable horses, which at that time the business demanded. He was an energetic and successful farmer, keeping his stock at 30 cattle and 40 sheep. He was gifted with a strong physique, was stout in stature, although less so, it is said, than his father Thomas Parker. He was a man of mind; was noted for his firm decision, and his strong, though pleasant, expression of countenance.

He believed in discipline and practised it with good government in his family. His words bespoke a sturdy, thoughtful character, and when he had anything to say everybody listened. Thus highly respected, his last years were, however, passed in feeble health. On this account he was unable to respond to the invitation of his native town on her sixtieth anniversary of the battle of Lexington. This was celebrated April 20, 1835, with eleven surviving actors present. At the commencement of the exercises it was announced with regret that Dea. Parker was absent, and the cause was duly stated that it was "on account of the infirmities of age." For a few years previous to the Deacon's decease his delight was to read the Bible constantly. He was able also to pick out any passage in it.

Mrs. Dorcas Parker d. "suddenly" (as is stated in the town records), Nov. 28, 1798. She was a most worthy lady and her loss was very widely lamented. He m. (2) Mrs. Mary (Binney) Rice, widow of Solomon Rice, who d. in Princeton, Sept. 25, 1794. He thus became stepfather of two children, Betsey and John P. Rice. The latter became a well known merchant in Boston. The wife, Mary, d. March 22, 1816. He d. Oct. 19, 1839, thus living to the ripe old age of 89. They were both interred, as was Mrs. Dorcas Parker, in the family row at the homestead burying-gound. The first three children were b. and bap. in Lexington. All were by first wife, Dorcas, save the last born, A. Dwight Parker.

Their children were:

Abijah Parker, b. in Lexington, May 28, 1773; d. Aug. 21, 1775.

103. Quincy Parker,* b. in Lexington, April 28, 1775; m. Patience Brooks of Princeton.

104. Betsey Parker, b. in Princeton, June 8, 1777; m. Benjamin Gould of Princeton.

105. Polly Parker, b. in Princeton, May 4, 1779; m. (1) Rufus Dodds of Princeton, (2) Dr. Isaac Warren of Princeton.

106. Lucy Parker, b. in Princeton, March 11, 1781; m. (1) Jonas Beaman of Princeton, (2) Edward Hanford of Camden, Me.

107. Ebenezer Parker, Jr., b. in Princeton, June 4, 1784; m. Hannah B. Merriam, then of Princeton.

108. Bitha Parker, b. in Princeton, July 26, 1786; m. Charles Folger of Camden, Me.

Aurelius Dwight Parker, b. in Princeton, April 23, 1803. He was admitted to the bar in Boston, where he figured prominently

* Ebenezer Parker and John Quincy Adams were boys together in Lexington, and were, it is said, intimately associated. At the birth of Mr. Parker's second child both he and Mr. Adams felt honored that *Quincy* should be his name.

as a lawyer for many years. He showed remarkable perception on points of law, his contemporaries learning to regard his opinion as one of the very best. He was perhaps more of a consultation lawyer than a declaimer. It was considered that he was one of the most learned lawyers in Boston. Ofttimes long practised members of the bar referred difficult technical points of law to Mr. Parker for his decision. He died unmarried.

34. Mary Parker *(Thomas,[5] Andrew,[4] John,[3] Hananiah,[2] Thomas[1])*, dau. of Thomas and Jane (Parrott) Parker, b. in Lexington, Dec. 25, 1758; bap. in Lexington, July 13, 1760; m. in Waltham, Oct. 5, 1775, Jonas Smith, b. in Waltham, Dec. 21, 1748, son of Jonas and Thankful (Fiske) Smith. This date of birth is as the family have it, the Waltham record says Nov. 21, 1747. He had brothers Elijah and Zachariah, whose families resided in Waltham, but their descendants are now scattered. Some are living in Lexington. Jonas Smith, the father, was b. June 7, 1719, the son of Zachariah, who was son of Jonathan. Jonathan was son of Thomas, who was born in England and came to this country 1635, with his father John. In this way we see that the ancestors of the Smith-Parker family branch which follows, and of the Smith-Parker family found on pages 68–73, were in a good measure the same.

At about 1777 Jonas and Mary Parker Smith removed to Princeton, took up 100 acres of her father's large estate of 600 acres, and they became his nearest neighbors. They lived upon that spot where Mrs. Stacia Harrington now resides. Their farm was transferred to Dea. Ebenezer Parker in 1794.

He was known as Lieutenant Smith. He d. May 9, 1814, "aged 66," thus he was born in the latter part of 1747. She d. Dec. 27, 1817, aged 59.

Their children were:

1. Sally Smith, b. Dec. 13, 1775; d. July 25, 1815.
2. Abijah Parker Smith, b. March 6, 1777; d. Sept. 29, 1778.
3. Abijah Parker Smith, b. Jan. 22 (or 12 as Princeton Records have it), 1779; m. 1802, Submit Howe, b. in Wilton, N. H., dau. of Israel and Submit (Keyes) Howe, later of Princeton. Mr. Smith was a shoemaker in Prince-

ton, where all his family were born. He afterwards removed to Waltham. Their children were:

- I. ABIJAH SMITH, m. and lived in Waltham.
- II. JONAS SMITH, lived in Rutland, d. by drowning, and left no issue.
- III. CHARLES SMITH, drowned in Rutland. Children:
  1. Henry Smith.
  2. Dana Smith.
  3. Lucy Smith.
  4. Thomas Smith.
  5. Israel Smith.
- IV. ELINOR SMITH, m. ——— Batchelder, and lived in Waltham.
- V. GEORGE SMITH, a farmer of Warwick.
- VI. PHEBE SMITH, m. ——— Garfield.
- VII. SARAH SMITH, m. ——— French, a lawyer of Waltham.
- VIII. WILLIAM SMITH.

4. WILLIAM SMITH, b. May 27 (Princeton Records read 23), 1781; m. Sept. 13, 1804, Lois Mirick, b. in Princeton, Oct. 24, 1785, dau. of John and Lois (Hobbs) Mirick of Princeton. He lived in Boston; kept a shoe store; d. in Sterling, July 18, 1855. Their children were:

- I. HARRIETT SMITH, b. Jan. 20, 1805; m. at Boston, Oct. 27, 1833, John G., b. in Sterling, March 22, 1804, son of Timothy and Sally (Smith) Hosmer. He was a chairmaker, and lived in Waltham. She still (1892) resides in Waltham in the 88th year of her age.
- II. LOIS SMITH, b. Nov. 30, 1806; m. ——— Wellington. She lived in Waltham and d. there several years since. She had four children.
- III. MOSES MIRICK SMITH, b. May 27, 1809; d. in Binghamton, N. Y. He left three sons.
- IV. WILLIAM SMITH, b. Feb. 24, 1811. Baptist minister in Chelsea. He d. soon after his ordination.
- V. THOMAS PARKER SMITH, b. Oct. 13, 1812. Dry goods merchant in Boston. Removed to West Medford, where he d., and left an issue.
- VI. SALLY SMITH, b. June 22, 1815; m. Horace A. Breed of Boston. They settled in West Medford, where they have both deceased. They left three children.
- VII. SOPHRONA MIRICK SMITH, b. May 29, 1817; d. in Sterling, unm.

5. JONAS SMITH, b. Aug. 3, 1783; d. Sept. 27, 1783.
6. JONAS SMITH, b. Nov. 22, 1784; d. May 22, 1786.
7. CYRUS SMITH, b. Aug. 3 (Princeton Records read 5), 1787; m. June 17, 1812, Prudence Wilder of Sterling, b. in Princeton; built the Estabrook House, kept the Wachusett House and was afterwards a farmer. He d. Oct. 3, 1861. She d. Dec. 12, 1871, aged 78. All their children were b. in Princeton:

I. FOSTER SMITH, b. Jan. 12, 1815; d. unm.

II. ADALAIDE BOWMAN SMITH, b. March 9, 1817; m. James F. Barnes, a native of London; removed to Wheeling, W. Va., where she d. about 1847. Their children were:

1. Adalaide Barnes, resides in Wheeling, W. Va.
2. Thyrza Barnes, m. Herman Schockey, and resides in Wheeling, W. Va.

III. MARY ANN SMITH, b. Nov. 9, 1818; m. Oct. 15, 1840, Eli, son of Seth and Polly (Hastings) Banister of Boylston, was a farmer and miller. He d. 1874. She resides at the homestead in Boylston. Their children were:

1. Linden Banister, b. Nov. 21, 1841; m. Elizabeth Maynard of Northborough. No issue.
2. Seth Banister, b. Oct. 23, 1845; m. Harriett Flagg of Boylston. He is a farmer in Boylston and has three sons.

IV. CATHARINE SMITH, b. May 1, 1821; d. in Princeton, aged about 45, unm.

V. LEONARD SMITH, b. June 23, 1822; m. Betsey, dau. of Nathan Farnsworth of Templeton. They lived in Templeton. Both are now deceased. He d. 1865. Their children were:

1. Leonard Farnsworth, removed to New Hampshire.
2. Lucy Farnsworth, d. Feb., 1866.
3. Adalaide Farnsworth, school-teacher in Boston.
4. Henry Marshall Farnsworth, resides at Templeton.

VI. JANE PARKER SMITH, b. Sept. 6, 1824; m. James S. Pinkham of Worcester, as his second wife. He was well known as an extensive carpet merchant. She resides in Worcester. No issue.

VII. FLAVILLE WILDER SMITH, b. June 23, 1826; m. Martha Pierce of Princeton. He d. without issue. She resides in Princeton.

VIII. LYDIA BABCOCK SMITH, b. March 9, 1832. Resides with her niece in Wheeling, W. Va., unm.

8. Jonas Smith, b. Aug. 5, 1790; m. (1) Oct. 24, 1814, Salome, b. in Princeton, April 8, 1796, dau. of Dr. Ephraim and Clarissa (Gale) Wilson of Princeton. They lived in Barre. He m. (2) Widow Mead, sister of his first wife, and had by both wives 12 children. The eldest child was Bradford Smith, who lived in Louisville, Ky.

9. Amos Smith, b. Dec. 29, 1791; m. Aug. 23, 1818, Betsey Gregory. He lived in Penfield, N. Y.; d. March 8, 1865. Their children were:

- i. Amos Smith, served in the Civil War, and is deceased.
- ii. Eliza Smith, d. in girlhood.
- iii. Dana Smith, lived in Webster, N. Y.
- iv. Charles Smith, d. in Chicago.
- v. Jones Smith, lived in Toronto, Ont.

10. Polly Smith, b. Jan. 2, 1794; m. Benjamin Buss of Sterling. They settled in Rutland, removed to Eastford, Conn., where she d. May, 1850. Their children were:

- i. Adaline Buss.
- ii. Frederick Buss, lives in Stockport, N. Y.

11. Ebenezer Smith, b. Dec. 3, 1798; d. June 11, 1873; m. at Princeton, Dec. 15, 1822, Anna Wilder, sister of Prudence Wilder of Sterling, b. May 27, 1790, dau. of Elihu and Prudence Wilder of that town. She d. April 15, 1870. They resided on his parents' place in the easterly part of the town, where he was a farmer. He represented the town in the Legislature for one year, was selectman two years and overseer of the poor at different times. Their child was:

- i. Addison Smith, b. in Princeton, May 28, 1827; m. (1) in Worcester, Oct. 28, 1856, Jeannette Brimner, of Yarmouth, N. S., b. in July, 1832; she d. Aug. 14, 1865; he m. (2) in Ghent, N. Y., Sept. 3, 1867, Martha, dau. of Jacob and Elizabeth New. He lived upon the old Smith place in Princeton for many years, where, in his early life, he and the Parker youths were boys together, and with whom he warmly associated. Later in life he removed to Southborough, where he now resides, a highly respected citizen. Children:

  1. Anna Smith, b. in Princeton, July 25, 1872. She is a teacher in Haverhill.
  2. Irving Smith, b. in Southborough, March 27, 1878.
  3. Jeannette Smith, b. in Southborough, Jan. 24, 1881.

35. Rhoda Parker *(Andrew,[5] Andrew,[4] John,[3] Hananiah,[2] Thomas[1])*, dau. of Dea. Andrew and Abigail (Jennison) Parker, b. in Lexington, June 19, 1760; m. 1785, Capt. Joseph Smith, a veteran soldier of the Revolution and a prominent citizen of Barre at the time. He was son of Joseph Smith of Sudbury, now Wayland, 16 miles west of Boston, and was one of a family of 13. Samuel, the oldest of this large family, was also a Revolutionary soldier, and owned a farm in Barre, where he d. in 1815.

Rhoda Parker, his worthy wife, survived him. She d. in Barre, May 1, 1814, aged 54. Her grandson wrote: "They were buried two miles north of Barre village, where they lie side by side." He was a man of much force of character and kind and indulgent to his family.

After the Revolution Lt. Smith held various town offices and was treasurer in 1792. He was an innholder. His first location was easterly of where E. W. Hemenway now lives and on the opposite side of the highway. In 1801 he erected a tavern of which he had charge about 12 years. This house is now used for a dwelling-house and is opposite the schoolhouse in old district No. 9.

As Capt. Smith was a prominent citizen of Barre, and his descendants are so numerous, the following brief biography is fitting for our genealogy. Jonas Smith, who m. Rhoda Parker, was b. Nov. 12, 1739. He enlisted in the Revolutionary army in Colonel Prescott's regiment, some time previous to the Battle of Bunker Hill. Prescott was one of the commanding officers in that battle, but the company to which Mr. Smith belonged was that day stationed northwest of the hill, toward Cambridgeport, to prevent those on the hill from being flanked. He afterwards went with the army to Long Island and White Plains, and was one of the 1,200 who stormed Fort Stony Point. He was with the army when it passed that winter of hardships at Valley Forge, where he had the small-pox and suffered terrible privations for his country. He afterwards went south with Washington and was in most of the principal battles, and at Yorktown when Cornwallis surrendered. He was Captain of a light infantry company in Col. Rufus Putnam's regiment, and was one of the officers called together by Washington when he delivered his farewell address. His company disbanded in 1783 and he returned to his home in Barre. He was 43 years of age at this time. Two years later he married Rhoda Parker at the age of 25. He owned a farm of 173 acres, being what is known as the "Rocking Stone Farm." A mention of the famous stone, from which the place takes its name, is made in the *Geological History of Mass.* He was also a Quartermaster in the Revolution, and served as Adjutant under Gen. Lincoln in the Shays' Rebellion. He was one of the school committee of Barre.

Their children were:

1. RUFUS SMITH, son of Capt. Joseph and Rhoda (Parker) Smith, b. in Barre, Nov. 8, 1787; m. (1) Nov. 21, 1811, Miriam Carruth of Barre, b. Sept. 6, 1788. He acquired a good education and was a school-teacher. They lived in Barre where George P. King now lives until about 1830, when he with his family removed to Cortland Co., N. Y. His wife d. Feb. 8, 1831, and he m. (2) in Cortland, N. Y., 1831, Orpha Sweet of McGrawville, N. Y., dau. of Stephen Sweet, b. Dec. 25, 1808. They lived first at McGrawville, N. Y., then Blodgett Mills. Mrs. Orpha (Sweet) Parker d. June 11, 1840, and he m. (3) Sept. 15, 1842, Mrs. Hannah (Lason) Gosper, b. Dec. 5, 1808, dau. of James and Hannah (Pembroke) Lason, then of Dryden, Tompkins Co., N. Y. He d. in Freetown, N. Y., June 17, 1877, aged nearly 89. She resides at Freetown Corners, N. Y. In Barre Rufus Smith taught school at the same district 18 terms in succession. He was a public spirited man, highly respected, and an active help in the Wesleyan Methodist Church in later years. He was a mason by trade. He was president of the Washingtonian Society of Cortland, N. Y., in its day. In politics he was a whig and abolitionist. He was a delegate to the presidential campaign of Polk and Dallas. He was influential toward temperance and anti-slavery; scarcely ever missed a town meeting or election, and went on foot four miles to the polls when over 85 years of age.

One of the many letters from him to cousin Josiah Smith of Barre is herewith preserved, showing the interest which he took in the political affairs of his time:

"DEAR COUSIN—These lines leave us enjoying as comfortable a share of health as can be expected in the down hill of life—I perceive by your letter that quite a number that I was well acquainted with have been called from time into eternity. A few more rolling suns and the same sad story will be told of us, the places that now know us will know us no more forever. * * * Tell your wife I have not forgotten her and my best wishes for her. I very often think of my scholars and think how much satisfaction I took while teaching the 'young idea how to shoot,' and where scholars took as much pains to learn and to obey the orders in school. You wrote of my keeping my politics that my father taught me while I was in my youth; that principle that he taught me was to do all the good I could for my

Country. That I have endeavored to keep in view. My motto is freedom to all people if they behave themselves well. Last fall the Republican party started and I liked their platform, and we had quite a large number in this county before the stated convention met at Syracuse. I was elected a delegate on the republican side. The Whigs met the next day in convention. We did nothing the first day but organize and be prepared for the Whigs for we expected a union of the two parties. Perrin H. McGraw, my sister Sally's son, was a delegate of the whig party. The whig party met and organized; sent a committee over to us to inform us they were ready to proceed—we sent a committee to them in like manner. Before uniting each delegation chose a committee of 16 on resolutions and a committee of 32 to report names of candidates for state officers. They then met, resolutions were read, and all of the whig party but two agreed; those two were silver greys. But it paid all costs to be there and hear the speeches that were delivered. One of the speakers was there from Kansas Territory. There were a great many that were formerly democrats that united with us and were put on the nominations, but we did not succeed on the election. The know-nothings carried the state by nearly 10,000. I hope the old Bay State will fall into the republican ranks and carry that state at the next presidential election, for we do not want to see Kansas kicked and cuffed any more. My respects to all my friends.

"Yours, etc.

"RUFUS SMITH.

"Blodgett Mills, Post Office, April 14, 1856."

His children were:

1. JOSEPH AARON SMITH, son of Rufus and Orpha (Sweet) Smith, b. in Lenox, Madison Co., N. Y., Oct. 1, 1833; m. in Sheridan, Chautauqua Co., N. Y., June 4, 1857, Hannah E. Nortrup, son of Absalom and Betey Nortrup, b. in Cortland, N. Y., June 3, 1833. He enlisted in 1862 for three years in the 145th Reg. of Penn. Vols. He was in every battle except Gettysburg up to Gen. Lee's surrender in 1865. He was struck in the back by an exploding shell at Fredricksburg, and wounded at Ream's Station. He enlisted as a private, and although acting as sergeant many times he would never take promotion. He often said that

he went out a private in the rear ranks and was going back the same. Mr. Smith is a dairyman of Chautauqua Co., N. Y. Their children were:

1. Orpha E. Smith, b. in Sheridan, N. Y., March 23, 1859; m. July 4, 1877, in Chautauqua, N. Y., Lyman Prindle. Their children were:
   - I. Willie M. Prindle, b. Oct. 24, 1879.
   - II. Myron J. Prindle, b. Aug. 2, 1881.
   - III. Blanch H. Prindle, b. June 14, 1883.
   - IV. Jesse R. Prindle, b. Feb. 20, 1887.
   - V. Anna C. Prindle, b. July 17, 1889.

   All in the town of Greenfield, Erie Co., Pa.
2. Rufus P. Smith, b. Feb. 10, 1867, in Harbour Creek, Erie Co., Pa.

II. MARY AMELIA SMITH, dau. of Rufus and Orpha (Sweet) Smith, b. in Lenox, Madison Co., N. Y., July 20, 1835; m. at Freetown, N. Y., Solomon F., son of Wesley and Sarah (Lake) Robertson of Freetown. He was b. in Freetown 1827. They reside at Freetown Corners. where he is a cooper and mail carrier. The children were all born in Freetown, N. Y.:

1. Rufus Randolph Robertson, b. 1854.
2. Charles Edward Robertson, b. 1856; m. in 1888.
3. Alliston Robertson, b. 1858; m. in 1882.
4. Ella E. Robertson, b. 1860.
5. Chauncy Herbert Robertson, b. 1865.

III. RUFUS PUTNAM SMITH, son of Rufus and Orpha (Sweet) Smith, b. in Lenox, Madison Co., N. Y., Aug. 20, 1837. He enlisted in the 76th N. Y. Vol. Inf. in 1861. He was the Colonel's orderly, and d. of a fever while in the service of his country, in camp at Washington, D. C., in the spring of 1862.

IV. AARON SMITH, son of Rufus and Orpha (Sweet) Smith, b. at Homer, N. Y., May 2, 1840; d. Aug. 5, 1840.

V. SARAH M. SMITH, dau. of Rufus and Hannah (Lason) (Gosper) Smith, b. at McGrawville, N. Y., Sept. 19, 1843; m. at Freetown, N. Y., Nov. 28, 1868, James D., son of Thomas and Betsey (Wright) Fish of Cincinnatus, N. Y. He is a farmer in Cortland, N. Y. They had a son and dau., twins, b. June 1, 1872, and d. in infancy.

VI. ANN MARIA SMITH, dau. of Rufus and Hannah (Lason) (Gosper) Smith, b. at McGrawville, N. Y., Jan. 9, 1846; d. Dec., 1853.

2. ABIGAIL SMITH, dau. of Capt. Joseph and Rhoda (Parker) Smith, b. in Barre, Aug. 16, 1789; m. in Barre, Jan. 5, 1812, Joseph Peckham of Petersham, b. June 18, 1788, son of John Peckham. He was a carpenter, wagon maker and blacksmith. They lived for a few years in Petersham, then removed to Homer, N. Y., and finally to Cortlandville, N. Y. Naturally quiet and retired in her disposition, she was a true Christian mother, and held a strong influence for the good over her large family of children. She d. May 14, 1871. He d. Aug. 22, 1875. Their daughter, Mrs. Louisa R. Seeber, writes: "Were my parents still living their living descendants would be seven children, 29 grandchildren, 63 great-grandchildren, and one great-great-grandchild, making just 100 in all."* Their children were:

I. ALMON PECKHAM, b. in Petersham, Nov. 1, 1812; m. at Allen, N. Y., Hannah Anstras, b. May 27, 1817, d. Feb. 23, 1875, dau. of Isaac and Hannah Peavy. He was a farmer in Allen and Friendship, N. Y., and is still living (1892). Their children were:

1. Ira D. Peckham, b. in Allen, N. Y., Feb. 27, 1841; resides at Richfield Springs, N. Y.
2. William Lester Peckham, b. in Allen, N. Y., Jan. 19, 1844; resides at Friendship, N. Y.

II. EDWIN PECKHAM, b. in Petersham, Sept. 28, 1814; m. at Belfast, N. Y., June 21, 1838, Sarah, dau. of Susan and William Sellon. He was a farmer, and lived first in Belfast, then in New Hudson, later in Eagle, and last in Pike, N. Y. The children were b. in Belfast, N. Y.:

1. Emeroy Peckham, b. April 5, 1839; resides at Pike, N. Y.
2. Alson N. Peckham, b. July 3, 1843; resides at Pike, N. Y.
3. Frank Peckham, b. April 3, 1846; resides at Freetown, N. Y.

III. ABIGAIL PECKHAM, b. in Petersham, May 18, 1816; m. in Allen, N. Y., Sept., 1840, George B. Hicks, b. Dec. 17, 1814, son of Phillipp and Mary (Thurbee) Hicks. They were farmers in New Hudson, N. Y., for more than 40 years, and now reside in the town of Eagle, Wyoming Co., N. Y. Their children were:

1. Willard Hicks, b. Dec. 21, 1842.
2. Louisa Hicks, b. Jan. 28, 1845; m. —— Roberts.
3. Mariette Hicks, b. Feb. 22, 1847.
4. Ellen Hicks, b. Oct. 22, 1849.

---

* Written at Texas Valley, N. Y., March 28, 1890.

5. Alonzo Hicks, b. March 13, 1851.
6. Leonora Hicks, b. April 4, 1853.
7. Julia Hicks, b. June 10, 1859.

IV. SALLY SMITH PECKHAM, b. in Cortlandville, N. Y., March 26, 1818; d. at age of 4 yrs. 8 mos. 4 days, Nov. 30, 1822.

V. HARRIETT PECKHAM, b. in Cortlandville, N. Y., Feb. 3, 1820; m. John Bennett, b. 1818, son of Nicholas and Martha Bennett. He d. April 3, 1871. Their children were:

1. Lydia Ann Bennett, b. June 6. 1848; m. Milo Tucker, and reside in Almond, N. Y.
2. Louise Bennett, b. Sept. 19, 1849; m. Daniel Coote, and reside in Angelica, N. Y.
3. Adelbert Bennett, b. April 1, 1851.
4. Franklin Bennett, b. March 26, 1853; d. Nov. 9, 1854.

VI. LAURISTON PECKHAM, b. in Cortlandville, N. Y., Feb. 5, 1823.

VII. RHODA LOUISA PECKHAM, b. in Cortlandville, N. Y., March 18, 1825; m. Nov. 2, 1851, Jacob, b. at Freetown, N. Y., son of Safrenas and Elizabeth (Shannon) Seeber. He d. April 6, 1889; was a farmer. She resides at Texas Valley, N. Y. All the children were b. in Freetown, N. Y.:

1. Eluette Seeber, b. Jan. 30, 1853; m. Nov. 17, 1875, George Brooks. They have one son, Charles D. Brooks.
2. Lucelia Seeber, b. Sept. 26, 1855.
3. Dewitt C. Seeber, b. Sept. 10, 1857.
4. Elbert M. Seeber, b. April 24, 1862.
5. Sibbie A. Seeber, b. July 13, 1866.
6. George Merton Seeber, b. Dec. 5, 1869. The above children are all deceased, except the youngest.

VIII. MARIETTE PECKHAM, b. in Cortlandville, N. Y., June 19, 1827; m. May 24, 1846, at Allen, Allegany Co., N. Y., Julius Spencer Graves, b. Nov. 21, 1822, at Blodgett's Mills, son of Asher and Achsah (Webster) Graves. He was a farmer of Freetown and Texas, Cortland Co., until 1866, when he removed to Clarence, Erie Co., N. Y., where he still resides. The following children were all b. in Freetown, N. Y.:

1. Justus H. Graves, b. June 10, 1847; resides at Chicago, Ill. } Twins.
2. Justin R. Graves, b. June 10, 1847; resides at Evanston, Ill. } Twins.
3. Abbie Evelyn Graves, b. Feb. 1, 1850; d. April 29, 1887.

4. Mary Elizabeth Graves, b. Aug. 25, 1855; resides at Evanston, Ill.
5. Stella Maria Graves, b. May 15, 1857; resides at East Clarence, N. Y.
6. Ernest Webster Graves, b. Oct. 2, 1861; resides at East Clarence, N. Y.
7. Melvin Wilbur Graves, b. Dec. 31, 1863; d. Aug. 18, 1865.

IX. CEPHAS B. PECKHAM, b. in Cortlandville, N. Y., July 7, 1829; m. in West Winfield, Herkimer Co., N. Y., Sarah E. Bentley, b. in West Winfield, Dec. 4, 1831. He is a farmer of Angelica, N. Y. Their son was:

1. Frank L. Peckham, b. in Caneadea, N. Y., Sept. 19, 1860. Resides at Angelica, N. Y.

X. AMELIA L. PECKHAM, b. in Cortlandville, N. Y., Feb. 15, 1833; m. in Allen, N. Y., Jan., 1854, Spencer Randall Franklin, son of John and Betsey (Miller) Franklin. He was a farmer and for a time constable in Allen, N. Y. Their children were:

1. Inez Gertrude Franklin, b. in Allen, N. Y., June, 1856.
2. Carrie Estell Franklin, b. in Faribault, Minn., July, 1858.
3. Jennie Abbie Franklin, b. in Faribault, Minn., Sept., 1862.

3. AARON SMITH, son of Capt. Joseph and Rhoda (Parker) Smith, b. in Barre, Nov. 4, 1791; m. Dec. 6, 1814, Sarah Allen Mason; b. Feb. 11, 1794, the dau. of Thaddeus, Esq., and Hannah (Allen) Mason of Barre. She was granddau. of Dea. John Mason, who with Dea. Andrew Parker were young men together in Lexington, and who in Barre were always hand-in-hand in all important affairs. Dea. Mason was the first representative to the General Court from Barre. A nephew of Sarah Allen Mason is still living—Thaddeus Mason Loring, Esq., of Cortland, N. Y. Their ancestors were doubtless the originators of most of the name in Mass.

They removed from Barre to Homer, N. Y., in 1816. He was Captain of a militia company there. They removed to Allen, N. Y., in 1838. He there held the office of ruling elder and deacon of the Church for 35 years, until his death, which occurred Feb. 1, 1862. "He no doubt (writes his son) inherited some of his Grandfather Parker's old time faith. An instance of his belief in direct answer to prayer is related by one of his old friends: 'One extremely dry season fires were raging all around us, and after he and others had done without avail all that human hands could do to stay their progress he dropped on his knees and prayed there in the midst of the fires for rain. And,' added the neighbor, 'it came almost immediately.'" He was a good influence in his town, and belonged to one of the first temperance societies organized in the country. Both he and his wife were partially paralyzed shortly before their deaths. She d. July 29, 1873. Their children were:

I. CAROLINE SMITH, b. in Barre, Oct. 6, 1815; m. March 18, 1835, Abel Webster of Fabius, N. Y., b. Sept. 17, 1809. They lived in Fabius and Allen, N. Y. She d. Dec. 12, 1872; he d. April 13, 1877. Children:

1. William S. Webster, b. in Fabius, N. Y., May 17, 1836.
2. Melvin A. Webster, b. in Allen, N. Y., July 16, 1843; m. Jan. 5, 1876, Maggie Reusch, b. in Wurtemberg, Germany, Aug. 4, 1849, dau. of Frederick and Margaret Reusch. He is a farmer in Angelica, N. Y.
3. Sarah E. Webster, b. in Fabius, N. Y., May 21, 1848; m. Jan. 25, 1874, Frank Walker, b. in Allen, N. Y., April 16, 1852, son of Lysander and Martha Walker. They have three children.
4. Byron A. Webster, b. in Allen, N. Y., July 26, 1860; d. at Chicago, Ill., Sept. 21, 1888.

II. ANDREW PARKER SMITH, b. in Homer, N. Y., Jan. 29, 1818; m. in Angelica, N. Y., Dec. 18, 1844, Sarah Ann Chaffee. He settled in Allen, N. Y., where he was both a farmer and a mason, which trade he had already mastered. He became the supervisor of the town of Allen, N. Y., which position he held for two years. In 1866 he bought a farm in Gratiot Co., Mich., and moved there with his family. As a most fitting tribute to his marked integrity of character, it need but be said that during the two years which he passed at his new home he held for one term the highest office in the township, was also superintendent of the Sunday-school and filled satisfactorily some minor offices. He d. of quick consumption, Dec. 30, 1868. Their children were:

1. Anna Maria Smith, b. Sept. 28, 1845; m. in Hubbardston, Mich., March 9, 1870, Charles R. Proctor, b. in Mesopotamia, O., Oct. 28, 1843, son of Peter and Harriett Proctor. She has in preservation a book bearing the title "Andrew Parker, 1776." This was one of the several diaries and account books which Dea. Andrew Parker kept during his busy life. Her father often spoke of it with worthy pride, saying, "That belonged to my great-grandfather, and from him I was named." She also has an old wooden canteen snd a powder-horn, which were carried by either Dea. Parker or Capt. Smith. She resides in Hubbardston, Mich.

2. Martha V. Smith, b. April 16, 1848; d. Aug. 15, 1876.
3. Mason A. Smith, b. Jan. 30, 1850.
4. Mary E. Smith, b. Sept. 3, 1851; d. March 19, 1869.
5. Milton A. Smith, b. Oct. 18, 1853; d. March 18, 1869.

III. WILLIAM MASON SMITH, b. in Homer, N. Y., April 14, 1821. He went with his parents to Allen, N. Y., in 1838, he himself walking the entire distance to drive the stock they took with them, and there helped to make a pleasant home of the new farm, which he and his father and brother owned together. The grounds around the house he planted full of forest trees, mainly evergreens, and in other ways made the place one delightful to remember. He m. in China (now Arcade), N. Y., May 8, 1855, Orilla Welles. They removed to Clinton Co., Mich., in 1865, where he d. on his farm near Hubbardston, June 7, 1872. He was very retiring in disposition and never sought or held many public offices. To his careful pains we are indebted greatly for the fulness and accuracy of the records and history of his own family and near relatives. He properly appreciated his ancestors, and in his family papers is written: "Grandfather Smith and wife, Great grandfather Allen and wife, also Great Grandfather Parker and wife were buried two miles north of Barre Village." Their children were:

1. Emma Caroline Smith, b. in Allen, N. Y., April 8, 1856; m. Oct. 15, 1878, Myron C. Goolthrite, b. in New York, Nov. 18, 1854.
2. Anna Louisa Smith, b. in Allen, N. Y., June 23, 1859; m. July, 1888, George R. Knowles, b. in N. Y. State, Jan. 3, 1862.
3. Sarah May Smith, b. in Allen, N. Y., May 3, 1861.
4. William Welles Smith, b. in Lebanon, Mich., Jan. 19, 1868.
5. Orilla Laverne Smith, b. in Lebanon, Mich., Jan. 15, 1870.

IV. ANN ELIZA SMITH, b. in Cortland, N. Y., Dec. 9, 1872; m. in Allen, N. Y., April 13, 1845, O. H. Walker, b. April 11, 1821, son of Erastus and Betsey B. (Porter) Walker. She d. Sept. 3, 1871, and left no issue. He resides at Angelica, N. Y.

4. SALLY SMITH, dau. of Capt. Joseph and Rhoda (Parker) Smith, b. in Barre; removed to Homer, N. Y., 1816; m. in Cortlandville, N. Y., Jan. 13, 1820, Harry McGraw, son of Samuel and Elizabeth (Whitman) McGraw. She was a devout Christian woman and a kind mother. Mr. McGraw

was a merchant of McGrawville. He was honored with several town offices, such as supervisor and assessor. He was also member of the Assembly, and the first postmaster of McGrawville, which office he held until his death, May 16, 1849. She d. May 1, 1874. All the children were b. in McGrawville:

I. LUCRETIA McGRAW, b. Jan. 11, 1821; m. Rev. E. B. Fancher. They reside in McGrawville, N. Y., and of their children these are living:

1. Ezra B. Fancher.
2. Edward P. Fancher.
3. Sarah L. Fancher Kinney.
4. Mary C. Fancher Jones.
5. Henry R. Fancher.
6. James R. Fancher.

II. PERRIN H. McGRAW, b. Dec. 26, 1822; m. at New Berlin, N. Y., April 26, 1848, Leonisia, b. June 9, 1824, in Solon, N. Y., dau. of Garrett and Philena Pritchard. He has been actively connected with his town and is a highly respected citizen of McGrawville, N. Y. He has been a merchant, produce dealer and manufacturer of corsets. Their children were:

1. Mary Louisa McGraw, b. Feb. 3, 1853; d. Dec. 16, 1865.
2. Albert Perrin McGraw, b. June 12, 1856; m. Jan. 18, 1882, Emiline N. Childs. They have one son:
   1. Charles Albert McGraw, b. Dec. 28, 1886.

III. PAMELIA McGRAW, b. Feb. 3, 1825; m. in McGrawville, N. Y., 1855, Henry M. Kingman, son of Oliver and Betsey Kingman. He is a merchant of McGrawville. They have one adopted dau., Carrie E. Kingman.

IV. MARINDA McGRAW, b. July 14, 1827; m. Sept. 5, 1860, in McGrawville, N. Y., Henry C., b. in Guilford, N. Y., Sept. 11, 1827, son of Leontes and Zilpha (Farnham) Hendrick. He is a physician. He was a surgeon in the Rebellion, 1861–65. He is president of the Board of U. S. Examining Surgeons, Cortland, N. Y. They reside in McGrawville, N. Y. They have one son:

1. Henry Delos Hendrick, b. Oct. 11, 1861.

V. DELOS McGRAW, b. Oct. 21, 1829. He is a merchant and produce dealer and resides in McGrawville, N. Y.

VI. LOUISA MARIA McGRAW, b. Oct. 21, 1832; d. Feb. 1, 1833.

36. Abigail Parker *(Andrew,[5] Andrew,[4] John,[3] Hananiah,[2] Thomas[1])*, dau. of Dea. Andrew and Abigail (Jennison) Parker, b. in Lexington, Jan. 29, 1762, came with her parents to Barre, 1763; m. Feb. 21, 1788, Nathan, b. in Barre, Nov. 1, 1763, son and eldest child of Jonathan and Hannah (Smith) Allen of Barre. They were among the very earliest settlers of "Rutland District," preceding Andrew Parker. He and brother Nehemiah Allen came from Lexington, and they may have caused Mr. Parker to locate with them. Jonathan Allen's wife was a native of Sudbury, where he m. her, took her to Lexington, and then proceeded to Barre with 40 apple trees and his young wife on the back of his horse! They made their way through the "District" by means of marked trees, and it is traditioned that until settlers became numerous they heard the howling of the wolves at night close to their very doors. Wrote Edwin Woods: "Jonathan Allen's memory shall live as long as there is an apple tree left in Barre." Mrs. Elizabeth Carter, Jonathan Allen's granddaughter, shortly before her death, remarked that she had often ate of the apples from these original trees. He lived at the north of the centre, on the same place with the same wife 60 years. He died aged 92, wife at 87, and had six children, whose *average age* at death was just 80 years. His brother Nehemiah Allen had ten children, four sons and six daughters, who reached at death the ages of respectively, 96, 96, 95½, 92½, 92, 84, 82, 80, 80, 78, making an average of 87!

Nathan and Abigail lived two miles northwest of the centre on the same place and in the same house lately occupied by their dau., Mrs. Carter. Moses and Josiah Allen lived in Barre and were brothers of Nathan Allen. Moses's son was the late distinguished Dr. Nathan Allen of Lowell. Nathan Allen, who m. Abigal Parker, was a farmer and was one of the most prominent men of Barre for a great many years. He was honored with all the offices in the gift of the town. He d. Aug. 16, 1831, aged 68; she d. Oct. 14, 1838, aged 77.

Their children were:

1. A child, unnamed, b. and d. April 11, 1789.
2. MARY ALLEN, b. in Barre, Feb. 17, 1790. She was unable to talk plain. She lived in Barre with her sister until her death. She d. unm. Jan. 26, 1865, aged 75 years.

3. Abigail Allen, b. in Barre, Feb. 4, 1793; m. Jan. 3, 1833, Alexander D., b. Sept. 23, 1785, son of Charles and Mary (Slocum) Dickinson, of Rhode Island. He was early in life a sea captain and later a farmer. Their children were:

i. Nathan Sumner Dickinson, b. in Barre, Aug. 31, 1836; m. Judith Holmes Prouty of Spencer. She was dau. of Pliny Prouty and Malissa Holmes. He enlisted in Co. C, 25th Mass. Reg., aged 27; was wounded in the battle of Cold Harbor, Va., June 3, 1864, and d. in the Harwood Hospital, Washington, D. C., Aug. 7, 1864. Buried in North Brookfield. Their children were:

1. George Sumner Dickinson, b. in Spencer; resides at North Brookfield.
2. Charles Levi Dickinson, b. in Spencer; resides at North Brookfield.

ii. Mary Abigail Dickinson, b. in Barre, Nov. 20, 1834; resides at Worcester.

4. Elizabeth Allen, b. in Barre, Aug. 31, 1795; m. April 23, 1834, at age of 34, Benjamin Goodnow Carter, b. in Petersham, Sept. 12, 1806, son of John and Ruth Carter of Petersham. He d. in Barre, Feb. 13, 1867, aged 60, and was buried in Petersham. They had no issue. She d. Sept. 19, 1890, at the age of 95. Her life was a very exceptional one, more than a repetition of that which our ancestors led two centuries ago. The old Nathan Allen place, which her father settled on in 1788, was located two miles northwest of Barre, not far from the Dea. Parker place. The old road which divided the farm was once populous with houses, but is now remote and forsaken. It was here she preferred to live, and did live, for 95 years, in the house built by her father, which still stands unchanged in appearance. She also preserved the old furniture as it was in her childhood.

She was never outside of her native town except on two occasions, once she went to Princeton and once to Gill. She travelled each time by private conveyance. Consequently it may be said that Mrs. Carter never saw a railroad train or a steamboat, and never even rode on a stage coach. When once questioned if she would not like to have seen something of the world, she replied, "No, some people like to ride on railroads, but home, sweet home is the place for me. Here my father and mother lived for 60 years of married life; in this house I was born; here I have lived for 95 years, and here I am to-day. There are but few now living who can say as much."

Her own home furnished a world of happiness to her and she never longed for foreign things. Her life was a most heroic example of contentment and Christian feeling. She clung dearly to the memories of her childhood days; spoke often of her honored and long-lived parents, and of her grandfather, Dea. Andrew Parker, "who made spinning wheels, and who wouldn't pay the minister for that kind of preaching in which he did not believe."

Until a few years before her decease she retained her full mental ability, and some years since she materially assisted, by means of her good memory, Edwin Woods in his popular *Memorial of Barre*. For the cheerful lesson which she teaches, for her generosity to all and devotion to home duty, she will long be remembered in Barre. Doubtless her long life was much prolonged by the watchful attention of her guardian and neighbor, Webster Washburn of Barre. The old home is a relic of antiquity in every way. She had no issue.

5. Nathan Allen, b. in Barre, Jan. 10, 1797; d. April 29, 1797.
6. Sumner Allen, b. in Barre, Jan. 31, 1798; d. April 27, 1822, aged 24, unm. He died of consumption caused by exposure while working in his sap orchard. Unlike his sister Mary, he lacked the free use of his limbs, but possessed good powers of speech.
7. Louisa Allen, b. in Barre, Dec. 4, 1801; m. Zebediah Allen, son of Samuel Allen. Samuel Allen was cousin to Nathan Allen. They lived on the Nathan Allen place after marriage. They had one son, but the parents both died and the child soon followed, having lived to the age of but a few weeks.

37. Sally Parker *(Andrew,[5] Andrew,[4] John,[3] Hananiah,[2] Thomas[1])*, dau. of Dea. Andrew and Abigail (Jennison) Parker, b. in Barre, March 17, 1765; m. Jonathan Mayhew of Phillipston. They lived in Phillipston and had a family of children, but who have already become extinct. She m. (2) ——— Robbins, who is remembered by the old residents of Phillipston as the one who played the big bass-viol in church. She d. in Phillipston.

The children, among whom were Nabby and Lyman Mayhew, never married. They settled in Phillipston for life and lived together for many years. He was a most constant attendant of the Church, a most strict adherer to his religion. Nabby and Lyman Mayhew are both buried in Phillipston.

38. **Bettey** (or **Betsey**) **Parker** *(Andrew,[5] Andrew,[4] John,[3] Hananiah,[2] Thomas[1])*, dau. of Dea. Andrew and Abigail (Jennison) Parker, b. in Barre, Jan. 13, 1766: m. Feb. 20, 1788, Paul Tobey, b. in Berkley, Sept. 6, 1761, son of Rev. Samuel and Bathsheba (Crocker) Tobey, and twin brother of Silas Tobey. He was one of a family of 12 children.* They removed to Chester, Vt. They lived first in a cabin; he cleared the land and built the house wherein they later lived. Mrs. Betsey (Parker) Tobey is remembered by her only surviving dau. as a smart, capable woman. She d. Dec. 30, 1808, and he m. (2) Feb. 4, 1813, Phebe Briggs. All the children, however, were by Betsey. He d. in Chester, Vt., Aug. 4, 1831. His death was very sudden. Standing in his grain field with a handful of grain, he received a shock and lived only a few hours.

---

*(The story of Parson Tobey's courtship has already been preserved in print in a paper called *The Christian.*) After Samuel Tobey was ordained pastor of the Church in Berkley, Mass., Nov. 23, 1737, being convinced of the truth of the scriptural doctrine, that it is not good for man to be alone, he very naturally looked about him to find a remedy for his isolation, and in this search he of course had the help and best wishes of his fair parishioners in general. Under the circumstances he became a frequent visitor at Mr. Crocker's, whose house was graced dy the presence of fine blooming daughters. Three of these daughters were usually in the room dressed in their best and ready to receive the young parson when he came, and to make his visits as agreeable to him as they were acceptable to them. The fourth daughter, Bathsheba, he seldom saw. Whether cümbered with much serving or shy of company, or what not, she managed to keep out of sight most of the time, though he would occasionally get a glimpse of her dress as she disappeared through the door on his arrival.

His curiosity was awakened by her shyness, and he thought, as he expressed it, that he would "like to see more of this coy bird," he therefore sought an interview with her, the result of which was that the three sisters who sat in the parlor with him had the honor of having the parson for a brother-in-law; while the parish register, still extant, bears the following record in parson Tobey's own handwriting: "Sept. 6, 1739, I was married to Bathsheba Crocker." They lived long together and she became the mother of 12 children, among whom some rose to high honor; and her grandchildren, who are still living, are among the merchant princes of Boston, of all of which we may say, as the parson said of his marriage, "I do not know as this would have taken place had she not been so shy."

Their children were:

1. SILAS TOBEY, b. June 10, 1789; d. May 29, 1795.
2. BETSEY TOBEY, b. Nov. 10, 1790; m. at age of 22, Otis Cook. They had ten children, seven living to maturity. They resided in Chester, Vt., and all the children were born there:
   - I. JAMES SPENCER COOK, b. Dec. 3, 1815; m. May 12, 1844, Philena Martin of Springfield, Vt. They had four children. He d. Aug. 31, 1887.
   - II. HARRIETT COOK, b. Feb. 24, 1818; m. Barnard Carlton of Ludlow, Vt. No issue.
   - III. SALMON COOK, b. May 4, 1820; m. Jan., 1847, Mary Bemis. They have one child.
   - IV. ELIZABETH COOK, b. Sept. 23, 1823; m. Feb., 1844, Fernando Baldwin of Andover, Vt. One child.
   - V. MARTHA COOK, b. Oct. 4, 1825; m. July 1, 1843, Leonard Redfield of Springfield, Vt. They have had seven children.
   - VI. THOMAS COOK, b. June 25, 1827; d. about 1850, unm.
   - VII. ABIGAIL TOBEY COOK, b. April 22, 1829; d. Jan., 1837.
3. ABIGAIL TOBEY, b. Oct. 31, 1792; m. in Chester, Vt., Jan. 10, 1811, Timothy, b. July 28, 1788, d. Dec. 15, 1865, son of Benoni and Sarah (Williams) Lockwood. He was a farmer, worked a shingle mill and resided at Springfield, Vt. She d. Aug. 26, 1828. Their children were:
   - I. A SON, b. Nov. 24, 1811; d. Dec. 10, 1811.
   - II. A SON, b. Dec. 26, 1812; d. Jan. 3, 1813.
   - III. HIRAM L. LOCKWOOD, b. March 3, 1814.
   - IV. NELSON H. LOCKWOOD, b. Aug. 25, 1816; d. Jan. 23, 1819.
   - V. ALVIN T. LOCKWOOD, b. Oct. 23, 1818.
   - VI. TIMOTHY P. LOCKWOOD, b. Jan. 11, 1821.
   - VII. ACHSAH A. LOCKWOOD, b. Aug. 30, 1823; m. at Springfield, Vt., Jan. 1, 1843, Sylvester, b. in Chester, Vt., Sept. 5, 1815, son of William and Rachel (Redfield) Ellison. He is a farmer at Springfield, Vt. They have two children:
     1. Achsah A. Ellison, b. Feb. 13, 1844.
     2. Azro D. Ellison, b. Jan. 29, 1853.
   - VIII. BATHSHEBA B. LOCKWOOD, b. Oct. 26, 1825.
   - IX. A SON, b. Aug. 8, and d. Aug. 12, 1827.
   - X. SILAS LOCKWOOD, b. July 28, 1828.

4. PAUL TOBEY, b. Nov. 21, 1794; d. April 22, 1815.

5. BATHSHEBA CROCKER TOBEY, b. March 30, 1797; d. May 7, 1829, unm.

6. SAMUEL TOBEY, b. May 6, 1800; d. May 12, 1884, unm.

7. A DAUGHTER, b. March 2, and d. May 12, 1802.

8. ANDREW PARKER TOBEY, b. Feb. 4, 1804; m. Jan. 28, 1840, Martha E. Boynton, b. in Weathersfield, Vt., July 17, 1820. He d. Jan. 17, 1877. Their children were:

   I. MARY E. TOBEY, b. Jan. 2, 1842.
   II. MYRON S. TOBEY, b. Nov. 20, 1843; d. July 5, 1886.
   III. EMMA E. TOBEY, b. June 16, 1847; resides at Chester, Vt.
   IV. PAULINA L. TOBEY, b. July 1, 1850; m. July 2, 1873, Hiland Chandler of Chester, Vt., and who d. Dec. 8, 1877. She resides at North Springfield, Vt.

9. SARAH TOBEY, b. Sept. 9, 1808; m. Jan. 2, 1837, Lincoln, b. in Springfield, Vt., Jan. 14, 1809, son of Peres Whitcomb of Cohasset, and wife Priscilla Litchfield of Scituate. He was a shoemaker and later a farmer. He resided in Springfield, Vt., where he d. Sept. 12, 1881, aged 72½ years. His widow (1890) still survives him in good health at 82 years of age. She was the last born and is the only surviving child of Paul and Betsey (Parker) Tobey. Their children were:

   I. ELLEN E. WHITCOMB, b. in Quechee, Vt., Sept. 9, 1839; m. George R. Hall. She d. Oct. 10, 1865, aged 26, without issue.
   II. JULIA M. WHITCOMB, b. in Quechee, Vt., Sept. 30, 1842; m. Henry F. Howe. She d. Oct. 13, 1862, aged 20. Their children were:
      1. Luman L. Howe.
      2. Lula M. Howe.
   III. GEORGIANNA WHITCOMB, b. in Springfield, Vt., June 20, 1845; m. Jan. 1, 1867, Charles E. Chandler. Their children were:
      1. Harry E. Chandler, b. July 12, 1869.
      2. Edward A. Chandler, b. Sept. 6, 1872; d. Oct., 1872.
      3. Nora G. Chandler, b. Dec. 12, 1875.
      4. Hellen W. Chandler, b. Aug. 26, 1877.
      5. Grace M. Chandler, b. June 25, 1880.
   IV. ANDREW L. WHITCOMB, b. Jan. 8, 1853; d. July 30, 1863.

39. Artemas Parker *(Andrew,[5] Andrew,[4] John,[3] Hananiah,[2] Thomas[1])*, son of Dea. Andrew Parker and Mary, his 2nd wife, b. in Barre, Aug. 5, 1786; m. ——— Spaulding. It is known that he lived in New Hampshire for a time, and from there removed to Chelmsford, Mass. But it is said he removed to Vermont, and that the descendants from his large family are still living in that State. It is known that the old Barre contingent were intimate with Parkers in Vermont, their relatives. At one time, Aunt Carter, as she was familiarly called, sent two family relics to her Parker relatives. One was Dea. Parker's large Continental hat with red and black plumes, and the other was an old cane. It is hoped that further research may finally reveal the history of this branch of the Parker family. It is known that one son was named Rodolphus Parker.

40. Mary Parker *(Josiah,[5] Josiah,[4] John,[3] Hananiah,[2] Thomas[1])*, dau. of Josiah and Mary (Monroe) Parker, b. in Woburn, Dec. 25, 1749; m. Sept. 29, 1774, John Gilmore. She was the first Parker of Lexington descent born in Woburn. They had two children born in Woburn, after which they removed from town.

John Gilmore, b. Feb. 4, 1775.
Mary Gilmore, b. May 27, 1779.

41. Josiah Parker, Jr. *(Josiah,[5] Josiah,[4] John,[3] Hananiah,[2] Thomas[1])*, b. in Woburn, Nov. 25, 1751; m. July 21, 1774, Hannah Gardner of Charlestown. He lived on or near his father's large estate on the west side of the town. He was very active in the stirring times of British oppression and did his best to secure the independence of the united colonies, as in many hard fought battles and several years of hardships and sufferings he risked both life and health in the cause. He belonged to the Woburn company of Minute-Men who marched to Lexington and Concord on the morning of the first outbreak of the war, and who intercepted the enemy at various points. He was with Capt. Wyman at the battle of Bunker Hill. He was several years in the service, was under Lt. Jos. Johnson at Cambridge in 1777, and with

Capt. Wyman endured the hardships and privations of 1778. He was a well beloved man and possessed a constitution of strength and health. His characteristics are plainly preserved by the epitaph upon his gravestone:

"In Memory of
Mr. JOSIAH PARKER,
who d. Jan. 20, 1830, a. 78.

"The man of charity extends
To all his helping hands
His Kindred, Neighbours, Foes and Friends,
His pity may command."

Mrs. Hannah (Gardner) Parker d. in Woburn at the age of 84, Jan. 14, 1838. The mother, Hannah,* was dau. of Henry, Jr., and Sarah (Noyes) Gardner of Charlestown, where she was b. Feb. 3, 1754. Henry, Jr., was grandson of Richard Gardner, the emigrant ancestor, who was in Charlestown at 1662. Her epitaph is also worth inserting:

"Look here my friend as you pass by
As you are now so once was I,
As I am now so you must be
Prepare for death and follow me."

Their children were:

109. JOSIAH PARKER, b. Nov. 6, 1774; m. Abigail Carter of Woburn.

110. HENRY PARKER, b. July 2, 1777; m. Abigail Hutchinson of West Cambridge.

111. HANNAH PARKER, b. March 19, 1779; m. Abel Richardson of Woburn.

112. POLLY PARKER, b. March 10, 1781; m. Caleb Richardson of Woburn.

BETSEY PARKER, b. 1785; "d. of canker rash, Feb. 26, 1795, aged 10 y." Woburn's Record of Deaths.

FREDERICK PARKER, b. 1786; "d. of canker rash, Feb. 28, 1795, aged 9 y." Woburn's Record of Deaths.

* She was b. in Charlestown, Feb. 3, 1754, dau. of Henry and second wife Lucy (Fowle) Gardner, being tenth in her father's family of twelve children. Lucy Fowle was dau. of Capt. John Fowle of Woburn, who was son of James. Henry Gardner was son of Henry and Elizabeth (Lane) Gardner, he (Henry) being son of Richard and Anna (Blanchard) Gardner of Woburn and Charlestown.

113. Electa Parker, b. May 4, 1794; m. Samuel C. Buckman of Woburn.

114. Betsey Parker, b. March 1, 1796; m. Jonathan Baldwin.

115. Frederick Parker, b. July 2, 1798; m. Nabby Thompson of Woburn.

42. Lydia Parker (*Josiah,5 Josiah,4 John,3 Hananiah,2 Thomas1*), b. in Woburn, Dec. 10, 1753; m. Aug. 24, 1772 (supposed), Jesse Wright, then of Woburn. They lived in Woburn a few years, where two children are recorded. Jesse Wright was with Capt. Wyman at the battle of Bunker Hill.

Lydia Wright, b. Jan. 6, 1774.

Jesse Wright, b. May 30, 1779.

43. Benjamin Parker (*Josiah,5 Josiah,4 John,3 Hananiah,2 Thomas1*), b. in Woburn, Jan. 30, 1756; m. May 12, 1779, Mehetable Tidd of Woburn, b. Dec. 13, 1759, dau. of Samuel and Phebe Tidd. He lived on the "West Side" in Woburn, near his father's homestead. The following list of children is transcribed from the original and excellently penned sheets of family records, now in possession of Mrs. Benjamin Wyer:

116. Benjamin Parker, Jr., b. Aug. 26, 1780; m. Sally Allen.

117. Joseph Parker, b. June 8, 1782; m. Betsey Richardson of Woburn.

118. Samuel Parker, b. Dec. 23, 1784; m. Lydia Thurston Allen.

119. Mehetable Parker, b. Oct. 23, 1786; m. Maj. Francis Johnson of Woburn.

Patty Parker, b. June 11, 1789; d. Nov. 14, 1811, aged 22.

120. Almira Parker, b Sept. 20, 1790; m. Nathan Johnson of Woburn.

121. Anna Parker, b. Sept. 9, 1791; m. Joshua Swan Robbins of West Cambridge.

Lucy Parker, b. Feb. 18, 1794; never married.

122. Lydia Parker, b. Aug. 15, 1796; m. Benjamin Wyer of Woburn.

123. Charlotte Parker, b. May 3, 1801; m. (1) Royal Caldwell; (2) Nathaniel Buck.

124. Fanny Parker, b. July 22, 1803; m. George Butters.

44. Edmund Parker (*Josiah,*[5] *Josiah,*[4] *John,*[3] *Hananiah,*[2] *Thomas*[1]), b. in Woburn, March 17, 1762; m. (1) April 5, 1790, Lydia Johnson of Woburn; she d. Feb. 3, 1801, and he m. (2) July 7, 1805, Mrs. Elizabeth Reed of Woburn. She d. in Feb., 1825, aged 62.

Like his Parker relatives he possessed a sound constitution and strong physique, which carried him through many hardships of service while fighting for his country. He served early with Capt. Green's R. I. regiment, and also a term in 1780. He lived among his kindred on the "West Side," dying June 28, 1840, aged 78.

> "Like a shock of grain ripe and seared,
> Removed from friends long endeared."

Their children were:

EDMUND PARKER, JR., m. March 21, 1816, Hannah Wyman of Woburn. They lived upon the "West Side" in the neighborhood of his relatives. They d. without issue.

THADDEUS PARKER, m. Feb. 6, 1821, Lydia Thompson of Woburn. He was b. on the "West Side" of Woburn; was a very strong man, possessing a remarkable constitution and great physical energy. He d. without issue aged about 90 years.

[Woburn Records show that an infant child of Edmund Parker d. Feb. 20, 1801.]

125. DAVID JOHNSON PARKER, m. Rebecca Carter of Wilmington.

MARY PARKER, m. in Woburn, Dec. 23, 1819, Dana Fay; they lived in Winchester and had no children.

45. Nathan Parker (*Josiah,*[5] *Josiah,*[4] *John,*[3] *Hananiah,*[2] *Thomas*[1]), b. in Woburn, Feb. 21, 1769; m. Nov. 10, 1793, Polly Richardson, b. Oct. 1, 1775, dau. of Reuben and Jerusha Richardson of Woburn. He was a dutiful son and became a highly respected citizen; but in his prime of life he was fatally injured by the fall of the Clapp house, which is best described in the records of the town, which read:

"From this accident, thirty or forty individuals, the strong men of our town, were wounded in an inconceivable number of ways."

This worthy inscription is upon his grave-stone:

In Memory of
Mr. NATHAN PARKER,
who d. July 19, 1807, Æt. 38.

"By a wound which he received by a fall of a frame of an House, he has left a widow and five children to lament the loss of one of the best of Husbands and Fathers; as a provider he was very remarkable for his attention to his Family, a very industrious & ingenious Tradesman, a real good neighbour, social and confident friend, very regular & Just in all his dealings & to conclude all his moral Virtues an Honest Man."

"O Death, thou Victor of the human frame
The soul's poor fabric trembles at thy name.
How long shall man be urged to dread thy sway
For those whom thou untimely take away?"

His widow m. Aug. 31, 1820, Seth Crosby of Billerica, and removed there.

126. POLLY PARKER, b. March 23, 1794; m. Joshua Reed, Jr., of Woburn.

CHILD, unnamed, d. 1796.

CAROLINE PARKER, b. 1805; d. in Woburn, May 31, 1826, aged 21.

CLARISSA PARKER, d. unmarried.

127. MARIA PARKER, m. Simon Adams of Lowell.

128. SUSANNA PARKER, m. Marshall Wyman of Woburn.

46. Anna Parker *(John,[5] Josiah,[4] John,[3] Hananiah,[2] Thomas[1])*, dau. of Capt. John and Lydia (Moore) Parker, b. in Lexington, Jan. 11, 1859; m. in Waltham, March 16, 1781, Ephraim Pierce, Jr., of Waltham. They lived in Waltham. There is in possession of her descendants a family tree wrought on canvas by the youngest daughter of the family, the growth of which is thereby represented. Within the two hearts at the base are inscribed the names of the father and mother, viz.:

"Epraim Pierce, b. Sept. 29, 1747—Anna Pierce, b. Jan. 11, 1749.
Married March 18, 1780."

From these united hearts springs the trunk of the tree, from whose branches are suspended five large apples, each containing a name and date, as follows:

"Lydia, born July 29, 1780.
Ephraim, born Oct. 1, 1782.
Nancy, born Nov. 22, 1784.
John, born Aug. 13, 1787.
Sibbyl, born Jan. 11, 1790."

1. LYDIA PIERCE, b. July 29, 1780; d. unm.
2. EPHRAIM PIERCE, b. Oct. 1, 1782; was drowned when a boy.
3. NANCY PIERCE, b. Nov. 22, 1784; m. Leonard Smith of Waltham, son of David. He was innkeeper in Waltham. Their children were:

  I. ANN AUGUSTA SMITH, d. 1829.
  II. JANE ISABELLA SMITH, b. Nov. 16, 1810; m. in Waltham, Dec. 25, 1834, Frederick Lawrence, b. Sept. 16, 1809; d. Feb. 13, 1876. He was a farmer in Waltham. Their children were:

    1. Ann Isabella Lawrence.
    2. Leonard Frederick Lawrence.
    3. Ellen Sophia Lawrence.
    4. Henderson Greene Lawrence.
    5. Nancy Jane Lawrence.

  III. LEONARD SMITH, b. Sept. 23, 1813; d. March 15, 1814.
  IV. ELVIRA SOPHIA SMITH, b. April 1, 1815; m. Horace Hammond, b. April 10, 1812; d. Jan. 2, 1880. She d. Feb. 10, 1872. He was owner and manager of Horse Car Railroad Works, Waltham, and Captain of the Waltham Artillery Co. Their children were:

    1. Child, unnamed, b. and d.
    2. Edward Horace Hammond, b. in Waltham, April 19, 1842; m. at Grand Rapids, Mich., May 18, 1887, Ada H., b. at Grand Rapids, Oct. 3, 1865, dau. of John and Helen M. (Lewis) Crissman. He is a practitioner of Christian Science Mind Healing. Residence, Grand Rapids, Mich.

  V. LEONARD PIERCE SMITH, b. Aug. 6, 1818; m. in Waltham, Jan. 12, 1855, Mary Jane Hale, b. March 26, 1827, dau. of John and Nancy. He was hotel keeper at Waltham. He d. 1866. Their children were:

    1. Leonard Smith, b. Dec. 17, 1855; d. Jan. 10, 1888.
    2. Jennie Maria Smith, b. June 23, 1857.

VI. ELLEN REBEKAH SMITH, b. Aug. 30, 1821; m. in Waltham, Dec. 4, 1845, Edward Lawrence Bond, b. in Wilmington, Sept. 10, 1817, son of Joseph and Lucy (Davis) Bond. He was a merchant in Boston for many years, and was the original manufacturer of the celebrated Bond crackers. He d. in Waltham, Feb. 9, 1891, aged 73 years. Their children were:

1. Edward Smith Bond, b. Oct. 13, 1846; d. Aug. 31, 1847.
2. Nancy Smith Bond, b. Jan. 24, 1848.
3. Ellen Rebekah Bond, b. March 15, 1849; d. Dec. 18, 1849.

VII. LYDIA SMITH, d. in nine weeks.

4. JOHN PIERCE, b. in Waltham, Aug. 13, 1787; m. Sarah Tewksbury. They resided in Chelsea. Their children were:

I. EPHRAIM PIERCE, b. June 16, 1813; d. June 2, 1833.

II. SARAH ANN PIERCE, b. Nov. 4, 1814; d. Oct. 17, 1834.

III. JOHN PAYSON PIERCE, b. March 26, 1818; m. Dec. 5, 1847, Augusta Putnam, dau. of David and Orpha Putnam of East Boston (Revere). Their children were:

1. John Theodore Parker Pierce, b. Oct. 17, 1848; d. Aug. 20, 1849.
2. Heman Winthrop Pierce, b. Nov. 25, 1850. He is an artist.

IV. LYDIA MARIA PIERCE, b. Jan. 12, 1821; m. Jan. 1, 1841, Joseph Fenno. He d. May 20, 1863. She d. in June, 1886. Their children were:

1. Thomas Lilley Fenno, b. Oct. 1, 1841; m. Addie E. Tucker.
2. Edward Augustus Fenno, b. Aug. 26, 1842; m. Sarah J. Derby.
3. Charles Francis Fenno, b. July 30, 1844; resides at Revere.
4. Sarah Pierce Fenno, b. Feb. 22, 1847; m. Fred. E. Proctor.
5. Walter Pierce Fenno, b. May 20, 1850; m. Emma E. Tucker.
6 Fred Austin Fenno, b. Feb. 5, 1853.
7. Morton Fenno, b July 6, 1855; d. Jan. 12, 1860.
8. Herbert Fenno, b. Aug. 17, 1858.
9. Parker Fenno, b. May 10, 1862.

V. ALMIRA LOUISA PIERCE, b. July 11, 1823; m. Oct. 29, 1844, Robert Aldersay Vinal of Somerville, son of Robert and Lydia (Stone) Vinal. The father, Robert, was son of Nathaniel Vinal of Scituate, where he lived until he went into business in Boston. Lydia Stone was dau. of John Stone of Charlestown, now Somerville. The family resides in Somerville. Children:

1. Almira Louisa Vinal, b. Feb. 6, 1846.
2. Robert Aldersay Vinal, b. Sept. 12, 1847.

3. Marie Augusta Vinal, b. Nov. 8, 1849.
4. Arthur Pierce Vinal, b. June 14, 1854.
5. Alice Montague Vinal, b. Oct. 29, 1856.
6. Charles Walter Vinal, b. Aug., 1861.

VI. ELIZABETH PAYSON PIERCE, b. June 25, and d. June 28, 1827.

VII. HENRY AUGUSTUS PIERCE, b. Nov. 29, 1828; d. Feb. 21, 1863, in a military hospital at Washington, D. C. He was an original member of Co. II, First Reg. Mass. Vols., and he took part in every engagement of his company from Bull Run to Fredericksburg.

VIII. AUGUSTA SMITH PIERCE, b. Sept. 26, 1830; m. Oct. 26, 1853, Quincy Adams Vinal (brother of Robert), son of Robert and Lydia (Stone) Vinal. They reside in Somerville. Their children were:

1. Anna Parker Vinal, b. Aug. 12, 1854.
2. Mary Lowell Vinal, b. June 16, 1856.
3. Martha Adams Vinal, b. Jan. 6, 1858.
4. Quincy Pierce Vinal, b. April 2, 1860.
5. Josephine Vinal, b. Oct. 30, 1861.
6. Sarah Augusta Vinal, b. Jan. 12, 1863.
7. Edward Lincoln Vinal, b. April 21, 1865.
8. Leonora Vinal, b. Dec. 15, 1866.
9. Isabelle Whitney Vinal, b. July 26, 1868.
10. Bertha Runey Vinal, b. Jan. 9, 1870.
11. Eva Neilson Vinal, b. Nov. 20, 1871.
12. John Henry Vinal, b. April 28, 1873.
13. Leslie Thorning Vinal, b. Oct. 29, 1878.

IX. EPHRAIM PIERCE, b. Feb. 20, 1834; enlisted Sept., 1861, in the Union army, was Capt. of Co. F, Third Reg., Minnesota Veteran Vols. He d. July 1, 1865, at Du Vulls Bluff, Ark.

5. SIBBYL PIERCE, b. in Waltham, Jan. 11, 1790; m. Horatio Bird. She d. about 1826, aged 36 years. Children:

I. HORATIO BIRD, b. about 1812; d. about 1842, aged 30 years. He left one dau., who went to Washington 45 years ago.

II. SIBBYL BIRD, b. about 1814; d. 1836, aged 22.

III. LYDIA BIRD, d. in infancy.

IV. OLIVER HAZARD PERRY BIRD, b. about 1821; was a sea-captain, when and where he d. is unknown to his relatives. He left two daughters, who were in Chelsea at the time of their mother's death about 40 years ago.

47. John Parker (*John*,[5] *Josiah*,[4] *John*,[3] *Hananiah*,[2] *Thomas*[1]), son of Capt. John and Lydia (Moore) Parker, b. in Lexington, Feb. 14, 1761; m. in Waltham, Feb. 17, 1784, Hannah Stearns, the dau. of Benjamin and Hannah (Seger) Stearns. She was the seventh of a family of eleven children, and was b. in Lexington, 1766. Hannah Seger was the descendant of Thomas Seger, or Seager, who came to Newbury before 1637.

"The descendants seem to have had a taste for frontier life. Nathaniel, of uncertain date, was one of the earliest settlers of Bethel, Maine; the Indians carried him off into Canada, as they did many another man and woman, when they could surprise them in the fields, driving them thence through the desolate gaps in the White Mountains, to make a bloody trail where now the summer streams of fashion and invalidism so easily flow. Nathaniel had a very hard time of it, which he must needs write about afterwards. Another member of this family enlisted during the Revolutionary War; was a sergeant in Capt. Bryant's company of artillery, and went through many an engagement. His captain lay mortally wounded after the battle of Brandywine, within the enemy's lines, whence he brought him away by night upon a litter, with two or three comrades helping, though he too had sustained a severe wound that day. Stories of the wilderness and of battle were told into greedy ears at the winter firesides of the Lexington families." *

John Parker was 14 when his father drew the first sword and captured the first weapon taken in the Revolution. He was too young to fight, but he helped all he could by carrying fresh water in wooden bowls to the thirsty soldiers.

John Parker was a stout able-bodied man, "uncommon strong," could endure cold and heat and abstinence from food and rest. He was a typical New England yeoman, a "quiet, thoughtful, silent, reading man, of strong sense, of great moral worth, reliable, honorable; worked every day and all day; kept good discipline in his family, governed easily; taught his children to speak the truth; always had a book in his hand in the evening." †

In consideration that John Parker and Hannah Stearns were the parents of the late Rev. Theodore Parker, world-

---

* Weiss' Biography of Rev. Theodore Parker.

† The testimony of his grandson, Rev. Columbus Greene, Esq.

famous for the advanced views of religion which he preached in his time, it is interesting to observe their characteristics. The following description of his parents comes mostly from Theodore, himself, an affectionate, grateful and revering son, who loved to speak of his parents; scarcely ever failed to record in his busy journal the anniversaries of their birth or death, and never made such record without dropping the tenderest words on their memories.

He was a skilful farmer, and had, perhaps, the best peach orchard in Middlesex, and adopted nearly all the improvements in farming that had proved valuable. But he was more of a mechanic than a farmer. Like his father, grandfather and great-grandfather before him, he was a worker in wood, was expert in making and repairing, and pursued his occupation of millwright and pumpmaker in his shop, while the farm work he left mainly to his boys. The shop was situated just above the house, it being the famous belfry tower from which rang the peals that awoke the Colonies to action in their glorious Revolution. He put brains into his work, originated new methods, "made his head save his hands." Theodore also informs us: "He was a man of much thought and reading, with fine power of speech, but *colloquial* and *orational*." "He was fond of mathematics, understood algebra and geometry, plane and solid, and was 'great at figures.'" He was also fond of metaphysics, psychology and all departments of intellectual and moral philosophy, and he had read all the English books upon philosophy. When he got into an argument, which was seldom, as controversy did not suit him, he was very effective. He was a great reader, rising before day in the winter to study, sleeping but about five hours; was nice and acute in metaphysical analysis; fond of Natural History, and well acquainted with the plants of Massachusetts. He was jovial and funny, but well mannered; no clownishness, profanity or indecency marred his humor. His townspeople had a saying, "John Parker has all the manners of the neighborhood."

Strength of mind is a characteristic of the Parker family. In this John Parker was no exception, he "was an independent thinker; in religion was a Unitarian, and in politics a

Federalist, when there were but five in the whole town. He was eminently just and magnanimous. fearless in the expression of opinion, often arbitrator in quarrels, was guardian of widows, etc., and administered estates, for there was no lawyer in town."

He took great pains with the intellectual and moral culture of his children. "Devoted to education," he was influential in bringing into the common schools a better class of teachers. He did not like poetry, but read the works of the leading authors. He disliked Paley and Edwards. "Paley left us no conscience," he used to say. He probably disliked Edwards because he left us no will, as will was a strong feature in the Parkers. He watched the heavens also, and made himself acquainted with the movements of the stars. His diligent study of the Bible made him formidable in theological debate.

Hannah Stearns was the daughter of a well-to-do farmer. Her son describes her as "a handsome woman. of slight form, flaxen hair, blue eyes and a singularly fresh and delicate complexion, more nervous than muscular." Her education was inferior to her husband's, her mind less positive and independent. Her favorite reading was the Bible and Hymn Book, but her mind was stored with passages of beauty from English literature. "She was imaginative, delicate minded, poetic, yet a very practical woman; far sighted and so nice in her perceptions and judgments that it used to startle me sometimes in the body and does now as I think of it." "She took great pains with the religious training of her children, but cared little for doctrines; no bigotry, no cant, no fear. Religion was love and good works. She had what I call piety, the ideal part of religion, love of God as well as morality."

Her rigid economy helped her to be generous to the poor. The father read aloud to his family in the evening. In this she took much delight, while she sewed and listened. This kept her supplied with food for thought. He read until the old, tall clock struck eight, then with a wave of his hand he dismissed the children to bed. When the children took their light and went to bed the day had still one grace in store for them, as they listened till their mother came up to see that they were well tucked in and to share the sweetness of their homely prayers. She was fond of romantic stories, of adventure among the Indians, some of which were printed in books, while others floated about in the form of legend. A fine memory enabled her to repeat these wild tales, and to carry about with her such literary stores as she had.

The drinking habits of the period were pure and simple, and highly commended. However, one of the first recorded instances of its disuse at funerals was at the house of Mr. Parker on the occasion of his grandmother's death, 1760. From this slight sketch it will be seen that John Parker was a man ahead of his time in both thought and action, and far ahead of his neighbors and countrymen. He well represented the Parker family of his time; intelligent, industrious, progressive, honorable, firm minded and independent.

She d. May 15, 1823, aged 59, and he d. Nov. 3, 1835, aged 74. From his note-book, entitled "John Parker's Book, 1788," is copied the following precise account concerning his family:

"Monday the 11th day of April, 1785, POLLY PARKER was born about 3 o'clock past midday." She m. June 25, 1816, Samuel Greene, who was a kind and affectionate mother-in-law to her sister's children. He d. Dec. 5, 1818, and she d. in Lexington in 1831.

"1786. JOHN PARKER was born Thursday, 12th day of October at 8 o'clock in the morning." He m. Maria Green of W. Cambridge.

"Tuesday, 2nd day of April, was born LYDIA PARKER, 25 minutes after seven o'clock in the evening;" she "departed this life April 25, between 4 and 5 o'clock in the morning in the year 1791, aged 2 years and 21 days. She died of the Quinsy."

129. "Tuesday, 15 day of March, 1791, HANNAH PARKER was born about 3 o'clock in the afternoon." She m. Samuel Green of Brighton.

130. "July 1, 1793, was born LYDIA PARKER on Monday Morning at five o'clock." She m. Isaac Herrick of Brighton.

"December 10, 1795, was born REBECCA PARKER between 2 and 3 of the Clock in the morning on Thursday." She d. Feb. 15, 1812, unm.

131. "November 5, 1798. ISAAC PARKER was born on Monday between the hours of 4 and 5 of the Clock in the afternoon." He m. Martha M. Miller.

"RUTH PARKER, born on Wednesday, the 12 day of November, 1800, in the morning between one & two of the clock." Died Dec. 27, 1812.

132. "July 16, 1803. HIRAM STEARNS PARKER was born on Saturday between the hours of 2 and 3 o'clock past midday." He m. Nancy Leavitt of New Hampshire.

"EMILY ANN PARKER born on Sunday, May the 11, 1806, between the hours of 4 & 5 in the afternoon." She m. Charles Miller of Somerville, and d. leaving no issue.

133. "August the 24th, 1810. Was Born THEODORE PARKER 5 minutes in the morning before three of the clock." He m. Lydia D. Cabot.

48. Isaac Parker (*John,[5] Josiah,[4] John,[3] Hananiah,[2] Thomas[1]*), son of Capt. John and Lydia (Moore) Parker, b. in Lexington, May 11, 1763. He seems to have inherited his father's military spirit, and very early in life arrayed himself against the British foe. He was fond of military adventures. When old enough to run with a musket he served in the Revolutionary war; he was in the battles of Saratoga and Yorktown, was in garrison at West Point in 1782 and 83, from whence an affectionate letter written his brother John Parker is still among the family records at Lexington, as is also a pass bearing date of Nov. 9, 1783, permitting "Nemiah Fowler, John Farrer, Titus Baker and Isaac Parker to Cross the Ferry and pass out in the Country and Return this Evening." He served many years in the Revolution, and seems to have continued steadily in the service from his first enlistment to the close of the war. After the war he removed to Groton, Mass., where he was a merchant, but failing in business he went to South Carolina, and married a lady of means at Charleston. He was living there up to 1820, the father of one son. This son m. and had one dau., but he came to an untimely end by the accidental discharge of a gun in his hand while gunning.

49. Ruth Parker (*John,[5] Josiah,[4] John,[3] Hananiah,[2] Thomas[1]*), dau. of Capt. John and Lydia (Moore) Parker, b. Dec. 7, 1765; m. Nov. 14, 1787, David Bent. He was the second or third son of Micah Bent who emigrated to Nova

Scotia, probably about the middle of the last century. They lived in Belisle, where, upon the old homestead, still reside several of their great-grandchildren, the children of Rufus, the third son. The descendants of both the Parkers and Bents are numerous in this and the adjoining counties, and they have in several instances intermingled by marriage. There were several other sons born unto the Micah Bent referred to above. Besides David there were William (whose son is Dr. W. H. Bent of Argyle, N. S.), and Stephen (whose grandson is J. G. H. Parker of Bridgetown. N. S., a lineal descendant of the ancient Parker line of Groton, Mass.). David Bent d. Aug. 16, 1831, aged 67 years. Ruth (Parker) Bent d. March 12, 1838, aged 73 years.

The children of David and Ruth (Parker) Bent were:

I. ASAPH BENT, now dead, m. Widow Vailes and had three children:

I. DAVID BENT, m. Suzan Stronach. They reside in Forest Glen, Annapolis Co., N. S. Children:

1. George Bent.
2. David Bent.
3. Susan Bent, m. George Stronach and had three children.
4. Ruth Bent, m. Hoyt Foster and had six children.

II. ISAAC BENT, now dead, m. Arminella Young. Children:

1. Abigail Bent, m. James Lettiney and is now deceased.
2. Louisa Bent.

III. RUFUS BENT, now dead, m. Ann Starrit. Children:

1. Sarah Ann Bent, now deceased, m. James Moore.
2. George Bent, now deceased, m. Mary Ann Inglis, and their children were: Frank Bent, A. Clifford Bent and five daughters. This family resides upon the old Bent homestead in Belisle, Annapolis Co., N. S.
3. David Bent, now deceased.
4. Zenas Bent, now deceased.
5. Elizabeth Bent, now deceased, m. Simeon Freeman and had three children.
6. Mary Bent, who resides in Belisle, N. S.
7. Edwin Bent, now deceased.
8. Caroline Bent, now deceased, m. Eli Boehner, and had two children.
9. Elizabeth Bent, resides in Somerset, Kings Co., N. S.

IV. ARATHUSA BENT, now deceased, m. Charles Barteaux.

v. ABIGAIL BENT, now deceased, m. Simon Starrit. Two children:

1. Euphenia Starrit, now deceased.
2. Amanda Starrit, m. Edmund Bent, is now deceased.

vi. REBECCA BENT, now deceased, m. Joseph Starrit. Children:

1. George Starrit, m. Emily Bentley, and has three children.
2. Benjamin Starrit, m. Clara Fowler, and has two children.
3. Stephen Starrit, now deceased.
4. David Starrit, now deceased, left two children.
5. John Starrit.
6. Abigail Starrit, now deceased.
7. Ruth Starrit, now deceased, m. Abel Wheelock.
8. Miriam Starrit, d. unm.

50. Rebecca Parker *(John,[5] Josiah,[4] John,[3] Hananiah,[2] Thomas[1])*, dau. of Capt. John and Lydia (Moore) Parker, b. in Lexington, June 28, 1768; m. May 29, 1803, Peter Clark of Watertown, now Belmont, whose first wife, Sarah Grant of Watertown, having died Jan. 1, 1800. He was the son of Thomas and Sarah (Bright) Clark of Watertown, whose ancestry is shown in "*The Genealogy of the Descendants of Hugh Clark of Watertown.*" He was a farmer, lived in that part of the town which is now Belmont, and d. May 2, 1859, aged 90. Peter Clark was intelligent and fond of reading, but better than all, endowed with a sweetness and liberality and a real courtesy which mere culture can never bring. Rebecca (Parker) Clark was a very worthy woman. She d. in Belmont, Jan. 10, 1851, aged over 82 years.

Their children were:

1. PETER BRIGHT CLARK, b. May 2, 1804; d. in Monroe, La., Sept. 9, 1834, unm.
2. ISAAC GRANT CLARK, b. Jan. 18, 1806; d. in Belmont, Dec. 8, 1861, unm.
3. HARRIETT REBECCA CLARK, b. Nov. 22, 1808; d. July 24, 1841, unm.
4. SARAH GRANT CLARK, b. March 10, 1810. She resides upon the old homestead in Belmont, unm.

51. Robert Parker *(John,[5] Josiah,[4] John,[3] Hananiah,[2] Thomas[1])*, son of Capt. John and Lydia (Moore) Parker, was b. in Lexington, April 15, 1771; m. Oct. 22,

1794, Elizabeth Simonds, who was b. in Lexington, July 4, 1772, the dau. of Joshua and Martha (Bowers) Simonds of Lexington. The father, Joshua Simonds, was one of the minute-men who met the British on the 19th of April, 1775. It was he who went into the meeting-house for powder, and finding himself cut off from his company, cocked his gun and placed the muzzle on an open cask of powder, resolved to blow up the church in case the British should enter it. The dau. Elizabeth was then but three years old. Robert Parker was a farmer and lived not far from his brother John Parker, Esq. He was remembered by his nephew, Rev. Theodore Parker, as a "tall, grave man." He lived in the west part of the town on what is now the Neville place, on the Concord road. Although a man of very quiet and gentle demeanor his influence for good was widely felt. He d. Dec. 31, 1840, aged 70. She d. April 11, 1849, aged 77. They were interred in the graveyard at Lexington. Her gravestone epitaph shows the motherly sentiment so characteristic of her:

"Father, I will that they also whom thou hast given me be with me where I am."

Their children were:

134. Mary Parker, b. Dec. 26, 1794; m. Isaac W. Lawrence of West Cambridge.

Josiah Parker, b. July 6, 1798; d. Dec. 25, 1840, unm.

Thomas Parker, b. March 16 and d. April 30, 1800.

135. Eliza Eleanor Parker, b. Sept. 20, 1804; m. Nathan Robbins of West Cambridge.

136. Almira Parker, b. Aug. 30, 1806; m. Joshua Robbins of West Cambridge.

Jonathan Simonds Parker, b. Aug. 8, 1808; d. Feb. 13, 1813.

137. Jonathan Simonds Parker, b. July 30, 1812; m. Abigail Tuttle of Lexington.

138. William Bowers Parker, b. Jan. 13, 1817; m. Elizabeth Garfield.

52. Susanna Parker (*Joseph,5 Josiah,4 John,3 Hananiah,2 Thomas1*), dau. of Joseph and Eunice (Hobbs) Parker, b. in Weston, Dec. 31, 1760. It is supposed that it was she who m. a Gregory, probably a Lincoln man, as it is known that one of the daughters of Joseph Parker m. one of that name. Where she lived is at present unknown; likewise her issue. Research among the Gregory family may soon reveal her posterity.

53. Levi Parker (*Joseph,[5] Josiah,[4] John,[3] Hananiah,[2] Thomas[1]*), son of Joseph and Eunice (Hobbs) Parker, was b. April 16, 1762. He was soon after living in Roxbury, as his venerable son, Isaac Parker of Chicago, informs us. He writes:

"My father, Levi Parker, was thirteen years old when the Battle of Bunker Hill was fought, which he witnessed. When he was seventeen he enlisted for the remainder of the war, and was a soldier over three years. He was given his discharge by Gen. Knox of Boston. After the war he went to Hubbardston to live and married my mother there. Her name was Mary Lyon. They lived there until they had six children, then they moved to Royalton, Vermont, where the other three were born."

The date of his marriage was Oct. 26, 1786. She was the dau. of Bazael and Mary Lyon of Hubbardston. He with cousins Hollis and Isaac Parker, who later settled in Shrewsbury and Westborough, respectively, lived in the same great division in Hubbardston, in the southeast corner of the town, which part was later set off to Princeton. His cousin Amos Parker lived in the other extremity of the town. Levi Parker was a mason by trade. Upon his removal to Royalton, Vt., he bought 100 acres of timber land, cleared it up and made a farm. He d. in Royalton, March, 1813. The widow, Mary (Lyon) Parker, went to live with her son-in-law, Horace Garfield, in Potsdam, N. Y., and there passed the remainder of her days. She d. there aged 88.

Children b. in Hubbardston:

139. Samuel Parker, b. March 4, 1787; m. Laurania Aikins.

140. Martha Parker, b. Nov. 19, 1788; m. Shubael Crandall of Connecticut.

141. Aaron Parker, b. Feb. 20, 1791.

Polly Parker, b. March 14, 1793; m. Horace Garfield. They had three sons; one still resides in Potsdam, N. Y.

John Parker, b. Aug. 7, 1795; d. April 7, 1825, unm.

Elisha Parker, b. Oct. 25, 1798; m. Alvira Colburn.

Children b. in Royalton, Vt.:

142. ANNA PARKER, b. April 13, 1801; m. David Paige.

MIRIAM PARKER, b. May 5, 1804; m. Harvey Edgarton. No issue.

143. ISAAC PARKER, b. Dec. 1, 1806; m. Mary Linsted of Barrington, Mass.

54. Lois Parker (*Joseph*,[5] *Josiah*,[4] *John*,[3] *Hananiah*,[2] *Thomas*[1]), dau. of Joseph and Eunice (Hobbs) Parker, b. in Lincoln, Nov. 17, 1763; int. of m. entered on Weston records to John Coburn of Weston, Sept. 14, 1782. He was a farmer and lived in Weston. He d. in June, 1796, and she m. 2nd, ——— Holbrook. She lived in that part of Lincoln through which the British troops marched on the famous 19th of April, and often related the story of the excitement of the family, as she described how she and the other "women folks" retreated to the woods on this occasion. She was then but 12 years old, and it plainly shows in which part of Lincoln was Joseph Parker's home.

All the children were b. in Weston:

1. SARAH COBURN, b. March 11, 1785; m. Thomas Heard of East Sudbury, now Wayland, where he was b. May 24, 1776. He d. in Waltham, March 7, 1832. She d. in Watertown, Sept. 4, 1809, leaving dau.:
   1. JANE E. HEARD, b. in Watertown, April 11, 1806; m. at Waltham, by Ralph Waldo Emerson, Aug. 24, 1834, Daniel Emerson of Waltham, son of Peter and Molly (Muzzy) Emerson. She d. Nov. 16, 1870. She was his second wife. He was b. in Sandown, N. H., Sept. 16, 1788. He came to Waltham in 1814, and d. there in 1874, after a residence of 60 years. He held no public office except school committee. He was a blacksmith and wheelwright. Their children were:
      1. Thomas Heard Emerson, b. in Waltham, March 20, 1836; m. Elizabeth Lord, dau. of W. W. and Lucy E. (Centre) Wellington, b March 3, 1843. They reside in Cambridgeport and have one dau.
      2. Warren Frank Emerson, b. July 29, 1839; m. June 1, 1870, Lillian, dau. of John C. and Elizabeth A. Thorp. They reside in Waltham and have two children.
      3. Sarah Jane Emerson, b. Sept. 12, 1841; resides in Waltham.
2. ABIJAH COBURN, b. Jan. 21, 1787; m. 1812, Lydia, dau. of Josiah and Mary (Flagg) Hastings. She d. in 1813. He m.

2nd, March 16, 1814, Sophia Hastings, sister of his first wife. She d. March 3, 1869. He was a boot and shoe manufacturer and farmer. He was selectman and representative to the General Court. He d. Feb. 4, 1861, aged 74. Children:

i. HENRY COBURN, b. Nov. 25, 1814; d. Oct. 14, 1815.

ii. ABIJAH COBURN, b. June 25, 1816. Resides on the homestead in Weston, unm. He has been a boot and shoe manufacturer and farmer. He was selectman, and assessor for several years.

iii. CHARLES COBURN, b. Nov. 24, 1817; m. (1) Jan. 1, 1843, Sarah P. Floyd. She d. Dec. 28, 1845, leaving dau. Sarah, and he m. (2) June 1, 1848, Jane M. Dyer, dau. of James and Anna M. Dyer of Boston. She resides in Cambridge. He d. April 25, 1890. Their children were:

1. Sarah E. Coburn, b. March 19, 1844; d. Jan. 4, 1861.
2. Anna M. Coburn, b. May 15, 1849; d. June 5, 1849.
3. Jeannie M. Coburn, b. Aug. 31, 1850; d. Sept. 3, 1850.
4. Anna M. Coburn, b. May 24, 1852; d. Jan. 23, 1859.
5. Jeannie M. Coburn, b. Feb. 24, 1856; is an assistant in the Harvard College Library.
6. Charles H. Coburn, b. May 17, 1865; d. Sept. 7, 1866.

iv. JOHN COBURN, b. Jan. 19, 1823; m. April 26, 1848, Emily Matilda Peirce, dau. of Benjamin and Almira (Harrington) Peirce of Weston. He resides in Weston. He has been librarian of the Weston Town Library for 31 years. She d. March 24, 1890. Children:

1. Elizabeth Sophia Coburn, b. Sept. 26, 1849; is an assistant in the Harvard College Library.
2. Emily Frances Coburn, b. Sept. 21, 1851.
3. George Henry Coburn, b. Aug. 27 and d. Aug. 28, 1853.
4. Agnes Peirce Coburn, b. Sept. 15, 1857; is an assistant in the Harvard College Library.
5. Mary Emma Coburn, b. July 5, 1861; d. Oct. 12, 1888.

v. HENRY COBURN, b. Aug. 10, 1826; d. Nov. 18, 1847.

vi. GEORGE COBURN, b. July 20, 1829; d. Aug. 22, 1847.

vii. CHARLOTTE SOPHIA COBURN, b. Nov. 5, 1836. She was a school teacher several years.

3. MARY COBURN, b. Oct., 1789; m. Nathan Russell of East Sudbury, now Wayland. They left no issue.

4. WILLIAM COBURN, b. about 1791; m. Maria Travis of Weston; d. in 1832. Two daughters and both m.

5. ISAAC COBURN, b. about 1793; d. at age of 19.

6. LOIS COBURN, b. about 1793; m. Charles Weston of Weston.

7. ELIZA HOLBROOK, b. in Weston; d. 1830, unm.
8. SAMUEL HOLBROOK, b. in Weston; d. in Reading. He was m. two times. His children were:
   - I. SAMUEL HOLBROOK; d. without issue.
   - II. LYMAN HOLBROOK; d. without issue.
   - III. JOSEPHINE HOLBROOK; m. ——— Nickols, and resides in Lynn.
   - IV. ELIZA HOLBROOK; m. ——— Aborn. She resides in Wakefield.
   - V. GEORGE HOLBROOK; resides in Provincetown.

55. Joseph Parker, Jr. (*Joseph,*[5] *Josiah,*[4] *John,*[3] *Hananiah,*[2] *Thomas*[1]), son of Joseph and Eunice (Hobbs) Parker, b. in Lincoln, Oct. 4, 1767; int. of m. entered on records of Weston, Oct. 16, 1791; m. Nov. 17, 1791, Polly* Fisk, dau. of Samuel and Mary Fisk of Weston. She was b. in Weston, March 6, 1771. Her father, Samuel Fisk, served in the opening of hostilities against England, 1775. They settled in Weston on a small farm, one-half mile south of the meeting-house. Here they passed the remainder of their lives, with the exception of a few years spent in Lincoln. He was a blacksmith as well as a farmer.

Their children were:

144. EUNICE PARKER, b. in Weston, Aug. 13, 1792; m. Cyrus Pratt of Needham.

MARY PARKER, b. in Lincoln, Jan. 19, 1794; "m. in Weston, April 4, 1816, Richard Hammond, son of Moses Hammond of Charlton. She d. in Charlton, Nov. 18. 1816, aged 23."†

WILLIAM PARKER, b. in Lincoln, March 5, 1795; d. in Weston, Sept. 22, 1798.

145. SOPHIA PARKER, b. in Weston, Oct. 6, 1796; m. Montgomery Haven of Shrewsbury.

WILLIAM PARKER, b. in Weston, Nov. 2, 1798; d. Oct. 13, 1801.‡

---

* As was then the custom this name was a substitute for Mary and she was known by both.

† From Joseph Parker's family Bible.

‡ An occurrence which "tries men's souls" was the sudden deaths of these two children. The son, William, a promising child of three years, died suddenly, and was buried on the second day following. The parents returned home only to find the baby, Joseph, Jr., dead also, having caught the same disease and having died as suddenly as his brother.

JOSEPH PARKER, JR., b. in Weston, Aug. 17, 1800; d. Oct. 15, 1801.

146. ISAAC PARKER, b. in Watertown, July 19, 1802; m. Lucy Dinsmore.

147. CYTHIA PARKER, b. in Weston, Jan. 15, 1810; m. in Waltham, Dec. 3, 1836, David M. Bathrick.

ADALINE PARKER, b. in Weston, March 7, 1814; d. in Weston, March 27, 1815.

56. **Elisha Parker** *(Joseph,[5] Josiah,[4] John,[3] Hananiah,[2] Thomas[1])*, son of Joseph and Eunice (Hobbs) Parker, b. in Lincoln, Sept. 10, 1775, twin brother with Rebecca Parker. His int. of m. stands upon the records of the town of Weston bearing date of Feb. 23, 1800. He was m. during the same year to Miss Jerusha Wentworth of Weston. They lived for several years in Maine, then settled in Stoughton, Mass., where he was a blacksmith and a well known and esteemed citizen.

Their children were:

148. CLOY PARKER, b. March 7, 1800; m. Caleb Carr of Easton.

149. ISAAC PARKER, b. April 23, 1802; m. Flavilla Crosbury.

150. ELISHA H. PARKER, b. April 17, 1805; m. Charlotte Skinner.

151. REBECCA R. PARKER; m. Martin Wales of Stoughton.

SAMUEL SAW PARKER, b. June 25, 1810.

152. HANNAH PARKER, b. Jan. 13, 1813; m. John Smith.

153. HIRAM PARKER, b. March 28, 1816; m. Rhody Freeman of Orleans.

154. JONATHAN CAPIN PARKER; m. Martha Briggs of Stoughton.

155. DAVID MANLEY PARKER; m. Mary Ann Andrews of Walpole.

57. **Rebecca Parker** *(Joseph,[5] Josiah,[4] John,[3] Hananiah,[2] Thomas[1])*, dau. of Joseph and Eunice (Hobbs) Parker, b. in Lincoln, Sept. 10, 1775; twin sister of Elisha Parker; m. in Weston, Dec. 13, 1796, Elisha Rand of Weston. He may have been the son of Benjamin Rand, who belonged to the company of minute-men from Weston, and served on several occasions in 1775.

58. **John Parker** *(Peter,[5] John,[4] John,[3] Hananiah,[2] Thomas[1])*, son of Peter and Ruth (Eaton) Parker, b. in Framingham, Nov. 16, 1762; m. 1781, Deborah Lamb, "who

was baptized 1760, dau. of Samuel Lamb of Framingham, whose great-grandfather, Thomas Lamb, came in the fleet with Winthrop in 1630. Samuel Lamb lived in the west part, north of the Lamb Hill, where a cellar-hole remains."*

John Parker lived in the southwest part of the town, northeast of Nathan Bridges, on the old way from the Bridges place, through the Goulding pasture, to George Nurse's. He was one of the first members of the Framingham Artillery Co., organized 1799. He removed, April 1, 1800, to Royalston, where the last four children of his large family were born. They lived in Royalston until 1834, when in Oct. the parents removed to Southborough to live with their son John Parker, Jr. He d. at this place March 10, 1838, and his wife followed him only five days later, March 15, 1838. In appearance John Parker was a well built man of about 5 feet 10 inches; his hair sandy, inclining to red. He was an intelligent looking man, ready and frank in speech. Although naturally quiet and thoughtful, he loved an argument and was a stirring talker with the gift of something like eloquence. He was a public spirited citizen, a most resolute Whig and a Free-Mason.

Their children were:

156. Nancie Parker, b. Dec. 11, 1782; m. Nathan Goddard of Athol.

Betsey Parker, b. March 17, 1785; d. July 16, 1796.

John Parker, b. April 22, 1787; d. June 18, 1796.

157. Mary Parker, b. June 2, 1789; m. Capt. John Forristall of Winchendon.

Deborah Parker, b. April 12, 1792; m. Jan. 8, 1839, Dea. Samuel Morse of Hopkinton. She d. April 26, 1865. She was an attractive and worthy lady. She left no issue.

158. Peter Parker, b. July 16, 1794; m. (1) Sarah Sawyer of Boylston.

Eliza Parker, b. Aug. 23, 1796; d. Jan. 30, 1803.

159. John Parker, b. June 16, 1798; m. Mary Ann Fales of Shrewsbury.

160. Ruth Parker, b. July 31, 1800; m. Capt. Nathan Leland of Holliston.

---

* Temple.

161. Abigail Parker, b. March 15, 1802; m. Newell Ware of Walpole.

162. Josiah Parker, b. July 31, 1804; m. Caroline Peck of Boylston.

163. Presson Parker, b. Oct. 24, 1807; m. Mary Newton of Southborough.

59. **Nathan Parker** *(Peter,*[5] *John,*[4] *John,*[3] *Hananiah,*[2] *Thomas*[1]*)*, son of Peter and Ruth (Eaton) Parker, b. in Framingham, Oct. 23, 1764; m. in Newton, March 17, 1791, Catharine Murdock of Newton, dau. of Aaron Murdock. Nathan Parker enlisted for the suppression of Shays' Rebellion; belonged to Framingham Artillery Co., and with wife were admitted to the Church 1792. He d. Aug. 17, 1826; she d. Nov. 1, 1836.

Their children were:

164. Harriett Parker, b. Oct. 10, 1793; m. Josiah Bigelow of Framingham.

Preston Parker, b. May 10, 1796; drowned Oct. 10, 1798.

165. Maria Parker, b. April 16, 1799; m. Abijah Fay of Southborough.

Preston Parker, b. Nov. 2, 1802; d. Aug. 20, 1804.

166. Peter Parker, b. June 18, 1804; m. Harriett Colby Webster.

Catherine Parker, b. Aug. 21, 1806; d. Oct. 30, 1842.

60. **Abigail Parker** *(Peter,*[5] *John,*[4] *John,*[3] *Hananiah,*[2] *Thomas*[1]*)*, b. in Framingham, Dec. 15, 1766; m. June 8, 1803, Lovell Howe of Marlborough. They removed to Southborough, where he was a farmer and bookbinder. They d. in Southborough.

Their children were:

1. Eliza Howe; d. unm.
2. Caroline Howe; d. unm.
3. Peter Parker Howe; m. Julia Newton of Southborough. He was a very conscientious and active worker, a man of pronounced character, and always distinguished by his strong will and independent ideas. Whatever he undertook he did with all his might. He took a lively interest in the education of the young. He was a school-teacher in Southborough for the

major part of his life. In his school he was very strict, allowing no deviation from study, but was a good teacher. All persuasion seldom changed the belief of Parker Howe. But he was an intellectual, sensible, sober man, and was ever ready for an argument with his own thoughtful ideas. He will not be forgotten. Associated with Dea. John Parker, the town of Southborough will long remember his name and his work. He was the right man in the right place. He lectured against intemperance, then a great evil in the town, and slavery. With Dea. Parker he held revival meetings. He worked hard and lived to see their causes triumph and the town improve from its former standard to one of the foremost rank in the State. He was selectman and representative and d. in 1869.

4. ABIGAIL HOWE; m. Charles Fales, b. in Shrewsbury, June 2, 1807, brother of Mary Ann Fales, whose name appears on page 163. They were children of Daniel and Sarah (Pratt) Fales of Shrewsbury. It is said that Daniel's father, Capt. Fales, was b. in Wales and was there educated as a physician. He lived afterwards in Shrewsbury, Mass., to almost the age of 100 years. His wife was the dau. of Pastor Mann of Wrentham. They had several children.

61. Ruth Parker *(Peter,[5] John,[4] John,[3] Hananiah,[2] Thomas[1])*, b. in Framingham, Jan. 8, 1769; m. Nov. 8, 1785, Joseph Bigelow, Jr., of Holliston. They lived in Holliston.

Their children were:

1. JOSIAH BIGELOW, b. Oct. 26, 1790; was captain of the Hopkinton militia company; m. March 20, 1821, Harriet Parker, his cousin. (No. 164.)
2. JOHN BIGELOW; d. aged about 23.
3. JOSEPH BIGELOW; m. ——— Wilson, dau. of Dr. John and Nancy Wilson of Hopkinton. They lived in Natick. They left no issue.
4. SALLY BIGELOW; m. Gilbert Dench Wilson, brother of Joseph Bigelow's wife. They settled in Southborough. When a young man he began teaching school and taught for 16 years. He was a well read and educated man. He was a farmer in Southborough. He was a strong supporter of anti-slavery. She d. March 27, 1864. Their children were:
   - I. GEORGE OVERING WILSON, b. May 24, 1820; d. 1864.
   - II. CHARLES BIGELOW WILSON, b. April 11, 1823; m. ——— Turner of Framingham; entered the business of Boyd & Corey, shoe manufacturers of Marlborough. He

became a silent partner and it is said he once saved the firm from a failure. He also enlarged and conducted the American House in Boston. He d. in 1885.

III. HENRY GILBERT WILSON, b. Nov. 7, 1830; m. and settled in Southborough, where he was a farmer. They removed to Northborough, where he now resides. Their son is the Rev. Lewis G. Wilson of Hopedale.

IV. WILLIAM WALLACE WILSON, b. Jan. 7, 1839; d. 1840.

5. RUTH BIGELOW; m. in Hopkinton, Jan. 20, 1818, Amherst Messenger, b. Oct., 1795, d. Feb., 1887, son of John and Margaret (Fisher) Messenger. He was a shoemaker. They lived (1) in Wrentham, (2) Ashland, (3) Sherborn, (4) Holliston, (5) Peru, Vt., and (6) Natick, Mass. He was justice of the peace for a number of years in Peru, Vt. She d. in Sherborn, March, 1828. He d. in Natick. Their children were:

I. EMILY WALDO MESSENGER, b. in Hopkinton, April 19, 1820; m. Sept. 29, 1842, Joseph Heywood Simonds, b. in Peru, Vt., May 19, 1818, son of David and Anna (Byam) Simonds. Their children were:

1. Albert Joseph Simonds, b. in Peru, Vt., Sept. 2, 1845; m. Lina Mills. He served in the late war three years; representative in 1890. Child:
   I. Mabel Edith Simonds, b. in Peru, Vt., July, 1878.
2. Ruth Eliza Simonds, b. in Peru, Vt.; d. in Natick.
3. Lewis Messenger Simonds, b. in Natick; d. in Natick.
4. Dexter Bigelow Simonds, b. in Peru, Vt.; d. in Peru, Vt.

II. SARAH ANN MESSENGER, b. in Hopkinton, Nov. 11, 1822; m. in Natick, Nov. 29, 1845, Dexter Washburn, b. in Natick, Oct. 30, 1820, son of Jedediah and Mita (Frost) Washburn. Their children were:

1. Janette Washburn, b. June 6, 1850; d. Aug., 1851.
2. Alice Washburn, b. Nov. 16, 1854; m. Nov., 1875, Silas Elijah Simonds, and has three children:
   I. Fred Washburn Simonds, b. Nov. 8, 1882.
   II. Jennie May Simonds, b. March 1, 1886.
   III. Warren James Simonds, b. Sept. 10, 1888.
3. Agnes Bigelow Washburn, b. March 2, 1858; m. Nov. 2, 1881, Walter Irving Fletcher, and has had three children:
   I. Harry Fletcher, b. and d. Dec. 24, 1883.
   II. Rollo Francis Fletcher, b. Sept. 3, 1887.
   III. Dexter Joshua Fletcher, b. Dec. 28, 1889; d. March 8, 1890.
4. Fannie Emily Washburn, b. March 6, 1866; m. June 3, 1886, Alvah Flansburg, and has three children:
   I. Pauline Flansburg, b. Nov., 1886; d. Dec., 1886.
   II. Robert Dexter Flansburg, b. Nov. 11, 1887.
   III. David Washburn Flansburg, b. July 8, 1889.

7. JOHN BIGELOW MESSENGER, b. 1826; m. Louisa Washburn. Their children were:

   I. CHARLES W. MESSENGER; resides in Natick.
   II. EMMA MESSENGER; m. W. Tilton.

8. CHARLES BIGELOW; m. ——— Francis; deceased.
9. GEORGE BIGELOW; m. April 17, 1831, Amy Learned. He d. Feb. 28, 1867. She d. Oct., 1887. Their children were:

   I. GEORGE BIGELOW, b. 1832; d.
   II. MARY BIGELOW, b. Nov. 24, 1836; d.
   III. ADELIZA BIGELOW, b. Oct. 10, 1839.
   IV. HARRIETT BIGELOW, b. Feb. 17, 1841.
   V. SUSAN BIGELOW, b. Oct. 11, 1844.

62. Experience Parker *(Peter,[5] John,[4] John,[3] Hananiah,[2] Thomas[1])*, b. in Framingham, Feb. 19, 1771; m. Feb. 3, 1797, Dea. Luther Haven of Framingham, b. April 15, 1770, son of Dea. Jesse Haven of Holliston. He came to Framingham, Dec. 21, 1791, to live with David Haven, Esq. He was one of the fifth generation in descent from Richard Haven, Esq., of Lynn, the emigrant ancestor. They lived in various places in Framingham, he bought the farm afterwards known as the Bigelow paper mill site, exchanged farms with Artemas Parker and Enoch Belknap. Removed to Rice's End, where they lived the remainder of their lives. He was deacon and representative. Mrs. Exprerience Haven d. Oct. 16, 1817. He m. again, this time to widow Anna Drury Rutter. He d. July 11, 1851.

Their children were:

1. CLARISSA HAVEN, b. Feb. 25, 1798; m. Dec. 19, 1822, Cornelius Morse, b. about 1797, son of Benjamin and Sarah (Claflin) Morse of Framingham. They settled in Framingham on the Hersey place, afterwards removed to Newton. He d. July 29, 1872, aged 74. She d. in 1877. Their children were:

   I. HORATIO MORSE, b. April 7, 1825.
   II. HENRY MORSE, b. Jan. 21, 1827; d. Oct. 28, 1855.
   III. CLARA MORSE.

2. RUTH EATON HAVEN, b. March 9, 1800; m. March 31, 1829, John C. Bixby, native of Hopkinton. They settled at Salem End on the Henry Brewer place; removed to Westborough

and West Newton, where he was station agent of B. & A. R. R. He d. in Lowell, 1882, aged 82. Children:

i. John Bixby; resides in West Newton.

ii. Henry L. Bixby; resides in West Newton.

3. Luther Haven, b. Aug. 14, 1806. Teacher in Leicester Academy; U. S. Collector; d. March 9, 1866, in Chicago.

4. George Haven; Supt. of New York Central R. R.; lived at Syracuse, N. Y., and Framingham; represented the town of Framingham for one or two years in the Legislature; d. in 1882, at Framingham.

63. Patty Parker *(Peter,[5] John,[4] John,[3] Hananiah,[2] Thomas[1])*, b. in Framingham, April 15, 1773; m. Nov. 1, 1793, Eleazer Bullard of Holliston.

Their children were:

1. Charles Bullard; was in business in Quincy Market, Boston, many years, and lived in Somerville.
2. Ruth Bullard; d. young.
3. Jemima Bullard; m. ——— Cutler of Holliston. Had five or six children.
4. Josiah Bullard.
5. Joseph Bullard.
6. Eleazer Bullard.

64. Sally Parker *(Peter,[5] John,[4] John,[3] Hananiah,[2] Thomas[1])*, b. in Framingham, March 25, 1775; m. April 21, 1800, William Eames of Holliston. He was a farmer, but was an invalid for 37 years. They lived and died in Holliston. She d. April 4, 1875, and he d. April 5, 1875.

Their children were;

1. Harriett Eames, b. July 29, 1801; d. in Framingham, Oct. 6, 1891, unm.
2. Millitiah Eames, b. May 5, 1803; d. in Ashland, unm., Jan. 12, 1882.
3. Sally Eames, b. Sept. 1, 1805; m. in Holliston, April 1, 1826, Daniel Ryder, b. 1795, d. April 5, 1875. She d. April 4, 1875. He was a farmer in Ashland. Their children were:

   i. Louisa Jane Ryder, b. Oct. 20, 1828; d. Jan. 20, 1833.

   ii. Charles Ferdinand Ryder, b. Oct. 9, 1830; d. Jan. 20, 1833.

III. SARAH RYDER, } twins, b. Oct. 7, and d. Oct. 8, 1832.
IV. NANCY RYDER, }

V. DANIEL BAINBRIDGE RYDER, b. May 23, 1834; m. Susan Gerrold of Boston; reside in San Jose, Cal. Children:

1. Bainbridge Lincoln Ryder.
2. Frank Ryder.
3. Louisa Jane Ryder.

VI. GEORGE WILLIAM RYDER, b. Sept. 24, 1836; m. Eliza Jane Hildreth of Lexington; reside in San Jose, Cal. Children:

1. Georgianna Ryder.
2. Jennie Ryder.
3. Lona Ryder; deceased.
4. Willie Ryder.
5. Irving Ryder.

VII. CHARLES HENRY RYDER, b. Aug. 7, 1839; d. May 23, 1862.

VIII. SARAH JANE RYDER, b. May 28, 1844; m. in Ashland, Dec. 10, 1867, Charles Eugene Loring, b. in Hopkinton, Aug. 8, 1842, son of John J. and Lucretia D. Loring. He is a farmer in Ashland. Children:

1. Mary Lucretia Loring, b. June 8, 1872.
2. Arthur Eugene Loring, b. Nov. 7, 1876.

4. MARY EAMES, b. Aug. 27, 1809; m. Reuben Dewing of Holliston. They lived in Holliston and had children. She d. Feb. 2, 1846. Children:

I. ELIJAH DEWING; m. Louise Willet of Holliston; lived and d. in Natick. One child:

1. Mary Louise Dewing.

II. MARY JANE DEWING; m. Wm. Henry Howard; lived in Braintree; d. Oct. 30, 1874. Children:

1. Maria Willet Howard.
2. Lizzie Willet Howard.

5. ANNIE EAMES, b. Dec. 11, 1814; m. Henry Bacon, b. Jan. 31, 1814, son of Henry Bacon of Quincy. Their children were:

I. WILLIAM HENRY BACON, b. July 14, 1845; m. in Memphis, Tenn., Feb. 10, 1872, Mattie E. Wilkins of Bangor, Me.

II. MARY ANNIE BACON, b. March 18, 1848. Resides in South Framingham.

III. CAROLINE ELIZABETH BACON, b. July 28, 1851; m. George H. Patch, b. in Lexington, Dec. 8, 1844. Corp. Patch, as he was called, was a very prominent member of the G. A. R. He was a soldier and orator. He was Corporal in Co. I, 19th Regiment. He delivered the oration at Gettysburg, Oct. 7, 1885; was Commander of the Department of Mass., G. A. R., and d. in South Framingham, July 26, 1887. Their two children are both deceased:

1. Willie Patch.
2. Adaline Patch.

65. Josiah Parker *(Peter,[5] John,[4] John,[3] Hananiah,[2] Thomas[1])*, b. in Framingham, April 26, 1779; "lived on the homestead with Nathan till 1828, when he built on the hill where Leander Barber now lives; admitted to Church, 1838; d. Feb. 26, 1854."* He bore the title of Captain. He m. April 8, 1804, Olive Stone, dau. of Dr. Elijah and Elizabeth (Lyndes) Stone of Framingham. She was b. in Framingham, July 22, 1799, one of a family of ten; admitted to the Church, 1815: d. in Framingham, July 4, 1826.

Their children were:

167. CHARLES PARKER, b. March 6, 1805; m. Mary H. Wallingford of Claremont, N. H.

OLIVE PARKER; d. young.

168. ELIZA ANN PARKER, b. July 17, 1810; m. Thomas Hastings, Jr.

169. EMILY PARKER, b. Nov. 17, 1813; m. Daniel Parmenter.

66. Artemas Parker *(Peter,[5] John,[4] John,[3] Hananiah,[2] Thomas[1])*, son and last surviving child of Peter and Ruth (Eaton) Parker, b. in Framingham, Dec. 20, 1781; m. Jan. 21, 1806. Almy Clark, "dau. of Rev. Edward and Elizabeth (Weaver-Look) Clark of Framingham. The father came to Framingham from R. I.; was minister of the Baptist Church 1781 to 1790, and from 1801 to 1809. Almy Clark was b. June 21, 1780. Artemas Parker bought, July 5, 1806, 71 acres, a part of the Brinley farm, of John Lovell; built the Dea. E. M. Capen house; in 1819 exchanged with Dea. Luther Haven for the Bigelow place in Ashland."† He belonged to the Framingham artillery company from its organization in 1799; and served in Capt. John Temple's

---

* Temple.

† *Same.*

company of artillery, in Col. William Edwards' regiment in the War of 1812. He d. in Framingham, Aug. 28, 1825. His wife d. Jan. 29, 1832, aged 52.

Their children were:

170. EDWARD C. PARKER, b. Sept. 26, 1806; m. Mary Leland of Holliston.

171. GEORGE SMITH PARKER, b. April 19, 1808; m. Mary Ann White.

172. CURTIS PARKER, b. June 28, 1810; m. Eliza J. Horton of Natick.

173. LORENZO PARKER, b. May 8, 1812; m. Mary E. Herrick of Portland, Me.

174. ELIZA JANE PARKER, b. June 6, 1817; m. David Washburn of Natick.

HENRY EMERSON PARKER, b. in Hopkinton, May 7, 1820; d. young.

67. Sally Parker (*Philemon,[6] Jonas,[5] Andrew,[4] John,[3] Hananiah,[2] Thomas[1]*), dau. of Philemon and Susan (Stone) Parker, was b. July 1, 1785. The records of Princeton, Mass., testify that the intention of marriage between Scannel Burt of Newton and Sally Parker of Princeton was entered May 3, 1807. He was b. in Westmoreland, N. H., May 3, 1782. They removed to Peru, Vt., where he was a farmer and where he d. Oct. 27, 1857, aged 75. She d. in Peru, Vt., Jan. 14, 1877, aged 92.

Their children were:

1. JOSEPH P. BURT, b. in Westmoreland, N. H., Nov. 10, 1807; d. unm.
2. ADLINE BURT, b. in Peru, Vt., Nov. 10, 1808; m. in Peru, Vt., Jan. 1, 1834, Capt. Cyrus Bailey, Jr., b. Sept. 23, 1804, son of Cyrus and Chloe (Burton) Bailey. She d. Nov. 6, 1848. He d. March 3, 1885. Their children were:
   - I. WARREN C. BAILEY, b. in Andover, Vt., June 10, 1835.
   - II. AUGUSTA A. BAILEY, b. in Andover, Vt., Aug. 14, 1836; d. July 11, 1841.
   - III. CALISTA A. BAILEY, b. Dec. 6, 1840; m. Orien Hutchins.
3. GRATIA M. BURT, b. Aug. 7, 1810; m. William Strong. Child:
   - I. SYLVESTER STRONG. He lived in Meriden, N. H., several years.

4. RODOLPHUS BURT, b. July 6, 1812; m. Elizabeth Hitchcock. He is deceased. She resides in East Saginaw, Mich. Their dau. was:

   I. SUSAN HITCHCOCK BURT; m. Edward Hayes. They reside in Bridgeport, Mich.

5. JOSHUA BURT, b. April 5, 1814; m. in Cambridgeport, Mass., Feb. 21, 1849, Rebecca Lakin, b. in Charlotte, Me., Dec. 8, 1823. He was a farmer. They lived in Peru, Vt. He d. in Bridgeport, Mich., Feb. 21, 1867. His wife survives him. All the children were b. in Peru, Vt.:

   I. CHELCIUS OTIS BURT, b. Dec. 30, 1850; d. March 21, 1871.

   II. MARIA CLINA BURT, b. Sept. 9, 1851; m. Joseph Jones, river captain. They reside in West Saginaw, Mich. Their children were:

      1. Alta Virginia Jones, b. June 13, 1875.
      2. Willard Burt Jones, b. July 7, 1882.
      3. Pearl Nida Jones, b. July 20, 1887.

   III. SARAH ADALINE BURT, b. Aug. 30, 1852; m. Peter H. Nichols. Child:

      1. Roy Leon Nichols, b. in East Saginaw, Mich., March 21, 1887.

   IV. MARCUS LUTHER BURT, b. July 6, 1854; m. Iona Becker of Bridgeport, Mich. He is a farmer at Bridgeport. They have seven children, all b. in Bridgeport:

      1. Evaline Ellen Burt, b. Dec. 20, 1876.
      2. Marcus Luthur Burt, b. Sept. 22, 1878.
      3. Alice Mabel Burt, b. Feb. 28, 1881.
      4. Chelcius Otis Burt, b. March 12, 1883.
      5. Glynn Malcom Burt, b. Nov. 23, 1885.
      6. Henry Ward Burt, b. Jan. 15, 1888.
      7. Vearner Burt.

   V. CHARLES HENRY BURT, b. July 6, 1856; m. Lizzie Hacket. He d. in Jackson, Mich., March 6, 1883. Child:

      1. Clarence Burt, b. Jan., 1883; d. May 10, 1883, aged 4 months.

   VI. ANNA REBECCA BURT; m. Frank E. Richards, conductor on the Michigan Central R. R. They reside in Bay City, Mich. Children:

      1. Edwin Frank Richards, b. in Detroit, Mich., Dec. 13, 1876.
      2. Charles Henry Richards, b. in Detroit, Aug. 8, 1879.
      3. Harrie Madison Richards, b. in West Bay City, Mich., Sept. 7, 1884.

   V. WILLARD ELMER BURT, b. Sept. 1, 1864. Resides in East Saginaw, Mich.

VIII. MARY ELLEN BURT; d. April 9, 1871.

6. JUSTIN BURT, b. May 7, 1816; m. in Goshen, Vt., Feb. 6, 1845, Nancy White, dau. of Jesse and Nancy White. He d. May 14. 1891, aged 75. He was a farmer. He lived upon the old Burt homestead in Peru. All the children were b. in Andover, Vt.:

I. LUTHER J. BURT, b. Aug. 18, 1847; d. in Andover, Vt., Sept. 12, 1854.

II. DORINDA V. BURT, b. Oct. 30, 1849. Resides in Peru, Vt.

III. ELWIN BURT, b. May 17, 1851; d. in Andover, Vt., June 8, 1852.

IV. SUSIE E. BURT, b. Feb. 2, 1857; m. Newton Lakin. Resides in Peru, Vt.

V. ELWIN L. BURT, b. June 8, 1864; m. Nellie Wyman.

7. SARAH BURT, b. March 20, 1818.

8. MARY ANN BURT, b. Sept. 18, 1819; d. March 23, 1827.

9. EZRA B. BURT, b. Dec. 22, 1821; m. Feb. 6, 1855, Clarissa, b. in Salisbury, Vt., Oct. 27, 1827, dau. of Henry and Abigail Alexander. He is a farmer of Salisbury, Vt. He is also Overseer of the Poor. Children:

I. AUGUSTUS E. BURT, b. Sept. 26, 1854.

II. ELLEN A. BURT, b. Dec. 2, 1856.

III. HATTY BURT, b. Aug. 6, 1865.

IV. GOSHEN M. BURT.

10. JONATHAN BURT, b. Nov. 22, 1823; d. Sept. 13, 1826.

68. Nancy Parker (*Philemon,*[6] *Jonas,*[5] *Andrew,*[4] *John,*[3] *Hananiah,*[2] *Thomas*[1]), dau. of Philemon and Susan (Stone?) Parker, b. Sept. 28, 1786; m. Timothy Wyman.

Their children were:

1. EMORY THOMAS WYMAN, b. July 28, 1803; m. Martha Davis.

2. EMELINE WYMAN, b. Sept. 30, 1807; m. Heman Wright.

3. JONAS WYMAN, b. Aug. 6. 1812; d. in infancy.

4. SUZAN ANN WYMAN, b. Nov. 4, 1814; m. Ebenezer Cary of Waltham.

5. CARLTON WYMAN, b. March 29, 1817.

6. JOSEPH PARKER WYMAN, b. in Swanzey, N. H., Aug. 4, 1818; m. Eunice L. Keith, b. Oct. 8, 1817, dau. of Samuel of Springfield, Vt. She d. in Springfield, Vt., May 27, 1885,

aged 67 years. He resides in North Springfield, Vt., is a carpenter and farmer. Children:

i. FREDERICK A. WYMAN, b. July 22, 1847; d. May 29, 1863.

ii. CHARLES E. WYMAN, b. Sept. 9, 1848. Resides in Cavendish, Vt. He is section master on C. V. R. R. He m. Margaret Morgan and has one son.

iii. ROYAL E. WYMAN, b. June 19, 1851. Resides in Perkinsville, Vt. He m. Annie Pike of Weathersfield, Vt., and has two sons and three daughters.

iv. GEORGE K. WYMAN, b. March 22, 1856; m. Eliza J. Rumrill of Springfield, Vt. He is a farmer and has one dau.

v. LIZZIE C. WYMAN, b. Aug. 22, 1857; d. Sept. 12, 1863.

vi. JAMES L. WYMAN, b. Oct. 22, 1859; m. Lottie I. Morgan of Springfield, Vt., and has one dau.

7. CALVIN WYMAN, b. Oct. 22, 1820; m. Millie Reed of Chester, Vt. } Twins.

8. LUTHER WYMAN, b. Oct. 22, 1820; m. Elizabeth Grant of Hardwick, Mass. }

9. JOHN DENSMORE WYMAN, b. Aug. 20, 1822; m. Susan Foster of Rutland, Vt.

69. Luther Parker *(Philemon,[6] Jonas,[5] Andrew,[4] John,[3] Hananiah,[2] Thomas[1])*, son of Philemon and Susan (Stone) Parker, was b. (twin with Calvin), April 7, 1796;* m. Jan. 1, 1822, Dolly Byam of Templeton, b. July 6, 1804, d. March 26, 1870. They settled in Chester, Vt., where he was a farmer. He d. in Chester, Oct. 3, 1840, aged 44 years.

All the children were b. in Chester:

GEORGE F. PARKER, b. Dec. 31, 1822; d. Sept. 2, 1823.

MARTHA A. PARKER, b. Dec. 10, 1824; m. May 28, 1845, Oscar W. Spalding, b. in Cavendish, Vt., Nov. 7, 1822. She d. March 18, 1880, leaving no issue.

175. SUSAN M. PARKER, b. March 10, 1826; m. Horace Thompson in Chester.

176. LUCINDA A. PARKER, b. June 3, 1827; m. Josiah Ayers of Windham, Vt.

---

*The records of Princeton show the births of Luther and Calvin. However, family tradition say that they were b. in Billerica, Mass. It may be that the Princeton record was only a transfer.

Luther Parker, b. March 1, 1829; d. June 30, 1833.

George Parker, b. Nov. 7, 1830; m. Oct. 19, 1854, Augusta A. Morrison, b. in Chester, Vt., March 11, 1835. He is a farmer and resides in Chester. No issue.

177. Sarah S. Parker, b. June 21, 1840; m. Alvin W. Davis.

70. Calvin Parker (*Philemon,[6] Jonas,[5] Andrew,[4] John,[3] Hananiah,[2] Thomas[1]*), son of Philemon and Susan (Stone) Parker (twin to Luther), was b. April 7, 1796. When ten years of age he went to live with his father's cousin, Dea. Ebenezer Parker of Princeton, where he remained as one of the family for many years. Then he removed to Chester, Vt., where his brothers had already settled. He was known for his honest, upright integrity and frugality, and his keenness of perception. He and Luther looked so near alike that many could not tell them apart. They were very good looking men. In Chester the brothers lived within two miles of each other, all being good livers, but not wealthy. They were all industrious farmers, but none of them professed Christianity. He m. at age of 31, May 8, 1827, Seba, dau. of Silas and Olive (Holbrook) Cutler, b. June 19, 1806, d. July 12, 1879. He d. Sept. 4, 1881, aged 85.

Their children were:

178. Mary Ann Parker, b. July 21, 1828; m. Silas F. Baldwin.

179. Olive A. Parker, b. Nov. 5, 1829; m. Silas J. Smith.

William A. Parker, b. June 16, 1832; d. Aug. 9, 1833.

180. Fannie E. Parker, b. April 18, 1835; m. Calvin W. Bates.

71. John Parker (*Philemon,[6] Jonas,[5] Andrew,[4] John,[3] Hananiah,[2] Thomas[1]*), son of Philemon and Susan (Stone) Parker, was b. in Princeton, June 11, 1798: m. Ellen Johnson, b. Feb. 14, 1802, d. Feb. 17, 1865, dau. of Asa and Ellen Hall Johnson. They settled in Chester, Vt. He was a farmer. He d. in Chester, Feb. 6, 1874.

Their children were:

181. James Parker, b. in Chester, Dec. 14, 1825; m. Sophia Hopkins.

Susan Parker, b. in Chester, June 14, 1831; d. March 14, 1872.

72. Lucinda Parker *(Amos,⁶ Amos,⁵ Andrew,⁴ John,³ Hananiah,² Thomas¹)*, dau. of Amos and Lucy (Robinson) Parker, was b. in Hubbardston; m. July 23, 1793, Nathaniel Bangs of Barre. He was a neighbor of Artemas Parker of that town. They continued to live upon their farm in Barre until 1795, when they sold out to Amos Parker and removed to Putney, Vt. She d. Feb. 2, 1803, leaving these children:

1. AMOS PARKER BANGS, b. Dec. 25, 1794; m. and removed to Cambridge, Vt. He had two children, who are now Mrs. Elvira Gilmore of Hyde Park, Vt., and Nathaniel Bangs of Hardwick, Vt.
2. AZARIAH BANGS, b. Dec. 7, 1797; m. and settled in Bakersfield, Vt., and has five children living:
   - Mrs. Louisa Gaugd, of East Evans, N. Y.
   - Mrs. Marietta Cableigh, of East Evans, N. Y.
   - Mrs. Adaline Holbrook, of Elmore, Vt.
   - Wm. Henry H. Bangs, of Elmore, Vt., who has three children.
   - Mrs. Orilla M. Graves, of Springfield, Mass.
3. LYSANDER BANGS, b. Jan. 15, and d. Jan. 22, 1803.

73. Joseph Parker *(Amos,⁶ Amos,⁵ Andrew,⁴ John,³ Hananiah,² Thomas¹)*, son of Amos and Lucy (Robinson) Parker, was b. in Hubbardston (1772?); m. Feb. 21, 1791, Relief Earle of Paxton, b. Sept. 12, 1778, dau. of Lt. Oliver and Mary (Earle) Earle of Paxton. This Oliver Earle's line was William,⁵ William,⁴ Ralph,³ William,² Ralph,¹ the emigrant ancestor. He was the common ancestor of a very large number of descendants of this illustrious name. He was a Rhode Island settler; an intelligent and prominent man. Oliver Earle lived in Paxton in the house still standing just north of the old William Earle or Joseph Penniman place. Oliver was a private in the company of minute men, who under the command of Capt. Phineas Moore "marched on the alarm, the 19th of April, 1775, from Paxton to Cambridge." He was afterwards lieutenant.

Joseph and Relief Parker removed about 1804 to Bakersfield, Vt. He accompanied his brother Amory and family, to whence their uncle Joseph Baker, Esq., awaited them. It is related on page 102 how Esquire Baker founded the town of

Bakersfield, and how his settlement there was quickly followed by his son-in-law Elisha Parker and Elisha's brothers Joseph and Amory.

The wife, Relief (Earle) Parker, d. in Bakersfield, June 2, 1854. He was a farmer. He was a resident of Bakersfield until his death, which occurred Jan. 1, 1861.

Their children were:

182. Amos Earle Parker, b. Feb. 26, 1802; m. Matilda Converse of Bakersfield.

183. Mary Robinson Parker, b. Jan. 5, 1804; m. Matthew Gray of Bakersfield.

184. Joseph Sumner Parker, b. Oct. 27, 1806; m. —— Hall.

Sophia Bigelow Parker, b. April 11, 1808; m. Dorastus Wright. They left no issue.

185. Euridicia E. Parker, b. April 25, 1811; m. Michael French of Barre, Vt.

186. Frederick Appleton Parker, b. June 14, 1813; m. Caroline Maxson of Squankum, N. J.

187. Betsey Lorinda Parker, b. Dec. 10, 1818; m. Oliver F. Stebbins of Bakersfield, Vt.

74. Sylvester Parker (*Amos,⁶ Amos,⁵ Andrew,⁴ John,³ Hananiah,² Thomas¹*), son of Amos and Lucy (Robinson) Parker, was b. in Hubbardston, May 31, 1774; removed to Vermont, and m. Feb. 6, 1800, Alice Davis, b. in Athens, Vt., June 7, 1778. They soon settled in Westminster, Vt., where they passed 20 years and where their children were born. Removing from Westminster the family settled in Lyndon, Vt., then in Derby, Vt., and finally in Westfield, Vt. She d. in Westfield, Aug. 28, 1838, aged 60 years, 2 months and 21 days. He d. at Troy, Vt., Dec. 8, 1843, at the age of 69 years, 6 months and 8 days.

Their children were:

188. Amos Parker, b. Dec. 29, 1800; m. Lorinda Fairbanks.

189. Joel D. Parker, b. Oct. 9, 1802; m. Lucy Wyman of Barnstead, P. Q.

Hollis Parker, b. March 9, 1806; d. Dec. 10, 1827.

190. Alice Parker, b. June 22, 1808; m. Henry Coburn.

191. Amory Parker, b. April 15, 1811; m. Susan Gilman of Lyndon, Vt.

12

192. Lucy Parker, b. May 24, 1813; m. John Alexander.
193. Rhoena Parker, b. July 24, 1815; m. Silas Howe.
Rhuhamah Parker, b. July 5, 1817; m. Alexander Coburn. They are both deceased and left no issue.
194. Samuel W. Parker, b. Dec. 27, 1820; m. Harriett Field of Bakersfield, Vt.

75. Patty Parker *(Amos,^{6} Amos,^{5} Andrew,^{4} John,^{3} Hananiah,^{2} Thomas^1)*, dau. of Amos and Lucy (Robinson) Parker, was b. in Hubbardston; m. ——— Felton and removed to Vermont.

They had one son:

1. Horatio Felton.

76. Dana Robinson Parker *(Amos,^{6} Amos,^{5} Andrew,^{4} John,^{3} Hananiah,^{2} Thomas^1)*, son of Amos and Lucy (Robinson) Parker, was b. in Hubbardston, Nov. 4, 1781; m. Nov. 19, 1806, Sarah, dau. of John and Sarah Davis Williams of Hubbardston. He succeeded to the homestead, where, in the west part of the town, he lived nearly the whole of his life. He was well educated, thoughtful and religiously inclined; a diligent student of the Bible, often indulging in theological discussions with zest; a loyal citizen and a democrat, though not a politician. He held no important public office, but was called upon to settle minor difficulties, and his opinion was highly regarded by all. He was a good singer and extremely fond of sacred music. His occupation was that of a farmer and he paid considerable attention to the propagation of fruit. The well known "Nonesuch" apple originated upon his farm. An apple tree was discovered by him—wild—in a swamp down in Newton. People liked the flavor. He secured grafts and started them on a tree in Conest's Valley, Hubbardston, and from this tree was the beginning of the cultivated apple. He thus introduced the popular "Hubbardston Nonesuch." This original tree looked well for over 50 years. He lived until nearly 82 years of age, a useful and respected citizen.

Their children were:

195. Lucinda B. Parker, b. March 9, 1807; m. Eli Grey.
196. Sarah Davis Parker, b. June 7, 1808; m. Oliver Hale.

JOHN WILLIAMS PARKER, b. March 5, 1810; m. Nancy F. Barr.

197. ELVIRA PARKER, b. Nov. 28, 1811; m. Seth P. Heywood.

JONAS PARKER, b. Oct. 30, 1813; m. Susan Ann Decker of Staten Island, N. Y.

198. SOPHRONIA PARKER. b. Nov. 25. 1815; m. Henry Humphrey.

LUCY ROBINSON PARKER, b. Nov. 13, 1817; m. Asa S. Hodge of Athol. They settled in Hubbardston, where she has since deceased. He survives her.

DENNISON ROBINSON PARKER, b. Aug. 15, 1819; m. Mary A. Vroome of Staten Island, N. Y.

199. MARY PARKER, b. July 11, 1821; m. George Raymond.

200. AMOS PARKER, b. Feb. 12, 1823; m. Lucy Shepherd.

201. MARTHA MARIA PARKER, b. July 9, 1825; m. Lysander Batchelder.

AMORY PARKER, b. Aug. 2, 1828. Went to California in 1852 by way of Cape Horn, was on the ill-fated steamer *Independence*, of whose 800 passengers 240 lost their lives. He staid several years but drifted home again. He lives at Hubbardston, unm.

GEORGE LEROY PARKER, b. June 12, 1830; d. Aug. 1, 1831.

202. SUSAN ELIZABETH PARKER, b. April 9, 1833; m. (1) David Heywood, (2) Lysander Batchelder.

77. Amory Parker (*Amos,[6] Amos,[5] Andrew,[4] John,[3] Hananiah,[2] Thomas[1]*), son of Amos and Lucy (Robinson) Parker, was b. in Hubbardston, Dec. 8, 1783; m. Lydia Parker, his cousin, who was b. March 8, 1784, dau. of Major Elisha Parker. They removed to Bakersfield, Vt., where some of his brothers, sisters and nephews were already settled. He d. April 5, 1823, at the age of 40. He was well esteemed, and his early death, coming in the midst of strength and usefulness, was deeply lamented. She d. May 15, 1858, aged 74.

Their children were:

LUCY ROBINSON PARKER, b. Oct. 18, 1808; unm. Removed with her sisters to Lowell.

203. AMOS ANDREW PARKER, b. Oct. 28, 1814; m. (1) Cynthia Pratt of Reading, Vt.

LYDIA MARIA PARKER, b. Dec. 14, 1817; removed to Lowell and d. Nov. 16, 1864, unm.

204. ELISHA SYLVESTER PARKER, b. Nov. 11, 1819; m. (1) —— Barnes.

SALLY A. PARKER, b. June 19, 1823; removed to Lowell; d. Sept. 17, 1841, unm.

78. Lucy Parker *(Amos,[6] Amos,[5] Andrew,[4] John,[3] Hananiah,[2] Thomas[1])*, dau. of Amos and Lucy (Robinson) Parker, was b. in Hubbardston; she m. Jan. 12, 1812, Silas Richardson, and lived in Sterling. She d. July 4, 1828, aged 40. He d. Jan. 24, 1833, aged 51.

Their children were:

1. Silas Richardson, who m.
2. Joshua Richardson, who m., removed to N. Y. and had children.
3. Reuben Richardson, who m.
4. Mary Richardson, who was unm.
5. Nahum Richardson, who lives single.
6. Amaranca Richardson, who m.

79. Joel Parker *(Isaac,[6] Amos,[5] Andrew,[4] John,[3] Hananiah,[2] Thomas[1])*, son of Isaac and Margery (Maynard) Parker, was b. in Hubbardston, Sept. 16, 1770; m. (1) Hannah Bond of Westborough, one of eleven children, b. May 3, 1776; d. Aug. 10, 1816. He m. (2) Feb. 6, 1817, Susannah Fay, b. June 14, 1779; d. July 24, 1858. They lived in Westborough. He was a very worthy and widely respected citizen. He was a miller, a deacon of the Church, and a moderator of the town meetings. He d. in Westborough, Nov. 6, 1853, aged 83.

Their children were:

Anna Osborne Parker, b. Jan. 1, 1797; d. Jan. 29, 1828.

205. Betsey Curwen Parker, b. Jan. 20, 1799; m. Elmer Brigham.

206. Hannah Sophia Parker, b. April 5, 1801; m. Orestes Forbush.

207. Achsah Forbes Parker, b. Sept. 2, 1803; m. Solomon T. Fay.

208. Elmina Augusta Parker, b. Nov. 16, 1806; m. Thomas H. Fayerweather.

Joel Lloyd Parker, b. March 21, 1809; d. Nov. 26, 1826.

209. Harriet Newell Parker, b. Aug. 16, 1815; m. Mendal G. Fosgate.

80. Gardiner Parker *(Isaac,[6] Amos,[5] Andrew,[4] John,[3] Hananiah,[2] Thomas[1])*, son of Isaac and Margery (Maynard) Parker, was b. in Hubbardston, March 14, 1772; m. Asenath

Sherman. He lived at different times in Westborough, Grafton and Northborough. He earned a local reputation as an inventor and manufacturer of clocks. For Westborough and Shrewsbury he made the town clocks which are still in use. He ended his life Feb. 16, 1816. His widow Asenath survived him.

He left one son:

210. PERLEY PARKER; m. Betsey Mellen of Westborough.

81. **Dea. Otis Parker** (*Isaac,[6] Amos,[5] Andrew,[4] John,[3] Hananiah,[2] Thomas[1]*), son of Isaac and Margery (Maynard) Parker, was b. in Hubbardston, April 1, 1774; m. about 1795, Polly Ann, b. Dec. 27, 1771, dau. of Daniel and Sarah Nourse of Westborough. They removed in 1804 to Hubbardston, where cousins were then living, and settled. She d. April 30, 1850, aged 78. He was a farmer; d. Feb. 27, 1855, thus living to the ripe old age of 82. He lived long and well to enjoy the harvest of the good seed which he had sown. Piety and public spirit were his guides.

Early in life Mr. Parker connected himself with the Church. In this he took an active interest, and was soon made deacon, by which title of respect he was ever afterward known. He was strong in his denunciation of intemperance. It was for such spirit of brotherly love which always flowed spontaneously from him that his associates learned to love him. His loving disposition and public spirit were a great blessing to the community, for by them he produced peace and good will with all. He was eminently a peacemaker: healed wounds between minister and parish, which not only testifies to his gift of ready speech, but his sound sense and judgment. His devout religious views were placed upon a sensible foundation. In the history of his town a description of much length is given of the influence which he held in the town on religious matters.

The following testimonial appeared at the time of his decease in a local paper of the town:

"All of us have known Dea. Otis Parker and can think of him only with respect and affection.

'Great not like Cæsar stained with blood,
But only great in doing good.'

"The friends of the temperance cause feel that they have lost a consistent advocate. For many years his whole influence has been on the side of temperance, and notwithstanding he had passed the prime of life and retired in a measure from its active duties, his pen has helped to fill our paper and his name has been given to aid and encourage the Ladies' Temperance Circle. Let us therefore cherish his memory and strive to imitate his example. May the mantle of his piety rest upon us, and may we like him endeavor to secure that 'Pearl of great price,' possessing which we shall be enabled to cast a good influence on others, and be prepared for a better world when time with us shall be no more."

Their children were:

ISAAC PARKER, b. in Westborough, Sept. 3, 1797; d. in Hubbardston, May 8, 1829, unm.

211. DANIEL PARKER, b. in Westborough, March 23, 1799; m. Polly White of Phillipston.

LUCY PARKER, b. in Westborough, July 15, 1801; d. in Hubbardston, Nov. 19, 1822, unm.

212. MARY NOURSE PARKER, b. in Westborough, Aug. 11, 1803: m. Alvin Waite of Hubbardston.

213. OTIS PARKER, b. in Hubbardston, Aug. 16, 1806; m. Eunice Allen.

SAMUEL AUSTIN PARKER, b. in Hubbardston, Oct. 20, 1810; m. Nov. 8, 1832, Ruth Ann Williams of Hubbardston. He d. in Hartford, Conn., Aug. 5, 1852, leaving no issue. She afterward m. Willard Cook of Chicago, Ill., and there d.

82. Capt. Jabez M. Parker (*Isaac,*[6] *Amos,*[5] *Andrew,*[4] *John,*[3] *Hananiah,*[2] *Thomas*[1]), son of Isaac and Margery (Maynard) Parker, was b. in Princeton, Aug. 9, 1776; m. in Framingham, April 15, 1798, Nancy Patterson, b. in Framingham, Feb. 18, 1771, dau. of David and Beulah (Clark) Patterson of that town. She was seventh in a family of fifteen children. The father, David, was a leading man in Framingham during the Revolutionary war. The family in 1783 removed to Boylston, but returned in 1799. The Patterson family of 15 made the good record of 14 who lived to be married, while the one died when an infant. David Patterson was great-grandson of the first of the line in America, James Patterson, who was one of the adherents of Charles II. James was in the Scottish army which was defeated in the battle of

Worcester by Cromwell, and he was transported to New England to be disposed by a sale for a term of years to defray expenses; arrived in Boston, May, 1652. In 1658 he settled in Billerica, where he died 1701.

Jabez Parker and wife removed to Phillipston, then called "Gerry," and where some of his posterity still reside. His location in Phillipston was probably caused by the fact that his uncle, Major Elisha Parker, was then residing there, in that part now known as "Golden Village." Jabez Parker bought land three miles distant in the north part of the town, on the ridge of land running west from Church Hill. It was a large farm, containing all kinds of land. The elevation commanded a view north and south. He was a member of the Church of Phillipston. In the military company he soon rose to rank. He was appointed Ensign in 1811 by Hon. Elbridge Gerry, Governor of Mass. In 1813 followed his promotion to Lieutenant, and in 1816 to the Captaincy of a company of infantry, given by his Excellency Caleb Strong.

Their children were:

214. Nancy Patterson Parker, b. May 2, 1799; m. James Wakefield of Marlborough, N. H.

215. Jabez M. Parker, b. Nov. 12, 1800; m. Azubah P. Powers of Phillipston.

216. Enoch Adams Parker, b. Jan. 14, 1802; m. Rebecca Gibbs.

217. Joel Dodge Parker, b. Aug. 17, 1804; m. Hannah Wood, native of Warwick.

218. Emily S. Parker, b. April 13, 1806; m. Isaiah White.

219. Beulah H. C. Parker, b. April 16, 1808; m. Walter Clapp.

220. Tulley Tollotson Parker, b. March 28, 1810; m. Arathusa Goddard.

221. James Maynard L. Parker, b. Sept. 3, 1812; m. Polly Kidder.

84. David Parker *(Isaac,[6] Amos,[5] Andrew,[4] John,[3] Hananiah,[2] Thomas[1])*, son of Isaac and Margery (Maynard) Parker, was b. in Westborough, May 1, 1785; m. Jan. 29, 1808, Betsey Eager of Northborough, b. June 21, 1789, d. in Barre, Feb. 22, 1869. They removed about 1810 to Barre, where he d. Aug. 10, 1832, aged 54 years.

Their children were:

MARTHA ELIZABETH PARKER, b. in Northborough, Feb. 28, 1809; d. in Barre, Oct. 15, 1841.

A son, unnamed, b. and d. Dec. 14, 1810.

FRANCIS EAGER PARKER, b. in Barre, June 11, and d. Oct. 8, 1812, in Westborough.

ANDREW PARKER, b. Sept. 21, 1813; d. April 4, 1881, in Cleveland, O., unm.

MARY LOUISA PARKER, b. in Northborough, Sept. 29, 1815; m. Dec. 29, 1846, John H. Knight of Worcester. Their children d. young. She d. in Worcester, Jan. 15, 1853, and he d. March 12, 1854.

DAVID PARKER, Jr., b. in Barre, June 24, 1817; m. in Fitchburg, July 22, 1848, Martha A. Deputron. He d. Oct. 19, 1855; she d. March 15, 1855. Their only child was Edgar D. Parker, who d. Dec. 20, 1852, aged 14 months.

222. HARRIET ANN PARKER, b. May 29, 1819; m. Nov. 16, 1841, John Walker of Holden.

223. PERSIS EAGER PARKER, b. May 8, 1821; m. June 13, 1843, Samuel N. Howe of Holden.

224. LUCY PARKER, b. Sept. 2, 1823; m. April 3, 1849, Lysander Crawford of Oakham.

ISAAC DAVIS PARKER, b. May 20, 1825; d. in Barre, April 27, 1841.

SARAH FAIRBANKS PARKER, b. July 31, 1827, in Barre; d. Jan. 6, 1891, aged 63.

CECILIA AUGUSTA PARKER, b. June 10, 1830; d. in Barre, Jan. 9, 1854.

85. Major Lewis Parker *(Isaac,[6] Amos,[5] Andrew,[4] John,[3] Hananiah,[2] Thomas[1])*, the last child and son of Isaac and Margery (Maynard) Parker, was b. in Westborough, March 1, 1787. His father d. when he was five, and his mother when nine. He first lived with his brother Gardiner Parker. After passing his boyhood upon his father's farm, he, still a youth, bound himself to learn the carpenter's trade. This was in Lancaster, and after serving his time he married at the age of 19. On the Sterling records we find: "Mr. Lewis Parker of Lancaster and Miss Elizabeth Seaver of Sterling were m. in Sterling, Nov. 30, 1806." They settled in the centre of the town. He was a successful builder and overseer of work on houses. He was also acquainted with the hat trade, at which business he devoted himself a part of the time.

He was stout in stature and a very good-looking man. He was sexton, but not a member of the Sterling Church. He favored the Universalist belief, which at his time was in its infancy. He was in the War of 1812. Enlisting as a private all went well in the company until they sighted the British troops, upon which their captain fled. The company thereupon chose Lewis Parker for their captain and placed him at their head. He was soon promoted to major, the title by which he was afterwards widely known. It seems that he, like some of his ancestors, was fearless, and often said that he would face the enemy if he dropped before them. He was offered the rank of major-general, which responsible position and rank of honor he was ready to accept, but his wife urged him to decline. Their family was already large and she valued his presence at home as a good influence for the children. He spoke of the honor which might thus be conferred upon him and family, but she replied, "What is honor to bringing up properly this large family of children?" Other and doubtless proper precautions could have been taken, but as they were all attached to their home he graciously yielded. He was a very hospitable man, having a large circle of friends, and his house was constantly sheltering or he and family entertaining a part of them. Mrs. Elizabeth (Seaver) Parker was a remarkable lady, of conscientious belief and a member of the Church. Mr. Parker highly appreciated his brothers and sisters and loved to pay tributes to their memory. He reverenced his sister Mrs. Green, and never ceased lamenting over the untimely decease of his brother Gardiner. He d. in Sterling, July 1, 1833, aged 46, and she d. in West Boylston, at her daughter's farm, Nov. 5, 1859, aged 76 years, 6 months.

Their children were:

225. Caleb Alexander Parker, b. Dec. 24, 1806.

226. Abigail Sawyer Parker, b. Oct. 15, 1809; m. Jan. 24, 1830, Joshua Buxton of Lowell.

Evelina Maynard Parker, b. Nov. 23, 1811; d. June 8, 1833, at Sterling.

227. Elizabeth Margaret Parker, b. Sept. 24, 1813; m. April 21, 1836, Gilbert H. Howe of Sterling.

228. Sarah Angeline Parker, b. Aug. 13, 1815; m. in Sterling, Nov. 10, 1836, John Phelps of West Boylston.

229. Lewis Livingstone Parker, b. Jan. 7, 1817. When quite young, he joined his brother Caleb A. Parker at Jackson, Miss., where he met with an accident, from which he d. on the evening of the 23d of Oct., 1841, "from the effects of a fall which he received in the morning from the giving away of some scaffolding, Mr. Lewis L. Parker of Sterling, Mass., aged 24 yrs. 9 mos. The deceased has long been known to our community, and his death is deeply lamented by all who knew him. His amiability and urbanity of manners, his natural warmth of feeling and correctness of deportment in all his dealings with his fellow-men endeared him to a numerous circle of friends, who will long cherish his memory and mourn his untimely dissolution. When a friend is stricken down in a moment—in the full bloom of health and young—while the heart is yet beating high with brilliant anticipations of the future, relatives and friends have cause indeed to mourn." He was buried in Jackson, Miss.

230. Hollis Gardner Parker, b. Sept. 30, 1818; m. Laura Goodrich of Hartford, Ct.

Mary Anne Capen Parker, b. March 31, 1820; d. in Pittsfield. March 5, 1834, unm.

Harrison Gray Otis Parker, b. Aug. 18, 1821; d. in Jackson, Miss., unm.

Thomas Sawyer Parker, b. April 15, 1823.

Lucy Parker, b. March 4, 1825.

86. Dr. Amos Parker *(Hollis,[6] Amos,[5] Andrew,[4] John,[3] Hananiah,[2] Thomas[1])*, son of Hollis and Louisa (Bragg) Parker, was b. in Hubbardston, Oct. 17, 1777; m. Elizabeth Whitney, dau. of the minister at Bolton. He succeeded to his father's homestead in Shrewsbury, living thereon during the lifetime of his parents, furnishing them a comfortable abode in their old age. He was known by the people of Shrewsbury as somewhat eccentric, for instance, it is said that he buried his small riches in bags around his house and farm for safe keeping and people are still in watch for "Dr. Parker's money bags." He finally removed to Bolton, where in the centre of the town his house still stands as he put it, and his old furniture, maps, books and pictures are as they were in his day. In Bolton he became a popular physician. Dr. Parker was a man of mind. He was well read and acquired a substantial education. He possessed a remarkably strong character. he was known as one who acted upon his own best views and feared not; was a good speaker and was one of the first to join the temperance movement, in which he took an active part. Dr. Parker was postmaster at Bolton for many years. At one time he was probably the oldest postmaster in the commonwealth.

Their children were:

ELIZABETH LYDIA B. PARKER, b. July 10, 1809; d. April 1, 1882, unm.

LOUISA JANE PARKER, b. Jan. 10, 1812; resides in Bolton, unm. She occupies the old Dr. Parker home located in the town centre. She preserves its ancient appearance, together with the ancient furniture, pictures and family treasures as they appeared in her childhood, when her father was living, making the homestead seem, as the visitor enters, as if he had stepped back into the 18th century.

87. **Mary Jennison Parker** *(Hollis,[6] Amos,[5] Andrew,[4] John,[3] Hananiah,[2] Thomas[1])*, dau. of Hollis and Louisa (Bragg) Parker, was b. in Hubbardston. July 31, 1780; m. (1) in Shrewsbury, Jan. 1, 1803, Josiah Harrington, b. in Worcester, Jan. 6, 1780, who came to Shrewsbury from Worcester when a lad and grew up in the family of John Rice, Sr. They had Josiah Harrington, Jr., b. in Hubbardston, Sept. 15, 1803. Josiah Harrington, the father, d. in Hubbardston, Oct. 7, 1803. The son m. Sylvia Smith of Lancaster, N. H.; had one son, Edward L. Harrington, b. in Lancaster, Oct. 1, 1836, and she d. there in 1838. Edward L. served in the Union army during the Civil war. Both he and his father are now deceased.

Mrs. Mary (Parker) Harrington m. (2) in Shrewsbury, April 10, 1805, Asahel, b. Feb. 6, 1775, son of Silas and Priscilla (Plympton) Allen. He was a cooper and farmer in Shrewsbury, where they lived up to about 1826, when the family removed to Lancaster, N. H., and where she d. Feb. 28, 1862. He d. in Berlin, Wis., Oct. 13, 1866, at the home of his son Waldo.

All the children were b. in Shrewsbury:

1. ASAHEL PLYMPTON ALLEN, b. May 4, 1806; m. Rebecca Bacon Haven of Boston; resided in Lancaster, N. H., where he owned a farm; he d. June 14, 1884. They had ten children:
   i. FREDERICK M. ALLEN, b. in Boston, 1832; d. Sept. 5, 1880.
   ii. EDWARD P. ALLEN, b. in Worcester, 1833; resides in Brookline.
   iii. HELEN R. ALLEN, b. in Lancaster, N. H., 1835; m. Daniel Sweet of Manchester, N. H.
   iv. SARAH E. ALLEN, b. in Lancaster, N. H., 1837; m. Joseph Cutting.
   v. MARY A. ALLEN, b. in Lancaster, N. H., 1840; m. Monroe Green of Shelburne, N. H.
   vi. WILLIAM H. ALLEN, b. 1842; d. in Washington, D. C., Feb. 8, 1863.
   vii. GEORGE L. ALLEN, b. 1844; resides in Wisconsin.
   viii. MARIA E. ALLEN, b. 1846; d. March 18, 1863.
   ix. ABBIE A. ALLEN, b. 1850; m. Alonzo Earle.
   x. ALICE L. ALLEN, b. 1853; m. D. W. Scribner of Portland, Me.
2. LUCY HEMENWAY ALLEN, b. Feb. 15, 1809; d. in Lancaster, N. H., April 18, 1842.
3. DANIEL WALDO ALLEN, b. May 17, 1811; he studied medicine, but early in life went west and spent most of his life upon a farm. By wife Marietta he had the following children:
   i. HENRY CLAY ALLEN, b. March 5, 1848.
   ii. CELESTIA ELIZABETH ALLEN, b. July 10, 1850; m. Rev. D. W. Day of Cleveland, O., and has had four children.
   iii. MARY MARIA ALLEN, b. Oct. 3, 1851.

   He m. (2) Lellice Boyle, by whom Lucy C. Allen was b. Sept. 7, 1856.
4. ELIZABETH WALDO ALLEN, b. Aug. 17, 1813; d. in Cleveland, O.

88. Silance Parker *(Hollis,[6] Amos,[5] Andrew,[4] John,[3] Hananiah,[2] Thomas[1])*, dau. of Hollis and Louisa (Bragg) Parker, was b. Oct. 17, 1786; m. Oct. 11, 1811, James Hall of Shrewsbury. He was a builder, and experienced, it is said, a remarkable occurrence. About the year 1828 he fell from near the top of the spire upon the roof of a meeting-house he was building in Sutton, and so indented it, by breaking one

of the rafters, as to obtain lodgment there until relieved. He was not sensibly injured, but soon went about his work. It is said, however, that he finally met his death in being struck by a falling beam. The family removed to Northborough about 1850, and he met his death the year following.

Their children were:

1. SARAH Z. HALL, b. Oct. 2, 1813; was school-teacher at Northborough.
2. LOUISA A. HALL, b. June 28, 1815.
3. JAMES M. HALL, b. July 22, 1817.
4. ANNA P. HALL, b. Nov. 13, 1819.
5. MARY J. HALL, b. Dec. 8, 1821.
6. WILLIAM E. HALL, b. April 26, 1824.
7. SILENCE M. HALL, b. April 16, 1832.

89. Betsey Parker *(Elisha,[6] Amos,[5] Andrew,[4] John,[3] Hananiah,[2] Thomas[1])*, dau. of Major Elisha and Sally (Baker) Parker, was b. March 25, 1782; m. April 25, 1810, Gardner Paige of Hardwick. They lived in Bakersfield, Vt. She d. Feb. 23, 1860. He d. Nov. 7, 1861.

Their children were:

1. GARDNER ADDISON PAIGE, b. in Bakersfield, Vt., April 23, 1811; m. May 27, 1835, Lydia B. Shattuck (b. also April 23, 1811) of St. Albans, Vt., dau. of Moses Shattuck of Townshend, Vt., and wife Hannah Bingham, a native of Rochester, N. Y. They removed, 1870, to Milford, Del., where he d. in Nov., 1888. His widow survives him. Their children were:
   - i. SENECA PAIGE, b. 1836; d.
   - ii. WORTHINGTON PAIGE, b. 1837; d.
   - iii. REED PAIGE, b. 1839.
   - iv. HANNAH PAIGE, b. 1841; m. —— Oaks.
   - v. LOUISA PAIGE, b. 1842; m. —— Smoot.
   - vi. MARION PAIGE, b. 1844; m. —— Green.
   - vii. GARDNER PAIGE, b. 1846.
   - viii. HARRIS L. PAIGE, b. 1850.
2. TIMOTHY S. PAIGE, b. Feb. 18, 1814; d. Oct. 16, 1817.
3. BETSEY M. PAIGE, b. April 5, 1817; m. (1) Dec. 29, 1842, Samuel Peckham of Broome, P. Q.; he d. July 1844, and she m. (2) Feb. 15, 1846, C. R. Parker of Lockport, N. Y. (No. 234, page 191). She d. May 7, 1853. She had dau. Mary Jane Peckham, who d. Aug. 29, 1866, aged 20 years.

4. ELISHA STILLMAN PAIGE, b. March 18, 1819; m. Betsey Soule of Fairfield, Vt. They had dau. Maria, now Mrs. Hawaigan.

5. MARY ANN LEE PAIGE, b. Feb. 17, 1822; m. Sept. 26, 1849, Edmund C., son of Ephraim Knight, who was son of Amos, of Shrewsbury, Vt., and Philander (Beaman) Knight, dau. of Sheldon Beaman of Milton, Vt. The family reside in Stanbridge, Canada. Their children were:

i. PAIGE KNIGHT, b. Dec. 31, 1850.

ii. CATHARINE KNIGHT, b. June 17, 1855; m. Sept. 26, 1877, Ernest M. Lambkin, and has three daughters.

iii. DAVID BROWN KNIGHT, b. Dec. 20, 1857; m. Dec. 17, 1879, Etta P. Rice, and has two daughters and two sons.

iv. STILLMAN PAIGE KNIGHT, b. May 3, 1860; m. Jan. 1, 1880, Julia Baker, and has two sons.

6. SARAH JANE PAIGE, b. May 27, 1824; m. Nov. 3, 1868, Henry Dean of Bakersfield, Vt. They reside in Bakersfield.

91. Elisha Parker *(Elisha,⁶ Amos,⁵ Andrew,⁴ John,³ Hananiah,² Thomas¹)*, son of Maj. Elisha and Sally (Baker) Parker, was b. Nov. 23, 1787; m. 1811, Eunice Dean of Barnard, Vt. Her parents were early settlers of Barnard from the town of Hardwick, Mass. He lived in Barnard four years; the remainder of his life was passed in Bakersfield, Vt. He d. April 15, 1847. His widow Eunice d. Sept. 21, 1884. He was stout in stature, and was blessed with a very hearty, happy disposition. Horseback riding was his favorite mode of conveyance and healthful exercise.

Their children were:

231. ELISHA H. PARKER, b. May 10, 1818; m. Alvira P. Ferrin.

232. MINERVA E. PARKER, b. May 13, 1827; m. Josiah Converse, a native of Brookfield, Mass.

233. ROBERT D. PARKER, b. May 6, 1834; m. Sarah Hawes of Auburn, Mass.

92. Elijah Parker *(Elisha,⁶ Amos,⁵ Andrew,⁴ John,³ Hananiah,² Thomas¹)*, son of Maj. Elisha and Sally (Baker) Parker, was b. Nov. 23, 1787; m. 1810, Rhody, younger dau. of Dea. Isaac Butler of Fairfield, Vt. She was seventh in descent from Dea. Richard Butler, whose name first appears on the records of Cambridge, Mass., in 1632; was a freeman there in 1634, and in 1636 was one of the company who went through the wilderness with Rev. Samuel Hooker and formed the settlement at Hartford, Ct. Elijah Parker removed with his family to New York State and settled in Cambria, where he d. Feb. 8, 1868. She survived him, her date of death being Nov. 6, 1873, at Lockport, N. Y. He was most highly respected by his fellow-citizens.

"Elijah Parker was one of the pioneers of this country; an industrious, careful, prudent man, and a law-abiding citizen. He accumulated a competency and lived long in the town of Cambria to enjoy it—a highly respected and honored member of the community."

All the children were b. in Bakersfield, Vt., except the youngest:

CHO LAURA PARKER, d. in infancy.

234. CHARLES ROLLIN PARKER, b. Jan. 5, 1814; m. (1) Portia Adelia Harmon.

235. CHO AUGUSTA PARKER, b. Aug. 10, 1815; m. Silas Hall, a native of Newburyport, Mass.

236. CAROLINE MIRANDA PARKER, b. March 16, 1818; m. Stephen Decatur Scovell.

MARTHA CORNELIA PARKER, b. Sept. 7, 1823.

AMANDA BOWDISH PARKER, b. Oct. 10, 1825; resides at Beach Ridge, N. Y. To her care and interest is indebted much of fulness of the genealogy of her family as shown in this volume.

237. ISAAC BUTLER PARKER, b. Nov. 19, 1829; m. Clarissa Gillet of Youngstown, N. Y.

238. FREDERIC DEFOREST PARKER, b. in Lewiston, N. Y., Aug. 10, 1830; m. Helen Nickols of Michigan.

93. Patty Parker *(Elisha,[6] Amos,[5] Andrew,[4] John,[3] Hananiah,[2] Thomas[1])*, dau. of Maj. Elisha and Sally (Baker) Parker, was b. in Bakersfield, Vt., May 3, 1790; m. Elijah Barnes as his second wife.

Her only child was:

1. ELIZABETH MARTHA BARNES, b. April 6, 1828. After her father's death she became a missionary teacher for the American Missionary Association to the Freedmen in the South, where she labored 17 years until her health failed her in 1882.

Jan. 18, 1883, she and Dea. H. M. Stevens of St. Albans, Vt., were m. Their m. life was short but very happy. She d. May 7, 1885.

94. James Sullivan Parker *(Elisha,[6] Amos,[5] Andrew,[4] John,[3] Hananiah,[2] Thomas[1])*, son of Maj. Elisha and Sally (Baker) Parker, was b. in Bakersfield, Vt., Aug. 1, 1798. He m. and had at least one dau., who became Mrs. Sarah E. Evans and lived in Washington, D. C.

95. Jonas Parker *(Elisha,[6] Amos,[5] Andrew,[4] John,[3] Hananiah,[2] Thomas[1])*, son of Maj. Elisha and Sally (Baker) Parker, was b. in Bakersfield, Vt., Sept. 15, 1800; m. Lima Freeman, b. in Barnard, Vt., Jan. 13, 1802, dau. of Joshua and Joan Freeman. They first settled in Bakersfield; removed to Moretown, Vt. He was a successful builder and a good farmer. He was well beloved by his associates, and a favorite with his brethren.

All the children were b. in Bakersfield, Vt.:

239. Rebecca Ann Parker, b. Sept. 29, 1825; m. Langdon Marshall of Brookfield, Vt.

240. Joshua Freeman Parker, b. Sept. 23, 1827; m. Caroline D. Seabury.

241. John Cortland Parker, b. March 15, 1831; m. Oliva M. Wheeler of Wallingford, Vt.

242. Lima Joan Parker. b. Aug. 11, 1836; m. April 26, 1875, Henry Fullerton of Waitesfield, Vt., and resides in Montpelier, Vt.

96. Abigail Parker *(Ephraim,[6] Amos,[5] Andrew,[4] John,[3] Hananiah,[2] Thomas[1])*, dau. of Ephraim and Abigail (Baker) Parker, was b. in Fitzwilliam, N. H., March 5, 1796; m. March 31, 1812, Joshua Worcester of Jaffrey, N. H.

Their children were:

1. Ephraim Parker Worcester, b. June 20, 1813; m. Nancy Gage, dau. of Jonathan Gage of Jaffrey, N. H. They reside in Pittsfield.
2. Emeline Parker Worcester, b. July 4, 1815; d. Oct. 23, 1886, aged 71. She never married, but for many years was a successful teacher of schools in Boston until she became too infirm to teach and then returned to her native place and died at the residence of her sister Abigail.

3. ABIGAIL WORCESTER, b. March 30, 1817; m. William Gage, son of Jonathan Gage of Jaffrey, N. H. He d. Sept. 12, 1842, aged 30, and she now lives on the old homestead in Fitzwilliam and successfully carries on the farm by the aid of all needed help.

4. JOSHUA WORCESTER, m. for a second wife Lydia Whipple of Richmond, N. H., by whom he had five children, to wit:

- I. MILTON WORCESTER.
- II. HANNAH WORCESTER.
- III. GEORGE ALBERT WORCESTER.
- IV. A child who d. in infancy.
- V. LYDIA WORCESTER.

97. Hannah Parker *(Nahum,[6] Amos,[5] Andrew,[4] John,[3] Hananiah,[2] Thomas[1])*, dau. of Judge Nahum and Mary (Deeth) Parker, was b. in Shrewsbury, Dec. 26, 1784; came to Fitzwilliam, N. H., with her parents in 1786; m. Luna Foster, Jr., of Fitzwilliam, Feb. 29, 1810. They lived at Fitzwilliam until 1815, when they removed to Westmoreland, N. H., and there resided the remainder of their days. She d. Aug. 7, 1863, aged 79½ years. He d. April 13, 1865.

Their children were:

I. BENJAMIN FRANKLIN FOSTER, b. in Fitzwilliam, N. H, in 1812; m. Sept. 30, 1832, Electa Beebe of Brattleborough, Vt. She lately d. They lived many years in East Westmoreland, N. H., and he now resides in Keene, N. H. Children:

- I. AMOS PARKER FOSTER; m. Sarah Gale. They reside in Austin, Texas, and have had two children.
- II. EUNICE P. FOSTER; m. George Abbot, and resides in Joliet, Ill.
- III. ADIN FOSTER; m. Nancy M. Perry, and resides in Gardner.
- IV. ELLEN D. FOSTER; m. Alfred D. Perry, and resides in Keene, N. H.
- V. ADDISON D. FOSTER; m. Malissa Perry. He went to the war of the Rebellion and d. in the service.
- VI. ALLISON D. FOSTER; m. Kate Wood, and resides in Natchez, Miss.
- VII. ELLA H. FOSTER; m. Frederick Wilson, and resides in Keene, N. H.
- VIII. ANSON F. FOSTER; m. Eldora H. Streeter, and resides in Keene, N. H.

2. Nahum Parker Foster, b. in Fitzwilliam, Feb. 10, 1814; d. May 9, 1875, aged 61; m. Emily Wilber. He was educated as a physician and took his degree of M.D. at Harvard University, and afterwards became a Baptist preacher, and practiced both professions with marked success to near the time of his death. Soon after his marriage he settled (1) at Unity, N. H., (2) at Cornish Falls, N. H., (3) at Stoughton, Mass., (4) at Burlington, Vt., and (5) at Montpelier, Vt. Here he was two years chaplain of the Legislature. On leaving Montpelier he took a voyage to Europe and visited various places of note, among which were Palestine, the Dead Sea, the pyramids of Egypt, etc., and on his return settled in New London, Ct., where he died. He left an estate of $30,000, and one daughter, who survives him. His wife died at New London a few years before his own death. He was a skilful doctor and an impressive preacher and lecturer. He had a most wonderful prepossessing appearance. He died suddenly in the full vigor of life from the effects of poison administered to him by mistake.

3. Mary Foster, b. in Westmoreland, N. H., Sept. 4, 1817; m. Edward R. Winchester, and lived in Westmoreland until his decease. She is living and has one son.

98. **Austin Parker** *(Nahum,[6] Amos,[5] Andrew,[4] John,[3] Hananiah,[2] Thomas[1])*, son of Judge Nahum and Mary (Deeth) Parker, was b. in Fitzwilliam, N. H., Jan. 24, 1787; m. Susan Martin of Gardner and settled in Westmoreland, N. H., and d. there Aug. 7, 1863, aged 76. His wife survived him a few years. Austin Parker was a good mechanic (a characteristic of the family branch), and was a carpenter as well as a farmer. He was for a long time surveyor. He was selectman and justice of the peace.

Their children were:

Marion M. Parker; now deceased.

Demaris C. Parker; now deceased.

243. Frederick A. Parker, b. 1822; m. Clara M. Hyland of Westmoreland, N. H.

Norman Parker; he was killed on the railroad.

99. **Amos A. Parker** *(Nahum,[6] Amos,[5] Andrew,[4] John,[3] Hananiah,[2] Thomas[1])*, son of Judge Nahum and Mary (Deeth) Parker, was b. in Fitzwilliam, N. H., Oct. 8, 1791. He

COL. AMOS ANDREW PARKER.

AGED 101, OCT. 8, 1892.

worked on his father's farm in the east part of the town until he was about 16 years of age, and not having a robust constitution turned his attention to classical studies and fitted for college. He was about a year under the tuition of the pastor of Fitzwilliam, Rev. John Sabin, and then went to the Academy at Amherst, N. H., and finished at the New Ipswich Academy. He entered the sophomore class at the University of Vermont, Feb. 3, 1811, and graduated in 1813. On his return to his native town he became storekeeper, but soon went to Virginia, where he staid three years as teacher in planters' families. Returning to his native State he commenced the study of law with James Wilson, senior, at Keene, and completed his course with Levi Champlain at Fitzwilliam, and was admitted to the bar of the Superior Court in 1821. He commenced the practice of law at Epping, N. H., and then went to Concord, N. H., where he became editor of the *New Hampshire Statesman*. While there he was ap pointed aid to Governor D. L. Morrill and enjoyed the title of Colonel. While he was serving in this capacity he had the pleasure of inviting Gen. Lafayette, then at Boston, to visit New Hampshire.

He removed to Concord in 1826, and soon after to New Market. In 1831 he located in Exeter and Kingston, and in 1836 returned to Fitzwilliam, after an absence of 16 years.

In April, 1879, he went to Glastonbury, Ct., and at that place and at Hartford he resided until 1888. He returned to his native town at the advanced age of 98 to spend the remainder of his days with his son.

These are the outlines of a busy life, and the details would fill a volume. A brief account of his life follows, in which I have made direct use of the venerable Mr. Parker's manuscript, written for this use at an age when we are accustomed to imagine a man as with one foot in the grave, and never with the ability to wield the pen with ease, and relate occurrences with accurate distinctness, yet these lines are the production of his vigorous intellect and active health at the great age of 99. He says:

"In the first place, it is needful to state I had the good fortune to have a father of a strong mind, firm convictions, steady in purpose, and a strict disciplinarian. Although restraint was sometimes disagreeable and even unreasonable, yet, surely, I ought to be thankful for all the restraints and teachings of early life, for to those I am indebted for the solid foundation of a long and busy life.

"My father would say, 'Children are not born with knowledge, but only with the capacity to achieve it and the only way to learn is to think, exercise mind and note passing events. The great difference found in men is mainly owing to one man's thinking while others think not, and that there is no natural connection between ideas and words, and therefore *words* must be learned in order to express our thoughts.' He would accordingly call me with spelling-book in hand to his side and teach me *how* to study. Following his careful instructions I soon found the benefit of it, for I was able to get my lessons perfect, so that in time I could readily spell all the words in the spelling-book. In the spelling down exercises I was always a standing scholar at the close. I gradually memorized all the words in the dictionary, which was of inestimable value to me in after life, as I had no need to look into a dictionary for spelling or definition." Mr. Parker also often relates the account of a little experience while still a small boy which much impressed him. At some entertainment a man exhibited his ability at memorizing, as each one in his audience named one object after another until 25 were named, he would then repeat them in the order named, forward or backward. Young Amos marvelled at this and so wrote the names down in order and found the man true to his word. He told the boy how he did it, to wit: by imagining each of the objects and placing them in a long row in order as the objects were named, and by practice, said he, you can so impress your mind as to remember them in order a long time. Young Amos found this to be practical, and he afterwards memorized in this manner. Up to this day he retains a tenacious memory, almost incredible for one of his extreme age. In his law practice this was very useful, as a conversation once heard he could repeat exactly, with no omissions or additions, and he still delights in repeating the conversations of his distinguished friends of the olden time. His anecdotes seem without number and are all interesting. After outgrowing Mr. Sabin's country school at Fitzwilliam he entered the New Ipswich Academy. He graduated from the Academy in 1809, 83 years ago! He then prepared for college and entered the sophomore class of the University of Vermont in Burlington, a year and a half ahead.

"I was deemed an unusually ready writer and composer and would finish a long composition in a short time. Although I might have a greater flow of words than others my compositions cost me many hours of intense thought. Be it known to all young men that no one is born a scholar, but to be one costs much time and labor.

"War with England was declared on the 18th day of June, 1812, and in a short time the town was full of soldiers. When I left at Commencement, in 1813, it was said there were seven thousand men. Captain Ezekiel Jewett of Rugby, afterwards Colonel, was then in command of a company. He was an early acquaintance of mine and often called at my room in college. He said he could assist me at any time when the army was not drilling or marching to visit the camp ground on the lake shore. All I had to do was to call on the officer of the day and call for Captain Jewett. He would come, take me over the lines and show all I wished to see in the camp. By his aid I witnessed many scenes new to me, some of which were painful. Not to go into all the particulars, I witnessed the pardon of two soldiers sentenced to be shot for desertion, two actually shot and one hanged. And that sufficed for a long life for I never have witnessed another execution.

"The Yankees had fitted up two sloops of war and the British had done the same thing and came out to Burlington and commenced firing at long shot, a challenge for a fight. The Yankees had pluck, hoisted all sail and bore down upon them. The British ships retreated, the wind was strong from the south and the Yankee ships gained upon them as they passed down the lake out of sight. Soon after we heard the booming of cannon in one continued roar for a few minutes and then all was silent. A short battle and complete victory on one side or the other. It was some days before we heard of the result, and then the Yankee sailors returned chop-fallen and mad. They had been fooled and lost their ships. The British ships had come out merely as a decoy, not intending any battle on the water, but went down the lake where it was narrow and the vessels must pass near the shore. All of a sudden a masked battery on the land opened upon them; that a surrender or cut to pieces was the only alternative. The British then had command of the lake and in a few days came out to Burlington with quite a fleet, the Yankee ships among them. No ships to meet them, but the Yankees had not been idle. Forty cannons had been placed on the lake shore, some of large size, to defend the city of Burlington. I was in the bell-deck of the college, some four hundred feet above the lake, and had a fine view of the whole scene. The British fleet came on slowly and with great caution. When about near enough to hit the city a flag of truce was hoisted on one of the ships, and a boat started for the shore. The American commander despatched a similar boat to meet it. They met, and in five minutes each boat returned to its own place. Immediately after the return of the boats the British gave a broadside, but the balls fell short, came nearer and fired again, the balls reached the shore. Then it was the Yankees gave them shot and shell from forty cannons on the shore. It is said that our guns were masked, except two or three, so that the British were not aware of their existence. Although the battle was more than a mile away I could see the balls in the air and when they struck the ships or water. The first volley cut sails of the ships and the ships also, and immediately a retreat was ordered, but as they were sailing vessels with a light wind their movements were slow, and as the guns from the shore continued firing the ships were more or less damaged. Soon they were at a safe distance, moved up into Shelburne Bay, took two or three small vessels there, and sailed back to Canada. A bloodless battle it seemed and no great mischief done, and yet it was an attractive scene from the place where I stood. Indeed, I know of no more splendid scene than at the balcony of the college. On the west the city, lake, islands and mountains beyond; on the east a long chain of the Green Mountains; and on the south and north an extended view of mountains and plains. But what is war? With all its glittering show and splendor it is but a savage affair, costing many lives and much property, and settles nothing.

"On Sundays the troops were under arms and marched miles away for exercise. As viewed from the college seven thousand men in platoons occupied two miles in length on the march.

"I never knew before what exhilarating music the drum and fife could make. The instruments seemed all in tune together and all together poured forth such a flood of music that would start a man into action if there was any life in him.

"I shortly entered into partnership with Maj. Pearson, a successful merchant of my native town. But in the fall of 1815 I decided to change my place and occupation. I travelled by stage to Albany, on to New York in the boat and to Philadelphia in the stage. From there to Baltimore in the stage and steamboat and without stopping passed on to Washington city in the stage. The war was over but we passed signs of the battle at Bladensburg, for the British soldiers had been so slightly buried that red coats, here and there, stuck out of the ground. At Washington city the capitol had been blown up and was in ruins. At Alexandria a man was employed to find a northern man to teach a planter's family living near Fredericksburg in Virginia. I passed on to Fredericksburg and soon found my place of destination, Holly Wood, on the northern neck, as the strip of land was called, between Chesapeake Bay and the Rappahannock river. The planter had some 300 slaves and 1,500 acres of land. I had a neat log school-house, well painted and finished inside, and eight scholars.

"In the beginning of the school I practiced the usual form of school-keeping in New England, but as I had only a few scholars and a year or more to teach, soon concluded to improve on the old plan as much as I could. New England schools were then, if not now, governed by strict authority, but I was determined to govern by kindness and succeeded even beyond my expectations. I soon gained the confidence and affection of all the scholars, for they found I was their true friend and anxious for their enjoyment of all rational pleasures. I aided them in getting and understanding their lessons, told them stories to illustrate and explain a sentiment; taught them the use of words, how to write and improve the memory, and then the duty of leading a true honest life and never needlessly giving any one pain, even to animals. Sometimes I joined them in walks over the plantation, looked on to see them play marbles and told them pleasant stories. In short, I had a model school, and the two years of my life were pleasant and as happy as they could be under the circumstances.

"On the 4th of July, 1816, I delivered an oration at a barbecue in a grove at Falmouth, Va. The performance was highly spoken of at the time, and a splendid notice appeared in the newspaper.

"I had a desire to see more of the State of Virginia before I left and bought a horse to take a trip and visit some of the beautiful scenes so well described in Jefferson's 'Notes on Virginia.' I passed over the Blue Ridge at Ashby Gap and had a splendid view of the Shenandoah Valley; went to Harper's Ferry, where the Potomac and Shenandoah meet and rush through the mountain, and where the United States Armory was in full operation. Satisfied with viewing this romantic spot I passed on through Charlestown, Winchester, Woodstock, New Market, to Port Republic and stopped at the hotel near the Wier and Madison caves. They are both in the same mountain and I visited them both. Wier's cave is much the larger and goes into the mountain half a mile. Madison's cave is well described by Mr. Jefferson, but Wier's was unknown in his day. Monticello, Mr. Jefferson's seat, is on a fine mountain, five miles distant from Charlottesville, and a branch of the Rappahannock river rushes by its base. Mr. Jefferson had a saw- and grist-mill on the stream, and I had a fine view of him there superintending his workmen. Montpelier, Mr. Madison's seat, is 20 miles north and his house stands a mile from the road."

Returning to New Hampshire Mr. Parker began the practice of law in Epping, N. H. Devoting a similar interest and thoroughness to this work, as was characteristic of him as a student and teacher, he achieved immediate success; won every case of law while there and soon enjoyed a large practice. At this time Isaac Hill published the *New Hampshire Patriot*, which had a large circulation and great influence. In an arbitrary manner the editor had so much offended some of the leading men of his own party that they started a sheet at Concord called the *New Hampshire Statesman* and wished to find an editor of sufficient power to successfully combat the *Patriot*. Mr. Parker was urged to accept this charge and he proved to be the proper man for the place. In regard to his life as editor he says:

"I left Epping with regret, for I had been very successful in law business and had many good friends, and felt I was leaving a certainty for an uncertainty, and so it proved, financially, but politically a success. At Concord I made a thorough investigation of the condition I had assumed and found I had a hard task before me. Isaac Hill was lord of all he surveyed, his paper had a large circulation and was full of advertisements. He did much more printing than his newspaper, was successful in business, had grown rich and asked no favors. And I, single handed, was expected to meet and successfully contend against such odds.

"Before I had time fairly to begin he made an onslaught on the *Statesman* and attempted to crush me at a blow. But in the end he had reason to feel discretion was the better part of valor, for the *Statesman* carried the State three successive times against him on the Governor and on the election of President of the United States. But I do not claim to be the author of all the vigorous editorials that were published in the *New Hampshire Statesman*. Ezekiel Webster, the brother of Daniel, freely wielded his vigorous pen, and *one article*, which caused a great sensation, was written by Daniel Webster, himself. Even the great lawyer, Jeremiah Mason, then of Portsmouth, N. H., lent a helping hand.

"'The war was carried into Africa,' and Mr. Hill at last treated me with due respect, showed me kind attentions and when I left Concord, bade me a friendly adieu."

In 1824 and 1825 Col. Parker was aid-de-camp to Gov. Morrill, during which time he rendered conspicuous service. Soon after Gen. Lafayette arrived in Boston in 1824 Col. Parker received an order from the Governor to invite the

General to visit the Granite State and to escort him from Boston to Concord, N. H. Lafayette had won the affection of all patriotic citizens, and was held by our people in the highest esteem of any man of foreign birth. It is little wonder that Col. Parker became very interested in his famous guest. The General once told him, in the best of good nature, that he was the most inquisitive man he had found in America. When about to depart from Concord, Lafayette, placing his arm around Mr. Parker and pressing him to his side, gave him a cordial invitation to visit him at his home in France. The Colonel thus describes his experience in the performance of his official duty:

"On the 21st of June, 1825, five days after the celebration at Bunker Hill, during which Gen. Lafayette placed the mortar on which the corner-stone was laid, I was in Boston prepared to escort the General to Concord. Besides the General, there were his son, George Washington Lafayette, his private secretary, Emile Lavassiur, and a servant.

"I had three carriages, a barouche drawn by four horses, a four-horse stage coach, and a two-horse covered carriage for baggage. When I was ready to call at the General's lodgings for him, an aid of the Governor of Massachusetts informed me that the honor of the State required that he should escort the guest to the State line at Methuen; so there was nothing for me to do but keep out of their way till that place was reached.

"Just then a Revolutionary veteran from Vermont who had attended the Bunker Hill celebration, and had been left by the stage, begged me for a ride as far as Concord. I took him in, unsuspicious of the consequences of my act, till we reached Malden.

"There we were welcomed by a great crowd, the bells ringing and cannon firing, bands playing, and people shouting, 'Welcome Lafayette.' They took the soldier at my side for Lafayette.

"I drove right into the crowd and said: 'This is not Gen. Lafayette; he will be here in an hour. This is an old Revolutionary veteran—give him three cheers, please.'

"They did so with a will. The veteran saluted and we passed on. On the way I had to make more than ten speeches before we reached Methuen.

"When the General arrived at Methuen he entered my barouche, the old soldier retiring to the stage coach. The General laughed heartily at my experience in speech-making, and laughingly proposed that for the rest of the way we alternate in making speeches, in order that he might have a rest.

"At all hotels, stores, villages and cross roads crowds had assembled to greet him. It was June and roses were abundant, and our carriage frequently became so encumbered with them that we were forced to unload them in solitary places. In every crowd men, women and children pressed enthusiastically forward, babies being frequently presented for the General to kiss.

"At one place a middle-aged woman put her arm about his neck and kissed him on the cheek, he returning the compliment. The air rang with applause and cheers, and all along the route the General would rise in the carriage, wave his hat and return thanks for the attentions, but he made no formal address till he reached Concord."

"For the evening reception the capitol and surrounding buildings were illuminated and a vast throng attended. At this levee I introduced my wife and first-born child, announcing his name to be George Washington. He shook hands with the wife, took the child in his arms, impressed a kiss on its cheek, looked at the mother and then at the child, and in a subdued voice said: 'I am reminded of the loved and the lost.' I knew he was thinking of his own beloved wife, his first born child and his noble friend, Washington—all dead!"

Many years later Mr. Parker published his reminiscences of that eventful trip in his "Recollections of General Lafayette," a work of great interest and of much historical value. His memory of the occasion and of the General is clear and distinct and his conversation concerning them is extremely entertaining.

In 1826 he removed to New Market, N. H., where he practiced law, taking a very active part in the social affairs of the place, and charged no fee for enforcing justice for those not possessed of worldly goods. He was very determined in his work of reform and the town of New Market owes much to his attentive interest and able leadership. It soon became known that the new lawyer would vindicate rights, money or no money. Speaking of his experience there he says:

"I then became aware how one man could chase a thousand tipplers and vagabonds, for they scattered and went elsewhere, as they found it was no place for them. It was manifest that the village had improved and that good order had taken the place of disorder and drunkenness."

At this time very little was known of the country west of the Mississippi. Col. Parker decided to devote a part of his life in exploring some of this large territory, stories about which were mostly conjecture, and make his trip of service to the public on his return. Even concerning what is now Michigan, Illinois, Missouri, Louisiana and Texas very little was definitely known. He writes as follows:

"I took the stage to Albany and then the canal-boat to Buffalo. Visited Niagara Falls, Detroit, and went by stage 200 miles to

St. Joseph on Lake Michigan and by boat to Chicago. There, in company with three young men, took a team and explored the upper portion of the State of Illinois as far as Rock river, then southerly to Peoria and then on steamboat to St. Louis. I rode in a steamboat to Natchez and from there on horseback into Texas beyond the Colorado river. I returned to the sea-coast at Velasco and sailed in a vessel to New Orleans. From there I came in a sailing vessel to Boston and home at Exeter; having been absent about five months, and travelled by land and water eight thousand miles.

"At this time emigration was rapidly increasing to the South and West. Many letters of inquiry were addressed to me and I at once wrote the book entitled 'Trip to the West and Texas.' The first 500 copies were so readily sold that a second edition was called for. Forty thousand copies were struck off and sold in a short time."

The book was very eagerly read by all. The following extract from his active pen, shows his interesting style, and the able manner in which he treated matters of deep research and thought. The second edition was published by William White of Concord, N. H., and B. B. Muzzey of Boston, Mass., in 1836, more than half a century ago.

"By diligent research," writes Col. Parker, "I have found *one* solitary copy, and in looking it over I find it so completely out of date that the southern and western portions of the United States have so completely changed that the book is useless now, as it can give no certain information of the present condition of the country. One thing, however, seems to be the same now as then, the great Mississippi valley, its rivers and tributaries, and, therefore, I copy an extract on that subject:

"The Mississippi river, which imparts a name and character to the great valley of the West, claims something more than passing notice. It rises in about the 48th parallel of latitude in wild rice lakes and soon becomes a large river. Sometimes it moves silently along over a wide, muddy channel, at others it glides swiftly over a sandy, and its waters as transparent as air, and again it becomes compressed to a narrow channel between high limestone cliffs, and foams and runs as it lashes the projecting rocks and struggles through. The Falls of St. Anthony, following the course of the river, is three hundred miles from its source. It is about half a mile wide and falls eighteen feet. Above the mouth of the Missouri its numerous large tributaries are the Wisconsin and Illinois from the east, and the Des Moines from the west. A little below 39° dashes in the Missouri river from the west, is a longer stream and carries more water than the Mississippi. Undoubtedly this is the largest tributary stream in the world, and from the facts that it has a longer course and carries more water, and gives its peculiar character to the united stream, it is claimed it ought to have given its name to the united stream and great valley of the West. In opposition to this claim it may be stated that the valley of the Missouri appears to be secondary to the Mississippi, has not the general direction of that river, joins it at right angles, and the direction of the Mississippi is the same above and below the junction. From these considerations it seems the Mississippi rightfully gives its name to the united stream and to the great valley from its source to the sea.

"The Missouri rises in the Rocky Mountains, nearly on the same parallel as the Mississippi itself. It is formed of three branches, called Jefferson, Madison and Gallatin, and the head waters of some of these are not more than a mile from the Columbia river which empties into the Pacific Ocean. These streams unite at the base of the mountain and become a foaming torrent, and is full of islands. It then passes through what is called 'The Gates of the Rocky Mountains.' The river appears to have torn for itself a passage for six miles through the mountains, and perpendicular cliffs of rock rise twelve hundred feet above the stream; the chasm is not more than three hundred feet wide, and the deep, foaming waters rush through with the speed of a race horse. For seventeen miles the stream becomes an almost continued cataract. The first fall is ninety-eight feet, the second nineteen, the third forty-seven, the fourth twenty-six. The river in a few miles assumes its distinctive character, sweeps briskly along in regular curves through limestone bluffs, boundless prairies and dark forests to its junction with the Mississippi. It has a current of four miles an hour, but is navigable for steamboats twenty-five hundred miles.

"The tributaries of the Missouri are many and large, the most important are the Yellow Stone, La Platte and the Ossage. The Yellow Stone rises in the same range of mountains as the main river, to which it has many points of resemblance. It enters the Missouri from the south eighteen hundred miles above its mouth and at the junction appears to be the largest river. It is sixteen hundred miles in length and boatable one thousand. Its shores are generally heavily timbered, its bottoms are wide and of the richest soil. Here the government has selected as a suitable place for a military post and an extensive park.

"The La Platte also rises in the Rocky Mountains, enters from the south, and measured by its meanders is two thousand miles in length. It is a broad, shallow stream, a mile wide at its mouth and not navigable except at high floods.

"The Ossage also enters from the south and is a large stream, boatable six hundred miles, and its headwaters interlock with the river Arkansas.

"The Gasconade enters from the south also, boatable for sixty miles and has on its banks extensive pine forests from which St. Louis is supplied with timber.

"The Missouri, measured from its highest source to the Gulf of Mexico, is longer than the Mississippi, and brings down more water, although it is not more than half as wide. It is at all times turbid or muddy, and gives to that river its own complexion. It dashes into the Mississippi fifteen miles above St. Louis, and gives its four-mile current to that stream to its mouth.

"Nearly two hundred miles below St. Louis comes in from the east the beautiful Ohio. At its junction it is as wide as the parent stream and far exceeds it in beauty, for it has clear water and a smooth and peaceful current. It is formed by the junction of the Alleghany and Monongahela at Pittsburgh. Beautiful streams come in on both sides in its course of eleven hundred miles to its mouth. And between these two points are a hundred islands, the most noted and beautiful is Blenerhassett Island of a hundred and eighty acres.

"Below the Ohio the most important tributaries are the White river, Arkansas and Red river, all entering from the west. The White river rises in the Black Mountains and is twelve hundred miles in length. The Arkansas, next to the Missouri, is the next largest tributary from the west, and twenty-five hundred miles in length. Its waters are at all times turbid and when the river is full are of a dark flame color.

"Eighty miles below Natchez comes in from the west Red river, though not as wide as the Arkansas it has as long a course and probably carries as much water.

"After receiving Red river the Mississippi carries its greatest volume of water. This, however, continues but for a short distance, for three or four miles below the mouth of Red river and on the same side is the first outlet of the Mississippi, and that carries off as much water as the Red river brings in. A small stream below this outlet on the east side comes into the Mississippi, called Bayou Sarah. The only eastern outlet is a small distance below Baton Rouge, called Ibberville, and passes its waters into Lake Maurepas. Two more outlets are on the west side called Bayou Plaquemine and Bayou La Stoube. The Mississippi then passes on between unbroken banks by the city of New Orleans and discharges the remainder of its waters through four mouths into the Gulf of Mexico, ninety miles below the city.

"The Mississippi is navigable for steamboats to the Falls of St. Anthony, a distance of twenty-two hundred miles. Below the falls the river becomes a placid, clear stream, with clean sand bars and fertile bottoms. Just below the entrance of the river Des Moines there is a rapid of nine miles, which impedes navigation at low water. Then the river is a mile wide to the mouth of the Missouri. There it receives double the water but is half as wide and wholly changes its character. Before its junction it has a current of only two miles an hour but when the Missouri pours into it its four-mile current of muddy waters it adds its own speed to the parent stream and it becomes a furious mass of muddy waters with sliding banks and jagged shores.

"When we descend from the Falls of St Anthony and behold the Mississippi swallowing up the rivers in its passage to New Orleans, we then become aware of the great mass of water it carries. From the mouth of the Ohio to its mouth it is eighty feet deep. The spring floods are usually about fifteen feet. at the mouth of the Ohio fifty feet, and at New Orleans only twelve feet. In these floods the bottom lands are overflowed. The medium width of these bottom lands above the Missouri is six miles, there to the Ohio eight miles, and from this point to New Orleans it is from thirty to fifty miles. These swamps at flood time are covered with water, and were it not for that circumstance and the outlets New Orleans would be many feet under water. The water at the city seldom rises above twelve feet and then has to be kept out of it by a levee or dike."

Mr. Parker has been three times married. While at college in Burlington he became acquainted with the accomplished daughter of the president of the college. Courtship in the midst of so many brother students was, we are assured, a very difficult matter. Yet at length after many trials and interferences they became engaged and were finally married in Medfield, Mass., Oct. 13, 1822. She was Miranda W., b. April 16, 1796: d. March 13, 1828, dau. of Daniel and Anna (Clark) Sanders of Medfield, Mass. They settled in Epping, N. H., as aforestated. Five years and five months they had lived together when the wife died.

His second wife was Mary McClary, dau. of Gen. Michael McClary of Epsom, N. H., famous for his brave leadership in the Revolutionary war. She was an efficient woman and a good housewife. She d. April 3, 1876, aged 81 years.

He m. third, April 9, 1879, Julia E. Smith of Glastonbury, Ct., b. May 27, 1792. She was famous for translating the Bible from the original Hebrew manuscript, which she had printed, and also for resisting "taxation without representation," as, like other women, she enjoyed no voice in public affairs. She had lived single previously and both were aged 86 at the time of their marriage. At this age Col. Parker was comparatively a man of 60, and the event shows the remarkable energy and exceptional courage of both parties. Seven years of pleasant married life were passed at the Smith estate in Glastonbury, Ct., where she d. March 6, 1886.

And now after a long eventful life he has returned to his native town to pass the remainder of his days. And Col. Parker's has been a life as full of activity as of years. He has held more offices and remained in office during a longer period than any other man in the State of New Hampshire. For 79 years a member of the bar, he was, during all but 20 years of the time, a justice of the quorum, holding commissions from 14 different governors, with all of whom he was intimately acquainted. He attended 13 sessions of the State legislature, was for eight years a trustee of the New Hampshire Asylum for Insane; for ten years first selectman of Fitzwilliam; member of the Legal Association of New York, and member of the New Hampshire Historical Society, besides holding many other positions of responsibility and trust.

In 1845 we find him actively engaged in forwarding the projected railroad between Boston and Burlington by way of Rutland. After aiding in obtaining charters for the Fitchburg and Cheshire road he brought the matter before the people of Vermont, addressing large crowds in Bellows Falls, Brandon, Rutland, Vergennes and Burlington. The Rutland and Burlington railroad was built and is to-day the Rutland division of the Central Vermont system.

When the Civil war broke out Mr. Parker was unable to enlist on account of his age but he furnished a substitute. Three of his sons went also, two returning in safety, while the third died in the service.

Besides the book of travels and the historical work on Lafayette already mentioned he published a book of poems in his eightieth year and wrote many stories, magazine articles and newspaper contributions.

As a public speaker Mr. Parker has also made his mark. In addition to Fast Day addresses, railroad, political and miscellaneous speeches Mr. Parker has delivered four Fourth of July orations, the first one being in 1816 at Falmouth on the banks of the Rappahannock in Virginia, one in Rockingham County, Vermont, and two at Fitzwilliam. Each of these orations were highly commended. One of the finest gems of its kind is an address on "Education," delivered at Rindge on October 17, 1843, before the Cheshire County Primary School Association. It is the result of experience, is full of common sense, is clear cut and vigorous. His address to his fellow-citizens at Fitzwilliam, Fast Day, 1862, in support of the civil war, was a very masterly oration and created enthusiasm.

At the time Esquire Parker quitted his profession he had practiced law the longest of any man in the State of New Hampshire. He is the oldest living graduate of any American college. At the election of Nov. 8, 1892, he arose from his bed, rode to the polls and in the village of his native town, at the age of 101 years, cast his ballot for President Harrison, the twentieth president for whom he has voted. It is the first known instance of such an event. But at such an extreme age we may well believe that the eye has grown dim and the feeble footstep very unsteady; yet up to 99 years he walked out every pleasant day. Sudden sickness has not spared him, particularly in his declining years, but a remarkable will power and a great desire to live has ever been his support in these afflictions. The retention of one's faculties to this extreme age is indeed worthy our study, as constant inquiries from the wondering public, of which he is the recipient, attest. Never far behind, he is ever interested in the changes and progress of the times, particularly in the social improvement which invention and education has accomplished in the remarkable epoch in which he has lived. In his opposition to intemperance and slavery; his aid in the introduction of railways, and in any other reforms which he has advocated during his long public service it has been his fortune to ever be on the right and winning side.

A patriarch of experience, observation and wisdom, his advice regarding longevity is quickly expressed: *Never eat, work, play or sleep to excess; keep a quiet mind*, and let it always have perfect influence over the body; let the mind be commander-in-chief. What activity and hope, what physical and mental vigor and manhood are depicted in this original note penned hastily at the age of 101!

"*Fitzwilliam, N. H., March 30, 1892.*

"But I am now Five-Score
And most six months more
And cannot ignore
A plain simple fact
That I cannot act
As in days of yore
When I was *three*-score,
And deeply deplore
That I can't do more.
And still I shall aim
To live and die game,
Perhaps put my name
On the Roll of Fame!
After all, what is FAME?
'Tis but a mere *name*.
Should the old man Amos,
Become *now* famous,
Would it help him to die?
If so, tell me why.
My solid intent
Is a *life well spent*.
And thus, I will end,
This letter I send,
To my distant Friend.

"AMOS A. PARKER,
"100 years old October 8, 1891."

Children of Amos A. Parker:

244. GEORGE WASHINGTON PARKER, b. in Concord, N. H., Aug. 14, 1824; m. Julia A. Deeth.

DANIEL CLARK SANDERS PARKER, b. in Medfield, Mass., Sept. 2, 1826; drowned in Troy, N. H., June 15, 1845. He was a very promising young man.

245. ANDREW PARKER, b. in New Market, N. H., March 2, 1828; m. Laura A. Morse of Winchendon.

246. MIRANDA SANDERS PARKER, b. June 10, 1829; m. June, 1855, Anson Smith of Fitzwilliam, N. H.

247. CHARLES HENRY PARKER, b. Sept., 1833; m. Jane S. Ballou of Richmond, N. H.

248. JOHN MCCLARY PARKER, b. Sept. 17, 1836; m. (1) Catharine H. Adams, (2) Abbie H. Kimball.

MARY ELIZABETH PARKER, b. 1839; d. July 17, 1870.

100. Capt. Ephraim Parker *(Nahum,[6] Amos,[5] Andrew,[4] John,[3] Hananiah,[2] Thomas[1])*, son of Judge Nahum and Mary (Deeth) Parker, was b. in Fitzwilliam, N. H., Aug. 18, 1793; m. Dec. 7, 1816, Lucy, b. June 3, 1795, dau. of Capt. David and Ruth (Mellen) Stone of Fitzwilliam. He was a millwright by trade in early life, was an excellent mechanic and made many inventions, many of them were valuable and are still in existence, but like most inventors made no money out of them. He was educated at New Salem Academy in Mass., and about the time of his majority he invented the machine for making and setting card teeth, which was then mostly used for domestic use, and proved to be a very valuable thing. He built mills in what is now called New Boston (part of Winchendon), Mass. In a few years he moved to the village of Fitzwilliam, where he was deputy sheriff for some years, also selectman, and there he worked at his trade of millwright and through that section of the country building many mills and becoming well known for his ability in this direction. He taught many apprentices the millwright trade. In 1836 or 1838 he bought a mill in Ashby, Mass., afterwards sold and moved to Ashburnham, Mass., still following the millwright business and speculating, buying and selling mill property in different places. From Ashburnham he moved to East Boston, bought a water-front and built a dry dock. From there he moved to Richmond, Va., after selling his dry dock, and bought the Woodruff patent right and started a large establishment for planing boards for building purposes. These were the first planing machines that were sent south. Later he moved his family to Rockford, Ill., but after a few months returned to Massachusetts and built large mills in Orange. He sold these and bought the cotton factory in Athol, and was very instrumental in getting the Vermont and Mass. R. R. through from Fitchburg to Brattleboro, Vt., holding meetings all along the line and publicly speaking in favor of the railroad, representing the town of Athol in the General Court in Boston. He was often chosen as moderator at town meetings. He was a great Biblical scholar. He was not only a man of great energy and enterprise but an able debater on almost any subject, especially religion and politics.

In Illinois his wife died in 1852 and was buried on the bluffs of the Mississippi river at Rock Island. He removed to Marlow, N. H., where his daughter, Mrs. Benjamin Coolidge, resided. Here he made many inventions, among which was a machine for turning and boring bobbins at one automatic operation. These machines are now in very extensive use. On his daughter's death he came to visit his son, Alfred A. Parker, at Orange, and in one week he had the third paralytic shock from which he died, and was there buried. He died Oct. 24, 1880, aged 87 years and two months. He retained his faculties in a marked degree to the very last.

Ephraim Parker was captain of a State Military Company at Fitzwilliam, N. H., and hence was known as Capt. Ephraim Parker through life. He was something of a lawyer, a prominent Anti-Slavery man and Washingtonian, and president of the society. He was called a man of marked ability, always living ahead of the times.

Their children were:

Julia Selina Parker, b. in Fitzwilliam, N. H.; m. Benjamin Coolidge (merchant), Dec. 22, 1842. She d. Oct. 7, 1880, in Marlow, N. H., at age of 62. leaving no children.

249. Alfred A. Parker, b. in New Boston (part of Winchendon), Mass., in 1823; m. March 30, 1857, Frances A. Whipple of Orange.

250. Edward Nelson Parker, b. in New Boston, in 1826; m. Miss Lackland of St. Louis, Mo. He d. 1883[?], in Missouri.

251. Charles Adams Parker, b. in Fitzwilliam, N. H., in 1833.

252. HORACE MILTON PARKER, b. in Fitzwilliam, N. H., in 1835.
253. ELIZA ANN PARKER, b. in Fitzwilliam, N. H., in 1838; m. Lucas C. Topping.
254. JANETTE FRANCES PARKER, b. in Ashby, Mass., in 1840; m. Marshall Thayer of Springfield.

101. Nahum Parker, Jr. *(Nahum,[6] Amos,[5] Andrew,[4] John,[3] Hananiah,[2] Thomas[1])*, son of Judge Nahum and Mary (Deeth) Parker, was b. in Fitzwilliam, N. H., March 16, 1797; m. —— Bean of Nottingham, N. H. He was a healthy child, but at the age of five years had a severe attack of the whooping cough which left him an invalid for life. He was a good musician and fine singer, and did much light work during life. He had a son and dau. He d. at Plaistow, N. H. The children lived in Manchester, N. H., and probably moved to Plaistow.

Selina Parker (see page 112) *(Nahum,[6] Amos,[5] Andrew,[4] John,[3] Hananiah,[2] Thomas[1])*, dau. of Judge Nahum and Mary (Deeth) Parker, was b. in Fitzwilliam, N. H., July 5, 1799; m. John Damon of Fitzwilliam, son of John Damon of Gardner, Mass. She lived at the southeast part of Fitzwilliam some five years after the death of her husband, then bought a home in the village where she resided until her death, July 2, 1888, aged 89. She left no issue.

102. Elmon Parker *(Nahum,[6] Amos,[5] Andrew,[4] John,[3] Hananiah,[2] Thomas[1])*, son of Judge Nahum and Mary (Deeth) Parker, was b. in Fitzwilliam, N. H., Jan. 20, 1802; m. Abigail M. Gray of Belfast, Me. He lived upon his father's homestead in Fitzwilliam until of age, then became clerk in Boston. He removed to Bangor, Me., in 1834, was an industrious and useful man; made a machine to saw shingles and clapboards. He lived in York Springs for a while, then went overland to California. He became a dentist, established a business there and died. He had four children, two sons and two daughters. The children did reside in Philadelphia.

103. Quincy Parker *(Ebenezer,[6] Thomas,[5] Andrew,[4] John,[3] Hananiah,[2] Thomas[1])*, son of Dea. Ebenezer and Dorcas (Monroe) Parker, was b. in Lexington, April 28,

1775; m. in Princeton, Patience, dau. of John Brooks, one of the sturdy pioneers of that town. He built a house adjoining the homestead to the east, by the side of the pond. This house was standing until recently. After living here a number of years he finally exchanged places for his father's farm in Rindge, N. H., where he with his family removed. After a large family had been born to them he suffered the fate of being badly gored by a bull. This he survived, but it affected his constitution, causing occasional hæmorrhage. A few years afterward while standing in the front doorway, with no particular excitement, he was taken with a hæmorrhage, which was the immediate cause of his death, which occurred Sept. 27, 1828.

Quincy Parker was a great worker. He was a strong, robust man and of great endurance. He possessed much inventive talent, but which by his early death he was prevented from developing. His widow removed to Providence, R. I., where she d. May 12, 1864, aged 85 years and 11 months.

Their children were:

THOMAS PARKER, b. in Princeton, Sept. 28, 1801; d. June 3, 1802.

255. THOMAS MAXWELL PARKER, b. in Princeton, April 26, 1803; m. Esther Luther of Swansea, Mass.

256. JOSEPH BROOKS PARKER, b. in Princeton, July 31, 1805; m. Mary Ann Morgan.

257. WILLIAM EATON PARKER, b. in Princeton, June 6, 1808; m. probably in Columbus, O.

PRISCILLA ELVIRA PARKER, b. in Princeton, April 26, 1809.

258. MARY PARKER, b. in Princeton, April 16, 1811; m. William Sweet of Providence, R. I.

QUINCY PARKER, Jr., b. in Princeton, Sept. 20, 1812; d. April 21, 1815.

259. IRA PARKER, b. in Princeton, April 16, 1814; m. Maria Haskell of Providence, R. I.

260. ELIZA PARKER, b. in Princeton, Oct. 20, 1815; m. Jonas Hunt of Providence, R. I.

261. SALLY PARKER, b. in Princeton, March 1, 1817; m. George B. Thomas.

262. ARTIMUS PARKER, b. in Princeton, Feb. 22, 1819; m. Susan Pierce of W. Boylston.

263. QUINCY PARKER, Jr., b. in Rindge, N. H., Jan. 12, 1821; m. Almira Kent of Eaton, N. Y.

264. EUNICE PARKER, b. in Rindge, Aug. 1, 1822; m. George Herrick.

104. Betsey Parker *(Ebenezer,[6] Thomas,[5] Andrew,[4] John,[3] Hananiah,[2] Thomas[1])*, dau. of Dea. Ebenezer and Dorcas (Monroe) Parker, was b. in Princeton, June 8, 1777 (the first birth of the Parker family in the town); m. Benjamin Gould of Princeton, native of Bolton. The deacon gave them the farm situated west of the present homestead estate, which was a part of the original purchase. They resided upon the place until 1815, when they with their family removed to Boston, where their son was janitor of the Boston City Hall. Upon their decease each were interred in the family burying-ground at Princeton.

Their children were:

1. DORCAS M. GOULD, b. Dec. 7, 1799; m. Henry R. Goodwin.
2. CYRUS P. GOULD, b. Nov. 11, 1802.
3. ERASTUS R. GOULD, b. Feb. 20, 1807.
4. MARY E. GOULD, b. July 26, 1810.
5. EBENEZER PARKER GOULD, b. Oct. 14, 1812; m. April 21, 1835, Susan Goodwin, b. Jan. 15, 1816, d. in Boston, Feb. 22, 1890. He was for about 20 years assistant janitor of Boston City Hall. He also served time on the "old night watch" police of Boston. He d. in Boston, Dec. 3, 1870. Children:
   - I. SUSAN W. GOULD; m. —— Merriam. Resides in E. Princeton.
   - II. ANNIE L. GOULD; resides in Chelsea.
   - III. GEORGE W. GOULD; m. April 17, 1864, Lizzie I., b. in New Bedford, June 16, 1854, dau. of William, Jr. and Susan B. Hammond. He has been for many years locomotive fireman, and resides at Cambridgeport. They have had seven children and two grandchildren. He served in the army of the U. S. in the late war.

105. Polly Parker *(Ebenezer,[6] Thomas,[5] Andrew,[4] John,[3] Hananiah,[2] Thomas[1])*, dau. of Dea. Ebenezer and Dorcas (Monroe) Parker, was b. in Princeton, May 4, 1779; m. (1) Rufus Dodd, b. in Princeton, Feb. 22, 1773, son of William and Anna (Child) Dodd. They removed to West-

minster, where he was a storekeeper. The father, William Dodd, is said to have been born in Bedford, but the records of that town show no light. Rufus Dodd's death occurred in Westminster, and she m. (2) Dr. Isaac Warren of Princeton, a young and very promising physician. He died, however, at the early age of 27, Sept. 14, 1815. The sweet memories of Mrs. Dodd are still cherished by those who knew her well. She was not only a kind mother but a noble wife and a dignified lady. She was a conscientious and christian woman, always particular in her teachings to her children, that they in future years might not part from honor and righteousness. She and her second husband, Dr. Warren, were buried in the "homestead" graveyard. She d. Oct. 10, 1857.

Her children were:

I. THEODORE SEDGWICK DODD, b. in Westminster, Oct. 28, 1803; removed to Maine; m. in Bucksport, Me., Feb. 11, 1834, Caroline, b. April 8, 1812, dau. of Samuel and Caroline (Elliott) Little. They settled in Bangor, where he became cashier of the Kenduskeag Bank, which position he held until shortly preceding his death. During all the 45 years which he served as cashier he performed the duties of his office in so faithful and accurate a manner that he was held in the highest esteem by the officers of the bank as well as by all others with whom his business led him. He was so exceedingly accurate that certain of those who worked with him said they never knew him to make a mistake. At the time of his resignation Mr. Dodd had been in office longer than any other cashier in the State. She d. Jan. 14, 1890. Children:

I. JULIA MARIA DODD, b. July 16, 1835; d. April 16, 1838.

II. MARY ELIZABETH DODD, b. Dec. 18, 1837.

III. HORACE SEDGWICK DODD, b. Dec. 13, 1839; m. in Bangor, Me., Oct. 25, 1864, Emily Lucretia, b. in Bangor, Feb. 18, 1840, dau. of Abner P. and Rebecca H. Guild. He is a cotton broker in Boston. Children:

1. Margaret Elliot Dodd, b. in Cambridge, Dec. 8, 1866.
2. Walter Sedgwick Dodd, b. in Cambridge, Feb. 5, 1868.
3. John Wellington Dodd, b. in Boston, March 29, 1876.
4. Rebecca Dodd, b. in Boston, May 31, 1881.

IV. CHARLES BAILEY DODD, b. May 26, 1848; d. Oct. 27, 1882.

V. HARRY WARE DODD, b. Oct. 18, 1849.

2. SARAH MARIA DODD, b. in Westminster; m. Caleb Strong Myrick, b. in Princeton, Oct. 28, 1802, son of Caleb and Lydia (Gregory) Myrick. He was a well-known and popular Princeton man. She was an excellent mother, a sincere and faithful woman. He d. Oct. 8, 1869. Children:

   I. CHARLES THEODORE MYRICK, b. in Princeton, Oct. 20, 1833; m. Nov. 20, 1858, Sarah P. Smith, b. in Princeton, Feb. 5, 1832, dau. of Francis H. and Susan (Fay) Smith. They reside in Worcester. Child:

      I. Harry Strong Myrick, b. in Worcester, May 17, 1862.

   II. CAROLINE DODD MYRICK, b. 1836; m. in Princeton, Edward C. Hartwell, son of Isaac and Susan Hartwell of Princeton. They have no issue.

   III. JOHN D. MYRICK, b. 1840; d. 1864. Enlisted at once upon the call for troops in the 25th Mass. Reg. for three months and later for three years. He was in many battles, was finally commissioned as an officer in the 31st U. S. colored regiment. While in battle at Olustee, near Jacksonville, Fla., he was valiantly leading his men with all speed possible and was singled out as a target for a sharpshooter. He was hit three times. One ball struck his watch, completely destroying it, but which did him no harm, another lodged in his shoulder, while the third was more serious. He died of his wounds soon after at Hilton Head, S. C. His name is patriotically inscribed on Worcester's beautiful soldiers' monument. His sword and watch are still in preservation in the Myrick family.

   IV. MARY W. MYRICK; d. Sept. 30, 1869, unm.

3. JULIA DODD, b. in Westminster; m. in Princeton, Horace Everett. They removed to Charlestown and had five children:

   I. MARY EVERETT; d. 1855.

   II. RUFUS EVERETT, who removed to Leavenworth, Kan.

   III. FANNIE EVERETT, who m. Edward Sawyer and settled in Newton.

   IV. STANWOOD EVERETT, a doctor in Boston.

   V. JULIA EVERETT, who m. and went to Nova Scotia.

4. ROSALINE WARREN, b. in Princeton; m. —— Foster. They reside in Fitchburg.

5. ISAAC WARREN, Jr., b. in Princeton, Aug. 9, 1815; m. He d. in Bernardston, April 7, 1879.

106. Lucy Parker *(Ebenezer,*[6] *Thomas,*[5] *Andrew,*[4] *John,*[3] *Hananiah,*[2] *Thomas*[1]*)*, dau. of Dea. Ebenezer and Dorcas (Monroe) Parker, was b. in Princeton, March 11, 1781; bap. in Lexington, July 22, 1781. Her intention of marriage, to Mr. Jonas Beaman, as entered upon the Princeton records, previous to publishing, bears date of Jan. 25, 1801. He was then a resident of Princeton; b. in Lancaster, Dec. 25, 1778, eldest son of Jonas and Rebecca (Whitcomb) Beaman. They removed to Camden, Me., where he pursued the trade of leather tanning. He d. Oct. 3, 1807, leaving two children. She m. (2) in 1809, Edward Hanford of Camden, Me., as his first wife. Locke in his *History of Camden* says:

"Major Edward Hanford was born, it is believed, in Norwalk, Conn. (about 1775). He came to Camden about the year 1806, and being a hatter worked at his trade. He afterwards went into trade.

"In time of the last war [of 1812] he was made a Lieut. and after peace was proclaimed he was promoted to the rank of Major, by which title everybody knew him. He was selectman one year and town clerk four years, and occupied other town offices.

"Affected with a disease of the heart it is supposed it induced the quietude of manner he evinced during the last score years of his life. However, he was, during all this time, in a store as proprietor, manager or clerk. He died in Belfast at the house of L. R. Palmer, Esq., his son-in-law, May 3, 1851, aged 76 years."

Her children were:

1. Edwin Beaman, b. in Princeton, Aug. 27, 1801; m. Sept. 28, 1829, Sarah, dau. of Moses Patten of Bangor, Me. He early entered into business and connected himself with the towns of Freedom, Camden, Bucksport and Brooks, where in 1829 he removed his store to the Head of the Tide. Removing to Belfast he, in company with Daniel Merrill, occupied the present store of A. D. Chase. In 1842 he removed to the present store of Augustus Perry, the two forming the firm of Beaman & Perry, which existed for 12 years. From that time Mr. Beaman was in business alone to the day of his death, which occurred March 30, 1880, a period of 54 years, making him the oldest trader in Belfast. He was an original incorporator of the Belfast Bank. He was a consistent and worthy member of the Congregational Church of Belfast since 1835, and for a large portion of the time held the office of deacon. Mr.

Beaman was held in high respect by his fellow-citizens and died greatly lamented by a large circle of friends acquired during his long and busy life. He left no children save an adopted daughter. His widow survives him.

2. JONAS BEAMAN, Jr., b. May 17, 1805; m. (1) Dec. 31, 1833, Martha M. Cook; she d. Jan. 3, 1859, and he m. (2) Sept. 7, 1859, Mary Weld of Sturbridge, whose home was very near the Brimfield line, and was a member of the Church at Brimfield. He settled in Hadley where he owned and worked a small farm; at about 1865 he moved to Princeton, taking a farm and there he died. Children:

   I. LUCY BEAMAN, now the wife of a physician in Black Rock, N. Y., if living.
   II. EDWIN(?) BEAMAN.
   III. DWIGHT BEAMAN.
   IV. JONAS BEAMAN, Jr.

3. MARY P. D. HANFORD, b. in Camden, Me., April 3, 1810; m. Dec. 25, 1849, Lemuel R. Palmer as his second wife, he having previously m. her sister Susannah. Their son was:

   I. JOSEPH H. PALMER, b. Nov. 22, 1850.

4. SUSANNAH R. HANFORD, b. June 17, 1812; m. Dec. 17, 1832, Lemuel R. Palmer. He was a ship carpenter, learning his trade in Camden. She d. Aug. 14, 1849, and he d. May 3, 1879. Children:

   I. Rev. EDWIN BEAMAN PALMER, b. Sept. 25, 1833; m. Thurza M. Field, native of Brunswick, Me. He is connected with the Congregationalist House in Boston.
   II. SUSAN MARIA PALMER, b. Sept. 7, 1835; m. James M. Craig, native of Windsor, N. S. They reside in Belfast.
   III. MARY ELIZA PALMER, b. Sept. 11, 1837; m. George F. Smith, native of Searsport, Me.
   IV. DWIGHT PARKER PALMER, b. Sept. 13, 1839; d. Sept. 2, 1841.
   V. DWIGHT PARKER PALMER, b. March 31, 1843; m. Mary E. Patterson of Belfast, Me.
   VI. LUCY A. E. PALMER, b. May 19, 1845.

5. LUCY A. HANFORD, b. May 19, 1814; m. Dec. 7, 1835, Nathaniel T. Eaton, sea-captain. He followed the sea until the last few years of his life, when he became a farmer in Camden. She d. Dec. 24, 1852, and he m. (2) Miss Nancy Heal, dau. of Peter and Eunice Heal of Camden. He d. May 25, 1870. His widow resides in Camden. Children:

The Princeton Parker Homestead.

I. ADELLA FRANCES EATON, b. Oct. 31, 1836; d. May 17, 1838.

II. EDWARD HANFORD EATON, b. May 27, 1840; m. 1886, Susan Sparling of Boston. They reside in Worcester.

III. LUCY HANFORD EATON, b. Dec. 27, 1844; d. Aug. 27, 1858.

IV. FRANK CHAPLIN EATON, who resides in Worcester.

107. Ebenezer Parker, Jr. (*Ebenezer,[6] Thomas,[5] Andrew,[4] John,[3] Hananiah,[2] Thomas[1]*). son of Dea. Ebenezer and Dorcas (Monroe) Parker, was b. in Princeton, June 4, 1784; intention of marriage entered for publication on Jan. 4, 1806; m. at age of 22, Feb. 27, 1806, Hannah B., b. in Concord, Mass., March 11, 1785, dau. of Capt. Amos and Deborah (Brooks) Merriam of Concord, who were m. in Lincoln, it being Deborah's native town, on Christmas Day, 1783. Hannah Brooks Merriam was thus first in a family of ten children. The father, Capt. Amos Merriam, d. Sept. 16, 1804, aged 44, and his widow m. (2) Stephen Mirick, who d. May 20, 1827. Deborah (Merriam) Mirick, d. Nov. 10, 1844. Ebenezer Parker remained upon the homestead until 1818, when he took up the place now known as the Princeton Poor Farm. This was a part of the original estate and but a short distance northeasterly from his old home. He was both a farmer and clothier. In his shop, at the outlet of the pond, he did a good business in coloring and smoothing. His customers were numerous and many came long distances with a year's supply of home-spun cloth at one time. After the destruction of the old homestead brick house by fire during the winter of 1835 he assumed charge of his father's estate. He then spent a few years in Ware; returning, he in company with his son, Frederick Parker, built upon the homestead site, the house now standing, it being the third built upon the site since 1777. What remained of the old farm after Deacon Parker's grants to his children and the many sales, was again improved with fresh vigor.

Ebenezer Parker was a man of sound intellect and of a strong, unimpeachable character. He was a very firm minded man and a conscientious citizen. He was chosen selectman in 1829. His district for the years of 1741, '42 and '43 elected him representative to the State Legislature. In personal appearance he was taller than his father, but inherited a strong and vigorous constitution. At the age of 75 his tall and manly figure stood firm and erect. He lived to the age of 85 years and 4 months, dying Oct. 25, 1869. He was an active member of the Church in Princeton.

The wife Hannah will be long remembered by the family. She was a loving mother, a perfect housekeeper and was blessed with a very attractive disposition. Her temperament was very calm, she was less nervous than Mr. Parker, and looked upon the difficulties of life in a more philosophical way. She lived happily and long, dying Aug. 31, 1876, at the age of 91 years, 5 months and 20 days.

Their children were:

265. LOUISA PARKER, b. Dec. 13, 1806; m. Eli Walker of Holden.

266. CHARLES AUGUSTUS PARKER, b. Aug. 18, 1808; m. Sylvia A. Moore.

267. FREDERICK PARKER, b. June 19, 1810; m. Eunice C. Howe of Princeton.

268. EBENEZER WARREN PARKER, b. Oct. 28, 1813; m. Chloe A. Parmenter of Oakham.

269. ADALINE PARKER, b. Oct. 24, 1815; m. Stephen H. Smith of West Boylston. } Twins.

270. AMOS PARKER, b. Oct. 24, 1815; m. Sarah Merrill of Beverly. }

271. GEORGE PARKER, b. Feb. 1, 1818; m. Emily R. Coller of Northfield. } Twins.

Child, unnamed, b. and d. Feb. 1, 1818. }

272. DEBORAH MERIAM PARKER, b. Sept. 9, 1819; m. Israel Howe of Princeton.

273. WILLIAM WHEELER PARKER, b. March 2, 1824; m. Emily Walker of Holden.

274. EDWARD HANFORD PARKER, b. Dec. 28, 1825; m. Mary C. Brown of Boylston.

LUCY MARIA PARKER, b. Sept. 10, 1828; d. March 7, 1829.

108. Bitha Parker *(Ebenezer,[6] Thomas,[5] Andrew,[4] John,[3] Hananiah,[2] Thomas[1])*, dau. of Dea. Ebenezer and Dorcas (Monroe) Parker, was b. in Princeton, July 26, 1786; m. Oct. 26, 1809, Capt. Charles Folger of Camden, Me., b. in Waldoborough, Me., Jan., 1780. They lived at Camden

EBENEZER PARKER, JR.

MRS. HANNAH B. (MERRIAM) PARKER.

for several years, Capt. Folger pursuing his marine vocation. Coming to Princeton they settled first upon the homestead place, then upon the farm shortly before occupied by Benjamin and Betsey (Parker) Gould. This is now the Brennan place. They resided there until his death, which occurred in Oct., 1857. She removed to Marlborough, and d. Nov., 1871.

Their children were:

1. CHARLES AUGUSTUS FOLGER, b. in Camden, Me., Jan. 16, 1811; m. in Buffalo, N. Y., Feb. 16, 1860, Louisa, b. in London, England, Nov. 13, 1839, dau. of James and —— (Potter) Baker of England. He was a merchant in Lockport, N. Y. He d. Nov. 28, 1873. Their children were b. in Lockport, N. Y.:

   I. CHARLES EDWARD FOLGER, b. Dec. 18, 1860.
   II. EMMA LOUISE FOLGER, b. Feb. 23, 1863.
   III. HATTIE ELIZABETH FOLGER, b. Sept. 6, 1866.

2. JOHN WALTER FOLGER, b. in Camden, Feb. 8, 1813.
3. GEORGE FRANCIS FOLGER, b. in Camden, July 15, 1815; m. Jan. 28, 1850, Eliza A., b. Sept. 14, 1825, dau. of Isaac and Susan (Davis) Hartwell of Princeton. They resided in Princeton, where he was a farmer. He d. March 14, 1881, and his widow survives. She resides in Worcester.
4. HENRY EDWARD FOLGER, b. in Princeton, May 23, 1820; m. (1) Louisa, dau. of Stillman and Susan (Beaman) Everett of Princeton.
5. LUCY JANE FOLGER, b. in Princeton, Aug. 23, 1825; m. May 11, 1843, Phineas Ross, b. in Sterling, Sept. 20, 1817, son of Amos and Hepsibeth (Bennett) Ross. He d. in Princeton. Oct. 18, 1867. She resides in Worcester. Children:

   I. ELLEN JANE ROSS, b. April 20, 1844; m. March 12, 1868, Staysia, b. Aug. 25, 1843, son of Charles and Mary J. (Seaver) Harrington. They reside upon the old Jonas Smith place in Princeton.
   II. THEODORE AUSTIN ROSS, b. Feb. 28, 1849; d. Aug. 5, 1859.
   III. CHARLES THURSTON ROSS, b. May 12, 1854. Resides in Worcester; organ maker.

6. CATHARINE LONG FOLGER, b. in Princeton, Oct. 10, 1828; m. Jan. 29, 1851, Erastus, son of James and Ruthalia (Carter) Dart of Moncton, Vt. They resided many years in Marlbor-

ough. Their dau., Alice Josephine Dart, d. at the age of six years. Mr. Dart d. in Marlborough, Oct. 28, 1872. She now resides with her sister in Worcester.

109. Josiah Parker, Jr. (*Josiah,*[6] *Josiah,*[5] *Josiah,*[4] *John,*[3] *Hananiah,*[2] *Thomas*[1]), son of Josiah, Jr., and Hannah (Gardner) Parker, was b. in Woburn, Nov. 6, 1774; m. Sept. 6, 1807, Abigail Carter, b. in Woburn, Sept. 15, 1781, dau. of Simon and Susanna Carter of Woburn, and by whom nine of his children were born. Removed to Wilton, N. H., where she d. Sept. 8, 1836, and he m. (2) in Woburn, Feb. 15, 1883, Mrs. Betsey S. (Eames) Converse of Woburn, by whom his last two children were born. He d. in Wilton, N. H., Nov. 29, 1852. She d. in Woburn, Dec. 3, 1881, aged 81 years, 3 months.

His children were:

275. Abigail Manning Parker, b. in Woburn, Jan. 6, 1808; m. James Burton.

276. Susan Richardson Parker, b. in Woburn, May 26, 1809; m. Lyman Stone.

277. Hannah Gardner Parker, b. in Woburn, Feb. 23, 1811; m. Jonathan Snow, after the decease of her sister Lydia.

278. Lydia Ann Parker, b. in Woburn, Aug. 5, 1813; m. Jonathan Snow.

279. John Flagg Parker, b. in Woburn, Dec. 27, 1815; m. Martha J. Jones.

280. Josiah Parker, b. in Wilton, N. H., April 10, 1819; m. Nancy M. Wyman.

281. Andrew Jackson Parker, b. in Wilton, N. H., May 26, 1821; m. Abbie A. Tapley.

Maria Louisa Parker, b. in Wilton, N. H., Oct. 24, 1823; m. Samuel R. Dolliver, who was b. in Marblehead. They reside in San Francisco, Cal. No issue.

Abram Parker, b. in Wilton, N. H., June 21, 1826; d. Aug. 8, 1832.

282. Albert Parker, b. in Wilton, N. H., April 12, 1839; m. Eliza H. Sawyer.

George Parker, b. March 2, d. March 24, 1841.

110. Henry Parker (*Josiah,*[6] *Josiah,*[5] *Josiah,*[4] *John,*[3] *Hananiah,*[2] *Thomas*[1]), son of Josiah, Jr., and Hannah (Gardner) Parker, was b. in Woburn, July 2, 1777; m. by the

Rev. Mr. Fiske of W. Cambridge, May 28, 1807, Abigail Hutchinson, b. Sept. 10, 1782, dau. of John Hutchinson of Charlestown. She was the sixth in generation in descent from George Hutchinson, Esq., who was an inhabitant of Charlestown in 1630, the line being thus: Abigail,[6] John[5] (whose second wife was Mary Fox), Thomas[4] of Cambridge (whose wife was Mary Ireland, dau. of Abraham Ireland and wife Abigail Greenland, both of Charlestown), Samuel[3] (whose wife was Sarah Fascitt), Nathaniel[2] (who m. Sarah Baker), and George,[1] the emigrant ancestor. She d. Aug. 17, 1876, aged 94 years and 9 months. He was a highly esteemed citizen, representing the town in the Legislature in the year 1839. He resided on the "West Side." He d. in Woburn, Feb. 7, 1862, aged 84 years, 7 months.

Their children were:

283. Oliver Hutchinson Parker, b. June 20, 1808; m. Patty Parker of Woburn (his cousin).

284. Martha Parker, b. Aug. 17, 1811; m. Charles Choate of Woburn.

285. Abigail Parker, b. March 26, 1814; m. William Winn of Burlington.

286. Louisa Parker, b. Dec. 14, 1816; m. John Weston of Woburn.

287. Maria Parker, b. July 5, 1819; m. George Winn of Burlington.

111. Hannah Parker *(Josiah,[6] Josiah,[5] Josiah,[4] John,[3] Hananiah,[2] Thomas[1])*, son of Josiah, Jr., and Hannah (Gardner) Parker, was b. in Woburn, March 19, 1779; m. April 28, 1808, Abel Richardson, b. Aug. 1, 1777. His father, Abel Richardson, was a tanner and shoemaker in Winchester, and his mother was Ann Tufts. He was known as Abel the fourth. He passed his life in Woburn, where he d. Jan. 5, 1854, in his 74th year. She d. in Woburn, Dec. 22, 1855, aged 76 years, 9 months. They had no children.

112. Polly Parker *(Josiah,[6] Josiah,[5] Josiah,[4] John,[3] Hananiah,[2] Thomas[1])*, son of Josiah, Jr., and Hannah (Gardner) Parker, was b. in Woburn; m. in Woburn, June 11, 1807, Caleb Richardson.

Their children were:

1. JOSHUA RICHARDSON, b. Feb. 25, 1808; unm.
2. MARY PARKER RICHARDSON. b. May 20, 1811; d. unm.
3. CALEB RICHARDSON, Jr., b. July 27, 1814; m. Jan., 1845, Amy Patience Taylor. She d. April, 1847. Child:
   1. GRANVILLE EUSTACE RICHARDSON, b. Nov. 21, 1845; m. Dec. 27, 1881, Susan M. Dean. Their son was:
      1. Frederick Wade Richardson, b. Nov. 27, 1882.
4. ABIGAIL RICHARDSON, b. May 28, 1817; m. July 8, 1847, Josiah Stratton of Woburn, son of Josiah and Sarah Stratton, b. in Woburn. She was b.. named and lived nearly all her life in the same house, which fronts the main street between Woburn and Winchester at a very enviable location. It was the old Caleb Richardson homestead. She lived in the old house 70 years, her entire life, with the exception of one year at the time of her marriage. She d. July 16. 1888, aged 71 years. At the opening of the War of the Rebellion Josiah Stratton enlisted from Woburn in Co. F of Hon. Henry Wilson's 22nd Mass. Reg. He was of a military spirit, had always belonged to the military companies of the town and proved himself to be a brave and true soldier. He was 44 years of age at his enlistment, which was much higher than the average, but he was a steady soldier upon the march and walked with a firm and manly carriage. He soon became Sergeant of the Co. The historian of the 22nd Reg., John L. Parker of Lynn, announces that he saw "Si Stratton, as he was familiarly called, June 22, 1862, upon the battle field of Gaines' Mills, Va., bravely fighting." This was the second of the famous Seven Days' Battles, and in this engagement, the Sergeant, who occupied a conspicuous and dangerous place, was the first to give the alarm to his Reg. that the "Rebs" were flanking them. His timely warning saved great loss to his company and perhaps his regiment. After this battle nothing more was ever heard of him. The State Records read: "*Josiah Stratton's service terminated June 22, 1862; caused by death while in Battle at Gaines' Mills.*" Children:
   I. GEORGE GARDNER STRATTON, b. Jan. 16, 1849; m. Dec. 20, 1876, Florence Leila Carter of Winchester, who d. upon the birth of their son, Oct. 2, 1877. He resides in Winchester, where he maintains his mother's old Richardson homestead. Child:
      1. Roscoe Carter Stratton, b. Oct. 2, 1877; d. July 12, 1878.
   II. JOSIAH FRANCIS STRATTON, b. Dec. 16, 1851; unm.

113. Electa Parker (*Josiah,*[6] *Josiah,*[5] *Josiah,*[4] *John,*[3] *Hananiah,*[2] *Thomas*[1]), dau. of Josiah, Jr., and Hannah (Gardner) Parker, was b. in Woburn, May 4, 1794; m. Feb. 16, 1813, Samuel Carter Buckman, the son of Samuel and Sarah (Cutter) Buckman of Woburn, and b. in Woburn, Nov. 10, 1789. He was a farmer and they lived in that part of Woburn which is now Winchester.

Their children were:

1. Samuel Carter Buckman, Jr., b. July 29, 1813. He is a wheelwright in Arlington, where he resides unm.
2. Electa Parker Buckman, b. May 16, 1815; m. Nathaniel Hill of Arlington. They had one child who d. young. She d. May 4, 1852.
3. James S. Buckman, b. Jan. 27, and d. April 11, 1819.
4. Lydia Ann Buckman, b. June 4, 1828; d. Aug. 28, 1877, unm.

114. Betsey Parker (*Josiah,*[6] *Josiah,*[5] *Josiah,*[4] *John,*[3] *Hananiah,*[2] *Thomas*[1]), dau. of Josiah, Jr., and Hannah (Gardner) Parker, was b. in Woburn, March 1, 1796; m. in Woburn, Dec. 29, 1825, Jonathan Baldwin, b. April 7, 1798, son of Reuben and Sarah Baldwin. He was a shoemaker and d. Jan. 11, 1881.

Their children were:

1. James Baldwin, b. Aug. 23, 1827; d. *about* Nov. 1, 1851, at Havana, Cuba, on his passage to California to try his fortune in the mines.
2. Marah Louise Baldwin, b. May 6, 1830; m. in Burlington, John Winn, b. July 3, 1828, son of Abel and Lydia Stearns (Lovering) Winn. He represented his town for one year in the State Legislature. She d. Oct. 11, 1852. He is a farmer in Burlington. Child:
    1. Marah Winn, b. June 13, 1852; m. in Woburn, Oct. 4, 1886, Frank Murray Pushee, b. in Lyme, N. H., March 12, 1844, son of Sylvester and Sarah (Emerton) Pushee. He is a farmer. They reside in Woburn. Child:
        1. Harold Baldwin Pushee, b. Jan. 16, 1890.

115. Frederick Parker (*Josiah,*[6] *Josiah,*[5] *Josiah,*[4] *John,*[3] *Hananiah,*[2] *Thomas*[1]), son of Josiah, Jr., and Hannah (Gardner) Parker, was b. in Woburn, July 20, 1798; m.

April 13, 1826, Nabby Thompson, sister of Gen. Thompson of Woburn. She was b. Jan. 20, 1803, the dau. of Major Abijah and Lydia Thompson. Frederick Parker succeeded to his father's homestead in the west part of the town, where he lived until shortly before his death. He was a farmer, a hard working man; was very orderly, he had a place for everything and everything must be in its place. He was once drawn juror and held at various times such town offices as school committee and street surveyor. He d. in Woburn, June 24, 1853, aged 54 years, 10 months. She d. March 31, 1879, aged 76 years.

Their children were:

LYDIA THOMPSON PARKER, b. June 11, 1827; d. Dec. 14, 1847.

288. FREDERICK CHANDLER PARKER, b. Jan. 16, 1829; m. M. Affie Hanson.

JOSIAH PARKER, b. Aug. 18, 1830; d. Feb. 25, 1832.

289. JOSIAH PARKER, b. Oct. 25, 1832; m. Sarah B. Hanson. } Twins.

290. HANNAH MARIA PARKER, b. Oct. 25, 1832; m. Walter Wellington. } Twins.

291. BETSEY FIDELIA PARKER, b. June 7, 1836; m. George Russell of Somerville.

292. MARTHA ANN PARKER, b. May 24, 1841; m. Joseph B. McDonald.

116. Benjamin Parker, Jr. *(Benjamin,[6] Josiah,[5] Josiah,[4] John,[3] Hananiah,[2] Thomas[1])*, son of Benjamin and Mehetable (Tidd) Parker, was b. in Woburn, Aug. 26, 1780. He m. 1801, Sally Allen, b. in Lincoln, Feb., 1780, the dau. of Phineas and Sally (Danforth) Allen. He removed after marriage to Fitchburg, where two of his children were born and removed afterwards to Harvard. Benjamin Parker was of medium height, had black hair and blue eyes and was called very handsome. But his life was short, as he died suddenly of bilious fever in the summer of 1806. He was a tanner and currier. She d. in Harvard, April 26. 1866, aged 86 years.

Their children were:

SALLY PARKER, b. Oct. 20, 1801; m. Sylvanus Jorden of Roxbury. He was a shoe manufacturer. She d. March, 1831, aged 29 years. He m. again.

293. Dorothy Flagg Parker, b. Jan. 2, 1804; m. Ephraim Barnard of Harvard.

294. Mehetable Parker, b. March 17, 1806; m. Jan. 19, 1830, Thomas Cummings of Hollis, N. H.

117. Dea. Joseph Parker *(Benjamin,[6] Josiah,[5] Josiah,[4] John,[3] Hananiah,[2] Thomas[1])*, son of Benjamin and Mehetable (Tidd) Parker, was b. in Woburn, June 8, 1782; m. Dec. 30, 1805, Betsey Richardson, b. Sept., 1788, the dau. of Josiah and Relief Richardson. For some time before his marriage he was connected with Tewksbury and was a resident of that town in 1805. He lived upon the West Side, was a shoemaker, a business in which many of his Woburn relatives became associated. He was blessed with a strong physique and was a highly respected citizen. He was very attentive to his family and a consistent christian. He was connected with the Church in Woburn, being a Universalist deacon. In the second burial-ground is his grave and gravestone epitaph which reads:

"In Memory of Dea. Joseph Parker,
who died Jan. 10, 1833, Æt 51.

"Blest is the man whose tender care
Relieves the poor in their distress,
Whose pity wipes the widow's tear,
Whose hand supports the fatherless.
We hear thy groans with deep surprise
And view thy wounds with weeping eyes.
Each bleeding wound, each dying groan
With anguish filled with pains unknown."

His widow Betsey d. in Woburn "of cholera,"* Sept. 21, 1855, aged 68 years and 10 months, thus she was b. in Sept., 1788.

Their children were:

Eliza Richardson Parker, b. Aug. 27, 1808; m. Warren Fox of Woburn.

Nathan Parker, b. Oct. 7, 1809; resides in Woburn, unm.

Mary Leathe Parker, b. March 10, 1811; m. in Woburn, May 29, 1828, Samuel Butters of Woburn. They had a dau. Mary

*Town records.

Isabell Butters, who d. of consumption, Dec. 20, 1860, aged 22 years, 7 months. The mother, Mary L. (Parker) Butters, d. Sept. 1, 1867, aged 56 years, 5 months.

PATTY PARKER, b. Oct. 12, 1812; m. March 4, 1834, Oliver H. Parker of Woburn. (See No. 283, page 224.)

295. JOSEPH ADDISON PARKER, b. July 7, 1815; m. (1) Rebecca J. Cutler of Woburn, (2) Emily Huse of Woburn.

296. ANN PARKER, b. Oct. 23, 1816; m. Elijah Marion of Burlington.

297. BENJAMIN PARKER, b. Jan. 25, 1820; m. Mary Waite of Woburn.

RUTH PARKER; d. 1874, unm.

118. Samuel Parker *(Benjamin,[6] Josiah,[5] Josiah,[4] John,[3] Hananiah,[2] Thomas[1])*, son of Benjamin and Mehetable (Tidd) Parker, was b. in Woburn, Dec. 23, 1784; m. in Fitchburg, 1804, Lydia Thurston Allen, b. in Fitchburg, Aug. 28, 1785, dau. of Phineas and Dorothy (Wooley) Allen of Lincoln. She was the oldest child of a third wife, and upon her birth was given to her aunt, Mrs. Thurston of Fitchburg, in whose house she was born. She always lived with her aunt's people, who had no children of their own. When married to Samuel Parker the ceremony was conducted in the same room in which she was born. Here they lived for 16 years and here in the same noted room were the seven children born. Finally removing (May 3, 1820) to Chenango Co., N. Y. They settled in the town of Otselic, where five more children were born to them. Samuel Parker was a joiner. In Fitchburg he was constable and collector. He belonged to the Fitchburg military company during the time of the War of 1812, but this company was not called out. He d. in Belvidere, Boone Co., Ill., Aug. 29, 1846. She d. Aug. 26, 1865.

Their children were:

298. SAMUEL THURSTON PARKER, b. in Fitchburg, June 11, 1805; m. Mary Bates.

BENJAMIN ALLEN PARKER, b. in Fitchburg, Dec. 31, 1806. He removed west. He m. and had children: Thomas A. Parker, Hosea Parker, and others.

299. LYDIA LUCRETIA PARKER, b. in Fitchburg, Oct. 4, 1808; m. William R. Orvis.

JOHN THOMAS PARKER, b. in Fitchburg, Oct. 27, 1810; removed with family to Otselic, N. Y.; m. Eunice Lindsay, b. in Milford, N. Y., Sept. 3, 1813, dau. of David and Jemime (Crane) Lindsay. He resides in Belvidere, Boon Co., Ill.

MARTHA ANN PARKER, b. in Fitchburg, Dec. 23, 1812; d. Dec. 25, 1812.

300. CHARLOTTE ELMIRA PARKER, b. in Fitchburg, June 8, 1814; m. William Wilbur.

HARRIET EMELINE PARKER, b. in Fitchburg, June 18, 1816; m. —— Miles. Children: Francis E. Miles, George B. Miles, and perhaps others.

301. FRANCIS EDWIN PARKER, b. in Fitchburg, May 3, 1819; m. Amanda M. Lindsay.

JOSEPH HENRY PARKER, b. in Otselic, N. Y., July 19, 1821; d. July 3, 1825.

302. ABIGAIL ELIZABETH PARKER, b. in Otselic, June 11, 1823; m. Dr. G. E. Lawrence.

303. ANN MARIA PARKER, b. in Otselic, Feb. 25, 1825; m. William Stover Wilcox of Smyrna, N. Y.

MARY ADALINE PARKER, b. in Otselic, Oct. 5, 1827; d. at age of 16.

DOROTHY CAROLINE PARKER, b. in Otselic, Aug. 3, 1832; m. —— Wegors, and had a dau., now Caroline (Wegors) Reed. The family reside in Herbert, Boon Co., Ill.

119. Mehetable Parker *(Benjamin,[6] Josiah,[5] Josiah,[4] John,[3] Hananiah,[2] Thomas[1])*, son of Benjamin and Mehetable (Tidd) Parker, was b. in Woburn, Oct. 23, 1786; m. in Woburn, Nov. 8, 1810, Major Francis Johnson, the son of Francis and Abigail (Brooks) Johnson of Woburn. He belonged to the military company of the town and had the title of Major, by which he was known. His brother was Nathan Johnson, who m. a sister of Mehetable Parker, and who also lived in Winchester, then Woburn. He was a blacksmith and d. of numb palsy, Nov. 16, 1846, aged 75 years.

Their children were:

1. FRANCIS JOHNSON, b. April 18, 1813; m. June 7, 1839, Elizabeth Monroe of Lexington. They were fourth cousins. From page 75 her ancient Monroe and Parker ancestry can be traced. They lived in Woburn, now Winchester. He was a blacksmith. He d. in Winchester, June 16, 1876. She resides in Lexington. Child:

I. ELIZABETH JOHNSON, b. in Winchester, Sept. 19, 1841; resides in Lexington.

2. BETSEY JOHNSON, b. Aug. 15, 1815; m. in S. Woburn (now Winchester), May 19, 1836, Samuel Martin Rice of Nahant, son of Jesse and Sally (Colman) Rice. They lived in Lynn and Winchester. He was a merchant and selectman. She d. in Winchester, April, 1856. He d. in Worcester, 1869, aged 54. Children:

I. SARAH ELIZABETH RICE, b. in Lynn, March 7, 1837; m. Henry C. Whitten of Winchester, and they have had six children.

II. ELLEN LOUISE RICE, b. in Woburn, Dec. 3, 1839; m. Albert Lane of Winchester. They have had four children.

III. CHARLES CUSHING RICE, b. in Woburn, Oct. 6, 1842; m. He went to Chicago, Ill., in 1866, and 1888 settled upon a ranch in Martinsdale, Mont., where he now resides.

IV. FRANK INMAN RICE, b. in Winchester, Sept. 6, 1851; d. in Chicago, Ill., Feb., 1875.

3. MEHETABLE JOHNSON, b. Oct. 23, 1824; m. Hon. Robert C. Cristy of Johnson, Vt., whose occupation is farming, but has been also selectman, assessor, representative, State Senator and county commissioner. They reside in Johnson, Vt., and have one son:

I. CHARLES CLARK CRISTY.

4. WARREN JOHNSON, b. Aug. 27, 1827; m. (1) Hannah Caroline, b. in Winchester, Feb. 15, 1830, d. April 21, 1882, dau. of Marshall Wyman and wife Susanna Parker, the dau. of Nathan Parker of Woburn. He m. (2) Oct. 8, 1885, Agnes, b. in Winchester, Aug. 27, 1843, dau. of William and Judith M. (Barker) Wescott of Winchester. Mr. Johnson has been selectman seven years and assessor four years. He resides in Winchester. Child:

I. MARY AGNES JOHNSON, b. Oct. 8, 1863; d. May 15, 1881.

Patty Parker (see page 144) *(Benjamin,[6] Josiah,[5] Josiah,[4] John,[3] Hananiah,[2] Thomas[1])*, dau. of Benjamin and Mehetable (Tidd) Parker, was b. in Woburn, June 11, 1789; d. Nov. 14, 1811, aged 22. Gravestone epitaph:

Sacred to the Memory of
Miss PATTY PARKER Dautr. of
Mr. Benjamin & Mrs. Mehetabel Parker
Who died Nov. 14, 1811, Æt 22.

"Taught in the Schools of Christ with Humble Mind
She breathed her last and left the world resigned.
Tis His to call our relations away,
Tis ours in sweet submission to obey."

120. Almira Parker (*Benjamin*,[6] *Josiah*,[5] *Josiah*,[4] *John*,[3] *Hananiah*,[2] *Thomas*[1]), dau. of Benjamin and Mehetable (Tidd) Parker, was b. in Woburn, Sept. 20, 1790; m. in Woburn, Nov. 2, 1819, Nathan Brooks Johnson, brother of Francis and son of Francis and Abigail (Brooks) Johnson of Woburn. He was a blacksmith and lived in Woburn, in the part which is now Winchester. He was deacon and selectman and d. June 28, 1871. She d. Jan. 12, 1879.

The children were all b. in Woburn:

1. ALMIRA JOHNSON, b. July 26, 1821; m. in Woburn, Sept. 19, 1844, Stephen Hall Cutter of Woburn, b. in S. Woburn, April 4, 1821, son of Stephen and Adeline (Wyman) Cutter. He is a lumber dealer and resides in Winchester. She d. Oct. 5, 1881. Child:
   1. ARTHUR HENRY CUTTER, b. Dec. 31, 1849; d. Oct. 7, 1851.
2. MARY JOHNSON, b. Jan. 26, 1823; resides in W. Medford, unm.
3. HARRIETT NEWALL JOHNSON, b. Oct. 4, 1829; d. Sept. 23, 1858, unm.
4. EDWARD PAYSON JOHNSON, b. Dec. 4, 1837; m. in Winthrop, June 1, 1865. Eliza S. Long, b. in Plymouth, Vt., July 29, 1840, dau. of Daniel and Eliza (Shewell) Long, both natives of Hartford Co., Maryland. He was a manufacturer of saddlery hardware. Resided in Montpelier, Vt. Child:
   1. ALFRED EDWARD CUTTER JOHNSON, b. in Montpelier, Sept. 29, 1882.

   The family were all together in a summer sojourn to the Vineyard and returned in the fatal car from which few lives escaped in the memorable railroad accident at Quincy, Mass., Aug. 19, 1890. Mr. and Mrs. Johnson were immediately killed and the son only lingered for a few hours, dying at the Quincy hospital. The family were well known and very highly respected in Montpelier, and their untimely and terrible death in this manner was a shock to their many friends, which is better imagined than described. The family were the only living descendants of Almira Parker and Nathan B. Johnson of Woburn. Thus this branch of the Parker-Johnson families became extinct. F. J. Johnson of Montpelier, a relative who accompanied the family on their summer trip, was also killed.

5. MARTHA ANN JOHNSON, b. Nov. 14, 1841; d. Jan. 6, 1878, unm.

121. Anna Parker (*Benjamin,[6] Josiah,[5] Josiah,[4] John,[3] Hananiah,[2] Thomas[1]*), son of Benjamin and Mehetable (Tidd) Parker, was b. in Woburn, Sept. 9. 1791; m. in Woburn, March 14, 1811, Joshua Swan Robbins of W. Cambridge, now Lexington. He was b. May 25, 1785, third child of a family of 15 children, the parents being Philemon and Sarah Swan Robbins of Lexington. He lived in Arlington; was a beef and poultry raiser: d. in Lexington, Aug. 3, 1817, where he is buried. She d. in Woburn while upon a visit to her father, July 30, 1814, aged 23 years.

Their children were:

I. JOHN ROBBINS, b. Aug. 3, 1811. After the early decease of his parents he went to live in the family of Dea. Joseph Parker of Woburn, his uncle, and there grew up as one of the family, becoming strongly attached to them. He m. Susan Allen Simonds, b. in Hillsborough, N. H., April 1, 1819, dau. of Daniel and Susan (White) Simonds. They reside in Woburn. Children:

I. JOHN WILLIAM ROBBINS, b. Nov. 26, 1837; shoemaker and musician; m. Mary S., dau. of Haskell and Mary (Dean) Bancroft of Woburn. He has three children:

1. Mary Alice Robbins; resides in Woburn.
2. William Byron Robbins; resides in Woburn.
3. Ida Robbins; resides in Woburn.

II. CHARLOTTE ANN ROBBINS, b. June 19, 1840; m. Joseph J. Knox of New Hampshire. He is a carpenter. They reside in Woburn and have children:

1. Lottie Lillian Knox.
2. Walter Knox.
3. Ethel Knox.

III. FRANK HARVEY ROBBINS, b. Jan. 10, 1849; m. Laura P. Weston, dau. of Asa Weston of S. Boston. He is

Assistant Bond Clerk, U. S. Custom House, Boston. They have children:

1. Cora May Robbins.
2. Susie White Robbins.
3. Bertha Phebe Robbins.
4. Florence Robbins.

IV. FRED SWAN ROBBINS, b. Feb. 3, 1858; unm.; is a musician at the Boston Theatre.

2. ANNA ROBBINS, b. in 1813; d. at age of 5 years, and was buried from her uncle's, Joseph Parker's, of Woburn, Jan. 23, 1819.

122. Lydia Parker *(Benjamin,[6] Josiah,[5] Josiah,[4] John,[3] Hananiah,[2] Thomas[1])*, dau. of Benjamin and Mehetable (Tidd) Parker, was b. in Woburn, Aug. 15, 1796; m. Nov. 15, 1814, Benjamin Wyer, b. in Woburn, May 19, 1790, the son of Edward and Lucy (Eaton) Wyer, who were m. March 20, 1788. Edward Wyer was probably from Charlestown, where his ancestor, Edward Wyer, from whom all of the name in America are descended, settled after coming from Scotland. He was a tailor; m. in 1648 to Elizabeth Johnson, and d. in Charlestown in 1693.

Benjamin Wyer was a bootmaker; lived in Woburn but finally removed to Lexington where he d. Lydia (Parker) Wyer d. in Woburn, Sept. 9, 1840, aged 44 years.

Their only child was:

1. BENJAMIN FRANKLIN WYER, b. in Woburn, Dec. 28, 1816; m. Nov. 24, 1842, Sarah Brown Page. He was a bootmaker and storekeeper, and d. in Woburn, Jan. 19, 1884, aged 67 years and 22 days. His wife was the sixth of a family of ten, was b. in Nashua, N. H., Feb. 2, 1822, the dau. of John and Lucy (Fitch) Page, natives of Bedford. Lucy Fitch was dau. of Dea. Moses Fitch of Bedford. Sarah B. Page Wyer resides in Woburn. Children:

I. LYDIA ANNETTE WYER, b. in Woburn, Jan. 5, 1846; d. Sept. 20, 1847.

II. SARAH ALLEN WYER, b. in Woburn, July 31, 1849; resides in Woburn.

Benjamin Wyer (son of Edward) had a brother, George Wyer, of Woburn, whose sons, Charles Wyer and Edward Francis Wyer, with their families reside in Woburn.

123. Charlotte Parker *(Benjamin,[6] Josiah,[5] Josiah,[4] John,[3] Hananiah,[2] Thomas[1])*, son of Benjamin and Mehetable (Tidd) Parker, was b. in Woburn, May 3, 1801; m. (1) Oct. 2, 1823, in Woburn. Royal Caldwell, then of Woburn. They lived in Burlington where he was a mechanic. She m. (2) March 25, 1845, Nathan Buck of Wilmington, now deceased and buried in Wilmington. She d. in Woburn, Dec. 23, 1871, and was buried in Woburn.

Her child was:

1. Calvin Caldwell, b. 1824; d. Dec. 31, 1841, at the age of 17 years.

124. Fanny Parker *(Benjamin,[6] Josiah,[5] Josiah,[4] John,[3] Hananiah,[2] Thomas[1])*, son of Benjamin and Mehetable (Tidd) Parker, was b. in Woburn, July 22, 1803; m. Dec. 23, 1824, George Washington Butters, b. in Woburn, June 28, 1799, son of Willard and Sarah (Caldwell) Butters of Woburn. He was a bootmaker and after the birth of his family removed to Methuen.

All the children were b. in Woburn:

1. Fannie Maria Butters, b. June 20, 1826; deceased.
2. Martha Butters, b. May 11, 1828; d. Aug. 12, 1873, unm.
3. George Albert Butters, b. July 7, 1830.
4. William Henry Butters, b. Feb. 10, 1834; m. in Derry, N. H., Jan. 21, 1866, Lucinda Perkins Nickols, dau. of Woodburn and Eliza K. Nickols, b. in Derry, July 3, 1834. They reside in Methuen. He is a farmer. Child:
   - i. George Henry Butters, b. in Methuen, Nov. 7, 1870.
5. Charles Butters, b. May 3, 1836; m. in Haverhill, Oct. 1, 1856, Catherine A. Webster, b. in Lynn, June 24, 1832, dau. of William and Matilda Webster. Children:
   - i. Carrie Parker Butters, b. in Haverhill, April 28, 1857; m. Wm. M. Webster of Bradford. Child:
     - 1. Carl Howard Webster, b. July 1, 1884.
   - ii. Charles Sumner Butters, b. in Haverhill, Aug. 3, 1861; m. Harriet Chase. Child:
     - 1. Frederick Butters, b. June 20, 1885.
6. Lucy Parker Butters, b. April 30, 1838; d. April 30, 1841.

125. David Johnson Parker *(Edmund,[6] Josiah,[5] Josiah,[4] John,[3] Hananiah,[2] Thomas[1])*, son of Edmund and Lydia (Johnson) Parker, was b. in Woburn; m. in Woburn, Jan. 5, 1815, Rebecca Carter of Wilmington. He d. in Woburn, Feb. 12, 1830.

Their children were:

DAVID PARKER, b. 1815; d. in Woburn, Feb. 17, 1819, aged 3½ years.

LYDIA PARKER, b. March 11, 1818; d. in Woburn, July 3, 1871, aged 53 years, unm.

JAMES PARKER, b. Sept. 17, 1819; m. Oct. 18, 1846, Mary Ann Laethe. He d. in 1872. She resides in San Francisco, Cal.

MARY PARKER, b. Sept. 7, 1823; m. Charles Swan of Woburn.

—— —— b. [probably] April, 1824, and d. same month.*

ELIZABETH PARKER, b. Jan. 12, 1825; m. 1844, Thomas Rice of Charlestown, son of Thomas and Sarah Rice, b. March 25, 1822. Their dau. was:

i. MARY ELIZABETH RICE, b. 1848; lived to the age of 19 years, 11 months, 7 days. She was a school-teacher; besides was a handsome and very promising girl. In four days' sickness, however, she d. with the spinal meningitis *upon the day set for her marriage!* The mother's residence, if living, is unknown.

DAVID BRADLEY PARKER, b. June 13, 1828; m. He is somewhere in the west, if living.

126. Polly Parker *(Nathan,[6] Josiah,[5] Josiah,[4] John,[3] Hananiah,[2] Thomas[1])*, dau. of Nathan and Polly (Richardson) Parker, was b. in Woburn, March 23, 1794; m. in Woburn, Aug. 4, 1812, Joshua Reed, Jr., b. in Woburn, July 24, 1790, the son of Joshua and Ann Reed of Woburn. He was a shoe manufacturer. She d. Jan. 7, 1834, aged 40 years. He d. of consumption, July 9, 1844, aged 82 years.

Their children were:

1. MARY P. REED, b. April 21, 1813; m. May 30, 1833, Samuel G. Neville. She d. Dec. 30, 1881. Children:

   i. HENRIETTA NEVILLE, b. July 4, 1836; d. March 15, 1840.

   ii. LEWIS W. NEVILLE, b. Aug. 7, 1838; m. March 16, 1862, Harriett F. Stevens.

* This birth is inserted on account of an entry in the Woburn town records, which reads: "——, a child of David Parker died April, 1824."

III. MARIETTA NEVILLE, b. March 11, 1841; m. Oct. 20, 1879, John Fickett.

IV. CHARLES H. NEVILLE, b. July 20, 1847; m. April 4, 1871, Bessie M. Maddison. They have six children.

V. ELIZABETH NEVILLE, b. May 13, 1851; m. June 30, 1875, Samuel Tripp Eldridge. They have four children.

VI. ANNIE M. NEVILLE, b. Dec. 11, 1857.

2. MARIA REED, b. Feb. 9, 1814; d. Jan. 18, 1815.

3. JOSEPH REED, b. April 19, 1817; d. in the west.

4. MARIA REED, b. April 1, 1819; m. March 12, 1853, Luther E. Hinckley. He d. Nov. 18, 1869, aged 47 years. She survives him. Their dau. was:

I. JOSEPHINE SMITH HINCKLEY, b. June 9, 1858.

5. SARAH ANN REED, b. June 10, 1821; m. in Woburn, Dec. 15, 1844, Aaron Thompson, son of Aaron and Rhoda (Lamb) Thompson, b. in Peacham, Vt., Dec. 9, 1816. He was supt. of the Woburn Gas Light Co. from 1855 to 1887. He d. June 18, 1888. She resides in Woburn. Children:

I. CAROLINE W. THOMPSON, b. April 20, 1846.

II. FANNIE THOMPSON, b. Oct. 1, 1848.

III. KATIE THOMPSON, b. Jan. 10, 1852; m. Oct. 26, 1876, F. A. Winn. Their dau. was:

1. Dora A. Winn, b. July 1, 1878.

6. HARRIET REED, b. Aug. 7, 1824; m. Nov. 20, 1842, Joseph B. Sawtelle of Woburn. He d. in Woburn, May 14, 1890, aged 70 years, 8 months. She resides in Woburn. Children:

I. HARRIET ALICE SAWTELLE, b. Dec. 20, 1843; d. April 10, 1846.

II. HARRIET ALICE SAWTELLE, b. Jan. 31, 1846; m. Aug. 4, 1864, Fred G. King. They have two children and two grandchildren.

III. EMMA L. SAWTELLE, b. May 2, 1848; m. Dec. 23, 1872, William Davis.

IV. JOSEPH E. SAWTELLE, b. Feb. 23, 1851; m. May 8, 1876, Harriett Newell.

V. NELLIE E. SAWTELLE, b. Jan. 18, 1854; d. Sept. 24, 1855.

VI. NELLIE M. SAWTELLE, b. Feb. 21, 1857; m. Nov. 14, 1877, Charles Dexter Wade. They have had three children.

VII. FRANK A. SAWTELLE, b. March 8, 1864; d. July 31, 1864.

127. Maria Parker (*Nathan,[6] Josiah,[5] Josiah,[4] John,[3] Hananiah,[2] Thomas[1]*), dau. of Nathan and Polly (Richardson) Parker, was b. in Woburn, July 9, 1801; m. 1829, Simon Adams, b. in Carlisle, Nov. 4, 1796, son of Timothy and Joanna Keyes Adams. He was a trader. They lived in Lowell. He was one year a member of the Mass. House of Representatives. He d. in Lowell, Sept. 7, 1847. She d. in Concord, Jan. 19, 1861.

The children were b. in Lowell:

1. Clara Maria Adams, b. Aug. 3, 1830; resides in Boston.
2. Mary Julia Adams, b. July 9, 1833; m. in Concord, Aug. 21, 1856, Abel Gardner Heywood, b. in Concord, June 12, 1835, son of Abel B. and Eliza (Lawrence) Heywood. He was an innholder; d. in Concord, Feb. 9, 1873. She d. in Worcester, Nov. 17, 1885. Child:
    - i. Annie Maria Heywood, b. in Concord, Oct. 3, 1861; m. in Boston, Dec. 28, 1882, Charles Howard Webber, b. Sept. 20, 1857, son of Moses H. and Susan D. (Burgess) Webber. Their children were:
        - 1. Velina Briard Webber, b. in Boston, Sept. 24, 1883.
        - 2. Ruth Webber, b. in Winthrop, March 11, 1890.
3. Elizabeth Bartlett Adams, b. Aug. 12, 1836; m. in Charlestown, June 12, 1861, George, b. in Roxbury, Dec. 9, 1836, son of Elisha and Henrietta (Mayo) Tolman. They reside in Concord. Mr. Tolman is a journalist. He is also an experienced genealogist, having spent a share of his life in this research for the benefit of Concord families, of whose genealogy he is the best authority. Their children were:
    - i. Adams Tolman, b. in Boston, April 15, 1862; m. in Roxbury, June 6, 1888, Harriett L., dau. of Daniel L. Giles of Concord. Their son was:
        - 1. Edward Mayo Tolman, b. in Concord, June 3, 1890.
    - ii. Mary Mayo Tolman, b. in Concord, Oct. 8, 1863; d. in Northfield, Vt., July 31, 1866.
    - iii. William Nickols Tolman, b. in Dorchester, Nov. 2, 1867.
    - iv. Charles Edward Tolman, b. in Concord, Sept. 12, 1871.
    - v. James Henry Tolman, b. in Concord, Aug. 29, 1876.

128. Susanna Parker *(Nathan,⁶ Josiah,⁵ Josiah,⁴ John,³ Hananiah,² Thomas¹)*, dau. of Nathan and Polly (Richardson) Parker, was b. in Woburn, July 28, 1799; m. in Woburn, April 10, 1821, Marshall Wyman, b. in Woburn, July 11, 1792, deacon, son of Daniel and Hannah Wyman. They lived in Woburn. He d. July 10, 1869. She d. Nov. 3, 1876.

Their children, all b. in So. Woburn, now Winchester, were:

1. HENRY MARSHALL WYMAN, b. Oct. 3, 1823; m. Emma Palmer of Boston. He is deceased and she is living in California. Children:
   - I. HENRY PARKER WYMAN; d. in Arlington, aged 22.
   - II. CHARLES CROSBY WYMAN; resides in California.
   - III. FRED ROSWELL WYMAN; d. in Chicago, Ill., aged 21.
   - IV. HERBERT EDWARD WYMAN; resides in Chicago, Ill.
2. WILLIAM AUGUSTUS WYMAN, b. Sept. 25, 1825; m. Lucy Fairbanks of Boston. He is deceased and she resides in Brooklyn, N. Y., where her family live also. Children:
   - I. HELEN ELOISE WYMAN.
   - II. MARSHALL FAIRBANKS WYMAN.
   - III. MAUD WYMAN.
3. NATHAN PARKER WYMAN, b. Feb. 14, 1828; d. of typhus fever, Sept. 29, 1845, aged 17 years.
4. HANNAH CAROLINE WYMAN, b. Feb. 15, 1830; m. Warren Johnson of So. Woburn, b. Aug. 27, 1827, son of Major Francis and Mehetable (Parker) Johnson (No. 119. See page 229 for Warren Johnson.) She had one dau.:
   - I. MARY AGNES JOHNSON, b. Oct. 8, 1863; d. May 15, 1881. The mother d. in Winchester the year following, April 21, 1882.
5. ABIGAIL FISKE WYMAN, b. May 4, 1833; she is deceased.
6. MARY ELIZA WYMAN, b. Jan. 11, 1835; d. aged 24.
7. SUSAN ANN WYMAN, b. Feb. 14, 1838; d. Sept. 1, 1876.
8. CLARA MARIA WYMAN, b. April 19, 1840; resides in Arlington.

John Parker (see page 153) *(John,⁶ John,⁵ Josiah,⁴ John,³ Hananiah,² Thomas¹)*, son of John and Hannah (Stearns) Parker, was b. in Lexington, Oct. 12, 1786; m. at the residence of her brother, Leonard Greene, in W. Cambridge, Harriet Maria Greene, b. in Weston.

Their children were:

EMELINE AUGUSTA PARKER; m. —— Gilman; resides 112 Broadway, Chelsea. She has filled responsible positions. A treasured family relic, Capt. John Parker's family Bible, is in her preservation. It was printed in 1769 and contains records in Capt. John's strong and legible hand. Its cost was five pounds.

CAROLINE ELIZA PARKER; m. George W. Stearns. She resides in Brookline.

JOHN BROOKS PARKER; resides in Everett.

129. Hannah Parker (*John,[6] John,[5] Josiah,[4] John,[3] Hananiah,[2] Thomas[1]*), dau. of John and Hannah (Stearns) Parker, was b. in Lexington, March 15, 1791; m. March 15, 1811, Samuel Greene,* then of Brighton, but a native of Weston. Samuel Greene went to Burlington, Vt., in 1815, where he was soon joined by his wife and two children. She d. there, however, Oct. 1, 1815. Her oldest sister, Mary Parker, was previously sent for. She arrived in time to witness the sad funeral, and assisted the family as she could. The year following, June 25, 1816, she and Samuel Greene were married. "A more kind and affectionate mother-in-law children never had." He d. Dec. 5, 1818, and she with the only surviving son returned to Lexington, where she d. at the homestead in 1831.

Their children were:

1. COLUMBUS GREENE, b. Feb. 13, 1812; m. 1839, Martha Dow Webber, who was b. in Rumney, N. H., May 6, 1811, dau. of Benjamin, whose father, Benjamin Webber, was one of the three men who in 1756 bought land on the south side of Baker's river, and were the first settlers of what is now the town of Rumney, N. H. It has already been shown that when a child of three years he accompanied his mother to Vermont in her removal there in 1815. Mr. Greene has several faint recollections of the journey. Upon the death of his parents his mother-in-law was anxious to place him under her father's, John Parker's, care, and they returned to Lexington in 1819. Being the oldest of Mr. Parker's grandchildren he became associated during his youth with many of the brave patriots who composed his great-grandfather's, Capt. Parker's,

* It is supposed that the families by the name in America of Greene who spell the name with the e final are descended from the same common ancestor.

Columbus Greene.

military company, who fought so hard for the blessings of liberty which they finally attained, and to whose accounts of adventures he was very fond of listening. He was but two years younger than Theodore Parker, and with him and some of the other sons of John Parker he worked, played and studied. They were boys together upon the old Parker homestead, then as previously well filled with youthful activity and hope. In speaking of his grandfather, Mr. Greene says: "I will only add that he was all to me that my father could have been if he had lived, and often said he knew no difference between me and his own children, and he certainly never manifested any, and in his declining years expressed a desire that I should remain with him, but I was too young to take the responsibility and wisely declined. His influence over me was a great blessing, which I shall never forget."

It was with sad heart he left his grandfather in 1832 at the age of 20 to reside in Lowell, and at his first opportunity signed a temperance pledge. In process of time the anti-slavery movement began, and opposition was so great for a time that it was only safe for the leaders to hold their meetings for consideration in private. However, while yet young, he identified himself with the cause, and through all the years has been a true friend of the colored race.

As might be expected this man had other conscientious beliefs. At this time he was a decided Unitarian and active in advocating their views; "but," to quote him exactly, "finally decided that I would say no more upon the subject of religion pro or con; would lay aside all opinions for the time being and sincerely read the New Testament to learn what it taught as necessary to salvation, and that I would pray to God to help me to learn the truth, and this absorbed my attention for months, and the result was I became a christian and united with the First Baptist Church in Lowell. It was a new era in my life; I became active in Church work; finally consented to my pastor's request to hold meetings in different places which he considered profitable, and thus years passed."

Columbus Greene was ordained pastor of the Baptist Church in Colchester, Vt., June 11, 1840. He enjoyed his work there and preached with success for about six years, when his health failing he engaged in the manufacture of furniture. In 1847 he removed to Montgomery, Vt., and engaged in a mercantile business. In 1849 he was instrumental in forming a division of the New England Protective Union. He was soon afterward appointed postmaster at the centre of the town and held the office for a period of 25 years; also filled some town offices, and during the Civil war drew the State pay for the soldiers. Upon the breaking out of the war in 1861 he did his best, publicly and privately, by orations, writing and personal influence, to stir up the fires of patriotism and defend the heritage our fathers gave us. He was a leader in his town, a man whose ability and righteous example was felt by all, and his name will live as long in Montgomery as the town itself. In 1863 and '64 he represented the town in the legislature, and was also elected in 1865, but did not serve. For more than 20 years he had charge of the Division store without the least disagreement among the officers, and succeeded beyond all expectations. He removed to Cazenovia, N. Y., in 1875, but after a few years removed to Washington, D. C., where he passed the remaining years of his life with his son. He d. in Washington, D. C., Aug. 2, 1892. His remains rest in Rock Creek Cemetery near that city. The mother survives.

1. Rev. SAMUEL H. GREENE, D.D., his only son, was b. Dec. 25, 1825; expecting to continue in business with his father was m. April 23, 1866, to Lucia A. Buzzell, but in January, 1868, commenced a course of study with the ministry in view at Madison University, N. Y. Graduating from the college and theological seminary he was ordained pastor of the Baptist Church in Cazenovia, N. Y., June 24, 1875. In 1879 he accepted a call from the Calvary Baptist Church in Washington, D. C., and began his pastorate in December. He has now served this Church 13 years and has been prospered in his labors. During his pastorate more than 1,350 persons have united with this Church. It is the largest white Protestant Church in Washington, save one. Rev. Mr. Greene has been honored with the degree of Doctor of Divinity by Norwich University, Rochester University and Colgate University, and is a trustee of the Columbian University. He has one son:

   1. Samuel Harrison Greene, Jr.

2. HARRISON GREENE, b. Jan. 9, 1814; d. Feb. 23, 1818.
3. SAMUEL PARKER GREENE, b. Sept. 16, 1815; d. Oct. 7, 1815.

130. Lydia Parker (*John,[6] John,[5] Josiah,[4] John,[3] Hananiah,[2] Thomas[1]*), dau. of John and Hannah (Stearns)

Mr. and Mrs. Isaac Parker.

Parker, was b. in Lexington, July 1, 1793; m. July 20, 1815, Isaac Herrick of Brighton. He was a butcher. He d. in Brighton.

Their children were:

1. LYDIA HERRICK, b. in Cambridge, June 9, 1817; m. in Brighton, Oct. 5, 1847, George Herrick (her cousin). Children:
   - I. ELLA P. HERRICK, b. May 31, 1852; m. in Everett, Benjamin H. Horne, Jr., son of Benjamin H. and Hannah H. (Cutter) Horne, b. in Brooklyn, N. Y., July 25, 1853. The children, all b. in Malden, were:
     1. Charles H. Horne, b. June 24, 1879.
     2. George B. Horne, b. July 27, 1883.
     3. Herbert P. Horne, b. March 7, 1887.
   - II. GEORGIANNA HERRICK, b. Dec. 25, 1855; d. Jan. 6, 1856.
2. JOHN ISAAC HERRICK, b. in Cambridge, Sept. 21, 1819; m. in Boston, Sept. 15, 1844, Rebecca Marsh of Boston, b. in Boston, Jan. 24, 1821, dau. of Joseph and Tryphosa C. (Parker) Marsh. He is a physician; resides in Marston, Wis. Their children were:
   - I. JOHN WILKINS HERRICK, b. in Detroit, Mich., Aug. 16, 1845.
   - II. SARAH PARKER HERRICK, b. in Detroit, Mich., Feb. 19, 1847; m. in New Lisbon, Wis., Sept. 16, 1875, ——— Whittemore. Their child was:
     1. Ethelwyn Whittemore, b. in Kansas City, Mo., June 7, 1879.

131. Isaac Parker (*John,[6] John,[5] Josiah,[4] John,[3] Hananiah,[2] Thomas[1]*), son of John and Hannah (Stearns) Parker, was b. in Lexington, Nov. 5, 1798; m. 1829, Martha M. Miller, b. in Hillsborough, N. H., June 29, 1801, dau. of James Miller (a native of Hillsbourgh; farmer, mason and miller), and wife Ann Macolley, who had ten children in Hillsborough, nine daughters and one son. Isaac Parker first drove the stage from Waltham to Boston, which he continued until 1832, when he returned to Lexington. He assisted his father in his declining years and settled on the old homestead. He was a farmer, knew also the trade of his ancestors, woodworking. He made many farm implements. He did a good business at pumpmaking.

Isaac Parker was esteemed as a man of character and a gentleman. He was assessor of the town of Lexington during the years 1846, '47, '48 and '50. He was slight but tall in stature, and lived to a ripe old age.

The mother (1892), in her ninety-second year, still resides at the old Parker homestead, a lady of remarkable industry and ability for one of her age. Her health is perfect, and her presence is a great blessing to the many visitors which the historical spot attracts. Her visitors' register contains many hundred names. Their first two children were born in Waltham and the remainder in Lexington. Their children were:

ISAAC MOORE PARKER, b. Nov. 10, 1829; d. about 1872.

304. MARTHA ANN PARKER, b. June 16, 1831; m. William W. Dingee of York, Pa.

FRANCES MARIA PARKER, b. Jan. 21, 1833; was a teacher.

CHARLES M. PARKER, b. Feb. 15, 1835; resides upon the homestead in Lexington. He enlisted from Lexington in the 24th Regiment in Aug., 1862, for three years, which he served in the Civil war. It is he who stands in the foreground in the picture, "The Lexington Parker Homestead."

JAMES THEODORE PARKER, b. Sept. 18, 1837; d. April 2, 1838.

EMILY R. PARKER, b. April 7, 1839; d. Aug. 6, 1858.

THEODORE JAMES PARKER, b. April 21, 1841. He resided upon the homestead in Lexington, where he d. unm., June 20, 1892, aged 54 years, 2 months.

GEORGE E. PARKER, b. Jan. 2, 1843; d. Oct. 6, 1857.

132. Hiram Stearns Parker *(John,[6] John,[5] Josiah,[4] John,[3] Hananiah,[2] Thomas[1])*, son of John and Hannah (Stearns) Parker, was b. in Lexington, Jan. 16, 1803; m. in Lexington, Jan. 1, 1828, Nancy Leavitt, b. in Amherst, N. H., April 7, 1803, dau. of Andrew and Elizabeth Leavitt of Amherst. They lived in Lowell, where he was a carpenter and builder. He d. in Lowell, Jan., 1852. She d. in Lowell, Feb. 22, 1889. Their children were:

305. ABIGAIL ANNA PARKER, b. Aug. 24, 1828; m. Charles William Rea of Hereford, P. Q.

THEODORE HENRY PARKER, b. Nov. 4, 1833; d. June 5, 1891.

EMMA FRANCES PARKER; resides in Lowell.

306. CHARLES LEAVITT PARKER, b. Aug. 1, 1839; m. Minnie Barker of Lowell.

307. SUSAN WEATHERBEE PARKER, b. Nov. 24, 1841; m. Col. George Edgar Wentworth of Lowell.

133. Theodore Parker (*John*,[6] *John*,[5] *Josiah*,[4] *John*,[3] *Hananiah*,[2] *Thomas*[1]), son of John and Hannah (Stearns) Parker, was b. in Lexington, Aug. 24, 1810, the youngest in a family of 11 children.

> "Let us do our duty in our shop or our kitchen, the market, the street, the office, the school, the house, just as faithfully as if we stood in the first rank of some great battle, and we knew that victory for mankind depended on our bravery, strength and skill."—*Theodore Parker.*

Theodore Parker, the distinguished American rationalistic preacher and social reformer, as a boy was richly endowed both intellectually and physically. At a very tender age he began to show a remarkable moral feeling and curiosity, which constantly grew as he increased in years. As has been shown, his father, John Parker, was an enterprising man of strong intellect as well as a prosperous farmer and mechanic; was studious, thoughtful and progressive; he was ahead of the age in which he lived.

Theodore's mother, Hannah (Stearns) Parker, was as remarkable in her way as the father was in his. She was an entertaining, poetic, loving, and very practical woman. She took great interest in the moral culture of her children. Conscience was her guide, gratitude and trust were interpreters to her of the ways of Providence.

Theodore began going to school when nearly six years old. He was distinguished as a scholar by his constant thirst for knowledge. In childhood he learned by heart and retained many pages of poetry, and knew at ten years of age the names of all the trees and plants familiar to Massachusetts. The plain district school-house was a mile distant by road, but was brought nearer by a short cut across the field and over the brook. Through the efforts of his father to secure good instructors, William Hoar White began teaching in 1820. He took home evening lessons which he always learned and wanted more. At the age of ten Mr. White led

NOTE. In parts of this sketch I have been materially assisted by both Rev. O. B. Frothingham's and John Weiss's authentic biographies of Rev. Theodore Parker, and by a masterly article from the pen of Rufus Leighton, Esq., 30 Pemberton Sq., Boston, written expressly for this genealogy. He is one of those still living who knew the great reformer well. THE AUTHOR.

him past the prescribed line of study and started him in Latin and Greek. A desire for verse-making attacked him when eight years old. His first composition on "The Starry Heavens" disappointed his teacher by being too short. The district school was open during the winter months only. He was all the time a devoted and constant reader. He read miscellaneously and everything. The extent of his reading was astonishing. Whatever the schoolmaster could lend, whatever the social or town library afforded, he devoured. The father brought home nothing that the boy did not appropriate. If the cautious parent put a volume away on a high shelf, judging it for some reason unfit for youthful eyes, the eyes espied it, and the hands reached it the instant the workshop absorbed the parental form. Before he was eight he had read the translations of Homer and Plutarch, Rollin's Ancient History and all the other volumes of history and poetry that circumstances afforded. His marvellously retentive memory, an inheritance from his mother, and which he later in life treasured and kept bright with diligent care, enabled him to remember all he had read and all the impressions which his active mind received. He was always studying in school and out. In the summer noons when others indulged in peaceful repose under the trees he refreshed his mind with books. The winter evenings and the summer mornings were long and the hours were faithfully used. At the academy he went through Colburn's Algebra in three weeks. The tuition for one term in this institute, Huntington's Lexington School, was four dollars. This was afforded by his self-denial in foregoing the accomplishment of dancing, which the boys and girls of his age were cultivating, in view of social festivities that were the ruling passion about that time. Between the culture of the two extremities, Theodore, on consideration, chose that of the head. In the humbler virtues of toil and economy his whole life was a school. He left no time for idleness, but he seemed to find time for everything. Whether in the field or in the workshop he studied Latin, Greek and mental philosophy. Nor were his studies confined to books. The stars interested him; the trees, the shrubs, the flowers of the neighborhood, the plants in cultivated gardens he visited, the foreign fruits he saw in the Boston market when sent there annually with the peach crop, all attracted his attention. The formation of the hills, their direction and slope; the minerals, rocks and stones that lay about, or those that were brought from a distance excited his curiosity. This constant thirst for knowledge of natural objects began in mere childhood. He strove to satisfy it every time an opportunity offered. He made it a rule to "explore a subject when curiosity is awake," and when unable to do so he noted the subject in his "Common Place Book" for future research.

He had his mother's aptitude for committing verses; could repeat a song from hearing it once, the Sunday hymn while the minister read it. He could carry several hundred lines in his memory so as to recite them at a sitting. In mature years, when his mind was burdened with stores, he could appropriate as many as a hundred and fifty lines of blank verse after a single reading. The gift of expression came to him as readily as the gift of acquisition. He had the political events of the country on his tongue's end while yet a schoolboy, and talked so intelligently about them that the political gossips of the town, assembled in Dudley's Tavern, often drew him out for the sake of hearing his opinion. At seventeen militia duties began and in these he was as active, prompt and efficient as in all the rest. There was always a touch of war-like spirit in him. The military reputation of the ancestor who was at Lexington Common and chafed under inaction at Bunker Hill was dear to his heart. He rose to rank in the company, clerk he certainly was, perhaps lieutenant.

He began his career of teaching at the early age of seventeen. The first winter, that of 1827, he took charge of the district school in Quincy; the second in North Lexington; the third in Concord; and the fourth in Waltham. He worked upon the farm during the summer, performing all kinds of farm work, helping his broad-shouldered father in his shop (the old Lexington belfry) mending wheels, repairing wagons, making pumps, wooden screws and wooden rakes with no less joy than he studied. He worked as if toil was his whole occupation; he studied as if study was his whole delight.

The day before his twentieth birthday, in August, 1830, he went away, telling no one whither he was going. His father had given him leave of absence from morning till night. Theodore walked to Cambridge (eight miles), was examined, passed examination, walked home and told his father, who had already retired for the night, that he had entered Harvard College. If the venerable parent wondered in the morning where his son was going, he wondered more at night on learning where he had been. "But, Theodore, I can not afford it." "Father, it shall cost you nothing. I will stay at home and keep up with my class." And this he did for a year, working on the farm as usual, and going over to Cambridge for his examination only.

Theodore opened a private school in Watertown in the spring of 1832. During the first year the scholars numbered 35. Subsequently it increased to 54. The charge was not high, five dollars a quarter, but rather than turn a deserving boy or girl away because the modest fee could not be paid, he would take the applicant gratis, and bestow as much care on him or her as on all the rest. Religion was the first interest with him; he was unhappy if he could not make his schoolboys feel its power and charm. He made the trees, flowers, birds and animals his texts as he rambled with the boys in the woods. He encouraged a thirst for general knowledge among his pupils, while he entertained them with unlimited information. He had a way of making scholars answer their own questions and remove their own difficulties, such as only complete masters of their art possess. During this time he also pursued his botanical studies. He walked to Cambridge and to Charlestown every Saturday afternoon for instruction in Hebrew.

In April, 1834, he took up a theological course at the Cambridge Divinity School. Here there was a chance for him to exercise his intellectual powers as much as he desired. He studied 14 hours a day. He met his expenses partly by teaching five private pupils in addition to his studies. He not only followed the usual course of study at the college, but made acquaintance with a large number of languages, including Hebrew, Chaldee, Syriac, Arabic, Coptic, Ethiopic, as well as the classical and the modern principal European languages, which last he learned to speak fluently. His power of getting at the secret of a language was wonderful. Hebrew he himself taught to a class of collegians. "The Swedish language is easy," he wrote, "and I expect to get much amusement and instruction from it. The Danish presents more difficulties than Swedish, and I shall not study it extensively, but soon make it give place to some other." The Russian he mastered sufficient to become acquainted with the dialect used by the priests. The German furnished him rich material for thought in theology and mental philosophy. He applied serious work to the Anglo-Saxon alphabet and on the derivation of the Celtic and Gothic tongues. He studied the rudiments of the ancient, the Indian and the heathen religions. Constantly adding to his immense store of knowledge, Theodore was looked upon by his fellow-students as "a prodigious athlete in his studies." His journal, which he commenced in 1835, and kept through life, throws a little light on the marvellous extent of his researches at this period. During the two months of November and December of that year the names of 65 volumes are given as having been read. Some were in German, others in Latin, Danish, Greek and including Dr. Channing's essay on slavery, which was an important seed, perhaps, of the tree which spread so widely in ten years. "At this time," writes his biographer, Rev. O. B. Frothingham, "Theodore's power of speech and of moral feeling was attracting attention. He was the best debater, though not the best writer, in the school; always speaking vigorously and to the point with an independence of thought, an enthusiasm of manner and a freshness that gave promise of greater pulpit power than was at first displayed."

After his year was up at the college Theodore prepared his mind for the great work which he from boyhood had craved to perform. He began preaching in Watertown to his old friends and neighbors with a success that surprised those who had heard only of his prodigious feats of learning. For several months he was a travelling minister, at first for a month in Barnstable, then in Northfield and Greenfield. Later he interested congregations in Portland, Lowell and Billerica. In

June, 1837, he accepted an offer of a pastorate in West Roxbury. While at Watertown he became superintendent of the Sunday-School. Among the teachers of the school was Miss Lydia Cabot, the only daughter of John Cabot of Newton. She resided with an aunt in Boston, but was boarding in Watertown at this time. An attachment grew up between them and they were married three years later, April 20, 1837. They settled on Spring Street. He lived very happily, diligently preaching and pursuing his studies and researches. In the pleasant weather he was much out of doors, planting and trimming in his garden. He took long walks, visiting Boston and the neighboring towns on foot, doing his ten, fifteen and twenty miles a day without fatigue. In summer his pedestrian exploits would have tasked the vigor of any but a very strong man. He once journeyed from New York to Boston on foot, making about 30 miles a day. He walked easily through the White Mountains, ascending Mount Washington from the Notch and back the same day, and starting off the next morning for Franconia. His healthy exercise, his mirthfulness, social temperament and the variety of his studies saved him from the oppression of overwork. He made weekly, even daily plans for his work, both physical and mental.

Up to this time he was only known as the promising Unitarian Minister of West Roxbury, whose congregation were delighted with his interesting sermons. But from his early boyhood he appears to have settled instinctively in his mind some of the vexing points of theology, and decided against the worst dogmas of the Orthodox Church. His future studies and researches strengthened this conviction and opened to him a boundless field of labor, requiring the highest character, the most inflexible determination, the firmest courage and endless self-denial on the part of who so might engage in it. Millions of men were to be emancipated from a belief in the terrible doctrines set forth by Calvin and his successors, which made their lives miserable and their future a matter of doubt, and brought under the benign influence of a form of religion which recognized God not as a capricious, malignant and revengeful being, but as the Father and Mother of us all, infinite in love, justice and mercy, and perfect in all his attributes; and which consisted not in observance of forms and belief in creeds, but in love to God and man. Others, also, who had discarded the Orthodox theology and had no settled belief in any form of religion, were to be shown that there was something better than the churches had hitherto offered for their spiritual help and guidance.

Gradually he came to the conviction that he must enter this field and this was to be his life-work. In 1837, not long after his settlement as minister of the Church at West Roxbury, he wrote two sermons on "The Historical, Scientific and Moral Contradictions of the Bible," and kept them in his desk for more than a year before he dared to preach them, and then did so with much doubt as to the result.

At a convention called in Groton in 1840 by Come-outers and Second Adventists, he said in a speech, that we must come back to what Jesus demanded, not a belief, but a life,—a life of love to God and love to man, and set forth distinctly the difference between mere dogmas and rational religion.

In 1841 he preached the famous South Boston sermon on the "Transient and Permanent in Christianity," which brought matters to a crisis between him and the Unitarian clergy. With few exceptions they turned upon him, refused him fellowship and declined to exchange pulpits with him. A torrent of opposition and abuse was poured out upon him from the press and the pulpit. But the opposition only served to make him more brave, to increase his zeal and determination. Although debarred from the aid or the encouraging helping hand from any of his brother ministers, he boldly took the reformer's stand against the religious shams and the social evils of the time; moreover, he was bound to overthrow them.

In the autumn of that year he delivered five lectures in Boston upon "Matters pertaining to Religion," in which he elaborated fully his ideas of God, of man, the relation between them, the Bible, the prevailing theology, and other matters collateral to these. He set forth freely, with great clearness and vigor, in his pulpit and the lecture room, the new views which had caused such an outcry, and gradually his hearers increased and his influence widened.

Theodore Parker was a natural reformer. The best blood

of New England ran in his veins. He inherited those lofty and sterling qualities which characterized his ancestors for many generations back, to which were added others peculiar to himself, not less lofty and admirable. By birth, by early training, by circumstances which compelled him to habits of industry and hard labor, by education and self-development in various forms, combined with his wonderful faculty for assimilating knowledge of all kinds, his keenness of conscience, his tenderness of heart and sympathy with the oppressed and suffering, his moral courage and unconquerable desire to enlist in their behalf and his marvellous ability to bring to bear his vast learning and scholarship in fighting their battles,—he was eminently fitted to engage in those great works of reform in which he labored so zealously and incessantly, and in which he achieved such grand success.

He was very open spoken at all times, and was too much self-sacrificed to his cause to fear the rebuke which popular opinion must give him. He was never backward to denounce forcibly any and all evils of Church and society; on the contrary he believed it effective and practiced it regardless of consequences. It was thus that he acquired his most stubborn enemies. One sentence from his first sermon in Melodian Hall shows us how he so easily achieved the commendation of the common people, but at the same time drew upon himself the strong enmity of the clergy:

"A Church truly Christian must lead the way in moral enterprises, in every work which aims directly at the welfare of man. But look at the Churches of this city: do they lead the Christian movements of this city,—the temperance movement, the peace movement, the movement for the freedom of man, for education; the movement to make society more just, more wise and good; the great religious movement of these times? Not at all."

Theodore was too generous hearted to allow any one sect to bound his sympathies. His religion was one of deeds, not creeds.

"My friends," said Theodore to an audience composed largely of ministers, "if you receive the notions about Christianity which chance to be current in your sect or Church solely because they are current, and if this is all your religion, alas for you! The ground will shake under your feet if you attempt to walk uprightly and like men. You will be afraid of every new opinion, lest it shake down your Church; you will fear, 'lest, if a fox, go up, he will break down your stone wall.' If on the other hand you take the true word of God, and live out this, nothing shall harm you. Men may mock; but their mouthsful of wind will be blown back upon their own face. . . . And alas for that man who consents to think one thing in his closet and preach another in his pulpit! Over his study and over his pulpit might be writ 'EMPTINESS'; on his canonical robes, on his forehead and right hand, 'DECEIT, DECEIT.'"

In short, he appealed to what was noble in man. All nature came in for a share in his worship; he showed how to practice direct prayerful communion at all times; taught duty by a marvellous example as well as advice: taught that man could make the inspiration of his own conscience his sure and constant guide. He loved to "apprehend religious truths directly from the Almighty without the mediation of sacrament, creed or Bible." He believed in the final redemption of the whole human race. His belief was that

"So a man is a Christian, it makes little difference whether he is a Calvinist or Lutheran, Papist or Protestant. We all know that each sect contains in its instructions enough of pure vital Christian advice to insure our salvation, so far as this depends upon ourselves or our fellow mortals."

His conscientious decisions were the result of his constant study, reflection, his strong mental philosophy and his great knowledge of men and things. He was a member of the Boston Association of Unitarian Ministers, who strongly criticized his religious views as not being confined to their sect. Theodore answered their attacks by an able letter of great length, therein declaring his principles, and nobly challenging any of their best speakers or writers to come forward and manfully discuss the great question on its merits. It was a challenge that was never answered and quiet was for some time restored. But the brotherhood forbid all exchanges with Mr. Parker on penalty of expulsion from the society. The people at large were now becoming interested.

His own words appropriately reveal the magnitude of his great undertaking, his indomitable will and courage.

"I feel it is a great work that I have undertaken. I know that so far as the ministers are concerned, I am *alone*,—all alone. But I have no ambition to gratify, and so neither fear the disgrace nor covet the applause they can give me. Blessed be these *iron* times! there is something for a man to do, and, still more, there is something for man to think.

. . . "If I had the presence of two men, I would be two ministers, one here, and the other in Boston. . . . I pray God for the permanence of my ability; I have greater deeds to do, greater deeds to dare. . . . I knew always the risks that I run in saying what was hostile to the popular theology. But I care not what the result is to me, I ask only a chance to do my duty. I know men will eye me with suspicion and ministers with hatred; that is not my concern. . . . The thought that I am doing my duty is of rich reward to me; I know of none so great. I see men stare at me in the street and point and say, 'That is Theodore Parker,' and look at me as if I were a *murderer*. Old friends, even parishioners, will not bow to me in the street. I knew all this would come. It has come from my religion; and I would not forego that religion for all this world can give. . . . Some of my relations, two or three hundred years ago, lost their heads for their religion. I am called on to no such trial, and can well bear my lighter cross. . . . I consider man's duty to be this,—*to do the most good and the least evil possible.* As for the consequences of such action, I fear them not; they lie not with me."

But a great part of Theodore Parker's fame as a preacher is associated with the Boston Music Hall. The society removed from the Melodian to their new place of worship Nov. 21, 1852. Here Theodore made his greatest power felt. In this spacious temple he could let in the world of mankind; it was the world he wanted. The assemblies were on the whole the most remarkable and nearly the largest that ever gathered statedly within four walls in America. He at once attracted and held a considerable body of earnest and truth-seeking men and women; and besides these, a large floating mass was drawn towards that centre, persons who were impelled by various motives, and who did not regard themselves as members of that Society, though many of them subsequently became so. For 14 years he occupied this position, preaching to the largest audience that gathered in any church in Boston, comprising all sorts and conditions of men, from the most cultured to the least,—each finding something to satisfy him. His earnestness and sincerity, his vast range of information, embracing every department of human knowledge, his wealth of illustration, his aptness in discriminating between shams and realities, his felicity of language, and his wonderful faculty in adapting his speech to the comprehension of listeners of all grades,—made his sermons a delight to the minds and a refreshment to the souls of those who heard them. He preached the "absolute religion," and its adaptation to every department and phase of human life and conduct, exposed the falseness and hollowness of the popular theology, held up to view and denounced the sins of the nation and of society,—war, slavery, intemperance, the degradation of women, covetousness and minor vices,—portrayed with masterly hand many prominent men of the nation, as warnings or examples, set up a lofty ideal of manhood and womanhood, and sought to bring all up to that high standard of virtue and excellence. The richness of his intellect, the sensitiveness of his conscience, the tenderness of his heart, the yearning of his soul for the "first good, first perfect and first fair," his love of truth, his hatred of wrong and injustice, his moral courage, his intense humanity, and his fervid piety, were expressed in his sermons and prayers, which lifted his hearers to a higher plane and gave them new life and strength and hope. None such had been heard in Boston before nor have been since.

His biographer, O. B. Frothingham, well known pastor of the Third Unitarian Church of New York, thus gives us a few interesting facts:

"Mr. Parker's central position commanded a broad view. He moved but little as he spoke; his hand only occasionally rose and fell on the manuscript before him as if to emphasize a passage to himself; but his person was motionless and his arm still. He was a scholar and a teacher, who addressed the individual understanding and the private conscience. He had no accessories of rite, symbol, ceremony, doctrinal or ecclesiastical mystery. His prayers were expressions of devout feeling, personal and tender, but without humiliation, superstition or the least recognition of dogma at beginning or end. The sermons were seldom less than an hour in length, often more; and were crammed with thought. To listen to him regularly was indeed a liberal education, not in theology or even in religion alone, but in politics, history, literature, science and art. His audiences were held in breathless attention by the spell of earnest thought alone, uttered in language so simple, that a plain man hearing him remarked on leaving the church, 'Is that Theodore Parker? You told me he was a remarkable man; but I understood every word he said.' His rule was to have no sentence that was above the comprehension of the simplest intelligence. The style was never dry; the sentences short and pithy; the language was fragrant with the odor of the fields, and rich with the juices of the ground.

"So fervent was his utterance, so natural and human his cry, that the flowers on the table before him colored his devout speech, and the voices of the animals blent easily with his own. One Sunday. a terrier dog, that had strayed into the hall, suddenly, in the midst of the prayer, lifted up a piercing bark. 'We thank thee, O Father of all, who hast made even the humblest dumb creature to praise thee after his own way!' responded the supplicating lips. He was preaching a discourse, one winter's day, on 'Obstacles.' Describing a man to whom obstacles are helps, he said, 'Before such a man all obstacles will'—at this instant a mass of frozen snow that had collected on the roof came down with a noise like thunder, that shook the building and startled the audience with a momentary feeling of dismay—'slide away like the ice from the slated roof,' said the preacher's reassuring voice."

He loved to preach; subjects crowded on him faster than he could deal with them. The Sundays were too few with him, rather than too many.

"Is it not sometimes a burden to the preacher to go through the devotional exercises of the Sunday?" asked one of his friends. "Never to me," was the reply. "The natural aptitude of my mind has always been prayerful. A snatch of such feeling passes through me as I walk in the streets, or engage in any work. I sing prayers when I loiter in the woods, or travel the quiet road; these founts of communion, which lie so deep, seem always bubbling to the surface; and the utterance of a prayer is at any time as simple to me as breathing."

A man of such commanding ability and genuine sympathy with mankind could not be spared from taking an active part in other movements for the amelioration and uplifting of the unfortunate and down-trodden. He was an early advocate of temperance and he entered into its encouragement with the same thoroughness and activity which characterized all his labors.

In 1845 he joined the anti-slavery leaders in their work, and from that time forward was one of the most conspicuous and indefatigable laborers in that field. He did an immense service in arousing and educating the conscience of the people, in impelling them to recognize and oppose the evils of slavery, and in enunciating and diffusing the principles and shaping the policy which found practical expression in the national politics, and which led ultimately to the overthrow of that gigantic wrong. He gave himself to this cause with all the ardor and thoroughness which characterized his efforts in the theological field, and lavished upon it all the wealth of his nature and acquirements. His writings upon this subject form a body of anti-slavery literature of great value for clearness and accuracy of statement, historical narrative and pertinent facts and statistics,—showing the rise and progress of slavery, and the development of the southern policy, and painting the evils of the institution in clear, bold colors; setting forth also the great American idea which gives to the Constitution and the Union their value and glory, and rebuking with just indignation the men in high places who betrayed that idea and imperilled the safety and prosperity of the country.

Politically, he vigorously opposed the Mexican war. He was bitterly opposed to the passage of the Fugitive Slave Law, which was accomplished in 1850. Every case of attempted rendition in Boston enlisted his personal activity. In June, 1854, when Anthony Burns, a fugitive, was captured and returned to his master, Mr. Parker delivered a stinging speech against the action and against the fugitive slave law to an anti-rendition meeting at Faneuil Hall. For this he was indicted on the charge of "resisting a U. S. officer in his attempt to execute process"; was arrested and tried. But Theodore made use of these circumstances to good advantage. He prepared an elaborate defence, which he printed and circulated. The charge was quashed upon a technicality, having produced no disgrace to Mr. Parker's reputation, as his enemies had desired. On the contrary, it was quite to his satisfaction, for his masterly speech and also his defence, entitled the "Trial of Theodore Parker for the Misdemeanor of a Speech delivered in Faneuil Hall against Kidnapping," was read by thousands throughout all the land who now began to take a lively interest in the anti-slavery movement.

His exposition of the wickedness and injustice of the Fugitive Slave Law, and his denunciation of it, and appeals to the higher law, when eminent clergymen, statesmen and merchants combined to uphold it and secure its enforcement, form a striking episode in the history of that eventful period. His speech and action, when the kidnappers came to Boston in search of their fugitive slaves, proved his courage and led to his indictment and the writing of his "Defence," a remarkable book, which will be of great value to the future historian. It contains the best account to be found of judicial and legal tyranny from the reign of James I. to the time of his own indictment.

At this time he began lecturing and preaching throughout the Northern States. His name was spoken of with esteem and with hate in every State; throughout every town. His printed sermons were sold by the thousand and read by the ten thousand.

His efforts for the suppression of poverty, drunkenness, ignorance, prostitution and crime, and the removal of their causes, were vigorous and unceasing; and the victims of these vices found in him a wise friend and helper. These matters are discussed with great efficiency and plainness in his books and are abundantly illustrated with facts and figures. His personal efforts, singly or in combination with others, for the benefit of these unfortunate classes, were without stint, and much of his time was consumed in that way.

The movement in behalf of the rights of woman and her equality with man found in him a hearty and eloquent advocate, and he was one of the foremost in denouncing the injustice of those who deny these rights, in exposing the fallacies of their arguments, and appealing to the common sense and justice of mankind to accord to her her proper position and an equal opportunity with man for culture, development and the exercise of her natural talents in various directions.

His biographical discourses were models of thoroughness and strength. While preparing his pulpit oration on John Quincy Adams he reviewed the statesman's whole career, read every speech, analyzed every argument, scrutinized every act, went behind every piece of public policy, and laid out the history so simply that the least instructed intelligence could understand it. Before writing the greatest discourse of them all, on Daniel Webster dead, he did more than this: he gleaned from all credible sources information in regard to Mr. Webster's private life and character; probed the secrets of his ancestry; read the principal works of distinguished authors, jurists and statesmen in England; studied again the orations of Demosthenes and Cicero in order to settle precisely in his own mind the rank of the great American as lawyer, statesman, orator and man. That wonderful oration was written at a heat. The preparation for it covered weeks and even years, but a few hours of solitary meditation in the country, after the statesman's death, fused the mass of material so completely that it ran like molten metal into the literary mould. The effect in the delivery was prodigious. The whole audience leaned forward in rapt attention, listening with breathless intensity; and when he spoke of his mourning for Webster, and cried in choking voice, "O Webster, Webster! my king, my king! would I had died for thee!" every eye was wet with tears.

He was the strongest man on any occasional platform on which he stood,—always presenting his views with a force of intellect, breadth of observation, homelike style of address and superabundance of information that quite overshadowed those whose lives had been spent in that special field of labor. His opinions were broader, more practical and nearer to common sense than the platform of the exclusive party with which he was working at the time. In every conflict between barbarism and true civilization he always was found on the side of the latter.

His preaching and other public speaking were not limited to Boston. As he became more known, he was in demand in the lecture-room and at gatherings of various kinds in New England and beyond. During the last ten years of his active life he lectured from eighty to a hundred times each year, his field comprising every Northern State east of the Mississippi, and once he spoke in a slave State, on slavery itself. Many invitations he was compelled to decline. The people heard him gladly and he made hosts of friends during these expeditions, comprising many of the best people in the various towns and overcame much of the prejudice existing against him.

He spoke on the subjects in which he was so deeply interested, mostly upon the various matters of reform to which he had given his life, directly and simply, and won his hearers to his side by his earnestness, candor and natural eloquence, and his happy faculty of presenting great themes—often dry and matter-of-fact in detail—in an attractive manner. As an illustration of this, one of his friends says:

"I have always remembered a certain lecture of his on the Anglo-Saxons as the most wonderful instance that ever came within my knowledge of the adaptation of solid learning to the popular inellect. There was nearly two hours of almost unadorned fact,—for there was less than usual of relief and illustration,—yet the lyceum audience listened as if an angel sang to them. So perfect was his sense of purpose and of power, so clear and lucid was his delivery, with such wonderful composure did he lay out, section by section, his historical chart, that he grasped his hearers as absolutely as he grasped his subject. Without grace or beauty or melody, his mere elocution was sufficient to produce effects which melody, grace and beauty might have sought for in vain."

The same friend, one of the few eminent classical scholars of New England, says:

"Theodore Parker was the only man with whom I could sit down and seriously discuss a disputed reading, and find him familiar with all that had been written upon it. I know for one, and there are many who will bear the same testimony, that I never went to Mr. Parker to talk over a subject which I had just made a specialty without finding that on that particular matter he happened to know, without special investigation, more than I did. This extended beyond books, as for instance any point connected with the habits of animals and the phenomena of out-door nature. Such were his wonderful quickness and his infallible memory that glimpses of these things did for him the work of years. It was in popularizing knowledge that his great and wonderful power lay."

Although he was one of the giants of learning his style is remarkable for its absence from all taint of scholastic and metaphysical terms. Speaking of his mental qualifications,

James Freeman Clarke, one of the few noble men and Unitarians who believed in the freedom of thought, and stood by Mr. Parker when the clergy of that faith denounced him, and remained his warm friend to the last, said of him:

"Some men's minds are filled with a great multitude of ill-assorted knowledges, crowded confusedly together like a mob around a muster-ground. Others have a very small number of very well arranged and drilled opinions, like a militia regiment thoroughly organized as regards its officers, but very thin as regards its rank and file. The thoughts, opinions, convictions, varieties of knowledge in Theodore Parker's mind are like a well-appointed and thoroughly organized army, with full ranks, beautiful in its uniforms and its banners, inspired by the martial airs of its music, complete in all arms,—infantry, cavalry, engineers, artillery,—marching to the overthrow of a demoralized and discouraged enemy."

His conversational power was marvellous. He could talk upon any subject, and astonished and fascinated every listener, pouring out a flood of various and delightful information, wit and wisdom, adapted to the needs and capacity of the hearer, and never failing to say the right thing in the right place. Thackeray said, when he came to America, that what he most desired was to hear Theodore Parker talk. In this phase of expression it has been said that he had no Anglo-Saxon rival except Macaulay, but he lacked the arrogance and impatience of opposition which characterized the great Englishman.

He had a very extensive correspondence with strangers and personal friends, among whom were eminent scholars and scientists in this country and Europe. The great leaders of the Republican party were his friends, and undoubtedly his influence was exerted through them on the momentous questions of the day. William H. Seward said of him: "In his grasp of the political issues of the times and their moral bearings he surpasses us all."

He was the most generous of men. His sympathies were world-wide and ever on the alert for the suffering and oppressed. Refugees from foreign lands, hunted slaves, poverty-stricken scholars, sorrowing women, all sorts of needy and unbefriended mortals came to him, and found in him a true friend and wise adviser. He helped them with money and lavished upon them what was of far more value.

Spiritually he was of immense service to thousands of earnest men and women who had fallen into indifference or unbelief in religious matters, a condition for which the false theology and low spiritual state of the Church were largely responsible. By the promulgation of his ideas he created a powerful revival of fundamental religion throughout the country; not by dealing with the mere superficial elements of human nature and character, as did the Calvinistic Churches in their so-called revivals. Their barbaric creeds, worldly policy and social inhumanities, and their interpretation of the Bible had repelled these people. His presentation of the natural religion, based on reason and the noblest instincts of humanity, drew them to his side, and they found a peace and satisfaction therein which they had not known before.

Mr. Parker's persistent and well-grounded attacks upon the popular theology, and exposition of its absurdities, together with the favor with which his teachings were received by a large class of people, were a constant source of annoyance and displeasure to the Churches which held to the old forms of belief, and many were the denunciations and warnings uttered from their pulpits against him and his heretical views. This feeling found remarkable expression during a season of revival in a prayer meeting held in Park Street Church, Boston, on Saturday, March 6, 1858, in which the Lord was besought to "remove him out of the way and let his influence die with him," to "send confusion and distraction into his study this afternoon, and prevent his finishing his preparation for his labors to-morrow," to "confound him so that he shall not be able to speak," to "induce the people to leave him and to come and fill up this house instead of that," to "put a hook in his jaws so that he may not be able to speak."

These supplications were admirably answered by Mr. Parker from his desk in the Music Hall, in two sermons preached on the 4th and 11th of April, on "A False and True Revival of Religion," and "The Revival of Religion which we Need." They furnished a striking instance of absolute, unvarnished truth-telling, and are full of unsparing criticism, pure morality and tender devoutness.

His last sermon, entitled "What Religion may do for a Man," was preached in Boston, January 2, 1859. On the morning of Sunday, January 9th, the illness from which he had been suffering for some years previous, the result of his multitudinous and incessant labors in so many fields of usefulness and exposures incident thereto, culminated in a hæmorrhage of the lungs. Consumption had been prevalent in his mother's family for a long time. The absolute necessity of stopping his work and devoting himself to an effort to restore his broken health was thus forced upon him in such a manner that he could not disregard the warning.

On the 3rd of February he left Boston never to return. He spent some weeks at Santa Cruz and other places in the West Indies, and then sailed for Europe, where he passed nearly a year, mainly in Switzerland and Italy, and died in Florence, May 10, 1860, tranquilly and beautifully, full of the trust and faith in God which he had so nobly preached. By his request his only funeral services consisted of the reading of the Beatitudes by his friend Mr. Cunningham. He lies in the Protestant Cemetery in Florence, a plain stone of gray marble over his grave, bearing his name and the dates of his birth and death. An American pine tree has also been planted there.

Up to the time when he was taken with hæmorrhage, the strong constitution inherited from the long line of hardy Massachusetts ancestors had preserved him through 40 years of constant application and toil; it had carried him triumphantly through hundreds of extraordinary exertions. The crisis was naturally severe. Experienced physicians declared the chances of recovery as one in ten. "If that is all I'll conquer," he replied, "I have fought ninety-nine against one,—yes, nine hundred and ninety-nine against one,—and conquered." Had he possessed a restful nature he might have recovered, but travelling was his element for continual mental occupation. He must know the name of every tree, read every new book, take daily excursions into the country wherever he was. He was constantly studying the habits, occupations and religion of the inhabitants, classifying the products, the minerals and the value of properties, thus becoming acquainted with the whole history of every country he visited. While at Santa Cruz he wrote his volume "Experience as a Minister." In Switzerland his health improved for a time. He wrote to a friend:

"I am still full of hope that the human mortal life will hold out long enough for me to hammer over again some of the many irons I have laid in the fire and got ready for the anvil. Indeed, I laid out my life to work publicly and hard till sixty, and then have a quiet afternoon till eighty for getting in my hay; but if the hour strikes at forty-eight, let not you nor me complain."

The last insertion in his journal states:

"When I die I wish to be buried in the old burying place at Lexington, where my fathers since 1709—four generations of them—have laid their venerable bones. I wish to be put near them.

"My life has failed of much I meant to hit, and might have reached, nay, should, had there been ten or twenty years left for me. But it has not been a mean life nor a selfish one. Above all things else I have sought to teach the true idea of man, of God, of religion, with its truths, its duties, and its joys. I never fought for myself nor against a private foe, but have gone into the battle of the nineteenth century and followed the flag of humanity. I would rather lay my bones with my father's in Lexington and think I may; but will not complain if earth or sea shall cover them up elsewhere."

But in Rome the winter was cold and damp. He wrote:

"Rome is the dampest city I was ever in. I have lost three pounds a week since I left Switzerland and have gained nothing but a great cough."

He welcomed the fair city of Florence with joy, although he well knew it was to be his last earthly home.

Thus passed away before he had reached his fiftieth birthday this unique and much-gifted man. No man was ever more cordially hated by such as upheld the errors, hypocrisies and iniquities which he exposed; none was ever more deeply and tenderly loved, by those who recognized his true greatness and manliness, or felt the magnetism of his influence. Those of his personal friends who survive hold him ever as a sacred memory in their hearts, and count it as the choicest of blessings that they were privileged to come within the charmed circle of his presence.

It is impossible to estimate at this time what he has accomplished in the various lines in which he worked. In the progress which has been made in the liberalizing of theology in all denominations his influence is so marked that it cannot be disputed. The Unitarians, who cast him out, have acknowledged their error, and now seek to retrieve their folly by honoring his memory. His portrait hangs in their hall, and his writings are printed and circulated by their association, with its imprint upon the title page. They have left behind the dogmas for attacking which they so eagerly denounced him. The various branches of the Orthodox Church, though not acknowledging the debt they owe to him, are moving in the same direction, and the modifications and humanizing of their creeds, which is continually in process, is unquestionably largely due to his efforts. Dean Stanley, when he came to America, said that Theodore Parker had contributed more to theological progress than any other religious thinker in this century. His anti-slavery work was a powerful factor in the abolition of slavery and in the triumph of the Union in the war of the Rebellion. The other reforms in behalf of which he labored owe much of their progress to his clear statement and able advocacy.

He was, said Emerson:

"A man who has put us all into his debt by his brave life and incessant labor in the cause of truth, freedom, good morals, religion and good sense, here and throughout the world; and whose single and unaided performances in behalf of learning and humanity might well put colleges and churches to shame. . . .

"New England put into him her choicest elements, made him as it were the incarnation of her characteristic genius. Her granite hills bequeathed to him their stern inflexibility; her climate gave him hardihood and health; her summer and winter left upon him their deposits of verdure and snow.

"Such was the largeness of his reception of facts and his skill to employ them, that it looked as if he were some president of council to whom a score of telegraphs were ever bringing in reports; and his information would have been excessive but for the noble use he made of it, ever in the interest of humanity. He had a strong understanding, a logical method, a love for facts, a rapid eye for their historic relations, and a skill in stripping them of traditional lustres.

"The vice charged against America is the want of sincerity in leading men. It does not lie at his door. He never kept back the truth for fear of making an enemy. It was his merit, like Luther, to speak tart truth when that was peremptory, when there were few to say it. But his sympathy for goodness was not less energetic. His commanding merit as a reformer is this,—that he insisted beyond all men in pulpits that the essence of Christianity is its practical morals; it is there for use, or it is nothing. . . .

"There were of course multitudes to censure and defame this truth-speaker. But the brave know the brave. . . .

"The sudden and singular eminence of Mr. Parker, the importance of his name and influence, are the verdict of his country to his virtues. We have few such men to lose. Amiable and blameless at home, feared abroad as the standard-bearer of liberty, taking all the duties he could grasp, he has gone down in early glory to his grave, to be a living and enlarging power, wherever learning, wit, honest valor and independence are honored."

Wendell Phillips said of him:

"No sect, no special study, no one idea bounded his sympathy, but he was generous in judgment where a common man would have found it hard to be so. He raised the level of sermons intellectually and morally. Other preachers were compelled to grow in manly thought and Christian morals in very self defence. No man ever needed to read any of his sentences twice to catch its meaning. None suspected that he thought other than he said or more than he confessed. He was far other than a bitter critic, though thank God for every drop of bitterness that came like a wholesome rebuke on the dead saltless sea of American life! Thank God for every Christian admonition that the Holy Spirit breathed through those manly lips. But if he deserved any single word, it was generous. Born on a New England farm in those days when small incomings made every dollar a matter of importance, he no sooner had command of wealth than he lived with open hands. Not even the darling ambition of a great library ever tempted him to close his ear to need. Go to Venice or Vienna, to Frankfort or to Paris, and ask the refugees who have gone back—when here friendless exiles but for him—under whose roof they felt most at home."

Moncure D. Conway of New York recently placed this tribute to his memory:

"Dr. Gannett, the great, though always fair, antagonist of Theodore Parker, has written of him: 'He was a very learned man and a tender, true-hearted man, honest and thorough.' The whole source of Parker's heresies is in that sentence. Because Parker was a very learned man he could not accept statements which criticism and scholarship had to him proved erroneous; because he was tender and true-hearted he rejected traditional conceptions which to him showed God heartless; because he was honest he spoke out what he believed. Those who once resisted his teachings, now favor his writings. While Boston society disowned him, he was of all men the most Bostonian. If Boston did not love Parker, Parker loved Boston. As an example of the transiency alluded to, Parker's concept of deity may be adduced. Nothing can be more perfect than his ideal of a deity supremely wise, loving and at work in all the laws of the universe, present in all events, minute or vast. Darwin, even more sweet and gentle than Parker, walked by facts rather than by faith, and he proved that the evils we had, though superficial and transient, were inherent in the very organization of nature. I believe the verdict must be that Parker was indeed tender to individuals, yet writing beneath the musket which another Captain Parker used at Lexington he felt himself struggling in a revolution against great religious and political oppressions; therefore his words were sometimes as hard as bullets, though each tore his heart as it went forth; but this is the inevitable inconsistency of all men who kneel to worship infinite perfection everywhere, then rise up to fight imperfection everywhere. There will some day be centennials of spiritual independence and of the union of religious colonies, and in that day every scrap of testimony concerning Theodore Parker will be searched for as is now every scrap relating to Washington. His will be a far greater name then than now, for it will take a century to sum up the results of his work. Theodore Parker! Thy work is achieved; thy congregation may be dismissed. We are free."

His relative and playmate in childhood, warm friend through life, Columbus Greene, Esq., says:

"While at the Divinity School at Cambridge I seldom saw him. I had left the old homestead and we were more widely separated, but we corresponded every month and we were familiar with each other's welfare. I visited him once while there, and when I asked him if he was taxed hard by the lessons assigned him, he replied, 'Oh no, it takes me about two hours.' He then showed me a list of the books he had read and what volumes he had written of the subjects treated and his opinions. The time was pleasantly spent at the Divinity School in some respects, while in others it was not. He entered the school in harmony with the Unitarian belief as generally held, but he gradually departed from it, and his sermons in the school were said to be dry and scholastic and called forth reproof from his professor. He differed so much from the doctrines taught that on 'Visitation Day' a certain D.D. said, that he had *no denominational character*, that he was an *eclectic*. Their frowns were more numerous than their smiles of approbation, but it did not move him from his fixed purpose to cling to what *he* believed to be *right*.

"His history after he entered the ministry, with its joys and sorrows, is clearly described by Weiss and Frothingham, but I wish to say that from his early youth he was conscientious, tenaciously attached to what he believed to be right, and the best scholar and the greatest reader I ever knew. The amount of his reading was marvellous, his passing through books was like a locomotive on a down grade with full head of steam and brakes off.

"His memory was remarkable; he retained what he read. In his library in Boston, worth $20,000, he could tell readily what each volume treated upon. A gentleman seeking for information upon a given subject, once called upon him to see if he had a book in his library that treated upon that subject, and as my memory serves me, he replied, 'No, but if you will go to the library at Harvard University in the northeast corner on the second shelf from the floor, and the third book from the corner, I think you will find it.'

"His organ of language was very fully developed. He once said to me 'Some people are troubled for words to express themselves, but as for me as much as five sets of words come up and I have to select from them.' He was naturally tender-hearted, diffident and retiring, but when he thought what was right was assailed he was brave as a Spartan. Circumstances would show him to be as tender as the kindest mother, or as argumentative as Webster in his reply to Hayne, or as terrible in denunciation as the cyclone that sweeps all before it. His father would have been pleased to have had him studied law, and for a time it was a question whether he should be a lawyer or a minister, but he soon decided that he could not conscientiously be a lawyer and he chose to be a minister. His aim from early life was not only to be learned, but to be useful to mankind, to do and defend what he believed to be right, if in so doing he stood alone. Being intimately acquainted with him I have no doubt but what he would have given up his life rather than to have ceased to cry out against what he believed to be wrong. I think he was the most fearless man I ever knew when almost overwhelmed by opposition. If any differ from me let them read his speeches and sermons when most public men were as quiet as those in the sepulchre; his sermon after the death of Webster, his speech in Faneuil Hall after the arrest of Anthony Burns, and his sermon after he was carried back to slavery, 'The New Crime against Humanity.' I admired him for his vivid conscience, his great ability, his devotion to what he believed was right and his fearlessness in defending it, however much he might suffer in so doing."

Some of the published works of Rev. Theodore Parker are:

Occasional Sermons and Speeches, 2 vols., 12mo, 1852.

Ten Sermons on Religion, 1853.

Sermons on Theism, Atheism and Popular Theology, 1853.

Additional Speeches, Addresses, etc., 2 vols., 12mo, 1855.

Trial of Theodore Parker for the "Misdemeanor of a Speech delivered in Faneuil Hall against Kidnapping," 1855.

Two Christmas Celebrations, 1859.

Experience as a Minister, 1859.

To these add the masterly pamphlet-sermons and addresses on "Immortal Life," on "The Perils of Adversity and Prosperity," "What Religion will do for a Man," "Lesson for a Midsummer Day," "The Function and Place of Conscience," the "Sermon of Poverty," "Of War," "Of Merchants," "The Chief Sins of the People," "The Power of a False Idea," of "The Perishing Classes," "The Dangerous Classes," "Great Cities," "The Dangers and Duties of Woman," "Crime," "Intemperance," and we have a partial list of his best sermons. He left unpublished about 1,000 sermons and lectures, among which is a series of lectures on great Americans, some of which are to be published. Different admirers of his works have privately compiled "Sermons and Lectures by Theodore Parker," amounting in all to about 18 different publications. Besides his autobiography by O. B. Frothingham, 'a more extensive one by John Weiss, and a third by A. Révielle of Paris, entitled "Theodore Parker, sa vie et sa Œuvres," 1865, and in English, London, Dec., 1865, 12mo. He left the chief part of all his very valuable library, 11,900 books and 2,500 pamphlets, to the Boston City Library.

Theodore Parker was a very affable man. His acquaintances included people of all classes of society and all kinds of people. He was easily approached, as he was very pleasant and genial in his countenance and temperament. His friends were everywhere, he seemed to know everybody. But little above the average height he was very firmly built and carried a rugged appearance. His wife continued to reside in Boston, where she died several years since. They had no issue.

134. Mary Parker *(Robert,[6] John,[5] Josiah,[4] John,[3] Hananiah,[2] Thomas[1])*, dau. of Robert and Elizabeth (Simonds) Parker, was b. in Lexington, Dec. 26, 1794; m. April 11, 1822, Isaac W. Lawrence, native of Lexington, b. Nov. 18, 1796, son of Phinehas and Polly (Wellington) Lawrence of Lexington. He d. Nov. 18, 1843. She d. Nov. 30, 1881.

Their children were:

1. ALBERT S. LAWRENCE, b. in Lexington, Jan. 1, 1823; d. Aug. 1, 1856.
2. HENRY L. LAWRENCE, b. in Lexington, Aug. 17, 1824; m. March 30, 1852, Lucy M. Ham of Rochester, N. H., b. in Rochester, Nov. 14, 1830. He and his brother are merchants at Faneuil Hall Market, Boston. All the children were b. in Lexington:
   - I. HELEN M. LAWRENCE, b. Dec. 27, 1852.
   - II. MARY A. LAWRENCE, b. Aug. 7, 1854.
   - III. ANNA LAWRENCE, b. May 9, 1857.
   - IV. ALICE S. LAWRENCE, b. Dec. 6, 1858.
   - V. HENRY D. LAWRENCE, b. Oct. 9, 1860.
   - VI. GERTRUDE A. LAWRENCE, b. Nov. 26, 1863.
   - VII. MINOT R. LAWRENCE, b. July 20, 1867.
   - VIII. GRACE LAWRENCE, b. Oct. 6, 1868; d. Aug. 10, 1869.
   - IX. EFFIE LAWRENCE, b. May 24, 1871; d. July 21, 1872.
   - X. DANA LAWRENCE, b. Dec. 5, 1875.
3. JOHN PARKER LAWRENCE, b. in Lexington, Dec. 27, 1830; m. July 15, 1860, Georgianna Williams of Boston, b. in Boston, April 3, 1823. Their children were:
   - I. ALBERT P. LAWRENCE, b. in Boston, July 31, 1863.
   - II. MARY H. LAWRENCE, b. in Boston, Oct. 15, 1864.
   - III. GEORGE L. LAWRENCE, b. in Boston, July 20, 1868.
   - IV. CHARLES H. LAWRENCE, b. in Cambridge, Oct. 16, 1869; d. Aug. 11, 1870.
   - V. BLANCHE L. LAWRENCE, b. in Cambridge, July 22, 1873.
4. THEODORE M. LAWRENCE, b. in Lexington, Jan. 5, 1837; m. Oct. 7, 1860, Sarah J. Luther of Boston, b. in Boston, Aug. 10, 1838, and d. Aug. 10, 1863. He d. Jan. 18, 1888. Their children were:
   - I. HENRY A. LAWRENCE, b. in Boston, Nov. 9, 1860; d. Oct. 3, 1861.
   - II. GRACE LAWRENCE, b. in Boston, Nov. 19, 1862; d. Jan. 4, 1863.

135. Eliza Eleanor Parker (*Robert,*[6] *John,*[5] *Josiah,*[4] *John,*[3] *Hananiah,*[2] *Thomas*[1]), dau. of Robert and Elizabeth (Simonds) Parker, was b. in Lexington, Sept. 20, 1804; m. April 12, 1829, Nathan Robbins of W. Cambridge, son of Nathan and Rebecca (Prentiss) Robbins of W. Cambridge, now Arlington. He had stalls in Faneuil Hall Market, where he dealt in poultry and wild game. He was one of the founders of the Faneuil Hall Bank, and was its president up to the time of his death.

Their children were:

1. EDWIN ROBBINS, b. in W. Cambridge, Jan. 9, 1832; m. 1852, Ellen S. Daniels, b. in W. Cambridge, Feb. 7, 1833, dau. of John P. and Elinor S. (Whittemore) Daniels. Children:
   - I. FRANK ROBBINS.
   - II. HENRY PARKER ROBBINS.
   - III. NELLY ROBBINS.
   - IV. NATHAN ROBBINS.
2. ORRIN ROBBINS, b. in W. Cambridge, Aug., 1835; d. in Philadelphia in 1868.
3. ALVIN ROBBINS, b. in W. Cambridge, Sept., 1837; m. Emma Deblois of W. Cambridge (now Arlington). Children:
   - I. AMELIA F. ROBBINS.
   - II. CLINTON A. ROBBINS.
   - III. CLARENCE ROBBINS.

136. Almira Parker (*Robert,*[6] *John,*[5] *Josiah,*[4] *John,*[3] *Hananiah,*[2] *Thomas*[1]), dau. of Robert and Elizabeth (Simonds) Parker, was b. in Lexington, Aug. 30, 1806; m. Oct. 1, 1837, Joshua Robbins of W. Cambridge.

Their children were:

1. J. MINOT ROBBINS, b. 1838; d. 1869, unm. He served in the War of the Rebellion, and was in business in Philadelphia, Pa.
2. A. LEONARD ROBBINS, who d. unm.
3. R. OSCAR ROBBINS; he m. and had at least two children, who are now living in Virginia. The parents are deceased.

137. Jonathan Simonds Parker (*Robert,*[6] *John,*[5] *Josiah,*[4] *John,*[3] *Hananiah,*[2] *Thomas*[1]), son of Robert and Elizabeth (Simonds) Parker, was b. in Lexington, July 30, 1812; m. Dec. 29, 1835, Abigail Tuttle, b. in Lexington,

Aug. 2, 1814, dau. of David and Abigail (Smith) Tuttle. The dau. Abigail was the *great-great-grand-dau.* of Lt. Josiah Parker, through Anna Parker, No. 14, Thomas Smith (page 72), and Abigail Smith Tuttle (page 72). See *Errata.* The father, David Tuttle, was b. in Winchendon, Dec. 2, 1782, son of Jedediah, a Revolutionary veteran.

Jonathan S. Parker was storekeeper. His place of business was the old location which G. W. Spaulding now occupies. He early associated himself with military affairs and became captain of the Lexington artillery. He filled the most important town offices, was treasurer five years, from 1839 to 1844, assessor of that town from 1850 to 1857, and 1859, and selectman three years.

Jonathan S. Parker was even when young a man to whom many of the town offices were entrusted, and must have proved worthy as he was ever ready to aid any good cause. He was a gentleman in the finest sense of the word, honest and fearless in his convictions. He was public spirited, genial, ready with a joke, fond of reading and in this way educated himself after his early leaving school. He was kind and helpful to any one in trouble, and although he died comparatively young his memory is still fresh in the minds of his many friends. Jonathan S. Parker was a man of mind, of true honor, of excellent business abilities and was a highly respected citizen. He d. in Lexington, July 5, 1859, and his widow d. April 4, 1860.

Their children were:

John Henry Parker, b. Sept. 16, 1836; d. Sept. 12, 1855.

Elizabeth Simonds Parker, b. Sept. 30, 1838; resides in Lexington, unm. She is a teacher in Boston, where she has taught in the grammar schools for 20 years.

Esther Tuttle Parker, b. Feb. 21, 1842; resides in Lexington, unm.

307. Abby M. Parker, b. April 23, 1847; m. Geo. H. Cutter of Arlington.

308. Georgiana Tuttle Parker, b. Oct. 12, 1849; m. Charles W. Converse of Woburn.

Emma Frances Parker, b. April 8, 1853. She is a teacher in Weymouth.

ELLEN HENRY PARKER, b. June 28, 1858; teacher for some years in Lexington; m. Sept. 2, 1891, George B. Grant of Boston; resides in Dorchester.

138. William Bowers Parker *(Robert,[6] John,[5] Josiah,[4] John,[3] Hananiah,[2] Thomas[1])*, son of Robert and Elizabeth (Simonds) Parker, was b. in Lexington, Jan. 13, 1817; m. in Lexington, Nov. 30, 1843, Elizabeth Garfield of Charlestown, whose parents were Emery Garfield of New Hampshire and Betsey Harrington of Lexington. They lived in Charlestown.

Their children were:

MARY ELIZA PARKER, b. Feb. 3, 1844; m. Sept. 20, 1864, Albert W. Lewis of Charlestown, son of Seth W., native of Claremont, N. H., and Sarah (Stone) Lewis, native of Weare, N. H. Their dau. was:

1. MARY ADELAIDE LEWIS, b. June 14, 1865; m. July 17, 1884, J. Eugene Hyland of Augusta, Me., and resides in Everett.

ALMIRA ROBBINS PARKER, b. Oct. 1, 1845; m. Thomas Faber of Everett, now residing in Weston. She d. Oct. 4, 1882. Their son was:

1. GEORGE W. FABER, b. July 31, 1870. Resides in Everett.

309. JOSIAH BOWERS PARKER, b. Aug. 31, 1848; m. Cristina Savage of Everett.

LUCIUS N. PARKER, b. April 7, 1851; d. May, 1856.

EDITH JOSEPHINE PARKER, b. Dec. 26, 1854; m. Edward Faber of Everett. She d. May 20, 1874, and her child has since died.

ELLEN E. PARKER, b. Feb. 26, 1860; d. Dec., 1867.

139. Samuel Parker *(Levi,[6] Joseph,[5] Josiah,[4] John,[3] Hananiah,[2] Thomas[1])*, son of Levi and Mary (Lyon) Parker, was b. in Hubbardston, March 4, 1787; m. in Potsdam, N. Y., Jan. 16, 1823, Lurania Akins, b. May 6, 1793, dau. of Nathaniel and Mary (Tupper) Akins. Samuel Parker was a farmer and lived in Potsdam. He d. in Potsdam, N. Y., May 6, 1855. She d. Nov. 24, 1879. In a local journal appeared the following complimentary obituary notice of Samuel Parker:

"There are few men who better deserve a note of commendation when they pass away from us than those strong and enterprising citizens who encountered the difficulties incident to new settlements, and whose industry serves to lay the foundation for generations to come. In this point of view our respected neighbor and friend now gone well deserves the tribute of a brief notice. Mr. Samuel Parker came from Royalton, Vt., to Potsdam, N. Y., in 1811, where the remainder of his life was spent. He was therefore one of the very earliest settlers of this point of St. Lawrence Co., and the community has known but few men who were from character and habits better fitted to encounter the hardships of a new settlement than was he. Untiring industry, indomitable perseverance, and strict moral integrity may be said to have been his ruling characteristics. He took up and subdued one of the largest farms in town and left a very comfortable estate to his family after him. He was highly respected and beloved by all who knew him, as a man of business he was honest and industrious, as a husband and father uniformly kind, as a neighbor always helpful and obliging. His funeral was attended by a very large concourse of mourning friends and neighbors, and by the Racket River Lodge of Free and Accepted Masons, No. 213, of which the deceased had been a highly respected member from 1813 to the day of his death. May the example of his great industry, his honest and useful life be followed by those who survive him."

Their children were:

310. Albert Parker, b. Oct. 19, 1823; m. —— Turner.
Anna Eliza Parker, b. May 29, 1826; d. Aug. 8, 1829.
Louis Parker, b. May 29, 1831; d. Aug. 7, 1861.

140. Martha Parker *(Levi,[6] Joseph,[5] Josiah,[4] John,[3] Hananiah,[2] Thomas[1])*, dau. of Levi and Mary (Lyon) Parker, was b. in Hubbardston, Nov. 19, 1788; m. 1812, Shubael Crandall, b. in Preston, Conn., Dec. 28, 1785. He moved with his father's family to Royalton, Vt. They removed to Pierrepont, St. Lawrence Co., N. Y., in 1817, where he purchased land in the then almost unbroken wilderness on which he resided until his death. He early became a member of the Presbyterian Church and was a sincere believer in the teachings of Jesus Christ until the close of his long life. He d. in Pierrepont, June 9, 1877, in the 92nd year of his age.

They had four children, who are all dead:

1. George Crandall; m. and had a dau. Ellen, now Ellen Squares.
2. Elizabeth Parker Crandall.

141. **Aaron Parker** *(Levi,[6] Joseph,[5] Josiah,[4] John,[3] Hananiah,[2] Thomas[1])*, son of Levi and Mary (Lyon) Parker, was b. in Hubbardston, Feb. 20, 1791; removed with family to Royalton, Vt.; m. in Howard, Steuben Co., N. Y.

Their children were:

SAMUEL PARKER; m. and had son Aaron, who is supposed to be living somewhere in the west.

ABIJAH PARKER(?).

MARTHA PARKER(?).

142. **Anna Parker** *(Levi,[6] Joseph,[5] Josiah,[4] John,[3] Hananiah,[2] Thomas[1])*, dau. of Levi and Mary (Lyon) Parker, was b. in Royalton, Vt., April 13, 1801; m. June 15, 1823, David Paige, b. April 19, 1796, son of Pierce and Anna (Durfee) Paige. They lived in Royalton, Vt.; removed to Downer's Grove, Ill. He was a clothier and farmer. He d. June 26, 1864. She d. June 8, 1879.

Their children were:

1. EDWIN PAIGE, b. and d. April 3, 1824.
2. GARDNER PAIGE, b. in Royalton, Vt., July 17, 1826; m. at Downer's Grove, Ill., June 17, 1852, Annis Weed Gilbert, b. in Castile, Wyoming Co., N. Y., April 27, 1828, dau. of Medad Parsons and Hannah (Hill) Gilbert. He was a farmer and for a time storekeeper. In Downer's Grove, Ill., he was police magistrate, assessor, collector of taxes and notary public. He d. in Downer's Grove, March 24, 1889. Children:
   - i. MARTHA VIRGINIA PAIGE, b. in Downer's Grove. Ill., Sept. 16, 1854; m. —— Miller. Children:
     1. Paige Miller, b. June 28, 1880.
     2. Clyde Orton Miller, b. March 1, 1883.
     3. Gertrude Rose Miller, b. July 8, 1886.
     4. George Samuel Miller, b. Feb. 9, 1889.
   - ii. ROSE A. PAIGE, b. in Wheaton, Ill., Nov. 28, 1856; resides at Downer's Grove, Ill.
   - iii. HANNAH G. PAIGE, b. in Downer's Grove, Ill., May 29, 1860; d. Dec. 13, 1865.
   - iv. ALZINA J. PAIGE, b. in Downer's Grove, Ill., Sept. 4, 1865; d. Nov. 19, 1865.
   - v. GERTRUDE M. PAIGE, b. in Downer's Grove, Ill., May 2, 1868; m. ——— Aunable(?).
3. MARY ALZINA PAIGE, b. April 25, 1829; m. in Downer's Grove,

Ill., Feb. 22, 1849, Washington Burdett Pratt, son of David and Electa (Alexander) Pratt. He was b. in Homer, N. Y., Sept. 24, 1827; d. in Durham, Butte Co., Cal., Dec. 25, 1879. He was a farmer and miller. She d. in Downer's Grove, Ill., March 4, 1856. Children:

i. ELLEN JOSEPHINE PRATT, b. in Grundy Co., Ill., March 1, 1850; m. Charles Clibourn. They reside in Decatur, Mo.

ii. EUGENE FRANKLIN PRATT, b. in Downer's Grove, Ill., June 23, 1851. He is m. and resides in Calistoga, Cal.

iii. Daughter, unnamed, b. and d. March, 1856.

143. Isaac Parker *(Levi,[6] Joseph,[5] Josiah,[4] John,[3] Hananiah,[2] Thomas[1])*, son of Levi and Mary (Lyon) Parker, was b. in Royalton, Vt., Dec. 1, 1806. He early removed to Ohio, where he lived 11 years. He m. in Cuyahoga Falls, Summit Co., O., Mary Linsted, then of Barrington, Mass. She was b. in Woodbridge, Suffolkshire, England, and came at four years of age with her parents from England and settled in Barrington, Mass. They removed to Chicago, Ill., where Isaac Parker still resides (1890) in the eighty-fourth year of his age. He was the youngest in the family of Levi Parker and is the only surviving child.

Their child was:

311. LUCY ANN PARKER, b. Dec. 17, 1838; m. Shubael Crandall.

144. Eunice Parker *(Joseph,[6] Joseph,[5] Josiah,[4] John,[3] Hananiah,[2] Thomas[1])*, dau. of Joseph, Jr. and Polly (Fisk) Parker, was b. in Weston, Aug. 13, 1792; m. in Weston, March 19, 1814, Cyrus Pratt, b. in Needham, Feb. 26, 1790, the sixth of the nine children of Deacon Samuel and Hepzibah Pratt of Needham. She d. in Needham, Aug. 16, 1834, aged 42. The family lived in Needham, where he was a farmer, but the town records fail to show the births of the children, who soon removed from town. He d. Sunday, March 26, 1871, a. 81.

Their children were:

1. SAMUEL PRATT, who d. young.
2. SAMUEL PRATT, b. 1818; d. Oct. 15, 1890. He was a nail manufacturer in Wareham.

3. JOSEPH PRATT, b. 1822; d. from an accident in Duncannon, Pa.
4. ISAAC PARKER PRATT, b. July 2, 1824; m. Feb. 1, 1846, Sophia Bird, b. in Chambly, Lower Canada, Nov. 8, 1828, dau. of Esther Bird. She d. in Brockton. Oct. 25. 1890. He resides in Brockton. Children:
   I. ROSWELL HENRY PRATT, b. in Bellingham, March 27, 1847; m. June 17, 1874, Ann J. Henry of Rockport, Me.
   II. HERBERT ALTON PRATT, b. in Bellingham, July 26, 1859; d. Dec. 29, 1864.
   III. FRANK PARKER PRATT, b. in Bellingham, Dec. 1, 1850; m. in Brockton, June 3, 1874, Mary Ada Cobb of Brockton.
5. EUNICE PRATT, b. 1826; m. Roswell Watkins. They lived in Boston. She survives and resides with her son-in-law in Wollaston. Children:
   I. LUCINDA WATKINS; m. William Plummer and lived in Wollaston.
   II. ETTA WATKINS; m. Fred Libby. They lived in Cambridge. They are both deceased.

   There were several children who d. young.
6. EDWIN PRATT, b. in Needham, Aug. 5, 1828; m. July 22, 1860, Caroline Patience Williams, b. March 7, 1840, dau. of Nathan A. and Esther B. (Haradon) Williams. He is a mental physician in Boston. Child:
   I. GRACE L. PRATT, b. Sept. 25, 1870; m. Feb. 10. 1891, Henry Jenkins of Malden.
7. WILLIAM HENRY PRATT, b. 1831; d. Oct. 27, 1845, aged 14.

145. Sophia Parker (*Joseph,*[6] *Joseph,*[5] *Josiah,*[4] *John,*[3] *Hananiah,*[2] *Thomas*[1]), dau. of Joseph, Jr. and Polly (Fisk) Parker, was b. in Weston, Oct. 6, 1796; m. at Shrewsbury, Dec. 4, 1817, Montgomery Haven, son of Samuel Haven, Jr., of Shrewsbury. She m. (2) in Waltham, Oct., 1832, Asa Luce, Jr., b. in Livermore Falls, Me., 1802, son of Asa and Hephzebeth (Weston) Luce. Asa Luce, senior, was probably a native of New Bedford, where his uncles were whalers, and his wife was a native of Weymouth. Asa Luce, Jr., with wife Sophia Parker settled in Livermore Falls, Me.

Their children, all b. in Livermore Falls, were:

1. FANNIE VALENTINE LUCE, b. Sept. 9, 1834; m. John Kennison of Jay, Me. They lived in Maine. She is deceased. He resides in Jay, Me. Children:

i. LAURA KENNISON; m. and resides in Livermore Falls, Me.
ii. ELIZA KENNISON; m. and resides in Livermore Falls, Me.

2. CHARLES DEMETRIAS LUCE, b. Dec. 23, 1835; m. Dec. 24, 1867, Joa Oakes Bruce, b. in Waltham, Aug. 10, 1844, dau. of Hiram and Hannah L. Bruce of Waltham. They reside in Waltham. He enlisted in Waltham in Co. H, 16th Mass., June 29, 1861, and was discharged Nov. 24, 1862. He was in Hooker's Division, Hentzleman's Corps, and was in the battles of Big Bethel, Fair Oaks, White Oak Swamp, Glendale, Malvern Hill, Second Bull Run and Chancellorsville.

3. HENRY BERNARD LUCE, b. June 10, 1837; m. Flavilla Emory, dau. of Rev. —— Emory of Auburn, Me. He d. Oct. 11, 1872, and she resides in Auburn, Me. He enlisted with his brother Charles D. Luce, and after his time expired he re-enlisted and served all through the war to its close. He was in all the battles in which his brother took part and in all which the Army of the Potomac were in afterwards. He was fifer for Hentzleman's Corps, and after re-enlisting was messenger of Gen. Sickles' staff. Child:

i. LILLIAN EMORY LUCE, b. June 18, 1871.

4. LAURA HAVEN LUCE, b. April 15, 1839; m. Myron Breuuer, son of Dr. Breuuer of Wilbraham. They have an adopted son Luther Breuuer.

5. SULLIVAN COOPER LUCE, b. Oct., 1841; enlisted in 1861 from Lewiston, Me., in Battery C. He was in all the battles of the Army of the Potomac up to the time when he was killed in the second day's fighting of the Battle of Gettysburg.

146. Isaac Parker (*Joseph,[6] Joseph,[5] Josiah,[4] John,[3] Hananiah,[2] Thomas[1]*), son of Joseph* and Mary (Fisk) Parker, was b. in Watertown, July 19, 1802; m. in Waltham, April 16, 1826, Lucy Dunsmore, b. in Lunenburg, March 13, 1807, dau. of Isaac and Lucy (Butterfield) Dunsmore of Lunenburg. Her father soon d. and when aged three she went to live with her grandfather, Enoch Cook of Westford, a Revolutionary

---

*The children of Joseph Parker, pages 161 and 162, as there found, are copied from Mrs. Joseph Parker's family Bible, which is in the possession of Isaac Parker's widow. Heading the list of children are three statements, to wit:

"Joseph Parker was born at Lexington, Oct. 4, 1767.

"Mary Fisk, wife of Joseph Parker, was b. at Weston, March 6, 1771.

"Mrs. Joseph Parker's Bible."

ISAAC PARKER OF WALTHAM.

veteran. She came to Waltham when 13 and has lived in sight of the bleachery at E. Waltham ever since. Isaac Parker came to Waltham when 19, in the year 1821. He was foreman of the packing and pressing at the bleachery, but he finally chose out-door work as more congenial and became a farmer. After his marriage he built the house in which his widow survives him. It stands at the corner of Willow and River Streets. He was a quiet, industrious man, fond of reading, and one of the earliest supporters of the town library. He gave a part of his farm to the town for the extension of River Street. He also owned the land situated between Gore Street and the Charles River, a part of which he gave to the Fitchburg R. R. Co. for the railroad there. He was a member of the Watertown Literary Organization which joined the Rumford Institute in Waltham. He was a very prominent and active member of that institute and for years took a very lively interest in its work.

Isaac Parker was a firm and unflinching believer in Masonry. In 1828 he took his Masonic degrees and was soon elected master. He was master of the Monitor Lodge 11 years, from Jan., 1847, to Nov., 1858, which is about three times as long as the administration of any other master of the lodge, and he was distinguished as the first master of Monitor Lodge who was ever presented with a past master's jewel. The lodge which bears his name was so named in honor to him—The Isaac Parker Lodge of Waltham. He was a man of the most unwavering integrity; his word was as good as his bond. He was wholly unostentatious, and he was a man of deep sense, sound learning and good judgment. He d. in Waltham, Oct. 1, 1875. His widow survives.

All the children were b. in Waltham:

312. Mary Hammond Parker, b. March 4, 1827; m. Shubael Treat.

313. Isaac Parker, Jr., b. March 4, 1829; m. Lydia Greenleaf Rowell.

George Parker, b. March 23, 1831; d. Nov. 20, 1832.

314. George Endicott Parker, b. Feb. 4, 1834.

Bernard Parker, b. Feb. 12, and d. May 5, 1836.

Charles Bernard Parker, b. July 17, 1838; d. Dec. 31, 1839.

315. Lowell Parker, b. April 24, 1840.

Joseph Parker, b. Feb. 3, and d. March 9, 1842.

Lucy Caroline Parker, b. Oct. 3, 1843; d. July 27, 1845.

316. Lucy Caroline Parker, b. June 9, 1846; m. Sept. 11, 1871, Warner W. Carpenter.

147. Cynthia* Parker *(Joseph,[6] Joseph,[5] Josiah,[4] John,[3] Hananiah,[2] Thomas[1])*, dau. of Joseph, Jr. and Polly (Fisk) Parker, was b. in Weston, Jan. 15, 1810; m. in Waltham, Dec. 3, 1836, David M. Batherrick, son of Timothy Batherrick of Westborough. They lived first in Waltham but soon removed to Weston. She d. in Weston, July 5, 1850.

Their children were:

1. Adaline Batherrick, b. 1837; d. in Weston, July 16, 1850, aged 13.
2. Elizabeth Batherrick; d. in Boston, aged about 20, unm.

148. Chloe Parker *(Elisha,[6] Joseph,[5] Josiah,[4] John,[3] Hananiah,[2] Thomas[1])*, dau. of Elisha and Jerusha (Wentworth) Parker, was b. in Weston, March 7, 1801; m. in Weston, April 20, 1823, Caleb Carr, b. July, 1797, son of Caleb[5] Carr of Easton, son of Eseck[4]. She d. in No. Easton, Dec. 10, 1882. She was an energetic and capable woman, and possessed rugged health until impaired by age. He was employed for 50 years by the Ames Shovel Co., N. Easton, Mass., and he d. March 28, 1887.

Their children were:

1. John H. Carr, b. April 9, 1824; m. (1) Mary Stoddard of Stoughton; she d. 1849, and he m. (2) Emily E. Willis of Easton, who d. July 17, 1889, and he m. (3) Sept. 21, 1889, Harriet N. Dow of Harwich. He is assistant foreman in the Ames Shovel Co., and resides in N. Easton. Children:
   - i. Lewis Carr, b. Nov. 28, 1851; d. July 28, 1852.
   - ii. Charles Carr, b. Oct. 10, 1853; d. March 4, 1854.
   - iii. Helen Carr, b. Feb. 11, 1855; m. June 26, 1878, John C. Wilder of Brockton, where they reside.
   - iv. Frank Carr, b. Feb. 12, 1861; m. Nellie Whiting of

*The name is spelled without the letter n in the mother's, Mrs. Joseph Parker's, Bible.

Whitman. They and their dau. Helen May Carr reside in Easton.

v. CALEB CARR, b. Nov. 1, 1866; d. Jan. 26, 1869.

2. ELIZA CARR, b. Nov. 6, 1825; m. Dec. 7, 1848, Hiram Williams of Easton, son of Larned Williams. They lived in N. Easton, where she d. Jan. 10, 1881. He survives. Children:

i. HENRY C. WILLIAMS, b. Oct. 26, 1849; m. Feb. 27, 1877, Mary H. Dunbar.

ii. EDITH WILLIAMS, b. Dec. 30, 1854; m. Nov. 9, 1880, Dr. George E. Woodbury of Brockton.

3. MARTIN WALES CARR, b. March 9, 1829; m. Dec. 22, 1858, Lucy E. Brackett of Quincy, b. July 3, 1838. He is a jewelry manufacturer in Boston, and resides in Somerville. Children:

i. LEWIS BRACKETT CARR, b. in N. Attleborough, May 31, 1860.

ii. EUGENE PARKER CARR, b. in Springfield, Jan. 31, 1864.

iii. FREDERICK MARTIN CARR, b. July 10, 1870.

iv. EMILY HOWARD CARR, b. Oct. 19, 1876; d. March 6, 1877.

v. HELEN DAMON CARR, b. Jan. 27, 1880.

vi. HOWARD WENTWORTH CARR, b. Jan. 30, 1881.

4. LEWIS CARR, b. Nov. 7, 1830; d. Jan. 13, 1851.

5. JERUSHA ANN CARR, b. Dec. 25, 1833; m. April 13, 1851, George H. Hartwell of W. Bridgewater, and reside in Cambridge. Children:

i. AMY HARTWELL.

ii. FANNIE HARTWELL.

6. SARAH F. CARR, b. March 25, 1836; m. (1) Oct. 5, 1854, Hannibal Wells of Easton, who d. Nov. 30, 1854, and she m. (2) March 15, 1863, Albert T. Reed, son of Rotheus A. and Ruhamah F. (Howard) Reed of Easton. They reside in Whitman. Children:

i. LILLIAN REED, m.

ii. FANNIE REED.

iii. ALICE REED.

iv. CHARLES REED, who d.

v. A son, unnamed.

vi. JENNIE REED.

7. HENRY CARR, b. Feb. 11, 1838; m. Nov. 1, 1863, Mary Elizabeth White, dau. of Sanford and Mary E. White of Easton. He is assistant foreman in the Ames Shovel Works, N. Easton, where he resides. Children:

i. LEWIS HENRY CARR, b. Sept. 22, 1867.

ii. EDWARD MARTIN CARR, b. Jan. 25, 1874.

8. LYDIA CARR, b. Dec. 7, 1840; m. (1) George Humphrey, (2) William Monroe. They reside in Lynn. Their dau. was:

i. BERTIE MONROE; m. and resides in Brockton.

149. Isaac Parker *(Elisha,[6] Joseph,[5] Josiah,[4] John,[3] Hananiah,[2] Thomas[1])*, son of Elisha and Jerusha (Wentworth) Parker, was b. in Weston, April 23, 1803; removed with his parents to Lincolnville, Me.; removed with them to Stoughton, Mass., about 1815; m. Nov. 9, 1825. by the Rev. Mr. Hawes of S. Boston, Flavila R. Crosby, b. in Carlisle, May 6, 1810, dau. of Rhoda Crosby. He removed (1) to Walpole, (2) to Needham, (3) to Newton, (4) to Cambridgeport, (5) to Stoughton, (6) to Canton, (7) in 1847 to Salem, where he d. Dec. 3, 1871. She survives him and lives in Salem. He was naturally a machinist. He learned the blacksmith trade. In Cambridgeport and Stoughton he and his brother Samuel made blind-hinges. In Salem he conducted a shop devoted to the manufacture of curriers' knives, and in which business he was succeeded by his son.

Their son was:

317. James Parker, b. in Stoughton, March 22, 1827; m. Martha A. Haskell of Deer Isle, Me.

150. Elisha Hobbs Parker *(Elisha,[6] Joseph,[5] Josiah,[4] John,[3] Hananiah,[2] Thomas[1])*, son of Elisha and Jerusha (Wentworth) Parker, was b. in Weston, April 17, 1805; removed with his family to Lincolnville, Me.; removed with them to Stoughton, Mass.; in Stoughton was a manufacturer of blind-hinges and one of the Stoughton Grenadiers.* While still a young man he removed to Connecticut and m. July 1, 1830, at E. Windsor, Ct., Charlotte Skinner of S. Windsor, Ct., dau. of Benjamin and Mary (Foster) Skinner, b. May 17, 1807. He settled in S. Windsor, Ct., where he was a boot manufacturer. He d. in S. Windsor, Aug. 25, 1845, aged 40. She d. March 25, 1883.

The children were all b. in E. Windsor, now S. Windsor:

Mary B. Parker, b. Sept. 13, 1831; m. May, 1849; d. Aug., 1858.

Louisa Catharine Parker, b. July 21, 1833; m. Jan. 21, 1851,

---

* The Stoughton Grenadiers have long taken a prominent part in the military social life of the town of Stoughton. Elisha H. Parker was one of the charter members, as was also Isaac Parker. The vacancy made by Elisha was filled by his brother Hiram Parker, who still belongs, and that caused by the removal of Isaac Parker was filled by his brother Jonathan C. Parker, while Charles Elbridge Parker succeeds to his father's membership.

William G. Tefft, b. in Windham, Ct., Oct. 1, 1819. He is a farmer in S. Windsor, Ct.

318. BENJAMIN SKINNER PARKER, b. Feb. 12, 1835; m. Julia Wolcott of Windsor, Ct.

319. FRANCES JANET PARKER, b. Dec. 8, 1836; m. Samuel S. Case.

ELLEN REBECCA PARKER, b. Nov. 20, 1840; m. in S. Windsor, Ct., Jan. 7, 1873, Edwin B. Ripley, b. in Blandford, Mass., son of John and Elizabeth Ripley. He is a farmer in S. Windsor, Ct.

320. EMMA SARAH PARKER, b. Jan. 4, 1843; m. Albert K. Fuller of Stafford, Ct.

CHARLOTTE MARIA PARKER, b. Feb. 1, 1845; m. July 14, 1892, Henry Brown of Feeding Hills.

151. Rebecca* Parker *(Elisha,[6] Joseph,[5] Josiah,[4] John,[3] Hananiah,[2] Thomas[1])*, dau. of Elisha and Jerusha (Wentworth) Parker, was b. in Lincolnville, Me., Sept. 18, 1807; m. Martin Wales, b. in Stoughton, Feb. 22, 1802, son of Joshua and Betsey Wales of Stoughton. She was an attractive lady, a very industrious and able woman. She was very ingenious. She excelled in fancy work, and her cone and shell work were also her pride. Martin Wales was a well-to-do and influential man; was president of the Brockton Bank, then N. Bridgewater, and his likeness adorned their bank-notes. He d. March 6, 1874. She d. Oct. 10, 1886.

Their children were:

1. MARY REBECCA WALES, b. June 5, 1829; m. Sept. 6, 1849, Caleb H. Packard of Campello. They have one adopted dau.
2. MARTIN WALES, Jr., b. Nov. 30, 1831; d. March 5, 1832.
3. MARTIN WALES, Jr., b. March 19, 1833; m. Jan. 2, 1853, Olive E. Wales of N. Bridgewater. He d. Dec. 17, 1864. She resides in Boston. Children:
   - I. EDWARD LEWIS WALES; m. and resides in N. Easton.
   - II. CHARLES LOWRY WALES; m. Caroline Wentworth of Stoughton. He is a railway conductor and resides in Stoughton.
4. GEORGE WALES, b. Sept. 25, 1835; m. (1) Oct. 16, 1856, Emily F. Richards of S. Weymouth; she d. Dec. 17, 1864;

*Rebecca Parker is recorded in the list of her parents' children with the middle initial R. But from the family papers it appears that she did not use a middle name.

m. (2) April 5, 1869, Mary A. Richards of S. Weymouth (niece of his first wife). He is a shoe merchant and resides in Stoughton. Children:

i. GEORGE ALBERT WALES, b. March 18, 1858.
ii. EMMA FRANCES WALES, b. May 11, 1870.

5. SETH WALES, b. Aug. 4, 1837; m. Oct. 2, 1864, Eudora Williamson of Stoughton, where they reside. Children:

i. SETH ELVA WALES.
ii. ARTHUR WALES.
iii. A dau., d. in infancy.
iv. BURTON WALES.
v. EDWIN FORREST WALES.
vi. CATHARINE REBECCA WALES.

6. LUCY MARIA WALES, b. July 3, 1839; m. Fisher Ames Copeland. Children:

i. HARRY ADDISON COPELAND; hotel keeper, Sea Isle City, N. J.
ii. MERTON FISHER COPELAND, who m. Caroline Packard of Brockton.

7. ADELAIDE FRANCES WALES, b. Nov. 5, 1845; m. Jan. 1, 1868, William Neale of Readfield, Me. He is a railway conductor and resides in Stoughton. She d. Dec. 31, 1882. Child:

i. MINNIE NEALE; d. at age of eight years.

Samuel Austin Whitney Parker (see page 162), *(Elisha,[6] Joseph,[5] Josiah,[4] John,[3] Hananiah,[2] Thomas[1])*, son of Elisha and Jerusha (Wentworth) Parker, was b. in Lincolnville, Me., July 25, 1810: removed about 1815 with his parents to Stoughton. Mass., where he m. Priscilla Tisdale Drake. b. in Stoughton, April 17, 1814, dau. of John and Hannah (Morse) Drake of Stoughton. He was a natural machinist, sharing the characteristic inventive genius of his family. He invented among other things the dinking machine for boot manufacturing and the turning machine. He invented, it is said, the first machine used on a boot. He lived in Stoughton. His widow survives him.

Samuel Parker was a large, fine looking man of six feet two inches in height, and stood very erect. From his several initials he was sometimes distinguished by the nickname of "Saw" Parker.

Their children were:

PRISCILLA DRAKE PARKER, b. Feb. 19, 1836; m. in Stoughton, 1856, William H. White, Jr., b. in Stoughton, 1835, son of William H. and Annie (Erskins) White of Stoughton. They reside in Stoughton. Children:

I. WILLIAM WHITNEY WHITE, b. in Stoughton, May 27, 1857.
II. ANNIE PRISCILLA WHITE, b. in Stoughton, May 5, 1862.

SAMUEL AUSTIN WHITNEY PARKER, Jr., b. Dec. 18, 1834; m. Hattie Wade of Brockton Heights. They reside in Stoughton. He with George Wales carried on the boot and shoe business in Stoughton in the Martin Wales building. He also kept the Hotel Parker for a while. Samuel Parker was a prosperous and very active citizen. He kept a market in Boston, when he suffered the misfortune of paralysis, and entrusted, to his financial loss, his large business to his help. Their son was:

I. AUSTIN PARKER, b. April, 1859; d. when a young man.

ESTELLE INEZ PARKER, b. May 4, 1845; m. 1866, Dr. W. E. C. Swan of Stoughton, native of S. Easton. She d. March 26, 1891, aged 45 years, 10 months, 22 days. Their son was:

I. CHARLES LOUIS SWAN, b. Dec. 19, 1867; resides in Stoughton.

152. Hannah Parker *(Elisha,[6] Joseph,[5] Josiah,[4] John,[3] Hananiah,[2] Thomas[1])*, dau. of Elisha and Jerusha (Wentworth) Parker, was b. in Lincolnville, Me., Jan. 13, 1813; m. in Stoughton, John Smith of Stoughton, a native of Portugal, b. 1811, and came when very young to this country with his brother Joseph C. Smith, who later settled in Cambridge. John Smith was first a ship rigger in Boston, afterward a shoemaker in Stoughton. He d. in Raynham, 1847. She remained a widow 14 years, when she m. (2) Eleazer Pratt of Weymouth. She d. in Weymouth about 1867.

The children of John and Hannah (Parker) Smith were:

I. JAMES ELISHA SMITH, b. in Stoughton, June 2, 1833; m. (1) Sophia Thomes, (2) Abbie Pope, (3) Sarah Kellogg, and resides in Athol.

The children of James and Sophia (Thomes) Smith were:

I. JOHN SMITH, b. 1865.
II. JAMES SMITH, b. 1867.
III. MARIA SMITH.

The children of James and Sarah (Kellogg) Smith were:

IV. IDA EVA SMITH, b. 1877.
V. ALICE LOUISA SMITH, b. Feb. 1, 1879.

vi. Edna Mabel Smith, } Twins.
vii. Flossie Smith, }

2. Betsey Maria Antoinette Smith, b. in Randolph, Oct. 27, 1837; m. Frederic Russell and resides in N. Easton. Child:
   i. Eveline D. Russell; m. H. E. French and resides in Neponset.

3. Joseph Creoister Smith, b. in Stoughton; m. Bridget Maguire, and has had:
   i. Cora Smith. ii. Flora Smith.

4. Sarah Jane Smith, b. in Stoughton; m. James Luther. They have a large family of children and reside in Taunton, where he is foreman of a locomotive factory.

5. Melissa Smith; m. John Dame. They lived in Hanover and are both deceased. Children:
   i. Alvin Dame; resides in Hanover.
   ii. Emma Dame; resides in Hanover.

The child of Eleazer and Hannah (Parker) (Smith) Pratt was:

6. Eleazer Pratt, Jr. He is living in Weymouth.

153. Hiram Parker *(Elisha,[6] Joseph,[5] Josiah,[4] John,[3] Hananiah,[2] Thomas[1])*, son of Elisha and Jerusha (Wentworth) Parker, was b. in Stoughton, March 28, 1816; m. Sept. 25, 1836, Rhody Freeman of Orleans, b. March 11, 1818, dau. of Jonathan and Eunice (Snow)[?] Freeman of Orleans. She d. of consumption, Nov. 21, 1848, and he m. (2) April 25, 1850, Sarah Irene Morse, b. in Roxbury, April 23, 1830, dau. of Amos and Abigail Barnet (Davenport) Morse. He learned the trade of shoemaking. He has been undertaker in Stoughton and sexton of the Universalist Church in all over 30 years. He is the mail-carrier of Stoughton.

The children of Hiram and Rhody (Freeman) Parker were:

Hiram Emmons Parker, b Nov. 4, 1837; d. July 13, 1859.
Mary Augusta Parker, b. Dec. 4, 1840; d. Jan. 13, 1841.
Albert Parker, b. June 1, 1844. He enlisted in the Civil War for two years; was taken prisoner and d. in 1865 in Andersonville stockade prison just before the close of the war.

The children of Hiram and Sarah I. (Morse) Parker were:

Cariella Parker, b. and d. Dec. 1, 1851.
Gertrude Parker, b. June 9, and d. July 24, 1856.

CHARLOTTE MORSE PARKER, b. Aug. 28, 1858; d. April 3, 1860.
WALDO PARKER, b. May 12, and d. June 19, 1862.
EVERETT PARKER, stillborn, May 30, 1866.

154. Jonathan Capin Parker *(Elisha,[6] Joseph,[5] Josiah,[4] John,[3] Hananiah,[2] Thomas[1])*, son of Elisha and Jerusha (Wentworth) Parker, was b. in Stoughton, April 23, 1820 (twin brother with David M.); m. in Lowell, Oct. 18, 1840, Martha Ann Briggs, b. in Stoughton, Jan. 23, 1822, dau. of Shepherd and Sally (Morris) Briggs of Stoughton. The father, Shepherd Briggs, was a manufacturer in Stoughton and Lowell.

Jonathan C. Parker was a natural mechanic with wood or iron. Besides that of a woodworker and machinist he knew also the shoemaker's trade. He lived in Stoughton all his days. He and his brother Samuel made the first steam engine that Samuel ever used. He conducted a machine shop in the manufacture of edge tools. He supplied all the shoemakers of Stoughton with knives, which were distinguished for their quality. He had the inventive genius of his people; was an intelligent looking, large and robust man of over 200 weight. He d. July 8, 1886. His widow survives.

Their children were:

321. CHARLES ELBRIDGE PARKER, b. May 21, 1844; m. Harriet A. Minzy of Brockton Heights.

322. ELISHA MELVILLE PARKER, b. April 18, 1848; m. Caroline Frances Coots of Stoughton.

155. David Manley Parker *(Elisha,[6] Joseph,[5] Josiah,[4] John,[3] Hananiah,[2] Thomas[1])*, son of Elisha and Jerusha (Wentworth) Parker, was b. in Stoughton, April 23, 1820 (twin brother with Jonathan C.); m. Mary Ann Andrews of Walpole. He was a shoemaker and d. in Stoughton, Feb. 5, 1890, aged 69 years, 9 months, 13 days.

Their dau. was:

MARY LAVINIA PARKER, who m. Hiram Smith of Stoughton. She d. aged about 22 and left no issue.

156. Nancie Parker *(John,[6] Peter,[5] John,[4] John,[3] Hananiah,[2] Thomas[1])*, dau. of John and Deborah (Lamb) Parker, was b. in Framingham, Dec. 11, 1782; m. in Royalston, 1802, Nathan Goddard, b. June 26, 1780. They lived first in Athol. Their home was near the Royalston line, but one-half mile from the Parker homestead in Royalston. Removed in 1806 to Bethlehem, N. H., where he resided the greater part of his time ever after. He was a farmer. He d. in Littleton, N. H., April 26, 1857, at the home of his dau., Mrs. Sally Strain. He was thus aged 76 years, 10 months. She d. in Littleton, N. H., Nov., 1865, aged 83.

Their children were:

1. ANNA GODDARD, b. in Athol, Oct. 6, 1803; m. Luke Aldrich of Littleton, N. H. She d. Feb., 1870. They had one dau.:
   i. MARIA ALDRICH; m. George Bacon.
2. ELIZA GODDARD, b. in Athol, Aug. 15, 1805; d. Feb. 5, 1886, unm.
3. JOHN GODDARD, b. in Bethlehem, N. H., July 15, 1807; m. April 15, 1835, Betsey Banfill of Dalton, N. H., and removed to Bethlehem, N. H. He d. July 28, 1887. Children:
   i. ELIZABETH GODDARD.
   ii. LEONORA S. GODDARD; m. —— Baker of Bethlehem, N. H., and resides in Littleton, N. H.
   iii. EMELINE GODDARD.
   iv. DANIEL GODDARD.
   v. ALBURN GODDARD; d. in the war of the Rebellion.
   vi. HENRY GODDARD.
4. MARY GODDARD, b. Jan. 31, 1810; m. Amasa Annis of Littleton, N. H., where they resided. She d. June, 1856, without issue. He is also deceased.
5. RHODA GODDARD, b. Oct. 3, 1812; m. in Bethlehem, N. H., Sept. 15, 1839, John Gordon of Littleton, N. H., b. in New Hampton, N. H., May 18, 1810, son of Jeremiah and Sally Gordon. He is a farmer. She now resides in Waterford Vt. Their seven children were all b. in Littleton, N. H.:
   i. AMASA N. GORDON, b. May 31, 1843.
   ii. MARY A. GORDON, b. Oct. 4, 1846; m. Freeman Morse, and resides in Waterford, Vt.
   iii. SALLY P. GORDON, b. Nov. 5, 1848; m. Jackson M. Perry, and have children, viz.:
      1. Georgianna Perry, b. Sept. 7, 1865.
      2. William Perry, b. Feb. 22, 1868.
      3. Frank G. Perry, b. Feb. 23, 1869.
      4. Jennie E. Perry, b. Dec. 3, 1871,

5. Mary E. Perry, b. Oct. 24, 1873.
6. Charles M. Perry, b. Nov. 6, 1874.
7. Hattie E. Perry, b. Nov. 8, 1875.
8. Carrie M. Perry, b. Feb. 28, 1877.
9. Allie B. Perry, b. May 11, 1878.
10. Willie B. Perry, b. July 12, 1879.
11. Harry G. Perry, b. Aug. 22, 1881.
12. Elsie L. Perry, b. Nov. 18, 1882.
13. Katie G. Perry, b. Dec. 2, 1884.
14. Ida M. Perry, b. April 18, 1887.

iv. George Gordon, b. Sept. 25, 1850.

v. Charles C. Gordon, b. June 28, 1852.

vi. Israel Gordon, b. April 8, 1854.

vii. Ellen I. Gordon, b. Jan. 1, 1857.

6. Peter Goddard, b. April 17, 1814; m. Emeline Banfill of Dalton, N. H. He d. March, 1889. They had one son:

i. H. P. Goddard, who resides in Franconia, N. H. No issue.

7. Abigail Goddard, b. Feb. 20, 1816; d. Aug., 1824.

8. Sally Goddard, b. Nov. 5, 1818; m. Aug. 29, 1838, Daniel Strain. He is deceased. She d. Dec. 1, 1888. They had seven sons and five daughters all but one son of whom lived to maturity. They are now widely scattered about the country. Their names were:

i. Ellen Strain; m. —— Brown and live in Vermont; no issue.

ii. Cornelius Hartwell Strain; resides in Littleton, N. H., and has sons:

1. Allie Strain. 2. Arthur Strain.

iii. John Parker Strain; d. unm.

iv. Jane Strain; m. Weston Lyons of Bath, Me. Their son is:

1. Harry Weston Lyons.

v. Catharine Eliza Strain; m. Court Spooner of Bethlehem. They live in Lisbon, N. H., and have children.

vi. Daniel J. Strain; m. Dora L. Adams, dau. of Jacob A. and Adelia B. Adams of Wilbraham. He is an artist in Boston; no living issue.

vii. Sarah C. Strain; m. James Long.

viii. Charles Strain; resides in Littleton, N. H., and has a family.

ix. Lyman Edward Strain; lived a few months.

x. Frank W. Strain; unm.

XI. HARRY STRAIN; resides in Littleton, N. H., and has a family.

XII. EVA C. STRAIN.

9. EVALINE GODDARD, b. Feb. 20, 1822; m. March 1, 1845, Albert Gilman of Bethlehem, N. H. She d. March 21, 1890. Their children were:

I. GEORGE GILMAN; m. —— Phillips, and resides in Bethlehem, N. H.

II. FRANK GILMAN.

III. MARY GILMAN.

157. Mary Parker *(John,[6] Peter,[5] John,[4] John,[3] Hananiah,[2] Thomas[1])*, dau. of John and Deborah (Lamb) Parker, was b. in Framingham, June 2, 1789; m. in Royalston, Oct., 1815, Capt. John Forristall of Winchendon, b. Feb. 23, 1787. He was a farmer in Winchendon, a captain of the militia and selectman for a number of years. He d. Oct. 16, 1862. She d. July 30, 1872.

The children were b. in Winchendon:

1. JOSEPH PARKER FORRISTALL, b. Oct. 24, 1816; m. in Winchendon, Aug. 30, 1842, Mary A. Flint, b. in Winchendon, Nov. 1, 1818. He is a farmer and lumberman and resides in Alstead, N. H. Their children were:

I. GEORGE PARKER FORRISTALL, b. Oct. 9, 1851; d. June 1, 1858.

II. FRANK M. FORRISTALL, b. April 22, 1857; m. June 19, 1878, and has three children:

1. Leslie Parker Forristall, b. May 4, 1879.
2. Florence M. Forristall, b. July 26, 1881.
3. Ralph W. Forristall, b. Oct. 6, 1888.

2. JOHN M. FORRISTALL, b. July 12, 1821; m. May 18, 1848, Mary J. Wright, b. in Vernon, Vt., April 9, 1823, dau. of Osmond and Sylvia Wright. He is foreman of construction on the Fitchburg Railroad, and resides in Ashburnham, Mass. Their children were:

I. FRED WRIGHT FORRISTALL, b. Aug. 7, 1850; m. June 3, 1874, Hattie A. Converse.

II. GEORGE BURROWS FORRISTALL, b. Feb. 4, 1861; d. June 18, 1873.

III. ABBIE JANE FORRISTALL, b. Sept. 17, 1862; m. John L. Clarke. They reside in Ashburnham. Child:

1. Ernest M. Clarke, b. Oct. 28, 1883.

3. CHARLES E. FORRISTALL, b. Dec. 17, 1823; m. June 27, 1850, Ann Augusta Whitney of Royalston. They lived in Winchendon. He d. Feb. 7, 1872. She d. Nov. 10, 1887. Children:

i. CLARENCE W. FORRISTALL, b. 1854; d. 1855.

ii. CHARLES WALTER FORRISTALL, b. March 12, 1860; resides in Royalston, unm.

4. ROSWELL M. FORRISTALL, b. Feb. 18, 1829; m. in Winchendon, Jan. 1, 1856, Mary Ann Lake, b. in Rindge, N. H., Jan. 5, 1833, dau. of John and Mary Ann Lake. She d. Feb. 1, 1890. He is a carpenter and resides in Winchendon; no issue.

Deborah Parker (see page 163), *(John,[6] Peter,[5] John,[4] John,[3] Hananiah,[2] Thomas[1])*, dau. of John and Deborah (Lamb) Parker, was b. in Framingham, April 12, 1792; was a most worthy lady of high ability. She during her early life took good care of her parents during their decline in life and devoted attentive service to her mother, an invalid from paralysis. She was seemingly well rewarded by the comfort which she bestowed, and always happiest when generously assisting or doing for others. Nearly a year after her mother's death she m. Jan. 8, 1839, Dea. Samuel Morse of Hopkinton. There were five sons and two daughters in his family, and, notwithstanding the necessary duties thus involved, the success of happiness, love and prosperity which crowned this marriage itself well attests her most excellent character and ability. She was a most conscientious and loving woman; was very popular with all her associates, who were ever pleased to speak a loving word in her memory. She d. April 26, 1865, aged 73. She left no issue.

158. Peter Parker *(John,[6] Peter,[5] John,[4] John,[3] Hananiah,[2] Thomas[1])*, son of John and Deborah (Lamb) Parker, was b. in Framingham, July 16, 1794; went when aged six with his father to Royalston, where he passed his early life and m. (1) 1824, Sarah Sawyer of Boylston. He succeeded to his father's homestead, farm and shingle-mill. He was a typical old-time shingle-maker. They were made in view of strength and durability, and were often carted long distances. On one occasion he transported a load from his farm to Hopkinton where he shingled the "coffee house" and these shingles remained upon the roof perfectly sound for 30 years. About 1836 he removed to Southborough, where he was a farmer, and soon after removed to Hopkinton. Mrs. Sarah (Sawyer) Parker d. 1830. He m. (2) in Hopkinton, Nov. 25, 1830, Emily Chamberlain of Hopkinton, dau. of Ebenezer Chamberlain. She d. about 1852.

Peter Parker was a stoutly built, good looking man of medium height, with black hair and sandy beard. He was a good mechanic by nature, and was more fond of work and business than learning. He loved to excel in his work. When engaged in the field it was his pride to let no one mow or hoe faster than he did. In politics he was a Whig and took a lively interest in the "Tippecanoe" campaign of 1840. He d. in Hopkinton, Oct. 30, 1862.

The children of Peter and Sarah (Sawyer) Parker were:

OWEN BOARDMAN PARKER, b. in Royalston, Jan. 5, 1826. He began to work at shoemaking at the age of 11, and has ever since followed this occupation. He resides in Worcester.

SARAH MOORE PARKER, b. in Royalston, March, 1828; resides in Hopkinton, unm.

The children of Peter and Emily (Chamberlain) Parker were:

323. HIRAM CHAMBERLAIN PARKER, b. in Hopkinton; m. Laurania Newton of Woodville.

324. MILTON BRIDGES PARKER, b. in Hopkinton, Feb. 17, 1834; m. Harriet Jane Ward of Hopkinton.

AMELIA PARKER, b. in Hopkinton; d. in Ashland at about the age of 12.

JAMES PARKER, b. in Hopkinton; killed when a child by a falling plank.

159. Dea. John Parker (*John,[6] Peter,[5] John,[4] John,[3] Hananiah,[2] Thomas[1]*), son of John and Deborah (Lamb) Parker, was b. in Framingham, June 16, 1798; m. Sept. 3, 1823, Mary Ann Fales, b. in Shrewsbury, Dec. 21, 1800, dau. of Daniel and Sarah (Pratt) Fales of Shrewsbury, and granddau. of Capt. Fales, native of Wales. Daniel Fales lived to the age of 99, and in Shrewsbury the old Fales homestead is still standing.

John Parker settled first in Holliston; second removed to Southborough, where he lived 20 years, and was a farmer; third removed to Holyoke, where he was instrumental in establishing the Second Baptist Church, of which he was senior deacon; fourth removed to Westfield; fifth to Holliston; sixth to Berlin, and he now resides in Malden at the advanced age of 94. It is well to chronicle with his name the characteristics and the rich harvests of this long and active life. He was always distinguished as a good talker and a man of very decided opinions. But his good nature was always overflowing. He took the lead on political and social questions. He will be remembered as not only a kind friend to all but an active missionary worker and a true christian man. He not only opposed the evils of his town, but he was determined to "weed out" what he could. With his cousin Peter Parker Howe he worked hard and well to improve the social standing of the town, and they were very successful. When he settled in Southborough it was an intemperate, noisy place. He approached men who were in the low depths of degradation, and as a friend and brother encouraged them to do better. His manner and argument were so effective that he seldom failed to produce an effect. He was an attractive speaker. He held meetings and led the singing, denounced intemperance and lectured on the blessings of the gospel. He was the means of establishing the Church in Southborough, of which he was made deacon. He made many speeches against slavery and intemperance. During his first stay in Holliston his example of teetotalism was the first known discard of liquor in that section. In politics he was a Whig, in religion a Baptist. When the Republican party was founded he helped form the first Republican party meeting ever held in Worcester. He was selectman. In 1840 his opposition to the Advent movement in his town at that time was strongly felt. After settling in Metcalf Village, Holliston, he was both farmer and shoemaker. During his stay he was a leading factor in the establishment of the Baptist Church there. His wife d. July 16, 1888. In his old age his retentive memory and characteristic vigor of life abide with him, and his interest in the im-

Dea. John Parker.

provement and welfare of mankind, which has distinguished him through life, is still an unfailing source of satisfaction.

Original poems by Rev. Dr. George C. Lorimer and Corp. George H. Patch were read upon the occasion of John Parker's golden wedding, Sept. 3, 1873. The following is an extract from Mr. Patch's donation:

"Know all by these presents, that friend Parker, Esquire,
Our dearly loved friend, who these lines did inspire,
Has faithfully lived in the marital bond,
For full fifty years, and been faithful and fond;
Upbearing the burdens and cares that assailed,
With a kind loving heart, that never has failed,
And his heart has always been cheerful and bright,
In the pure steadfast beams of domestic delight:
And tho' met by misfortune, has not felt its harm,
While the loved ones at home were left to his arms.
Who while mingling freely with the world and its strife,
Has allowed no defilement to disfigure his life,
And so we can trust him without any fears
That he'll do just the same for the next fifty years.

"You see his hair parts much wider to-day
Than when he was basking in youth's noontide ray,
And you see his kind eyes in integrity fail,
As father Time's hand his vigor assails.
But his heart is as young as when long ago
He felt it throb quick with youth's springtime glow.
And freshly and brightly its influence cheers,
Despite the oncoming of gathering years.

"Three cheers for a Parker; may his coronet shine
With the wreath that our kindly affection entwines;
May the sweet flowers that spring 'mid the air of his home,
Be wet with the dewdrops from *God's heavenly* dome."

Their children were:

ELIZA ANN PARKER, b. June 7, 1824; m. Burley Collins of Southborough. He d. Nov. 7, 1853. She d. Sept. 19, 1856. The whole family were buried in Westborough. They had one son:

1. DEWITT COLLINS; d. Sept. 19, 1853.

325. CHARLES FALES PARKER, b. Aug. 1, 1826; m. Julia A. Brigham of Milwaukee, Wis.

JOANNA WHITING PARKER, b. June 16, 1833; m. June 19, 1857, Milton Day of Westfield. They settled in Westfield; removed to Berlin, where he was a shoemaker and farmer and where he d. July 1, 1889. She now resides with her aged father in Malden at the home of her brother John H. Parker.

326. John Henry Parker, b. Sept. 14, 1835; m. Annie E. Gilmore of Boston.

Ellen D. Parker, b. June 22, 1837; d. Dec. 23, 1838.

327. Sarah Letitia Parker, b. Dec. 17, 1839; m. Homer E. Sawyer of Bradford, Vt.

160. Ruth Parker *(John,[6] Peter,[5] John,[4] John,[3] Hananiah,[2] Thomas[1])*, son of John and Deborah (Lamb) Parker, was b. in Royalston, July 31, 1800; m. in Holliston, Sept. 12, 1821, Capt. Nathan Leland of Holliston. She was an interesting conversationalist, an attractive and most worthy lady. She, like her sister Deborah, m. a widower, and like her sister's family, it was often jokingly remarked by the step-children that they never knew such a good mother-in-law. He was a farmer of Holliston, representative to the Mass. Legislature, selectman and captain of the militia. He d. in Holliston, 1842, aged 74. She d. in Erie, Pa., April 27, 1856. Charles, Simeon and Warren Leland, the three well known and popular landlords of the Metropolitan, New York city, were nephews of Capt. Nathan Leland.

Their children were:

1. John Parker Leland, b. April 22, 1822; m. Lydia Morgan of Holliston, dau. of Jonathan Morgan. They lived in Hollis ton for a few years, after which they removed to Gangese, Mich. They are both deceased. Children:
   - i. Everard Leland; resides in Toledo, O.
   - ii. Nathan Leland.
   - iii. Emma Leland; m. and resides in Michigan.
   - iv. George Leland. And probably others.
2. George Ames Leland, b. May 9, 1824; d. at age of 13 months.
3. Leander Fales Leland, b. May 21, 1826; m. in Springfield, Sarah Price, dau. of Nathan Price of New York city. She d. in Marlborough, Feb., 1890. He enlisted in 1861 in Co. K, 27th Mass. Reg. and served three years, mostly under Gen. Foster's command. He was given much picket duty and was generally sent to the remotest outposts, positions of much trust and danger. During his service he was offered a captaincy, but he preferred to remain a private. The most trying time was the forced march from Newberne to Goldsboro, N.

C., during which occurred the battle of Whitehall, and about 16 days constant marching with but few hours' sleep at any time. They were also besieged at Little Washington, N. C., for 17 days. He resides in Whitman. Children:

i. STARK LELAND; m. Josephine Kimball of Holliston, dau. of Ebenezer Kimball. He is superintendent of a shoe factory in Calais, Me., and has two children:

1. Frank Leland. 2. Leroy Leland.

ii. GEORGE LELAND; who lived three years.

iii. and iv. Two children, who d. in infancy.

v. BERTHA LELAND; resides in Calais, Me., unm.

4. ERASTUS DARWIN LELAND, b. Sept. 13, 1828; m. Serena Morgan (sister of Lydia Morgan). She d. and he m. (2) Harriet ——; she d. and he m. again. He resides in Lanark, Ill., and has three children, one of whom is named Effendi Leland.

5. POLLY LELAND, b. June 27, 1831; m. in Springfield, Nov. 1, 1852, Henry Foulds, b. in Arnold, Eng., Jan. 28, 1826. They removed to Lanark, Ill., where he was postmaster the 16 years preceding his death. She resides in Burlington, Ia. Their children were:

i. ALICE CAREY FOULDS, b. in Springfield, Mass., March 30, 1854.

ii. LIZZIE MORSE FOULDS, b. in Wooster, O., June 14, 1858.

iii. THOMAS FOULDS, b. in Martin, O., Dec. 9, 1860.

iv. MARY FOULDS, b. in Milford, Mass., April 17, 1865.

v. HENRY MORSE FOULDS, b. in Lanark, Ill., March 31, 1869.

vi. EUNICE FOULDS, b. in Lanark, Ill., July 26, 1873.

161. Abigail Parker *(John,[6] Peter,[5] John,[4] John,[3] Hananiah,[2] Thomas[1])*, dau. of John and Deborah (Lamb) Parker, was b. in Royalston, March 15, 1802; m. Jan. 1, 1829, Newell Ware of Walpole, b. 1806, son of Capt. Nathan and Eunice (Smith) Ware of Walpole. She was a very capable woman. He was a farmer and a very retired man. They lived in Walpole but later removed to Ashland. She d. in Walpole, Aug. 29, 1864. He d. in Ashland, May 10, 1884.

Their dau. was:

1. ELIZABETH DEBORAH WARE, b. Nov. 21, 1829; m. in Boston, March 18, 1857, Elisha Morse of Hopkinton, b. Feb. 20, 1830,

son of Dea. Samuel and Catharine (Sloan) Morse. He was a bookbinder. Lived in Hopkinton; removed to Ashland, 1865; removed to Worcester, 1886, where he d. May 29, 1888. She resides in Worcester. He was a soldier in Co. K, 44th Mass. Reg., in which he served nine months. Their children were:

i. MARTHA ELIZABETH MORSE, b. in Westborough, March 29, 1860; d. Aug. 31, 1861.

ii. GEORGE NEWELL MORSE, b. in Walpole, Jan. 31, 1863. He is a music teacher in Worcester, Mass.

162. Josiah Parker *(John,[6] Peter,[5] John,[4] John,[3] Hananiah,[2] Thomas[1])*, son of John and Deborah (Lamb) Parker, was b. in Royalston, July 31, 1804; m. in Royalston, March 4, 1835, Caroline Peck, b. in Royalston, dau. of Bonona Peck, Esq. She was a school teacher. He m. (2) 1857, Harriet May of Winchendon. He was a most industrious man, worked every day and all day at his trade of crimping and treeing boots at which he was a very capable workman. The family lived in Ashland. Mrs. Harriet (May) Parker d. in Southville, Feb., 1884. He d. in Southville, March 21, 1886.

His children were:

328. MARY JANE PARKER, b. Jan. 14, 1836; m. Edgar W. Lane.

329. SYLVANUS A. PARKER, b. May 11, 1838; m. Mary Etta Gates of Stowe.

ELLEN FRANCES PARKER, b. in Hopkinton, Aug. 4, 1840; d. June 16, 1842.

ARTHUR LEROY PARKER, b. Jan. 5. 1842; m. Caroline Gay of Hopkinton; d. Aug. 20, 1871. He served three years in the Union army. Their son was:

i. WALTER A. PARKER, b. Feb. 2, and d. July 2, 1866.

330. ROSETTA FRANCENA PARKER, b. June 16, 1845; m. Morris Flint of Marlborough.

331. JOHN FRANCIS PARKER, b. Aug. 20, 1849; m. Mary C. Gassett.

332. ELLA ANNETTE PARKER, b. Dec. 16, 1850; m. Edward E. Leighton.

163. Presson Parker *(John,[6] Peter,[5] John,[4] John,[3] Hananiah,[2] Thomas[1])*, son of John and Deborah (Lamb)

Parker, was b. in Royalston, Oct. 24, 1807: m. Mary Newton, b. in Southborough, Jan. 22, 1816, dau. of Abel and Laurania (Rice) Newton of Southborough. She was one of a family of 12 children. They removed to Ashland. Removing west he d. in Bloomington, Ill., Oct. 8, 1858. Presson Parker was a large, handsome, well formed man, six feet in height, and wore a heavy, black beard. The family had the severe misfortune of losing all their children but one before reaching the age of 25 years. She still resides in Marlborough with her son.

Their children were:

Infant, b. and d.

GEORGE PRESSON PARKER, b. May 6, and d. July 31, 1838.

333. LYSANDER PRESSON PARKER, b. in Worcester, Oct. 2, 1839; m. Eleanor Wilkins of Marlborough.

MINERVA ANN PARKER, b. in Southborough, Oct. 18, 1841; m. Dec. 25, 1864, William B. Wetherby of Marlborough; d. April 6, 1866. No issue.

GEORGIETTE MARION PARKER, b. in Sutton, Jan. 10, 1844; m. May 28, 1865, Daniel B. Bigelow; d. Jan. 17, 1867. No surviving issue.

ROLAND EVERETT PARKER, b. in Southborough, Aug. 4, 1847; d. Jan. 30, 1854.

164. Harriet Parker *(Nathan,[6] Peter,[5] John,[4] John,[3] Hananiah,[2] Thomas[1])*, dau. of Nathan and Catharine (Murdock) Parker, was b. in Framingham, Oct. 10, 1793; m. March 20, 1821, Josiah Bigelow, b. Oct. 26, 1790. He was a carpenter and they lived in Framingham. He was the son of Joseph and Ruth (Parker) Bigelow of Holliston, thus making him cousin to Harriet Parker. She d. Nov. 2, 1861. He d. July 22, 1863.

Their children were:

1. JOHN PRESTON BIGELOW, b. Feb. 14, 1822.
2. HENRY W. BIGELOW, b. Oct. 21, 1824; m. (1) Mary Langell.
3. CATHARINE A. BIGELOW, b. Sept. 8, 1827; m. Aug. 31, 1853, Job T. Perry, native of Belfast, Me. He owned the mills in Framingham, near F. A. Billings's. The family removed to Somerville. He d. April, 1884. Their children were:
   - i. EVERETT T. PERRY, b. Nov. 27, 1854.
   - ii. HATTIE MARIA PERRY, b. Oct. 13, 1858.
   - iii. CATHARINE E. PERRY, b. Dec. 22, 1860.

4. Josiah Q. Bigelow, b. June 18, 1828; d. young.
5. Charles E. Bigelow, b. June 2, 1830; m. Marcia E. Terrell. He d. Dec. 15, 1885.
6. Josiah Q. Bigelow, b. Feb. 6, 1836.

165. Maria Parker *(Nathan,[6] Peter,[5] John,[4] John,[3] Hananiah,[2] Thomas[1])*, dau. of Nathan and Catharine (Murdock) Parker, was b. in Framingham, April 16, 1799; m. Dec. 9, 1819, Abijah Fay of Southborough. He was a farmer in Framingham. They adopted one dau., but left no children.

166. Dr. Peter Parker *(Nathan,[6] Peter,[5] John,[4] John,[3] Hananiah,[2] Thomas[1])*, son of Nathan and Catharine (Murdock) Parker, was b. in Framingham, June 18, 1804. In his youth he exhibited a remarkable thirst for knowledge and power of attaining it, together with an untiring industry and worthy ambition. He was an enthusiastic student from boyhood and early showed a preferment for missionary labors. He graduated from Yale College in 1831, after which he took up a course in the medical department from which he graduated in 1834 with the title of M.D. He was licensed to preach Aug., 1833.

Peter Parker was a renowned missionary, theologian, doctor and surgeon, and conspicuous in the early diplomatic relations between his country and China. His ability was not bounded by one profession. Wherever he went or whatever his duties his associates felt the blessing of his presence or beheld the improvement of his touch.

Having studied theology, in which profession he took a deep interest, he was immediately appointed by the American Board of Commissioners of Foreign Missions as missionary physician to China. He was ordained by the Second Presbytery of Philadelphia, May 16, 1834. He embarked for China June 3, and reached Canton Oct. 29. At Canton he established a hospital. It was originally intended to treat only those affected with the diseases of the eye, in which Dr. Parker was an expert, but soon applicants suffering from other ailments were admitted, and the first year he had taken in 2,000. The medical ability of Dr. Parker was a marvel. The natives appreciated his wonderful cures and showed him the greatest respect and gratitude. He also preached to the inmates of the hospital. He was the first known white man who ever saw the face of the Emperor of China. This was occasioned by the Emperor's illness, which necessitated Dr. Parker's educated skill.

A worthy account of Dr. Peter Parker is by J. H. Temple, Esq., historian of Framingham, in which he thus writes knowingly of his deceased neighbor and friend:

"Soon after reaching Canton he went to Singapore to study the Fuhkeen Dialect; returned to China, Aug., 1835, and Nov. 4 opened the Ophthalmic Hospital in Canton, originally intended for diseases of the eye but soon became, by force of circumstances, more general in its character. In 1837, Dr. P. visited Lew Chew and Japan, in the ship *Morrison*, to return to their homes some shipwrecked Japanese sailors. He was one of the founders of the Medical Missionary Society of China, and, for many years, president of the same.

"On the breaking out of the Opium War between England and China—at which date upwards of 12,000 cases had been treated at the Canton Hospital—Dr. Parker returned to America. visiting, also, England and Scotland. As a direct result of his efforts. a widespread interest was awakened in his work; auxiliary societies were formed, and the sum of $6,000 was secured for the purposes of the Medical Missionary Society.

"In Washington, D. C., March 29, 1841, Dr. Parker married Miss Harriet Colby Webster, dau. of John Ordway and Rebecca Guild (Sewall) Webster of Augusta, Me., and returned to China in 1842,—Mrs. P. being the first foreign lady to reside in Canton. In 1844, with the consent of the Pru. Com. of the Am. Board, he accepted the appointment, by Hon. Caleb Cushing, U. S. Minister to China, of Chinese Secretary and Interpreter to the Legation. An historical fact of interest may here be recorded: A *projet* of a treaty had been prepared by Mr. Cushing, and translated into Chinese, prior to the arrival at Canton of the Imperial Commissioner, Ke Ying. This *projet* was referred to deputies named by each of the two Commissioners, to be examined in detail. One of the Chinese deputies was Pwan Tze Shing, son of Pwan Ting-kwa, a Hong merchant, from whom Dr. Parker (one of the American deputies) had successfully removed a large polypus in each nostril, and whose mother had also been his patient. When, in the progress of their examination, the deputies came to the 17th Article, which granted to Americans the right to rent sites and construct houses and places of business, also hospitals and cemeteries, Pwan Tze Shing—evidently as a graceful tribute of acknowledgment to the benefactor of his parents, as well as a public recognition of the claims of the Christian religion—proposed to add, 'and temples of worship.' The added clause was adopted, and was accepted by the Commissioners, and became a provision of the treaty. Whether the prompting of personal gratitude, or of a broader motive, this suggestion prepared the way for the Imperial Rescript of Dec. 28, 1844, granting toleration to Christianity throughout the Chinese Empire.

"In 1845 Dr. Parker was appointed by our government Secretary of Legation and Chinese interpreter, at which date his connection with the Am. Board of Missions ceased, though he continued his labors at the Hospital till 1855, when 53,000 names of patients had been entered on its roll. He then returned to America; but was soon appointed U. S. Commissioner, with plenipotentiary powers, to revise the treaty of 1844. He reached China in December, and after two years' service returned to the U. S. in 1857. He afterward resided in Washington, though a love for his native town induced him to purchase the paternal homestead in Framingham, where his summers were passed.

"Dr. Parker was made a corporate member of the A. B. C. F. M. in 1871; was elected Regent of the Smithsonian Institution in 1868; and was appointed in 1871 by the Evangelical Alliance, one of the American delegates to Russia, to memorialize the Emperor in behalf of religious liberty in the Baltic provinces."

Biographical notices of Dr. Peter Parker are also found in all standard encyclopædias and in the History of Middlesex Co., Mass. He d. in Washington, D. C., Jan. 10, 1888.

Their only child was:

334. Peter Parker, b. in Washington, D. C., June 13, 1859.

167. Charles Parker (*Josiah,[6] Peter,[5] John,[4] John,[3] Hananiah,[2] Thomas[1]*), son of Josiah and Olive (Stone) Parker, was b. in Framingham, March 6, 1805; m. May 16, 1830, Mary H. Wallingford of Claremont, N. H., b. in Dublin, N. H., 1806, dau. of Ebenezer Blodgett and Mary (Hildreth) Wallingford. He succeeded to his father's new homestead in Framingham; removed to Illinois; removed to Bridgewater; bought an estate in Framingham Centre; removed to Roxbury, where he d. Jan. 16, 1885. He felt an interest in his genealogy, and to him much of the credit is due for the fulness of the Parker records in the History of Framingham. He properly appreciated the worth of his ancestors' noble lives and observed the many abilities which they had transmitted to their descendants. He was an enterprising and public-spirited citizen. Mrs. Mary H. Parker d. March 1, 1870, aged 64.

Their children were:

335. Charles W. Parker, b. June 27, 1831; m. Mary Jane Schoff of Newburyport.

Josiah S. Parker. b. Jan. 13, 1834; d. Dec. 22, 1838.

Elizabeth Leman Parker, b. July 4, 1835; m. Nathan D. Robinson of Bridgewater.

336. Edgar Parker, b. June 7, 1840; m. Frances Ames Hyde of Bridgewater.

168. Eliza Ann Parker *(Josiah,[6] Peter,[5] John,[4] John,[3] Hananiah,[2] Thomas[1])*, dau. of Capt. Josiah and Olive (Stone) Parker, was b. in Framingham, July 17, 1810; m. in Framingham, Nov. 4, 1835, Thomas Hastings, Jr., b. in Framingham, April 18, 1809, son of Thomas and Nancy (Abbott) Hastings of Framingham. He d. June 6, 1886. She resides in Cambridgeport.

Their children, all b. in Framingham, were:

1. Courtland Evarts Hastings, b. March 21, 1843; m. in Chelsea, Florence Hubbard of Chelsea, dau. of Charles Hubbard. He resides in New York city, where he is in the wholesale jewelry business. Children:

   i. Lillian Hastings, b. Jan. 16, 1873.

   ii. Alice Hastings, b. April, 1874.

2. Frederic Ashburton Hastings. b. Sept., 1845; m. Jan. 15, 1872, Elizabeth Dow Ladd, b. in Newton, Feb. 4, 1846, dau. of William H. and Hannah B. (Goodridge) Ladd. He was of Portsmouth, N. H., and she was of Haverhill. Children:

   i. Ella May Hastings, b. in Jamaica Plain, June 18, 1873.

   ii. Clarence Frederick Hastings; b. July 2, 1877; d. Nov. 21, 1877.

   iii. Fred Parker Hastings. b. in Brighton, Aug. 9, 1878.

3. Ella Webster Hastings, b. Oct. 11, 1849; m. Nov. 25, 1875, John Langdon Chapman, son of Eben and Eliza Chapman, b. in York, Me., Nov. 24, 1844. They reside in Cambridgeport.

169. Emily Parker (*Josiah,*[6] *Peter,*[5] *John,*[4] *John,*[3] *Hananiah,*[2] *Thomas*[1]), dau. of Josiah and Olive (Stone) Parker, was b. in Framingham, Nov. 17, 1813; m. Daniel Parmenter. She possessed good musical talent. They lived in Framingham, where they have both deceased.

They had one son:

1. DANIEL PARMENTER, who served in the Union army. It is said that he was shot in a Rebel prison while attempting to send a letter home. He was a graduate of Norwich (Vt.) University.

170. Edward C. Parker (*Artemas,*[6] *Peter,*[5] *John,*[4] *John,*[3] *Hananiah,*[2] *Thomas*[1]), son of Artemas and Almy (Clark) Parker, was b. in Framingham, Sept. 26, 1806; m. May 17, 1832, Mary Leland, b. in Holliston, April 6, 1808, dau. of James and Betsey Leland of Holliston. He settled in Holliston in the east part of the town, where he built the house in which he still lives, adjacent to E. Holliston station. He was a farmer and station agent, which latter position he held for a great many years and which has now passed to his son. His wife d. Aug. 31, 1879. He was the last survivor of his family and d. in E. Holliston, Feb. 3, 1893, aged 86 years.

Their children were:

337. JAMES EDWARD PARKER, b. Feb. 19, 1834; m. Susan Mason of Southbridge.

JOSEPH STODDARD PARKER, b. March 28, 1839; m. just previous to his enlistment, Clara Thompson. Enlisted in 1862 for nine months in the 44th Mass. Reg. He served a part of the time at Port Royal, S. C. He is conductor on Pullman excursion cars.

171. George Smith Parker (*Artemas,*[6] *Peter,*[5] *John,*[4] *John,*[3] *Hananiah,*[2] *Thomas*[1]), son of Artemas and Almy (Clark) Parker, was b. in S. Framingham, April 19, 1808; m. in New Scotland, N. Y., Oct. 14, 1829, Mary Ann White of Albany, N. Y., b. in New Scotland, N. Y., Sept. 2, 1816, dau. of Cobert and Sarah White. After three children were b. to them in Albany, N. Y., they removed May 7, 1837, to Holliston, where he was a shoemaker and where he d. Aug. 1, 1875. She d. in Medway, Nov. 23, 1887.

Their children were:

George Smith Parker, Jr., b. Oct. 2, 1832; m. Mary Skahal.

338. Melvina Parker, b. Dec. 9, 1834; m. (1) Alvin B. Batchelder, (2) William Batchelder.

339. Eliza Jane Parker, b. Feb. 2, 1837; m. Luther H. Turner.

Mary Emeline Parker, b. Sept. 15, 1839; d. in Holliston, Aug. 5, 1841.

James William Parker, b. March 27, 1842; m. in St. John, N. B., Catharine C. Godsoe. They had three children.

340. Charles Augustus Parker, b. Aug. 15, 1844; m. Eliza A. Pettis of Holliston.

341. Henry Emerson Parker, b. Oct. 13, 1849; m. Ellen E. M. Jones of Medway.

Edward Lorenzo Parker, b. July 2, 1852; d. in Chicago, Ill., Nov. 20, 1872.

172. Curtis Parker *(Artemas,[6] Peter,[5] John,[4] John,[3] Hananiah,[2] Thomas[1])*, son of Artemas and Almy (Clark) Parker, was b. in Framingham, June 28, 1810; m. April 5, 1832, Eliza Jane Horton, b. April 14, 1810, dau. of William and Hannah (Rice) Horton of Natick. He settled in Natick, where he d. Dec. 25, 1873. She d. in Natick, May 28, 1888.

Their children were:

Sumner Wheelock Parker, b. Dec. 10, 1835; d. Dec. 8, 1841.

342. Althea Wheelock Parker, b. Nov. 21, 1843; m. John Lovett Sanger of Natick.

343. Sumner Horton Parker, b. Jan. 7, 1848; m. Emma Jane Fay of Natick.

173. Lorenzo Parker *(Artemas,[6] Peter,[5] John,[4] John,[3] Hananiah,[2] Thomas[1])*, son of Artemas and Almy (Clark) Parker, was b. in Framingham, May 8, 1812. He learned bookbinding of O. Boynton of Framingham, after which he settled in Holliston and m. April 10, 1837, Mary E. Herrick, b. in Portland, Me., Dec. 29, 1812, dau. of Moses and Mary (Cogswell) Herrick. Moses Herrick was in the War of 1812 and d. soon after its close. Mary Cogswell was dau. of William Cogswell of Lunenburg. Lorenzo Parker was a printer and bookbinder. He kept a bookstore in Holliston for many years, but in his later years he was a farmer. He lived on the place where his widow still resides. He d. July 11, 1887.

174. Eliza Jane Parker *(Artemas,[6] Peter,[5] John,[4] John,[3] Hananiah,[2] Thomas[1])*, dau. of Artemas and Almy (Clark) Parker, was b. in Framingham, June 6, 1817; m. in Natick, Dec. 17, 1834, David Washburn, b. March 7, 1815, son of Jedediah and Mitta Frost Washburn of Natick. He was engaged in the shoe business most of his life. They lived in Natick. She d. March 12, 1884. He d. Aug. 17, 1887.

Their children were:

1. ALMY CLARK WASHBURN, b. Sept. 27, 1835; m. (1) Jan. 1, 1856, Charles M. Felch of Natick, where they resided. He d. and she m. (2) Dec. 12, 1866, George W. Lewin. They removed to Fall River, where she d. Oct. 9, 1888, and where he still resides. Children:

   I. CHARLES SUMNER FELCH, b. Jan. 2, 1858; m. Nov. 26, 1884, Stella Daniels; resides in Felchville, Natick, and has one dau.:

      1. Mabel Louise Felch, b. Sept. 10, 1886.

   II. JENNIE ALMY FELCH, b. Dec. 26, 1857; m. George Winslow. They reside in Steep Brook, Fall River, and have:

      1. Charles Winslow. 2. Beula Winslow.

   III. FANNIE LEWIN; resides in Fall River, unm.

2. ROMANZO NERIDIN WASHBURN, b. July 4, 1839; m. Aug. 22, 1865, Annie Church of Augusta, Me. They lived in Natick, where he d. March 22, 1887. She resides in Salem. Children:

   I. LORENZO PARKER WASHBURN; resides in Salem.
   II. WALTER REYNOLDS WASHBURN; lived two or three years.

3. MARY ELIZA WASHBURN, b. April 4, 1845; m. Sept. 6, 1865, Sylvanus Stewart of Haverhill, where they reside and have one son:

   I. ERNEST L. STEWART, b. Feb. 27, 1867; m. Bertha Eastman; resides in Haverhill. Child:

      1. Effie Stewart.

4. OSCAR JEDEDIAH WASHBURN, b. Jan. 28, 1850; m. in Sherborn, Jan. 8, 1876, Emma Jane Leland, dau. of Amariah and Martha (Anderson) Leland, b. in Eden, Me., Nov. 1, 1852. He is a dentist and resides in Natick. Their child was:

   I. DAVID LELAND WASHBURN, b. in Natick, Nov. 16, 1879.

175. Susan M. Parker (*Luther,*[7] *Philemon,*[6] *Jonas,*[5] *Andrew,*[4] *John,*[3] *Hananiah,*[2] *Thomas*[1]), dau. of Luther and Dolly (Byam) Parker, was b. in Chester, Vt., March 10, 1826; m. in Cavendish, Vt., Dec. 24, 1849, Horace Thompson of Chester, b. in Chester, May 16, 1825. They reside in Cavendish.

Their children were:

1. William P. Thompson, b. in Cavendish, Vt., Aug. 20, 1855; m. Nov. 28, 1878. He is overseer in a woolen factory.
2. Hattie M. Thompson, b. July 10, 1860; m. April 22, 1883, Alva T. Pierce of Cavendish.

176. Lucinda A. Parker (*Luther,*[7] *Philemon,*[6] *Jonas,*[5] *Andrew,*[4] *John,*[3] *Hananiah,*[2] *Thomas*[1]), dau. of Luther and Dolly (Byam) Parker, was b. in Chester, Vt., June 3, 1827; m. Sept. 12, 1850, Josiah Ayers, b. in Windham, Vt., April 29, 1819, son of James Ayers of Windham. He was a farmer in West Pawlet, Vt., where he d. Feb. 5, 1890.

Their children were:

1. Horace J. Ayers, b. Aug. 13, 1851; m. Jan. 7, 1873, Ella Hicks, dau. of Daniel and Arathusa (Johnson) Hicks. Children:
   - i. Addie L. Ayers, b. Jan. 28, 1876; d. Aug. 16, 1888.
   - ii. Mardie R. Ayers, b. Aug. 24, 1882.
2. George J. Ayers, b. Oct. 26, 1855; m. Feb. 17, 1878, Ida M. Woodard, dau. of Marcelar and Mary A. (Miller) Woodard. Their daughters were:
   - i. Isma C. Ayers, b. Aug. 15, 1879.
   - ii. Grace P. Ayers, b. July 3, 1882.
   - iii. May B. Ayers, b. July 5, 1884.
   - iv. Leslie J. D. Ayers, b. July 19, 1886.
3. Addie L. Ayers, b. Aug. 20, 1867; d. March 5, 1870.

177. Sarah S. Parker (*Luther,*[7] *Philemon,*[6] *Jonas,*[5] *Andrew,*[4] *John,*[3] *Hananiah,*[2] *Thomas*[1]), dau. of Luther and Dolly (Byam) Parker, was b. in Chester, Vt., June 21, 1840; m. April 5, 1868, Alvin W. Davis.

178. Mary Ann Parker (*Calvin,*[7] *Philemon,*[6] *Jonas,*[5] *Andrew,*[4] *John,*[3] *Hananiah,*[2] *Thomas*[1]), dau. of Calvin and Seba (Cutler) Parker, was b. in Chester, Vt., July 21, 1828;

m. May 1, 1849, Silas F. Baldwin, b. Oct. 4, 1822, son of Nahum and Philinda (Harvey) Baldwin. He is a farmer in Chester, Vt.

Their children were:

1. Elsie M. Baldwin, b. Feb. 23, 1853; m. Feb. 15, 1884, S. Lincoln Hutchinson of New York City.
2. Oscar S. Baldwin, b. March 26, 1856; d. March 30, 1879.
3. William P. Baldwin, b. May 6, 1870.

179. Olive A. Parker (*Calvin,*[7] *Philemon,*[6] *Jonas,*[5] *Andrew,*[4] *John,*[3] *Hananiah,*[2] *Thomas*[1]), dau. of Calvin and Seba (Cutler) Parker, was b. in Chester, Vt., Nov. 5, 1829; m. March 12, 1856, Silas J. Smith, b. Jan. 7, 1825, son of William and Ruth (Blodget) Smith. He is a farmer in Chester Depot, Vt.

They have one dau.:

1. Grace O. Smith.

180. Fannie E. Parker (*Calvin,*[7] *Philemon,*[6] *Jonas,*[5] *Andrew,*[4] *John,*[3] *Hananiah,*[2] *Thomas*[1]), dau. of Calvin and Seba (Cutler) Parker, was b. in Chester, Vt., April 18, 1835; m. March 21, 1855, Calvin W. Bates, b. March 25, 1832, son of James and Mary (Grimes) Bates. She d. Feb. 22, 1889.

Their children were:

1. Forest C. Bates.
2. Cora F. Bates.

181. James Parker (*John,*[7] *Philemon,*[6] *Jonas,*[5] *Andrew,*[4] *John,*[3] *Hananiah,*[2] *Thomas*[1]), son of John and Ellen (Johnson) Parker, was b. in Chester, Vt., Dec. 14, 1825; m. (1) Sept. 2, 1850, Sophia Hopkins, b. in Springfield, Vt., Sept. 26, 1835, dau. of Jotham and Esther (Perry) Hopkins. She d. June 30, 1863, and he m. (2) March 23, 1864, Susan Balch. He is a farmer and resides in Chester, Vt.

The children of James and Sophia (Hopkins) Parker were:

344. Emma S. Parker, b. in Chester, Vt., Aug. 17, 1851; m. Henry Philips.

George E. Parker, b. in Springfield, Vt., March 26, 1855.
Abbie M. Parker, b. in Springfield, Vt., Sept. 11, 1857.
345. Nellie L. Parker, b. in Springfield, Vt., March 31, 1860; m. Tyler Putnam. } Twins.
Nettie L. Parker, b. in Springfield, Vt., March 31, 1860. }

The children of James and Susan (Balch) Parker were:

Frederic C. Parker, b. Dec. 14, 1864.
346. Lizzie A. Parker, b. April 23, 1866; m. Gilford Ellison.
Julia A. Parker, b. Aug. 29, 1871.

182. Amos Earle Parker (*Joseph*,[7] *Amos*,[6] *Amos*,[5] *Andrew*,[4] *John*,[3] *Hananiah*,[2] *Thomas*[1]), son of Joseph and Relief (Earle) Parker, was b. in Hubbardston, Feb. 26, 1802; m. Feb. 25, 1829, Matilda Converse of Bakersfield, by whom the first two children were born. She d. July 26, 1832, and he m. (2) June, 1833, Eunice W. Reid, by whom he had four children. Her father was a native of Townshend, Vt. She d. at the birth of her last child, July 24, 1842. He m. (3) Jan. 1, 1844, Roxanna McAllister of Enosburg, Vt., no issue. She is still living, but he d. Sept. 25, 1881.

When at the age of two years he removed with his parents to Bakersfield, Vt. At 24 he with about 20 other young men gathered at St. Albans, where they on Jan. 1, 1826, started for New York with 22 yoke of oxen and 19 carts. They were on the road 22 days in this journey; they then filled in low land for building purposes, which land is now in the business part of the city. He then engaged in the carpenter's trade, and during his three years' stay assisted as far as possible in the growth of this great city. Returning to Bakersfield he was during the 23 years there a farmer, except the three years when he kept the hotel in Bakersfield. He then bought a farm in Fletcher, Vt. While in Fletcher he was honored with all the offices in the gift of the town. He was selectman for four or five years. In 1863 he was a recruiting officer and he gladly gave to the new soldier his commission of $15 for each recruit. He represented his town in the Legislature in 1862 and '63, also at the extra session to ratify the Emancipation Proclamation. He returned to Bakersfield in 1867, where he held various offices of trust until his death, which occurred Sept. 25, 1881. He was a large, finely proportioned man, five feet eleven in height, and his usual weight being about 200. In habits he was temperate in all things, as he neither used liquors of any kind, tea, coffee or tobacco. He was a keen critic and a despiser of shams, but large in charity and full of original wit that made him a welcome guest in any society or company.

The children were b. in Bakersfield:

HOLLIS PARKER, b. May, 1830; d. May 19, 1832.

347. FANNY M. PARKER, b. May 11, 1832; m. Ralph Madison Blaisdell.

348. HOLLIS REID PARKER, b. Aug. 1, 1835; m. Mary M. Morrow of Pennsylvania.

349. JANE A. PARKER, b. June 20, 1838; m. Reuben H. Blackstone.

SUMNER EARL PARKER, b. Oct. 28, 1839; killed at the storming of Fredericksburg Heights, May 3, 1863. He was unm.

350. WORCESTER R. PARKER, b. July 24, 1842; m. (1) Emma F. Chase of Fletcher, Vt., (2) Hattie Pearson of Bakersfield, Vt.

183. Mary Robinson Parker (*Joseph,[7] Amos,[6] Amos,[5] Andrew,[4] John,[3] Hananiah,[2] Thomas[1]*), dau. of Joseph and Relief (Earle) Parker, was b. in Hubbardston, Jan. 5, 1804; m. Matthew Gray of Bakersfield, Vt. She lived and d. in Bakersfield.

They had five children, of whom two survive:

1. SENECA GRAY.
2. MARY ANN GRAY; m. —— Cheeseman, and resides in Cambridge, Vt.

184. Joseph Sumner Parker (*Joseph,[7] Amos,[6] Amos,[5] Andrew,[4] John,[3] Hananiah,[2] Thomas[1]*), son of Joseph and Relief (Earle) Parker, was b. in Bakersfield, Vt., Oct. 27, 1806; m. —— Hall and removed to New York city, where they resided and where she d. April, 1885. He was twice m. He is deceased. He was a dealer in milk.

Their only child was:

CORNELIA SUSAN PARKER, b. in New York city, Dec. 22, 1832; removed after the death of her parents to Bakersfield, Vt., and m. in 1857, Henry Warner French of Barre, Vt., where she afterwards resided. She d. April 4, 1885; he d. Sept., 1874. Child:

1. Adell May French, b. in Barre, Vt., July 2, 1859; m. Sept. 29, 1881, —— Ball of Barre, Vt., where she resides and has one son:

1. Frank Warner Ball, b. Aug. 18, 1882.

Sophia Bigelow Parker (see page 177), (*Joseph,[7] Amos,[6] Amos,[5] Andrew,[4] John,[3] Hananiah,[2] Thomas[1]*), dau. of Joseph and Relief (Earle) Parker, was b. in Bakersfield, Vt., April 11, 1808; m. Dorastus Wright. They are both deceased, but left one dau.:

1. Amanda Wright.

185. Euridicy E. Parker (*Joseph,[7] Amos,[6] Amos,[5] Andrew,[4] John,[3] Hananiah,[2] Thomas[1]*), dau. of Joseph and Relief (Earle) Parker, was b. in Bakersfield, Vt., April 25, 1811; m. July 4, 1845, Micha French, b. in Barre, Vt., Jan. 2, 1803. They lived in Barre, Vt., where she d. April 27, 1865, and he d. May 9, 1888.

Their children were:

1. Colman Sumner French, b. Nov. 27, 1847; m. in Chicago, Ill., March 12, 1872, Abbie L. Southgate, dau. of Richard and Martha (Alden) Southgate. He is station agent at Hampton, Ia. Their son was:

1. Fred Porter French, b. July 27, 1877.

2. Alfred B. French, b. April 29, and d. Aug., 1830.
3. Fred O. French, b. Oct. 10, 1855; m. at Clinton, Mo., May 16, 1887, Bertha Custer, b. in London, O., Dec. 25, 1860, dau. of Berthier J. and Nellie (Tyler) Custer. He is bookkeeper for the Iowa Central Railroad Co. at Marshalltown, Ia.

186. Frederick Appleton Parker (*Joseph,[7] Amos,[6] Amos,[5] Andrew,[4] John,[3] Hananiah,[2] Thomas[1]*), son of Joseph and Relief (Earle) Parker, was b. in Bakersfield, June 14, 1813; removed to New York city; m. Caroline Maxson of Squankum, N. J. He was a hackman in New York. He is deceased. She resides at Lakewood, N. J.

Their children were:

351. Joseph Albert Parker, b. Aug. 1, 1842; m. Samantha Wing Price.

352. Christianna Parker, b. Jan. 17, 1844; m. Emil Neesen of Brooklyn, N. Y.

353. SARAH PARKER; m. Henry Calenberg of Brooklyn, N. Y.
354. GEORGE PARKER; m. Louisa Ross.

187. **Betsey Lorinda Parker** (*Joseph,[7] Amos,[6] Amos,[5] Andrew,[4] John,[3] Hananiah,[2] Thomas[1]*), dau. of Joseph and Relief (Earle) Parker, was b. in Bakersfield, Vt., Dec. 10, 1818; m. July 7, 1845, Oliver F. Stebbins, son of Jotham Stebbins of Bakersfield. They lived first in Worcester, Mass., where their three children were born, and second in Athol. He is deceased. She resides in W. Medford with her son.

Their children were:

1. ADELBERT O. STEBBINS, b. May 3, 1846; d. April 29, 1861.
2. MERRIT E. STEBBINS, b. Feb. 22, 1848; d. July 30, 1850.
3. HERBERT WARNER STEBBINS, b. March 15, 1857. He was graduated from Dartmouth College in the class of '78; then entered the Theological Seminary at Andover, from which he was graduated in 1882. He is a Congregational minister. He m. Sept. 23, 1886, Anna L. Spear.

188. **Amos Parker** (*Sylvester,[7] Amos,[6] Amos,[5] Andrew,[4] John,[3] Hananiah,[2] Thomas[1]*), son of Sylvester and Alice (Davis) Parker, was b. in Westminster, Vt., Dec. 29, 1800; m. at Newark, Vt., June 8, 1825, Lorinda Fairbanks, b. April 17, 1802. They lived in Lyndonville, Vt. She d. Aug. 26, 1859. He d. Dec. 8, 1873.

Their children were:

SARAH ANN PARKER, b. Aug. 22, 1826; d. Aug. 16, 1846.
355. HORACE F. PARKER, b. in Kirby, Vt., Oct. 6, 1829; m. Mary Mianda Cole of Charleston, Vt.
HARRIET W. PARKER, b. Feb. 9, 1833; d. Sept. 18, 1835.
ABNER R. PARKER, b. May 7, 1835. Enlisted Nov. 19, 1863, in Co. B, 11th Reg., Vt. Vol. Heavy Artillery, was wounded in the battle at Cedar Creek, Va., Oct. 19, 1864. He returned to the hospital at Brattleboro, Vt., but getting worse was sent home the 5th of May, and d. July 31, 1865, aged 30 years.
356. SOPHIA W. PARKER, b. Nov. 5, 1837; m. Joseph H. Smith.
357. ANN ELIZABETH PARKER, b. Nov. 1, 1840; m. Josiah D. Smith.

189. **Joel D. Parker** (*Sylvester,[7] Amos,[6] Amos,[5] Andrew,[4] John,[3] Hananiah,[2] Thomas[1]*), son of Sylvester and Alice (Davis) Parker, was b. in Westminster, Vt., Oct. 9,

AMOS PARKER.

1802; m. Dec. 13, 1827, Lucy Wyman of Barnstead, P. Q. They settled in Hatley, Can. He d. in Hatley, Nov. 29, 1881, aged 79, and his widow, Lucy Wyman Parker, survives him at Hatley, and enjoys vigorous health at the advanced age of 87.

Their children were:

358. Adaline L. Parker, b. March 1, 1829; m. Asahel P. Parker.
359. Levi E. Parker, b. Aug. 5, 1830; m. Maria Howe.
360. Amanda M. Parker, b. June 23, 1836; m. Alfred Ives.
361. Edwin W. Parker, b. March 13, 1842; m. Adella Gordon.
362. Alba W. Parker, b. June 18, 1845; m. Ethel Emery.
363. Orville H. Parker, b. June 1, 1848; m. Betsey Bowen.
Alice F. Parker, b. May 29, 1854; m. Sept. 3, 1880, H. F. Barlow of Lennoxville, P. Q., b. Nov. 14, 1849, son of Horace (who d. in St. Johnsbury, Vt., 1883) and Rachel (Glidden) (of Waterville, P. Q.) Barlow. He is a general store-keeper in Magog, P. Q., where they reside.

190. **Alice Parker** *(Sylvester,[7] Amos,[6] Amos,[5] Andrew,[4] John,[3] Hananiah,[2] Thomas[1])*, dau. of Sylvester and Alice (Davis) Parker, was b. in Westminster, Vt., June 22, 1808; m. April 27, 1828, Henry Coburn, b. Aug. 3, 1799; d. Feb. 18, 1870. She d. Sept. 6, 1887.

Their children were:

1. Hollis P. Coburn, b. Nov. 24, 1828; m. March 25, 1860, Flora A. Stiles, dau. of Wm. R. Stiles of Albany, Vt. They have:
   i. Clarence E. Coburn, b. Sept. 22, 1861; m. Lucy E. Gallup. They reside in N. Troy, Vt., and have a son:
      1. Harry A. Coburn.
   ii. Sidney R. Coburn, b. Oct. 13, 1869; m. July 25, 1888, Jennie Smith. They reside in Barton, Vt.
   iii. Avis F. Coburn, b. Oct. 23, 1872; d. Feb. 25, 1879.
   iv. Roy W. H. Coburn, b. Jan. 20, 1881.
2. Alice P. Coburn, b. March 25, 1833; d. Feb. 27, 1835.
3. Lucy Rosaline Coburn, b. in Lyndon, Vt., Dec. 6, 1835; m. Dec. 22, 1863, in Albany, Vt., Hiram M. Hunter, b. Aug. 11, 1838, son of Ira and Nancy Hunter of Albany, Vt. He is a farmer in East Albany, near Irasburgh, Vt. Their dau.:
   i. Alice L. Hunter, b. in Albany, Vt., April 4, 1867; m. Sept. 12, 1889, George A. Sawyer.

191. Amory Parker (*Sylvester,*[7] *Amos,*[6] *Amos,*[5] *Andrew,*[4] *John,*[3] *Hananiah,*[2] *Thomas*[1]), son of Sylvester and Alice (Davis) Parker, was b. in Westminster, Vt., April 15, 1811; m. Nov. 10, 1841, Susan Gilman of Lyndon, Vt. They settled at Island Pond, Vt., where they still reside.

They have two children:

ALBERT PARKER, b. 1843; unm. Resides at Island Pond, Vt., where he is in the employ of the Grand Trunk R. R.

NELLIE PARKER; m. George W. Warner, and resides at Washburn, Byfield Co., Wis.

192. Lucy Parker (*Sylvester,*[7] *Amos,*[6] *Amos,*[5] *Andrew,*[4] *John,*[3] *Hananiah,*[2] *Thomas*[1]), dau. of Sylvester aud Alice (Davis) Parker, was b. in Westminster, Vt., May 24, 1813; m. Nov. 1, 1836, John Alexander, b. Aug. 14, 1812, d. Aug. 10, 1881, son of Abram Alexander, who was a private in the war of 1776, and who d. May 23, 1851, aged 92, and whose wife lived to the age of 86. She d. June 20, 1865, and he m. (2) Feb. 8, 1866, Mrs. Laura Dalgson.

The children of Lucy Parker were:

1. WILLIAM W. ALEXANDER, b. May 21, 1839; d. March 29, 1842.
2. ABRAM ALEXANDER, b. April 30, 1841; m. July 20, 1874, Sarah M. Scranton. They reside in Cambridgeport, and have had:
   - i. LUCY ALEXANDER, b. Feb. 2, 1877; d. aged five weeks.
   - ii. GEORGIA ALEXANDER, b. April 15, 1879.
3. BETSEY A. ALEXANDER, b. May 9, 1843; m. Feb. 11, 1864, J. H. M. Cochran. He d. Aug., 1885, without issue. She resides in Santa Ana, Cal.
4. LUCY JANE ALEXANDER, b. Sept. 14, 1845; d. April 29, 1865.
5. CHARLES HENRY ALEXANDER, b. Feb. 3, 1853; d. May 12, 1874.

193. Rhoena Parker (*Sylvester,*[7] *Amos,*[6] *Amos,*[5] *Andrew,*[4] *John,*[3] *Hananiah,*[2] *Thomas*[1]), dau. of Sylvester and Alice (Davis) Parker, was b. in Westminster, Vt., July 24, 1815; m. Jan. 1, 1840, Silas N. Howe, then of Westfield, Vt., b. in Ludlow, Vt., Oct. 23, 1811, son of Silas and Phebe (Newell) Howe, native of Holden, Mass. He was the fifth in a family of eleven children (b. between 1802 and 1822), some of whom removed to the State of Vermont. He was a farmer.

They lived in Troy, Vt., from whence they removed to Irasburg, Vt., March 8, 1854, where she d. July 6, 1881, and he d. Oct. 30, 1887.

Their children were:

1. Edward Sylvester Howe, b. in Troy, Vt., March 7, 1846; m. Sept. 17, 1868, Lavina Hammond of Coventry, Vt., b. in Coventry, Sept. 17, 1849. They reside at Barton Landing, Vt.
2. George Newell Howe, b. in Irasburg, Vt., Sept. 10, 1871.

194. Samuel W. Parker (*Sylvester,*[7] *Amos,*[6] *Amos,*[5] *Andrew,*[4] *John,*[3] *Hananiah,*[2] *Thomas*[1]), son of Sylvester and Alice (Davis) Parker, was b. in Westminster, Vt., Dec. 27, 1820. He with his brother Amory are the only surviving members of the family of nine children of Sylvester and Alice (Davis) Parker. He was the youngest, and although in his infancy seemed the most delicate of all, yet since has developed a very strong and rugged physique. He was six months old when his parents removed to Lyndon, Vt., where he lived 14 years. His early education was the plain, scanty instruction which the place and the limited means of the family afforded. He was, to quote his own words, "a better trout catcher than scholar." From early childhood he showed, as was necessary for one in his circumstances, an energetic and worthy application for work and industry. Removing from Lyndon to Derby, Vt., he worked on his father's farm living with and supporting his parents in their old age, also working at carpentering summers and chopping cord wood winters at 25 cents a cord, finally leaving for pastures new he took passage at Burlington for Whitehall, N. Y., on the first steamboat he ever saw; thence proceeded to Albany and from there by canal packet to Buffalo, a distance of 300 miles in seven days; thence by steamboats through lakes Erie, St. Clair, Huron and Michigan to Southport, which is now Kenuska, Wis. There he was first a carpenter, and later a maker of pipe organs. Being ingenious with tools and having a fine ear for music he continued in the latter business until 1847, when he returned to Bakersfield, Vt. He then, in 1848, m. Harriet Field, dau. of Ebenezer W. and Adah (Davis) Field of

SAMUEL W. PARKER.

Bakersfield and settled in Coventry, Vt. He was a successful mechanic, made pianos, wagons and sleighs, also made and repaired furniture. He made four trips annually through the settled portions of the State in tuning pianos and organs.

He removed with his family to Newport, Vt., in 1869, where he opened the music store which is still conducted by his successors. Ever an enterprising and public-spirited citizen, he has taken a personal part in the development of the West and South. He is thus very widely known and is as highly esteemed by all. In temperament his genial nature, hospitality and good will are ever bubbling to the surface. He has by his great industry and good judgment accumulated a very goodly estate from the smallest of beginnings. Owing to his interest and pains is partly due the fulness of the records of his own and allied families in this genealogy.

Their children were:

George O. Parker, b. Nov. 6, 1848; was drowned in Dec., 1859.

Homer E. Parker, b. May 4, 1858; d. June 15, 1862.

364. Eliza E. Parker, b. Aug. 5, 1853; m. Nov. 6, 1874, Edward H. Boden.

Florence E. Parker, b. Dec. 29, 1860; m. May 11, 1882, George H. Newland. They have no issue.

195. Lucinda Bangs Parker *(Dana,[7] Amos,[6] Amos,[5] Andrew,[4] John,[3] Hananiah,[2] Thomas[1])*, dau. of Dana R. and Sarah Davis (Williams) Parker, was b. in Hubbardston, March 9, 1807; m. in Hubbardston, Aug. 28, 1832, Eli Gray, son of Simeon and Sarah (Treadwell) Gray of Templeton. They lived in Templeton, where she d. Dec. 30, 1856. He m. (2) Mrs. Maria E. Hutchinson, who survives. He d. at the age of 83 years, Jan. 17, 1889.

Their children were:

1. Infant dau., b. and d. June 8, 1833.
2. Marshall E. Gray, b. Aug. 27, and d. Oct. 11, 1834.
3. Lucinda Sophia Gray, b. Sept. 21, 1835; m. May 12, 1855, Leonard Hunting, b. in Hubbardston, March 19, 1826, son of Lemuel and Polly (Baker) Hunting of Hubbardston. They reside in Worcester. Their children were:
   1. Lewis Pratt Hunting, b. in Templeton, Aug. 13, 1856; m. Nov. 13, 1878, Josephine Williams of Templeton,

dau. of James Williams. He resides near Baldwinsville. Their children were:

1. James Hunting. 2. George Hunting. 3. Herbert Hunting.

II. LUCINDA MARIA HUNTING, b. in Phillipston, July 1, 1857; d. Jan. 30, 1858.

III. ADA LOUISA HUNTING, b. in Templeton, April 5, 1860; d. Nov. 13, 1861.

IV. FREDERICK M. HUNTING, b. in Templeton, Aug. 13, 1863; resides in Worcester.

V. ELI ADELBERT HUNTING, b. in Templeton, Oct. 25, 1864; m. Minnie Merritt of Templeton, dau. of John Merritt. They reside in E. Templeton. No surviving issue.

VI. LEONARD LESLIE HUNTING, b. in Templeton, Jan. 5, 1867; resides in Worcester.

VII. CHARLES EVERARD HUNTING, b. in Templeton, Aug. 12, 1872.

VIII. ALICE EFFIE HUNTING, b. in Templeton, June 18, 1875; d. Aug. 16, 1876.

4. ELI ELBIA GRAY, b. Sept. 17, 1836; m. (1) in Fitzwilliam, May 29, 1862, Rebecca Elizabeth Newton, b. March 5, 1845, d. May 10, 1873, dau. of Asa and Rebecca Prescott (Dolbear) Newton. They had three children. He m. (2) Emma Briggs, b. May 20, 1844, dau. of Franklin and Lydia (Johnson) Briggs. He was a teamster in Templeton. Children:

I. HATTIE LUCINDA GRAY, b. in Templeton, June 20, 1863; m. in Baldwinsville, March 2, 1881, Fredric S. Coy, b. in East Cambridge, July 10, 1858, son of Horace S. and Lucy E. (Babb) Coy. He is a hotel-keeper.

II. WILLIAM NEWTON GRAY, b. in Templeton, May 13, 1866; m. —— Houghton of Athol. They reside in Baldwinsville and have a son and dau.

III. MABEL EVELINA GRAY, b. in Templeton, July 19, 1868; m. Frank Smith of Templeton.

5. SIMEON DENNISON PARKER GRAY, b. Dec. 6, 1841; m. (1) March 27, 1864, Almanza S. Clayton, and had:

I. ALICE CLAYTON GRAY, b. Feb. 15, 1869.

II. HERBERT GRAY, b. Jan. 29, and d. July 28, 1871.

m. (2) Feb. 20, 1873, Susan E. Knowlton, and had:

III. EDITH GODDARD GRAY, b. Jan. 9, 1874.

IV. ANNA LOUISA GRAY, b. July 14, and d. Aug. 23, 1876.

V. EVA MARIA GRAY, b. Jan. 16, 1880.

6. Amos Wilberforce Gray, b. April 6, 1843. He enlisted as a recruit in Co. C, 27th Reg., Mass. Vols., in March, 1862. In April he joined his regiment near Newberne, N. C. Through the summer they were kept in that vicinity on guard duty. He was eight months in the service when he was taken sick and d. in the hospital at Washington, N. C., Dec. 5, 1862, at the age of 19 years.
7. Infant son, b. and d. March 15, 1846.
8. John Marshall Gray, b. April 6, 1847; m. Joanna Wood. He d. Sept. 24, 1880, and left no issue.

196. Sarah Davis Parker *(Dana,[7] Amos,[6] Amos,[5] Andrew,[4] John,[3] Hananiah,[2] Thomas[1])*, dau. of Dana R. and Sarah Davis (Williams) Parker, was b. in Hubbardston, June 7, 1808; m. March 18, 1830, Oliver Hale of Hubbardston, son of Luther Hale, who came from Leominster to Hubbardston about 1788, m. three times and had a family of 15 children, Oliver being the ninth, b. Sept. 28, 1804. In the midst of life, while en route for San Francisco, he was drowned off the southern coast of California by wreck and burning of steamer *Independence* in 1853, and was buried on Magdelena Island with 240 others who perished out of 800 passengers. He d. Feb. 16, 1853. His brother-in-law, Amory Parker, who now lives in Hubbardston, was on the same ship. She still resides in Hubbardston with her children.

The three brothers, John Williams, Jonas and Dennison Robinson Parker, sons of Dana R. Parker, removed to New York city early in life. The issue of John W. as far as is known appears above. Jonas Parker m. Susan Ann Decker, and Dennison R. Parker m. Mary A. Vroome, both of Staten Island, N. Y. They each left families in or near New York city, but whose present whereabouts I am unable to state. Jonas Parker went to S. Carolina about 1874; he was in Aiken, S. C., in 1886, and his dau. m. there. He is probably deceased. He had a son whose name was probably Amos Parker, who is supposed to be living in the vicinity of New York city.

Dennison Robinson Parker is deceased. He had two daughters, who are supposed to be married, and it is supposed that one lives in the vicinity of Boston.

"Of Dana R. Parker's descendants," writes one of them, "I can only say that they are in about as widely scattered pursuits at present as any I ever knew: bankers, railway managers, civil engineers, doctors, lawyers, steamboat men and manufacturers. Had I the time I could write quite a history of their pursuits. I should say, however, that I never knew a politician among them. They are travelled, having been from Maine to California, where some are now. Some are silver mining in Mexico."

Their children were:

1. JOHN OTIS HALE, b. April 2, 1831; m. Nov. 7, 1860, Lucy Browning of Hubbardston. He d. Dec. 8, 1873, and she d. Jan. 28, 1878. They left five children:
   - I. ABBY CALISTA HALE, b. July 21, 1862.
   - II. OLIVER HALE, b. Dec. 12, 1863.
   - III. JOSHUA BROWNING HALE, b. June 14, 1864.
   - IV. JOHN OTIS HALE, b. Dec. 1, 1866.
   - V. LUCY DORRIT HALE, b. Aug. 18, 1868.
2. SARAH MARIA HALE, b. Aug. 3, 1833; m. Aug. 31, 1862, Luke Davis of Boston. He d. Aug. 29, 1883, leaving no issue. She resides in Newton.
3. MINERVA F. HALE, b. June 27, 1837; resides in Hubbardston.
4. CATHERINE SWAN HALE, b. June 8, 1841; unm. } Twins.
5. CLARA SWAN HALE, b. June 8, 1841; unm. }
6. SETH P. HALE, b. Feb. 12, 1846; m. Dec. 2, 1867, Abby Bennett of Hubbardston. She d. March 8, 1888. Child:
   - I. WILLIAM BENNETT HALE, b. May 14, 1871.

John Williams Parker (see page 179), *(Dana,[7] Amos,[6] Amos,[5] Andrew,[4] John,[3] Hananiah,[2] Thomas[1])*, son of Dana R. and Sarah Davis (Williams) Parker, was b. in Hubbardston, March 5, 1810; removed to New York city or vicinity; m. Jan. 1, 1837, Nancy F. Barr of New York city, b. in New York city, 1817. She d. July 30, 1847. He d. about 1874.

Their children were:

GEORGE W. L. PARKER, b. Jan. 20, 1840; was twice m.; was a steamboat man and lived in East New York, L. I.

MARY L. PARKER, b. Dec. 26, 1841; m. William A. Heywood (see page 322).

197. Priscilla Elvira Parker *(Dana,[7] Amos,[6] Amos,[5] Andrew,[4] John,[3] Hananiah,[2] Thomas[1])*, dau. of Dana R. and Sarah Davis (Williams) Parker, was b. in Hubbardston, Nov. 28, 1811; m. Aug. 31, 1835, Seth P. Heywood of Barre, son of the Heywood family of Shrewsbury and connected with the Worcester, Gardner and Fitchburg families of this name. His mother, Alice (Pratt) Heywood, was also a native of Shrewsbury. Seth P. Heywood and wife settled in Barre and had two sons. She d. Dec., 1876, aged 65 years, and he

m. her sister, Martha Maria Parker (see No. 201), and resides in Barre Plains.

Their children were:

1. WILLIAM AUSTIN HEYWOOD, b. Jan. 13, 1841; m. Mary L. Parker, b. Dec. 26, 1841, dau. of John Williams and Nancy F. (Barr) Parker (see page 321). She d. April 20, 1862, and he m. (2) Amanda Sanderson of Barre. They reside in Springfield and have one son:
   1. FRANK A. HEYWOOD, in the employ of the B. & A. R. R.
2. PHINEAS HEYWOOD, b. July 9, 1845; m. Nov. 8, 1864, Hattie Louisa King, dau. of Charles and Harriet D. King, both of Rutland. He is station agent at Barre Plains. Children:
   1. HATTIE ELVIRA HEYWOOD, b. Oct. 11, 1868; d. March 17, 1889.
   11. ERNEST PRATT HEYWOOD, b. Jan. 24, 1876.

198. Sophronia Parker *(Dana,[7] Amos,[6] Amos,[5] Andrew,[4] John,[3] Hananiah,[2] Thomas[1])*, dau. of Dana R. and Sarah Davis (Williams) Parker, was b. in Hubbardston, Nov. 26, 1815; m. June 21, 1836, Henry Humphrey of Athol Centre, b. Nov. 7, 1795, d. Jan. 9, 1882. He was son of Dr. Royal and Eusebia Humphrey. He was the second physician of Athol. Dr. Royal Humphrey was son of Rev. James Humphrey, who was the first minister of Athol, where he was settled in 1750. She resides in Athol Centre.

Their children were:

1. HENRY M. HUMPHREY, b. March 21, 1837; d. in infancy.
2. HENRY M. HUMPHREY, b. Aug. 10, 1840; m. Oct. 18, 1866, Abbie F. Holton. He represented his district in the Legislature of 1882, and was chairman of Athol's School Committee for four years. Their children were:
   1. JOHN H. HUMPHREY, b. Aug. 6, 1867; m. Nov. 12, 1890, Clara H. Ward of S. Carolina.
   11. HELEN M. HUMPHREY, b. Sept. 7, 1870.
3. HELEN A. HUMPHREY, b. Jan. 3, 1844; d. in infancy.

199. Mary Parker *(Dana,[7] Amos,[6] Amos,[5] Andrew,[4] John,[3] Hananiah,[2] Thomas[1])*, dau. of Dana R. and Sarah Davis (Williams) Parker, was b. in Hubbardston, July 11,

1821; m. May 5, 1842, George Raymond of Westminster. They are both deceased.

Their son was:

1. JOSEPH L. RAYMOND, b. June 14, 1857; m. Nov. 19, 1878, Clara L. Miller, b. Jan. 26, 1861, dau. of George W. and Susan P. (Brooks) Miller. They reside in Westminster. Their children were:

   i. LOUIS RAYMOND, b. May 11, and d. June 1, 1880.
   ii. ARTHUR N. RAYMOND, b. Feb. 10, 1887.
   iii. ALICE F. RAYMOND, b. Dec. 17, 1888.

200. Amos Parker *(Dana,[7] Amos,[6] Amos,[5] Andrew,[4] John,[3] Hananiah,[2] Thomas[1])*, son of Dana R. and Sarah Davis (Williams) Parker, was b. in Hubbardston, Feb. 12, 1823; m. April 2, 1844, Lucy M. Shepard of Oakham, b. April 29, 1825 or 6, dau. of Samuel Shepard. Amos Parker d. in Worcester, Mass., Oct. 29, 1849.

Their only son was:

AMOS E. PARKER, b. in Barre Plains, Nov. 1, 1848; m. Oct. 15, 1874, Ruth Eleanore Dorsey, b. in Roxbury Mills, Howard Co., Md., dau. of John Alrastus Dorsey, Esq., Judge of Orphan's Court, Howard Co., Md. He is a physician. They reside in Philadelphia, Pa.

201. Martha Maria Parker *(Dana,[7] Amos,[6] Amos,[5] Andrew,[4] John,[3] Hananiah,[2] Thomas[1])*, dau. of Dana R. and Sarah Davis (Williams) Parker, was b. in Hubbardston, July 9, 1825; m. July 2, 1844, Lysander Batchelder of Athol. He d. March 20, 1872, aged 49 years, 7 months, 14 days. She m. (2) Aug., 1877, Seth P. Heywood, widower of her sister Priscilla Elvira Parker (No. 197). They reside in Barre.

The children of Lysander and Martha Maria (Parker) Batchelder were:

1. HULDAH M. BATCHELDER, b. Feb. 12, 1846; m. George W. Richey. She is deceased.
2. ANGELA BATCHELDER, b. May 6, 1852; m. John C. Dalton, Jr. They reside in Salem. No issue.

202. Susan Elizabeth Parker *(Dana,[7] Amos,[6] Amos,[5] Andrew,[4] John,[3] Hananiah,[2] Thomas[1])*, dau. of Dana R. and Sarah Davis (Williams) Parker, was b. in Hubbardston, April 9, 1823; m. Oct. 6, 1848, Henry Burr Howells of New York city, native of Hartford, Ct., son of William A. and Alice M. Howells. He d. May 12, 1889. She is a noted songstress; resides in San Francisco.

Their children were:

1. Charlotte Elizabeth Howells, b. April 17, 1852; m. Henry Kunz of San Francisco. Their son:
   1. Charles H. B. Kunz.
2. Vera Amoretta Howells, b. Nov. 7, 1854; m. Robert E. Astell, a resident of Canada. They have a dau:
   1. Lottie E. Astell, b. Feb. 27, 1877.
3. Theodore H. Northrup Howells, b. Feb. 7, 1865; m. Beppie B. Lee of Weaverville, Cal.
4. Edward E. Northrup Howells, b. May 30, 1866.
5. Grace Aguilla Howells, b. May 30, 1871.
6. Ralph Burr Howells, b. May 22, 1873.

203. Amos Andrew Parker *(Amory,[7] Amos,[6] Amos,[5] Andrew,[4] John,[3] Hananiah,[2] Thomas[1])*, son of Amory and Lydia (Parker) Parker, was b. in Bakersfield, Vt., Oct. 28, 1814. He removed from the northern part of the State to Cavendish in April, 1835. He m. in Cavendish, May 4, 1837, Cynthia Pratt, b. in Reading, Vt., April 28, 1811, dau. and sixth child in the family of nine children, of Luther and Susanna (Childs) Pratt. Luther Pratt was a native of Fitchburg and his wife was the third dau. of David and Lydia (Stearns) Childs, who both settled in Westminster about 1775. Luther Pratt was brother to Levi Pratt and son of David Pratt, both of Fitchburg. Her sister, Nancy (Childs) Ward, the youngest of this family of nine children, was b. July 20, 1790, and is still living. She is a very remarkable lady and retains her memory well. She resides in Amsden, Vt., with her grandson Charles Ward.

Cynthia Parker d. Nov. 14, 1857. Mr. Parker afterwards m. in Reading, Vt., Feb. 24, 1859, Almira Foster, b. in Reading, July 11, 1813, dau. of George Foster, a native of

Dudley, Mass. Traditions in her family show that seven brothers of the name of Foster came from England at an early day and that her family were among the descendants of one of them. Her mother, Willaba (Chamberlain) Foster, was dau. of Abiel Chamberlain, was b. in Woodstock, Ct., Aug. 29, 1772, and a descendant also of the Peak and Ainsworth families. The children of Mr. Parker were all b. before the decease of his first wife, Cynthia. He has great-grandchildren.

Mr. and Mrs. Parker settled in Cavendish where they resided for over 20 years. He remained on the same farm till he m. the second time, then, in 1860, he settled in Reading, Vt., her native place, where they still reside. He is a farmer in S. Reading, Vt.

The children of Amos Andrew and Cynthia (Pratt) Parker, all b. in Cavendish, Vt., were:

EARL PARKER, b. Oct. 30, 1838; d. May 4, 1840.

LYDIA ANN PARKER, b. June 15, 1840; m. April 9, 1861, Joseph H. Adams, son of Samuel H. and Salome F. (Seaver) Adams of Cavendish, Vt. They reside at Cavendish. No issue.

365. SARAH EMILY PARKER, b. Aug. 9, 1841; m. Lewis Russell.

AMORY EARL PARKER, b. Oct. 22, 1842; d. July 18, 1843.

DANE PARKER, b. Dec. 11, 1843; d. Nov. 3, 1846. } Twins.

DENNISON PARKER, b. Dec. 11, 1843; served in the war of 1861, enlisting when quite young. He d. in the Brigade Hospital at Union Mills, Va., June 21, 1863, of typhoid pneumonia. } Twins.

LUCRETIA JANE PARKER, b. Dec. 2, 1845; d. Nov. 30, 1846.

HELEN MARIA PARKER, b. July 7, 1847; d. Aug. 31, 1865.

366. MARY FRANCES PARKER, b. May 9, 1849; m. Lyman L. Howard.

MARTHA AUGUSTA PARKER, b. May 4, 1851; d. Sept. 13, 1870.

367. GEORGE W. PARKER, b. Nov. 25, 1854; m. Mary E. Rist.

204. Elisha Sylvester Parker (*Amory*,[7] *Amos*,[6] *Amos*,[5] *Andrew*,[4] *John*,[3] *Hananiah*,[2] *Thomas*[1]), son of Amory and Lydia (Parker) Parker, was b. in Bakersfield, Vt., Nov. 11, 1819; m. a Miss Barnes for his first wife. They removed to New York city, afterwards lived in Mamaroneck, N. Y. He was a butcher in early life, later a farmer. He d. about 1885, and his second wife d. July, 1889.

His children were:

GEORGE A. PARKER; he served in the war for the Union, and has been a showman in New Haven. Ct.

HARRY M. PARKER; he is the originator and conductor of the well-known Parker's Circus d'Canine; he has educated a troupe of remarkably well-trained dogs and has for years exhibited them with ability and success.

205. Betsey Curwen Parker (*Joel,*[7] *Isaac,*[6] *Amos,*[5] *Andrew,*[4] *John,*[3] *Hananiah,*[2] *Thomas*[1]), dau. of Joel and Hannah (Bond) Parker, was b. in Westborough, Jan. 20, 1799; m. May 14, 1823, Dea. Elmer Brigham of Westborough, b. Sept. 8, 1798; d. March 3, 1871. They lived in Westborough, where she d. Nov. 29, 1875. He was a farmer.

Their children were:

1. ELLEN ELIZABETH BRIGHAM, b. March 3, 1824; m. May 12, 1847, David W. Hill of Westminster. She d. Sept. 13, 1848, leaving no issue. He resides in Westminster.
2. JANNETTE HANNAH BRIGHAM, b. Jan. 9, 1827; m. April 6, 1848, Archelaus M. Howe of Westborough, b. April 21, 1823, son of Luther and Lucy (Brigham) Howe, a native of Vernon, Vt. Their children were:
   - I. ARTHUR L. HOWE, b. Nov. 27, 1848; d. Oct. 13, 1849.
   - II. ELMER PARKER HOWE, b. Nov. 1, 1851. He is a lawyer in Boston.
3. MERRICK PUTNAM BRIGHAM, b. March 9, 1829; m. May 21, 1851, Sarah E. Wellington. He d. Dec. 10, 1875. She resides in Attleborough. Their children were:
   - I. EDWARD BRIGHAM; m. Elizabeth Brightman of Fall River. They reside in Attleborough and have four children.
   - II. SABRA BRIGHAM; m. George Cole. They reside in Attleborough and have children:
     - 1. Ralph Cole. 2. Edith Cole.
   - III. WALTER BRIGHAM; m. Julia Briggs. He is deceased. Their son was:
     - 1. Charles Brigham.
   - IV. ALFRED BRIGHAM; resides in Attleborough; is m. and has two children.
4. ANNA PARKER BRIGHAM, b. Sept. 18, 1832; m. Feb. 3, 1853, Charles A. Harrington. He resides in Westborough. She d. Feb. 26, 1870. No issue.

5. Sophia Augusta Brigham, b. July 10, 1837; d. April 17, 1842.
6. Susan Parker Brigham, b. Jan. 4, 1840; d. Oct. 14, 1863.
7. Charles Elmer Brigham, b. March 14, 1842; m. March 2, 1866, Ellen Davis. He d. July 28, 1877. No issue.
8. Calvin Lloyd Brigham, b. July 30, 1844; m. (1) Oct. 11, 1866, Mary Millerson Brown. She d. April 6, 1875, and he m. (2) June, 1875, Ethie Burpee of Sterling. He has one dau.:
   1. Alice A. Brigham, b. May 10, 1868.

206. Hannah Sophia Parker *(Joel,[7] Isaac,[6] Amos,[5] Andrew,[4] John,[3] Hananiah,[2] Thomas[1])*, dau. of Joel and Hannah (Bond) Parker, was b. in Westborough, April 5, 1801; m. Nov. 3, 1826, Orestes Forbush of Westborough, b. 1797; d. June 21, 1846. She d. July 26, 1833.

Their children were:

1. Lorenzo P. Forbush, b. Oct. 11, 1827; d. young.
2. Andrew P. Forbush, b. Nov. 11, 1829; m. (1) —— Ward of Princeton; m. (2) —— Davis. He resides in Princeton.

207. Achsah Forbes Parker *(Joel,[7] Isaac,[6] Amos,[5] Andrew,[4] John,[3] Hananiah,[2] Thomas[1])*, was b. in Westborough, Sept. 2, 1803; m. April 10, 1826, Solomon T. Fay, b. Aug. 21, 1803, son of Benjamin Fay. He d. Nov. 11, 1872. She d. in Westborough, Aug. 9, 1891, at the age of nearly 88. She had 28 grandchildren, 23 of whom are living.

Their children were:

1. Henry Clinton Fay, b. March 4, 1827; m. Carrie E. Tallman. He is the pastor of the Congregational Church of N. Reading and resides in Somerville. They have children.
2. George Ellis Fay, b. in Shrewsbury, Jan. 13, 1829; m. April 10, 1851, Eliza Ward, b. in Framingham, April 5, 1829, dau. of Putnam and Betsey Ward, who were both natives of Southborough. They reside in Westborough. Their children were all b. in Westborough:
   - i. Charles Ellis Fay, b. Dec. 9, 1852; m. Ella Dale of E. Exeter, Me., and have:
     1. Avis Arvilla Fay, b. in E. Exeter, Me., Nov. 24, 1881.
     2. Mildred Fay, b. in E. Exeter, Me., June 23, 1884.
   - ii. Austin Hamilton Fay, b. Oct. 21, 1857; m. Capitolia Aseneth Thompson. They have one dau.:
     1. Ethel Aseneth Fay, b. in Boston, Sept. 9, 1880.

III. EVANGELINE LOUANA FAY, b. Feb. 6, 1874; m. Oct. 12, 1891, Everett L. Metcalf of Butte City, Mont.

3. ABBIE ANN FAY, b. Nov. 28, 1830; m. April 7, 1855, Burt Newman, b. in S. Egremont, Mass., Sept. 29, 1827, son of Samuel and Permelia (Curtis) Newman. Children:

I. HENRY DEXTER NEWMAN, b. in Shakopee, Scott Co., Minn., Feb. 5, 1856; d. Aug. 11, 1884.

II. ANNIE SHERRARD NEWMAN, b. in Alton, Ill., Dec. 9, 1857.

III. SAMUEL CURTIS NEWMAN, b. in Delavan, Ill., Nov. 13, 1862; m. in Kenosha, Wis., Sept. 3, 1891, Alice Fellows. Their dau. was:

1. Amy Fay Newman, b. Sept. 4, 1892.

IV. EMMA NEWMAN, b. in Delavan, Ill., June 7, 1867; m. Aug. 4, 1892, Elmer E. Giles.

V. FRED NEWMAN, b. in Delavan, Ill., Jan. 17, 1870.

4. S. DEXTER FAY, b. Jan. 15, 1833; m. Aug., 1860, Mrs. Mary Atwood (Robbins) Merriam, b. in Plymouth, April 11, 1833, dau. of Chandler and Elenor (Holmes) Robbins of Plymouth. They reside in Westborough and their children were:

I. LOUISE FRANCES FAY, b. June 10, 1860; d. July 2, 1885.

II. FRED DEXTER FAY, b. May 8, 1870; d. Sept. 18, 1876.

5. SUSAN AUGUSTA FAY, b. June 23, 1835; d. Aug. 12, 1837.

6. JOEL PARKER FAY, b. March 30, 1838; m. Oct. 9, 1867, Susan E. Capen. Resides in Westborough. They have two children. One dau., Gracie.

7. FRANCIS TAYLOR FAY, b. Nov. 6, 1840; m. (1) Julia Hamlin, and had four children; m. (2) Jennie Holmes, and has three children. Resides in Stamford, Ct.

8. SUSAN AUGUSTA FAY, b. July 19, 1843; d. Oct. 6, 1863.

9. CHARLES GILBERT FAY, b. March 27, 1846; d. Sept. 23, 1862.

10. SARAH MARIA FAY, b. March 5, 1848; m. in Westborough, Nov. 25, 1870, Edward F. Mellen, b. in Ashland, Sept. 9, 1849, son of Isaac and Sarah Mellen. He is a locomotive engineer. Their children were:

I. EDDIE N. MELLEN, b. in Ashland, April 20, 1874; d. June 6, 1878.

II. RALPH W. MELLEN, b. in Ashland, Aug. 5, 1879.

III. EDITH L. MELLEN, b. in Boston, April 8, 1883; d. June 28, 1884.

11. MARTHA STOWE FAY, b. May 9, 1850; m. Wilmot B. Rice. They reside in Stamford, Ct., and have four children.

208. Elmina Augusta Parker (*Joel,*[7] *Isaac,*[6] *Amos,*[5] *Andrew,*[4] *John,*[3] *Hananiah,*[2] *Thomas*[1]), dau. of Joel and Hannah (Bond) Parker, was b. in Westborough, Nov. 16, 1806; m. April 10, 1827, Thomas Hubbard Fayerweather of Westborough (grandson of Thomas), b. May 16, 1806; d. Feb. 23, 1879. She d. Oct. 21, 1861. The Fayerweather family has long been prominently connected with the growth of the town.

Their children were:

1. John Lloyd Fayerweather, b. Sept. 27, 1827; d. Oct. 30, 1892, unm.
2. Charles Hubbard Fayerweather, b. April 22, 1830; m. Harriet Fay. They have had two daughters:
   - i. Elizabeth Augusta Fayerweather, b. April 25, 1854; d. Feb. 23, 1889.
   - ii. Nellie Hubbard Fayerweather, b. Oct. 1, 1859; m. Charles Piper and resides in Boston.
3. George Thomas Fayerweather, b. Aug. 27, 1840; m. Nellie Brown of Westborough. He d. March 8, 1893. Children:
   - i. Frank R. Fayerweather; in the Custom House, Boston.
   - ii. John Harrison Fayerweather; res. Westborough.
4. Henry Edward Fayerweather, b. April 26, 1843; m. Mary Bennett of Worcester. He was connected with the Worcester police force for several years, and since has been truant officer of the Public Schools of Worcester.

209. Harriet Newell Parker (*Joel,*[7] *Isaac,*[6] *Amos,*[5] *Andrew,*[4] *John,*[3] *Hananiah,*[2] *Thomas*[1]), dau. of Joel and Hannah (Bond) Parker, was b. in Westborough, Aug. 16, 1815; m. in Westborough, April 19, 1834, Mendal Gilbert Fosgate of Berlin, b. in Vermont, May 16, 1809, son of Mendall and Sally (Spofford) Fosgate. He d. in Washington, D. C., Feb. 2, 1885. She d. July, 1869.

Their children were:

1. Harriet Parker Fosgate, b. in Amherst, Aug. 27, 1835; m. (1) in Berlin, Nov. 21, 1852, William L. Eager of Northborough, son of Nahum and Sally Eager. Children:
   - i. Walter Ward Eager, b. in Fitchburg, March 6, 1855.
   - ii. Harry Lewins Eager, b. in Fitchburg, Aug. 14, 1857.
   - iii. Fannie Louise Eager, b. in Fitchburg, Aug. 6, 1862.

iv. HERBERT LAWRENCE EAGER, b. in Fitchburg, Dec. 9, 1864.

v. ARTHUR WILLIAM EAGER, b. in Fitchburg, Dec. 29, 1871.

Mrs. Harriet Parker (Fosgate) Eager m. (2) in Westborough, July 2, 1878, Curtis Harrington, b. in Westborough, Jan. 6, 1835, son of Samuel A. and Catharine Harrington. They reside in Westborough, where he is a farmer. Child:

vi. ROBERT CURTIS HARRINGTON, b. June 14, 1881.

2. MARTHA AUGUSTA FOSGATE, b. in Keene, N. H., April 17, 1837; m. Robert H. Reed. She d. Sept. 19, 1883. He resides in Boston. Children:

i. CHARLES REED. ii. FRANK REED.

3. LOUISE GILBERT FOSGATE, b. in Northborough, Jan. 12, 1845; m. (1) —— Putnam; m. (2) Charles A. Harrington of Westborough (brother of Curtis Harrington). She d. 1889. Their children were:

i. WALTER HARRINGTON. ii. HATTIE HARRINGTON.

210. Perley Parker (*Gardiner*,[7] *Isaac*,[6] *Amos*,[5] *Andrew*,[4] *John*,[3] *Hananiah*,[2] *Thomas*[1]), son of Gardiner and Asenath (Sherman) Parker, was b. in Grafton; m. Betsey Mellen of Westborough, and settled in Hopkinton.

Their children were:

368. EMILY PARKER, b. Sept. 11, 1818; m. John Crooks of Hopkinton.

369. GARDNER PARKER, b. May 13, 1821; m. Mary L. Sawyer of Gloucester.

370. J. MELLEN PARKER, b. March 30, 1829; m. Sarah Curtis of Hopkinton.

JOSHUA PARKER.

211. Daniel Parker (*Otis*,[7] *Isaac*,[6] *Amos*,[5] *Andrew*,[4] *John*,[3] *Hananiah*,[2] *Thomas*[1]), son of Dea. Otis and Polly Ann (Nourse) Parker, was b. in Westborough, March 23, 1799; m. Jan. 13, 1829, Polly White, b. Aug. 16, 1804, d. Feb. 13, 1866, dau. of Abel and Sarah (Wood) White of Phillipston. They later in life removed to Greenwich Village, but all the children were b. in Hubbardston. He was a man of strong body and mind. He was a miller; a man of sterling integrity, more of deeds than words, and a humble follower of Jesus, his Saviour, whom he trusted to the last. He d. in Greenwich, Aug. 13, 1885, at the age of 86.

Their children were:

SUSAN PARKER, b. Feb. 18, 1831; d. Sept. 5, 1863.

MARY PARKER, b. Jan. 27, 1833; m. (1) March 5, 1863, Henry T. Sears of Greenwich, who d. in Amboy, Ill., Oct. 3, 1866; m. (2) Aug. 12, 1868, Samuel B. Estey of Greenwich, who d. Oct. 31, 1888. She resides in Phillipston. The dau. of Henry T. and Mary (Parker) Sears was:

1. NELLIE MAY SEARS, b. April 28, 1865.

MELISSA PARKER, b. Aug. 7, 1834; d. Dec. 9, 1855.

371. SARAH PARKER, b. Oct. 15, 1835; m. Henry C. Work of Hartford, Ct.

DANIEL WEBSTER PARKER, b. Sept. 26, 1837; d. July 24, 1840.

ISAAC PARKER, b. Sept. 12, 1839; d. July 29, 1840.

372. DANIEL WEBSTER PARKER, b. June 13, 1841; m. Fannie E. Morse.

LUCY AUGUSTA PARKER, b. Oct. 30, 1843; resides in Greenwich Village.

HARRIET ELIZABETH PARKER, b. May 9, 1845; resides in Greenwich Village.

373. ABEL OTIS PARKER, b. Dec. 20, 1847; m. Mrs. Fannie E. M. Parker.

212. Mary Nourse Parker (*Otis,*[7] *Isaac,*[6] *Amos,*[5] *Andrew,*[4] *John,*[3] *Hananiah,*[2] *Thomas*[1]), dau. of Dea. Otis and Polly Ann (Nourse) Parker, was b. in Westborough, Aug. 11, 1803; m. Dec. 29, 1825, Alvin Waite of Hubbardston. She d. Oct. 16, 1833.

Their children were:

1 and 2. Their two oldest children d. in infancy.

3. AUGUSTA WAITE, b. in Hubbardston; d. in Worcester, at about the age of 18.

4. CLARENDON WAITE, b. Dec. 16, 1830; a graduate of Brown University in 1852, and of Andover Theological Seminary in 1856, studied six months in the University of Halle, Prussia; he was ordained and installed in Rutland, Feb. 25, 1858. During the winter of 1864–65 he did good service in the Freedmen's Bureau, N. C. The winter of 1866–67 was spent in Cuba in search of health. He had accepted a professorship in Beloit College and was on his way thither when he was seized with an attack from which he died Dec. 16, 1867. During his ministry of eight years in Rutland 84 persons joined the Church there,

and this statement is not even an indication of his success, though in some measure a tribute to his faithfulness. In Salem he won quickly the strong love of his people, which was shown in their thoughtful and generous deeds towards him and his. It were hard to tell whether by thoughtfully studied and carefully written sermons or by warm hearted pastoral work he accomplished most for the Lord he loved. He m. June 16, 1858, Harriet G. Baker, dau. of James and Lydia (Goulding) Baker of Phillipston. She resides in Worcester. Their children were:

i. ANNA MARY WAITE, b. in Rutland, Aug. 18, 1862.

ii. FLORENCE SHERMAN WAITE, b. in Rutland, Aug. 19, 1865; m. June 5, 1890, George Arthur Smith of Worcester.

213. Otis Parker, Jr. *(Otis,[7] Isaac,[6] Amos,[5] Andrew,[4] John,[3] Hananiah,[2] Thomas[1])*, son of Dea. Otis and Polly Ann (Nourse) Parker, was b. in Hubbardston, Aug. 16, 1806; m. Nov. 4, 1829, Eunice Allen, b. April, 1813, d. Oct. 13, 1855. He d. Sept. 1, 1876.

Their children were:

374. LUCY PARKER, b. Nov. 25, 1830; m. (1) James Baker of Worcester; m. (2) Charles Lester of Wisconsin.

A son, b. and d. May 11, 1832.

375. AVALINA PARKER, b. June 21, 1833; m. Joseph Willard Rice of Hubbardston.

376. ELMER PARKER, b. Aug. 30, 1836; m. Sarah J. Hallock of Connecticut.

ELIZABETH L. PARKER, b. July 23, 1842; m. Oct. 8, 1862, John G. Allen of Pittsfield, Vt.

MINAR R. PARKER, b. Oct. 4, and d. Oct. 13, 1848.

214. Nancy Patterson Parker *(Jabez,[7] Isaac,[6] Amos,[5] Andrew,[4] John,[3] Hananiah,[2] Thomas[1])*, dau. of Capt. Jabez M. and Nancy (Patterson) Parker, was b. May 2, 1799; m. June(?), 1830, James Wakefield of Marlborough, N. H. (as his second wife), b. in Reading, 1782, son of Thomas and Elizabeth (Hardy) Wakefield. He d. in Marlborough, May 21, 1864. He was a farmer. He lived first in Roxbury, N. H., where by his first wife, Hannah Hemenway, he had several children, among whom was the distinguished Cyrus Wakefield, b. 1811, benefactor and namer of the town of Wakefield, Mass., that part of old Reading from which the Parker family sprung. James Wakefield lived later in Marlborough, N. H. He was a justice of the peace, selectman and representative. Mrs. Nancy (Parker) Wakefield d. 1848.

Her dau. was:

i. Julia Wakefield; m. in Marlborough, N. H., Oct. 1, 1851, Obed Gilman Dort, b. in Surry, N. H., Jan. 25, 1828, son of Lois Bemis and Elizabeth Dort of Surry, N. H. She met her death in the steamboat *West Point* collision and disaster on the Potomac, Aug. 13, 1862, in which other New Hampshire ladies together with 80 soldiers lost their lives. She was returning from a visit to her husband, Major Dort, at Newport News, Va., where he was in the service of the 6th N. H. Reg. stationed there with Burnside's army. The son Arthur, of six years, who was with her, was also drowned. The sorrowful event cast an added gloom over the people of this portion of the State to their already many misfortunes of war.

Major O. G. Dort came to Keene in 1840 and learned the carriage painter's trade, and in 1852 commenced the druggist business, following it practically until 1875, and from that date has been engaged in the banking business. In 1861 he raised company E of volunteers and joined the 6th Reg. N. H. Vols. as Captain, afterwards promoted to Major; served with the Burnside expedition in N. Carolina, Virginia and Maryland. After the loss of his wife and oldest child he resigned and returned home to care for the remaining child and his druggist business. He is president of the Citizens' National Bank of Keene, N. H. Their children, all b. in Keene, were:

i. Arthur Wakefield Dort, b. Feb. 25, 1856; d. Aug. 13, 1862.

ii. Frank Gilman Dort, b. Dec. 17, 1857; m. Jan. 14, 1885, Kate Bardwell Cobb of Putney, Vt. They reside in Keene. Their son:

1. Robert Gilman Dort, b. Aug. 10, 1892.

iii. Mary Ellen Dort, b. Feb. 13, 1861; d. Nov. 27, 1861.

215. Jabez M. Parker, Jr. *(Jabez,[7] Isaac,[6] Amos,[5] Andrew,[4] John,[3] Hananiah,[2] Thomas[1])*, son of Capt. Jabez M. and Nancy (Patterson) Parker, was b. Nov. 12, 1800; m. Azubah P. Powers, b. 1811, dau. of Oliver Powers of Phillipston. They resided in various places, but mostly on his father's place, to which he succeeded and owned when he died, in the north part of the town. They both d. in 1865. The place is now owned by Mr. Lovewell. He was a farmer and stonecutter.

Their children were:

ISAAC MYRON PARKER, b. in Phillipston, Nov. 17, 1829; d. Dec. 26, 1847.

377. ADDISON LESLIE PARKER, b. in Phillipston, June 28, 1831; m. Dec. 15, 1854, Mary Melvina Buxton.

378. ISABELLA BROWN PARKER, b. in Roxbury, N. H., Feb. 17, 1834; m. 1855, Asa B. Turner.

JAMES HENRY PARKER, b. in Phillipston, Feb. 12, 1841; d. April 15, 1859.

216. Enoch Adams Parker (*Jabez,[7] Isaac,[6] Amos,[5] Andrew,[4] John,[3] Hananiah,[2] Thomas[1]*), son of Capt. Jabez M. and Nancy (Patterson) Parker, was b. in Phillipston, Jan. 14, 1802; removed to Sullivan, N. H., where he taught school, and was m. to Rebecca M. Gibbs, b. in Sullivan, March 27, 1803, dau. of Dalphon and Asenath (Fay) Gibbs. The parents were natives of Sturbridge, Mass., where the father was b. Aug. 12, 1777; m. about 1800 and removed to New Hampshire, finally settling in Marlow, N. H., where he d. 1859, aged 82. Dolphon, one of the nine children, resides in Worcester, Mass. He traces the genealogy of the Gibbs family back to Matthew Gibbs, who emigrated from Fenton or Venton, Darlington Parish, England, and settled in Charlestown, Mass. He was a planter. He later removed to Sudbury, being one of the original proprietors of the town. The genealogical descent became Matthew,[1] John,[2] Thomas,[3] John[4] of Sudbury, Jonathan[5] of Sturbridge, Dalphon[6] of Marlow, N. H., and Dalphon[7] of Worcester, Mass. Enoch Parker had a farm of 100 acres in Roxbury, N. H., was selectman, and d. July, 1839. She d. Feb. 26, 1854.

Their children were:

379. PHERONA E. PARKER, b. July 7, 1834; m. John S. Leach of Rockingham, Vt.

PHEDRAS E. PARKER, b. Feb. 20, 1837; drowned May 23, 1852.

380. PERRY ANDER PARKER, b. Nov. 30, 1838; m. Mary Russel of Gilsum, N. H.

217. Joel Dodge Parker *(Jabez,[7] Isaac,[6] Amos,[5] Andrew,[4] John,[3] Hananiah,[2] Thomas[1])*, son of Capt. Jabez M. and Nancy (Patterson) Parker, was b. in Phillipston, Aug. 17, 1804. His boyhood was passed upon his father's farm in the north part of the town. He was a skilful mechanic and builder, so following his inclinations he built a shop for manufacturing purposes, locating where is now "Golden Village," a short distance south of the centre of the town, thus putting to use the valuable water power of this section. He made improvements and additions and later built the brick factory which has assisted in the growth of this village. He took up the old Major Parker homestead (then in possession of Nathaniel Powers), one of the oldest settled localities of the town. Here his son J. Damon Parker resides.

Their children were:

381. JOEL DAMON PARKER, b. May 7, 1836; m. Dec. 26, 1864, Catharine M. Whitney.

JASON GOULDING PARKER, b. March 27, 1840; d. Oct. 26, 1864, while in the service of the Union army.*

HANNAH MARIA PARKER, b. June 24, 1843; d. Oct. 22, 1864.

218. Emily Sophia Parker *(Jabez,[7] Isaac,[6] Amos,[5] Andrew,[4] John,[3] Hananiah,[2] Thomas[1])*, dau. of Capt. Jabez M. and Nancy (Patterson) Parker, was b. in Phillipston, April 13, 1806; m. March 3, 1834, Isaiah White, son of William and Esther (Maynard) White, b. in Marlborough, N. H., July 13, 1809. He was a direct descendant of Peregrine White of Pilgrim fame. He d. Sept. 25, 1837. She d. May 28, 1867. He was a painter.

---

* He enlisted at St. Louis, Mo., in Dec., 1861, joining Co. C, 1st Mo. State Militia. He was with his regiment a short time doing Provost Guard duty in St. Louis, then was detailed as Orderly for Gen. Schofield. By order of the Brig.-Gen. he was detailed June 11, 1862, as clerk in the Asst. Adjt.-General's Office, Head Qrs. Dist. of Mo. He remained there (being re-detailed when Maj.-Gen. Curtis took command, when they became the Head Qrs. of the Department of the Missouri), until his death, which occurred Oct. 26, 1864. His detail was the oldest one in St. Louis at that time. After his regiment took the field he applied several times for leave to join his regiment, but was held at Head Qrs. during all his service, much to his disapproval.

Their children were:

1. RODOLPHUS HARVEY WHITE, b. Feb. 15, and d. April 4, 1835.
2. EMILY ELMIRA WHITE, b. July 9, 1836; m. April 7, 1857, George Hills Smith, b. in Alstead, N. H., Aug. 7, 1835, son of Ralph E. and Bia (Hale) Smith. He is a machinist and they reside in Harrisville, N. H. Children:
   - I. WILLIE HALE SMITH, b. Feb. 13, and d. Feb. 25, 1858.
   - II. ANNA LOUISE SMITH, b. March 12, 1859; m. Jan. 5, 1881, William D. Morrison of Marlow, N. H. Child:
     - 1. Helen Morrison, b. Nov. 23, 1887.
   - III. ETHEL BIA SMITH, b. Sept. 24, 1865; m. Feb. 3, 1883, Herbert A. Davis of Keene, N. H. Children:
     - 1. Bertram Stuart Davis, b. Sept. 3, 1883.
     - 2. Alice Harriet Davis, b. Aug. 2, 1888.
   - IV. SARAH BELLE SMITH, b. Sept. 22, 1867; m. Dec. 25, 1886, Alvin W. Davis of Keene, N. H. She d. Nov. 7, 1888.
   - V. HARRIETT BUSS SMITH, b. Jan. 27, 1870; m. March 9, 1889, George M. Towns of Keene, N. H. Their son:
     - 1. Charles Henry Towns, b. Jan. 9, 1893.
   - VI. BERTHA INEZ SMITH, b. Feb. 3, 1873.
   - VII. LEON HENRY SMITH, b. July 16, 1875.
   - VIII. MARGARET LILLIAN SMITH, b. Dec. 31, 1877.

219. Beulah H. C. Parker (*Jabez,*[7] *Isaac,*[6] *Amos,*[5] *Andrew,*[4] *John,*[3] *Hananiah,*[2] *Thomas*[1]), dau. of Capt. Jabez M. and Nancy (Patterson) Parker, was b. in Phillipston, April 21, 1809; m. Nov. 25, 1836, Walter Gunn Clapp of Holden, b. Dec. 27, 1812, now living (1889) at Cambridgeport, a descendant of Thomas Clapp, who came from England in 1633. (See Clapp Family in America, published by David Clapp & Son, Boston, Mass.). She d. Jan. 9, 1864.

Their children were:

1. ALPHONSO LAROY CLAPP, b. in Phillipston, Oct. 26, 1837; m. Dec. 22, 1862, Harriet Augusta Rose. He d. May 30, 1874. Two children:
   - I. CHARLES IRVING CLAPP, b. in Troy, N. Y., Dec. 13, 1866; d. Oct. 28, 1867.
   - II. FRED. WHITNEY CLAPP, b. in Worcester, July 25, 1869.
2. ADDIE I. CLAPP, b. in Worcester, Oct. 28, 1839; m. 1872, Hiram Parker. One child:

i. WARREN BELDING PARKER, b. in Rochester, Aug. 3, 1873.

3. ELAM SMALLEY PHÆDON CLAPP, b. in Worcester, Jan. 5, 1842. Entered the Sophomore class of Troy University when 17 years of age; graduated second in his class in July, 1862; enlisted same day he graduated in Co. H, 125th New York Infantry, as a private; promoted to Corporal before leaving the city, afterwards promoted to Lieutenant for bravery at the battle of Gettysburg; was wounded at Chancellorsville at the battle of the Wilderness, May 12, 1864; died from the effects of his wounds, June 5, 1864. He was a very intelligent young man, finely educated and was a gentleman. In all of the engagements in which his regiment participated he distinguished himself for bravery.

4. LILLIAN EDNA CLAPP, b. in Phillipston, July 18, 1844; m. Jan. 1, 1869, Sylvester Nelson Gardner of Troy (a descendant of the martyr John Rodgers). Their children were:

i. WARREN SYLVESTER GARDNER, b. Sept. 22, 1869.

ii. ELAM LAROY GARDNER, b. May 11, 1872.

iii. BEULAH EDNA GARDNER, b. Feb. 16, 1875; d. Dec. 13, 1882.

iv. HOWARD NELSON GARDNER, b. May 23, 1877; d. Dec. 12, 1882.

v. ERNEST HOWARD GARDNER, b. Feb. 12, 1885; d. July 16, 1886.

221. James M. L. Parker *(Jabez,[7] Isaac,[6] Amos,[5] Andrew,[4] John,[3] Hananiah,[2] Thomas[1])*, son of Capt. Jabez M. and Nancy (Patterson) Parker, was b. in Phillipston, Sept. 3, 1812; m. in Roxbury, N. H., April 1, 1835, Polly Kidder, b. in Roxbury, N. H., Aug. 19, 1816, dau. of Aaron and Persis B. Kidder. She d. in Forestville, Wis., Jan. 7, 1868. He was a carpenter and joiner by trade, also machinist. He resided in Phillipston, Mass.; Roxbury, Peterborough, Hillsborough and Marlborough, N. H.; and Racine, Ahnapee and Forestville, Wis. He held the offices of superintendent of schools, town clerk, supervisor and justice of the peace. He d. in Forestville, Door County, Wis., Sept. 25, 1877.

Their children were:

JAMES ANSEL PARKER, b. in Roxbury, N. H., June 25, 1836. He was one of the crew of the whaling schooner *Virginia*, which was lost at sea in Aug., 1854, with all on board. He was unm.

382. AMINE CECELIA PARKER, b. in Hillsborough, N. H., July 12, 1839; m. George Fowles of Ahnapee, Wis.

NANCY PATTERSON PARKER, b. in Phillipston, Dec. 26, 1842; d. June 4, 1857, in Ahnapee, Wis.

ROSELL REONE PARKER, b. in Phillipston, June 28, 1845; d. July 4, 1857, in Ahnapee, Wis.

383. MAYNARD TILLOTSON PARKER, b. in Roxbury, N. H., Oct. 30, 1850; m. Mary Overbeck of Ahnapee, Wis.

222. Harriet Ann Parker *(David,[7] Isaac,[6] Amos,[5] Andrew,[4] John,[3] Hananiah,[2] Thomas[1])*, dau. of David and Betsey (Eager) Parker, was b. in Barre, May 29, 1819; m. Nov. 16, 1841, John Walker, native of Holden, b. March 3, 1815, son of John and Eunice (Metcalf) Walker of Holden. She d. March 16, 1878. He resides in Barre, where he is a farmer.

Their children were:

1. JOHN ALFRED WALKER, b. Oct. 31, 1842; m. Jan. 19, 1867, Bessie Whitcomb of Boxborough. They reside in Boxborough. Their children were:
   - I. MARTHA JANE WALKER; m. Burpee Steele and reside in Leominster. They have children:
     1. Clifton Steele. 2. Russell Steele.
   - II. MARION WALKER. She resides in Leominster.
   - III. BERTHA WALKER; m. John Perzanzon. They reside in Boxborough.
   - IV. BESSIE ISORA WALKER.
   - V. HENRY W. WALKER.
   - VI. DAVID PARKER WALKER.
2. HARRIET ELIZABETH WALKER, b. Nov. 21, 1843; m. Nov. 11, 1865, Harlow Foskett of Westminster. He d. June, 1870. She resides in W. Rutland. Their children were:
   - I. WALLACE H. FOSKETT, b. Sept. 25, 1866; m. Nov. 18, 1889, Etta Himes, b. Jan. 11, 1870, dau. of Edwin and Mary (Leonard) Himes of Hubbardston. They reside in Worcester and have:
     1. Harold Eugene Foskett, b. Jan. 20, 1891.
     2. Della May Foskett, b. June 30, 1892.
   - II. FRED E. FOSKETT, b. 1868; d. in Florida, aged 19, 1877.
3. LUCY MARIA WALKER (twin of Harriet Elizabeth Walker), b. Nov. 21, 1843; m. May 7, 1865, Charles Dennison Robinson

of Barre, b. Nov. 25, 1836, son of Marshall P. and Mary Elizabeth (Perry) Robinson of Barre. They reside in Worcester. Their children were:

i. ARTHUR C. ROBINSON, b. March 28, 1866; m. Dec. 17, 1890, Elmina M. Cole of Worcester, b. March 24, 1866. They reside in Cambridgeport.

ii. ALBERT D. ROBINSON, b. April 27, 1867; m. March 26, 1892, Louise E. Hamberger of Willimantic, Ct. They reside in Worcester.

iii. MARY L. ROBINSON, b. Sept. 7, 1870; d. Oct. 27, 1870.

iv. GEORGE P. ROBINSON, b. Oct. 27, 1871.

v. HATTIE L. ROBINSON, b. Dec. 5, 1875.

4. GEORGE CHAMBERLAIN WALKER, b. Sept. 4, and d. Oct. 20, 1845.

5. ANDREW McFARLAND WALKER, b. Aug. 14, 1846; resides in W. Rutland, unm.

6. GEORGE FREDERICK WALKER, b. June 30, and d. Aug. 20, 1852. } Twins.

7. GEORGIETTA FLORENCE WALKER, b. June 30, and d. Sept. 20, 1852. } Twins.

8. DAVID PARKER WALKER, b. July 4, 1855; d. Jan. 5, 1876.

9. MARTHA DAVIS WALKER, b. March 11, 1861; m. March, 1882, Lewis Freeman, and reside in Spencer. No children.

223. Persis Eager Parker *(David,[7] Isaac,[6] Amos,[5] Andrew,[4] John,[3] Hananiah,[2] Thomas[1])*, dau. of David and Betsey (Eager) Parker, was b. in Barre, May 8, 1821; m. June 13, 1843, Samuel N. Howe of Holden.

They had one child:

1. CECILIA HOWE, who d. at the age of 1 year, 8 months.

224. Lucy Parker *(David,[7] Isaac,[6] Amos,[5] Andrew,[4] John,[3] Hananiah,[2] Thomas[1])*, dau. of David and Betsey (Eager) Parker, was b. in Barre, Sept. 2, 1823; m. April 3, 1849, Lysander Crawford of Oakham, b. Feb. 2, 1824. They lived in Barre, where he was a farmer and where he d. April 16, 1884. She resides in Barre.

Their children were:

1. SAMUEL P. CRAWFORD, b. March 13, 1850; d. Dec. 14, 1852.
2. CLARE E. CRAWFORD, b. June 17, 1853; d. April 4, 1854.
3. EMMA A. CRAWFORD, b. July 15, 1860; resides in Barre.

225. Caleb Alexander Parker *(Lewis,[7] Isaac,[6] Amos,[5] Andrew,[4] John,[3] Hananiah,[2] Thomas[1])*, son of Major Lewis and Elizabeth (Seaver) Parker, was b. in Sterling, Dec. 24, 1806.

While still a young man he went to New Orleans, La., in the early thirties. After a few years' residence in that city he removed to Jackson, Miss., where for some years he successfully prosecuted his business of builder and contractor, erecting the Mississippi State Capitol, the State Insane Asylum, Hinds County Court House and other public buildings. He also built a part of the New Orleans, Jackson and Great Northern Railroad, now the Illinois Central. He went to New Orleans again in 1859 to live, and many of the finest edifices in that city were erected by him, among them the St. Louis Hotel.

He d. in New Orleans, Nov. 29, 1891, aged 85 years. He was a resident of Mississippi and Louisiana for more than 50 years. The funeral took place from the residence of his son, Colonel C. Harrison Parker.

"The cause of his death was old age, a wearing out of the body which had spent a long and busy life. He had been failing for weeks, but with the indomitable energy which ever characterized the man he would not yield even to the grim destroyer himself and lived for days after he was thought to be in the throes of actual dissolution. Once before he displayed the same characteristic. More than 50 years ago, while foreman of one of the volunteer fire companies, exposure at a fire brought on an attack of pneumonia, from which his physician said he could not recover; but the iron constitution had not then been sapped by age and the will of the man conquered death itself and he recovered.

"He was much respected by those who knew him for his courage, his openness of character, his attachment to his friends and his many other stirling qualities. He leaves children and grandchildren who are scattered throughout the Union. He was an old and valued member of the Masonic fraternity, which paid to his memory the last sad tribute of respect by returning his body to the earth beneath the shadow of the acacia."

He had a family of several children, who are in active life throughout the South and West.

226. Abigail Sawyer Parker *(Lewis,[7] Isaac,[6] Amos,[5] Andrew,[4] John,[3] Hananiah,[2] Thomas[1])*, dau. of Major Lewis and Elizabeth (Seaver) Parker, was b. in Sterling, Oct. 15, 1809; m. Jan. 24, 1830, Joshua Buxton of Lowell, b. Dec. 28, 1799, the youngest son of Ebenezer and Susanna Buxton of N. Reading. They settled in Woburn, where he was a cabinetmaker. They finally removed to Stetson, Me., where he was a farmer until his decease, which occurred Feb. 13, 1877. Mrs. Abigail S. Buxton still survives him, residing in Stetson, Me.

Their children were:

1. SUSAN JANE BUXTON, b. in Sterling, Dec. 4, 1830; is a dressmaker and resides in Woburn.
2. GEORGE PARKER BUXTON, b. in Woburn, Oct. 15, 1832; d. June 12, 1862.
3. JOSHUA THOMAS BUXTON, b. in Woburn, Oct. 25, 1834; m. in Hampden, Me., Dec. 23, 1865, Mariah Emery, b. Feb. 23, 1838, dau. of John and Sarah (Fernald) Emery. He is a farmer and they reside in Woburn. Their children were:
   - I. GEORGE BUXTON, b. April 8, 1866; d. Jan. 25, 1875. } Twins.
   - II. FRANK BUXTON, b. April 8, 1866. } Twins.
   - III. HARRY BUXTON, b. Dec. 15, 1868; d. Jan. 31, 1875.
   - IV. WILLIAM BUXTON, b. April 2, 1870.
   - V. LEWIS BUXTON, b. June 17, 1873; d. Feb. 5, 1875.
   - VI. EDWARD BUXTON, b. Jan. 23, 1876.
4. ANN ELIZABETH BUXTON, b. in Woburn, Sept. 18, 1837; m. Charles Starkey of Stetson, Me. He is a merchant. They reside in Natural Bridge, N. Y. Their children were:
   - I. EDGAR POE STARKEY. He is connected with railroad work.
   - II. CHARLES STARKEY. He is a storekeeper with his father.
   - III. MARY STARKEY.

Evelina Maynard Parker (see page 185) *(Lewis,[7] Isaac,[6] Amos,[5] Andrew,[4] John,[3] Hananiah,[2] Thomas[1])*, dau. of Major Lewis and Elizabeth (Seaver) Parker, was b. in Sterling, Nov. 23, 1811. She was a very promising and beautiful young lady; was a dressmaker. In May, 1833, she wet her feet in going to a neighbor's house and, it being a warm day, she remained in a room where there was no fire until her feet were dry. From effects of this she died in a fortnight, June 8, 1833. Hers was the first death of a young lady which had occurred in the town for a long time. Her handsome face was enclosed with black hair and curls, and she was already engaged to Reuben Sawyer, who always felt downcast after her death. Her loss was widely felt throughout the township and a very large gathering attended her funeral.

227. Elizabeth Margaret Parker *(Lewis,[7] Isaac,[6] Amos,[5] Andrew,[4] John,[3] Hananiah,[2] Thomas[1])*, dau. of Major Lewis and Elizabeth (Seaver) Parker, was b. in Sterling, Sept. 24, 1813; m. April 21, 1836, Gilbert Hamilton Howe of Sterling, b. March 6, 1810. They lived in the centre for several years; removed then to Minneapolis, Minn., where she d. Jan. 18, 1882, and where he still resides with his son, William Parker Howe.

All of the children were b. in Sterling:

1. MARY AUGUSTA HOWE, b. Jan. 8, 1838; m. Nov. 4, 1860, in Sterling, James Henry Little, b. in Shirley, Mass., June 29, 1838. She d. July 4, 1877; he d. Sept. 18, 1879. Children:
   - I. JANE ELIZABETH LITTLE, b. Nov. 12, 1861; d. Sept. 8, 1884.
   - II. CARINA HAMMOND LITTLE, b. Feb. 16, 1866; m. Jan. 18, 1887, in Minneapolis, Minn., William Shutte Marshall. They reside in Omaha, Neb.
   - III. ARTHUR WILSON LITTLE, b. Aug. 8, 1867; resides in Superior, Wis.
   - IV. ORA HOWE LITTLE, b. June 25, 1869; m. Nov. 5, 1887, Seymour A. Miller, who d. May 7, 1888. She resides in Minneapolis, Minn.
   - V. MARY HELEN LITTLE, b. June 24, 1875.

2. HENRY GILBERT HOWE, b. April 23, 1839; m. (1) May 2, 1865, Josephine L. Bartlett, dau. of Perley Bartlett. She d. Jan. 16, 1866, in Minneapolis, Minn., and he m. (2) Dec. 2, 1868, in Putnam, Ct., Louise Ann Willett, b. in Hartford, Ct., Feb. 22, 1839. He is now (1890) in Tombstone, Ariz., an engineering and mining expert, U. S. Deputy Mineral Surveyor and mine owner. Their children were:

i. GERTRUDE DEAN HOWE, b. in Minneapolis, Oct. 15, 1869; m. Sept. 26, 1889, in Tombstone, Ariz., Edward Warren Perkins.

ii. CHARLES WILLETT HOWE, b. in Chicago, Ill., Nov. 29, 1872; d. July 8, 1873.

iii. ALVAN WILLETT HOWE, b. in Chicago, Nov. 25, 1873.

iv. LOUISE ROGERS HOWE, b. in Chicago, Sept. 3, 1876.

3. CHARLES LEWIS HOWE, b. Nov. 13, 1841; d. May 1, 1861.

4. WILLIAM PARKER HOWE, b. Sept. 7, 1846. He is editor and proprietor of the important commercial periodical, *The Trade Reporter*. He resides in Minneapolis, Minn.

5. PETER OSGOOD HOWE, b. Oct. 8, 1848; d. Jan. 22, 1861.

6. SILAS WALTER HOWE, b. Aug. 15, 1850; d. Jan. 29, 1861.

7. HERBERT KENDALL HOWE, b. Feb. 18, 1853; d. April 23, 1861.

8. THOMAS PRENTICE ALLEN HOWE, b. Jan. 23, 1855; resides in Minneapolis, Minn. He is Assistant Consulting Engineer of the Great Northern Railway Co., St. Paul, Minn.

9. ANNIE ELIZABETH HOWE, b. Aug. 13, 1857; d. Aug. 22, 1858.

228. Sarah Angeline Parker (*Lewis*,[7] *Isaac*,[6] *Amos*,[5] *Andrew*,[4] *John*,[3] *Hananiah*,[2] *Thomas*[1]), dau. of Major Lewis and Elizabeth (Seaver) Parker, was b. in Sterling, Aug. 13, 1815; m. in Sterling, Nov. 10, 1836, John Phelps of W. Boylston, b. June 23, 1810, son of Abijah and Maria Phelps of W. Boylston. They settled on Malden Hill in W. Boylston, where he carried on a farm of 120 acres in a very successful manner. He was a thorough temperance man from boyhood, and a member of the Congregational Church of the town from the age of 19 until his decease, which occurred May 30, 1859, from consumption. His widow, Mrs. Sarah Phelps, conducted the place for ten years following, devoting herself to the good of her family and the farm. She has long been a constant member of the Church in W. Boylston, in which place she still resides.

Their children were:

1. ANGELINA PARKER PHELPS, b. Oct. 29, 1837; d. March 20, 1857.

2. HENRY LEWIS PHELPS, b. Nov. 13, 1839; m. May 6, 1869, Mary Ella Brown of W. Boylston, b. in Oakdale, June 19, 1852, dau. of Dexter (of Sterling) and Rhoda Russell (Lawrence) Brown of Weld, Me. He conducts the Phelps farm on Malden Hill, W. Boylston, where they reside. Children:

i. Henry Edward Phelps, b. May 24, 1870.
ii. Mary Augusta Phelps, b. Jan. 12, 1872; d. Dec. 30, 1874.
iii. Minnie Addie Phelps, b. July 21, 1876; d. Oct. 28, 1883.
iv. Charles Walter Phelps, b. Dec. 9, 1879; d. Nov. 5, 1883.
v. Ella May Phelps, b. April 10, 1883; d. Sept. 18, 1883.
vi. Annie Maude Phelps, b. Dec. 15, 1888; d. April 2, 1890.

3. Emily Caroline Phelps, b. Aug. 2, 1842; m. in W. Boylston, Nov., 1866, William Franklin Davis, b. in Ashby, June 30, 1846, son of Jonathan P. and Emily M. (Mansfield) Davis. They reside in Worcester, where he is a watchman. Children:
i. Nellie Loretta Davis, b. in Leominster, Oct. 19, 1867.
ii. Nettie Angeline Davis, b. in Leominster, July 23, 1869.
iii. Ruby Lura Davis, b. July 2, 1884.

4. Ellen Louise Phelps, b. April 4, 1846; d. Nov. 13, 1863.

5. Sarah Elizabeth Phelps, b. Sept. 14, 1849; m. in W. Boylston, May 27, 1868, Josiah Samuel Davis, b. in Ashby, Jan. 8, 1844, brother of William Franklin Davis. He lived in Fitchburg, where he conducted a bakery and restaurant. He d. July 27, 1886. She resides in Fitchburg. Children:
i. Sarah Annie Davis, b. June 5, 1869; m. Fred A. Lewis of Worcester, where they reside.
ii. Frank Henry Davis, b. May 3, 1883.
iii. Raymond Walter Davis, b. March 4, 1885.

6. John William Phelps, b. Jan. 23, 1852; m. May 16, 1878, Addie M. Colby Adams, b. in Nashua, N. H., Jan. 27, 1858, dau. of John Q. and Amanda (Farmer) Adams of Nashua. Her parents, who were b. Nov. 22, 1830, and Jan. 8, 1837, respectively, d. before she was five years and she grew up in her aunt Colby's family, which caused a change in the name. They reside in Fitchburg. Their children were:
i. Mira Addie Phelps, b. March 14, 1879.
ii. Minnie Alice Phelps, b. Nov. 11, 1885.

230. Hollis Gardner Parker *(Lewis,[7] Isaac,[6] Amos,[5] Andrew,[4] John,[3] Hananiah,[2] Thomas[1])*, son of Major Lewis and Elizabeth (Seaver) Parker, was b. in Sterling, Sept. 30, 1818; m. in Hartford, Ct., May 4, 1847, Laura A. Goodrich, dau. of Jared and Abigail Goodrich. He is a merchant in Manchester, Ct. She d. March 4, 1879.

Their children were:

George Hollis Parker, b. in Hartford, Ct., Feb. 21, 1851; d. 1855.
Laura Ann Parker, b. in Philadelphia, Pa., March 16, 1856; d. Sept. 5, 1857.
Ella Goodrich Parker, b. in Philadelphia, Pa., Jan. 28, 1859.
384. Charles Duffield Parker, b. in Philadelphia, Pa., June 19, 1861; m. Julia Skipper.
William Lewis Parker, b. in Buckland, Ct., Jan. 18, 1868.
Grace Adams Parker, b. in Buckland, Ct., July 10, 1873.

Mary Anne Capen Parker (see page 186) (*Lewis,[7] Isaac,[6] Amos,[5] Andrew,[4] John,[3] Hananiah,[2] Thomas[1]*), dau. of Major Lewis and Elizabeth (Seaver) Parker, was b. in Sterling, March 31, 1820. She went to live with Dr. Willard Parker of Woodstock, Vt., when quite young, removing with the Doctor's family to Pittsfield, Mass., where she lived several years, then to Cincinnati, O., where she d. March 5, 1834. This was the well known Dr. Willard Parker who later settled in New York city. He was descended from the emigrant ancestor, Abraham Parker of Chelmsford.

Lucy Adams Parker (see page 186) (*Lewis,[7] Isaac,[6] Amos,[5] Andrew,[4] John,[3] Hananiah,[2] Thomas[1]*), dau. of Major Lewis and Elizabeth (Seaver) Parker, was b. in Sterling, March 4, 1825; m. in Hartford, Ct., Mr. Gourly of Worcester. They removed to Pittsfield, Mass., where she later died. She d. in Troy, N. Y. Her middle name arose from the coincidence of her date of birth with the inauguration of President John Quincy Adams. She had two children, who both died young and are buried in Worcester.

231. Elisha H. Parker (*Elisha,[7] Elisha,[6] Amos,[5] Andrew,[4] John,[3] Hananiah,[2] Thomas[1]*), son of Elisha and Eunice (Dean) Parker, was b. in Barnard, Vt., May 10, 1818; m. Sept. 27, 1847, Alvira P. Ferrin, b. in Morristown, Vt., June 24, 1826. They resided in Morristown until 1879, when he removed to Middlefield, Ct., where he resides.

Their children were:

Julia A. Parker, b. Sept. 8, 1848; deceased.
John F. Parker, b. Sept. 20, 1850; resides in Middlefield, Ct.
Lizzie A. Parker, b. July 22, 1854; resides in Middlefield.

232. Minerva E. Parker *(Elisha,[7] Elisha,[6] Amos,[5] Andrew,[4] John,[3] Hananiah,[2] Thomas[1])*, dau. of Elisha and Eunice (Dean) Parker, was b. in Bakersfield, Vt., May 13, 1827; m. March 3, 1850, Josiah Converse, b. in Brookfield, Oct. 15, 1797, and came with his father to Bakersfield, in 1804. She resides in Bakersfield.

Their children were:

1. CHARLES CONVERSE, b. July 6, 1851.
2. ELISHA H. CONVERSE, b. July 8, 1853; d. June 8, 1854.
3. MARIA E. CONVERSE, b. Sept. 1, 1856; d. Aug. 7, 1889, leaving two sons.
4. CHENEY A. CONVERSE, b. March 30, 1858.
5. BURTON H. CONVERSE, b. June 19, 1860; d. Feb. 19, 1864.

233. Robert D. Parker *(Elisha,[7] Elisha,[6] Amos,[5] Andrew,[4] John,[3] Hananiah,[2] Thomas[1])*, son of Elisha and Eunice (Dean) Parker, was b. in Bakersfield, Vt., May 6, 1834. He removed to Worcester, Mass., and m. Sarah Hawes of Auburn. They lived in Worcester. Robert D. Parker was a strong, hearty man, a characteristic of his Parker relatives. His brother Elisha was also gifted with a remarkable physique in his younger days. The former was known to carry upon his back and up three flights of stairs a sugar barrel filled with coal. Robert D. Parker died from an accident at Lincoln Square in Worcester. He jumped from the team which he was driving and seizing a runaway horse by the bridle he succeeded in stopping him, but while thus engaged was dashed against a passing train and killed. His widow resides in Worcester.

Their children were:

ELIZABETH PARKER; m. Frank M. Muzzy, and resides in Chicopee.

RALPH H. PARKER, b. Jan. 26, 1866. He is a letter-carrier in Worcester.

CLARE PARKER.

LEE RAYMOND PARKER. He is a farmer in Barre.

BIRNEY PARKER.

234. Charles Rollin Parker *(Elijah,[7] Elisha,[6] Amos,[5] Andrew,[4] John,[3] Hananiah,[2] Thomas[1])*, son of Elijah and Rhody (Butler) Parker, was b. in Bakersfield, Vt., Jan. 5, 1814; m. (1) July 4, 1834, Portia Adelia Harmon, b. Jan.

21, 1815. He shared to a considerable extent in the arduous and manifold privations, often severe, of those who changed the dense forests of our country into an orchard, blossoming like the garden of the Lord. In this school he learned those habits of industry, economy and prudence which enabled him to overcome the great difficulties which stood in the way of his life's success. After his marriage he engaged in the lumber business in Niagara County, N. Y. His company ultimately failed and Charles R. Parker lost all his property. Penniless and burdened with a family he commenced the study of law. For a time he was clerk in the office of Ransom & Holmes. After his admission to the bar he became a successful practitioner of his profession and practiced in what is now the city of Lockport, N. Y., for nearly 50 years, without a stain upon his moral or professional character. By his industry, his close attention to business and his economy he accumulated not only a competence but a very considerable estate. He was prompt in the discharge of his duties, a safe counsellor and a trustworthy employee. Whatever he undertook was carefully attended to and well done. He was not gifted with eloquence, on the contrary he had an impediment in his speech which forbid his entering into that portion of legal practice in which lawyers are most conspicuous to the public, the trial of litigated causes. He was content to shun the paths in which he could not shine. He had a discriminating legal mind, good common sense and sound judgment, and above all he was an honest man, "The noblest work of God."

Mrs. Portia A. H. Parker d. Dec. 21, 1842, and he m. (2) Feb. 14, 1843, her sister, Marcia Ann Harmon, b. Nov. 22, 1824, d. Oct. 10, 1845. He m. (3) Mrs. Betsey Maria (Paige) Peckham, his cousin, of Bakersfield, Vt. She d. May 7, 1853, and he m. (4) Nov. 10, 1853, Harriet Newhall, b. in Conway, Mass., Dec., 1818, dau. of Daniel Newhall. He d. May 6, 1887.

His children were:

385. Charles Fessenden Parker, b. June 6, 1836; m. (1) Mary Dickerman of New Haven, Ct.; (2) Kate Isadore Shipman of Girard, Pa.; (3) Mary F. Ball of Columbus, O.

Clinton Ranson Parker, b. Oct. 15, 1839; d. May 8, 1843.

ALBERT BUTLER PARKER, b. Feb. 18, 1842; m. Mary Kellogg of Leslie, Mich. Their only child was:

i. CHARLES ROLLIN PARKER; d. in South Haven, Mich., March 12, 1888, aged 8 years and 6 months.

ADELIA PARKER (twin of Albert), b. Feb. 18, 1842; d. 1843.
ANN ADELIA PARKER, b. May 8, 1845; d. Aug. 26, 1854.
MARY JANE PARKER, b. Nov. 29, 1846; d. Aug. 25, 1866.

235. Cho Augusta Parker *(Elijah,[7] Elisha,[6] Amos,[5] Andrew,[4] John,[3] Hananiah,[2] Thomas[1])*, dau. of Elijah and Rhody (Butler) Parker, was b. in Bakersfield, Vt., Aug. 10, 1815; m. Feb. 5, 1834, Silas Hall, b. Oct. 8, 1805, son of Ralph and Mary Hall of Newburyport, Mass. He d. June 1, 1883.

Their children were:

1. HERMAN D. HALL, b. in Cambria, Dec., 1834. He is in business in Gunnison, Col.
2. JOHN N. HALL, b. in Pendleton, Dec., 1836. He is in business in Gunnison, Col.
3. ADDISON PARKER HALL, b. in Pendleton, Oct., 1839; m. 1863, Celia Warren of Tonawanda, N. Y. She d. 1880. Their surviving children are:
   i. MARY JANE HALL, b. July, 1866.
   ii. ADDIE AUGUSTA HALL, b. Oct., 1872.
4. CAROLINE AUGUSTA HALL, b. Dec., 1841; m. Nov. 25, 1863, Rev. Edward Payson Marvin, a descendant of Reynold Marvin of Lyme, Ct. They reside in Lockport, N. Y., and have four children:
   i. CORNELIA FRANCES MARVIN, b. 1864; m. Dec., 1885, Albert McDonnell, and have a dau.:
      1. Cho Augusta McDonnell, b. Feb. 2, 1888.
   ii. EDWARD PAYSON MARVIN, Jr., b. 1868.
   iii. WALTER CLARK MARVIN.
   iv. WILLIAM ROY MARVIN.
5. CAROLINE A. HALL, b. Nov., 1845; d. May 28, 1864.
6. CHARLES W. HALL, b. Dec., 1848; m. May, 1876, Rachel Cowles, and have had the following children:
   i. WILLIS HAROLD HALL, b. May, 1877.
   ii. CHARLES RALPH HALL, b. 1879; d. 1883.
   iii. LEE BUTLER HALL, b. Dec., 1883.

7. Henry C. Hall, b. May, 1852; m. Sept., 1876, Addie Denning. Their children are:
   i. Emerson D. Hall, b. Jan., 1878.
   ii. Raymond Hall, b. May, 1882.

8. Alice M. Hall, b. July, 1854; m. Nov., 1879, Dr. John W. Corman. Their children were:
   i. John Wesly Corman, Jr., b. and d. 1882.
   ii. Bruce Corman, b. June, 1883.
   iii. Percy Corman, b. Sept., 1884.
   iv. Alice Corman, b. March, 1888.

236. Caroline Miranda Parker *(Elijah,[7] Elisha,[6] Amos,[5] Andrew,[4] John,[3] Hananiah,[2] Thomas[1])*, dau. of Elijah and Rhody (Butler) Parker, was b. in Bakersfield, Vt., March 16, 1818; m. June 17, 1840, Stephen Decatur Scovell, whose mother was Annah Saxe, descended from the House of Saxe-Coburg, Germany. He was first cousin to John G. Saxe, the poet. They settled in Vermontville, Mich., where he d. Jan., 1850. She m. (2) June 18, 1851, Argalus Sprague of Vermontville, where they reside.

Her children were:

1. Josiah T. Scovell, b. July 29, 1841; m. Dec. 25, 1877, Joanna Jameson of Lafayette, Ind. He was 20 years a professor in the State Normal School at Terra Haute, Ind. He is a doctor by profession and is now practicing in Terra Haute. Children:
   i. Gada M. Scovell, b. Jan. 4, 1879.
   ii. Ralph R. Scovell, b. June 24, 1884.
   iii. Robert Scovell, b. Aug. 11, 1887.

2. Augusta A. Scovell, b. July 18, 1843; d. Jan. 18, 1869.
3. William P. Scovell, b. June 1, 1846; d. Feb. 16, 1848.
4. Alice L. Scovell, b. April 29, 1848; d. Feb. 28, 1852.
5. Amanda C. Sprague, b. Oct. 26, 1853.
6. Ernest E. Sprague, b. Aug. 7, 1855; m. Ezra Potter of Vermontville, Mich. They have two sons:
   i. George Clare Sprague, b. June 21, 1884.
   ii. Milton W. Sprague, b. Aug. 11, 1886.

7. Frederic P. Sprague, b. Nov. 7, 1858; m. Carrie Sackett. Their children are:
   i. Augusta Scovell Sprague, b. Sept. 24, 1879.
   ii. Lelia Sprague, b. May 18, 1881.
   iii. Rollin Argalus Sprague, b. Dec. 18, 1882.

237. Isaac Butler Parker *(Elijah,[7] Elisha,[6] Amos,[5] Andrew,[4] John,[3] Hananiah,[2] Thomas[1])*, son of Elijah and Rhody (Butler) Parker, was b. in Bakersfield, Vt., Nov. 19, 1827; m. Oct., 1851, Clarissa Gillett of Youngstown, N. Y. He was a lawyer and had just settled at Marshalltown, Ia., when he d. Dec. 26, 1862.

Their children were:

EDWARD GILLETT PARKER, b. in Warsaw, Ill., Dec. 11, 1852; m. (1) Oct. 18, 1882, Tryphenia Pierson, b. 1860. She d. Feb. 12, 1885, and he m. (2) March 8, 1888, Elizabeth Kane of Canandaigua, N. Y., b. Sept. 3, 1854. He is continuing the law office of his uncle, C. R. Parker, Esq.

WILLIS FREDERICK PARKER, b. in Mitchell, Ia., April 2, 1859. He is a lawyer in Helena, Col.

CLARA AMANDA PARKER, b. in Mitchell, Ia., June 22, 1861. She is a teacher in Oneida, N. Y.

238. Frederic Deforest Parker *(Elijah,[7] Elisha,[6] Amos,[5] Andrew,[4] John,[3] Hananiah,[2] Thomas[1])*, son of Elijah and Rhody (Butler) Parker, was b. in Lewiston, N. Y., Aug. 10, 1830; m. in Battle Creek, Mich., Dec., 1854, Helen Nickols. He d. Nov., 1856.

Their son was:

FREDERICK B. PARKER, b. Dec., 1855; m. Jan. 5, 1881, in Brooklyn, N. Y., Jennie Sarle. He d. in Maker, Col., Dec. 11, 1888, and she d. in Brooklyn, N. Y., Dec. 12, 1888. Their son was:

i. HOWARD SARLE PARKER, b. Jan., 1882.

239. Rebecca Ann Parker *(Jonas,[7] Elisha,[6] Amos,[5] Andrew,[4] John,[3] Hananiah,[2] Thomas[1])*, dau. of Jonas and Lima (Freeman) Parker, was b. in Bakersfield, Vt., Sept. 29, 1825; m. Sept. 1, 1848, Langdon A. Marshall, and lived in E. Brookfield, Vt., until her death, which occurred April 5, 1888. He d. April 8, 1890.

Their children were:

1. EUGENE LANGDON MARSHALL, b. Aug. 6, 1850; m. Aug. 19, 1873, Alma Reed. He d. Aug. 2, 1880. Children:

   i. ANNA EMILY MARSHALL, b. July 12, 1877.

   ii. EUGENE LANGDON MARSHALL, b. March 10, 1879.

2. LIMA MATILDA MARSHALL, b. Nov. 2, 1858; m. April 14, 1879, Eugene V. Price, and have one dau.:
   1. LIMA MARCIA PRICE, b. Sept. 7, 1883.
3. MINNIE SPRAGUE MARSHALL, b. Sept. 21, 1879.

240. Joshua Freeman Parker (*Jonas,[7] Elisha,[6] Amos,[5] Andrew,[4] John,[3] Hananiah,[2] Thomas[1]*), son of Jonas and Lima (Freeman) Parker, was b. in Bakersfield, Vt., Sept. 23, 1827; m. April 7, 1853, Caroline D. Seabury. They reside in Moretown, Vt.

Their child was:

GEORGE L. PARKER, b. in Moretown, Vt., March 11, 1866.

241. John Cortland Parker (*Jonas,[7] Elisha,[6] Amos,[5] Andrew,[4] John,[3] Hananiah,[2] Thomas[1]*), son of Jonas and Lima (Freeman) Parker, was b. in Bakersfield, Vt., March 15, 1831; m. (1) May 3, 1857, Oliva M. Wheeler of Wallingford, Vt. She d. and he m. (2) July 8, 1863, Abigail P. Wheeler of Wallingford.

His children were:

FRANKLIN J. PARKER, b. Nov. 30, 1858; m. (1) Oct. 29, 1870, Mary Hathaway of East Montpelier, Vt. She d. and he m. (2) March 17, 1875, Elia Bennett of Calais, Vt.

CARRIE O. PARKER, b. Oct. 7, 1864.

243. Frederick A. Parker (*Austin,[7] Nahum,[6] Amos,[5] Andrew,[4] John,[3] Hananiah,[2] Thomas[1]*), son of Austin and Susan (Martin) Parker, was b. in Westmoreland, N. H., 1822; m. Clara M. Hyland, b. in Westmoreland. He resides in Gardner, where he is a mechanic.

Their children were:

FRANK F. PARKER. He resides in Gardner, unm.

MARION M. PARKER.

Child, unnamed, b. and d.

244. George Washington Parker (*Amos A.,[7] Nahum,[6] Amos,[5] Andrew,[4] John,[3] Hananiah,[2] Thomas[1]*), son of Col. Amos A. and Miranda (Sanders) Parker, was b. in Concord, N. H., Aug. 14, 1824; m. Oct. 26, 1848, Julia A. Deeth, b. Nov. 2, 1828, dau. of Lyman and Julia (Chapin)

Deeth. He was for a long time station agent at Fitzwilliam, N. H. They reside in Halifax, Mass.

Their children were:

ELLEN MIRANDA PARKER, b. in Fitzwilliam, July 17, 1849; m. in Fitzwilliam, June 20, 1871, Herbert C. Keith, b. in E. Bridgewater, Oct. 18, 1848, son of Freedom and Minerva (Holmes) Keith. They reside in E. Bridgewater.

386. DANIEL DEETH PARKER, b. in Fitzwilliam, June 29, 1851; m. Abby S. Holmes of Halifax, Mass.

387. GEORGE AMOS PARKER, b. in Fitzwilliam, April 28, 1853; m. Jennie W. Richardson of Halifax, Mass.

388. CAROLINE SANDERS PARKER, b. in Fitzwilliam, May 30, 1855; m. Benjamin F. Thrasher of Halifax, Mass.

JULIA FRANCES PARKER, b. in Fitzwilliam, April 28, 1861; m. Feb. 22, 1890, Edward Heywood Sawin of Gardner, Mass., b. Feb. 25, 1829, son of Levi Heywood and Lucy (Putnam) Sawin of Gardner. She graduated from Smith College, Northampton, Mass., in the class of '83.

245. Andrew Parker *(Amos A.,[7] Nahum,[6] Amos,[5] Andrew,[4] John,[3] Hananiah,[2] Thomas[1])*, son of Col. Amos A. and Miranda (Sanders) Parker, was b. in New Market. N. H., March 2, 1828; m. Feb. 12, 1851, Laura S. Morse, b. May 2, 1829, dau. of Isaac and Frances (Stevens) Morse of Winchendon. They reside in Brooklyn, N. Y. They have no children.

246. Miranda Sanders Parker *(Amos A.,[7] Nahum,[6] Amos,[5] Andrew,[4] John,[3] Hananiah,[2] Thomas[1])*, dau. of Col. Amos A. and Mary (McClary) Parker, was b. June 10, 1829; m. June, 1855, Anson Burt Smith of Fitzwilliam, b. July 25, 1825. He was a prominent merchant in Winchendon for many years, where he d. Oct. 18, 1888. She resides in Winchendon.

Their children were:

1. FREDERICK PARKER SMITH, b. Aug. 4. 1859; m. June 4, 1884, H. Isabel Snelling of Boston. She d. May 19, 1888, and he now resides in Boston.
2. CHARLES H. SMITH, b. July 26, and d. Aug. 6, 1860.
3. HERBERT ANSON SMITH, b. Oct. 25, 1861; d. Feb. 28, 1875.

247. Charles Henry Parker (*Amos A.*,[7] *Nahum*,[6] *Amos*,[5] *Andrew*,[4] *John*,[3] *Hananiah*,[2] *Thomas*[1]), son of Amos A. and Mary (McClary) Parker, was b. in Amesbury, Mass., Sept., 1833; m. Nov. 23, 1859, Jane S. Ballou, b. June 17, 1836, d. Jan. 6, 1862, dau. of James and Polly (Handy) Ballou of Richmond, N. H. He enlisted in the 10th N. H. regiment in 1861. After a service of nine months he d. at Beute La Rosse, La., and was there buried.

Their dau. was:

ADA PARKER, b. Nov. 5, 1860. She resides in Keene, N. H.

248. John McClary Parker (*Amos A.*,[7] *Nahum*,[6] *Amos*,[5] *Andrew*,[4] *John*,[3] *Hananiah*,[2] *Thomas*[1]), son of Amos A. and Mary (McClary) Parker, was b. in Kingston, N. H., Sept. 17, 1836; m. (1) Oct. 17, 1865, Catharine A. Adams, b. June 25, 1840, d. March 19, 1869, dau. of Capt. Jonathan S. and Abigail (Tower) Adams; m. (2) Sept. 21, 1870, Abbie H. Kimball, b. Jan. 10, 1838, dau. of John and Jane S. (Richardson) Kimball.

He enlisted in the 3rd N. H. Reg. in July, 1861, and served constantly three years and three months, until toward the close of the war. The losses of this regiment ranked among those of the State next to the 5th. He was in the sieging of Fort Wagner, was before Petersburgh, Drewrey's Bluff, Secessionville, S. C., and in many other important engagements. He was promoted from private to orderly sergeant, second lieutenant, first lieutenant, adjutant and sometimes led the company as captain. Mr. Parker has been several years moderator of the town meetings of Fitzwilliam, like his father and grandfather before him, the three generations making a total of over 30 years. He has been for many years a merchant in Fitzwilliam, where they reside.

His children were:

HELEN ADAMS PARKER, b. Aug. 6, 1866.
FRANCIS RICHARDSON PARKER, b. July 19, 1873.

249. Alfred A. Parker (*Ephraim*,[7] *Nahum*,[6] *Amos*,[5] *Andrew*,[4] *John*,[3] *Hananiah*,[2] *Thomas*[1]), son of Capt. Ephraim and Lucy (Stone) Parker, was b. in New Boston (part of

Winchendon), Mass., 1823; m. in Orange, March 30, 1857, Frances A. Whipple of Orange, b. Sept. 19, 1834, d. Nov. 6, 1891, dau. of John Rice and Martha (Holbrook) Whipple. While still young he removed in 1838 to St. Louis, Mo., where he became engaged in mercantile pursuits. He removed in 1864 from St. Louis to Orange, Mass., where he now resides, and where he has been engaged in mercantile business up to the present time.

Their children were:

ALFRED WHIPPLE PARKER, b. in St. Louis, Mo., Jan. 22, 1859; d. in Orange, Dec. 17, 1887.

JOHN RICE PARKER, b. in Orange, Sept. 9, 1861; m. Jan. 1, 1887; d. Dec. 19, 1889, without issue.

MARY POWERS PARKER, b. in Orange, March 14, 1865.

MARTHA FRANCES PARKER, b. in Orange, Dec. 6, 1867.

250. Edward Nelson Parker *(Ephraim,[7] Nahum,[6] Amos,[5] Andrew,[4] John,[3] Hananiah,[2] Thomas[1])*, son of Capt. Ephraim and Lucy (Stone) Parker, was b. in Marlow, N. H., April 7, 1822; m. in St. Louis, Feb. 7, 1848, Louisa Moore Lackland, b. in Frederickton, Md., Feb. 6, 1826, dau. of Dennis and Eliza Lackland. She d. Nov. 12, 1869.

Edward N. Parker came to St. Louis about 1843 and engaged in the business of merchant tailoring and gentlemen's furnishing goods. After the death of his wife he went to Washington, Mo., and was editor of the *Franklin County Observer* until shortly before his death, which occurred April 28, 1881, of pneumonia, and he was buried in Washington.

Their children, all b. in St. Louis, were:

EVA LOUISA PARKER, b. Dec. 28, 1849; d. Sept. 10, 1850.

389. DENNIS LACKLAND PARKER, b. April 28, 1851.

MARGARET ANN PARKER, b. Oct. 22, 1852; d. Nov. 4, 1854.

390. MARGARET ANN PARKER, b. Aug. 31, 1854.

391. LULU LOUISA PARKER, b. Oct. 25, 1856.

EDWARD NELSON PARKER, b. Dec. 10, 1859; d. June 6, 1860.

MARY SUSANNAH PARKER, b. April 21, 1860. She resides in Baltimore, Md., unm.

251. Charles Adams Parker *(Ephraim,[7] Nahum,[6] Amos,[5] Audrew,[4] John,[3] Hananiah,[2] Thomas[1])*, son of Capt. Ephraim and Lucy (Stone) Parker, was b. in Fitzwilliam, N.

H., 1833. Lived in St. Louis and Rock Island, where he was in the mercantile business. From Rock Island he went to California. He later became editor and publisher of a daily paper in Virginia City, Nevada. He was president and treasurer of various mining companies. In 1882, when last heard from, he was at White Pine Mines in Nevada, unmarried. It is supposed that he is not living.

252. Horace Milton Parker *(Ephraim,[7] Nahum,[6] Amos,[5] Andrew,[4] John,[3] Hananiah,[2] Thomas[1])*, son of Capt. Ephraim and Lucy (Stone) Parker, was b. in Fitzwilliam, N. H., 1835. He went to St. Louis and also engaged in the mercantile business in Illinois and Sulphur Springs, Mo. He was twice married. Both wives are deceased, leaving no children.

253. Eliza Ann Parker *(Ephraim,[7] Nahum,[6] Amos,[5] Andrew,[4] John,[3] Hananiah,[2] Thomas[1])*, dau. of Capt. Ephraim and Lucy (Stone) Parker, was b. in Fitzwilliam, N. H., 1838; m. in St. Louis, Jan. 6, 1852, Lucas C. Topping, b. in Chatham, Mass., 1823, son of John and Patience Topping. He has been a merchant in St. Louis. They now reside in Wichita, Kan., where he is a wholesale lumber dealer.

Their son is:

1. CHARLES PARKER TOPPING, b. in St. Louis, Oct. 5, 1863.

254. Janette Frances Parker *(Ephraim,[7] Nahum,[6] Amos,[5] Andrew,[4] John.[3] Hananiah,[2] Thomas[1])*, dau. of Capt. Ephraim and Lucy (Stone) Parker, was b. in Ashby, Mass., 1840; m. Marshall Thayer of Springfield, Mass.

Their dau. was:

1. GRACE THAYER, who is m. and is living in Boston.

255. Thomas Maxwell Parker *(Quincy,[7] Ebenezer,[6] Thomas,[5] Andrew,[4] John,[3] Hananiah,[2] Thomas[1])*, son of Quincy and Patience (Brooks) Parker, was b. in Princeton, April 26, 1803; m. Aug. 9, 1829, in Providence, R. I., Esther Cole Luther, b. Aug. 4, 1802, d. Nov. 27, 1845, dau. of Mary and Theophilus Luther of Swansea, Mass. They resided in Providence, where he d. Dec. 9, 1884.

Their children were:

FRANCES MARIA PARKER, b. April 27, 1830; m. Feb., 1861, Edward S. McCashland. She d. June 12, 1862, at Newtown, Ill.

HELENA AUGUSTA PARKER, b. Oct. 18, 1832; m. Jan. 18, 1853, William Eddy of Providence, R. I., b. Jan. 17, 1823. They reside in Providence.

392. BENJAMIN THOMAS PARKER, b. March 22, 1836; m. Charlotte A. Saunders of Augusta, Me.

ESTHER LOUISA PARKER, b. Feb. 18, 1838; d. July 10, 1839.

256. Joseph Brooks Parker (*Quincy,*[7] *Ebenezer,*[6] *Thomas.*[5] *Andrew,*[4] *John,*[3] *Hananiah,*[2] *Thomas*[1]), son of Quincy and Patience (Brooks) Parker, was b. in Princeton, July 31, 1805; m. Oct. 16, 1833, Mary Ann Morgan, b. in Brimfield, Dec. 28, 1809, dau. of Calvin and Polly (Forbush) Morgan. He settled in the house which he built for himself in W. Boylston, which stands near the grist-mill at the junction of the roads. He was a true and active student in the teachings of Christ and a devoted follower of Him, his Master. In July, 1835, he was chosen deacon of the Orthodox Congregational Church in W. Boylston. He later removed to Clinton, residing near the depot in the house which his family still occupy and where he d. His widow survives.

Aside from his home training. his early education was limited to the common district school of his town. At the age of 15 he was apprenticed to Joel Howe, a blacksmith of Princeton, with whom he remained six years. Completing his apprenticeship he entered the machine shop of Samuel Flagg of Oakdale. In this position he developed at once an uncommon tact for his new employment, for within a year he was appointed foreman of the shop, on account of which some of the senior workmen refusing to work under so young a man resigned; but his apparent ability as a mechanic held for him his position and his manly demeanor won back his disaffected shopmates and made them ever after his true and faithful friends. His engagement with Mr. Flagg terminating he commenced the machine business on his own account, occupying the shop formerly occupied by Mr. Flagg. Meanwhile, E. B. Bigelow, then of W. Boylston, and since so distinguished as an inventor, had conceived the idea of building a loom for weaving counterpanes. In his struggle to bring forth the invention he sought the aid of Deacon Parker. The coming together of these two men resulted in the formation of a company to complete the undertaking and put the loom in operation. The company consisted of E. B. Bigelow, Dea. Parker and Eli Holbrook, all young men of about the same age. This loom, however, was not a success. The company wanting means to carry on the work further the enterprise was for a time abandoned, though they fully believed in the final success of the work. From this the inventive genius of E. B. Bigelow was turned to his coach lace loom, which at once came to better results. This loom was built by Dea. Parker and put in operation at Shirley Village, and later was removed to Clinton. In 1840 Dea. Parker removed his business to Providence, R. I. The success of the Messrs. Bigelow being assured, they, with others, formed a company, purchased the water power in Clinton, built a machine shop and made extensive preparations for operating their new inventions. After the trial of other machinists to build their machinery the Bigelows again sought the aid of Dea. Parker. He came from Providence to Clinton and was put in charge of the new machine shop built by the Clinton Company. This new position brought more fully his mechanical ability to the test. Following the coach lace loom came the reconstruction of the counterpane looms then running, but which had not done satisfactory work. These were all rebuilt, resulting in the manufacture of a much improved fabric. Following these were the gingham and Brussels carpet looms, each of which was the *first loom of its kind ever in operation*. All these were made under Dea. Parker's supervision. All were new, there being no models to work from or workmen experienced in that line of machinery building. Everything was wrought out step by step without the suggestion or the aid of others. In the coach lace loom was found the germ of the Brussels carpet loom which was brought to its present state of perfection only by the protracted study of years. To invent or make such a masterpiece of machinery is honor enough for any man and justly entitles him to lasting fame. The idea of a machine being given him he could make it, which oftener than otherwise is the most difficult part to perform. In 1851 Dea. Parker went to England to superintend the setting up of Brussels carpet looms. He returned after eight months. Soon after he built a manufactory in Clinton. His business at once increased; the machine shop was doubly enlarged and under his management it became an important business interest of Clinton, and it is still conducted under the name of The J. B. Parker Machine Co. His strong points as a man of business were his strength and clearness of mind. These were seen in everything. United with his intense application this quality was invaluable to him as a machinist. He was a man of superior judgment. This also appeared in all matters of every-day life. He was every man's counsellor though he never wore a title. In his business few men were his equal as a judge of machinery. Young men esteemed it a privilege to be taught the trade of a machinist by him. His ideal of a machine was perfection. Great care was taken to make every machine perfect. Nothing was allowed to leave his shop that was not so. This had much to do with his success in after life. His attention to all the details of his business was unremitting. He trusted nothing to others. And as it was continuously on the increase it was almost a matter of necessity that he be more and more industriously occupied with its cares and management. In the summer of 1859 he and his family spent a day at the seashore in York, Me., which up to that time was the only holiday of the kind he had enjoyed. Few men are identified with the almost model town of Clinton more than Dea. Parker. In the variety and extent of his manufactures, in its rapid growth and continued prosperity he took a constant and bore a conspicuous part. And could the town be photographed in its moral as well as in its material aspects it would appear that he was even more an important factor in it. A man of clear head, sound judgment and Christian character that always commanded respect and confidence. He with others did the most valuable pioneer service in laying the foundations of the moral and religious institutions of the town. He exerted a strong influence over young men and by his counsel and example was most useful in aiding them to make a good start in life. Though sufficiently conservative he was a man of reform, always headed in the right direction, always standing for the best things, no man ever doubting how he would talk or what he would do when the common good was at stake.

Their children were:

MARY ISADORE PARKER, b. in W. Boylston, Oct. 7, 1836; d. in Lancaster, July 14, 1845.

HENRIETTA EVELINE PARKER, b. in Lancaster, Sept. 5, 1841; d. in Lancaster, July 1, 1843.

MARY ISADORE PARKER, b. in Lancaster, June 6, 1844; resides with her mother in Clinton.

393. HENRIETTA EVELINE PARKER, b. in Lancaster, July 29, 1847; m. Charles Murdock of W. Boylston.

257. **William Eaton Parker** *(Quincy,7 Ebenezer,6 Thomas,5 Andrew,4 John,3 Hananiah,2 Thomas1)*, son of Quincy and Patience (Brooks) Parker, was b. in Princeton, June 6, 1808. He was very fond of travel and adventure. He went West, locating finally in Columbus, O., where he m.

Unfortunately little is known of this family. His life was doubtless an active and interesting one, worthy of longer insertion here, if the facts could only be ascertained. He had several children, of whom a daughter is supposed to be living. Two of his children died of scarlet fever, and William Parker, his son, was killed in the war of the Rebellion. He, the son, joined McClellan's army and was killed at the battle of the Wilderness, where he was fighting in the foremost ranks.

Priscilla Elvira Parker (see page 213), *(Quincy,7 Ebenezer,6 Thomas,5 Andrew,4 John,3 Hananiah,2 Thomas1)*, dau. of Quincy and Patience (Brooks) Parker, was b. in Princeton, April 26, 1809. She was teacher in the High School, Providence, R. I. She was a very kind hearted and worthy lady. For many years before her death she kindly assumed the care of the children of her then deceased sister, Mrs. Eunice Herrick. She d. Nov. 6, 1872, aged 63, and was buried in the family grave-yard at Princeton.

259. **Ira Parker** *(Quincy,7 Ebenezer,6 Thomas,5 Andrew,4 John,3 Hananiah,2 Thomas1)*, son of Quincy and Patience (Brooks) Parker, was b. in Princeton, April 16, 1814; m.

Maria Haskell, dau. of Moses and Kezia (Warner) Haskell of Providence, R. I., the latter being of the Warner family of Seekonk, Mass. He was a very industrious, hard-working man; like his family was a good mechanic and enjoyed agriculture as a recreation. He d. in Ashburnham.

Their children were:

HANNIBAL PARKER; d. young.
394. CHARLES HANNIBAL PARKER, b. March 22, 1839; m. Abby J. Rockwood of Ashburnham.
GILBERT J. PARKER; d. young.
395. ALFRED WRIGHT PARKER, b. June 5, 1844; m. Clara Hallet of Yarmouthport.
396. JULIA MARIA PARKER; m. Edward Safford.
JOSEPHINE R. PARKER; deceased.
397. FRANK HERBERT PARKER, b. in E. Boston, July 24, 1852; m. Marietta Story of Newburyport.

260. **Eliza Parker** (*Quincy*,[7] *Ebenezer*,[6] *Thomas*,[5] *Andrew*,[4] *John*,[3] *Hananiah*,[2] *Thomas*[1]), dau. of Quincy and Patience (Brooks) Parker, was b. in Princeton, Oct. 20, 1815; m. in Providence, R. I., Dec. 16, 1840, Jonas Hunt, b. in Boylston, April 29, 1810, son of David and Nancy (Cutting) Hunt of Boylston. They removed to Clinton, where he was a machinist, and where he d. Aug. 20, 1892. She d. April 20, 1892, the last survivor of her family of 13 children. David Hunt of Boylston was b. in Sudbury, Feb. 12, 1784. Nancy Cutting was b. in Boylston, July 30, 1784. William Hunt was the first of the name in New England. He was b. in 1605; came from Yorkshire, Eng., and settled early in Concord, Mass. From him was descended Isaac of Sudbury, Isaac, Isaac, Isaac, then Uriah of Boylston, who was the father of David above mentioned.

Their children were:

1. ELIZABETH LAROCHE HUNT, b. in Providence, R. I., Oct. 14, 1842; m. in Clinton, Oct. 2, 1873, Salem Wilder of Sterling, b. in Templeton, Aug. 30, 1842, son of Thomas W. and Martha B. Wilder. They reside in Clinton, where he is a belt maker. Their dau. is:
    1. ETHEL LOUISE WILDER, b. in Clinton, Jan. 1, 1879.

2. Hanford Lavier Hunt, b. in Clinton, May 12, 1846; m. in Southbridge, Aug. 26, 1874, Flora Booth, b. in Baldwinsville, N. Y., March 27, 1849, dau. of Thomas and Elizabeth Booth. He is a clothing merchant in Willimantic, Ct., where they reside. Their children were:
   i. Harry L. Hunt, b. in Willimantic, Nov. 12, 1877.
   ii. Willie B. Hunt, b. March 13, 1880; d. Aug. 10, 1886.
3. Alice Louise Hunt, b. in Clinton, Oct. 16, 1848. She is a teacher of art in Ann Arbor, Mich.
4. Mary Emma Hunt, b. in Clinton, Dec. 29, 1854; m. June 22, 1882, Eben H. Bailey, son of Oliver and Judith (Howe) Bailey of Rowley, Mass. They reside in Boston.

261. Sally Parker *(Quincy,[7] Ebenezer,[6] Thomas,[5] Andrew,[4] John,[3] Hananiah,[2] Thomas[1])*, dau. of Quincy and Patience (Brooks) Parker, was b. in Princeton, March 1, 1817; m. Sept. 28, 1847, George Brown Thomas of Providence, R. I. They settled on the west side of that city. He was a member of the old firm of "Thomas and Co.," tailors, and d. Feb. 18, 1875. Owing to her excellent memory and regard for her family many interesting items and important dates have been added to this genealogy. She resides on Warren Street, Providence, with her dau. and son-in-law, John Davis.

Their children were:

1. Anna Louise Thomas, b. Sept. 28, 1848; m. June 8, 1870, John Edward Davis of Providence. Their children were:
   i. Jane Louise Davis, b. Jan. 13, 1872.
   ii. Bessie Alice Davis, b. Nov. 12, 1873.
   iii. Blanche Nathalie Davis, b. Nov. 20, 1877.
2. Frederick Parker Thomas, b. Jan. 9, 1853; d. May 20, 1854.
3. Clarence Frederick Thomas, b. Nov. 20, 1857; resides in Providence, unm.

262. Artimus Parker *(Quincy,[7] Ebenezer,[6] Thomas,[5] Andrew,[4] John,[3] Hananiah,[2] Thomas[1])*, son of Quincy and Patience (Brooks) Parker, was b. in Princeton, Feb. 22, 1819; m. Susan Pierce of W. Boylston. They soon removed to Boston, and later to Kansas with the early settlers of that State. When the Kansas War broke out he was journeying from Columbus, O., and a curious experience he had. While proceeding through Kansas on horseback his attention was attracted by a mob, and curious to know its meaning hastened into its midst. He was immediately supposed to be one of the leaders of the mob, was arrested by the authorities and imprisoned for three months. Later he gathered his family together at Columbus and there settled. He d. Oct. 8, 1864. She was b. in Sutton, Mass., the dau. of John and Lucy (Carroll) Pierce, who owned a large farm there, and had a family of six sons and six daughters, of whom the only surviving one is William N. Pierce, Esq., of W. Boylston. Another of the brothers was Rev. John W. Pierce, a Congregational minister of Highgate, Vt.

Their children were:

SUSAN EMILY PARKER, b. Oct. 10, 1848; m. Sept. 21, 1872, William H. Ward, and removed to Skowhegan, Me. They have:

1. WALTER NEWELL WARD, b. July 17, 1875.
2. ETHEL CARROLL WARD, b. July 20, 1880.
3. ESTELLA PARKER WARD, b. March 14, 1883.
4. WILDER WHEELER WARD, b. March 9, 1885.

263. Quincy Parker, Jr. *(Quincy,[7] Ebenezer,[6] Thomas,[5] Andrew,[4] John,[3] Hananiah,[2] Thomas[1])*, son of Quincy and Patience (Brooks) Parker, was b. in Rindge, N. H., Jan. 12, 1821. Most of his childhood days were spent in Rindge, but he was for a while in Princeton and Boylston. At 14 he started out to earn his own living, and at 16 he determined to learn the moulder's trade, entering the High Street Foundry, Providence, R. I., in which city his mother was living. The trade he mastered in two years. Wishing to see something of the world he left home and let himself as a sailor on the whaleship *New England* of Poughkeepsie, N. Y., bound for S. America. He felt perfectly at home on board ship and easily distinguished himself among his fellow-sailors. Prizes were offered by the captain for the one who first saw the whale. He was the first to win the prize. He loved to race his companions about the rigging, being exceptionally quick and strong. For six years he cruised at sea and visited Talquehama, Callao, Lima and all places of any note along the

QUINCY PARKER, JR.

coast of S. America. Like many sailors much might be said about his travels, his narrow and miraculous escapes from drowning, sunstrokes, etc. In the employ of the Peruvian government he explored the Andes Mts. and the wild parts of Peru. After satisfying his love for romantic adventure and witnessing many wonderful things he shipped for home. The captain of the vessel was a tyrant and was soon universally hated by the crew. While at sea he safely escaped from the ship and came the remainder of the way upon other vessels.

Returning home to Providence he gave his mother and friends a great surprise, as they had received no word from him and all supposed him dead. In Providence he again worked at the moulder's trade, at which he was a very efficient workman, and continued at the Franklin Foundry for 24 years. In 1848 he was m. to Almira Kent of Eaton, N. Y. They settled upon Smith Hill in Providence, where he still resides. Since the death of Milton Parker, his youngest son, he has engaged in the florist business at his home, besides being the maker of *Parker's Premium Tomato Catsup*. Mrs. Almira (Kent) Parker, after a severe illness, d. Jan. 30, 1888. He m. (2) Nov. 20, 1889, Emerancy Kent, sister to his late wife.

His children were:

398. EUGENE COSTELLO PARKER; m. Adelia O. Barker.
ALMIRA EUNICE PARKER; resides with her father in Providence.
399. CLARA EMU PARKER; m. Lorenzo Dupony.
MILTON PARKER; d. at age 18.
EUGENE B. PARKER, b. March 28, 1849; d. Feb., 1850.
QUINCY K. PARKER, b. Jan. 1, 1853; d. Aug., 1855.
A child, b. and d. April 8, 1861.

264. Eunice Parker *(Quincy,[7] Ebenezer,[6] Thomas,[5] Andrew,[4] John,[3] Hananiah,[2] Thomas[1])*, dau. of Quincy and Patience (Brooks) Parker, was b. in Rindge, N. H., Aug. 1, 1822; m. George Herrick. He won for himself the title of Colonel. He was a volunteer in the R. I. State militia; was active in many engagements and was wounded at the battle of Gettysburg. She d. 1849.

Their children were:

1. EDWIN THOMAS HERRICK, b. in Providence, R. I., March 28, 1846; m. Jennie Knight, an adopted dau. of Edwin Knight. Their children are:

    I. FANNIE HERRICK; aged 15.

    II. GEORGE HERRICK; aged 11.

2. MARY EMMA HERRICK, b. in Providence, March 20, 1848; m. (1) in Providence, May 21, 1874, James H. McClenthan, son of James H. and Caroline V. McClenthan. She m. (2) in Minneapolis, Minn., April 14, 1887, Watson S. Taylor, son of Hector J. and Maria Taylor, b. in Jefferson, N. Y., May 5, 1850. He is superintendent of the Red River Lumber Co. and they reside in Crookston, Minn. Her children, all b. in Minneapolis, were:

    I. MABEL MCCLENTHAN, b. Oct. 15, 1876.

    II. FREDERICK H. MCCLENTHAN, b. Aug. 18, 1880; d. July 3, 1881.

    III. HERRICK MCCLENTHAN, b. Feb. 18, 1882.

265. Louisa Parker *(Ebenezer,[7] Ebenezer,[6] Thomas,[5] Andrew,[4] John,[3] Hananiah,[2] Thomas[1])*, dau. of Ebenezer, Jr., and Hannah B. (Merriam) Parker, was b. in Princeton, Dec. 13, 1806; m. April 10, 1828, Eli Walker, b. March 2, 1802, son of Hezekiah and Lucy (Raymond) Walker of Holden. They lived first near the homestead in the house adjoining that of Israel Howe; second, in W. Boylston, being principally upon that place which is still occupied by their family. She d. Feb. 24, 1884, her death resulting from a fall. He belonged to a sturdy and long lived family. In his eighty-fourth year, then still smart and active, but very deaf, he was struck by a railway train, causing his death, June 9, 1886. All who knew him felt the loss of a kind neighbor and a valuable citizen.

Their children were:

1. MELVILLE WALKER, b. Dec. 14, 1828; d. March 21, 1829.

2. JULIA MARIA WALKER, b. Feb. 3, 1830; m. May 4, 1852, Lovell A. Lesure, son of Simeon of Uxbridge and Hopy (Lovell) Lesure of W. Boylston. He is well known as a carriage maker and resides in Oakdale, where she lived until her decease, which occurred Aug. 5, 1889. Uniting in early life with the Baptist Church she filled with great Christian activity and zeal many important offices in the Church and

mission circles while faithfully fulfilling with love and devotion all her home duties as wife, mother and friend. She was a very active member and treasurer of the Woman's Christian Temperance Union, and her words of encouragement did much to cheer the hearts of her co-laborers. Dea. Lovell Lesure m. (2) Sept., 1890, Mrs. Sarah Martin of West Boylston. The children of Julia Maria (Walker) Lesure were:

i. CARRIE MARIA LESURE, b. Jan. 23, 1860; m. Sept. 10, 1885, Alfred H. Evans, son of Rev. William H. and M. (Barber) Evans. Their children were:

1. Helen Barber Evans, b. Sept. 12, 1886.
2. Ada Lesure Evans, b. July 23, 1887.
3. Ralph Curtis Evans, b. Jan. 9, 1892.

ii. WALDO HASKELL LESURE, b. Oct. 14, 1866; m. Sept. 26, 1889, Annie G. Hastings, dau. of George M. W. and Olive (Lord) Hastings. They have one son, b. Sept. 16, 1890.

iii. ADA CHILSON LESURE, b. Aug. 2, 1872; d. Sept. 27, 1876.

Their adopted son was:

HERBERT STEARNS LESURE, b. Oct. 22, 1850; adopted May 5, 1857; son of Abijah and Clarissa M. (Waterman) White. He is m. and resides in Worcester.

3. HARRIET SOPHIA WALKER, b. Jan. 27, 1832; d. Jan. 18, 1850.

4. MARY LOUISA WALKER, b. Feb. 24, 1834; m. April 12, 1854, Milton K. Howe, son of William and Eunice (Robbins) Howe of Princeton. Their children were:

i. EDGAR R. HOWE, b. June 19, 1855. He is an optician in Worcester.

ii. WALTER ARVINE HOWE, b. Aug. 25, 1858; d. April 6, 1863.

5. MELVILLE EDWARD WALKER, b. Feb. 23, 1836; m. in W. Boylston, Nov. 19, 1865, Louise Hutchinson of W. Sutton, b. in Oxford, Nov. 15, 1845, dau. of Stephen and Evelyn (Jenks) Hutchinson. They reside in Los Angeles, Cal., where he is a florist. Children:

i. CLARENCE M. WALKER, b. in W. Boylston, Aug. 27, 1866; d. Aug. 10, 1867.

ii. MAY WALKER, b. in W. Boylston, May 13, and d. May 15, 1868.

iii. LOLITA GERTRUDE WALKER, b. in W. Boylston, March 16, 1871; d. June 27, 1871.

iv. LOLITA WALKER, b. in W. Boylston, Dec. 4, 1872; m. April 23, 1891, Bernard Berg. Child:

i. Clifford W. Berg, b. Feb. 1, 1892.

v. WALTER WALKER, b. in Pawtucket, R. I., March 16, 1880; d. June 16, 1881.

6. EMILY ADLINE WALKER, b. Sept. 3, 1840; m. April 17, 1861, Rutillius Dana, son of George and Ora (Newton) Dana of W. Boylston. They reside in W. Boylston and have one dau.:

i. LILA GERTRUDE DANA.

7. WILLIAM RAYMOND WALKER, b. May 22, 1843; m. July 15, 1868, Mary Bailey, b. in England, Oct. 10, 1843, dau. of Robert and Elizabeth (Butcher) Bailey of England. They reside in W. Boylston and have children:

i. FRANKLIN ELI WALKER, b. Aug. 24, 1873.

ii. ALICE ELIZABETH WALKER, b. July 3, 1875.

iii. FREDERICK BAILEY WALKER, b. Jan. 15, 1878.

iv. HOWARD WILLIAM WALKER, b. May 29, 1883.

8. ANNA EUDORA WALKER, b. Sept. 9, 1849; m. in S. Dedham, Mass., Nov. 22, 1871, Edward Ross, b. in Preston, England, Feb. 21, 1847, son of Alexander and Hannah (Tuson) Ross of England. They reside in W. Boylston, where he is a mechanic. They have had three children:

i. DILLON WALKER ROSS, b. in W. Boylston, Sept. 23, 1872; d. July 17, 1880.

ii. ALIDA LOUISA ROSS, b. in W. Boylston, Feb. 4, 1876.

iii. WALTER WYMAN ROSS, b. in W. Boylston, Jan. 1, 1884; d. March 2, 1886.

266. Charles Augustus Parker *(Ebenezer,[7] Ebenezer,[6] Thomas,[5] Andrew,[4] John,[3] Hananiah,[2] Thomas[1])*, son of Ebenezer, Jr., and Hannah B. (Merriam) Parker, was b. in Princeton, Aug. 18, 1808; m. Dec. 18, 1834, Sylvia A. Moore,* dau. of John and Sirena Moore of Princeton. They settled upon a part of the homestead estate. The house which he built by the north side of the pond is still standing and here

* She was sister to Dr. George W. Moore, who d. in Amherst, N. H., Sept. 8, 1866, whose eminence as a physician was well known. Another brother was Humphrey Moore, Esq., who d. in Baltimore, Dec., 1886, who gave a considerable portion of his property to found the "Humphrey Moore Institute" for the benefit of young men, which gives promise of doing good work for Baltimore.

Mrs. Sylvia Parker still resides. The location shares the natural beauties of the old homestead. While yet a young man he was school teacher at the district school near the homestead for several terms. From his manhood to the time of his early death he was a subject of asthma. He was, notwithstanding, very industrious and ambitious, and possessed much mechanical talent and ability. He was thus prevented, however, from maturing the plans of life which he had desired to follow and in which he would have doubtless been successful. He d. in Princeton, Sept. 5, 1854, aged 46 years.

Their children were:

400. Lucy Maria Parker, b. Nov. 8, 1835; m. Thomas R. Howe.

401. Sarah Ann Parker, b. March 14, 1839; m. Milton K. Howe.

402. George Washington M. Parker, b. Aug. 19, 1841; m. Laura D. Hamilton.

403. William Dwight Parker, b. Jan. 27, 1844; m. Margaret Smith of Worcester.

Mary French Parker, b. Aug. 5, 1846; d. Aug. 23, 1851.

Ellen Moore Parker, b. March 5, 1850; d. Aug. 29, 1851.

404. Emma Frances Parker, b. Sept. 23, 1853; m. Warren F. Bartlett of Rutland.

267. Frederick Parker (*Ebenezer,[7] Ebenezer,[6] Thomas,[5] Andrew,[4] John,[3] Hananiah,[2] Thomas[1]*), son of Ebenezer, Jr., and Hannah B. (Merriam) Parker, was b. in Princeton, June 19, 1810; m. Nov. 28, 1833, Eunice C. Howe, b. Aug. 13, 1812, eldest dau. of William and Eunice (Robbins) Howe of Princeton. He passed his boyhood partly upon the homestead and partly upon that place which is now the Princeton Poor Farm. In 1837, he with his father, Ebenezer Parker, Jr., assumed charge of the old place, and with that place was identified all his life. He was a man of true and thorough character, was remarkably firm minded and positive in his beliefs. He was an able and successful farmer, a kind father and a true friend. He was selectman and assessor, also representative for his town in the Centennial year, thus making three successive generations upon whom this honor was tendered. He d. Sept. 4, 1883, at the age of 73. His widow is still living upon the homestead.

CHARLES AUGUSTUS PARKER.

FREDERICK PARKER.

Their children were:

405. CHARLES WILLIAM PARKER, b. Feb. 1, 1837; m. Inez Bullard.

406. AMOS MILTON PARKER, b. Sept. 12, 1839; m. (1) Anna J. Frizell; m. (2) Esther A. Holt.

HENRY A. PARKER, b. June 12, 1843; enlisted at the age of 19 in Co. K, 53d Reg. He d. while in the service of his country at Arsenal Hospital, Baton Rouge, La., from injury and sickness, at the age of 20 years and 14 days.

EUNICE H. PARKER, b. July 5, 1851; m. Oct. 23, 1889, Levi Cushman, b. Jan. 29, 1848, son of Levi and Cordelia (Hall) Cushman of Buckfield, Me. He was for a number of years a stock raiser in Grant and Diamond Counties, Oregon. They reside upon the Parker homestead in Princeton.

268. Ebenezer Warren Parker *(Ebenezer,[7] Ebenezer,[6] Thhomas,[5] Andrew,[4] John,[3] Hananiah,[2] Thomas[1])*, son of Ebenezer, Jr., and Hannah B. (Merriam) Parker, was b. in Princeton, Mass., Oct. 28, 1813; m. May 26, 1840, Chloe

---

The Parker and Howe families of Princeton have often intermarried. The name is an old one in Holden and Princeton. The first of the name who lived in Princeton was Israel Howe, native of Sudbury. His first ancestors in America were John and Mary Howe, who settled in Sudbury about 1640. They had children, one of whom was Samuel,[2] whose son David[3] had a son David, Jr.[4] David, Jr., had a son Israel, all which successive generations were born in Sudbury. This Israel Howe married Submit Keyes of Shrewsbury and lived first in Wilton, N. H., where their four children were born, and second in Princeton, where they removed in May, 1785. Israel Howe d. Oct. 25, 1816, and wife Submit Oct. 28, 1816. Their children were: 1. Israel, Jr. 2. Eleanor, who m. William Soulale of Boylston. 3. William, who m. March 29, 1811, Eunice Robbins. 4. Submit, who m. in 1802, Abijah Parker Smith, grandson of Thomas Parker of Princeton. (See page 122.)

William and Eunice (Robbins) Howe lived in Princeton and had the following children:

1. Eunice Howe, b Aug. 23, 1812; m. Frederick Parker of Princeton (No. 267).
2. Adaline Howe, b. Sept., 1814; m. William Joslin of Leominster. Their son, William Joslin, resides very near the old Parker homestead in Princeton, and has four children.
3. Israel Howe; m. Deborah Parker of Princeton (No. 272).
4. William Howe; m. Cornelia Everett and settled in Millbury. They have one son.
5. Thomas R. Howe, b. Sept. 30, 1821; m. Lucy Maria Parker, dau. of Charles A. Parker of Princeton.
6. Charles S. Howe; d. in Leominster of typhoid fever, unm.
7. Milton K. Howe, b. Sept. 7, 1827; m. (1) Mary Louisa Walker, dau. of Louisa Parker (No. 265); m. (2) Sarah Ann Parker (No. 401), dau. of Charles A. Parker of Princeton.

EBENEZER WARREN PARKER.

A. Parmenter, b. Sept. 11, 1817, dau. of Solomon Parmenter, Jr. They removed in 1856 to Urbana, Ill. The place was at that time an unbroken prairie. The town of Urbana has since been subdivided and the name of that part in which they are settled changed to Philo. Here he still resides and is a farmer.

Their three children were b. in Princeton:

407. Mary Adelia Parker, b. Jan. 27, 1842; m. Pascal P. Parkman of Northfield.

Emma Elvesta Parker, b. Dec. 7, 1846; d. Dec. 7, 1849.

Ebenezer Calvin Parker, b. Sept. 7, 1850; m. July 3, 1872, Martha E. Baker, b. in Bellfontaine, O., Sept. 1, 1851, dau. of Reuben and Susan (Kunbrough) Baker. They reside in Philo, Ill. He is proprietor of the Philo Exchange Bank, and is an active and public spirited citizen.

Louisa Florence Parker, b. Nov. 23, 1858.

269. Adaline Parker *(Ebenezer,[7] Ebenezer,[6] Thomas,[5] Andrew,[4] John,[3] Hananiah,[2] Thomas[1])*, dau. of Ebenezer, Jr., and Hannah B. (Merriam) Parker, was b. in Princeton, Oct. 24, 1815 (twin of Amos); m. Sept. 17, 1844, Stephen Smith, b. Jan. 27, 1816, son of John Smith, native of Southborough, and Martha (Hastings) Smith, native of Boylston. They settled in W. Boylston, where she resided until her death which occurred May 23, 1876. He experienced an active life in town affairs. His service of selectman, assessor and overseer of the poor amounted altogether to 30 years. He m. (2) Mrs. Abby Florilla (Beaman) Keyes, b. in Princeton, Aug. 2, 1823, dau. of Phineas and Phebe (Merriam) Beaman. Her mother, Phebe Merriam, was sister to Hannah B. Merriam, and Phineas Beaman was a near relative of Jonas Beaman, who m. Lucy Parker. He d. in W. Boylston, June 17, 1891. She d. in W. Boylston, May, 1891.

Her children were:

1. Edna Carlona Smith, b. Oct. 9, 1852; m. Sept. 25, 1877, Oscar S. Whittemore, son of Woodbury and Nancy (Lawrence) Whittemore of Ballston, N. Y. They reside in Bridgeport, Ct. Children:
    1. Edith A. Whittemore, b. Aug. 7, 1879; d. Dec. 24, 1885.

II. HAROLD O. WHITTEMORE, b. Sept. 9, 1880.

2. JOHN SMITH, b. Sept. 3, 1856; m. Jan. 17, 1882, Fannie A. Keyes, dau. of Ezra S. and Abby F. (Beaman) Keyes of E. Princeton. They reside in W. Boylston and have children:

I. CHESTER MILTON SMITH, b. July 25, 1884.

II. MYRTIS F. SMITH, b. Feb. 11, 1891.

270. **Amos Parker** *(Ebenezer,[7] Ebenezer,[6] Thomas,[5] Andrew,[4] John,[3] Hananiah,[2] Thomas[1])*, son of Ebenezer, Jr., and Hannah B. (Merriam) Parker, was b. in Princeton, Oct. 24, 1815 (twin of Adeline); m. in Lowell, Aug. 15, 1842, Sarah Merrill, b. in Dunbarton, N. H., Jan. 22, 1818, dau. of Richard and Sarah (Whipple) Merrill. She was a native of Ipswich, Mass. He was a native of Dunbarton and son of Richard, who was a lieutenant in the Revolutionary war, and a native of England, coming to this country when very young in company with his father Richard. Amos Parker learned the chairmaking trade, which was then carried on by hand, and worked at this in E. Princeton; later he was employed in a cotton mill in Ware, from whence he became an overseer in the Massachusetts Mills in Lowell. Removing to Worcester he made farm implements in the Court Mills. Following his marriage the first 15 years were mostly passed upon farms in Princeton, the second 15 following upon farms in Sterling. During this time he conducted the town farm in Princeton five years; that of Sterling three years, and the Princeton Parker homestead place for a few years. They removed to Worcester in 1874, where they reside.

Their children were:

A dau., b. and d. in Princeton, June 26, 1844.

FRANK ELLINGWOOD PARKER, b. in Worcester, July 21, 1849; d. July 3, 1851.

ABBY DANE PARKER, b. in Princeton, Sept. 11, 1851; m. Eben D. Blood.

A son, b. and d. in Princeton, 1852.

A son, b. and d. in Princeton, Sept., 1853.

HATTIE LOUISE PARKER, b. in Sterling, May, 1855; d. Dec. 12, 1856.

HATTIE FRANCES PARKER, b. in Sterling, Aug. 13, 1856; m. Frederick J. Miller, and resides in Worcester.

271. George Parker *(Ebenezer,[7] Ebenezer,[6] Thomas,[5] Andrew,[4] John,[3] Hananiah,[2] Thomas[1])*, son of Ebenezer, Jr., and Hannah B. (Merriam) Parker, was b. in Princeton, Feb. 1, 1818 (twin); m. Sept. 14, 1841, Emily R. Collar, dau. of Rev. Hezekiah and Rhody (Robbins) Collar of Northfield, Mass. They lived in Lowell and for a few years upon the Princeton homestead. In 1856 he accompanied his brother, E. Warren Parker, to Urbana, Ill., but soon returned. They removed in 1874 to E. Blackstone, where they resided up to the time of his death, which occurred Jan. 20, 1893, aged 74 years, 11 months, 20 days. He was a man of high conscientiousness of character, a kind father, quiet and retiring in his nature, and most highly esteemed as a man and a friend.

Their children were:

408. Walter E. Parker, b. in Princeton, Sept. 29, 1847; m. (1) Anna Elliott, (2) Lida Willis, (3) Mary Beetle.

Herbert Parker, b. in Lowell, April 23, 1850. He was freight transfer clerk in the employ of the Providence and Worcester R. R. for a few years preceding his death, which occurred Jan. 23, 1873.

272. Deborah Merriam Parker *(Ebenezer,[7] Ebenezer,[6] Thomas,[5] Andrew,[4] John,[3] Hananiah,[2] Thomas[1])*, dau. of Ebenezer, Jr., and Hannah B. (Merriam) Parker, was b. in Princeton, Sept. 9, 1819; m. Nov. 16, 1841, Israel Howe, son of William and Eunice (Robbins) Howe of Princeton. The fact is remarkable that three brothers and sisters of the Parker family and their two nieces married to four brothers and sisters of the Howe family. Israel and Deborah Howe settled in the immediate vicinity of the homestead place, where she resided until her decease, which occurred March 12, 1889. She was a most efficient and praiseworthy woman. She possessed a tenacious memory and felt a loving interest in all her relatives and friends. Mr. Howe was a farmer. He d. in Hartford, Ct., March 21, 1893. Their dau. was:

Ella R. Howe, b. Dec. 13, 1848; m. Benjamin W. Kenyon of Provincetown. They reside in Hartford, Ct., where he is a designer and painter.

Of the ten marriages in the family of Ebenezer and Hannah B. (Merriam) Parker, those of Louisa Walker, Ebenezer W., George and Amos were ripened after the half century into Golden Weddings, while Frederick Parker's death preceded his fiftieth anniversary of marriage but two months.

George Parker.

273. Rev. William Wheeler Parker *(Ebenezer,*[7] *Ebenezer,*[6] *Thomas,*[5] *Andrew,*[4] *John,*[3] *Hananiah,*[2] *Thomas*[1]*)*, son of Ebenezer, Jr., and Hannah B. (Merriam) Parker, was b. in Princeton, March 2, 1824; m. Aug. 27, 1847, Emily Walker, dau. of Joel and Diedamia Walker of Holden. Joel Walker is still living in great preservation of health. Eli Walker was his brother.

On leaving home Mr. Parker was employed in F. H. Kinnicutt's hardware store in Worcester for a year and a half. He prepared for college at Monson Academy and Williston Seminary. He finished his college course by private instructors. After a business life of four years in Clinton he entered Andover Theological Seminary, from which he graduated in 1858. He first preached in York, Me., for two years as an evangelist, then received a call to Cambridge, Mass., and was there installed pastor of the Church on Second Street. He left Cambridge to go into the army to take charge of the Christian Commission Work in the 10th Corps (Gen. Butler's). After the war was over he was next installed over the Union Church in Groton. This gave way to Williamsburg, his last settlement. He has since preached continuously, but in different places. He has resided in W. Boylston since 1872.

Their *adopted* son was:

WILLIAM E. PARKER; m. Feb. 14, 1883, Luna Florence Keyes, dau. of Ezra Sawyer and Florella (Beaman) Keyes. He is a machinist and resides in Worcester.

274. Edward Hanford Parker *(Ebenezer,*[7] *Ebenezer,*[6] *Thomas,*[5] *Andrew,*[4] *John,*[3] *Hananiah,*[2] *Thomas*[1]*)*, son of Ebenezer, Jr., and Hannah B. (Merriam) Parker, was b. in Princeton, Dec. 28, 1825. His boyhood was passed upon the homestead place. He procured the common school education which the district school afforded. During his youth he warmly associated with the young men of the school and town, and is said to have been the fleetest runner and the best swimmer among them. At the age of 17 he apprenticed himself to Mason H. Morse, a well known builder of Worcester, of whom he learned the carpenter's trade. He later worked with Alzirus Brown of Worcester. At the age of 26 he m.

EDWARD H. PARKER.

MRS. MARY C. (BROWN) PARKER.

Jan. 12, 1851, Mary Calista Brown, b. in Boylston, March 13, 1832, dau. of Joel and Lucy (Whitney) Brown of Boylston. She resides in Worcester. Joel Brown was a native of Concord, and Lucy Whitney a native of Bolton.* Mr. Parker made Worcester his residence save for two years passed in Urbana, Ill. His death, hastened by accident, occurred Feb. 26, 1874, aged 47. He was a man of much judgment and intellect, firmness of integrity and purpose, and of true generosity and good will. He was a very efficient and active workman.

Their children, all b. in Worcester, were:

410. ARTHUR AUGUSTUS PARKER, b. April 5, 1855; m. Lida E. Denton of Jersey City, N. J.

411. CLARENCE EDWARD PARKER, b. April 4, 1860; m. Jennie See of Hastings-on-Hudson, N. Y.

412. EDWARD HENRY PARKER, b. Jan. 4, 1867; m. Lena A. Converse of Oxford, Mass.

THEODORE PARKER, b. Sept. 8, 1869. He is the compiler of this genealogy.

275. Abigail Manning Parker (*Josiah,[7] Josiah,[6] Josiah,[5] Josiah,[4] John,[3] Hananiah,[2] Thomas[1]*), dau. of Josiah, Jr., and Abigail (Carter) Parker, was b. in Woburn, Jan. 6, 1808; m. June, 1832, James Burton, b. in Woburn, April 18, 1809. They reside in Wilton, N. H.

Their children were:

1. JOHN BURTON, b. June 26, 1833; d. Nov. 5, 1857.
2. JAMES BURTON, b. Jan. 6, and d. April 30, 1835.
3. MARTHA P. BURTON, b. March 7, 1836; m. Nov. 9, 1859, Charles G. Blanchard of Greenville, N. H. She d. July 1, 1882. He resides in Greenville. They had two children, who reside in Greenville:
   1. EZRA L. BLANCHARD, b. in Wilton, N. H., Dec. 5, 1863; m. in Woonsocket, R. I., Sept. 10, 1890.

*Potter's genealogy of Concord families shows that the ancestral lineage of Joel Brown[6] was: Lieut. Samuel[5] and Elizabeth (Brown) Brown, Dea. Ephraim[4] and Abigail (Wheeler) Brown, Thomas[3] and Hannah (Potter) Brown, Thomas[2] and Ruth (Jones) Brown, Thomas[1] and Bridget Brown. This Thomas, the emigrant ancestor, was settled in Concord in 1641. Lieut. Samuel and Elizabeth (Brown) Brown were third cousins. Joel Brown was the last of their family of 11. David Brown, late of Worcester, and Alzirus Brown of Worcester, were sons of Joel.

ii. PERLEY R. BLANCHARD, b. in Milford, N. H., April 22, 1873.

4. ABBIE F. BURTON, b. July 29, 1837; m. Jan. 1, 1863, Solon Tarbell of Hancock, N. H. She d. May 27, 1887. He resides in Peterborough, N. H. No issue.

5. EMILY A. BURTON, b. Sept. 21, 1839; m. June 14, 1864, William H. Hopkins, b. Aug. 30, 1838, son of Benjamin Hopkins. They have two children, and reside in Wilton, N. H.

6. MARIETTA H. BURTON, b. Aug. 28, 1841; m. (1) April 24, 1863, George W. Eaton, who d. Aug. 16, 1876; m. (2) Jonathan P. Snow, who was b. Nov. 9, 1848. They reside in Somerville.

7. AUGUSTA M. BURTON, b. May 26, 1843; m. Nov. 2, 1865, Irving S. Farnsworth, son of Albert Farnsworth. They reside in Franklin and have one child.

8. JAMES A. BURTON, b. Feb. 8, 1846; d. Dec. 23, 1856.

9. JOSIAH H. BURTON, b. April 3, 1847.

10. CLARISSA J. BURTON, b. Nov. 14, 1848.

11. LYDIA L. BURTON, b. April 5, 1850; m. Willis H. Edson, native of Canada. They reside in Plymouth, and have one child.

276. Susan Richardson Parker (*Josiah,*[7] *Josiah,*[6] *Josiah,*[5] *Josiah,*[4] *John,*[3] *Hananiah,*[2] *Thomas*[1]), dau. of Josiah, Jr., and Abigail (Carter) Parker, was b. in Woburn, May 26, 1809; m. Lyman Stone, b. in Nelson, N. H. He d. Nov., 1882. She d. Oct., 1883, leaving no issue.

277. Hannah Gardner Parker (*Josiah,*[7] *Josiah,*[6] *Josiah,*[5] *Josiah,*[4] *John,*[3] *Hananiah,*[2] *Thomas*[1]), dau. of Josiah, Jr., and Abigail (Carter) Parker, was b. in Woburn, Feb. 23, 1811; m. in Worcester, Sept. 24, 1850, Jonathan Snow, b. in Brewster, April 1, 1813, son of David and Mercy (Clark) Snow. His first wife was Lydia Parker, sister of the above. He was a blacksmith and master mechanic. They lived in various places, finally settling in Milford, N. H., where he d. March 4, 1889. She survives him and resides in Milford, N. H.

Their children were:

1. AMELIA SNOW, b. in Worcester, June 18, and d. June 21, 1852.
2. EMMA JOSEPHINE SNOW, b. in Worcester, June 30, 1853.

278. Lydia Ann Parker (*Josiah,*[7] *Josiah,*[6] *Josiah,*[5] *Josiah,*[4] *John,*[3] *Hananiah,*[2] *Thomas*[1]), dau. of Josiah, Jr., and Abigail (Carter) Parker, was b. in Woburn, Aug. 5, 1813; m. Nov. 14, 1844, Jonathan Snow (see No. 277), son of David and Mercy (Clark) Snow. She d. March 4, 1849, and left three children. He m. (2) her sister, Hannah Gardner Parker (see No. 277). He d. in Milford, N. H., Feb. 28, 1889.

Their children, all b. in Concord, N. H., were:

1. Anne Louisa Snow, b, Sept. 6, 1845; d. July 20, 1864.
2. Adaline Frances Snow, b. May 4, 1847; d. July 14, 1864.
3. Jonathan Parker Snow, b. Nov. 19, 1848; m. Marietta H. Burton (his cousin), dau. of James and Abigail (Parker) Burton (see page 378). They reside in Somerville. No issue.

279. John Flagg Parker (*Josiah,*[7] *Josiah,*[6] *Josiah,*[5] *Josiah,*[4] *John,*[3] *Hananiah,*[2] *Thomas*[1]), son of Josiah, Jr., and Abigail (Carter) Parker, was b. in Woburn, Dec. 27, 1815, m. March 29, 1845, in Wilton, N. H., Martha Jane Jones, b. in Wilton, Dec. 27, 1815 dau. of Asa and Lucy Jones.

Their children were:

Ella Evora Parker, b. in Woburn, April 21, 1847; m. in Groton, Nov. 26, 1889, Thomas Gilson Hemenway, son of Phineas and Ann (McGraw) Hemenway of Groton.

Everett Leland Parker, b. in Woburn, Jan. 22, 1849; d. in Woburn, Jan. 9, 1854.

Marion Jane Parker, b. in Woburn, Dec. 20, 1856; m. in Groton, Oct. 25, 1888, Maynard Sumner Prescott, b. in Dunbarton, N. H., April 20, 1854, son of George Washington and Susan Walker (Marshall) Prescott of Dunbarton. He is a poultry breeder in Montvale.

280. Josiah Parker (*Josiah,*[7] *Josiah,*[6] *Josiah,*[5] *Josiah,*[4] *John,*[3] *Hananiah,*[2] *Thomas*[1]), son of Josiah, Jr., and Abigail (Carter) Parker, was b. in Wilton, N. H., April 10, 1819; m. Jan. 26, 1847, Nancy M. Wyman, b. in Woburn, Jan. 10, 1823, dau. of Abel and Maria Wyman of Woburn. He d. Jan. 22, 1880, and the family reside in Woburn.

Their children were:

JOSIAH WYMAN PARKER, b. May 28, 1847.
MARY FRANCES PARKER, b. June 29, 1849.
AUSTIN WILBER PARKER, b. April 14, 1863.
LILLIAN WINTHROP PARKER, b. April 28, 1866.

281. Andrew Jackson Parker (*Josiah,*[7] *Josiah,*[6] *Josiah,*[5] *Josiah,*[4] *John,*[3] *Hananiah,*[2] *Thomas*[1]), son of Josiah, Jr., and Abigail (Carter) Parker, was b. in Wilton, N. H., May 26, 1821; m. Nov. 29, 1847, Abbie A. Tapley, b. in Wilton, March 2, 1823, dau. of Nancy and Gilbert Tapley of Wilton. They reside in Wilton. To Mr. Parker's interest and pains is largely due the fulness of the records of the Wilton Parkers. He is a carriage builder.

Their son was:

CHARLES PARKER, b. in Worcester, Aug. 10, 1852; m. April 15, 1883, Grace M. Wright, b. Sept. 3, 1856, dau. of John and Malissa Wright of Stoneham. They reside in Cambridge.

282. Albert Parker (*Josiah,*[7] *Josiah,*[6] *Josiah,*[5] *Josiah,*[4] *John,*[3] *Hananiah,*[2] *Thomas,*[1]), son of Josiah and Mrs. Betsey (Converse) Parker, was b. in Wilton, N. H., April 12, 1839; m. in Woburn, Nov. 2, 1862, Eliza A. Sawyer, b. in Amesbury, July 8, 1839, dau. of John and Nancy Sawyer, then of Salisbury. He is a carriage blacksmith, residing in Merrimac, Mass.

Their children were:

WILLARD ALBERT PARKER, b. in S. Amesbury (now Merrimacport), Dec. 25, 1863. He resides in Nashua, N. H.
FREDERIC EAMES PARKER, b. in S. Amesbury (now Merrimacport), Dec. 8, 1866. He resides in Merrimac.
GEORGE ATHERTON PARKER, b. in Merrimacport, July 26, 1878.

283. Oliver Hutchinson Parker (*Henry,*[7] *Josiah,*[6] *Josiah,*[5] *Josiah,*[4] *John,*[3] *Hananiah,*[2] *Thomas*[1]), son of Henry and Abigail (Hutchinson) Parker, was born in Woburn, June 20, 1808; m. in Woburn, March 4, 1834, Patty Parker (his cousin), b. in Woburn, Oct. 12, 1812, dau. of Joseph and Betsey (Richardson) Parker. At the age of 20, upon the event of his grandfather's death, Jan. 20, 1829, he carried the sad news to his uncle Josiah at Wilton, N. H., where the latter was then living. He walked the entire distance, about 50 miles, all in one day, and in this unpleasant season of the year. He d. in Woburn, Nov. 1, 1867, aged 59 years, 4 months.

Their children were:

413. JOSEPH HENRY PARKER, b. Sept. 16, 1836; m. Henrietta M. Young.

OLIVER GARDNER PARKER, b. Feb. 23, 1837; d. March 21, 1870.

414. MARTHA PARKER. b. Oct. 20, 1841; m. Joseph Linnell.

Child, unnamed, b. and d. Nov. 14, 1845.

284. Martha Parker *(Henry,7 Josiah,6 Josiah,5 Josiah,4 John,3 Hananiah,2 Thomas1)*, dau. of Henry and Abigail (Hutchinson) Parker, was b. in Woburn, Aug. 17, 1811; m. Charles Choate.

Their child was:

i. MARTHA PARKER CHOATE, b. in Woburn, May 12, 1833; m. Aug. 9, 1855, Osgood Johnson of Worcester. He is deceased. She resides in Woburn with her dau.:
   i. HELEN JOHNSON.

285. Abigail Parker *(Henry,7 Josiah,6 Josiah,5 Josiah,4 John,3 Hananiah,2 Thomas1)*, dau. of Henry and Abigail (Hutchinson) Parker, was b. in Woburn, March 26, 1814; m. William Winn of Burlington, b. April 8, 1809, son of William and Abigail (Walker) Winn.

Their child was:

i. WILLIAM H. WINN; m. (1) Nov. 11, 1863, Josephine Harriet Dow of Woburn, dau. of Stephen and Celinda Dow. She d. March 24, 1870, and he m. (2) Elizabeth J. Pollock. They reside in Woburn. Children:
   i. FRED HARTWELL WINN, b. Nov. 10, 1873.
   ii. A dau., b. and d. Sept. 6, 1876.

286. Louisa Parker *(Henry,7 Josiah,6 Josiah,5 Josiah,4 John,3 Hananiah,2 Thomas1)*, dau. of Henry and Abigail (Hutchinson) Parker, was b. in Woburn, Dec. 14, 1816; m. Jan. 10, 1839, John Weston, b. Sept. 5, 1814, son of Jeremy and Priscilla (Perkins) Weston. They lived in Woburn, where he was a milkman and farmer, and where he d. Oct. 3, 1873. She resides in Woburn.

Their children were:

1. HELEN LOUISA WESTON, b. Aug. 29, 1840; m. April 26, 1859, Phineas G. Hanson of Woburn. They reside in Woburn on Cambridge Street, near the site of the old Parker homestead. He is a farmer. Their children were:
   - I. FLORA LOUISA HANSON, b. Aug. 22, 1860.
   - II. HOWARD WESTON HANSON, b. March 6, 1865; d. Sept. 1, 1868. in Lexington.
   - III. HELEN MARIA HANSON, b. Jan. 6, 1870; d. July 5, 1872.
   - IV. MARIA ALICE HANSON, b. Aug. 24, 1875.
   - V. JOHN WESTON HANSON, b. April 2, 1878.
2. JOHN HENRY WESTON, b. Jan. 10, 1843; m. Jan. 10, 1870, Ella Rowena Hanchett, b. in Natick, Dec. 25, 1849, dau. of William T. and Ede R. (Childs) Hanchett. He is a milkman and resides in Somerville. Their children were:
   - I. HOWARD HANCHETT WESTON, b. in Somerville, Oct. 3, 1871.
   - II. JOHN DANA WESTON, b. July 30, 1875.
3. MARY FRANCES WESTON, b. May 19, 1846; d. young.
4. CHARLES LEWIS WESTON, b. Nov. 24, 1848; resides in Natick, unm.

287. Maria Parker (*Henry,[7] Josiah,[6] Josiah,[5] Josiah,[4] John,[3] Hananiah,[2] Thomas[1]*), dau. of Henry and Abigail (Hutchinson) Parker, was b. in Woburn, July 5, 1819; m. Dec. 10, 1844, George Winn, b. in Burlington, Mass., Nov. 12, 1811, son of Abel and Ruth (Richardson) Winn. He was a farmer and d. in Woburn, Dec. 25, 1878. She survived him nearly ten years. She d. in Woburn, Nov. 23, 1888.

Their children were:

1. ALICE MARIA WINN, b. March 14, 1846; m. in Woburn, Jan. 18, 1871, Frank Murray Pushee, b. in Lyme, N. H., March 12, 1844, son of Sylvester and Sarah (Emerton) Pushee. She d. in Woburn, June 4, 1883, and he m. (2) Marah B. Winn, dau. of John and Marah (Baldwin) Winn. The children of Frank M. and Alice (Winn) Pushee were:
   - I. ETTA MARIA PUSHEE, b. in Nashua, N. H., March 14, 1875.
   - II. GEORGE WINN PUSHEE, b. in Woburn, April 25, 1880; d. May 12, 1882.

iii. WALTER FRANK PUSHEE, b. in Woburn, May 28, and d. July 28, 1883.

iv. HAROLD B. PUSHEE, b. Jan. 16, 1890.

2. ABBIE LOUISA WINN, b. Jan. 10, 1856; d. in Woburn, March 28, 1867.

288. **Frederick Chandler Parker** (*Frederick,[7] Josiah,[6] Josiah,[5] Josiah,[4] John,[3] Hananiah,[2] Thomas[1]*), son of Frederick and Nabby (Thompson) Parker, was b. in Woburn, Jan. 16, 1829; m. June 30, 1857, Martha Abbie Hanson, b. in Peabody, Jan. 26, 1833, dau. of Isaac (of Wakefield, N. H.) and Eliza (of Peabody) (Batchelder) Hanson. He was one year selectman. He built the residence on Canal Street, where he now resides and where he conducts a business of leather currying.

Their children were:

415. LYDIA THOMPSON PARKER, b. April 4, 1858; m. J. Herbert Richardson.

WILLIAM CHANDLER PARKER, b. Aug. 11, 1863; m. Aug. 7, 1886, Charlotte M. Kelley. He has been captain of Co. G, 5th Reg. Inf., M. V. M. (Woburn Mechanic Phalanx).

MARY WELLINGTON PARKER, b. Jan. 21, 1868.

289. **Josiah Parker** (*Frederick,[7] Josiah,[6] Josiah,[5] Josiah,[4] John,[3] Hananiah,[2] Thomas[1]*), son of Frederick and Nabby (Thompson) Parker, was b. in Woburn, Oct. 25, 1832 (twin brother of Hannah Maria Parker); m. Nov. 17, 1864, Sarah B. Hanson, b. in Peabody, Jan. 6, 1840, sister to Martha Abbie Hanson, and resides in Woburn.

Their son is:

FRANK FLANDERS PARKER, b. March 4, 1871.

290. **Hannah Maria Parker** (*Frederick,[7] Josiah,[6] Josiah,[5] Josiah,[4] John,[3] Hananiah,[2] Thomas[1]*), son of Frederick and Nabby (Thompson) Parker, was b. in Woburn, Oct. 25, 1832 (twin sister of Josiah Parker); m. Jan. 6, 1852, Walter Wellington. b. in Lexington, Dec. 3, 1824, son of Marshall and Elizabeth (Kimball) Wellington, and grandson of William of Waltham, and resides in E. Lexington.

Their children were:

1. Charles Walter Wellington, b. Oct. 13, 1853.
2. Abbie Elizabeth Wellington, b. Feb. 1, 1856.
3. Marion Elizabeth Wellington, b. Oct. 17, 1866.
4. Arthur Bryant Wellington, b. Aug. 26, 1870.

291. Betsey Fidelia Parker *(Frederick,[7] Josiah,[6] Josiah,[5] Josiah,[4] John,[3] Hananiah,[2] Thomas[1])*, dau. of Frederick and Nabby (Thompson) Parker, was b. in Woburn, June 7, 1836; m. Feb. 26, 1857, in Woburn, George Russell, b. in Charlestown, now Somerville, June 22, 1836, son of William Adams and Keziah (Teele) Russell. They reside in Woburn on Cambridge Street, very near her childhood home, the old Parker homestead of Woburn.

Their children were:

1. Emma Thompson Russell, b. in Somerville, Dec. 14, 1857; m. in Somerville, Feb. 26, 1879, Charles Henry Hartshorn of Medford. Child:
   1. Edward Russell Hartshorn, b. in Medford, Aug. 5, 1879; d. in Woburn, Aug. 5, 1880.
2. Carrie Russell, b. in Woburn, Oct. 19, 1861; m. in Woburn, June 1, 1887, Charles Edward Sutherland of Woburn.
3. Josie Russell, b. in Somerville, Sept. 19, 1863.
4. George Parker Russell, b. in Somerville, Aug. 28, 1868.
5. William Adams Russell, b. in Somerville, June 9, 1874.

292. Martha Ann Parker *(Frederick,[7] Josiah,[6] Josiah,[5] Josiah,[4] John,[3] Hananiah,[2] Thomas[1])*, dau. of Frederick and Nabby (Thompson) Parker, was b. in Woburn, May 24, 1841; m. in Woburn, July 14, 1863, Joseph Belknap McDonald, b. in Danville, Vt., June 28, 1839, son of William B. and Eunice P. (Wyman) McDonald. They reside in Woburn. He is a lumber dealer in Boston and the coal dealer of Woburn.

Their children, both b. in Woburn, were:

1. Fred Wyman McDonald, b. May 25, 1867.
2. Joseph Belknap McDonald, Jr., b. July 7, 1878.

293. Dorothy Flagg Parker (called also Dolly) *(Benjamin,[7] Benjamin,[6] Josiah,[5] Josiah,[4] John,[3] Hananiah,[2] Thomas[1])*, dau. of Benjamin, Jr., and Sally (Allen) Parker, was b. in Fitchburg, Jan. 2, 1804; m. in Harvard, May 27,

1827. Ephraim Barnard of Harvard, b. March 19, 1805, son of Phineas and Betsey (Whitney) Barnard. He was a shoemaker and farmer in Harvard, where all of the children were born. She d. July 30, 1854. He d. April 11, 1883.

Their children were:

1. ELIZA ANN WILLARD BARNARD, b. March 30, 1828; m. Nov., 1851, John Wright of Charlestown. She d. March 7, 1852.
2. SARAH PARKER BARNARD, b. April 13, 1830; m. in Harvard, March 29, 1853, George Whitney of Stow, b. Oct. 28, 1823, son of Asa and Sally (Brooks) Whitney. They reside in Harvard, where he is a farmer. Children:
   i. FREDERICK A. WHITNEY, b. in Stow, April 8, 1858.
   ii. GEORGIANA WHITNEY, b. in Harvard, June 21, 1871.
3. EPHRAIM AUGUSTUS BARNARD, b. Aug. 28, 1832; d. of consumption, June 26, 1853.
4. EMELINE JANE BARNARD, b. July 28, 1835; m. in Harvard, Feb. 4, 1864, Vandola E. Whitcomb of Littleton, b. in Littleton, Jan. 11, 1830, son of Emory Vandola and Sophia (Foster) Whitcomb. They reside in Bolton.
5. LUTHER ALLEN BARNARD, b. Dec. 24, 1837; m. Antoinette L. Taylor of Boxborough, dau. of Varnum and Mary (Bowers) Taylor. He d. of consumption, Nov. 17, 1867. They had a dau. who d. young. His widow married again and resides in W. Acton.
6. ABIGAIL MARIA BARNARD, b. May 27, 1840; m. in Hudson, Charles Frank Stone of Littleton, b. in Groton, Oct. 17, 1831, son of Nathaniel (native of Groton) and Lydia (Page) Stone (native of Shirley). They reside in Littleton, where he is a farmer.
7. HENRY ALBERT BARNARD, b. Nov. 30, 1842; m. Jan. 10, 1866, Ann Augusta Gates of Leominster, b. in Leominster, Nov. 16, 1848, dau. of Edwin and Ann B. Gates. They reside in Leominster. Children:
   i. CORA MABEL BARNARD, b. in Leominster, April 8, 1868.
   ii. CHARLES EDWIN BARNARD, b. March 20, 1873.
8. WALDO GARDNER BARNARD, b. Dec. 11, 1848; d. of consumption, Oct. 19, 1870.

294. Mehetable Tidd Parker (*Benjamin*,[7] *Benjamin*,[6] *Josiah*,[5] *Josiah*,[4] *John*,[3] *Hananiah*,[2] *Thomas*[1]), dau. of Benjamin, Jr., and Sally (Allen) Parker, was b. in Harvard,

March 17, 1806; m. Jan. 19, 1830, Thomas Cummings of Hollis, N. H., b. Aug. 22, 1805, son of Thomas and Mary Cummings. They lived in Harvard, where he was a farmer the greater part of his life. He was also a shoemaker. He d. March 20, 1885, and she resides with her son in Somerville.

Their children were:

1. Benjamin Thomas Cummings, b. in Boston, Nov. 26, 1830; d. Jan. 30, 1834.
2. Charles Henry Cummings, b. Nov. 7, 1834; m. Oct. 28, 1856, Helen S. Farnsworth of Harvard, dau. of Jerome and Lydia Farnsworth. They lived first in Harvard, now in Somerville. He is a clerk in Chandler's dry goods house, Boston. Children b. in Harvard:
   i. Arthur Thomas Cummings, b. April 20, 1859; m. Sept., 1882, Laura Leavitt of Bangor, Me. They reside in Somerville.
   ii. Cecil Henry Cummings, b. March 3, 1865. Resides in Omaha, Neb., unmarried.

Eliza Richardson Parker (see page 228) (*Joseph,[7] Benjamin,[6] Josiah,[5] Josiah,[4] John,[3] Hananiah,[2] Thomas[1]*), dau. of Dea. Joseph and Betsey (Richardson) Parker, was b. in Woburn, Aug. 27, 1808; m. May 17, 1827, in Woburn, Warren Fox, b. in Woburn, Jan. 16, 1804, son of Capt. William and Arathusa (Munroe) Fox. They lived on the West Side of the town. The Fox homestead stood on Lexington Street, near the old Parker farm. It is now unoccupied and is a part of the Colburn farm. Warren Fox was a leather dresser. She d. Oct. 21, 1886, and he d. Jan. 22, 1887.

Their children were:

1. Warren Parker Fox, b. May 13, 1829; m. June 16, 1853, Maria N. Newhall, b. in Woburn, March 13, 1833, dau. of Alfred A. and Margery Fowle (Thompson) Newhall. The father was b. in Lynn, March 8, 1809, and the mother in

---

Arathusa Munroe, the wife of Capt. William Fox, was b. in Lexington, March 10, 1773, dau. of Nathan and Elizabeth (Harrington) Munroe (see page 74). Nathan, the father, was son of Marrett and Deliverance (Parker) Munroe; she, Deliverance, being dau. of Lieut. Josiah Parker of Lexington and sister of Capt. John Parker of Lexington and Lieut. Josiah Parker of Woburn.

Woburn, April 26, 1810. Mr. Fox resides on Kilby Street in Woburn. Their children were:

i. CLARA MARIA FOX, b. Sept. 19, 1855; resides in Woburn.

ii. EVERETT PARKER FOX, b. Sept. 10, 1860; m. Nov. 29, 1882, Elona S. Dennis of Boston, dau. of Ward and Caroline (Parker) Dennis of Lewiston, Me. She d. Aug. 29, 1892. He resides in Woburn. Child:

i. Elona Sybil Fox, b. in Woburn, Aug. 28, 1884.

iii. JOHN WILLIAM FOX, b. Feb. 14, 1863; m. Nov. 18, 1885, Carrie Belle Cook. They reside in Woburn. Child:

i. Mildred A. Fox, b. Sept. 15, 1887.

2. MARY ELIZA FOX, b. Sept. 10, 1832; m. in Woburn, March 19, 1857, John Samuel Wheeler, b. in Bolton, June 3, 1833. They lived in Woburn, where he still resides. She d. April 9, 1889, leaving no issue.

3. SARAH JANE FOX, b. June 30, 1835; m. (1) Silas Nowell Bedelle of Somerville; m. (2) in Woburn, Jan. 24, 1872, Mosely N. Brooks. She d. Nov. 24, 1885. Her children were:

i. JOSEPH WARREN BEDELLE, b. in Woburn, Jan. 3, 1856; m. Rebecca Louis Fowle, b. Sept. 20, 1858, dau. of Josiah L. and Rebecca Fowle of Woburn. He is a leather dresser in Fitchburg.

ii. MARY BROOKS, b. in Woburn, Dec. 12, 1872; d. July 20, 1873.

iii. WINTHROP BROOKS, b. Sept. 3, 1874; d. Aug. 25, 1875. } Twins.

iv. WALDO BROOKS, b. Sept. 3, 1874. He lives with his uncle, Charles Brooks, in Franconia, N. H. } Twins.

4. CELINDA THOMPSON FOX, b. July 27, 1840; m. in Woburn, April 24, 1864, Jacob C. Whitcher. He d. She resides in Woburn. Their children were:

i. ARTHUR WARREN WHITCHER, b. Oct. 3, 1865.

ii. JACOB FRANKLIN WHITCHER, b. March 31, 1869; d. Dec. 7, 1875.

iii. JENNIE ELIZA WHITCHER, b. Dec. 13, 1870; d. May 23, 1882.

iv. MARY CELENDA WHITCHER, b. Oct. 29. 1874.

v. CARRIE LOUISE WHITCHER, b. Jan. 28, 1877.

295. Joseph Addison Parker (*Joseph,[7] Benjamin,[6] Josiah,[5] Josiah,[4] John,[3] Hananiah,[2] Thomas[1]*), son of Dea. Joseph and Betsey (Richardson) Parker, was b. in Woburn, July 7, 1815; m. Dec. 31, 1839, Rebecca Jane Cutler, dau.

of Amos and Rachel (Flagg) Cutler of Lexington, later of Mason, N. H. She was b. in Lexington; d. in Woburn, April 14, 1849. He m. (2) in Woburn, June 11, 1854, Emily Hewes, native of Fairlee, Vt. They reside in Woburn, where Mr. Parker has always lived. He is a leather dresser.

Their children were:

JOSEPH ADDISON PARKER, Jr., b. Oct. 16, 1840. He entered the service of the Union army, and d. in Woburn, Oct. 19, 1861, from the effects of the battle of Bull Run.

MARIA JANE PARKER, b. Aug. 8, 1845; d. April 8, 1881.

296. Ann Parker (*Joseph,[7] Benjamin,[6] Josiah,[5] Josiah,[4] John,[3] Hananiah,[2] Thomas[1]*), dau. of Dea. Joseph and Betsey (Richardson) Parker, was b. in Woburn, Oct. 23, 1816; m. in Woburn, June 4, 1840, Elijah Marion of Burlington, b. Dec. 28, 1812, son of John C. and Martha (Carter) Marion. He was highway surveyor, overseer of the town farm of Burlington and a representative to the General Court in 1872. They lived in Burlington, where he was a farmer. She d. March 20, 1879. He d. June 19, 1884.

Their children were:

1. ELIJAH PARKER MARION, b. in Burlington, Dec. 28, 1841; m. in Woburn, June 24, 1878, Evelyn E. Manning, b. in Burlington, July 3, 1845, dau. of William and Elizabeth (Shedd) Manning. They reside in Woburn, where he is a garden farmer. Children:
   - I. EDITH EVELYN MARION, b. in Woburn, June 22, 1879.
   - II. GUY ELWOOD MARION, b. in Woburn, March 25, 1882.
2. ANN ELIZABETH MARION, b. in Woburn, May 14, 1843; m. Oct. 5, 1865, John Pollock of Woburn. She resides in Burlington with her daughters:
   - I. IDA POLLOCK.
   - II. HARRIET POLLOCK.
3. CHARLES EDWARD MARION, b. in Woburn, Aug. 16, 1846; m. in Chelsea, Oct. 12, 1870, Kate Downs, b. in Westbrook, Me., May 10, 1845, dau. of Samuel W. and Irene Downs. He is a farmer in Burlington. Their children were:
   - I. HENRY ELMER MARION, b. in Woburn, Sept. 15, 1871.
   - II. FRANCIS HERBERT MARION, b. in Woburn, Sept. 29, 1876.
   - III. EVERETT HANCOCK MARION, b. in Burlington, Jan. 6, and d. April 8, 1882.

iv. EMILY ELVA MARION, b. in Burlington, April 11, 1883.

4. WILLIAM CHESTER MARION, b. in Burlington, May 23, 1852. He resides in St. Paul, Minn.

5. ELLA CHESTINA MARION, b. in Burlington, Dec. 7, 1854. She resides in Burlington.

297. Benjamin Parker (*Joseph,*[7] *Benjamin,*[6] *Josiah,*[5] *Josiah,*[4] *John,*[3] *Hananiah,*[2] *Thomas*[1]), son of Dea. Joseph and Betsey (Richardson) Parker, was b. in Woburn, Jan. 25, 1820; m. in Woburn, Nov. 19, 1846, Mary Elizabeth Waitt, b. in Malden, Sept. 10, 1828, dau. of James and Deborah Waitt. They lived on Bedford Street in Woburn. He was a currier.

Their children were:

ELIZABETH FRANCES PARKER, b. Sept. 11, 1847; m. in Woburn, Nov. 24, 1886, Capt. John William Ellard of Woburn, b. Dec. 9, 1854, son of William and Elizabeth A. Ellard. He is a leather splitter and stock raiser. They reside in Woburn. He was for two years Capt. of the Woburn Mechanic Phalanx.

416. BENJAMIN FRANKLIN PARKER, b. Sept. 8, 1850; m. Mary M. Childs of Woburn.

417. SUSAN EMMA PARKER, b. April 21, 1854; m. Clarence M. Crowell.

418. LUCY AUGUSTA PARKER, b. Jan. 24, 1858; m. Asa W. Boutwell of Woburn.

HERBERT WALLACE PARKER, b. Nov. 1, 1869.

298. Samuel Thurston Parker (*Samuel,*[7] *Benjamin,*[6] *Josiah,*[5] *Josiah,*[4] *John,*[3] *Hananiah,*[2] *Thomas*[1]), son of Samuel and Lydia Thurston (Allen) Parker, was b. in Fitchburg, Mass., June 11, 1805; removed with the family to Otselic, N. Y.: m. in Smyrna, N. Y., Oct. 16, 1829, Mary Bates, b. Feb. 19, 1806, in Nova Scotia, dau. of Daniel and Sally (Hinman) Bates. He was a carpenter and farmer. He d. March 17, 1860. She d. Nov. 30, 1873.

Their children were:

419. SAMUEL DWIGHT PARKER, b. Dec. 29, 1830; m. Hannah R. Congdon.

THOMAS LEROY PARKER, b. in Georgetown, N. Y., Sept. 18, 1832; m. in Belvidere, Boone Co., Ill., Oct. 7, 1855, Amanda E. Brown, b. in Parkman, Ohio, Oct. 6, 1835, eldest dau. of Alonzo and

Hannah Brown. He went to Illinois in Sept., 1853. He was a farmer; moved to Clayton Co., Iowa, in 1858. He enlisted in Co. B, 21st Reg., Iowa Inf. Vols., in Aug., 1862. He participated in five battles, viz.: Port Gibson (Magnolia Hills), Champion Hill, Black River Bridge, Vicksburg and Jackson, all in Mississippi. He d. while on a furlough, Sept. 30, 1863. He had no issue. She resides at Strawberry Point, Iowa.

420. Henry Norton Parker, b. in Georgetown, N. Y., June 16, 1834; m. (1) Hannah M. Glynn, (2) Mary A. Cooley, (3) Martha Bowers Cady.

421. John Lasson Parker, b. in Georgetown, N. Y., July 6, 1836; m. Lydia A. Vanhovenburgh.

422. Lucy Lizzette Parker, b. in Smyrna, N. Y., July 17, 1838; m. Lewis Jones.

Mary Parker; d. young.

423. Albert Monson Parker, b. in Madison, Co., N. Y., Oct. 10, 1843; m. Elizabeth Van Zandt.

424. Edwin Eugene Parker, b. in Madison Co., N. Y., Dec. 5, 1846; m. Nellie Heath.

425. William Charles Addison Parker, b. in Otselic, N. Y., Aug. 5, 1849; m. Emma O. Crandall.

Benjamin Allen Parker (see page 229) *(Samuel,[7] Benjamin,[6] Josiah,[5] Josiah,[4] John,[3] Hananiah,[2] Thomas[1])*, son of Samuel and Lydia Thurston (Allen) Parker, was b. in Worcester, Mass., Dec. 31, 1806. He removed at an early age with his parents to Chenango Co., N. Y., and when of age to Chardon, Ohio. In 1863 he visited Kansas, and in 1864 moved his family to Spring Hill, Johnson Co., Kansas, where he d. July 10, 1870, and now lies in the cemetery at Spring Hill. He m. about 1831 or 1832 Orpha Stebbins, b. in Longmeadow, Mass., Jan., 1814. She removed to Chardon, Ohio, when only two years old. She d. at Chardon, Oct., 1890.

Their children were:

Harriet Parker; d. at 11 years of age.

426. Thomas Allen Parker, b. in Chardon, O., Nov. 18, 1834; m. Margaret Ann Lindsey.

Charles Burr Parker; d. at nine years of age.

Martha Jane Parker; d. at two years and eleven months.

427. Hosea Stebbins Parker; m. Martha D. Wilson.

428. Mary Louisa Parker; m. Benjamin Sprague.

299. Lydia Lucretia Parker (*Samuel,*[7] *Benjamin,*[6] *Josiah,*[5] *Josiah,*[4] *John,*[3] *Hananiah,*[2] *Thomas*[1]), dau. of Samuel and Lydia Thurston (Allen) Parker, was b. in Fitchburg, Oct. 4, 1808; m. in Smyrna, N. Y., William Riley Orvis, b. April 17, 1803, son of Joseph and Mabel Orvis. He was a farmer. They lived in Sumner, Ia., where he d. Aug., 1892. They had ten children.

1. LUCY A. ORVIS, b. March 19, 1825; m. Richard J. Quinlan. He was a shoemaker. He d. and she m. (2) Joseph W. Mertz, b. May 10, 1813. He has been a farmer in Odebolt, Ia., where they still reside. Her children were:
   - I. THOMAS B. QUINLAN, b. in Sherburne, N. Y., April 4, 1845; resides in Covington, Ia., where he is a merchant and postmaster, and has three children.
   - II. FRANK B. QUINLAN, b. in Sherburne, N. Y., May 10, 1847; resides in Shurdon, Green Co., Iowa, where he is a farmer. He has four children.
   - III. JAMES R. QUINLAN, b. in Schoolcraft, Mich., Dec. 29, 1849; resides in Sherwood, Branch Co., Mich. He has three children.
   - IV. MIRIAM L. QUINLAN, b. in Schoolcraft, Mich., May 2, 1851; m. and resides in Coldwater, Mich., and has three children. } Twins.
   - V. FREDERICK D. QUINLAN, b. in Schoolcraft, Mich., May 2, 1851; resides in Wayland, Allegan Co., Mich. } Twins.
   - VI. ELLEN QUINLAN, b. in Schoolcraft, Mich., Nov. 10, 1855; m. Joseph Henton. He is a farmer near Farnhamville, Calhoun Co., Ia.
2. LOTTIE A. ORVIS; m. in Fayette, Ia., Dec. 3, 1879, William T. Wade, b. in Elizabeth, N. J., Dec. 27, 1818. They reside in Sumner, Ia., where he is a farmer.

300. Charlotte Elmira Parker (*Samuel,*[7] *Benjamin,*[6] *Josiah,*[5] *Josiah,*[4] *John,*[3] *Hananiah,*[2] *Thomas*[1]), dau. of Samuel and Lydia Thurston (Allen) Parker, was b. in Fitchburg, June 8, 1814; m. 1830, William Wilbur. She d. June 11, 1831, leaving a daughter four weeks old. She grew up in her grandmother's, Mrs. Samuel Parker's, family. Her name was:

1. ELLEN MARIA WILBUR, b. May 13, 1831. She removed West with some of her relatives. She m. Henry Dennis and d. in Chicago, Ill. She had three children.

Harriet Emeline Parker (see page 230) *(Samuel,[7] Benjamin,[6] Josiah,[5] Josiah,[4] John,[3] Hananiah,[2] Thomas[1])*, dau. of Samuel and Lydia Thurston (Allen) Parker, was b. in Fitchburg, June 18, 1816; m. Nov. 30, 1834, Lorenzo Dow Miles, b. March 4, 1812, son of William and Charity Miles. They lived in Otselic, N. Y., where he d. Feb. 23, 1891. She d. in Otselic, N. Y., Oct. 2, 1883. He was a farmer. He was assessor for three years.

Their children, all b. in Otselic, N. Y., were:

1. FRANCIS E. MILES, b. July 2, 1835; m. Emma Bishop. She d. Aug., 1882. He resides in Otselic, N. Y. Children:
   - i. CHARLES MILES.
   - ii. LAMOTT MILES.
   - iii. ADELBERT MILES.
   - iv. FLOYD MILES.
2. HENRY A. MILES, b. July 13, 1837; m. Sept. 13, 1857, Rebecca Ann Kinzon, b. Nov. 7, 1839; d. Oct., 1880. He d. Oct. 6, 1862. They had one child:
   - i. CARRIE FLORENCE MILES, b. Feb. 24, 1862; m. Feb. 15, 1880, William Conley of Smyrna, N. Y. Children:
     1. Lucy H. Conley, b, Nov. 29, 1880.
     2. Nellie E. Conley, b. July 22, 1882.
     3. Lois R. Conley, b. Dec. 15, 1885.
3. ORPHA E. MILES, b. June 1, and d. Aug. 28, 1839.
4. GEORGE B. MILES, b. Oct. 10, 1840; m. Jan. 29, 1868, Rebecca Ann (Kinzon) Miles, his brother's widow. He resides in Otselic, N. Y. He is a farmer. Their son:
   - i. BURTON P. MILES, b. March 3, 1870; m. June 21, 1891, Nora E. Brown of Otselic, N. Y. They have a son:
     1. Max Merton Miles, b. June 3, 1892.

301. Francis Edwin Parker *(Samuel,[7] Benjamin,[6] Josiah,[5] Josiah,[4] John,[3] Hananiah,[2] Thomas[1])*, son of Samuel and Lydia Thurston (Allen) Parker, was b. in Fitchburg, May 3, 1819; m. in Lebanon, N. Y., Aug. 24, 1843, Amanda Minerva Lindsay, b. Nov. 4, 1819, dau. of David and Jemima (Crane) Lindsay. She d. in Belvidere, Ill., Jan. 19, 1872. He was a farmer in Boone Co., Ill., until shortly before his wife's death, when they removed to Belvidere, Ill. He m. (2) Mrs. Nancy Powell. He d. Dec. 19, 1876, in Belvidere, Ill.

Their children were:

EMMA MATILDA PARKER, b. in Cook Co., Ill., April 3, 1848; d. Jan. 29, 1869.

429. MARY ELLEN PARKER, b. in Lake Co., Ill., May 13, 1851; m. Stephen Abraham.

302. Abigail Elizabeth Parker *(Samuel,[7] Benjamin,[6] Josiah,[5] Josiah,[4] John,[3] Hananiah,[2] Thomas[1])*, dau. of Samuel and Lydia Thurston (Allen) Parker, was b. in Otselic, N. Y., June 11, 1823; m. in Otselic, N. Y., June 16, 1840, Dr. G. E. Lawrence, b. in Oneonta, Otsego Co., N. Y., Nov. 18, 1816, son of Charles and Hannah Lawrence. He d. in Smyrna, N. Y., Aug. 8, 1887. She resides in Smyrna.

Their children were:

1. EDWARD FAYETTE LAWRENCE, b. in Sherburne, Chenango Co., N. Y., April 15, 1843; m. Oct. 20, 1870, Emily S. Wells of Evansville, Ind., b. in Madison, Ind., March 14, 1841, dau. of Hiram K. and Emily S. Wells. He is assistant business manager of the *Elmira Advertiser*, N. Y. Their children were:
   - I. E. WINIFRED LAWRENCE, b. in Norwich, N. Y., Feb. 7, 1875.
   - II. HARRY LAWRENCE, b. in Smyrna, N. Y., June 4, 1877.
2. MARY AMELIA LAWRENCE, b. in Sherburne, Chenango Co., N. Y., Aug. 9, 1846; m. Feb. 28, 1868, Floyd Brooks of Smyrna, N. Y. They have children:
   - I. MAY MALISSA BROOKS.
   - II. CHAUNCY D. BROOKS.
   - III. FLORENCE AMELIA BROOKS.
3. LEWIS ADELBERT LAWRENCE, b. in Sherburne, Chenango Co., N. Y., Aug. 17, 1851; d. Aug. 3, 1873.
4. FRANK JAMIA LAWRENCE, b. in Smyrna, N. Y., March 25, 1855.
5. FREDDIE LAWRENCE, b. in Smyrna, N. Y., July 16, and d. Sept. 11, 1862.

303. Ann Maria Parker *(Samuel,[7] Benjamin,[6] Josiah,[5] Josiah,[4] John,[3] Hananiah,[2] Thomas[1])*, dau. of Samuel and Lydia Thurston (Allen) Parker, was b. in Otselic, N. Y., Feb. 25, 1825; m. in Smyrna, March 25, 1847, William

Stover Wilcox, b. in Smyrna, Aug. 28, 1821, son of Thomas and Jemima (Stover) Wilcox. He was a farmer and d. in Smyrna, May 4, 1869. She resides in Woodhull, N. Y.

Their children were:

1. LAURA ANN WILCOX, b. in Smyrna, N. Y., Dec. 29, 1847; m. in N. Norwich, N. Y., May 22, 1870, Edwin G. Brown, son of Sylvester G. and Rebecca (Martin) Brown. They reside in Woodhull, Steuben Co., N. Y. Their children were:
   - I. LYNN D. BROWN, b. Oct. 8, 1871.
   - II. EVA MARIA BROWN, b. Feb. 17, 1873.
   - III. BERTHA BROWN, b. April 14, 1885.

2. DELIA AVARENA WILCOX, b. in Otselic, N. Y., July 1, 1849; m. in Smyrna, N. Y., Nov. 8, 1870, Lawrence H. Goodrich, son of Eleazer and Hannah (Way) Goodrich. They reside in Norwich, N. Y. Their children were:
   - I. LENA A. GOODRICH, b. Sept. 28, 1871.
   - II. CORA E. GOODRICH, b. April 25, 1873.
   - III. ETTA H. GOODRICH, b. Nov. 5, 1875.
   - IV. WILLIE O. GOODRICH, b. April 26, 1877.
   - V. CLARA V. GOODRICH, b. April 29, 1878.
   - VI. LYNN E. GOODRICH, b. July 28, 1883.
   - VII. DEAN GOODRICH, b. Jan. 24, 1885.

3. ELLA MARIA WILCOX, b. in Otselic, N. Y., April 20, 1852; m. in Smyrna, N. Y., Dec. 16, 1874, Everett A. Dodge, son of William and Mary Ann (Colton) Dodge. They reside in Brooklyn, Ct. Their dau. was:
   - I. ANNA BELLE DODGE, b. March 14, 1889.

4. CORA ELIZABETH WILCOX, b. in Smyrna, N. Y., Dec. 3, 1857; m. in Sherburne, N. Y., Oct. 9, 1877, George F. Harrington, son of Ezekiel and Emeline (Alexander) Harrington. They reside in Norwich, N. Y. Their children were:
   - I. LEWIS E. HARRINGTON, b. July 29, 1884.
   - II. PEARL W. HARRINGTON, b. Nov. 8, 1887.

5. HATTIE AMELIA WILCOX, b. in Smyrna, N. Y., July 4, 1860; m. in Smyrna, Sept. 27, 1882, George W. Sumner, son of Daniel and Mary (Smith) Sumner.

6. WILLIAM STOVER WILCOX, b. in Smyrna, N. Y., April 11, 1862; m. in Lebanon, Madison Co., N. Y., Jan. 31, 1884, Ella J. Gavin, dau. of John Gavin. They reside in Brooklyn, Ct. Their son was:
   - I. GEORGE S. WILCOX, b. Aug. 19, 1885.

7. KATIE BELLE WILCOX, b. in Smyrna, N. Y., July 11, 1868; m. June 29, 1892, Horace D. Covell of Pomfret Landing, Ct., where they reside.

304. Martha Ann Parker (*Isaac,[7] John,[6] John,[5] Josiah,[4] John,[3] Hananiah,[2] Thomas[1]*), dau. of Isaac and Martha M. (Miller) Parker, was b. in Lexington, June 16, 1831; m. Oct., 1855, William W. Dingee of Philadelphia Co., Pa. They reside in Racine, Wis.

Their children were:

1. GERTRUDE PARKER DINGEE, b. Nov., 1857.
2. THEODORE PARKER DINGEE, b. Jan., 1863: d. Dec., 1869.

305. Abigail Anna Parker (*Hiram S.,[7] John,[6] John,[5] Josiah,[4] John,[3] Hananiah,[2] Thomas[1]*), dau. of Hiram S. and Nancy (Leavitt) Parker, was b. in Lowell, Aug. 24, 1828; m. in Lowell, July 17, 1850, Charles William Rea, b. Nov. 10, 1827, in Hereford, P. Q., eldest son of Alexander and Betsey Rea. They lived many years in Toronto, Ont. They reside in Everett, Mass. He is a carpenter.

Their children were:

1. EMMA MATILDA REA, b. in Lowell, Aug. 24, 1851.
2. ANNIE ISABEL REA, b. in Lowell, May 19, 1853; m. in Compton, P. Q., June 6, 1877, George H. Reneau.
3. CHARLES HENRY REA, b. in Lowell, Jan. 12, 1856.
4. GEORGE FRÄZIER REA, b. in Lowell, Feb. 24, 1858.
5. ALEXANDER REA, b. in Lowell, May 20, 1859.
6. ALLAN REA, b. in Lowell, Nov. 2, 1861.
7. FREDERICK PARKER REA, b. in Compton, P. Q., March 17, 1863; m. Feb. 14, 1888, Mary Augusta Kennedy. Their children are:
   - I. MARY KATHLENE REA, b. March 5, 1889.
   - II. FREDERICK REA, b. Oct., 1890.
   - III. MARGUERITE GENEVIEVE REA, b. July 4, 1892.
8. HIRAM MILES REA, b. in Compton, P. Q.
9. MINNIE SUSIE REA, b. in Compton, P. Q., Aug. 21, 1867.
10. ABBIE NANCY LOUISE REA, b. in Compton, P. Q., Jan. 11, 1870; m. Jan. 26, 1889, William James Hanson Bastard. Child:
    - I. DONALD REA HANSON BASTARD, b. Jan. 10, 1890.

306. Charles Leavitt Parker *(Hiram S.,[7] John,[6] John,[5] Josiah,[4] John,[3] Hananiah,[2] Thomas[1])*, son of Hiram S. and Nancy (Leavitt) Parker, was b. in Lowell, Aug. 1, 1839; m. in Nashua, N. H., Oct. 23, 1867, Maria Barker, b. in Sandwich, Mass., Sept. 25, 1847, dau. of John and Rebecca (McLane) Barker of Sandwich. They reside in Lowell.

Their children were:

ARTHUR LEAVITT PARKER, b. Jan. 19, and d. Feb. 7, 1872.
HIRAM THEODORE PARKER, b. Aug. 9, 1873.
CHARLES HENRY PARKER, b. March 4, 1876; d. April 19, 1878.
JOHN LEAVITT PARKER, b. Jan. 4, 1879.
LEONA BELL PARKER, b. Nov. 22, 1881; d. April 22, 1885.
MINNIE GRAVES PARKER, b. Aug. 10, 1884; d. Jan. 16, 1887.
ANNIE REA PARKER, b. Oct. 28, 1887.

307. Susan Weatherbee Parker (see page 244) *(Hiram S.,[7] John,[6] John,[5] Josiah,[4] John,[3] Hananiah,[2] Thomas[1])*, dau. of Hiram S. and Nancy (Leavitt) Parker, was b. in Lowell, Nov. 24, 1841; m. in Lowell, March 19, 1864, George Edgar Wentworth of Lowell, b. in Alstead, N. H., March 14, 1842. He was a scholar at the Franklin School in Lowell. Enlisting as a private in the 30th Mass. Reg., he was appointed to the Lieut. Colonelcy of the 88th U. S. Colored Reg., which position he honored with his high courage as an officer and warm hearted humanity. He was severely wounded and carried to his grave one bullet which could not be extracted. He was a most efficient soldier and he won the confidence of his superiors. He was offered a captaincy, which he declined. He was a gentleman of refined manners and considerable culture of mind and heart and was a public spirited citizen. He was Collector of Internal Revenue and Clerk of the U. S. Courts at Pensacola, Fla., at the time of his death, Oct. 14, 1881. Mrs. Wentworth resides in Pensacola.

Their children were:

1. NANCY LOUISA WENTWORTH, b. in Lowell, Aug. 13, 1869.
2. ALICE KATE WENTWORTH, b. in Pensacola, Fla., Aug. 3, 1871.
3. ELLIE GRACE WENTWORTH, b. in Pensacola, March 16, 1875.
4. GEORGE PARKER WENTWORTH, b. in Pensacola, June 18, 1877.
5. WARREN PIERCE WENTWORTH (twin of Emma Annie), b. in Pensacola, March 25, 1879.

6. EMMA ANNIE WENTWORTH (twin of Warren Pierce), b. in Pensacola, March 25, 1879.

Theodore Henry Parker (see page 244) *(Hiram S.,[7] John,[6] John,[5] Josiah,[4] John,[3] Hananiah,[2] Thomas[1])*, son of Hiram S. and Nancy (Leavitt) Parker, was b. in Lowell, Nov. 4, 1833. He was educated in the public schools of Lowell. The pure patriotism which ever burned within him led him to enlist upon the outbreak of the Civil War in the 6th Mass. Reg., Capt. Hanson, Co. B, and was in the service nine months, during all of which time he acquitted himself as a brave and true soldier. After his return he was a book-keeper in Boston for 15 years. In 1886 his health failed and he declined gradually until his death. He was a talented and much gifted man; possessed a most tenacious memory, was fond of books and was a great reader. He was thus, in a measure, like his uncle, the Rev. Theodore Parker. He was a favorite with all; was generous to a fault and belonged to a Masonic order in Boston. He d. June 5, 1891.

307. Abby M. Parker (see page 272) *(Jonathan,[7] Robert,[6] John,[5] Josiah,[4] John,[3] Hananiah,[2] Thomas[1])*, dau. of Jonathan S. and Abigail (Tuttle) Parker, was b. in Lexington, April 23, 1847: m. Feb. 17, 1869, George H. Cutter of Arlington, son of Jefferson and Sarah E. (Thorpe) Cutter of Arlington, formerly W. Cambridge. They reside in Lexington.

Their children were:

1. FRANK P. CUTTER, b. Jan. 25, 1870.
2. HENRY E. CUTTER, b. Nov. 9, 1871; d. July 22, 1873.
3. HARRY N. CUTTER, b. March 25, 1875.

308. Georgiana Tuttle Parker *(Jonathan,[7] Robert,[6] John,[5] Josiah,[4] John,[3] Hananiah,[2] Thomas[1])*, dau. of Jonathan S. and Abigail (Tuttle) Parker, was b. in Lexington, Oct. 12, 1849; m. Aug. 14, 1872, Charles William Converse, b. in Woburn, July 29, 1849, son of Charles S. and Joanna Converse of Woburn. He d. in Marietta, Ga., March 26, 1888. She resides in Woburn.

Their children were:

1. CHARLES ATHERTON CONVERSE, b. Sept. 1, 1873; d. July 29, 1878.

2. Wallace P. Converse, b. Jan. 9, 1876.
3. Helen M. Converse, b. July 18, 1883; d. in Marietta, Ga., Oct. 22, 1887.

309. Josiah Bowers Parker (*William B.*,[7] *Robert*,[6] *John*,[5] *Josiah*,[4] *John*,[3] *Hananiah*,[2] *Thomas*[1]), son of William Bowers and Priscilla E. (Garfield) Parker, was b. in Charlestown, Aug. 31, 1848; m. July 17, 1873, Christina Alice Savage of Everett, dau. of Patrick and Ann (Doroty) Savage, natives of Ireland. They reside in Everett.

Their children were:

William Bowers Parker, b. April 23, 1874.
Henry Joseph Parker, b. July 23, 1876; d. Jan. 21, 1888.
Theodore Otis Parker, b. Dec. 26, 1878.
Anna Josephine Parker, b. Feb. 13, 1882; d. Jan. 11, 1888.
Mary Alice Parker, b. April 1, 1885.

310. Albert Parker (*Samuel*,[7] *Levi*,[6] *Joseph*,[5] *Josiah*,[4] *John*,[3] *Hananiah*,[2] *Thomas*[1]), son of Samuel and Lurania (Aikins) Parker, was b. in Potsdam, N. Y., Oct. 19, 1823; m. in Potsdam, Nov. 1, 1848, —— Turner, b. in Watertown, N. Y., May 25, 1828, dau. of Thomas and Polly (Gleason) Turner. He is a mechanic and resides in Potsdam.

Their children were:

Anna Elizabeth Parker, b. July 23, 1852; m. Gilbert J. Lemon.
Morton Louis Parker, b. July 9, 1853; m. Alice R. Hawkes.
Nellie Foster Parker, b. Oct. 28, 1865.

311. Lucy Ann Parker (*Isaac*,[7] *Levi*,[6] *Joseph*,[5] *Josiah*,[4] *John*,[3] *Hananiah*,[2] *Thomas*[1]), dau. of Isaac and Mary (Linsted) Parker, was b. Dec. 17, 1838; m. Shubael Crandall of New York State. They removed to Pierrepont, N. Y., then to Potsdam, N. Y., where they reside.

Their children were:

1. Minnie Crandall; d. aged 21.
2. Edith Crandall; m. Aug. 19, 1889; d. Nov. 17, 1889.
3. Jessie Crandall.

312. Mary Hammond Parker (*Isaac*,[7] *Joseph*,[6] *Joseph*,[5] *Josiah*,[4] *John*,[3] *Hananiah*,[2] *Thomas*[1]), dau. of Isaac and Lucy (Dunsmore) Parker, was b. in Waltham, March 4,

1827; m. (1) July 2, 1845, Shubael Treat. They lived in Waltham in the house, still standing, which he built. He d. and she m. (2) in Victoria, Vancouver Island, B. C., May, 1867, Mortimer Lewis. They reside in San Francisco, Cal.

Her children were:

1. MARY HARRIET TREAT, b. July 1, 1846; m. Aug. 25, 1864, Warren Lane Pope of Waltham. They reside in Waltham.
2. FRANCENA MARIA TREAT, b. Jan. 28, 1848; m. in Waltham, Dec. 24, 1868, Frederick Richard Eaton of Newton, b. in Boston, June 11, 1847, son of William Green and Elizabeth (Boylston) Eaton. They reside in Waltham. He is a mechanic. Their son was:
    1. WARREN MOSELY EATON, b. in Waltham, June 11, 1884.
3. CHARLES SHUBAEL TREAT, b. Aug. 13, 1850; d. Nov. 30, 1851.

313. Isaac Parker, Jr. *(Isaac,[7] Joseph,[6] Joseph,[5] Josiah,[4] John,[3] Hananiah,[2] Thomas[1])*, son of Isaac and Lucy (Dunsmore) Parker, was b. in Waltham, March 4, 1829; removed to Seattle, Puget Sound, Washington, where he m. Sept. 9, 1867, Lydia Greenlief Rowell, b. in Bangor, Me., Aug. 20, 1845, dau. of Stephen and Mary (Caldwell) Rowell. He first went to San Francisco, Cal., early in 1850. He later went to Mexico, where he superintended mining machinery. He was later in similar work at Gold Hill, Cal. At the time he set up his lumber mill in Seattle there were but two others in that territory. He went to the territory when the first settlements were being made; the country and society were then in a very primitive form. He is a mechanical engineer for which he served an apprenticeship with Hinkley & Drury of Boston in 1846. He was appointed in 1872 Government Inspector of Steamship Boilers for Puget Sound District. He was elected in 1888 City Treasurer of Seattle for one term. He is prominently connected with the Masonic bodies. He became a Mason in Feb., 1867, and has filled positions of honor and degree in the lodges of Seattle. They reside in Seattle.

Their children were:

GEORGE FREDERICK PARKER, b. in Seattle, Oct. 17, 1868; m. in Portland, Oregon, Aug. 20, 1892, Hattie Howe, and resides in Boise City, Idaho.

BEN STEPLER PARKER, b. Sept. 9, 1870.
ISAAC CURTIS PARKER, b. April 5, 1879.

314. George Endicott Parker *(Isaac,[7] Joseph,[6] Joseph,[5] Josiah,[4] John,[3] Hananiah,[2] Thomas[1])*, son of Isaac and Lucy (Dunsmore) Parker, was b. in Waltham, Feb. 4, 1834. He commenced the trade of a machinist at the shop of Mr. Pettis, Newton Upper Falls; removed to Springfield; removed to Colt's Armory, Hartford, Ct., where he remained nine years, taking contracts for pistol frames and parts of the revolving rifle. He removed to Newark, N. J., in 1864, where he resides and conducts a machine shop for model and experimental jobbing work. He is unmarried.

315. Lowell Parker *(Isaac,[7] Joseph,[6] Joseph,[5] Josiah,[4] John,[3] Hananiah,[2] Thomas[1])*, son of Isaac and Lucy (Dunsmore) Parker, was b. in Waltham, April 24, 1840. At the age of 14 he went to sea, and on his first trip went to S. America: on his second to Antwerp; third to England; fourth around the "Horn" to California and Puget Sound, where he was a steamboat engineer. He then joined his brother at Gold Hill, Cal., and became engineer on the mining engines there. From California he went to Newark, N. J., where he joined his other brother in the machine business, now known by the name of Parker & Co. He resides in Newark, unmarried.

316. Lucy Caroline Parker *(Isaac,[7] Joseph,[6] Joseph,[5] Josiah,[4] John,[3] Hananiah,[2] Thomas[1])*, dau. of Isaac and Lucy (Dunsmore) Parker, was b. in Waltham, June 9, 1846; m. in Waltham, Sept. 11, 1871, Warner Wells Carpenter, b. in Linden, Vt., March 23, 1842, son of Ira and Hannah (Skinner) Carpenter. Ira Carpenter was a well known music teacher. They reside in Waltham. He is a postal clerk on the Boston and Troy R. P. O.

Their children were:

1. HAMILTON LOWELL CARPENTER, b. Sept. 26, 1842.
2. LUCY BLANCHE CARPENTER, b. April 3, 1875; she lived one week.
3. GEORGE WARNER CARPENTER, b. June 8, 1876.
4. ISAAC PARKER CARPENTER, b. Sept. 10, 1878.

317. James H. Parker (*Isaac,[7] Elisha,[6] Joseph,[5] Josiah,[4] John,[3] Hananiah,[2] Thomas[1]*), son of Isaac and Flavila R. (Crosby) Parker, was b. in Stoughton, March 22, 1827; m. Oct. 9, 1852, Martha A. Haskell, b. in Deer Isle, Me., Jan. 25, 1831, dau. of Edward Y. and Martha M. (Haskell) Haskell. They reside in Cambridgeport. He is a machinist.

Their children were:

FRANK HENRY PARKER, b. in Charlestown, Nov. 9, 1855; m. Nov. 9, 1877, Eliza A. Spofford of Deer Isle, Me., dau. of William and Lucy Spofford. They lived in West Newton, from whence they removed to San Juan Del Rio, Mex., where they reside. Child:

1. ALICE ELIZA PARKER.

NELLIE ROSETTA PARKER, b. at Deer Isle, Me., Aug. 26, 1872; m. April 9, 1892, Charles A. Jarvis of Cambridgeport, b. March 10, 1872, son of Amos B. and Ellen A. (Joy) Jarvis of Cambridgeport. They reside in Cambridgeport.

318. Benjamin Skinner Parker (*Elisha,[7] Elisha,[6] Joseph,[5] Josiah,[4] John,[3] Hananiah,[2] Thomas[1]*), son of Elisha H. and Charlotte (Skinner) Parker, was b. in S. Windsor, Ct., Feb. 12, 1835: m. (1) in S. Windsor, Sept., 1858, Julia Wolcott of Windsor, dau. of Hiram Wolcott; m. (2) in Windsor, April, 1871, Mary Ford. They reside in S. Windsor, where he is a farmer. At the time of his father's decease he was still a boy, but he took charge of the farm and has conducted it from that time. His valuable estate of 100 acres is well known throughout his section, and he is a leading tobacco farmer. He is sexton of the village, is one of the school committee, and is a carpenter as well as a farmer. He is a staunch democrat; is well known as a man of sound sense and judgment, good nature and hospitality.

Their son:

HARRY VENNER PARKER, b. in S. Windsor, Jan. 27, 1872.

319. Frances Janet Parker (*Elisha,[7] Elisha,[6] Joseph,[5] Josiah,[4] John,[3] Hananiah,[2] Thomas[1]*), dau. of Elisha H. and Charlotte (Skinner) Parker, was b. in S. Windsor, Ct., Dec. 8, 1836; m. in Hartford, Ct., Jan. 18, 1856, Samuel S. Case, b. in Killingworth, Ct., March 9, 1827, son of Rev. William Case. They removed in 1869, and reside at Oak Park, Ill.

Their children were:

1. MARY PARKER CASE, b. in S. Windsor, April 26, 1857; m. Joel Gurley of Chicago, Ill.
2. FANNIE ANTOINETTE CASE, b. in S. Windsor, Jan. 12, 1859.
3. NELLIE MARIA CASE, b. in S. Windsor, March 24, 1861; m. Frank Durkee of Lake Geneva, Wis. Their children were:
   - I. MAURICE DURKEE, b. at Lake Geneva, March 24, 1884.
   - II. MARGERIE DURKEE, b. at Lake Geneva, Aug. 9, 1886.
4. KITTIE WARD CASE, b. in S. Windsor, Feb. 1, 1863; m. Channing Taylor of Chicago, Ill. Their child was:
   - I. OTTILENE TAYLOR, b. at Oak Park, Ill., Nov. 17, 1886.
5. OTTILENE STOUGHTON CASE, b. at Oak Park, Dec. 9, 1873.

320. Emma Sarah Parker (*Elisha,*[7] *Elisha,*[6] *Joseph,*[5] *Josiah,*[4] *John,*[3] *Hananiah,*[2] *Thomas*[1]), dau. of Elisha H. and Charlotte (Skinner) Parker, was b. in S. Windsor, Jan. 4, 1843; m. in Hartford, Ct., July 16, 1869, Albert K. Fuller, b. in Stafford, Ct., May 6, 1843, son of Robert S. and Hannah (Bugbey) Fuller. They reside at Feeding Hills, Mass., where he was postmaster four years. He is a merchant.

Their children were:

1. BERTIE E. FULLER, b. in Windsor, May 5, 1870; d. at Feeding Hills, Mass., Feb. 29, 1884.
2. JENNIE EMMA FULLER, b. in Windsor, May 18, 1874.
3. ALBERT EDWARD FULLER, b. in W. Hartford, Ct., Oct. 16, 1877.

321. Charles Elbridge Parker (*Jonathan C.,*[7] *Elisha,*[6] *Joseph,*[5] *Josiah,*[4] *John,*[3] *Hananiah,*[2] *Thomas*[1]), son of Jonathan Capin and Martha Ann (Briggs) Parker, was b. in Stoughton, May 21, 1844; m. in Stoughton, July 14, 1867, Harriet Abbie Minzy, b. in N. Bridgewater (now Brockton Heights), July 14, 1849, dau. of George W. (of Dorchester) and Harriet (Lynnfield) Minzy (of E. Stoughton, now Avon). Mr. Parker served an apprenticeship to the carpenter's trade, which he learned, and became a cabinet maker. He entered the service of the J. J. Phinney Counter Co. and has remained with them 24 years, repairing and building machines. He is one of the Stoughton Grenadiers. He is constable. He is also connected with the Masonic and Odd Fellow fraternities.

Their children were:

CHARLES EVERETT PARKER, b. in Stoughton, March 31, 1870; m. July 26, 1892, Nellie Hallett Reynolds, dau. of George (of New York city) and Ellen (Churchill) Reynolds (native of Stoughton). They reside in Stoughton. He is a woodworker.

ETTA ABBIE PARKER, b. in Stoughton, April 21, 1877.

322. Elisha Melville Parker *(Jonathan C.,[7] Elisha,[6] Joseph,[5] Josiah,[4] John,[3] Hananiah,[2] Thomas[1])*, son of Jonathan Capin and Martha Ann (Briggs) Parker, was b. in Stoughton, April 18, 1848; m. March 31, 1869, Caroline Frances Coots of Stoughton, b. in Dorchester, June 29, 1850, dau. of William and Sarah (Dwinnel) Coots of Stoughton. They reside in Stoughton. He is a storekeeper.

Their children were:

MELVILLE AUGUSTUS PARKER, b. June 24, 1870.

CARRIE MATTIE PARKER, b. Feb. 25, 1885.

323. Hiram Chamberlain Parker *(Peter,[7] John,[6] Peter,[5] John,[4] John,[3] Hananiah,[2] Thomas[1])*, son of Peter and Emily (Chamberlain) Parker, was b. Oct. 5, 1833; m. Hannah Laurania Newton of Woodville, b. in Hopkinton, Feb. 16, 1845, dau. of Charles and Hannah M. Newton. They reside near Woodville, Hopkinton.

Their children were:

LOUIS FRANCES PARKER, b. in Hopkinton, April 21, 1861; d. 1863, aged 17 months, 11 days.

FLORENCE GERTRUDE PARKER, b. in Hopkinton, June 1, 1873.

EDWIN OWEN PARKER, b. in Hopkinton, Aug. 16, 1875.

CHARLES OTIS PARKER, b. in Hopkinton, July 29, 1878.

324. Milton Bridges Parker *(Peter,[7] John,[6] Peter,[5] John,[4] John,[3] Hananiah,[2] Thomas[1])*, son of Peter and Emily (Chamberlain) Parker, was b. in Hopkinton, Feb. 17, 1834; m. in Hopkinton, Sept. 20, 1854, Harriet Jane Ward, b. in Hopkinton, June 12, 1834, dau. of Sylvester and Cynthia Ward. He d. May 9, 1863. She d. in Hopkinton, May 9, 1866.

Their children were:

430. MILTON AUGUSTUS PARKER, b. Sept. 2, 1855; m. Mae Hapgood of Cambridge.

MARY A. PARKER, b. March 30, 1857; d. in Framingham, 1873.

FRANK A. PARKER, b. Sept. 25, 1859; removed to Clyde, O., where he m. Dec. 19, 1883, Flora Eva Stevenson, dau. of B. W. and Elizabeth A. Stevenson. They reside in Clyde, O. Mr. Parker is a farmer.

EMMA MEHETABLE PARKER, b. Nov. 13, 1861. She was adopted when very young. Her name was thus changed. She is married.

325. Charles Fales Parker (*John,[7] John,[6] Peter,[5] John,[4] John,[3] Hananiah,[2] Thomas[1]*), son of Dea. John and Mary Ann (Fales) Parker, was b. Aug. 1, 1826; m. in Milwaukee, Wis., April 12, 1855, Julia A. Bingham of Milwaukee, b. in Rochester, N. Y., March 5, 1834, dau. of John Bingham, b. in Chesterfield, N. H., July 1, 1790, and Lucy Gage, his wife, b. in Norway, N. Y., Feb. 6, 1798. He is manager of the Metal Last and Tree Co., 88 Lincoln Street, Boston.

Their children were:

LUCY MARY PARKER, b. in Boston, Feb. 12, 1856; m. in Boston, Feb. 7, 1877, Warren B. Hopkins, son of Samuel B. and Rebecca Hopkins. They reside in Boston, where he is a wholesale clothing merchant on Summer Street. Children:

1. ANNIE LOUISE HOPKINS, b. in Boston, Jan. 21, 1878.
2. ETHEL MAY HOPKINS, b. in Boston, Oct. 31, 1881.
3. ALICE HOPKINS, b. in Boston, Oct. 9, 1886.

LILA ANN PARKER, b. Nov. 6, 1857; m. in Malden, Oct. 6, 1886, Harry P. Ballard of Malden (brother of Minnie Waters Ballard), son of Capt. Henry A. and Lydia (Brown) Ballard of Malden. They reside in Malden. Child:

1. EDITH P. BALLARD, b. in Malden, Dec. 30, 1887.

GRACE LOUISE PARKER, b. Sept. 4, 1864; m. in Wollaston, Oct. 10, 1888, Frank E. Wallis, b. in Eastport, Me., June 14, 1862, son of Richard C. and Sarah H. Wallis. They reside in Montclair, N. J. Child:

1. RICHARD PARKER WALLIS, b. in Montclair, N. J., Aug. 31, 1889.
2. CHARLES P. WALLIS, b. in Montclair, N. J., March 22, 1893.

326. John Henry Parker (*John,[7] John,[6] Peter,[5] John,[4] John,[3] Hananiah,[2] Thomas[1]*), son of Dea. John and Mary Ann (Fales) Parker, was b. Sept. 14, 1835; m. March 30, 1859, Annie E. Gilmore. They reside in Malden. He conducts the boot and shoe business of John H. Parker, 103 Bedford Street, Boston. He removed to Brookfield in 1861 and was during the time of the war superintendent of the factory of the well known boot and shoe firm of Kimball, Robinson & Co. He removed from Brookfield to Holliston in 1863, and from thence to Malden in 1864. At this date he became the partner with his brother in the firm of Charles F. Parker &. Co., Boston. The name has since been changed to John H. Parker & Co. He united in 1856 with the First Baptist Church in Boston. He has ever since taken an active part in religious work. He is also an active temperance advocate and a public spirited citizen. He is superintendent of the Sunday School in Malden. He was warden nine years and has been auditor of the Industrial Aid Society of Malden since its foundation 17 years ago.

Their children were:

ELLEN LETITIA PARKER, b. May 21, 1860; m. Oct., 1889, Benjamin S. Cudworth of Malden, son of Jesse Cudworth. They reside in Melrose. Children:

1. ROBERT PARKER CUDWORTH, b. Oct. 31, 1891.
2. DOROTHEA CUDWORTH, b. April 7, 1893.

431. JOHN FREEMAN PARKER, b. July 15, 1862; m. Minnie Waters Ballard of Malden.

CHARLES LINCOLN PARKER, b. April 12, 1865.

ANNA MABEL PARKER, b. May 26, 1870.

MARY CAROLINE PARKER, b. March 19, 1872; m. Dec. 2, 1891, Harry E. Converse of Malden, son of Hon. E. S. Converse. They reside in Malden.

HARRY DAY PARKER, b. Feb. 12, 1875.

327. Sarah Letitia Parker (*John*,[7] *John*,[6] *Peter*,[5] *John*,[4] *John*,[3] *Hananiah*,[2] *Thomas*[1]), dau. of Dea. John and Mary Ann (Fales) Parker, was b. Dec. 17, 1839; m. Oct. 28, 1858, Homer E. Sawyer of Bradford, Vt. He d. in New Orleans, Oct. 12, 1867. She d. in Nerva, near Genoa, Italy, Jan. 4, 1888, and was buried in Holliston. She was a talented musician. She was a prominent singer. She secured the best musical education that London and Paris could afford. She sang at the Handel and Haydn Society in Boston and for 13 years at Dr. Webb's Congregational Church, Tremont Street, Boston.

Their children were:

1. ANNA BELLE SAWYER, b. Oct., 1863; d. Jan. 8, 1865.
2. HOMER EUGENE SAWYER, b. Aug. 8, 1866; m. Nov. 24, 1890, Mary Buckley of Detroit, Mich. They reside in Malden. He is assistant superintendent in the Boston Rubber Co. Child:
   1. HOMER EUGENE SAWYER, b. April 8, 1892.

328. Mary Jane Parker *(Josiah,[7] John,[6] Peter,[5] John,[4] John,[3] Hananiah,[2] Thomas[1])*, dau. of Josiah and Caroline (Peck) Parker, was b. Jan. 19, 1836; m. Edgar N. Lane. They reside in Stoughton.

Their children were:

1. CARRIE P. LANE, b. Sept. 28, 1854; m. May 9, 1877, Frank M. Packard of Brockton. Child:
   1. LAILA E. PACKARD, b. Sept. 13, 1878.
2. EMORY E. LANE, b. June 20, 1856; m. Nov. 10, 1877, Mary J. Howe of Randolph. They reside in Stoughton. Child:
   1. EDWARD E. LANE, b. July 22, 1878.
3. GEORGE C. LANE, b. Jan. 15, 1860.
4. ELMER E. LANE, b. Dec. 26, 1861; m. and resides in Stoughton.
5. ELIZA N. LANE, b. June 12, 1867; d. young.
6. ALICE N. LANE, b. Oct. 16, 1869; resides in Stoughton.
7. BERT L. LANE, b. Sept. 2, 1876.

329. Sylvanus H. Parker *(Josiah,[7] John,[6] Peter,[5] John,[4] John,[3] Hananiah,[2] Thomas[1])*, son of Josiah and Caroline (Peck) Parker, was b. in Southborough, May 11, 1838; m. April 20, 1859, Mary Etta Gates, b. in Stowe, April 9, 1840, dau. of Ephraim and Lydia (Wolcott) Gates. Mr. Parker enlisted July 29, 1861, in the 13th Reg., from Marlborough, for three years. He was connected with the Army of the Potomac, was in Slaughter Mountain and Second Bull Run; discharged for disability, but afterward re-enlisted in 1864 and was stationed at Baltimore for three months. He resides in Marlborough.

Their children were:

STEPHEN ROLAND PARKER, b. in Marlborough, July 9, 1860; resides in Marlborough.

CAROLINE OLIVIA PARKER, b. in Stowe, Jan. 28, 1862; d. May 23, 1877.

Lizzie Frances Parker, b. in Marlborough, July 16, 1863; m. Robert E. Toomes of Boylston.

Floria May Parker, b. in Berlin, Sept. 15, 1876.

330. Rosetta Francena Parker (*Josiah,*[7] *John,*[6] *Peter,*[5] *John,*[4] *John,*[3] *Hananiah,*[2] *Thomas*[1]), dau. of Josiah and Caroline (Peck) Parker, was b. in Ashland, June 16, 1845; m. in Fayville, Jan. 9, 1865, Walter Morris Flint, b. in Lowell, Jan. 1, 1833. They reside in Marlborough.

Their children, all b. in Marlborough, were:

1. Minnie Parker Flint, b. May 19, 1866.
2. Walter Morris Flint, b. June 26, 1872.
3. Arthur Francis Flint, b. Dec. 30, 1880.

331. John Francis Parker (*Josiah,*[7] *John,*[6] *Peter,*[5] *John,*[4] *John,*[3] *Hananiah,*[2] *Thomas*[1]), son of Josiah and Caroline (Peck) Parker, was b. in Ashland, Aug. 20, 1849; m. in Westborough, Nov. 16, 1861, Mary E. Gassett. He d. in Westborough. She m. again and resides in Winnemissett, Fla.

His children were:

Arthur L. Parker, b. Oct. 13, 1873; d. Aug. 28, 1874.

Normon Francis Parker, b. Aug. 18, 1875.

332. Ella Annette Parker (*Josiah,*[7] *John,*[6] *Peter,*[5] *John,*[4] *John,*[3] *Hananiah,*[2] *Thomas*[1]), dau. of Josiah and Caroline (Peck) Parker, was b. in Ashland, Dec. 16, 1850; m. in Ashland, Nov. 16, 1869, Edward E. Leighton, b. in Mt. Vernon, Me., May 13, 1847, son of Nathaniel and Mary Leighton. They reside in Westborough. He is a carpenter.

Their children were:

1. Edward P. Leighton, b. in Ashland, Dec. 1, 1870; m. and has a dau.:
   1. Iva B. Leighton, b. March 4, 1892.
2. Lester L. Leighton, b. in Mt. Vernon, Me., Nov. 7, 1872.
3. Daisy G. Leighton, b. in Southville, Feb. 21, 1881.

333. Lysander Presson Parker (*Presson,*[7] *John,*[6] *Peter,*[5] *John,*[4] *John,*[3] *Hananiah,*[2] *Thomas*[1]), son of Presson and Mary (Newton) Parker, was b. in Worcester, Oct. 2, 1839. He enlisted May 9, 1861, aged 21, in the volunteer service of his country for three years. He served in Co. I,

13th Reg., Mass. Vols. He was promoted to corporal Nov. 1, 1862, and served as color guard until Feb. 1, 1864, when he was promoted to 3rd sergeant and soon after to 1st sergeant. He was very actively engaged with his regiment. He was in all the engagements in which his regiment figured up to June, 1864, when in the battle before Petersburgh he was wounded in the hand by a bursting shell. He was taken prisoner at Gettysburg, July 1, 1863, but was paroled three days later. During this period of service (May 9, 1861—June, 1864) he took part in 25 battles and skirmishes, among which were 12 important battles, viz.: Cedar Mountain, Second Bull Run, Chatilly, Antietam, First and Second Fredericksburg, Chancellorsville, Gettysburg, Wilderness, Spottsylvania, Cold Harbor and Petersburg. He was in City Point Hospital until July 17, 1864, when he returned to his regiment. He was discharged Aug. 1, 1864. He m. Oct. 2, 1867, Eleanor Wilkins, b. Feb. 1, 1843, dau. of Louis and Phebe Wilkins of Marlborough. They reside in Marlborough.

Their children were:

GERTRUDE LILLIAN PARKER, b. March 25, and d. Oct. 2, 1871.
PRESSON LEWIS PARKER, b. Oct. 5, 1872.
GEORGE EVERETT PARKER, b. Oct. 7, 1877.
RALPH ALBERT PARKER, b. June 1, 1879.
LULA MAUD PARKER, b. Jan. 14, 1882.

334. Peter Parker *(Peter,[7] Nathan,[6] Peter,[5] John,[4] John,[3] Hananiah,[2] Thomas[1])*, son of Dr. Peter and Harriet Colby (Webster) Parker, was b. in Washington, D. C., June 13, 1859; m. in Washington, June 5, 1890, Fanny Stuart Wilson, b. in Washington, Jan. 24, 1868, dau. of William Van Syckle and Marie (Stuart) Wilson. He resides in Framingham.

335. Charles Wallingford Parker *(Charles,[7] Josiah,[6] Peter,[5] John,[4] John,[3] Hananiah,[2] Thomas[1])*, son of Charles and Mary Hildreth (Wallingford) Parker, was b. in Framingham, Mass., June 27, 1831. His father's farm, where he passed his boyhood, was the original Parker homestead of the Framingham branch; it was where John Parker, who came from Lexington, settled, and the farm had been in the posses-

sion of the family for more than 150 years. He was educated in the district school and Framingham Academy. At the age of 16 he was employed in a small retail clothing store in Worcester in which Addison Macullar and George B. Williams were salesmen. Two years later Mr. Macullar opened a similar store on his own account, and Charles Parker went with him as store boy, salesman and book-keeper, the only employé. In Feburary, 1852, the firm's name being Macullar & Williams, they established a house in Boston for the manufacture of clothing for wholesale, retaining their Worcester retail store, and Mr. Parker came to Boston as book-keeper for the firm. After three removals the firm became located at 192 Washington Street, and at this time Mr. Parker was admitted to the firm, the name being made Macullar, Williams & Parker. In 1864 they removed to the present site, into a new store built for them by the trustees of the Joshua Sears estate. This was destroyed in the great fire of 1872, and the present larger and finer structure was completed in 1874. In 1880 their quarters were enlarged by the addition of the adjoining store, formerly occupied by Palmer & Bachelder. Mr. Williams retired from the house in 1879 and the firm name became Macullar, Parker & Company. Mr. Parker's business connection with Mr. Macullar continued for over 45 years, and their house has long occupied a foremost position in its special line in New England. In February, 1893, this great store, covering 11,000 feet of land, was purchased by Mr. Parker for the continued use of his firm. He is much interested in letters and art and has travelled extensively abroad. He was m. in Chelsea, Nov. 30, 1854, to Mary Jane Schoff, b. in Newburyport, Aug. 6, 1832, dau. of Charles E. and Ann (Huse) Schoff.

Their children were:

MARY PARKER, b. Aug. 26, 1856.

CHARLES SCHOFF PARKER, b. March 23, 1860.

HERMAN PARKER, b. Jan. 2, 1866; m. April 15, 1891, Lillian H. Percival of Boston.

ALLSTON PARKER, b. June 20, 1869; d. Feb. 6, 1870.

ROSS PARKER, b. June 17, 1871.

Elizabeth Leman Parker (see page 303) (*Charles,[7] Josiah,[6] Peter,[5] John,[4] John,[3] Hananiah,[2] Thomas[1]*), dau. of Charles and Mary Hildreth (Wallingford) Parker, was b. in Framingham, July 4, 1835; m. June 2, 1859, Nathan Dyer Robinson of Bridgewater. She d. in Roxbury, Nov. 8, 1885.

Their children were:

1. Harry Parker Robinson, b. June 22, 1861.
2. Edward Standish Robinson, b. Aug. 19, 1863.
3. Helen Wallingford Robinson, b. April 3, 1865; d. Dec. 15, 1868.
4. Nathan Stone Robinson, b. Nov. 28, 1866.
5. Channing Robinson, b. May 5, 1869.
6. Ethel Robinson, b. Jan. 13, 1873; d. Jan. 31, 1874.
7. Waldo Pierce Robinson, b. Feb. 18, 1875; d. Dec. 16, 1879.
8. Charles Edgar Robinson, b. March 5, 1876.
9. Elizabeth Dyer Robinson, b. March 31, 1884.

336. Edgar Parker (*Charles,[7] Josiah,[6] Peter,[5] John,[4] John,[3] Hananiah,[2] Thomas[1]*), son of Charles and Mary Hildreth (Wallingford) Parker, was b. in Framingham, June 7, 1840. He graduated from the Norwich Military University in 1859, and as M.D. from Harvard University in 1863. He then entered the army as assistant surgeon in the 13th Mass. Inf. He was taken prisoner twice and was severely wounded at the Battle of Gettysburg. He was in practice at Saxonville, Mass., 1866–70. He relinquished the practice of medicine in 1870 and adopted portrait painting as a profession, in which he achieved great success and a world-renowned reputation. Edgar Parker was a man of marked and general ability. He continued in his profession as an Artist, at his studio on Washington Street, Boston, returning daily to his home in Bridgewater, until he retired on account of his health, which was in the service of his country so roughly exposed. The painting of Charles Sumner which hangs in the State House is one of his works. He m. Jan. 28, 1864, Frances Ames Hyde of Bridgewater, dau. of Joseph A. Hyde. He d. in Bridgewater, April 9, 1892.

Their child was:

Joseph Hyde Parker, b. Dec. 12, 1865; d. May 24, 1866.

Edgar Parker.

337. James Edward Parker (*Edward C.*,[7] *Artemas*,[6] *Peter*,[5] *John*,[4] *John*,[3] *Hananiah*,[2] *Thomas*[1]), son of Edward C. and Mary (Leland) Parker, b. Feb. 19, 1834; m. Nov. 6, 1855, Susan Mason, b. April 13, 1833, dau. of Oliver and Maria Mason of Southbridge. He lived for 30 years in Framingham and Westborough, during which time he was in the straw hat business and was a manufacturer of straw hats a part of that time. He now resides in E. Holliston, where for nine years he has been station agent and postmaster.

Their children were:

BESSIE MARIA PARKER, b. in Westborough, Nov. 27, 1864.
EDWARD OLIVER PARKER, b. in Westborough, Oct. 23, 1868.

George Smith Parker (see page 305) (*George S.*,[7] *Artemas*,[6] *Peter*,[5] *John*,[4] *John*,[3] *Hananiah*,[2] *Thomas*[1]), son of George S. and Mary A. (White) Parker, was b. in Albany, N. Y., Oct. 2, 1832; m. in Framingham, Oct. 10, 1853, Mary A. Skahal. He resides in W. Medway, Mass. They have had seven children, of whom two are living:

1. GEORGE HENRY PARKER.
2. EVA L. PARKER.

338. Melvina Parker (*George S.*,[7] *Artemas*,[6] *Peter*,[5] *John*,[4] *John*,[3] *Hananiah*,[2] *Thomas*[1]), dau. of George S. and Mary Ann (White) Parker, was b. in Albany, N. Y., Dec. 9, 1834; m. (1) in Medway, May 24, 1854, Alvin B. Batchelder; m. (2) William Batchelder, who is also deceased.

Children by her first marriage were:

1. FRANCIS BATCHELDER.
2. ELIZA J. BATCHELDER.

339. Eliza Jane Parker (*George S.*,[7] *Artemas*,[6] *Peter*,[5] *John*,[4] *John*,[3] *Hananiah*,[2] *Thomas*[1]), dau. of George S. and Mary Ann (White) Parker, was b. in Albany, N. Y., Feb. 2, 1837; m. in Holliston, Aug. 15, 1852, Luther H. Turner, b. in Dedham, Oct. 22, 1832, son of Sabin and Deborah (Shephard) Turner. He was a ladies' hat bleacher. She resides in Chicago, Ill.

Their children were:

1. HERBERT W. TURNER, b. in Holliston, Oct. 5, 1858; m. Matilda Grimm.

2. Nellie Louise Turner, b. in Holliston, April 13, 1861; deceased.
3. Arthur Warren Turner, b. in Holliston, May 8, 1864; deceased.
4. Henry Luther Turner, b. in Holliston, March 17, 1866; m. Sophia Louise Kramer. Their child:
   1. Matilda Magdelene Turner, b. Jan. 27, 1888.
5. Ernest Sabin Turner, b. in Chicago, Ill., Feb. 20, 1868; deceased.
6. Mabel Eliza Turner, b. in Chicago, Sept. 1, 1870; deceased.
7. Frankie Turner, b. in Chicago, March 20, 1873; deceased.

340. Charles Augustus Parker (*George S.*,[7] *Artemas*,[6] *Peter*,[5] *John*,[4] *John*,[3] *Hananiah*,[2] *Thomas*[1]), son of George S. and Mary Ann (White) Parker, was b. in Holliston, Aug. 15, 1844; m. in Ashland, Aug. 7, 1864, Eliza A. Pettiss, b. in Sherborn, Nov., 1848, dau. of George E. and Sarah Pettiss. She d. in Oct., 1880. Mr. Parker was a leather cutter in Holliston. He enlisted for three years' service March 1, 1862, in the First Unattached Co., Mass. Heavy Artillery, in which he served. He resides in Togus, Me.

Their children were:

Warren W. Parker, b. July 13, 1867.
Alfred C. Parker, b. June 17, 1872.
Mabel Parker, b. Aug. 7, 1874.

341. Henry Emerson Parker (*George S.*,[7] *Artemas*,[6] *Peter*,[5] *John*,[4] *John*,[3] *Hananiah*,[2] *Thomas*[1]), son of George S. and Mary Ann (White) Parker, was b. in Holliston, Oct. 13, 1849; m. in Woonsocket, R. I., May 22, 1870, Ellen E. M. Jones, b. in Medway, Aug. 29, 1852, d. in Holliston, Sept. 1, 1880, dau. of Ellen M. and John Paul Jones. Mr. Parker is overseer in a shoe factory in Medway.

Their children were:

Harrison Walter Parker, b. in Holliston, Feb. 11, 1871; m. July 18, 1889, Nellie K. Ainslee, b. in Cohasset, Nov. 11, 1866, dau. of Edward P. and Eleanor (Runey) Ainslee.
Bertha Ellen Parker, b. in Holliston, Oct. 10, 1874.

342. Althea Wheelock Parker (*Curtis*,[7] *Artemas*,[6] *Peter*,[5] *John*,[4] *John*,[3] *Hananiah*,[2] *Thomas*[1]), dau. of Curtis and Eliza Jane (Horton) Parker, was b. in Natick, Nov. 21,

1843; m. in Natick, Nov. 19, 1868, John Lovett Sanger, native of Framingham, where his parents, Edwin and Harriet (Boynton) Sanger, are still living. He is a descendant of Richard Sanger, the emigrant ancestor of the name, who was among the early settlers of Sudbury and Watertown. He is in the shoe manufacturing business. They reside in Natick.

Their children were:

1. ESTELLE SANGER, b. and d. Oct. 1, 1870.
2. TALBOT PARKER SANGER (adopted son), b. Oct. 1, 1870; d. July 24, 1871.
3. HERBERT BOYNTON SANGER (adopted son), b. March 27, 1870.
4. FLORENCE VIRGINIA SANGER, b. July 16, and d. Dec. 8, 1872.
5. EDWIN TOWNSEND SANGER, b. Dec. 14, and d. Dec. 15, 1874.

343. Sumner Horton Parker (*Curtis,*[7] *Artemas,*[6] *Peter,*[5] *John,*[4] *John,*[3] *Hananiah,*[2] *Thomas*[1]), son of Curtis and Eliza Jane (Horton) Parker, was b. in Natick, Jan. 7, 1848; m. Nov. 21, 1873, Emma Jane Fay, b. in Grafton, Sept. 26, 1853, dau. of Wyman Fay. They lived in Natick. He d. May 28, 1886.

Their children were:

ETHEL ALTHEA PARKER, b. in Melrose, April 2, 1874.
SUMNER WYMAN PARKER, b. Aug. 26, 1876.

344. Emma S. Parker (*James,*[8] *John,*[7] *Philemon,*[6] *Jonas,*[5] *Andrew,*[4] *John,*[3] *Hananiah,*[2] *Thomas*[1]), dau. of James and Sophia (Hopkins) Parker, was b. in Chester, Vt., Aug. 17, 1851: m. Henry Philips.

Their dau. was:

1. BELLE PHILIPS, b. Oct. 30, 1878.

345. Nellie L. Parker (*James,*[8] *John,*[7] *Philemon,*[6] *Jonas,*[5] *Andrew,*[4] *John,*[3] *Hananiah,*[2] *Thomas*[1]), dau. of James and Sophia (Hopkins) Parker, was b. in Springfield, Vt., March 31, 1860; m. Tyler Putnam.

Their children were:

1. ADEN PUTNAM, b. June 28, 1875.
2. SOLON PUTNAM, b. May, 1877.
3. ARTHUR PUTNAM, b. July, 1879.
4. JOHN PUTNAM, b. Feb. 22, 1885.

346. Lizzie A. Parker (*James,*[8] *John,*[7] *Philemon,*[6] *Jonas,*[5] *Andrew,*[4] *John,*[3] *Hananiah,*[2] *Thomas*[1]), dau. of James and Susan (Balch) Parker, was b. April 23, 1866; m. Gilford Ellison.

Their dau. was:

1. BERTHA ELLISON, b. Jan. 8, 1887.

347. Fanny M. Parker (*Amos E.,*[8] *Joseph,*[7] *Amos,*[6] *Amos,*[5] *Andrew,*[4] *John,*[3] *Hananiah,*[2] *Thomas*[1]), dau. of Amos Earle and Matilda (Converse) Parker, was b. in Bakersfield, Vt., May 11, 1832; m. March 16, 1858, Ralph M. Blaisdell, b. May 14, 1813, son of Daniel and Mary Blaisdell of N. Cambridge, Vt. They reside in E. Fletcher, Vt.

Their son was:

1. LEON PARKER BLAISDELL, b. April 1, 1861.

348. Hollis Reid Parker (*Amos E.,*[8] *Joseph,*[7] *Amos,*[6] *Amos,*[5] *Andrew,*[4] *John,*[3] *Hananiah,*[2] *Thomas*[1]), son of Amos Earle and Matilda (Converse) Parker, was b. in Bakersfield, Vt., Aug. 1, 1835; m. Mary M. Morrow of Penn., b. 1845, They reside in Chicago, Ill. They have one daughter.

349. Jane A. Parker (*Amos E.,*[8] *Joseph,*[7] *Amos,*[6] *Amos,*[5] *Andrew,*[4] *John,*[3] *Hananiah,*[2] *Thomas*[1]), dau. of Amos Earle and Matilda (Converse) Parker, was b. in Bakersfield, Vt., June 20, 1838; m. July 17, 1859, Reuben H. Blackstone, b. June 27, 1834, son of Daniel Blackstone, a native of Maine. The original ancestry of this family in America were the three brothers of this name who, it is said, came from England and settled in Maine. Mr. Blackstone served in the late war, from which he contracted disease, owing to the hardships which he endured. He d. in N. Groton, N. H., Oct. 20, 1884.

Their children were:

1. SUMNER EARLE BLACKSTONE, b. Jan. 2, 1868; is now practicing law in E. Saginaw, Mich.
2. SUSIE BELLE BLACKSTONE, b. Oct. 20, 1874.

Sumner Earl Parker (see page 310) (*Amos E.,*[8] *Joseph,*[7] *Amos,*[6] *Amos,*[5] *Andrew,*[4] *John,*[3] *Hananiah,*[2] *Thomas*[1]), son of Amos Earle and Matilda (Converse) Parker, was b. Oct.

28, 1839. He enlisted in Co. H, Second Vt. Reg., in 1861. He was with his regiment in every battle in which it was engaged until he fell at the storming of Fredericksburg Heights. One-half hour of intense suffering and the loyal soldier breathed his last. With his last breath he said to his comrades, "Tell father I died at my post." His was one noble life among the many given for his country in the hour of peril.

350. Worcester R. Parker *(Amos E.,[8] Joseph,[7] Amos,[6] Amos,[5] Andrew,[4] John,[3] Hananiah,[2] Thomas[1])*, son of Amos Earle and Matilda (Converse) Parker, was b. in Bakersfield, Vt., July 24, 1842; m. (1) Feb. 13, 1867, Emma F. Chase, youngest dau. of Isaac N. Chase of Barre, Vt., and who was of the same family as Chief Justice Chase of the U. S. Court. She d. Dec. 12, 1872, and he m. (2) Hattie Pearson, youngest dau. of Charles and Jane (Greenleaf) Pearson, and reside in Fletcher, Vt. Mrs. Jane G. Pearson is still living, being the only survivor of the remarkable family of 22 children. Mr. Parker is a farmer.

The dau. of Worcester R. and Emma F. (Chase) Parker was:

EUNICE M. PARKER, b. Sept. 30, 1871.

351. Joseph Albert Parker *(Frederick A.,[8] Joseph,[7] Amos,[6] Amos,[5] Andrew,[4] John,[3] Hananiah,[2] Thomas[1])*, son of Frederick A. and Caroline (Maxson) Parker, was b. Aug. 1, 1842; m. in New York city, Dec. 31, 1860, Samantha Wing Price. They reside in Philadelphia, Pa.

Their children were:

432. CHARLES FREDERICK PARKER, b. March 4, 1864; m. Emma Kunzig.
GEORGE WASHINGTON PARKER, b. July 14, 1867.
JOSEPH ALBERT PARKER, b. Nov. 1, 1868.
IDA FRANCES PARKER, b. Aug. 26, 1870; d. March 28, 1873.
ROBERTA BAYNE PARKER, b. Nov. 6, 1874; d. March 28, 1885.
JAMES BENJAMIN B. PARKER, b. Feb. 6, and d. May 14, 1880.
THEODORE DE KLINE PARKER, b. June 12, 1881.
JOHN RICHARD PARKER, b. June 21, 1885.

352. Christianna Parker *(Frederick A.,[8] Joseph,[7] Amos,[6] Amos,[5] Andrew,[4] John,[3] Hananiah,[2] Thomas[1])*, dau. of Frederick A. and Caroline (Maxson) Parker, was b. Jan. 17, 1844; m. June 10, 1867, Emil Neesen, son of Baldwin and Bertha Neesen of Brooklyn, N. Y., where they reside.

Their children were:

1. OTIE NEESEN, b. Oct. 28, 1869.
2. VICTOR NEESEN, b. Sept. 2, 1872.
3. HARRY NEESEN, b. Aug. 20, 1874.
4. FLORENCE NEESEN, b. July 3, 1877.

353. Sarah Parker *(Frederick A.,[8] Joseph,[7] Amos,[6] Amos,[5] Andrew,[4] John,[3] Hananiah,[2] Thomas[1])*, dau. of Frederick A. and Caroline (Maxson) Parker; m. Nov. 30, 1862, Henry Calenberg, well known as a manufacturer of pianos, of Brooklyn, N. Y. They reside in New Rochelle, N. Y.

Their children were:

1. EMMA LOUISE CALENBERG, b. Sept. 23, 1863.
2. HENRY CALENBERG, b. Oct. 1, 1865.
3. SARAH CALENBERG, b. Oct. 21, 1867.
4. MARY IDA CALENBERG, b. June 4, 1871.
5. LILLIE CALENBERG, b. July 31, 1874.
6. BLANCHE IRENE CALENBERG, b. Oct. 22, 1879.
7. EDNA MARION CALENBERG, b. Nov. 6, 1883.

355. Horace F. Parker *(Amos,[8] Sylvester,[7] Amos,[6] Amos,[5] Andrew,[4] John,[3] Hananiah,[2] Thomas[1])*, son of Amos and Lorinda (Fairbanks) Parker, was b. in Kirby, Vt., Oct. 6, 1829; m. in Charlestown, Vt., May 30, 1853, Mary Mianda Cole, b. March 25, 1832, dau. of Lathrop Cole of Charlestown. They reside in Denver, Col.

Their children were:

CORA I. PARKER, b. in Charlestown, Vt., Dec. 4, 1855; m. Jan. 2, 1876, C. W. Warner of St. Johnsbury, Vt. They reside in Denver, Col.

AMOS L. PARKER, b. in Hatley, P. Q., Feb. 20, 1860; m. in Danville, Vt., June 11, 1884, Nanena S. Chaffee. They reside in Denver, Col.

356. Sophia W. Parker *(Amos,[8] Sylvester,[7] Amos,[6] Amos,[5] Andrew,[4] John,[3] Hananiah,[2] Thomas[1])*, dau. of Amos and Lorinda (Fairbanks) Parker, b. Nov. 5, 1837; m. in E.

Burke, Vt., March 11, 1857, Joseph H. Smith, b. Sept. 10, 1833, son of Olney Smith and grandson of Eric Smith. They reside in Lyndonville, Vt.

Their children were:

1. ELEANOR A. SMITH, b. June 24, 1859; m. Jan. 1, 1884, Frank H. Davis. Their children:
   - I. FRED E. DAVIS, b. Jan. 1, 1886.
   - II. WILLIE H. DAVIS, b. May 17, 1889.
2. WILLIAM H. SMITH, b. Feb. 20, 1863; d. March 18, 1886.
3. HERBERT B. SMITH, b. Jan. 8, 1871; d. June 9, 1880.

354. George F. Parker (*Frederick A.*,[8] *Joseph*,[7] *Amos*,[6] *Amos*,[5] *Andrew*,[4] *John*,[3] *Hananiah*,[2] *Thomas*[1]), son of Frederick A. and Caroline (Maxson) Parker; m. April 28, 1874, Louisa Ross, b. in New York, Aug. 7, 1854, dau. of Wendall and Eva Ross, and resides in New York city. Mr. Parker is in the piano business.

Their children, all b. in New York city, were:

GEORGE EDWARD PARKER, b. April 30, 1875.
CARRIE EVA PARKER, b. Aug. 3, 1876; deceased.
ARTHUR WENDALL PARKER, b. July 29, 1878; deceased.
FREDERICK ANDREW PARKER, b. June 18, 1880.
EVA K. PARKER, b. Sept. 29, 1881.
FERDINAND CHARLES PARKER, b. June 11, 1886.
SADIE KATH PARKER, b. Nov. 19, 1888.

357. Ann Elizabeth Parker (*Amos*,[8] *Sylvester*,[7] *Amos*,[6] *Amos*,[5] *Andrew*,[4] *John*,[3] *Hananiah*,[2] *Thomas*[1]), dau. of Amos and Lorinda (Fairbanks) Parker, was b. Nov. 1, 1840; m. in E. Burke, Vt., May 26, 1858, Josiah D. Smith, and reside in Burke.

Their children were all b. in Newark, Vt.:

1. MARY L. SMITH, b. Jan. 13, 1864; m. Jan. 1, 1884, Frank B. Garfield of Newark, Vt. They have two children:
   - I. LULU M. GARFIELD, b. Sept. 22, 1884.
   - II. LEON GARFIELD, b. Jan. 23, 1886.
2. CHARLES L. SMITH, b. Nov. 14, 1871.
3. EDWARD J. SMITH, b. Jan. 19, 1873.

358. Adaline L. Parker (*Joel D.*,[8] *Sylvester*,[7] *Amos*,[6] *Amos*,[5] *Andrew*,[4] *John*,[3] *Hananiah*,[2] *Thomas*[1]), dau. of Joel

D. and Lucy (Wyman) Parker, was b. in Hatley, P. Q., March 1, 1829; m. Asahel P. Parker, son of Daniel and Cynthia (Huntington) Parker. Daniel was son of Thomas and Betsey (Porter) Parker, who came in 1800 from "Charleston No. 4" to Compton, P. Q. Asahel and Adaline Parker reside in Hatley.

They have one dau.:

VELARIA A. PARKER, b. Oct. 31, 1851; m. Frank W. Maloney. They have one son:

1. PERCY H. MALONEY, b. Jan. 15, 1878.

359. Levi E. Parker *(Joel D.,[8] Sylvester,[7] Amos,[6] Amos,[5] Andrew,[4] John,[3] Hananiah,[2] Thomas[1])*, son of Joel D. and Lucy (Wyman) Parker, was b. in Hatley, P. Q., Aug. 5, 1830; m. Maria Howe. He is a general merchant in Hatley, where he resides.

They have one son:

LINDSAY E. PARKER.

360. Amanda M. Parker *(Joel D.,[8] Sylvester,[7] Amos,[6] Amos,[5] Andrew,[4] John,[3] Hananiah,[2] Thomas[1])*, dau. of Joel D. and Lucy (Wyman) Parker, was b. in Hatley, P. Q., June 23, 1836; m. Oct. 15, 1869, Alfred Ives of Hatley, b. Oct. 3, 1822, son of Harley and Martha (Sleeper) Ives. They reside in Hatley.

They have one dau.:

1. MYRTIE IVES, b. Sept. 1, 1874.

"Harley Ives' paternal grandfather's name was Joseph Ives. He m. Clarissa Hall. They were both from Meriden, Ct., and came to Canada in 1793. The family have no authentic account of their ancestry, but tradition says they were among the early emigrants to the New England colonies. He was a man of energy and his posterity with hardly an exception have been intelligent and useful members of the community, some of whom have occupied prominent positions in public life. We find them generally identified with the different branches of the Christian Church. His (Alfred's) maternal grandfather's name was Hezekiah Sleeper. A family of this name came from England about the year 1700 and settled in New Hampshire. The branch of this family described in this sketch remained loyal to the government of England during the struggle of the Colonies for independence. And Hezekiah Sleeper, then a child, removed early in life to Vermont, where he married Hannah Batchelder. Not satisfied with the government and laws they came in 1801 to Canada and settled in Stanstead. Mr. Sleeper was a captain of militia and took an active part in the War of 1812 in organizing companies to defend the border against invasion. This couple lived to see their ten children, five girls and five boys, grown up and settled in life. No one in the community was more esteemed than Mr. Sleeper. He died the 23rd of Sept., 1849, at the age of 79 years. His wife lived to see her great-great-grandchildren and died in Aug., 1871, at the age of 93. The oldest child, a daughter, married Harley Ives of Hatley, neither of whom are living."

361. Edwin W. Parker *(Joel D.,[8] Sylvester,[7] Amos,[6] Amos,[5] Andrew,[4] John,[3] Hananiah,[2] Thomas[1])*, son of Joel D. and Lucy (Wyman) Parker, was b. in Hatley, P. Q., March 13, 1842; m. May 6, 1868, Adella H. Gordon, dau. of John Gordon and granddau. of Phineas Gordon of New Hampshire. Mr. Parker began active life at the age of 20, when for six years he was a successful teacher and teacher of music. He then entered the mercantile business in company with his brother, L. E. Parker, and continued for ten years. The four years following he was in business alone in Hatley, after which he with his family removed to Martinville, Que., and opened trade in a general store which has been successful. Mrs. Parker is president of the W. C. T. U. Mr. Parker and his wife are both earnest workers in the temperance cause.

Their children were:

EDWIN GORDON PARKER, b. April 23, 1869.
ALBERT L. PARKER, b. May 23, 1871.
JOHN J. PARKER, b. Feb. 22, 1877.

362. Alba W. Parker *(Joel D.,[8] Sylvester,[7] Amos,[6] Amos,[5] Andrew,[4] John,[3] Hananiah,[2] Thomas[1])*, son of Joel D. and Lucy (Wyman) Parker, was b. in Ayers Flat, P. Q., June 18, 1845. When of age he engaged himself as head clerk of a Minnesota hotel, which position he held two and one-half years. Returning home he was with his brother, Levi E. Parker, in the mercantile business for one year, until Nov., 1872, when he became connected with the Passumpsic R. R.

At first telegraph operator, express agent and spare station agent he soon became regular station agent, which position he held for 15 years. Mr. Parker, characteristic of his family, has always been a very busy man. While at Ayers Flat 15 years he had in connection with his railroad business a general store, was engaged very extensively in buying and selling hemlock bark and railroad wood and ties, and was sheriff for five years. Resigning in Nov., 1887, he raised an excursion party of 46 which he brought through to the Pacific coast. Since that time he has been engaged in the mercantile business, at present at Los Angeles, Cal., where he and his family reside. He m. July 2, 1875, Ethel Emery, b. May 24, 1859, dau. of Lucius Emery, a well-to-do farmer of Canada.

Their children were:

BERTHA M. PARKER, b. July 5, 1876.
FREDERICK E. PARKER, b. Feb. 22, 1878.
GERTRUDE M. PARKER, b. April 14, 1880.

363. Orville H. Parker (*Joel D.*,[8] *Sylvester*,[7] *Amos*,[6] *Amos*,[5] *Andrew*,[4] *John*,[3] *Hananiah*,[2] *Thomas*[1]), son of Joel D. and Lucy (Wyman) Parker, was b. June 1, 1848; m. Sept. 10, 1872, Betsey Ann Bowen, b. Sept. 10, 1850, dau. of Benjamin F. and Mary (Putney) Bowen of Compton, Canada, and granddau. of Joseph Bowen of Compton and Caleb Putney, native of Peacham, Vt. He is a farmer in Hatley, P. Q.

Their children were:

WALTER DAVIDSON PARKER, b. June 26, 1873.
MARY ANN PARKER, b. April 24, 1875.
EDNA LUELLA PARKER, b. July 30, 1877.
CORA LOUISE PARKER, b. July 27, 1878; d. Feb. 25, 1879.
ELSIE RHOENA PARKER, b. March 16, 1881.
LEON HERBERT PARKER, b. Dec. 9, 1883.
ETHEL FLORENCE PARKER, b. Jan. 5, 1889.

364. Eliza E. Parker (*Samuel*,[8] *Sylvester*,[7] *Amos*,[6] *Amos*,[5] *Andrew*,[4] *John*,[3] *Hananiah*,[2] *Thomas*[1]), dau. of Samuel W. and Harriet (Field) Parker, was b. Aug. 5, 1853; m. Nov. 6, 1874, Edward H. Boden. They reside in Duarte, Los Angeles Co., Cal. He is a cultivator of oranges.

Their children were:

1. Grace F. Boden, b. May 12, 1878.
2. Susie H. Boden, b. Nov. 27, 1883.
3. Bertha G. Boden, b. June 6, 1885.

365. Sarah Emily Parker *(Amos A.,[8] Amory,[7] Amos,[6] Amos,[5] Andrew,[4] John,[3] Hananiah,[2] Thomas[1])*, dau. of Amos A. and Cynthia (Pratt) Parker, was b. in Cavendish, Vt., Aug. 9, 1842; m. in Cavendish, June 9, 1864, Lewis Russell, b. Sept. 21, 1821. They reside in Cavendish.

Their children were:

1. Lydia Maria Russell, b. March 10, 1865; m. in Cavendish, Feb. 4, 1883, Elmer Buck, b. Jan. 3, 1839. One dau.:
   1. Addie Alice Buck, b. Oct. 30, 1886.
2. Julia Emma Russell, b. Oct. 15, 1867.
3. Martha Ann Russell, b. March 10, 1870; m. in Chester, Vt., April 29, 1889, Albert H. Reed, b. in Andover, Vt., April 13, 1869.
4. Flora Lena Russell, b. Sept. 17, 1876.

366. Mary Frances Parker *(Amos A.,[8] Amory,[7] Amos,[6] Amos,[5] Andrew,[4] John,[3] Hananiah,[2] Thomas[1])*, dau. of Amos A. and Cynthia (Pratt) Parker, was b. in Cavendish, Vt., May 9, 1849; m. March 23, 1871, Lyman Howard of Windham, Vt. They reside in N. Windham, Vt.

They have two children:

1. Levi Joseph Howard, b. in Rockingham, Vt., Dec. 25, 1872. } Twins.
2. Lyma Andrew Howard, b. in Rockingham, Vt., Dec. 25, 1872. } Twins.

367. George W. Parker *(Amos A.,[8] Amory,[7] Amos,[6] Amos,[5] Andrew,[4] John,[3] Hananiah,[2] Thomas[1])*, son of Amos A. and Cynthia (Pratt) Parker, was b. in Cavendish, Vt., Nov. 25, 1854; m. Oct. 13, 1880, Mary E. Rist, b. Feb. 7, 1850, in No. 14, Warren Co., N. Y., dau. of Elijah and Mary Rist. Elijah Rist was a native of Reading, Vt., while his wife Mary was b. in No. 13, Warren Co., N. Y., March 13, 1821. Mr. Parker is a farmer in So. Reading, Vt.

Their children are:

William Darius Parker, b. Jan. 1, 1886.
Lois Alzina Parker, b. July 8, 1889.

368. Emily M. Parker *(Perley,[8] Gardiner,[7] Isaac,[6] Amos,[5] Andrew,[4] John,[3] Hananiah,[2] Thomas[1])*, dau. of Perley and Betsey (Mellen) Parker, was b. in Hopkinton, Sept. 11, 1818; m. in Northborough, Feb. 10, 1841, John Crooks of Hopkinton. He was a boot and shoe cutter. They reside in Hopkinton.

Their children were:

1. John Parker Crooks, b. Aug. 29, 1846; m. Dec. 24, 1868, Jennie O. Grout. They reside in N. Brookfield. Children:
   - i. Emmie L. Crooks, b. Oct. 15, 1870; m. Aug. 28, 1888, Arthur Thompson of N. Brookfield, and had two children.
   - ii. Henry B. Crooks, b. Nov. 10, 1872.
   - iii. Stearns Crooks, b. March 29, 1875.
   - iv. George F. Crooks, b. Oct. 15, 1879.
   - v. Florence Crooks, b. May 12, and d. Aug. 10, 1882.
2. Stearns S. Crooks, b. April 30, 1851; m. Sept. 12, 1875, Carrie Coryell of Detroit, Mich. Children:
   - i. John S. Crooks, b. July 6, 1878.
   - ii. Fred Crooks, b. Sept., 1878; d. June, 1879.

369. Gardner Parker *(Perley,[8] Gardiner,[7] Isaac,[6] Amos,[5] Andrew,[4] John,[3] Hananiah,[2] Thomas[1])*, son of Perley and Betsey (Mellen) Parker, was b. in Hopkinton, May 13, 1821; m. Dec. 9, 1844, Mary L. Sawyer of Boston, b. in Gloucester, Dec. 5, 1823, dau. of Capt. George P. and Judith R. Sawyer. He was a trader in Hopkinton and a dealer in horses. He is now a slate dealer and proprietor of the Parker House in Poultney, Vt.

Their children, all b. in Hopkinton, were:

433. Emma Eliza Parker, b. Nov. 2, 1845; m. Roswel I. Frail of Hopkinton.

Mary Carrie Parker, b. March 20, 1847; m. in Poultney, Vt., May 13, 1874, Martin D. Cole. They removed to Castleton, Vt., where he was cashier of the bank, and where she d. Nov. 8, 1878. He survives her. No children.

434. George Gardner Parker, b. in Hopkinton, Oct. 25, 1849; m. Mandana Hyde of Poultney, Vt.

435. Edgar Vinton Parker, b. in Hopkinton, Aug. 18, 1855; m. Lillie C. Butterworth.

370. J. Mellen Parker *(Perley,[8] Gardiner,[7] Isaac,[6] Amos,[5] Andrew,[4] John,[3] Hananiah,[2] Thomas[1])*, son of Perley and Betsey (Mellen) Parker, was b. in Hopkinton, March 30, 1829; m. Sarah L. Curtis of Hopkinton.

Their son:

CURTIS PARKER, b. in Hopkinton, Sept. 4, 1854.

371. Sarah Parker *(Daniel,[8] Otis,[7] Isaac,[6] Amos,[5] Andrew,[4] John,[3] Hananiah,[2] Thomas[1])*, dau. of Daniel and Polly (White) Parker, was b. in Hubbardston, Oct. 15, 1835; m. Jan. 1, 1857, Henry C. Work of Hartford, Ct. She d. Oct. 2, 1882. He d. June 7, 1884.

Their children were:

1. WALDO F. WORK, b. in Chicago, Ill., Oct. 2, 1857; d. in Greenwich Village, July 2, 1871.
2. WILLIE L. WORK, b. in Hyde Park, Ill., Dec. 10, 1861; d. July 22, 1862.
3. ELLEN L. WORK, b. in Hyde Park, Ill., Oct. 9, 1863; m. Robert Austin of Brooklyn, N. Y., where they now reside.
4. CLARA E. WORK, b. in Vineland, N. J., April 13, and d. Aug., 1868.

372. Daniel Webster Parker *(Daniel,[8] Otis,[7] Isaac,[6] Amos,[5] Andrew,[4] John,[3] Hananiah,[2] Thomas[1])*, son of Daniel and Polly (White) Parker, was b. in Hubbardston, June 13, 1841; m. Aug. 7, 1865, Fannie E. Morse. He d. Oct. 10, 1875, and she m. June 7, 1880, his brother, Abel Otis Parker, and resides in Greenwich Village.

Their children were:

FRANK LEON PARKER, b. Oct. 1, 1868.
CHARLES MORSE PARKER, b. Jan. 28, and d. May 14, 1871.

373. Abel Otis Parker *(Daniel,[8] Otis,[7] Isaac,[6] Amos,[5] Andrew,[4] John,[3] Hananiah,[2] Thomas[1])*, son of Daniel and Polly (White) Parker, was b. in Hubbardston, Dec. 20, 1847; m. June 7, 1880, Fannie E. (Morse) Parker (widow of Daniel Webster Parker) of Greenwich. They reside in Greenwich Village.

Their son:

WEBSTER MORSE PARKER, b. July 4, 1883.

374. Lucy Parker *(Otis,[8] Otis,[7] Isaac,[6] Amos,[5] Andrew,[4] John,[3] Hananiah,[2] Thomas[1])*, dau. of Otis and Eunice (Allen) Parker, was b. in Hubbardston, Nov. 25, 1830; m. (1) May 1, 1849, James S. Baker of Worcester, b. in Stamford, Vt., Nov. 26, 1827, son of Bazaleel C. (native of Salem, Mass.) and Mary I. (Brown) Baker (native of Cape Cod). He was an iron moulder. He d. Jan. 7, 1859. Mrs. Lucy (Parker) Baker m. (2) Sept. 16, 1860, Charles Lester of Wisconsin, b. in Sandy Creek, N. Y. They reside in Adrian, Minn., where he is a farmer.

The children of James S. and Lucy (Parker) Baker were:

1. Cecelia L. Baker, b. Jan. 18, 1851; d. of consumption, March 6, 1872.
2. Edna A. Baker, b. Sept. 24, 1853; d. of consumption, Aug. 6, 1868.
3. James H. Baker, b. Sept. 26, 1855. He lives in Adrian, Minn.
4. Henrietta M. Baker, b. Jan. 10, 1858; d. of dropsy, Dec. 21, 1868.

The children of Charles and Mrs. Lucy (Parker) (Baker) Lester were:

5. Esther A. Lester, b. Sept. 2, 1861; m. Feb. 21, 1882, Erastus R. Gibbs. She d. of consumption, Jan. 2, 1891, leaving three sons:
   i. Roy R. Gibbs, b. July 30, 1883.
   ii. Otis W. Gibbs, b. March 6, 1885.
   iii. Ora H. Gibbs, b. Oct. 9, 1889.
6. William O. Lester, b. Feb. 10, 1866; m. Nov. 1, 1891, Bell Osher. He is editor of *The Citizen*, Hecla, So. Dakota. They have dau.:
   i. Cora Esther Lester, b. Aug. 12, 1892.
7. Amanda I. Lester, b. June 11, 1867; d. July 14, 1869.
8. Elmer R. Lester, b. Aug. 28, 1870.

375. Avalina Parker *(Otis,[8] Otis,[7] Isaac,[6] Amos,[5] Andrew,[4] John,[3] Hananiah,[2] Thomas[1])*, dau. of Otis and Eunice (Allen) Parker, was b. in Hubbardston, June 21, 1833; m. in Hubbardston, Nov. 19, 1854, Joseph Willard Rice of Hubbardston, b. April 7, 1822, son of Ralph Rice. They removed (1) to Worcester, Mass., (2) to Crawford Co., Wis., from whence he enlisted and served in the War of the

Rebellion. He was wounded in battle and died two weeks afterwards from its effects, Dec. 13, 1862. Mr. Rice was a carpenter and millwright. She m. (2) Barnett Daywitt of Wisconsin. They removed to Minnesota. She d. in Windom, Minn., July 13, 1878. He d. May, 1886.

The children of Joseph W. and Avalina (Parker) Rice were:

1. JOHN WILLARD RICE, b. in Milwaukee, Wis., Nov. 20, 1856; m. in Amo, Cottonwood Co., Minn., May 3, 1886, Charity L. Clough, b. in Jackson, Minn., Dec. 1, 1866. She d. May 27, 1888. He is a carpenter and resides in Windom, Minn. Their son:
   i. JESSE WILLARD RICE, b. in Windom, Minn., March 8, 1887.
2. FREDERICK OTICE RICE, b. in Crawford Co., Wis., Nov. 28, 1859; d. Nov. 21, 1862.
3. HARRIET ELIZABETH RICE, b. in Crawford Co., Wis., June 20, 1861.

The children of Barnett and Avalina (Parker) (Rice) Daywitt were:

4. ALVIN B. DAYWITT, b. in Crawford Co., Wis., April 1, 1865.
5. CORA E. DAYWITT, b. in Crawford Co., Wis., June 28, 1867; m. Feb., 1882, James Ward. Their children are:
   i. AVA WARD. ii. ALLIE WARD. iii. JENNIE WARD.

376. Elmer Parker *(Otis,[8] Otis,[7] Isaac,[6] Amos,[5] Andrew,[4] John,[3] Hananiah,[2] Thomas[1])*, son of Otis and Eunice (Allen) Parker, was b. in Hubbardston, Aug. 30, 1836; m. Sarah J. Hallock, b. in New Milford, Ct., April 30, 1837, dau. of Russell and Sally (Whitehead) Hallock. They settled first in Ashland; removed to Worcester, where they now reside. He enlisted from Templeton, Aug. 5, 1862, in Co. D, 13th Mass. Reg. He served two years, being discharged Aug. 1, 1864. He was most of the time on detached service. He was 11 months assistant steward at Alexandria, for seven months he had charge of the deserters' eating quarters. Mr. Parker is a woodworker.

Their son:

OTIS R. PARKER, b. July 28, 1866. He resides in Worcester.

Elizabeth L. Parker (see page 332) (*Otis,[8] Otis,[7] Isaac,[6] Amos,[5] Andrew,[4] John,[3] Hananiah,[2] Thomas[1]*), dau. of Otis and Eunice (Allen) Parker, was b. in Hubbardston, July 23, 1842; m. in Rochester, Vt., Oct. 8, 1862, John G. Allen of Sterling, b. May 22, 1833, son of Nathan and Harriet (Greenleaf) Allen. They reside in Sterling.

Their children were:

1. Charles O. Allen, b. July 28, 1864; m. in Pittsfield, Vt., March 12, 1888, Effie Martin of Pittsfield, Vt.
2. Hattie E. Allen, b. June 20, 1867.
3. Miner S. Allen, b. Aug. 6, 1873.
4. Frank E. Allen, b. May 17, 1875.
5. Alice L. Allen, b. April 8, 1878.
6. Archie Allen, b. July 14, 1882.
7. J. Winfield Allen, b. March 24, 1884.

377. Addison Leslie Parker (*Jabez,[8] Jabez,[7] Isaac,[6] Amos,[5] Andrew,[4] John,[3] Hananiah,[2] Thomas[1]*), son of Jabez M. and Azubah P. (Powers) Parker, was b. in Phillipston, June 28, 1831; m. Nov. 15, 1854, Mary M. Buxton. They reside in Keene, N. H.

Their children were:

Henry Eugene Parker, b. in Phillipston, March 22, 1859; m. Dec. 25, 1884, Sadie E. Towne, b. Aug. 23, 1858. Their son:

1. Eugene Henry Parker, b. in North Adams, June 9, 1886.

Ida Elmira Parker, b. in Phillipston, Oct. 31, 1861; d. 1874.

Earnest Leslie Parker, b. in Keene, N. H., Jan. 22, 1867; m. July 14, 1888, Bertha C. Tasker, b. June 16, 1869. Their dau.:

1. Ida Bertha Parker, b. in Attleborough, Aug. 14, 1889.

Alice Mary Parker, b. in Keene, N. H., Feb. 26, 1873.

378. Isabella Brown Parker (*Jabez,[8] Jabez,[7] Isaac,[6] Amos,[5] Andrew,[4] John,[3] Hananiah,[2] Thomas[1]*), dau. of Jabez M. and Azubah P. (Powers) Parker, was b. in Roxbury, N. H., Feb. 17, 1834; m. 1855, Asa B. Turner. They reside in W. Gardner.

Their children were:

1. Hattie E. Turner, b. 1856; m. 1877, Frank P. Sawyer, and reside in Clinton.
2. Herbert L. Turner, b. and d. 1863.

379. Pherona E. Parker *(Enoch,[8] Jabez,[7] Isaac,[6] Amos,[5] Andrew,[4] John,[3] Hananiah,[2] Thomas[1])*, dau. of Enoch A. and Rebecca (Gibbs) Parker, was b. July 7, 1834: m. Sept. 2, 1857, John S. Leach, son of Joseph Leach of Rockingham, Vt., and Jerusha Allen of Hopkinton, N. H., natives of Sturbridge, Mass. They reside in Westminster, Vt.

Their children were:

1. EMMA E. LEACH, b. Sept. 11, 1858.
2. WALTER P. LEACH, b. March 26, 1860.
3. HERBERT W. LEACH, b. Dec. 27, 1861.
4. JOHN E. LEACH, b. Feb. 6, 1864.

380. Perry Ander Parker *(Enoch,[8] Jabez,[7] Isaac,[6] Amos,[5] Andrew,[4] John,[3] Hananiah,[2] Thomas[1])*, son of Enoch A. and Rebecca (Gibbs) Parker, was b. in Roxbury, N. H., Nov. 30, 1838; m. in St. Charles, Ill., March 22, 1861, Mary Russell, b. in Gilsum, N. H., July 17, 1838, dau. of Joseph B. and Sidia (Farr) Russell. He is a teamster. They reside in Aurora, Ill.

Their children are:

436. RICHARD E. PARKER, b. in Keene, N. H., Oct. 5, 1861; m. Hattie Grout.

437. CARRIE B. PARKER, b. in Westminster, Vt., Nov. 8, 1863; m. Gilbert C. Sibley.

438. ELLA M. PARKER, b. in Sugar Grove, Ill., March 9, 1865; m. Frank McCannon.

LILLA E. PARKER, b. in Sugar Grove, Ill., Oct. 22, 1871.

KATIE M. PARKER, b. in Plainfield, Ill., Jan. 24, 1874.

381. Joel Damon Parker *(Joel,[8] Jabez,[7] Isaac,[6] Amos,[5] Andrew,[4] John,[3] Hananiah,[2] Thomas[1])*, son of Joel Dodge Parker, was b. May 7, 1836; m. Dec. 26, 1864, Catharine M. Whitney, b. in Dorchester, Dec. 26, 1843, dau. of Francis N. and Catharine (Bird) Whitney. They reside in Phillipston upon the old homestead formerly owned by Major Elisha Parker. Mr. Parker is a manufacturer of chairs in what was formerly the cotton factory.

Their children were:

JASON DAMON PARKER, b. Oct. 2, 1865; d. April 13, 1878.

EDWARD MYRON PARKER, b. Sept. 23, 1869.

FRANCIS WOOD PARKER, b. Sept. 12, 1872.
ALICE EDNA M. PARKER, b. July 2, 1885.

382. Amine Cecelia Parker (*James M. L.,*[8] *Jabez,*[7] *Isaac,*[6] *Amos,*[5] *Andrew,*[4] *John,*[3] *Hananiah,*[2] *Thomas*[1]), dau. of James M. L. and Polly H. (Kidder) Parker, was b. in Hillsborough, N. H., July 12, 1839; m. George Fowles. They reside in Forestville, Door Co., Wis.

Their son:

GEORGE ANSEL MAYNARD PARKER FOWLES.

383. Maynard Tillotson Parker (*James M. L.,*[8] *Jabez,*[7] *Isaac,*[6] *Amos,*[5] *Andrew,*[4] *John,*[3] *Hananiah,*[2] *Thomas*[1]), was b. in Roxbury, N. H., Oct. 30, 1850; m. July 1, 1880, at Ahnapee, Wis., Mary A. Overbeck, b. in Lake Mills, Wis., Nov. 25, 1854, dau. of Rev. Henry and Hannah F. (Vollmer) Overbeck.

Maynard T. Parker came with his parents to the West about the year 1854, first settling at Racine, Wis., removing with his parents from that city to Ahnapee, then called Wolf River, in 1855, and has ever since been a resident of that place. He received such common school training as was obtainable in a Western town in those days, later spending some time as a student at Ripon College. He was for a time after leaving school engaged in teaching; later took up the study of law and was admitted to practice in October, 1879, and has since practiced his profession. Mr. Parker was engaged in newspaper work as one of the editors and proprietors of *The Ahnapee Record*, from 1881 to 1884. He has held several offices of honor and trust, among them being that of city clerk, which office he held for several terms. He was city attorney two terms, and held the office of district attorney of Kewaunee County by appointment of Gov. Rusk. He is now serving his fifth term as mayor of the city of Ahnapee, having been five times elected to that office without opposition. Mr. Parker is a senior member of the law firm of Parker & Decker, solicitors of the Ahnapee & Western Railway Company. Besides the practice of law he is engaged in several business enterprises, being a stockholder and the present secretary of the Ahnapee Veneer and Seating Company, and is also engaged in the insurance and real estate business. Mr. Parker is a Republican in politics and is secretary of the Republican Club of his city.

Their children were:

MABEL CECELIA PARKER, b. in Ahnapee, Wis., Aug. 20, 1881.
EDGAR JAMES PARKER, b. in Ahnapee, April 19, 1886.
IONE LOUISE PARKER, b. in Ahnapee, Nov. 23, 1888.

384. Charles Duffield Parker *(Hollis G.,[8] Lewis,[7] Isaac,[6] Amos,[5] Andrew,[4] John,[3] Hananiah,[2] Thomas[1])*, son of Hollis Gardner and Laura A. (Goodrich) Parker, was b. in Philadelphia, Pa., June 19, 1861; m. in Atlanta, Ga., Dec. 22, 1879, Julia A. Skipper, b. in Charaw, N. C., Sept. 10, 1856, dau. of Edmond and Nancy Skipper. C. D. Parker is a cabinet workman and joiner.

Their children were:

GRACE PARKER, b. in Atlanta, Ga., Feb. 15, and d. June, 1881.
HOLLIS EDMOND PARKER, b. in Atlanta, March 28, 1883.
WILLIAM ALEXANDER PARKER, b. in Atlanta, April 3, 1885.
BLANCHE AIDELE PARKER, b. in Chattanooga, Tenn., July 15, 1887; d. March 20, 1888.

385. Charles Fessenden Parker *(Charles R.,[8] Elijah,[7] Elisha,[6] Amos,[5] Andrew,[4] John,[3] Hananiah,[2] Thomas[1])*, son of Charles R. and Portia A. (Harmon) Parker, was b. June 6, 1836; m. (1) in Mt. Carmel, Ct., Jan. 1, 1864, Mary E. Dickerman. She d. at Dansville, N. Y., April 14, 1865. He m. (2) Dec. 12, 1865, Kate Isadore Shipman, dau. of Rev. Charles L. Shipman of Girard, Erie Co., Pa. She d. in Lockport, N. Y., Oct. 12, 1875. He m. (3) in Washington, D. C., May 29, 1878, Mary F. Ball, eldest child of John D. Ball of Columbus, O. They reside in Chattanooga, Tenn.

The child of Charles F. and Kate I. (Shipman) Parker was:

LUNA ADELIA PARKER, b. in Girard, Pa., Jan. 15, 1870.

386. Daniel Deeth Parker *(George W.,[8] Amos A.,[7] Nahum,[6] Amos,[5] Andrew,[4] John,[3] Hananiah,[2] Thomas[1])*, son of George Washington and Julia A. (Deeth) Parker, was

b. in Fitzwilliam, N. H., June 29, 1851; m. March 20, 1877, Abby S. Holmes of Halifax, dau. of Martin and Jane Standish Holmes. Daniel D. Parker graduated in class of '76 from the New Hampshire Agricultural College. They reside in Halifax.

Their children were:

LAURA ABBY PARKER, b. in Gardner, Oct. 17, 1878; d. March 1, 1881.
DANIEL HOLMES PARKER, b. in Gardner, Jan. 5, 1882.
MIRIAM HOLMES PARKER, b. in Gardner, Jan. 18, 1885.
A daughter, b. Sept. 8, 1884.
HELEN HOLMES PARKER, b. in Halifax, Sept. 8, 1887.

387. George Amos Parker (*George W.*,[8] *Amos A.*,[7] *Nahum*,[6] *Amos*,[5] *Andrew*,[4] *John*,[3] *Hananiah*,[2] *Thomas*[1]), son of George Washington and Julia A. (Deeth) Parker, was b. in Fitzwilliam, N. H., April 28, 1853; graduated in class of '76 from Massachusetts Agricultural College; m. Dec. 6, 1876, Jennie W. Richardson, b. Oct. 12, 1851, dau. of Andrew and Harriet N. (Waterman) Richardson of Halifax, Mass. They reside in Halifax.

Their children were:

ARTHUR PARKER, b. in Poughkeepsie, N. Y., Sept. 6, 1877.
ANDREW RICHMOND PARKER, b. in Poughkeepsie, June 12, 1881.
ROBERT LYMAN PARKER, b. in Halifax, July 16, 1886.

388. Caroline Sanders Parker (*George W.*,[8] *Amos A.*,[7] *Nahum*,[6] *Amos*,[5] *Andrew*,[4] *John*,[3] *Hananiah*,[2] *Thomas*[1]), dau. of George Washington and Julia A. (Deeth) Parker, was b. in Fitzwilliam, N. H., May 30, 1855; m. Oct. 20, 1880, Benjamin F. Trasher, b. in E. Bridgewater, Oct. 6, 1852, son of Benjamin Burse and Abigail Vaughn (Bryant) Trasher. They reside in Halifax, Mass.

Their children were:

1. MERTICE PARKER TRASHER, b. in Gardner, Nov. 29, 1881.
2. FRANCIS PARKER TRASHER, b. in Gardner, Aug. 10, 1885.
3. CAROLINE MILDRED TRASHER, b. in Gardner, April 12, 1888.

389. Dennis Lackland Parker (*Edward N.*,[8] *Ephraim*,[7] *Nahum*,[6] *Amos*,[5] *Andrew*,[4] *John*,[3] *Hananiah*,[2] *Thomas*[1]), son of Edward Nelson and Louisa M. (Lackland)

Parker, was b. in St. Louis, Mo., April 28, 1851; m. in St. Louis, July 8, 1873, Jennie R. Mahoney of Washington, Mo. He is a passenger conductor on the Missouri Pacific R. R., and resides in Washington, Mo.

Their children, all b. in Washington, Mo., were:

LULU MAUD PARKER, b. May 19, 1874.
MAGGIE MARY PARKER, b. Oct. 25, 1875.
EDNA NELSON PARKER, b. May 1, 1885.

390. Margaret Ann Parker *(Edward N.,[8] Ephraim,[7] Nahum,[6] Amos,[5] Andrew,[4] John,[3] Hananiah,[2] Thomas[1])*, dau. of Edward N. and Louisa M. (Lackland) Parker, was b. in St. Louis, Mo., Aug. 31, 1854; m. May 2, 1878, James M. Beecher. He is in the insurance business.

Their children were:

1. SAMUEL EDWARD BEECHER, b. Feb. 21, 1879.
2. WILLIAM LACKLAND BEECHER, b. Sept. 22, 1881.
3. WALTER DENNIS BEECHER, b. Sept. 24, 1885.
4. MAI LEDGEWOOD BEECHER, b. Jan. 12, 1890.

391. Lulu Louisa Parker *(Edward N.,[8] Ephraim,[7] Nahum,[6] Amos,[5] Andrew,[4] John,[3] Hananiah,[2] Thomas[1])*, dau. of Edward N. and Louisa M. (Lackland) Parker, was b. in St. Louis, Mo., Oct. 25, 1856; m. in St. Louis, April 30, 1880, James W. Owens of Washington, Mo. He is an attorney at law. They reside in Washington, Mo.

Their children are:

1. EMILY ELIZABETH OWENS, b. May 6, 1881.
2. LULU LOUISA OWENS, b. Jan. 10, 1882.
3. HELEN OWENS, b. July 20, 1888.

392. Benjamin Thomas Parker *(Thomas M.,[8] Quincy,[7] Ebenezer,[6] Thomas,[5] Andrew,[4] John,[3] Hananiah,[2] Thomas[1])*, son of Thomas Maxwell and Esther C. (Luther) Parker, was b. in Providence, R. I., March 22, 1836; m. in Boston, July 25, 1862, Charlotte Augusta Saunders, b. June 3, 1837, dau. of Jonas B. and Sarah H. Saunders of Augusta, Me. They reside in Medford, Mass.

Their children were:

CHARLES SUMNER PARKER, b. May 8, 1863; d. Jan. 5, 1868.
BENJAMIN AUSTEN PARKER, b. Oct. 24, 1864; m. in Reading, Oct. 30, 1888, Emma Florence Adams, b. Feb. 25, 1861, dau. of Benjamin Franklin and Mehitable (Foster) Adams. They reside in Wakefield.

393. Henrietta Eveline Parker (*Joseph,*[8] *Quincy,*[7] *Ebenezer,*[6] *Thomas,*[5] *Andrew,*[4] *John,*[3] *Hananiah,*[2] *Thomas*[1]), dau. of Dea. Joseph and Mary Ann (Morgan) Parker, was b. in Lancaster, July 29, 1847; m. in Clinton, by Rev. William Murdock, May 18, 1871, Charles C. Murdock, son of David C. and Adaline (King) Murdock of W. Boylston. He is book-keeper and treasurer of the J. B. Parker Machine Co. They reside in Clinton.

Their children were:

1. EVELYN LOUISE MURDOCK, b. Aug. 14, 1874.
2. CORA ALICE MURDOCK, b. March 28, and d. Aug. 31, 1878.
3. HARRISON PARKER MURDOCK, b. Dec. 11, 1880.
4. ANNA MORGAN MURDOCK, b. Jan. 25, 1883.

394. Charles Hannibal Parker (*Ira,*[8] *Quincy,*[7] *Ebenezer,*[6] *Thomas,*[5] *Andrew,*[4] *John,*[3] *Hananiah,*[2] *Thomas*[1]), son of Ira and Maria (Haskell) Parker, was b. in Providence, R. I., March 22, 1839; m. Abby J. Rockwood of Ashburnham, b. Dec. 20, 1839, dau. of George Rockwood, formerly of Wilton, N. H., and Anna Baldwin Stickney, native of Townsend. He enlisted in Co. G of the 21st Mass. Reg. in Aug. of 1861, for three years service. His companions were his Ashburnham friends. The sturdy qualities in Mr. Parker were soon recognized, and upon leaving Worcester was appointed sergeant. After eight months of service he received the commission of lieutenant. During this short time he was in seven important engagements, including the Battle of Antietam, where, Sept. 17, 1862, he was wounded in both legs by one shot. He came home, but in two months he was again following his regiment, in time to take part in the Battle of Fredericksburg. Finally, his wounds troubling him, he resigned his commission and returned home. Mr. Parker is a man of powerful strength and vigorous constitution. It is interesting that notwithstanding all the engagements, rough marches, exposure and excitement which his company passed through, and his own extra duties on account of his commissions, he was, up to the time of his misfortune at Antietam, improved in health, and had increased his weight 50 pounds. Mr. Parker is under six feet in stature, but is very largely and firmly built.

Their children were:

WINONA PARKER, b. in Ashburnham, June 18, 1867. } Twins.
WINIFRED PARKER, b. in Ashburnham, June 18, 1867. }
CHARLES BRUND PARKER, b. in Chelsea, Jan. 4, 1871.

395. Alfred Wright Parker *(Ira,[8] Quincy,[7] Ebenezer,[6] Thomas,[5] Andrew,[4] John,[3] Hananiah,[2] Thomas[1])*, son of Ira and Maria (Haskell) Parker, was b. in Providence, R. I., June 5, 1844; m. Aug. 22, 1871, Clara Hallett, b. Oct. 26, 1845, dau. of Benjamin Hallett, 2nd, of Yarmouthport. He is connected with the Boston Bridge Works. They have since 1883 resided in Waltham.

Their dau.:

MARY PARKER, b. Sept. 14, 1872.

396. Julia Maria Parker *(Ira,[8] Quincy,[7] Ebenezer,[6] Thomas,[5] Andrew,[4] John,[3] Hananiah,[2] Thomas[1])*, dau. of Ira and Maria (Haskell) Parker, was b. in E. Boston, July 27, 1848; m. Edward Safford. They lived at Mt. Auburn, Mass., and Strafford, N. H. She is deceased.

Their children were:

1. LOIS MARIA SAFFORD.
2. EDWARD SAFFORD. He d. young.
3. CLARENCE SAFFORD.

397. Frank Herbert Parker *(Ira,[8] Quincy,[7] Ebenezer,[6] Thomas,[5] Andrew,[4] John,[3] Hananiah,[2] Thomas[1])*, son of Ira and Maria (Haskell) Parker, was b. in E. Boston, July 24, 1852; m. Jan. 31, 1877, Marietta Story, b. Aug. 2, 1850, dau. of Elisha Story of Newburyport. He and his brother Alfred are employed in the Boston Bridge Works. He resides in Cambridgeport.

Their children were:

EULALIA PARKER, b. Aug. 16, 1878.
CLARA PARKER, b. June 25, 1882.

398. Eugene Costello Parker (*Quincy,*[8] *Quincy,*[7] *Ebenezer,*[6] *Thomas,*[5] *Andrew,*[4] *John,*[3] *Hananiah,*[2] *Thomas*[1]), son of Quincy and Almira (Kent) Parker, was b. in Providence, R. I.; m. Aug. 29, 1871, Adelia O. Barker.

Their children were:

WILLIAM QUINCY PARKER, b. March 15, 1872.
CHARLES EUGENE PARKER, b. Jan. 26, 1873.
LOUIS FRANCES PARKER, b. June 10. 1874.
MABEL TRAVERS PARKER, b. Aug. 26, 1875.
FREDERICK THOMAS PARKER, b. Feb. 17, 1877.

399. Clara Emu Parker (*Quincy,*[8] *Quincy,*[7] *Ebenezer,*[6] *Thomas,*[5] *Andrew,*[4] *John,*[3] *Hananiah,*[2] *Thomas*[1]), dau. of Quincy and Almira (Kent) Parker, was b. in Providence, R. I.; m. Sept., 1876, Lorenzo Dupouy, native of Cuba, and resides in Providence, R. I.

Their children were:

1. RAPHAEL SALVADOR DUPOUY, b. March 18, 1877.
2. MILTON AMEJIO DUPOUY, b. Aug. 17, 1880.

400. Lucy Maria Parker (*Charles A.,*[8] *Ebenezer,*[7] *Ebenezer,*[6] *Thomas,*[5] *Andrew,*[4] *John,*[3] *Hananiah,*[2] *Thomas*[1]), dau. of Charles Augustus and Sylvia A. (Moore) Parker, was b. in Princeton, Nov. 8, 1835; m. June 8, 1858, Thomas R. Howe, son of William and Eunice (Robbins) Howe of Princeton. They reside in Holden, where he is a farmer.

Their children, b. in Holden, were:

1. WALDO EMERSON HOWE, b. May 13, 1859; d. Oct. 27, 1865.
2. WALTER THOMAS HOWE, b. Oct. 17, 1866. He is a clerk in Worcester, Mass.

401. Sarah Ann Parker (*Charles A.,*[8] *Ebenezer,*[7] *Ebenezer,*[6] *Thomas,*[5] *Andrew,*[4] *John,*[3] *Hananiah,*[2] *Thomas*[1]), dau. of Charles Augustus and Sylvia A. (Moore) Parker, was b. in Princeton, March 14, 1839; m. Nov. 24, 1864, Milton K. Howe (see page 370). They reside in Worcester.

Their dau. was:

1. MARY LOUISA HOWE, b. Nov. 6, 1868; d. Sept. 16, 1869.

402. George Washington M. Parker (*Charles A.*,[8] *Ebenezer*,[7] *Ebenezer*,[6] *Thomas*,[5] *Andrew*,[4] *John*,[3] *Hananiah*,[2] *Thomas*[1]), son of Charles Augustus and Sylvia A. (Moore) Parker, was b. in Princeton, Aug. 19, 1841; m. Dec. 14, 1866, Laura D. Hamilton, b. in Augusta, Ga., Oct. 24, 1844. They reside in Champaign, Ill.

Their children were:

ANNIE ELIZA PARKER, b. in Alexandria, La., Oct. 23, and d. Nov. 15, 1867.
HARVEY E. PAKKER, b. in Champaign, Ill., Feb. 1, 1869.
NETTY F. PARKER, b. in Champaign, May 13, 1871.
CARRIE E. PARKER, b. in Champaign, Nov. 23, 1873.
GEORGE A. PARKER, b. in Champaign, Jan. 3, 1876.
CALTON W. PARKER, b. in Urbana, Aug. 28, 1878.
WALTER G. PARKER, b. in Champaign, Aug. 25, 1886.

403. William Dwight Parker (*Charles A.*,[8] *Ebenezer*,[7] *Ebenezer*,[6] *Thomas*,[5] *Andrew*,[4] *John*,[3] *Hananiah*,[2] *Thomas*[1]), son of Charles Augustus and Sylvia A. (Moore) Parker, was b. in Princeton, Jan. 27, 1844; m. Dec. 25, 1866, Margaret Smith, b. in Newport, R. I., July 1, 1838, dau. of Morton and Mary (Knowles) Smith. He is an organ maker.

Their children were:

LOUIS D. PARKER, b. June 12, and d. July 20, 1872.
HERBERT DWIGHT PARKER, b. Sept. 26, 1877.
CHARLES AUGUSTUS PARKER, b. June 3, and d. Aug. 24, 1884.

404. Emma Frances Parker (*Charles A.*,[8] *Ebenezer*,[7] *Ebenezer*,[6] *Thomas*,[5] *Andrew*,[4] *John*,[3] *Hananiah*,[2] *Thomas*[1]), dau. of Charles Augustus and Sylvia A. (Moore) Parker, was b. in Princeton, Sept. 23, 1853; m. Dec. 24, 1888, Warren F. Bartlett of Rutland. They reside in Plainfield, N. J. Mr. Bartlett is a machinist.

Their daughter:

1. EDITH MARION BARTLETT, b. in Plainfield, N. J., Aug. 23, 1892.

405. Charles William Parker (*Frederick*,[8] *Ebenezer*,[7] *Ebenezer*,[6] *Thomas*,[5] *Andrew*,[4] *John*,[3] *Hananiah*,[2] *Thomas*[1]), son of Frederick and Eunice (Howe) Parker, was b. in

Princeton, Feb. 1, 1837; m. Oct. 12, 1859, Inez Bullard, dau. of Hiram Bullard, then of Littleton, N. H. They lived (1) in Worcester, where he was for a while one of the common council of that city. Later they removed to Princeton and settled upon the homestead, where they still reside.

Their only son:

CHARLES FREDERICK PARKER, b. March 25, and d. Sept. 13, 1863.*

406. Amos Milton Parker (*Frederick*,[8] *Ebenezer*,[7] *Ebenezer*,[6] *Thomas*,[5] *Andrew*,[4] *John*,[3] *Hananiah*,[2] *Thomas*[1]), son of Frederick and Eunice (Howe) Parker, was b. in Princeton, Sept. 12, 1839; m. April 18, 1861, Anna J. Frizell, b. in Norwich, Ct., Sept. 28, 1837, dau. of Lorenzo and Priscilla Frizell. His school advantages were those of his native town and the Millbury Academy. At the age of 16 he became clerk in the store of F. L. Cutting, Oakdale, and the year following, 1856, entered the employ of A. Y. Thompson, dry goods merchant of Worcester, with whom he remained until the war of the Rebellion. Believing his duty was at the front he immediately enlisted, knowing not for how long a service or whether he was to receive pay for so doing. His company was the Worcester City Guards, Capt. A. B. R. Sprague. The day after his enlistment he was married. Upon the famous April 19 his company proceeded first to Annapolis and second to Fort McHenry. Here violent sickness of malarial typhoid fever prevented his further service with his company and confined him to the hospital. His very vigorous constitution enabled him to reach home alive in company with his brother Charles. He was confined to his bed until Christmas time and was unable to work for three years. But still fired with patriotism he attempted to re-enlist again in the 53d and 57th Mass. Regiments respectively, in the former of which he was offered a commission, but was twice rejected. In 1865, however, he raised a company of

* This son made at that time four generations who were all living upon the homestead. Hiram Bullard was son of Daniel Bullard of Linesboro, N. H., who in 1820 travelled through the wilderness upon ox-sleds by the aid of marked trees and settled in Hyde Park, Vt. He d. 1869, aged 79, a respected and worthy citizen. Hiram Bullard spent the last portion of his life upon the Parker homestead in Princeton.

Amos M. Parker.

militia and was its captain, under a commission issued by Gov. John A. Andrew. He was also a member of the old "State Guard," of which he was lieutenant in 1870 and '71. After 1864 he was connected with the clothing and furniture business until 1868, the latter part of which time the company was known as Parker, Denny & Co. The ten years following he was general agent of the Mass. Mut. Life Ins. Co., since when he was auctioneer and appraiser several years, and later with the furniture house of Putnam & Sprague. In 1888 he was elected one of the city assessors for three years and in 1891 was re-elected for a second term.

Mr. Parker was commander of Post 10, G. A. R., in 1869 and in 1889. He is a member of Montacute Lodge of Master Masons, is also a member of Blake Lodge, Knights of Pythias, and his Church relations are with the First Universalist Church of Worcester, of which parish he is one of the trustees.

Mrs. Anna C. Parker, after a sickness of five years, d. July 3, 1888. Mr. Parker m. (2) Sept. 18, 1889, Esta A. Holt, b. in Denmark, Me., June 27, 1850, dau. of Joseph and Mehetable (Miller) Holt.

The children of Amos M. and Anna C. (Frizell) Parker were:

FREDRIC MELVILLE PARKER, b. Dec. 20, 1863; m. in Bellefontaine, O., July 13, 1892, Kittie H. Cranston, b. Feb. 3, 1868, dau. of George and Mary (Sanderson) Cranston. He is a designer for the Worcester Carpet Works, in which city he resides.

HENRY WALFORD PARKER, b. April 2, and d. Aug. 27, 1868.

HARRY NICHOLS PARKER, b. June 3, 1872. He is a clerk in the Quinsigamond National Bank of Worcester.

407. Mary Adelia Parker *(Ebenezer,[8] Ebenezer,[7] Ebenezer,[6] Thomas,[5] Andrew,[4] John,[3] Hananiah,[2] Thomas[1])*, dau. of Ebenezer Warren and Chloe (Parmenter) Parker, was b. in Princeton, Jan. 27, 1842; m. June, 1860, Pascal P. Parkman of Northfield. He d. Jan. 13, 1869, and she d. Aug. 12, 1874.

Their children were:

1. EMMA SARAH PARKMAN; m. Sept. 10, 1877, Irving A. Baker of Bellefontaine, O. Children:

Walter E. Parker.

i. FRANKLIN ARTHUR BAKER.
ii. ROY PARCHAL BAKER.
iii. HARRY ARCHIBALD BAKER.

2. CHARLES ELVESTER PARKMAN.
3. WILLIAM WARREN PARKMAN.

Abby Dane Parker (see page 373) *(Amos,[8] Ebenezer,[7] Ebenezer,[6] Thomas,[5] Andrew,[4] John,[3] Hananiah,[2] Thomas[1])*, dau. of Amos and Sarah (Merrill) Parker, was b. in Princeton, Sept. 11, 1851; m. in Sterling, Nov. 29, 1871, Eben D. Blood, b. in Deering, N. H., April 20, 1850, son of Eben Preston and Eliza Jane (Dix) Blood. They reside in Sterling Junction. He is engineer for the Old Colony R. R.

Their children were:

1. FRANK HENRY BLOOD, b. Aug. 15, 1872.
2. ALICE ELIZA BLOOD, b. Oct. 28, 1873.
3. HARRY EARNEST BLOOD, b. March 29, 1876.
4. ARTHUR PRESCOTT BLOOD, b. Jan. 30, 1878.
5. SADIE BERNICE BLOOD, b. June 24, 1883.
6. FLORENCE BERTHA BLOOD, b. Oct. 22, 1885.
7. PERCY EBEN FRANCIS BLOOD, b. Oct. 20, 1887.

408. Walter Edward Parker *(George,[8] Ebenezer,[7] Ebenezer,[6] Thomas,[5] Andrew,[4] John,[3] Hananiah,[2] Thomas[1])*, son of George and Emily R. (Collar) Parker, was b. in Princeton, Sept. 29, 1847; m. (1) Oct. 12, 1870, Anna Augusta Elliott of Woonsocket, R. I., dau. of Nathaniel and Olive A. (Jenks) Elliott. She d. Feb. 24, 1875. He m. (2) May 2, 1877, Alida Charlotte Willis, b. in N. Dana, Mass., Jan. 26, 1849, dau. of Rev. John H. and Charlotte (Gleason) Willis of College Hill. He m. (3) Jan. 1, 1888, Mary Bradley Beetle of Lawrence, dau. of John and Harriet (Brown) Beetle of Nantucket. Mr. Parker resides in Lawrence. With his parents he passed the four years from 1857 to 1861 in Illinois, from whence the family returned to New England and settled in Woonsocket, R. I. Early in 1863 he entered the employment of the Social Mill, Woonsocket, as office clerk, while he continued his studies and attended school. This lasted two years, after which he devoted his whole time to the mill duties, save a few months which he spent at a drawing school in Boston at about this time. Starting with the Social Mill when but a mere boy he worked his way steadily and with persistent energy to responsible positions. On Oct. 27, 1876, he became superintendent of the Globe Mill of Woonsocket, which continued until April 1, 1881, when he left the Globe Mill to take charge of the cotton department of the Pacific Mills* in Lawrence, and later, Jan. 1, 1887, was made agent of all the mills of the Pacific Corporation, in which capacity he still serves. While in Woonsocket he was elected member of the town council and president of the council for one year. He was a director in the Producer's National Bank for 14 years. In Lawrence, upon the organization of the Merchants' National Bank, he was made the Vice-President and a member of its board of directors. He has for several years been a member of the board of trustees of Essex Co. Savings Bank and is now Vice-President of that institution. He was President of the New England Cotton Manufacturers' Association in 1889, '90 and '91, and is a member of the American Society of Mechanical Engineers. He was made a Mason in 1869, and was master of Morning Star Lodge of Woonsocket in 1877, and commander of the Woonsocket Commandery of Knights Templar for two years.

Child of Walter E. and Anna A. (Elliott) Parker:

HERBERT S. PARKER, b. Oct. 18, 1874.

Child of Walter E. and Alida C. (Willis) Parker:

HELEN PARKER, b. June 27, 1878.

410. Arthur Augustus Parker *(Edward H.,[8] Ebenezer,[7] Ebenezer,[6] Thomas,[5] Andrew,[4] John,[3] Hananiah,[2] Thomas[1])*, son of Edward H. and Mary C. (Brown) Parker, was b. in Worcester, April 5, 1855; m. Sept. 16, 1882, Lida Eliza Denton, b. May 13, 1858, dau. of James W. and Sarah

---

*The Pacific Mills rank among America's greatest factories. They are devoted to the making and printing of cotton and worsted into calicoes and delaines. They were incorporated in 1853 with a capital of $1,000,000; increased in 1855, 1858 and 1862 to $2,500,000. Probably no mill is known throughout the country at large as the Pacific, which has succeeded for many years in keeping at the front and whose diversified fabrics have won for it the popularity fairly earned.

EDWARD H. PARKER.

ARTHUR A. PARKER. CLARENCE E. PARKER.

THEODORE PARKER.

A. (Lovell) Denton.* He is fence agent of the Washburn & Moen Mfg. Co., conducting the construction of the wire fencing contracts of this corporation. Resides in Jersey City, N. J.

Children:

WALTER DENTON PARKER, b. and d. April 3, 1885.
ARTHUR DENTON PARKER, b. Sept. 4, 1886.
RALPH AUGUSTUS PARKER, b. May 25, 1889.
MARY LOVELL PARKER, b. and d. Jan. 21, 1891.
MARY GRACE PARKER, b. May 3, 1892.

411. Clarence Edmund Parker (*Edward H.*,[8] *Ebenezer*,[7] *Ebenezer*,[6] *Thomas*,[5] *Andrew*,[4] *John*,[3] *Hananiah*,[2] *Thomas*[1]), son of Edward H. and Mary C. (Brown) Parker, was b. in Worcester, April 4, 1860; m. Aug. 26, 1886, Jennie E. See, b. in Yonkers, N. Y., Sept. 27, 1864, dau. of Benjamin A. and Ellen† (Lafarge) See‡ of Yonkers, N. Y. The parents of Benjamin A. See were David and Elizabeth (Austin)

*James W. Denton was son of Ebenezer Denton of Braintree, Mass., whose wife was Eliza W. Hollis, daughter of Capt. John Hollis of Braintree, and a lady of great worth. She was a descendant of Peregrine White of Pilgrim fame. Two brothers, William and Rev. Paul Denton, are said to have come from England and settled in Plymouth Co. as early as 1638. Rev. Paul Denton removed to Long Island, while William Denton became the ancestor of the Dentons of Braintree. Lida E. Denton is sister to Prof. James Edgar Denton of Jersey City, N. J.; and the father, James W. Denton, has been for many years an instructor in the Hoboken Institute of Technology.

Sarah A. Lovell was daughter of Stephen Lovell of Weymouth, Mass., in which town lived each of her successive ancestral generations from her own back to the Lovell ancestor of 1635, who came from Weymouth, England.

†Ellen Lafarge was born in Hastings-on-Hudson, N. Y., Aug. 5, 1827, dau. of Isaac and Jane Lafarge.

‡Benjamin A. See still enjoys rugged health in his advanced age of 82. The Lafarge family in America have come from two brothers, so attested by tradition, who sought America for the free worship of their Protestant beliefs. One of them settled in the Hudson River valley, where his descendants are more or less numerous at the present day. Many of them were active in the Colonial Revolution and rendered all possible service to the common cause. In their section, that part of the State adjacent to New York city, occurred much contest, and in this hotbed of the struggle which lasted so long were many personal experiences and trials of the Lafarge family. The great-grandfather lived in the neighborhood of Dobbs Ferry. His farm was near the Hessian camp and suffered accordingly. The family were obliged to keep their food in a secret spaceway under the kitchen floor. The homestead was but a few miles from either White Plains or from the place where Maj. André was taken.

See. Mr. Parker resides in Yonkers, where he is a fence manufacturer.

Their dau.:

Elsie Ellen Parker, b. in Yonkers, N. Y., June 12, 1889; d. Feb. 16, 1892.

412. Edward Henry Parker (*Edward H.*,[8] *Ebenezer*,[7] *Ebenezer*,[6] *Thomas*,[5] *Andrew*,[4] *John*,[3] *Hananiah*,[2] *Thomas*[1]), son of Edward H. and Mary C. (Brown) Parker, was b. in Worcester, Jan. 4, 1867; m. Sept. 9, 1886, Lena A. Converse, dau. of Hiram S. and Delia A. (Moffitt) Converse of Oxford. Since 1884 he has been connected with the Washburn & Moen Mfg. Co. of Worcester, in which city they reside.

Their dau.:

Myrtis Idella Parker, b. Aug. 7, 1887.

413. Joseph Henry Parker (*Oliver*,[8] *Henry*,[7] *Josiah*,[6] *Josiah*,[5] *Josiah*,[4] *John*,[3] *Hananiah*,[2] *Thomas*[1]), son of Oliver H. and Patty (Parker) Parker, was b. in Woburn, Sept. 16, 1836; m. Dec. 4, 1867, Henrietta M. Young, b. in Woburn, June 25, 1840, dau. of Sumner and Mary A. Young.

Their son:

Joseph Henry Parker, Jr., b. April 16, 1871.

414. Martha Parker (*Oliver*,[8] *Henry*,[7] *Josiah*,[6] *Josiah*,[5] *Josiah*,[4] *John*,[3] *Hananiah*,[2] *Thomas*[1]), dau. of Oliver H. and Patty (Parker) Parker, was b. in Woburn, Oct. 20, 1841; m. Joseph Linnell, b. in Orleans, Jan. 25, 1836, son of Gould and Paulina Linnell of Orleans. They reside in Woburn.

Their son:

1. James Houston Linnell, b. in Woburn, Sept. 24, 1874.

415. Lydia Thompson Parker (*Frederick C.*,[8] *Frederick*,[7] *Josiah*,[6] *Josiah*,[5] *Josiah*,[4] *John*,[3] *Hananiah*,[2] *Thomas*[1]), dau. of Frederick Chandler and Martha A. (Hanson) Parker, was b. in Woburn, April 4, 1858; m. J. Herbert Richardson.

Their dau.:

1. Grace Parker Richardson, b. March 16, 1881.

416. Benjamin Franklin Parker (*Benjamin,*[8] *Joseph,*[7] *Benjamin,*[6] *Josiah,*[5] *Josiah,*[4] *John,*[3] *Hananiah,*[2] *Thomas*[1]), son of Benjamin and Mary Elizabeth (Waitt) Parker, was b. in Woburn, Sept. 8, 1850; m. in Woburn, Dec. 24, 1878, Mary M. Childs, b. March 24, 1854, dau. of Prentiss and Esther F. Childs. They reside in Woburn.

Their children:

LOUIS FRANKLIN PARKER, b. Aug. 11, 1879.
EARNEST ELMORE PARKER, b. Dec. 13, 1880.
WILLIAM CHESTER PARKER, b. Aug. 24, 1883.
ELSIE MAY PARKER, b. Feb. 21, 1888.

417. Susan Emma Parker (*Benjamin,*[8] *Joseph,*[7] *Benjamin,*[6] *Josiah,*[5] *Josiah,*[4] *John,*[3] *Hananiah,*[2] *Thomas*[1]), dau. of Benjamin and Mary Elizabeth (Waitt) Parker, was b. in Woburn, April 21, 1854; m. in Woburn, Feb. 2, 1875, Clarence M. Crowell, b. on Martha's Vineyard Island, March 21, 1849, son of Capt. Joseph M. and Abbie P. Crowell. They reside in Woburn.

Their children:

1. BENJAMIN PARKER CROWELL, b. Aug. 2, 1877.
2. HARRY EDMUND CROWELL, b. Aug. 9, 1880.
3. FRED GILBERT CROWELL, b. Aug. 24, 1886.
4. BERTHA WALLACE CROWELL, b. Sept. 16, 1889.

418. Lucy Augusta Parker (*Benjamin,*[8] *Joseph,*[7] *Benjamin,*[6] *Josiah,*[5] *Josiah,*[4] *John,*[3] *Hananiah,*[2] *Thomas*[1]), dau. of Benjamin and Mary Elizabeth (Waitt) Parker, was b. in Woburn, Jan. 24, 1858; m. in Woburn, Feb. 6, 1889, Asa W. Boutwell, b. Dec. 4, 1863, son of Asa and Lorinda A. Boutwell. They reside in Woburn.

Their son:

1. DANA SYLVESTER BOUTWELL, b. in Woburn, May 21, 1890.

Dorotha Caroline Parker (see page 230) (*Samuel,*[7] *Benjamin,*[6] *Josiah,*[5] *Josiah,*[4] *John,*[3] *Hananiah,*[2] *Thomas*[1]), dau. of Samuel and Lydia Thurston (Allen) Parker, was b. in Otselic, N. Y., Aug. 3, 1832; m. in Chicago, Ill., March 30, 1854, Henry Wiggers, b. in Mariensee, Hanover, Germany, June 2, 1829, son of William and Caroline (Hulke)

Wiggers. He d. in Chicago, Feb. 5, 1851. She d. in Chicago, March 30, 1854. He was a manufacturer of and dealer in mouldings.

Their children were:

1. EMMA WIGGERS, b. Oct. 19, and d. Oct., 1852.
2. CAROLINE ALIDA WIGGERS, b. Feb. 23, 1854; m. in Spring, Boone Co., Ill., Feb. 22, 1876, Fred Augustus Reed, b. in Spring, Jan. 8, 1855, son of Hon. George and Eliza Ann (Wait) Reed. He is a farmer and they reside in Herbert, Boone Co., Ill. Their children, all b. in Spring, Ill., were:
   i. MYRTIE MAUD REED, b. Nov. 19, 1876; d. Aug. 28, 1881.
   ii. ALBERT EUGENE REED, b. Dec. 23, 1878.
   iii. EARL VICTOR REED, b. Aug. 24, 1882.
   iv. PEARL ELIZA REED, b. June 14, 1885.
   v. THOMAS GLEN REED, b. Aug. 27, 1887.

419. Samuel Dwight Parker (*Samuel T.,*[8] *Samuel,*[7] *Benjamin,*[6] *Josiah,*[5] *Josiah,*[4] *John,*[3] *Hananiah,*[2] *Thomas*[1]), son of Samuel Thurston and Mary (Bates) Parker, was b. Dec. 29, 1830; m. Oct. 27, 1850, Hannah R. Congdon, b. in Pompey, N. Y., Sept. 1, 1833, dau. of William and Ervilla Congdon. He resides in De Ruyter, N. Y., where he is a farmer.

Their children:

ELMERA E. PARKER, b. in De Ruyter, N. Y., March 27, 1854; d. Sept. 19, 1872.

EVA MAY PARKER, b. Oct. 2, 1860; m. Oct. 10, 1878, A. Clendening. She d. May 31, 1879, leaving a son:

i. ANDO I. CLENDENING, b. Oct. 30, 1879.

420. Henry Norton Parker (*Samuel T.,*[8] *Samuel,*[7] *Benjamin,*[6] *Josiah,*[5] *Josiah,*[4] *John,*[3] *Hananiah,*[2] *Thomas*[1]), son of Samuel Thurston and Mary (Bates) Parker, was b. in Georgetown, N. Y., June 16, 1834; m. (1) March 15, 1857, Hannah M. Glynn; m. (2) Dec. 31, 1861, Mary A. Cooley, b. Jan. 22, 1841; m. (3) March 12, 1889, Martha Bowers Cady. He is a farmer in New Woodstock, N. Y.

His children:

MACIUS I. PARKER, b. in Smyrna, N. Y., Jan. 8, 1863.

439. MARY ELLEN PARKER, b. in Smyrna, June 21, 1864; m. April 19, 1884, Frank M. Cash.

SARAH ADALAIDE PARKER, b. in Smyrna, Nov. 2, 1865; m. Oct. 29, 1890, Edward Knickerbocker.

440. ALICE AMANDA PARKER, b. in Smyrna, Aug. 10, 1868; m. Dec. 27, 1883, George Hitchcock.

MYSON HENRY PARKER, b. in Smyrna, June 4, 1872.

EDNA MAY PARKER, b. in Smyrna, Dec. 7, 1881.

421. John Lasson Parker (*Samuel T.*,[8] *Samuel*,[7] *Benjamin*,[6] *Josiah*,[5] *Josiah*,[4] *John*,[3] *Hananiah*,[2] *Thomas*[1]), son of Samuel Thurston and Mary (Bates) Parker, was b. in Georgetown, N. Y., July 6, 1836; m. in Georgetown, Feb. 11, 1864, Lydia A. Vanhovenburgh, b. in Schenectady, N. Y., Aug. 6, 1838, dau. of William and Jane Vanhovenburgh. He is a carpenter in Smyrna, N. Y.

Their son:

CLINTON DEWITT PARKER, b. in Georgetown, N. Y., Sept. 20, 1866.

422. Lucy Lizzette Parker (*Samuel T.*,[8] *Samuel*,[7] *Benjamin*,[6] *Josiah*,[5] *Josiah*,[4] *John*,[3] *Hananiah*,[2] *Thomas*[1]), dau. of Samuel Thurston and Mary (Bates) Parker, was b. in Smyrna, N. Y., July 17, 1838; m. in De Ruyter, Madison Co., N. Y., June 1, 1865, William Lewis Jones, b. in Smyrna, N. Y., July 9, 1839, son of John I. and Sarah (Lewis) Jones. He was a farmer. He d. Sept. 28, 1872. She resides in Smyrna, where all the children were born.

Their children were:

1. MINNIE LAVERNA JONES, b. March 19, 1867; m. in Smyrna, N. Y., Feb. 3, 1887, John S. Weaver. She d. Dec. 29, 1888.
2. EUGENE LUZERNE JONES, b. Nov. 4, 1868.
3. FLOY LANETTE JONES, b. June 8, 1870.

423. Albert Monson Parker (*Samuel T.*,[8] *Samuel*,[7] *Benjamin*,[6] *Josiah*,[5] *Josiah*,[4] *John*,[3] *Hananiah*,[2] *Thomas*[1]), son of Samuel Thurston and Mary (Bates) Parker, was b. in Madison Co., N. Y., Oct. 10, 1843; m. in Sioux City, Ia., Aug. 13, 1869, Elizabeth Van Zandt, b. in Cincinnati, O., April 21, 1840, dau. of Jacob and Sarah Van Zandt. They reside in S. Sioux City, Neb.

Their children:

CHARLES A. PARKER, b. May 5, 1870.
SARAH E. PARKER, b. March 6, 1872.
GEORGE O. PARKER, b. June 20, 1875.

424. Edwin Eugene Parker (*Samuel T.,[8] Samuel,[7] Benjamin,[6] Josiah,[5] Josiah,[4] John,[3] Hananiah,[2] Thomas[1]*), son of Samuel Thurston and Mary (Bates) Parker, was b. in Madison Co., N. Y., Dec. 5, 1846; m. in Willow, Union Co., Dak., July 7, 1867, Nellie Heath, b. in Upper Canada, April 2, 1839, dau. of Mitchell and Jeannett Heath. Mr. Parker is a house-mover. He resides in Sioux City, Ia.

Their children:

HARRY V. PARKER, b. in Covington, Neb., March 8, 1872.
FRED PARKER, b. Dec. 7, 1874.

425. William Charles Addison Parker (*Samuel T.,[8] Samuel,[7] Benjamin,[6] Josiah,[5] Josiah,[4] John,[3] Hananiah,[2] Thomas[1]*), son of Samuel Thurston and Mary (Bates) Parker, was b. in Otselic, N. Y., Aug. 5, 1849; m. in Smyrna, N. Y., Dec. 22, 1869, Emma O. Crandall, b. in Smyrna, June 9, 1854, dau. of Timothy D. and Amy E. Crandall. They reside in Norwich, N. Y. He is a car repairer.

Their children:

LIZZIE M. PARKER, b. May 26, 1871; m. in Norwich, N. Y., Nov. 12, 1890, Oliver M. Jones. Their son:

1. HAZEL JONES, b. in Norwich, N. Y., Nov. 19, 1891.

MARY E. PARKER, b. Sept. 4, 1874.
CHARLES E. PARKER, b. Jan. 8, 1877.
L. BELLE PARKER, b. Sept. 6, 1880.

426. Thomas Allen Parker (*Benjamin A.,[8] Samuel,[7] Benjamin,[6] Josiah,[5] Josiah,[4] John,[3] Hananiah,[2] Thomas[1]*), son of Benjamin Allen and Orpha (Stebbins) Parker, was b. in Chardon, O., Nov. 18, 1834; m. in Fayette Co., O., Aug. 27, 1857, Margaret Ann Lindsey. At 17 years of age he began teaching in the public schools, and going to school a term occasionally when he could save enough money to pay his way; was a member of the Hiram Eclectic Institute (afterwards Hiram College) during the fall terms of both 1853 and '54, while Gen. Garfield was a student there. From there he went to Fayette Co., O., and was appointed a member of the Board of County Examiners, which position he resigned on removing to Kansas, after teaching two years in the public schools and conducting a normal school one year at Bloomingburg, Fayette Co., O. April 1, 1860, he first beheld the prairies of Kansas, since which time his avocations have been various, sometimes teaching, sometimes farming, keeping a hardware store, surveying, etc., etc.

Their children:

EVA CORA PARKER, b. June 2, 1859.
CHARLES CARLOS PARKER, b. April, 1861; d. Aug., 1864.
MARY ELIZABETH PARKER, b. Jan. 10, 1868.
FREDERICK LE GRANGE PARKER, b. Nov. 13, 1873.
MINERVA MAUDE PARKER, b. April 7, 1878.

427. Hosea Stebbins Parker (*Benjamin A.*,[8] *Samuel*,[7] *Benjamin*,[6] *Josiah*,[5] *Josiah*,[4] *John*,[3] *Hananiah*,[2] *Thomas*[1]), son of Benjamin Allen and Orpha (Stebbins) Parker; m. in Spring Hill, Kan., Sept. 11, 1867, Martha D. Wilson, b. in Blount Co., Tenn., Oct. 21, 1844, dau. of Alexander M. and Mary Jane Wilson. He was a farmer in Spring Hill, Kan. For about ten years preceding his death he was sergeant in the Home Militia, also clerk in the school district one term. He d. in Spring Hill, July 28, 1875. His widow survives him in Melvern, Osage Co., Kan.

Their children were:

441. MARY EMOGENE PARKER, b. in Spring Hill, Kan., Aug. 24, 1869; m. John Stucker.
ALLEN WILSON PARKER, b. Aug. 3, 1873; d. Jan. 23, 1874.
HOSEA ROBERT PARKER, b. Dec. 4, 1874.

428. Mary Louisa Parker (*Benjamin A.*,[8] *Samuel*,[7] *Benjamin*,[6] *Josiah*,[5] *Josiah*,[4] *John*,[3] *Hananiah*,[2] *Thomas*[1]), dau. of Benjamin Allen and Orpha (Stebbins) Parker; m. Benjamin Sprague. She d. Dec. 23, 1873, and was buried at Spring Hill, Kan. He was a telegraph operator. They lived at Tye Siding, Wyoming, on the Union Pacific R. R.

Their children were:

1. ORRIE SPRAGUE; m. George Dobbins, and resides in Marceline, Mo.
2. JOHN SPRAGUE; d. young.

429. Mary Ellen Parker *(Francis E.,[8] Samuel,[7] Benjamin,[6] Josiah,[5] Josiah,[4] John,[3] Hananiah,[2] Thomas[1])*, dau. of Francis Edwin and Amanda M. (Lindsay) Parker, was b. in Lake Co., Ill., May 13, 1851; m. in Belvidere, Ill., Feb. 17, 1869, Stephen Abraham, b. in New York city, Oct. 1, 1848, and resides in Genoa, Dekalb Co., Ill. He was deputy sheriff and town constable.

Their children:

1. EMMA M. ABRAHAM, b. in Spring, Boone Co., Ill., Nov. 22, 1869; d. Jan. 27, 1872.
2. WILLIS L. ABRAHAM, b. in Spring, Dec. 24, 1870.
3. LINDSAY ABRAHAM, b. in Spring, June 26, 1872.
4. EDWIN ABRAHAM, b. in Spring, April 17, 1874.
5. FREDERICK S. ABRAHAM, b. in Genoa, Dekalb Co., Ill., Oct. 27, 1876.

430. Milton Augustus Parker *(Milton B.,[8] Peter,[7] John,[6] Peter,[5] John,[4] John,[3] Hananiah,[2] Thomas[1])*, son of Milton B. and Harriet J. (Ward) Parker, was b. Sept. 2, 1855; m. in Cambridge, Oct. 21, 1885, Mae Hapgood of Cambridge, dau. of Oliver and Mary J. (Sanderson) Hapgood.

Their children were:

CHESTER CURTIS PARKER, b. in Cambridge, Aug. 6, and d. Dec. 11, 1886.
ROY MILTON PARKER, b. in Charlestown, Oct. 3, 1887.
HAROLD BRYANT PARKER, b. in Natick, Dec. 22, 1892.

431. John Freeman Parker *(John H.,[8] John,[7] John,[6] Peter,[5] John,[4] John,[3] Hananiah,[2] Thomas[1])*, son of John Henry and Annie E. (Gilmore) Parker, was b. in Brookfield, July 15, 1862, and soon removed with his parents to Malden. After his school life in that city he studied the practical side of the shoe business at his father's manufactory. He afterwards took charge of the manufacturing and the customers' departments. He was one of the first members of Co. L, 5th Reg., M. V. M., rising from private by competitive drill to corporal

LIEUT. JOHN F. PARKER.

sergeant and finally commissioned first lieutenant. He m. Oct. 24, 1888, Minnie Waters Ballard of Malden, dau. of Capt. Henry A. and Lydia (Brown) Ballard. Lieut. Parker was appointed military instructor at the Malden High School, serving in that capacity to the time of his death, occurring June 5, 1890. His sickness of typhoid fever was brief. He was well and favorably known, and his death while in the full vigor of early manhood caused profound sadness. He was very thorough and proficient in whatever he undertook, and was a man of great promise. He was buried at Forestdale Cemetery, Malden, Mass.

Their dau.:

MARJORIE GILMORE PARKER, b. Nov. 24, 1889.

George Henry Parker (see page 411) (*George S.*,[8] *George S.*,[7] *Artemas*,[6] *Peter*,[5] *John*,[4] *John*,[3] *Hananiah*,[2] *Thomas*[1]), son of George Smith and Mary A. (Skahal) Parker, was b. in Sucotock, Mich., Oct. 7, 1856; m. Jan. 12, 1878, in E. Medway, now Millis, Nancy E. Ross, b. in Natick, July 24, 1860, dau. of Roswell P. and Helen L. (Lawrence) Ross. They reside in W. Medway.

Their dau.:

HELEN LOUISA PARKER, b. in Medway, April 3, 1879.

Eva L. Parker (see page 411) (*George S.*,[8] *George S.*,[7] *Artemas*,[6] *Peter*,[5] *John*,[4] *John*,[3] *Hananiah*,[2] *Thomas*[1]), dau. of George Smith and Mary A. (Skahal) Parker; m. Amos Hurd, and resides in W. Medway, Mass.

432. Charles Frederick Parker (*Joseph A.*,[9] *Frederick A.*,[8] *Joseph*,[7] *Amos*,[6] *Amos*,[5] *Andrew*,[4] *John*,[3] *Hananiah*,[2] *Thomas*[1]), son of Joseph A. and Samantha W. (Price) Parker, was b. in Philadelphia, Pa., March 4, 1864; m. Emma Kunzig. They lived in Philadelphia, where their children were born. To improve his health he removed to San Francisco, where they resided. He was a very promising and successful teacher there, when very sadly, while swimming on July 20, 1890, he ventured out too far and was drowned.

Their children were:

1. BERTIE PARKER. 2. WALTER PARKER.

433. Emma Eliza Parker *(Gardner,[9] Perley,[8] Gardiner,[7] Isaac,[6] Amos,[5] Andrew,[4] John,[3] Hananiah,[2] Thomas[1])*, dau. of Gardner and Mary L. (Sawyer) Parker, was b. in Hopkinton, Nov. 2, 1845; m. May 8, 1865, Roswel I. Frail of Hopkinton. They reside in Hopkinton.

Their children are:

1. MARY CARRIE FRAIL, b. in Hopkinton, Jan. 11, 1869.
2. GARDNER PARKER FRAIL, b. in Hopkinton, March 26, 1872.

434. George Gardner Parker *(Gardner,[9] Perley,[8] Gardiner,[7] Isaac,[6] Amos,[5] Andrew,[4] John,[3] Hananiah,[2] Thomas[1])*, son of Gardner and Mary L. (Sawyer) Parker, was b. in Hopkinton, Oct. 25, 1849; m. Oct. 7, 1869, Mandana Hyde of Poultney, Vt. They reside in Poultney, where Mr. Parker is in the slate business.

Their children are:

FRED HYDE PARKER, b. in Poultney, Vt., May 7, 1872.
THEODORE JOHN PARKER, b. in Poultney, May 2, 1876.
MARY CARRIE PARKER, b. in Poultney, Aug. 18, 1878.
RAYMOND ARTHUR PARKER, b. in Poultney, May 11, 1881.

435. Edgar Vinton Parker *(Gardner,[9] Perley,[8] Gardiner,[7] Isaac,[6] Amos,[5] Andrew,[4] John,[3] Hananiah,[2] Thomas[1])*,. son of Gardner and Mary L. (Sawyer) Parker, was b. in Hopkinton, Aug. 18, 1855; m. in Warren, May 12, 1880, Lillie C. Butterworth. They reside in Poultney, Vt. He is a slate dealer.

Their children are:

WARREN HENRY PARKER, b. in Poultney, Vt., Jan. 23, 1883.
ALBERT WILLIAM PARKER, b. in Poultney, Jan. 20, 1885.
EDITH MARION PARKER, b. in Poultney, March 17, 1887.
GARDNER VINTON PARKER, b. in Poultney, June 16, 1890.
CARL PARKER, b. in Poultney, Nov. 16, 1892.

Henry E. Parker (see page 426) *(Addison L.,[9] Jabez M.,[8] Jabez M.,[7] Isaac,[6] Amos,[5] Andrew,[4] John,[3] Hananiah,[2] Thomas[1])*, son of Addison L. and Mary M. (Buxton) Parker, was b. in Phillipston, March 22, 1859; m. Dec. 24, 1884, Sadie E. Town of Keene, N. H. He is a railroad engineer and resides in Fitchburg.

Their children are:

EUGENE H. PARKER, b. June 9, 1886.
GRACE PARKER, b. July 2, 1891.

Earnest L. Parker (see page 426) *(Addison L.,[9] Jabez M.,[8] Jabez M.,[7] Isaac,[6] Amos,[5] Andrew,[4] John,[3] Hananiah,[2] Thomas[1])*, son of Addison L. and Mary M. (Buxton) Parker, was b. in Keene, N. H., Jan. 22, 1867; m. July 14, 1887, Bertha E. Tasker of Providence, R. I. He is a druggist and resides in Everett.

Their children are:

IDA B. PARKER, b. Aug. 14, 1889.
LESLIE PARKER, b. March 1, 1891.

436. Richard E. Parker *(Perry A.,[9] Enoch,[8] Jabez,[7] Isaac,[6] Amos,[5] Andrew,[4] John,[3] Hananiah,[2] Thomas[1])*, son of Perry Ander and Mary S. (Russell) Parker, was b. in Keene, N. H., Oct. 5, 1861; m. in Bellows Falls, Vt., June 24, 1890, Hattie Grout. They reside in West Fitchburg, Mass.

Their children:

RUBY PARKER, b. April 17, 1880.
PERRY E. PARKER, b. Feb. 23, 1891.

437. Carrie B. Parker *(Perry A.,[9] Enoch,[8] Jabez,[7] Isaac,[6] Amos,[5] Andrew,[4] John,[3] Hananiah,[2] Thomas[1])*, dau. of Perry Ander and Mary S. (Russell) Parker, was b. in Westminster, Vt., Nov. 8, 1863; m. in Manchester, Ia., Dec. 16, 1884, Gilbert C. Sibley, b. in Penn., Feb. 7, 1862, son of John and Emily Sibley, now of Owego, N. Y. They reside in Mt. Vernon, S. Dak.

Their children:

1. STELLA SIBLEY.
2. HARRY SIBLEY.
3. WILLIE SIBLEY.
4. BESSIE SIBLEY.

438. Ella M. Parker *(Perry A.,[9] Enoch,[8] Jabez,[7] Isaac,[6] Amos,[5] Andrew,[4] John,[3] Hananiah,[2] Thomas[1])*, dau. of Perry Ander and Mary S. (Russell) Parker, was b. in

Sugar Grove, Ill., March 9, 1865: m. in Aurora, Ill., March 14, 1881, Frank McCannon, b. in Essex, Vt., June 15, 1857, son of Thomas and Sarah McCannon of Burlington, Vt. They reside in Sugar Grove, Ill.

Their children:

1. May A. McCannon, b. April 26, 1880.
2. Maude C. McCannon, b. Jan. 1, 1882.
3. Mattie McCannon, b. Aug. 14, 1884.
4. Benjamin McCannon, b. Sept. 5, 1886.
5. Minnie McCannon, b. Oct. 20, 1888.

439. Mary Ellen Parker (*Henry N.*,[9] *Samuel T.*,[8] *Samuel*,[7] *Benjamin*,[6] *Josiah*,[5] *Josiah*,[4] *John*,[3] *Hananiah*,[2] *Thomas*[1]), dau. of Henry Norton and Mary A. (Cooley) Parker, was b. in Smyrna, N. Y., June 21, 1864; m. April 19, 1884, Frank M. Cash.

Their children:

1. Earl Cash.
2. Eva Cash.

440. Alice Amanda Parker (*Henry N.*,[9] *Samuel T.*,[8] *Samuel*,[7] *Benjamin*,[6] *Josiah*,[5] *Josiah*,[4] *John*,[3] *Hananiah*,[2] *Thomas*[1]), dau. of Henry Norton and Mary A. (Cooley) Parker, was b. in Smyrna, N. Y., Aug. 10, 1868; m. Dec. 27, 1883, George Hitchcock.

Their children:

1. Henry Hitchcock, } b. July 18, 1887.
2. Harry Hitchcock, }

441. Mary Emogene Parker (*Hosea S.*,[9] *Benjamin A.*,[8] *Samuel*,[7] *Benjamin*,[6] *Josiah*,[5] *Josiah*,[4] *John*,[3] *Hananiah*,[2] *Thomas*[1]), dau. of Hosea Stebbins and Martha D. (Wilson) Parker, was b. in Spring Hill, Kan., Jan. 24, 1869; m. in Lyndon, Osage Co., Kan., Sept. 12, 1888, John Martin Stucker, b. in Emporia, Kan., Feb. 10, 1867, son of Eli and Hannah Stucker. He is a farmer. They reside in Melvern, Kan.

Their children are:

1. Gale Edwin Stucker, b. in Melvern, Kan., June 28, 1889.
2. Raymond Eli Stucker, b. in Melvern, Feb. 24, 1891.

Col. C. Harrison Parker (see page 340) *(Caleb A.,[8] Lewis,[7] Isaac,[6] Amos,[5] Andrew,[4] John,[3] Hananiah,[2] Thomas[1])*, son of Caleb Alexander Parker, was b. in Jackson, Miss. From his early manhood he has followed the profession of journalism. He has held prominent positions on many of the leading journals of New Orleans, and has secured along with his acknowledged great energy reputation as an uncompromising reformer. In 1881 he was editor-in-chief of the *Picayune*, and he inaugurated a fight in the Democratic party which culminated in the election of Gov. Nichols in 1888. He was appointed State Tax Collector by Gov. Nichols. He was one of the organizers of the Anti-Lottery League, and was chosen chairman of the executive committee and conducted the correspondence incident to the organization of the movement throughout the State. He organized a company organizing the *New Delta*, and he has been the editor and manager of that paper since its foundation. The *New Delta* fought the combined daily press of the State, backed as it was by Lottery millions; but its cause, though one of the most unequal, was one of the most gallant in the history of journalism.

HOMESTEAD RECOLLECTIONS OF REV. THEODORE PARKER.

A fragment of an autobiography by the late Rev. Theodore Parker, which was commenced at Rome shortly before his death, is printed here in its original condition. When he found that he could write no more he closed the manuscript with a caveat to the reader, which was printed in the commencement of the first volume of the "Life and Correspondence of Theodore Parker," by John Weiss. It is of much interest to our family and is reprinted here.

N. B. Caveat Lector.—This will require careful rewriting, and as it stands may contain many errors of detail, for I write it when too ill to read and with no memoranda to aid me. I should like to consult the deeds of the early settlers in my neighborhood to learn the original ownership of land, the date of the houses and the names of the places like "the great meadow." Few men, if any, will remember the name, but I have found it in old deeds.

I began this at Rome, March 16, 1860. It is not likely I shall get far in it. I have waited more than a year for strength to begin it and now commence at my weakest point.

The material and human surroundings about a man in his early life have a strong and abiding influence upon all, especially on those of a sensitive disposition, who are both easily affected by such externals and rather obstinate in retaining the impression made on them.

Of the Material Surroundings.

About 1710 my grandfather's grandfather, John Parker, then somewhat advanced in life, with a part of his grown up children removed from Reading, where a family of Parkers had settled about 1640, to the Cambridge Farms, since called Lexington, where he had bought a considerable quantity of land with one small house upon it, probably of logs. The next year he built him a large and commodious house and furnished it with the usual out-buildings necessary for a farmer's business. The situation was pleasant, a considerable valley, a mile or more in length and half a mile wide, with a fresh meadow at the bottom, called in deeds of the time "the great meadow," wound among hills tall and steep on the western and northern side, while on the south and east the hills were of less height and more gradual in their slope. Indeed, it is the general character of the hills in that part of the country to be steep on their southern and eastern side, and of gradual ascent on the opposite side. A brook steals through the valley or percolated through the soft, spongy meadow, and following a continuation of the valley it falls into Charles river at length. The stream was then much larger than at present, for now the hills have nearly all been stripped of their trees and the meadows drained, and the brook is proportionally shrunk, except when a sudden melting of snow floods the meadow and restores it to more than its original size. Near the upper end of this valley, in about the centre of his farm lot, the old settler built his house, in which children to the fourth generation were born to him. It stood about 80 or 100 feet above the present surface of the great meadow on the southeast side of a high hill, which gently sloping in front of the house rose steep and abrupt behind.

As the old man at sunrise stood at the front or south door of his new house on some fine October morning of 1712 he could see but a single house, and that half or three-quarters of a mile off, the other side of the valley, two other columns of pale blue smoke in that direction might tell him of other neighbors, while not far off in the same valley were two others, hid by wooded hills, in a different direction one more house had been built earlier than his own, but on the north side of the hill which sheltered him.

Agriculture was at a low stage, that part of the country was covered with thick woods, and when the farmer cut down or girdled the trees and run the ground over with fire the land must have looked as we see it now in parts of New Hampshire and Vermont, like "the abomination of desolation." However, he planted many apple trees, importing them from England, but they had not been grafted and so many of them bore sorry specimens of fruit. Many of those which it is said he set out were standing in my boyhood. He, or his son Josiah, who succeeded to a part of his lands at Lexington, planted also locust trees, whose white blossoms used to fill the air with sweetness in June. He also brought lilac bushes, a common ornament about the houses of New England in the last century, and planted a barberry bush, which in my boyhood had grown to prodigious dimensions, besides having increased and multiplied and replenished that part of the earth with its descendants.

In the rear of the house was a monstrous elm which endangered the building and was removed as a nuisance, that was a full-grown tree in the days of my grandfather's grandfather; other huge oaks and elms once stood close by but they had all perished before my birth, and only a white ash with a great round top stood at the northwest corner of the house. It was planted by my grandfather and was the largest tree of its kind I remember ever to have seen in New England. Huge boulders lay scattered about along the valley and its tributaries, some were of the hard, bluish greenstone which forms the skeleton of all the hills in that neighborhood, but others were of whitish granite, brought many miles from their original site to the northwest of that locality. Loose stones abounded, indeed, a more unattractive piece of land for a farmer to work could scarcely be found than that whole section for miles around in all directions. There were stones enough within a foot of the surface to fence all the land into acre lots, each surrounded with a strong "balance wall."

The most common trees were numerous species of oak, the white pine, the pitch pine, and a variety of it called the yellow pine, the hemlock and spruce; on the rocky hill sides the juniper or red cedar, and in the swamp the cypress or white cedar; maples, the white or gray, black and yellow birches, the elm, white and black ashes, poplars, buttonwood, walnuts, chestnut, beech, sassafras and wild hop or hop-hornbeam, willows; three species of sumach occurring on the homestead, indeed, most of the trees of New England grow within a few miles of my home.

The handsome flowering shrubs and plants of New England could mostly be found in the immediate neighborhood, the shadbush, the rhodora, the viscous or white azalea, the pink flowered species was farther off, the numerous cornels, though only a single instance of the large flowering cornel, the several viburnums and the andromedas, the narrow leaved kalmia, and even the broad leaved kind, grew in a thicket in the vicinity, the choke cherries, the sporæas, both pinkish-white flowered and the other with steeple-shaped purple spikes, wild roses and sweet briars, the clethra, blossoming from July to October. In the meadows spongy with soft mosses were the arathusas and the cymbidium and the rarer painted cup, successively disclosing their native beauties, while a little later the pitcher plant offered its curious flower and leaf to the most careless eye. The cranberry bore in midsummer its rich pale-red flowers and covered whole acres, from whence the farmer hoped, often vainly, to win as fair a harvest to season his winter food. The beautiful water lily grew abundantly in a shallow pond, not far off, and also in many brooks of sluggish water, nay, it did not refuse the benediction of its presence in ill-formed ditches whence peat had been cut for fuel or for manure. Here the fringed gentian, not then to be seen, has happily since taken up its abode, the soapwort gentian was uncommon, the trilliums rare, but along the brooksides the cardinal flowers hung out their brilliant colors.

On the hard land saxifrage and columbine grew on the sunny side of all the red rocks. Blue violets and white were to be had everywhere, the yellow species were rarer and anemones nodded their handsome heads on the south side of every wall where nature had her own way. In the woods the lady's slipper hung out its mysterious beauty; the several pyrolas opened their blossoms, they with the ground pine, the partridge berry, the boxberry or Mitchella, kept a green life in the woods under the snow all winter through. What need to mention the humbler beauties of the New England flora, such as the meadow pride, the white cicely, the craneflower and the buttercups. There were also red lilies and yellow, some of them stately and queen-like plants, on a single stalk. I have seen 49 buds and blossoms, nor should the humbler name of the dogtooth-violet be forgotten in the names of its liliaceous sisterhood. My sisters cultivated the crimson peony, white and yellow narcissus, daffodils, white and red roses of the most delicious fragrance.

In the thick, dark swamps corki-fungi grew on the trunks of old maples, but more especially on the white birches, and curious puff balls shot up in the hot, muggy nights of summer and in two days became mysteriously as large as a quart bowl, while the usual variety of other fungi sprung up in their appropriate places, and the Indian pipe of seeming make and mould, while lichens, some as large as a modern Kossuth hat, covered the north side of rocks and trees.

My ancestors had planted the white locust not far from the house and a beautiful grove had grown up; some of the trees were very large and sweetened the air for a week or two in June and the grass all the summer through. When the autumn came—

> "Every bush did put its glory on
> Like a gemmed bride."

How red the maples were, how yellow the birches and the walnuts and what richly tinted leaves did the chestnut shake down!—last of New England trees to blossom and bearing the richest, sweetest fruit the savage found in the austere land. Even the ivy and the poison dogwood were clad in more glory than the Queen of Sheba intent on wooing the King of Israel's son; nay, Solomon himself in all his glory was not arrayed like one of these. From the middle of May when the introduced trees, the plum, peach, cherry, apple and pear, began to bloom till the middle or end of October, the eye need not seek a landscape of humble, quiet New England beauty more attractive than this, and all winter long the white pines, which seemed so cool and attractive in July and August, had a warm, motherly look and told of life still sleeping in them, around them, everywhere.

Of the Human Surroundings.

At the age of 45 my grandfather, Capt. John Parker, died on the 17th of September, 1775. He was sick on the day of the Battle of Lexington but did his duty from 2 A. M. till 12 at night. On the 17th of June he was too ill to be allowed to enter the turmoil of the Battle of Bunker Hill, so he discontentedly commanded troops who did no fighting that day. He was never well afterwards and an epidemic dysentery in September found him an easy prey; he died at an early age for his long lived family and left three sons and four daughters, with a widow who died at the respectable age of 92, passing a portion of the last 47 years of her life in a second marriage which both she and her children had bitter cause to repent. The respectable property of Capt. John Parker was wasted, the relict obliged to take her new husband and his children home to be supported on "the widow's thirds." When my father married Hannah Stearns, the daughter of a neighboring farmer, he went back to the original homestead to take care of his mother while he should support his handsome young wife and such family as might happen. It was the day of small things—he wore home-made blue yarn stockings at his wedding, and brought his wife home over the rough winding roads, riding in the saddle of his tall gray horse, with her upon a pillion. The outfit of furniture did not bespeak more sumptuous carriage—the common plates were of wood; the pitcher, mugs, teacups and saucers were of coarse earthenware, while the great carving dishes were of thick well kept pewter. The holiday service "for company" was of the same material. Yet a few costly wine glasses were not wanting and two long-necked decanters, a few china teacups and saucers of the minutest pattern, and the pride of the buffet a large china bowl. Besides the young bride could show patchwork bedquilts and counterpanes, and a pretty store of linen towels, and a tablecloth of the same, white as the snow, and spun, woven and bleached by her own laborious hands; and her father raised the flax which her brother pulled, and rotted, and broke, and swingled, and hackled and combed. Hannah made their work into linen.

In the course of many years ten children had been born to John and Hannah (one had slipped out of life an infant) when their fourth son and eleventh child came into the world on the 24th of August, 1810, lagging a little more than five years after his youngest, and afterwards his favorite, sister. I think I was the last child born in the old house, which then numbered just 100 years.

1. In my earliest childhood the family at home consisted (to begin in the order of age) of my father's mother, more than 80 at my birth. A tall, stately, proud-looking woman: she occupied an upper chamber, but came down stairs to dinner—other meals she took in her own room—and sat at the head of the table on the woman side thereof, opposite my father, who kept up the ancient Puritan respect for age—always granting it precedence. She busied herself chiefly in knitting and puttering about the room, but passed the Sundays in reading the large Oxford quarto Bible of her husband, bought for the price of more than one load of hay, delivered up at Boston. She had also the original edition of the "Puritan Hyme Book" printed at Cambridge, which was much in her hands. She read the newspapers, the *Columbian Centinel*, which then appeared twice a month; but common mundane literature she seldom touched. It was a part of my childish business to carry the drink to my venerable grandmother, twice a day, at 11 A. M. and 4 P. M., this was flip in cool weather, and in spring or summer was *toddy* or *punch*, the latter was, however, more commonly reserved for festive occasions.

2. Next were my father and mother: grave, thoughtful, serious and industrious people. From an ancestry of five generations of his own name, who had died in New England, my father had inherited a strong and vigorous body; in his youth there was but one man in town who could surpass him in physical strength and few who were his equal. He could endure cold and heat and abstinence from food and rest to a degree that would be thought impossible by men brought up in the effeminate ways, which so often are thought to be the curses of civilization. He was a skilful farmer, though as he lived not on his own land, but on the widow's thirds, he was debarred from making costly improvements in the way of buildings, fences and apple trees, which are long in returning profit to him that plants. But he yet contrived to have, perhaps, the best peach orchard in the County of Middlesex, to graft valuable kinds of fruit upon the old trees and to adopt nearly all the improvements in farming as they were tested and found valuable. He was also an ingenious mechanic; his father and grandfather were mechanics as well as farmers and did all kinds of work in wood, from building saw-mills, cider-mills, pumps, to making flax spinning-wheels and turning wooden bread bowls of maple stumps. He had religiously kept the tools of his father and grandfather, and like them continued to do all kinds of ordinary jobs; indeed, both he and they were such mechanics as men must be in a new country, and should not be in one where industry is more elaborate and able minded men are ready to turn their hands to anything. Mechanical talent was hereditary in the family for several genera-

tions, and appeared in my remote relations, and even among women, on whose shoulders this mantle seldom falls. My father was a thoughtful man, turning his large and active brain and his industrious hand to the mechanical and agricultural work before him; he was an originator of new and short ways of doing many things and made his head save his hands. In this respect his father and grandfather resembled him.

His education—his schooling ended when the Revolution begun—was of course much neglected, but he was an uncommonly good arithmetician, often puzzling the schoolmasters with his original problems. Works on political economy and the philosophy of legislation were favorites with him. He had learned algebra and geometry, and was familiar with the use of logarithms. He read much on Sundays, in the long winter evenings, sometimes in the winter mornings before it was light and in the other intervals of toil. His favorite works were history—that of New England he was quite familiar with—biography and travels, but he delighted most of all in works of philosophy which give the *rationale* of the material of the human world; of course he read much of the theology of his times, and the literature of progressive minds found its way to the farmer's kitchen. He had no fondness for poetry. In his latter years his reading was chiefly of novels, not to instruct, but to amuse the old man, whose mortal life was all behind him. His fathers before him had been bookish men.

My mother, a woman of slight form, flaxen hair, blue eyes and a singularly fresh and delicate complexion, more nervous than muscular, had less education than my father. Her reading was confined mainly to the Bible, the hymn-book, stories of New England captives among the Indians, of which there were many in the neighborhood, some in manuscript and perhaps never printed. Ballads and other forms of poetry gave her a great delight. Of course the newspapers passed through her busy hands. My father often read aloud to her and the rest of the family in the long winter evenings, while her fingers were occupied with sewing or knitting, making or mending. She was industrious, as indeed were all the women of the neighborhood, but like them found opportunities, though too rare, for social enjoyment with them. Dinner was always at noon, and after that was over and its paraphernalia put in order, the household work was done, and a more comely dress took the place of the blue check of the morning.

She was eminently a religious woman. I have known few in whom the religious instincts were so active and so profound, and who seemed to me to enjoy so completely the life of God in the soul of man. To her the Deity was an Omnipresent Father, filling every point of space with His beautiful and loving presence. She saw Him in the rainbow and in the drops of rain which helped compose it as they fell into the muddy ground to come up grass and trees, corn and flowers. She took a deep and still delight in silent prayer —of course it was chiefly the more spiritual part of the Old Testament and New Testament that formed her favorite reading, the dark theology of the times seems not to have blackened her soul at all. She took great pains with the moral culture of her children—at least with mine.

3. Come the brothers and sisters, nine in number, and one in infancy laid away in the grave. Some of these were much older than I and had gone to seek their fortunes in the various trades and callings of the time. There was still a houseful at home; all of them but three had a decided fondness for literature; they read all the good books they could lay their hands on, and copied the better parts. At school they were always among the best scholars.

4. The uncles and aunts come next. On my father's side there were two uncles and twice as many aunts; one of the former, a farmer not far off, a tall, grave man; the other, a more restless character, had served many years in the Revolutionary war; he was in the battles of Saratoga and Yorktown, had failed in business, gone to South Carolina, and married a woman of some property in Charleston, where he then lived, the father of one son. Of the aunts, one was a maiden, an uncommonly intellectual woman; another was a widow living in an adjoining town, while two were the wives of farmers, one living in Nova Scotia, the other in Watertown not far off. On the maternal side, there was one aunt, a strange, eccentric woman, and ten uncles, rejoicing in the names of Asahel, Jepthah, Noah, Ammi, Ishmael, Habakkuk and the like, which if not euphonious, are at least scriptural. They were farmers and laborers, some rich and some poor.

Besides, the brothers and sisters of my grandmother still continued to live, though aged people. Other relations from the Parker side of the family dwelt in more remote towns who occasionally paid my father a visit, in special one very old and tall man, to whom he surrendered the head of the table and invited to say grace.

5. The neighbors about us were farmers: a shoemaker lived a mile off on one side and a blacksmith within two miles on the other. These were generally, perhaps universally, honest, hard-working men: they went to meeting Sundays, morning and afternoon. "Their talk was of bullocks and they were diligent to give the kine fodder." In their houses, generally neat as good houswifery could

make them, you would find the children's school-books, commonly a "singing book," Billings Collection, or some other, perhaps a hymn book, and always a good quarto Bible kept in the best room, sometimes another Bible, inherited from some Puritanic ancestor, these with an almanack hung in the corner of the kitchen chimney made up the family library. Perhaps a weekly or semi-weekly newspaper was also taken and diligently read. Two families not far off were exceptions to this poverty of books. Yet now and then the life of some great thief, like Stephen Burroughs, or some pirate or highway man, would show itself. In other parts of Lexington, "on the great road" in "the middle of the town," perhaps there was a better show of books. I only speak of my immediate neighborhood.

From Birth till the age of Eight.

On the 24th of August, 1810, early on a hot, sweltering morning, I came into this world of joys and sorrows. It seems one of my sisters thought an eleventh child improbable, for she had finished the "Family Tree" with the tenth, five years older than myself. However, a place was soon found for the new comer, both in the needle-work and the hearts of the household. As the youngest child it may be supposed that I was treated with uncommon indulgence, and probably received a good deal more than a tenth part of the affection distributed. I remember often to have heard neighbors say, "Why, Miss Parker, you 're spilin' your boy! He never can take care of himself when he grows up." To which she replied, "She hoped not," and kissed my flaxen curls anew.

Among the earliest things I remember is the longing I used to feel to have the winter gone, and to see the great snow banks sometimes, when new-fallen, as high as the kitchen window, melt away in front of the house. I loved though to run in the snow barefoot and with only my night shirt on, for a few minutes at a time. When the snow was gone the peculiar smell of the ground seemed to me delicious. The first warm days of spring, which brought the blue birds to their northern home and tempted the bees to try short flights, in which they presently dropped on the straw my provident father had strewn for them over the snow about their hives, filled me with emotions of the deepest delight. In the winter I was limited to the kitchen, where I could build cob houses or form little bits of wood into fantastic shapes. Sometimes my father or one of my brothers would take me to the shop where he pursued his toilsome work, or to the barn, where the horse, the oxen and the cows were a perpetual pleasure. But when the snow was gone and the ground dry I had free range. I used to sit or lie on the ground in a dry and sheltered spot and watch the great yellow clouds of April that rolled their huge masses far above my head, filling my eye with their strange, fantastic, beautiful and ever changing forms and my mind with wonder at what they were and how they came there.

But the winter itself was not without its in-door pleasure, even for a little fellow in brown, home-spun petticoats. The uncles and aunts came in the sleighs full of cousins, some of whom were of my own age, to pass a long afternoon and evening, not without abundant good cheer and a fire in "the other room," as the humble parlor was modestly called. They did not come without a great apple or a little bag of shagbarks, or some other tid-bit for Mrs. Parker's baby, for so the youngest was called after he ceased to merit the name. Nay, father and mother often returned these visits, and sometimes took the baby with them; because the mother did not like to leave the darling at home, or perhaps she wished to show how stout and strong her eleventh child had come into the world.

I must relate one example to show, as well as many more, the nice and delicate care she took of my moral culture. When a little boy in petticoats in my fourth year, one fine day in spring my father led me by the hand to a distant part of the farm, but soon sent me home alone. On the way I had to pass a little "pond-hole," then spreading its waters wide: a rhodora in full bloom—a rare flower in my neighborhood and which grew only in that locality—attracted my attention and drew me to the spot. I saw a little spotted tortoise sunning himself in the shallow water at the root of the flaming shrub. I lifted the stick I had in my hand to strike the harmless reptile; for though I had never killed any creature, yet I had seen other boys out of sport destroy birds, squirrels and the like, and I felt a disposition to follow their wicked example. But all at once something checked my little arm and a voice within me said, clear and loud, "It is wrong!" I held my uplifted arm in wonder at the new emotion—the consciousness of an involuntary but inward check upon my actions,—till the tortoise and the rhodora both vanished from my sight. I hastened home and told the tale to my mother and asked what was it that told me it was wrong. She wiped a tear from her eye with her apron, and taking me in her arms, said, "Some men call it conscience, but I prefer to call it the voice of God in the soul of man. If you listen and obey it, then it will speak clearer and clearer and always guide you right. But if you turn a deaf ear or disobey, then it will fade out little by little and leave you all in the dark and without a guide. Your life depends on heeding this little voice." She went her way careful and troubled about many things, but doubtless pondered them in her motherly heart; while I went off to wonder and think it over in my poor childish way. But I am sure no event in my life has made so deep and lasting an impression on me.

Thus it closes, but not abruptly, with the incident which marked the opening of his religious consciousness, for the life itself flows naturally on, drawing in both experience and education to make the whole of his career an amplification of the story, as he set free and vindicated in himself and others, the Life of God in the Soul of Man.

OBITUARY OF MRS. REV. THEODORE PARKER.

"Mrs. Lydia D. Parker, widow of Theodore, the eminent divine, died at her residence, 142 Chandler Street, Saturday evening. Mrs. Parker was a daughter of John Cabot and was born in Newton, 1814. Mrs. Parker was possessed of a tender and confiding nature, which coupled with her sympathetic and philanthropic spirit caused her to be dearly beloved by her large circle of friends and acquaintances. She was a prominent member of the Twenty-Eighth Congregational Society, which her husband founded and exercised a pastoral care for during his lifetime. She was very domestic in her habits and essayed but little in the literary line although she rendered her husband excellent service in the way of copyist and when his biography was compiled assisted the historian to a great extent in deciphering the manuscript of her husband, who was an indifferent penman.

"Some 18 months since she met with a severe accident, being knocked down by a team in the street in which she lived, and since then was confined to the house nearly all the time. Her remains were interred at Mt. Auburn."

THE WILL OF LYDIA D. PARKER.

William D. Bowditch of Brookline and Wendell Phillips were the executors of the will of the late Lydia D. Parker, widow of Rev. Theodore Parker. No bonds were required of them. The will is dated April 25, 1879. The chief public interest is in the first two sections of the will, which are as follows:

"First. To the city of Boston I give all my books which I do not otherwise dispose of by memorandum herein disclosed, that they may be deposited for use in the Public Library of Boston with the other books which my late husband bequeathed to said library, upon the conditions affixed to his bequest. The study desk and table is also to be deposited at my death in the Public Library, also the marble bust of my late husband by Story; and I do desire the same to be placed near the books bequeathed by him to the said library; also the crayon portrait of my late husband by Cheney; also the one of myself.

"Second. To Franklin B. Sanborn of Concord, Mass., I give all the manuscripts, sermons and lectures, bequeathed to me by my late husband, all copyrights and extensions of copyrights that may be in my possession at my decease; all note books, bound and unbound, all journals, letters and diaries, and the literary property generally, to do with as he shall see fit; also the blocks of wood engravings in Weiss's Biography of Theodore Parker; also the stereotype plates."

In the remainder of her will a large number of bequests of small sums of money are made to her relatives and friends. To Juliette Frances Ridlar, a member of her family, she gave $10,000, her piano, silverware, including the large silver candlestick given her by her husband in 1853, and her personal wardrobe. To George C. Cabot, once her husband's ward, $7,000, to be held in trust for the benefit ot his children—also silverware and her husband's gold pencil case and pen. To Mary T. Drew, her esteemed friend, $5,500. To Miss Hannah E. Stevenson the large inkstand which for many years had stood on Mr. Parker's desk. To Emeline P. Gilman of Chelsea the silver cup given to Mr. Parker by his Watertown pupils in 1834. All the residue of her household furniture, plate, engravings and pictures and all articles in her dwelling house, not specially bequeathed in her will she left to Sarah W. Jackson and Juliette Frances Ridlar, in trust, to give and distribute as she requested in a memorandum which was enclosed in her will. According to this, the furniture in the house, which came from Mrs. Parker's family, the Cabots, was all to be returned to her brother, who lived in Lawrence. The remaining articles, connected with herself and Mr. Parker, are most of them divided between her nephew, George C. Cabot of South Boston, and her adopted daughter, Mrs. Wardell of North Andover, formerly Miss Etta Ridlar. To her housekeeper, Mary Drew, who had lived with her about 30 years, she left a portion of the rest, and then distributed the articles which Theodore Parker mostly used and which were connected most closely with his daily life and studies, to Mrs. Robert E. Apthrop, Miss Hannah E. Stevenson, Miss Caroline C. Thayer and sister, Miss Sarah Jackson and sister, Mrs. Willey and Miss Carew of Weymouth, Wendell Phillips and Miss

Kate Johnson of Andover, sister of the Rev. Samuel Johnson. To Mrs. Ralph Waldo Emerson she left the very fine photograph of Mr. Emerson which always hung in Mr. Parker's parlor, and to Mr. John Brooks Parker,.formerly treasurer of the Eastern Railroad, and nephew of her husband, she left the Parker family Bible. The residuary legatees were Juliette Frances Ridlar, who received half of the property, and the legal heirs of Theodore Parker.

GENEALOGY OF REV. THEODORE PARKER.

As arranged by him at about 1850.

FIRST GENERATION.

[1]**Thomas Parker** m. **Amy ——.**

born 1609 (epitaph in Reading graveyard). Sailed from London, March 11, 1635, adm. freeman 1637, one of seven who founded the 1st Church at Reading abt. 1645; died Aug. 12, 1683.

She died Jan. 15, 1690.

SECOND GENERATION.

[2]**Hananiah Parker** m. (1) **Elizabeth ——.** (2) **Mary (Bright) Bursham.**

of Reading, born 1638; died March 18, 1723-4.

She was living in 1731.

THIRD GENERATION.

[3]**John Parker** m. **Deliverance ——.**

of Reading, b. Aug. 3, 1664. He moved from Reading to Lexington and died there Jan. 22, 1740-1.

She died at Lexington, March 10, 1717-18.

FOURTH GENERATION.

[4]**Lt. Josiah Parker** m. **Hannah Stone.**

of Lexington, born April 11, 1694; m. Dec. 28, 1718; died Oct. 8, 1756.

Probably the Hannah S., Wat. Gen., p. 585, d. of Nath. S. and —— Hinckley, who was dau. of Gov. Hinckley.

FIFTH GENERATION.

[4]**John Parker** m. **Mary Moore.**

of Lexington, b. July 13, 1729; m. May 22, 1755.

T. P.'s memo. of Lydia Moore.

SIXTH GENERATION.

[4]**John Parker** m. **Hannah Stearns.**

of Lexington, b. Feb. 7, 1761; m. in Waltham, Feb. 17, 1785.

SEVENTH GENERATION.

1. Mary.
2. John.
3. Hannah.
4. Lydia.
5. Lydia.
6. Rebecca.
7. Isaac.
8. Ruth.
9. Hiram S.
10. Emily Ann.
11. Theodore.

FIRST GENERATION.

[5]**Charles Stearns** m. (1) **Hannah ——,** who d. in Watertown. (2) **Rebecca Gibson.** June 22, 1654, dau. of John and Rebecca G. of Cambridge.

Adm. freeman May 6, 1646.

SECOND GENERATION.

[6]**John Stearns** m. (1) **Judith Lawrence.** (2) April 2, 1713, **Mary Norcross.**

(Carpenter), b. in Cambridge, Jan. 24, 1656; died in Lex. Feb. 22, 1722.

THIRD GENERATION.

[7]**Benjamin Stearns** m. **Hepsibah Shattuck.**

bap. June 22, 1690; m. Sept. 6, 1721.

b. 1687, widow of Nathaniel Shattuck and dau. of John Hastings. She m. Shattuck April 14, 1714.

FOURTH GENERATION.

[7]**Benjamin Stearns** m. **Hannah Segar**

b. in Lexington, Dec. 27, 1728; m. in Newton, Sept. 11, 1754.

of Newton, b. Jan. 25, 1736, the 10th and youngest child of Ebenezer and Ruth (Burrage) Segar.

FIFTH GENERATION.

1. Asahel.
2. Habbakuk.
3. Nahum.
4. Martha.
5. Ishmael.
6. Noah.
7. Hannah married John Parker.
8. Hiram.
9. Jepthah.
10. Ammi.
11. Elisha.

Notes.

[Hepsibah (Hastings) (Shattuck) Stearns,[3] John Hastings,[2] Thomas H.[1] of Ipswich.]

Benjamin Stearns of Lexington. See Genealogies and History of Watertown, p. 137.

Hannah Segar. See Jackson's Hist. of Newton, p. 404. Hannah,[5] Ebenezer,[4] Job[3] and Mary, Henry[2] and Mary (Bishop), Thomas Segar[1] of Newbury.

---

[1] T. P.'s MSS., p. 125. [2] Wat. Gen., 524, note. T. P.'s MSS. [3] Wat. Gen., p. 524, note. Bridgeman's Pilgrims of Boston, p. 136-7. Gen. and History of Watertown, p. 558-9. [4] Wat. Gen., 524. [5] Wat. Gen., 552. [6] Wat. Gen., 553. [7] Wat. Gen., p. 558.

THE FOLLOWING TO PAGE 480 ARE COPIES OF ANCIENT PAPERS STILL IN THE PRESERVATION OF THE PARKER FAMILY.

DEA. THOMAS PARKER, 1688.

NOVEMBER: 6th 1688: IN REDDING

The bounds of Deacon Thomas Parkers 2nd devision loot in the Comon Land to note the Hundred acres bounded on the sowe east Corner a white oack by Clarks and Samul Fitches slodg marked I P and sowtherly on hede of Loots Adam Calson Thomas Burnap John Eatton to a maple marked H P: I E I F so northerly to a maple marked H P I F N G and then Eastwarly to a maple In the swamp H P N G and so Eastwardly to a high black oack on a Rocky hill with a heap of stones about it marked H P N G ner onkl John Parkers loot.

JOHN PARKER TO NATHANIEL PARKER—1705.

TO ALL PEOPLE TO WHOM THISE PRESENTS SHALL COM John Parker of Redding in ye County of Middlesex within her Majties Province of the massachusets bay in Newingland Joyner Sendeth Greeting Know ye yt he ye said John Parker for and in Consideration of a Valluabl sum of mony to him in hand paid at or before ye enseal ing & delivery of these pressents by Nathanil Parker of Redding Jun cooper in ye county of middlesex above sd ye Resepth wherof ye sd John Parker to his full Content & Satisfaction doth here by Acknoledge and their of and of Evry part and parcill their of doth acquit Exonerate and discharge him ye sd Nathanil Parker his Heirs Executors and Administrators for ever by these presents Hath given granted bargained sould aliened enfeoffed and confirmed and by these presents Doth fully frely clearly & absolutely give grant bargain sell alien Enfeoffe and confirm unto him the said Nathanill Parker his heirs and Asigns for ever Eleven achors of Upland mor or lees Lying in ye bounds of Redding and is a second devison lot and ye thirty Second lot & Lyeth ner Samuel Hitches sledg so caled ye South East corner being a whit oack marked TP and HP and so southarly on ye heds of ye Lots to a mapl tree marked TP and HP at ye south west corner and so to a litle pitch pine on a Rocky knol at ye nor west corner and so norwarly by ye Land of Nathanil goodwin to a hep of stone about a black oak marked HP and TP on a Rocky knoull at ye nor east corner which was Laid out to Decon Thomas Parker of Redding and now in ye posesion of John Parker above s^{d} TOGETHER with all ye profits privelidges Rights comodities appurtinances what so evr their unto be Longing or in any kind appertaining

TO HAVE AND TO HOLD ye Eleven acors mor or less as above s^{d} with all other ye a bove barganed premises unto him the s^{d} Nathanill Parker Jun his heirs Assigns to his and their only proper use benifit and behoofe forevr &c ye s^{d} John Parker for himselfe his heirs Executtors and Adminstrators Doth hearby Covenant promis and grant to and with ye s^{d} Nathanill Parker his heirs and asignes in manr following that is to say that att ye time of ye ensealing and delivering of thes presents to the s^{d} John Parker hath in himselfe full pouer good Right and Lawfull authority to grant bargain sell and convey and a dower ye same as a for s^{d} and that ye said Nathanil Parker his heirs and asignes shall and may from hence forth and for evre her aftr by force and vertue of thes presents Lawfuly peacably and quieatly have hold use ocupie poses and injoy ye above granted premeses with their appurtinances and evry part their of with out ye lest denial interuption or Evacuation of him the s^{d} John Parker: or Deliverance his wife their heirs excutours Adminstratours or asignes or of any other persons whom so evr claming and having any Lawfull right their too or Intrest their in IN WITNESS wher of the s^{d} John Parker and Deliverance his wife in Testemony of heir free and voluntary consent to this act and deed of her husband her unto set their hands and seals ye twenty sixt day of April Anno Dominie one thousand sevn hondred and five and in the ffourth year of the Rain of our souvraign Lady Queen Anne

Sined sealed and Delivered
In the presents of us — John Parker

BENJAMIN BURNAP — DELIVERANCE PARKER
WILLIAM BRIANT
WILIAM SAWYER his x mark 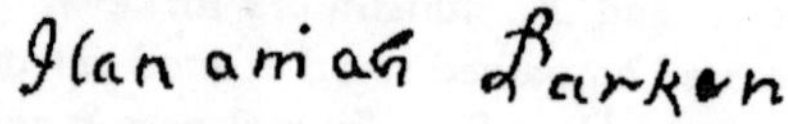

Middlss June 6 1705
then John Parker personly apered
befor mee the subskriber one of her
majty Justises of the pece for the
County afors^{d} and acknoledged this Instrumnt
to be his act and deed

J$^{o}_{n}$ BREWER

Charles Towne July 10th 1708 Reced and accordingly
Entened with the Registry of Deeds &c for midl^{x}
Lib 140 A= pag 555 By SAM^{LL} PHIPPS Reg

JOHN CUTLER'S DEED TO JOHN PARKER—1712.

TO ALL PEOPLE to whom this present Deed of Sale shall Come Greeting, Now KNOW YEE, that I John Cutler Junr: of Cambridge In the County of middlesex in the Province of the massachusetts Bay In New England husbandman for & in Consideration of one hundred and thirty pounds currant mony of New England to me in hand well & truly paid by John Parker Senr: of Redding in sd: County Joiner, the receipt whereof I do by these presents acknowledge unto my full satisfaction, & of & from every part & parcel thereof do fully absolutely and for ever acquitt & discharge him the sd: John Parker, his heirs, execr: & assigns by these presents HAVE Given, granted, bargained, sold, aliened, enfeoffed, & confirmed, & do by these presents Give, grant, bargain, sell, aliene, enfeoff, Convey and Confirm unto him the sd: John Parker one certain messuage, or tenement lying & being situate In Cambridge abovesd: in the farm, containing one small mansion house, & about Sixty Acres of Land more or less and is bounded westerly by Leftn: Cutler from a black oak in the norwest corner to a black oak at a corner in Watertown Line, Southerly upon sd: Watertown Line Partly, & partly by sd: Cutler, southeast, & east upon Danl: White, & northerly partly by John Stone, & partly by Thomas Cutler; TO HAVE, and TO HOLD sd: Lands so bounded, or however otherwise bounded, or reputed to be bounded with all the fences, edifices, wood, water wayes, easments, & emoluments whatsoever, with all other the Rights, Titles, priveledges & appurtenances to the same belonging unto him the sd: John Parker his heirs, execs: & assigns and to his & their sole proper use benefitt, & behooff for ever. And I the sd: John Cutler do hereby Covenant promise & engage that before and untill the sealing & delivery of these presents I am the sole and proper owner of the above granted premises with each of their appurtenances, and that I have in myself good right full power and Lawfull Authority to Convey the same as aforesd: and that the same are free & clear acquitted and discharged of & from all other and former Gifts, Grants, bargains, Sales Leases, Mortgages, Thirds, Intails, & Incumbrances whatsoever, and that it shall & may be Lawfull for him the sd: John Parker his heirs, execrs: & assigns from time to time & at all times for ever hereafter TO HAVE, hold, use, Improve, occupy, possess & enjoy the same, peacably & Quietly without the Lawfull Lett, Suitt, denial, or disturbance, contradiction, or expulsion of me the sd: John Cutler, my heirs, execrs: or assigns, or any other person or persons by from or under me or my procurement. And the Sale hereof as abovesd: I will for ever WARRANT save harmless & defend from all manner of persons makeing any Lawfull claim thereunto, and will make perform, and execute all such other & further Act, & Acts, thing & things, Device & devises as is in Law or Equity can be devised, advised, or required for the Confirmation hereof according to the Laws & Customs of this Province. IN WITTNESS whereof I the s[d]: John Cutler with Hannah my now married wife have hereunto putt our hands & seals this third day of June, Anno Dom[i]: one thousand seven hundred & twelve, In the eleventh year of her Maj[es]: Reign.

Signed, Sealed, & delivered
In presence of
JOHN MASON.
THOMAS CUTLER.

JOHN CUTLER Jun[r]. [SEAL.]
his + mark
HANAH CUTLER [SEAL.]
her + mark

Midle[sx] ss Redding y[e] 25 June 1712 John Cutler jun[r] personally appeared before me y[e] subscriber one of her Majesties Justices of y[e] Peace for s[d] County & acknowledged this above written instrument to be his voluntarie act & deed. JNO. PRESCOT.

Charlestown: July: 5th: 1712: Reced and accordingly entered wth y[e] Records of Deeds &c for Middlesex: Lib: 16°, pag[e] 104—105. By SAM[ll] PHIPPS, Reg[r].

JOHN PARKER'S DEED TO JOSEPH BROOKS—1725.

TO ALL PEOPLE to whom these presents Shall Come Greeting, Know yee, that I John Parker of Lexington in y[e] County of middlesex in y[e] Province of y[e] Massachusets bay In New England Joiner, for & in Consideration of Six hundred pounds In good bills of Credtt: of y[e] Province aforesd: to me in hand well and truly paid by Joseph Brooks of Weston in y[e] County aforesd: husbandman, the receipt whereof I do by these presents Acknowledge unto my full satisfaction, & of & from every part and parcel thereof do fully absolutely & for ever Acquitt, and discharge y[e] s[d]: Joseph Brooks his heirs, Exec: Adminr: by these presents. HAVE Given, granted bargained, sold, aliened, enfeoffed & Confirmed, & do by these presents Give, grant bargain, sell, aliene, enfeoff, Convey, & Confirm to him y[e] s[d]: Joseph Brooks one certain messuage or tenement lying in Lexington aforesaid Containing one mansion house, one barn, two outhouses, & one hundred Acres of Land more or Less, bounded Westerly by Benjamin Cutler. from a stake and stones strait to y[e] corner of y[e] wall that divides between John & Josiah Parker, that is to say up to y[e] westerly end of y[e] wall as far as tis now built. Southerly by John & Josiah Parker by y[e] s[d]: wall & by a maple to y[e] Ditch in Palfrys meadow, & so as the ditch runs to Daniel Whites Land. Easterly &

Northerly by Daniel White. Southerly by ye ditch of andrew Parkers meadow, & so round as ye trees are marked & partly by y^e same, to a stake & stones, next to Daniel Whites Land, and so directly to y^e mark tree between Daniel White, John Stone and Matthew Bridge. North East by Matthew Bridge to a walnut marked, so to a red oak marked: which is Palfrys corner. Northerly by Palfry to a walnutt $mark^t$, North East by Palfry to a black oak & so to Andrew Parkers wall; then tis bounded by Andrew Parker as y^e fence stands that divided between him & his father to Joseph Stones Land, then Northerly by Joseph Stone as y^e fence stands to $Benj^n$: Cutlers Corner, TO HAVE and TO HOLD s^d: messuage with all y^e buildings, fences, profitts, priveledges, & Conveniences to y^e same belonging unto him y^e s^d: Joseph Brooks his heirs Exec: & Adminrs: and to his & their sole proper use, benefitt and behooff for ever. And I the sd: John Parker do hereby Covenant & engage that at ye executing of these presents, I am the sole & proper owner of ye above granted premises, and that ye same are free & clear Acquitted & discharged of & from all other & former gifts, grants, bargains, sales, Leases mortgages Thirds Intails, & Incumbrances whatsoever, excepting a way reserved thro ye premises for Josiah Parker his heirs & assigns to Lexington meeting house thro Gates or bars, & Liberty for Andrew Parker to Fetch hay from his meadow thro y^e premises. And the said John Parker doth grant to y^e sd: Joseph Brooks his heirs & Assigns a bridle way which he hath reserved thro Andrew Parkers Land to meeting. and a way or passage thro s^d: John Parkers Land to Watertown. and the sale hereof as $aboves^d$: I will for ever Warrant and defend from all manner of persons makeing any Lawfull Claim thereunto. free & clearly to Hold use Improve, occupy, possess & enjoy y^e same peacably & quietly without the Lawfull Lett, Suitts, denial or contradiction of me y^e s^d: John Parker my heirs or assigns, or any other person or persons by from or under me or my procurement. and will make perform & execute all such other & further Act, & Acts for ye Confirmation hereof to ye said Joseph Brooks his heirs or Assigns as by his & their Council learned in ye Law shall be devised, advised, or required. In Wittness whereof I the s^d: John Parker with Sarah my wife have hereunto putt our hands, & seals this twenty seventh day of March Anno Dom^i: one thousand, seven hundred & twenty five in ye eleventh year of his Maj^{es}: Reign.

Signed sealed, & delivd: JOHN PARKER
In presence of
JOHN HANCOCK
EBENEZR HANCOCK

JOHN PARKER'S BOND TO JOHN PARKER, 1737.

Know all Men by these Presents y^{t} I JOHN PARKER of Framingham in ye County of Midd^{lx} in ye Province of ye Massachu^{s}: Bay in New England Yeoman am holden & firmly Bound & obliged unto John Parker of Lexington in ye County above s^{d} turner in ye Penal sum of thirty Pounds Currunt mony of New England to ye which Payment well & truly to Be made & Don unto him ye s^{d} John Parker his heirs Execrs: Admrs: asigns or Lawfull Attorny I Binde myself my heirs Execrs Admrs: firmly by these Presents Sealed with my seal this second Day of march anno Dom one thousand Seven hundred & thirty seven Eight & in ye Eleventh Year of his majesties Reign.

The Condition of this above written Obligation is such that if ye above Bounden John Parker his heirs Execrs Admrs: or Assigns Shall well & truly Pay or Caus to be Paid unto him ye s^{d} John Parker his heirs Execrs Admrs: asigns or Lawfull Attorny ye full & Just Sum of fifteen Pounds Currnt mony of New England or Good Bills of Creddet on ye Province above s^{d} of ye old tenour at on or Before ye twenty fift Day of Desember next Insuing ye Date hereof & that without fraud or furder Delay then this obligation to Be void and of none Efect But Else to Remain in full force Power and Vertue.

Signed Sealed & Delivered
in Presents of us

Josiah Parker John Parker

MARY PARKER

AGREEMENT BETWEEN JOHN PARKER, ANDREW PARKER AND JOSIAH PARKER, 1739-40.

Know all men By these Presents that we John Parker and Andrew Parker Do fully & freely Consent and agree that Josiah & John Parker. ju: or their heirs or assigns shall have full Right and Lawfull authority to take Emproove & Injoy for Ever all ye Moovable Estate Belonging to John Parker my Hon^{erd}: father of what kind or nature soever it may be and we Likewise Promise that we will not either Directly nor in Directly keep or Conseal any thing or things that shall or may at any time appear to be ye s^{d}: John Parkers movable Estate upon Penalty of Paying all Damage^{s}: that may arise by our withholding any of ye Goods of ye nature above s^{d}

Except all such moveblcs as are needed for house keeping which at ye Deacese of our Hon^{erd}: Parents: John Parker & Sary his wife are to be Eaqualy Divided Between Andrew: Josiah & John Parker or their heirs

As Witness our Hands and Seals this fourth Day of January 1739/40

DAVID MEAD	JOHN PARKER [SEAL.]
JABEZ KENDALL	ANDREW PARKER [SEAL.]

[The following is the copy of a Royal decree issued to Capt. John Parker of Lexington. It was one of the Stamp Act documents so unwelcome to the unrepresented colonists. It is preserved at Lexington.]

G. R.

Province of
Maſſachuſetts-Bay.

[ROYAL SEAL.]

The Honorable HARRISON GRAY, *Eſq;*

Treasurer and Receiver-General for His Majeſty ſaid Province.

To JOHN PARKER, *Conſtable or Collector of Lexington,* Greeting, &c.

BY Virtue of an Act of the Great and General Court or Aſſembly of the ſaid Province, begun and held at Boſton, *on Wedneſday the* Twenty-ſeventh *Day of* May, 1767, *in the Seventh Year of His Majeſty's Reign, entitled,* An Act for apportioning and aſſeſſing the Sum of *Forty Thouſand Pounds,* &c.

THESE are in His Majeſty's Name to will and require you to collect all and every the Sums of Money mentioned in the Liſt or Liſts of the Tax or Aſſeſsment of your Town, Diſtrict, Pariſh or other Place, made by the Aſſeſſors or Selectmen of the ſaid Town, Diſtrict, Pariſh or other Place, and committed to you to collect: Amounting in the whole to the Sum of

Seventy Eight pounds nineteen shillgs & 10 $^3/_4$

In Manner following: That is to ſay, To collect the whole of each reſpective Sum aſſeſſed on each particular Perſon, ſet down in the faid Lift or Lifts, fo that you duly pay in the Sum-Total of the faid Lift or Lifts unto, and make up and iffue your Accompt of the Whole thereof with Myfelf, His Majefty's Treafurer and Receiver-General of His Revenue within this Province, my Deputy or Deputies, or Succeffors in the faid Office, at or before the Thirtieth Day of *March* next, which will be in the Year of our Lord *One thoufand feven hundred and fixty-eight.* And in Cafe any Perfon or Perfons shall refufe or neglect to pay the feveral Sum or Sums, whereat he or they are fet at in the faid Affefsment, and to pay the fame upon demand made, it shall and may be lawful for you, and you are hereby authorifed and required for Non-payment, to deftrein the Perfon or Perfons fo refufing or neglecting, by his or their Goods or Chattles; and the Diftrefs or Diftreffes fo taken, to keep for the Space of Four Days, at the Cost and Charges of the Owner thereof; and if the Owner does not pay the Sum or Sums of Money fo affeffed upon him, within the faid Four Days, then the faid Diftrefs or Diftreffes to be forthwith openly fold at an Outcry, by you for the Payment of the faid Money, Notice of fuch Sale being pofted up in fome public Place in the fame Town, Diftrict, Parish or other Place, Twenty-four Hours before-hand; and the Overplus coming by the faid Sale (if any there be) over and above the Charges of taking and keeping the Diftrefs or Diftreffes, to be immediately reftored to the Owner. And if any Perfon or Perfons affeffed as aforefaid, shall refufe or neglect to pay the Sum or Sums fo affeffed, by the Space of Twelve Days after Demand thereof, where no fufficient Diftrefs can or may be found, whereby the fame may be levied; in every fuch Cafe, you are to apply yourfelf unto Two or more of the Affeffors within your Town, Diftrict, Parish or other Place, for Warrant to commit fuch Perfon or Perfons to the common Goal, as the Law directs. And where any Perfon or Perfons shall remove from your Town, not having firft paid the refpective Sums or Proportion fet upon him or them in faid Tax or Affefsment, you are hereby authorifed and impowered to demand the Sum or Sums affeffed upon fuch Perfon or Perfons, in what Town or Place foever he or they may be found within this Province; and upon Refufal or Neglect to pay the fame, to deftrein the faid Perfon or Perfons, by his or their Goods and Chattles, as aforefaid; and for want of fuch Diftrefs to commit the Party to the common Goal, there to remain until Payment be made of the Sum or Sums fo fet upon him, with all Charges arifing by reafon of fuch Commitment.

And hereof you are not to fail, upon the Pains and Penalties as may in fuch Cafe by Law be inflicted on you.

GIVEN under my Hand and Seal at Bofton, *the* Seventh *Day of* November, 1767, *in the Eighth Year of the Reign of our Sovereign Lord* GEORGE *the Third, of* Great Britain, *&c. KING.*

☞ *AS there will be a Neceffity for the above Money to be in the Treafury, by the 30th of March, to enable me to difcharge the Government's Securities, that will about that Time become due; You are therefore ordered ftrictly to obey this Warrant.* } H GRAY

CAPT. JOHN PARKER'S WIDOW'S DOWER.

Middlesex ss. To the Honorable John Winthrop Esq[r] Judge of Probate for said County

Sir, in observance of the Commission from your Honor to us directed, which is herewith exhibited, we have apprized the real estate whereof John Parker late of Lexington in said County gentleman deceased, died seized & possessed, containing about One Hundred & Twenty acres, lying in the towns of Lexington & Waltham with a dwelling house, barn & work-shop standing thereon, bounded Southerly by lands of Isaac Pierce, Jonas Smith, Jonas Dix, Sam[l] Fisk, Isaac & Silas Stearns, & the heirs of Ebenezer White deceased; Easterly by lands of Jonas Smith, Jonas Dix Esq[r], Isaac Pierce, Samuel Fisk, the heirs of Ebenezer White, & Thomas Parker; Northerly on land of Thomas Parker aforesaid; & Westerly by lands of Abijah Child & Isaac Pierce aforesaid; apprized at One Thousand & Five Hundred Pounds £1500. .0. .0 Having thus Perfected our Inventory we proceeded & set off to Lydia the widow of the deceased as her right of dower, the westerly end of the dwelling house, the westerly end of the barn, as far as the east side of the floor, together with about forty acres of land lying partly in the town of Lexington & partly in the town of Waltham, bounded westerly by lands of Abijah Child & Isaac Pierce; southerly by lands Isaac Pierce, Jonas Smith, Jonas Dix Esq, Sam[l] Fisk, Isaac & Silas Stearns; Easterly by lands of Jonas Smith, Jonas Dix Esq, Isaac Pierce, & Samuel Fisk; & elsewhere on the two thirds of said Farm, as follows; viz. Beginning at the West end of a stone wall in the meadow on the line between the towns of Waltham & Lexington, thence turning & running northwesterly to a white oak tree marked near a spring, Thence to the corner of the stone wall by the spring, thence running with the wall on the easterly side of the close until it comes to the northerly corner thereof, thence turning westerly & running to a stake & heap of stones near the barn on the front thereof, thence turning & running to & through the barn on the east side of the floor (reserving a privilege in said floor for the Owners or Occupants of the two thirds of said farm to use and improve the floorway for carting in stover, grain, threshing, &c, with convenient room for passing & repassing with a team for that purpose) thence turning & running westerly with said barn to the northwest corner thereof, thence running southwesterly to a stake & heap of stones at the corner of a wall at the Cowyard, thence turning & running Westerly with said wall to a stake & heap of stones, thence turning & running northerly across the center of the well to the center of the front door of the dwelling house, thence thro' the center of the chimney to a stake & heap of stones three feet north of said house (both the Possessors of the thirds & two thirds to have the privilege of using the entry & front stairs of said house) thence running three feet distant from said house to the southwest corner thereof, thence turning & running westerly with the stone wall to the corner thereof, thence running northerly with the wall to the corner thereof, then running westerly with said wall to the corner, thence running Northerly to the corner thereof, & thence turning & running southwesterly with said wall until it connects the land of Abijah Child aforesaid; valued at Five Hundred Pounds

JONAS DIX
JOHN BRIDGE
THADDEUS PARKER

Nov. 4th 1778

We assent to the foregoing apprizal & Division
LYDIA PARKER
LYDIA PARKER junr

Middlesex 10 Nov. 1778, I accept of this return & order the same to be recorded.

J WINTHROP J Prob

Copy examined, Attest

JAMES WINTHROP Regr

ELISHA HEDGE TO THOMAS PARKER.

TO all People to whom thefe Prefents shall come, Greeting.

Know Ye, That I ELISHA HEDGE of Malbrough in the County of middelsex in the province of the Mafachufsetts Bay For and in Confideration of the Sum of thirteen Hundred and thirty pounds to me in Hand before the Enfealing hereof, well and truly paid by THOMAS PARKER of Lexinton in the County of middelsex gentleman the Receipt whereof I do hereby acknowledge, and myfelf therewith fully fatisfied and contented; and thereof, and of every Part and Parcel thereof, do exonerate, acquit and difcharge the faid

Thomas His Heirs, Executors and Adminiftrators, forever by thefe Prefents: HAVE given, granted, bargained, fold, aliened, conveyed and confirmed; and by thefe Prefents, Do freely, fully and abfolutely give, grant, bargain, fell, aliene, convey and confirm, unto him the faid Thomas His Heirs and Affigns forever. one fertin tract or persal of Land Sittuate and Being in Prinstown Contaning Fore Hundred Acres Together with the Road Pafsing Thro the fame and is bounden as follows Viz: Begening at a mark[t] tree on the North Sid of the Road By Mr Oaks his land thence Norly to a mark[t] Tree on the North Sid of the Brook thence Bounding on Said Brook Till it Comes to Shrewfbury old line thence Norwefterly on land of Re[vd.] Israel Loring Thence Northerly By Said Lorings land tell it Coms to Land of one Walle Thence round Said Walles land Tell it comes to land of Nathan Jones Thence Bounded on Said Jones tell it comes to land of Jofeph Abbot Thence to land of one Goodenough Thence to land of one Curtice Thence to Rutland Line to land that Dr Hervy Sold to Nathan Jones Thence Bound by said Okes land tell it coms to where it first Began, Containing all the Land that the said Mr Hedge ones in Princtown

To have and to hold the faid granted and bargained Premifes, with all the Appurtenances, Privileges and Commodities to the faid belonging, or in any wife appertaining to him the faid thomas his Heirs and Affigns forever. To his and their only proper Ufe, Benefit and Behoof forever. And I the faid Elisha for myself my Heirs, Executors and Adminiftrators, do Covenant, Promife and Grant to and with the said thomas His Heirs and Affigns, that before the Enfealing hereof, I am the true, fole and lawful Owner of the above-bargained Premifes, and am lawfully feized and poffeffed of the fame in my own proper Right, as a good, perfect and abfolute Eftate of Inheritance in Fee Simple: And have in myfelf good Right, full Power and lawful Authority, to grant, bargain, fell convey and confirm faid bargained Premifes in Manner as aforefaid: And that he the faid thomas His Heirs and Affigns, shall and may from Time to Time, and at all Times forever hereafter, by Force and Virtue of thefe Prefents, lawfully, peaceably and quietly Have, Hold, Ufe, Occupy, Poffefs and Enjoy the faid demifed and bargained Premifes, with the Appurtenances, free and clear, and freely and clearly acquitted, exonerated and difcharged of, from all and all Manner of former or other Gifts, Grants, Bargains, Sales, Leafes, Mortgages, Wills, Entails, Jointures, Dowries, Judgments, Executions, or Incumbrances of what Name or Nature foever, that might in any Meafure or Degree obftruct or make Void this prefent Deed.

Furthermore, I the faid Elisha for myfelf my Heirs, Executors and Adminiftrators, do Covenant and Engage the above-demifed Premifes to him the faid thomas his Heirs and Affigns, againft the lawful Claims or Demands of any Perfon or Perfons whatfoever, forever hereafter to Warrant, Secure and Defend by thefe Prefents. in witneff hear of I have hereunto fet my hand and feal this Ninth Day of April Anno Dominio one thoufand feven Hundred and Seventy Seven

Signed Sealed & delivered
in prefuence of Us — ELISHA HEDGE [SEAL]
EBENEZER PARKER
ANTIPAS BRIGHAM

Worcefter fs. April 29 1778
Elisha Hedge Subfcriber to this Inftrument
acknowledged the same to be his free act & Deed
Col JOHN WOOLSON J[s] Pace

Worcester fs Sep[r] 8 1779 Rec[d] & Recorded with the
Records of Deeds for s[d] County Libro 83 page 6
NATH. BALDWIN Regr

MILITARY HISTORY.

From first to last throughout the long struggle for Independence the Parker name ranks prominently in patriotism, bravery and service. Let the towns of Reading and Lexington testify to this assertion. From Reading there were 15, all bearing the name of Parker, who responded to the alarm from Lexington upon the opening of hostilities, April 19, 1775. Fathers, sons, brothers, uncles, nephews and cousins—all these were represented among them. They all did good service on that day and many of them for a long period in some part of the war. On the various stones which mark the resting-places of these men who served in the wars from King Phillip's to the last in our history, we read the titles which they so gallantly earned, —colonels, captains, lieutenants, sergeants and ensigns. From early times the colonists were obliged to be very familiar with their flintlocks and muskets. They carried their heavy "firelocks" from house to field, to town or to church and always kept them handy in the house at night. In many of the early settlements the struggle for existence from nature on one side and savage foes on the other was fatal. It is no wonder that this constant schooling made them defensive and quick to respond to duty's call.

From the wars with King Phillip to the Revolution was a period of 100 years of almost successive warfare and untold stories of endurance, hardship and courage. An interesting tale it would make were we able to relate here the part in this history which the Parker name has acted.

Capt. James Parker of Groton, Mass., was an Englishman. He was one of the founders of the town. He was a very active and brave officer in the earliest wars of the colony with the Indians. He was also a deacon. His son James was killed by the Indians, July 27, 1694. John Parker, the first settler of Parker's Island, now Georgetown, Me., had many dealings with the Indians. But with his son John he was, however, driven from the island by the Indians and killed by them at the second destruction of the town of Falmouth, May, 1690.

We note by the dying words of Jonathan Parker (page 30) that he had served in a war, probably that of King Phillip.

Hananiah Parker of Reading must have been at some time in active defence of his colony, as he was lieutenant of the Reading military company in this period of frequent warfare. His son John Parker had no military title so far as is known. It has been seen, however, how John's son, Hananiah, served in Queen Anne's war with the French in 1712 (see page 40). John Parker's son Josiah was a lieutenant. He was an active and efficient officer and participated in much service. His sons were Josiah, John, Thaddeus and Joseph, one of whom, at least, was in the French and Indian war at the taking of Quebec in 1759. His cousin, Peter Parker of Framingham, was in this war in the year 1757.

In the French and Indian War of 1757 the following men were from Reading: Asa Parker, Phineas Parker, Jonah Parker, all in the troop of horse, Ephraim Parker, Ebenezer Parker, Green Parker, Benjamin Parker.

Those of the family in Lexington who responded to the roll call of Capt. Parker on the morning of the alarm which opened the Revolution were Thaddeus Parker (see page 88), Jonas Parker (see page 49), Ebenezer Parker (see page 117) and necessarily Capt. John Parker. They were all members of the organized and well drilled company "The Lexington Minute Men." They saw very active service that day and for several periods thereafter.

The following show extracts of the rolls of the three companies of militia in the town of Reading, belonging to the regiment commanded by Col. David Greene of Reading, as they stood April 19, 1775: First Parish Company—Ebenezer Parker, Thomas Parker, Jr., Thomas Parker, Sr. Second Parish Company—David Parker, Samuel Parker. Third Parish Company—Lt. Jonas Parker, Asa Parker, Wm. Parker, Daniel Parker, Jr., Benjamin Parker, Caleb Parker, Ædmund Parker, Ephraim Parker, 2nd, Aaron Parker, Isaac Parker, Daniel Parker, Sr., Ephraim Parker. The Reading men were in the hottest of the fight and were among the first, if not the first, to begin the battle on the retreat of the British. It is remarkable that they all escaped uninjured.

In the following records are extracts copied from the official muster-rolls, archives, etc., of the State of Massachusetts, to be found at the State House, Boston.

"The muster roll of Capt. John Bridge's company in Col. Eleazer Brooks' regiment on command at Roxbury, March 4, 1776:" Thomas Parker, Jonas Parker, Sergt. Ebenezer Parker and others. This Thomas Parker was the Lexington Thomas of page 57, and Sergt. Ebenezer was his son. Jonas Parker was Thomas's nephew, son of Jonas Parker who was killed by the British at the Lexington fight the year preceding. (See No. 23, page 51).

We have no records of military service of Amos Parker of Shrewsbury (page 52). But he had a family of seven sons, all of whom served more or less in the Revolutionary war, except the youngest, who was too young for service. The son, Elisha Parker (see page 102), is first found in Capt. Job Cushing's company, in Hon. Artemas Ward's regiment. With him were Sergt. Jonathan Harrington, Isaac Harrington, Simon Parker and many other names.

Dea. Andrew Parker of Barre (see page 62) was lieutenant of the first company of Barre militia at the opening of the Revolution, and probably marched with it upon the Lexington alarm, 1775.

On "A pay roll of Capt. John Maynard's company in Col. Job Cushing's regiment of Mass. Bay who marched on Y^e Alarm to Still-water for 30 days under the command of Lieut.-Col. Wheelock, Sept. 29, 1777:" is found Nahum Parker. With him were Timothy Bragg and others. Israel Allen, Jr., of Shrewsbury, enlisted into the Continental army for a longer service.

Upon the Bennington alarm Asa Parker, Israel Allen, Jr., Israel Allen, 3rd, Jonathan Harrington and others marched in Capt. John Maynard's company from Shrewsbury. John Parker of Shrewsbury, who was like Asa of different family lineage than Nahum Parker, marched with the Shrewsbury company to Cambridge upon the Lexington alarm, and then offered his services for the united colonies for a long period.

We also find "A pay roll of Capt. Asa Rice's company in Col. Job Cushing's regiment of militia from Shrewsbury, where they were ordered to march to Manchester upon an alarm and were discharged at Bennington:" John Parker, Nahum Parker, Caleb Parker, John Bragg, Jonas and Josiah Stone and others.

The archives show that Nahum Parker (see page 106) also served in the Rhode Island campaign from May 4 to July 4, 1777, for which he received a bounty from the State.

"An abstract of pay due to Capt. Nathaniel Wright's company in Col. Luke Drury's regiment of militia from the command of Mass. for service done at West Point in the year 1781:" Lt. Hananiah Parker from Westborough, John Parker of Southborough, Nahum Parker from Shrewsbury, Lt. Jonathan Harrington of Shrewsbury, Benj. Harrington of Westborough, Reuben Ross of Sterling, Enoch Roper of Sterling and others.

Ebenezer Parker, Sergeant (see page 118), appears on "The roll of a detachment of a company of militia of Lexington, commanded by Capt. John Parker, on command at Cambridge from May 6, 1775, to May 10, inclusive, by order of the Committee of Safety." He was also at the battle of Bunker Hill.

On "A pay roll of Capt. George Minot's company in Col. Samuel

Bullard's regiment of Mass. Bay militia in the Northern Army, 1777, Aug. 14 to Nov. 30:" is found Philemon Parker (see page 95). There were also Isaac Pierce, Solomon Pierce, John Hosmer, Wm. Bond and others.

In State archives we find: "Sir, It is the Desire of the Committee of Safety that you march one half of your company to Cambridge forthwith to parade before the church meeting house and to persue such orders as you shall receive from the General from time to time. Thos. Gardner, Col. To Capt. John Parker."

Josiah Parker of Woburn (see page 77) was lieutenant of the Woburn militia. His brother was Capt. John Parker of Lexington (see pages 79 to 87), whose praiseworthy defensive action on the famous 19th of April, 1775, ushered in the war in an honorable manner, and marked the opening of a new epoch in the world's history. Thaddeus Parker of Lexington was another brother (see pages 89 and 90). He was in the earliest struggles for independence and later served eight months in the Jerseys under Gen. Washington. He died of consumption in 1789. The other brother was Joseph Parker of Lincoln (page 91). His sons, both Levi (No. 53, pages 91 and 158) and Joseph, Jr. (No. 55), were Revolutionary veterans, as was also Isaac Parker, son of Capt. John.

Levi Parker served first with Capt. Stearns of Princeton in his large company three months in 1780.

This note from the undersigned is found in the archives: "Capt. Stearns. Sir,—Please pay to Sergt. John Brigham the bearer hereof the wages due to me for service done in your company at North Castle Last Summer. If any allowance for Gun and blanket please to pay him that also—And his Receipt shall be your discharge from your friend & Servant, Levi Parker. Princeton, Mass., Apr. 30, 1781."

And again, "The following is a return of the hire and bounty which has been advanced by the town of Princeton for the purpose of hiring men for the term of three years, which were required by a resolve of the General Court of the 2nd of Dec., 1780. To Levi Parker £30. hard money." Then follows James Thompson, Ephraim Norcross, Sam'l Ball, Benj. Stearns, Thomas, James and John Ramar, amounting to £240. "And to each of the above mentioned soldiers 12 three-year old cattle, estimated at £6. 0. 0. each, which amounts to £576. 0. 0. To Jonas Beaman one hundred hard Dollars and thirteen three-year old Cattle est. at £6. 0. 0. each. £78. 0

30.

108.

"Also the eight soldiers first mentioned are entitled to one horned creature three years old each by agreement of the Committee although it is not mentioned in their receipts which amounts to £48. 0. 0. hard money.

"Also the Above s^d Encouragement was engaged to be sent to Camp to the Soldier at Two Different times which journeys we estimate at £50.

"The whole acc't amounts to £1022. 0. 0.

BENJ. HOLDEN } Selectmen
SARDY MASON } of
BOAZ MOORE } Princeton.''

An accompanying sheet shows "We the subscribers do hereby certify that we have each one for himself Re'cd as an encouragement to enlist into the Continental Army for the term of three years in hard money and in the towns security one hundred dollars and twelve three year old cattle of a middling size. Princeton, May 2, 1781. Levi Parker, James Thompson, Sam'l Ball, Ephraim Norcross and Benj. Stearns.

"Joseph Parker, Jr., of Lincoln [see page 161] enlisted for three years' service July 4, 1781, aged 16, four feet, 10 inches high, light complexion, light hair, light eyes, occupation, farmer, and residence Lincoln."

"Isaac Parker of Lexington [see page 154] enlisted for a term of three years, March 2, 1781, aged 18. He was 5 ft., 7 inches, dark complexion, dark hair, dark eyes, a farmer by occupation and residence Lexington." From official list of men from County Middlesex who enlisted agreeably to a resolve of the Court of Dec. 2, 1780.

Of the names with whom the Parkers of Lexington and their descendants married we find on the alarm list of soldiers from Watertown under Col. Thomas Gardner, these and many others: Abraham, Ephraim and Isaac Pierce, Josiah, James and Jonas Smith, Jr., John, Nathan and Jonas Viles, John, Jonas, Phineas and George Lawrence and Ephraim Hammond.

In Woburn in Capt. Joshua Walker's company under command of Col. David Greene of 2nd regiment were: Corp. Isaac Burton, Isaac Pierce, Abel Winship, Timothy Winn, Jr., and Increase Winn, James Thomson, Jr., and the following who bore the name of Johnson: Ensign Joseph, 3rd, Abijah, Jonathan, Jonathan, Jr., William, William, Jr., Azel and Shuball.

Familiar names other than Parker in Capt. John Bridge's company of Lexington men on command at Roxbury, March 4, 1776, were Ebenezer, Samuel, William, Stephen and John Munroe, Joseph

Mason, Simon and Henry Winship, Joel Viles, Lt. Joseph and Joshua Simonds.

Capt. Timothy Paige of Hardwick commanded the Hardwick company which marched to Bennington to re-enforce the Continental Army under Gen. Gates, 1777.

Among those who marched to Roxbury from Holliston on the alarm, April 19, 1775, were Nathan, Asa, John and Elijah Bullard and Daniel Leland.

We also find, "Holliston, Jan. 20, 1781."

"In Capt. Ezra Eames' company, Col. Abner Perry's regiment, in R. I. service" were: Ezra Eames, Aaron Eames, Timothy Leland, Jesse Forristall, Isaac Bullard, Eli Bullard. Asaph Leland, Joseph Morse, James Morse, Ephraim Bigelow, Joseph Bigelow, Wm. Haven, Henry Bullard, Henry Leland, John Leland. From July 28, 1780, to Aug. 7, 1780.

Eleazer Bullard appears under Capt. Daniel Taylor's men, dated Oct., 1782.

"Framingham. John Parker, Jr., private, enlisted July 28, 1780, discharged Aug. 4, 1780, in Capt. David Brewer's company in Col. Abner Perry's regiment, being the tenth company in said regiment, who marched to the State of Rhode Island."

The Eames family were well represented as is attested by the Framingham alarm roll. There were Capt. Jesse, Sergt. John, Gershom, Jotham and Nathaniel.

Grant Haven and Jotham Eames of Framingham were in the service several months.

Nathan Allen of Barre (page 136) was in the service more than once. On one occasion he was in Capt. Sibley's company in Col. Drury's regiment, in the year 1781. He marched Aug. 13, and arrived in camp Aug. 22. With him in this campaign was Elijah Robinson of Barre and others.

William Dodd of Princeton appears on the rolls of Capt. Manassah Sawyer's company in Col. Dike's regiment, Sept. 1 to Dec. 1, 1776.

"Waltham, March 4, 1776. Muster roll of Capt. Abraham Pierce's military company in Waltham, called out by Col. Samuel Thatcher in his regiment, who marched at the taking possession of Dorchester Hills: Samuel Stearns, Ezra Pierce, Wm. Bridge, Benjamin Pierce, Elijah Lawrence, John Lawrence, David Smith."

Condensed records of service of the non-commissioned Parkers of Massachusetts in the Revolutionary war, as shown by Vol. 54 of the Mass. Archives:

	COMPANY.	REGIMENT.	RESIDENCE.
Samuel Parker,	Phineas Cook,	Thomas Gardner,	Newton.
Henry Parker,	"	"	"
Nathaniel Parker,	"	"	"
Abraham Parker,	"	"	"
Daniel Parker,	Isaac Hall,	"	Stoneham.
Caleb Parker,	Barnabus Dodge,	Sam'l Gerrish,	Wenham.
Thomas Parker,	Enoch Chapin,		W. Springfield.
John Parker,	Abiathar Angel,	Dav. Brewer, May 15,	Gageborough.*
Samuel Parker,	John Davis,	James Frye, May 6, '75,	Methuen.
Free Parker,	Nath'l Gage,	"	Bradford.
Joseph Parker,	Benjamin Ames,	"	Andover.
Colton Parker,	"	"	"
Michael Parker,	Benj. Farnum,	"	"
John Parker,	"	"	"
Sergt. John Parker,	"	"	"
Benjamin Parker,	"	" drummer,	"
Enoch Parker,	"	"	"
Phineas Parker,	"	"	"
James H. Parker,	Wm. Campbell,	Eben'r Learned,	Sutton.
John Parker,	Thos. Drury,	John Nixon,	Spencer.
Abraham Parker,	Joseph Stebbins,	Jona. Brewer,	Whately.
Joseph Parker,	John Black,	"	Sudbury. Corp.
Josiah Parker,	"	"	Barre.
Stephen Parker,	Abel Thayer,	John Fellows,	Weston.
John Parker,	John Wright,	David Brewer,	New Provid'ce.†
Jacob Parker,	Amos Walbridge,	"	Stafford.
Wm. Parker,	Levi Rounseul,	"	Freetown.
James Parker,	Isaac Colton,	"	Springfield.
Daniel Parker,	Peter Ingesol,	"	Sheffield ‡
Isaac Parker,	Joshua Parker,	Wm. Prescott,	Westford.
John Parker,	"	"	"
Lemuel Parker,	Asa Lawrence,	"	Groton.
Eleazer Parker,	"	"	"
Nehemiah Parker,	"	"	"
Lemuel Parker,	"	"	" fifer.
Levi Parker,	"	"	" drummer.
Abijah Parker,	John Nutting,	"	Pepperell. Sergt.
Abel Parker,	Robt. Longley,	Asa Whitcomb,	Shirley.
John Parker,	"	"	"
William Parker,	Edmund Bemis,	"	Westminster.
Asa Parker,	Joel Fletcher,	Eph'm Doolittle,	Templeton.
Francis Parker,	Josiah Stearns,	"	Leominster
Oliver Parker,	Sam'l Kilton,	John Patterson,	Natick.
James Parker,	Joseph Morse,	"	" fifer.
"	"	"	" private.
Ichabod Parker,	Sam'l Sloan,	"	East Hoosack.
Nathaniel Parker,§	"	"	"

* Then in Berkshire.
† Then a town in Berkshire County.
‡ Deserted June 28.
§ On command to Quebec.

	COMPANY.	REGIMENT.	RESIDENCE.
Samuel Parker,	Archaelus Towne,	Eben'r Bridge,	———
Silas Parker,	John Ford,	"	Chelmsford.
John Parker,	"	"	"
Benjamin Parker,	"	"	"
William Parker,	Peter Coburn,	"	Methuen.
Ebenezer Parker,	John Bacheller,	"	Reading.
Jonas Parker,	"	"	"
David Parker,	"	"	"
Corp. Nathan Parker,	"	"	"
Corp. Joseph Parker,	"	"	"
Simeon Parker,	Benj. Walker,	"	Chelmsford.
Daniel Parker,	George Gould,	Paul D. Sargent,	Salem.
Phineas Parker,	John Wood,	"	Woburn.
Abijah Parker,	David Bradish,	Edm'd Phinney,	Falmouth.
John Parker,	Hart Williams,	"	Gorham.
John Parker,	Job Cushing,	Jona. Ward,	Shrewsbury.
Josiah Parker,	Daniel Barnes,	"	Marlboro.
Jacob Parker,	Moses Whiting,	Wm. Heath, Apr. 28, '75,	Roxbury.
Noah Parker,	Edw'd P. Williams,	"	Roxbury.

The Archives show these records of service in the volume of non-commissioned officers and privates of the Continental army.

	REG.	M. D.		RESIDENCE.	COMPANY.
Gideon Parker,	1	44—18		Stockbridge, D. W. S.	Capt. Stoddard.
Abijah Parker,	1	48—0	D. W.*	Boston Mills. Recd $20 bounty.	
John Parker,	2	43—0	D. W.	Easton.	4th Co.
Daniel Parker,	3	36—0	3 yrs.	Malden.	Child.
Joshua Parker,	4		D. W.	Groton. Recd. 50.	
Joseph Parker,	4	25—0	D. W.	England.	Learned.
Jesse Parker,	6	36—0	3 yrs.	Brimfield.	Toogood.
Jesse Parker,	7	47—0	D. W.	Brookfield.	Coburn.
John Parker,	7	5—19	3 yrs.	Chelmsford. killed.	Capt. Ballard.
Joshua Parker,	7		D. W.	Groton. Recd. $50.	
Samuel Parker,†	8	30—16	3 yrs.	Pepperell. Recd. 50.	Capt. Brown.
Edmond Parker,	8	36—0	3 yrs.	Pepperell. Brown.	Varnum.
Oliver Parker,	8	12—16	3 yrs.	Chelmsford.	Varnum.
Jackson Parker,	8	36—0	3 yrs.	Newton.	Wiley.
Daniel Parker,	8	31—0	D. W.	Haverhill.	Wiley.
Benjamin Parker,	9	6—14	D. W.	Andover.	Major's Co.
David Parker,	10	36—0	3 yrs.	Watertown.	
William Parker,	10	36—0	3 yrs.	Winchendon.	3rd Co.
George Parker,	10	48—0	D. W.	Boston. Recd. $20.	4th Co.
William Parker,	11	35—29	3 yrs.	Andover.	Abbot.
John Parker,	11	36—0	3 yrs.	Falmouth.	Clark.
Nathaniel Parker,	13	4—0	3 yrs.	Gorham. dead.	Lt. Inf. Co.
Nathaniel Parker,	13	6—0	D. W.	Watertown.	Woodbridge Co.
William Parker,	14	9—21	3 yrs.	Falmouth. dead.	6th Co.

* Enlisted during the war. † Invalid.

	REG.	M. D.		RESIDENCE.		COMPANY.
David Parker,	15	35—21	3 yrs.	Harvard.		Munro.
John Parker,	15	34—23	3 yrs.	Gorham.	Recd. $50.	Brown.
Eleazer Parker,	15	36—0	3 yrs.	Harvard.		Brown.
Charles Parker,	16	36—0	3 yrs.	Waldoboro.		Lt. Inf. Co.
Elias Parker,*		4—2	D. W.	Boston.		Sargeant.
Josiah Parker,*		36—0	3 yrs.	Natick.	Recd. $50.	Burbeck.
Samuel Parker,*		47—0	D. W.		Recd. $200 bounty.	Burbeck.
Thomas Parker,*		48—0	D. W.	Greenwich.		Buckland Co.

"List of the officers of militia in the State of Massachusetts Bay: The following is a list of the field officers of the several regiments of militia in this colony, as chosen by the House," viz.:

Lt. William Parker, 2nd Regiment of Essex.

Lieutenants John and Jonathan Parker, 4th Regiment of Essex.

Capt. Enos Parker, 7th Regiment of Essex.

Lt. Aaron Parker, 6th Middlesex.

Lt. John Parker, 1st Company, 4th Regiment of Essex.

Capt. Enos Parker, 8th Company, Col. Simonds' Regiment of Essex.

Lt. Nathaniel Parker, 3rd Company, 7th Middlesex, Col. Simeon Spaulding.

Lt. Benjamin Parker, Jr., 9th Company, 2nd Regiment of York. He received a promotion in 1780.

Lt. Thomas Parker, 3rd Company, 1st Regiment of Worcester.

Capt. Jordon Parker of company stationed at Georgetown, of Lincoln Co. (Me.).

Ebenezer Parker, Jr., was 2nd lieutenant in 2nd Company, 4th Regiment of Plymouth.

Daniel Parker was ensign in Col. Michael Jackson's regiment in the expedition to Penobscot, 1780.

Abel Parker was 2nd lieutenant of the Middlesex and Worcester brigade of the guards raised by the State to do duty in and around Boston, under Maj.-Gen. Gates and Maj.-Gen. Heath, and detached from same to re-enforce Continental Army for three months.

Lt. Abijah Parker was likewise detached from Middlesex militia to re-enforce Continental Army for three months.

Lt. Levi Parker received a promotion in the 7th Regiment, commanded by Lt.-Col. Brooks.

Lt. Elias Parker received a promotion while serving in 1st Regiment, commanded by Lt.-Col. J. Vose.

John Parker was 2nd lieutenant in Boston Regiment, 1780.

Under date of June 10, 1789, is recorded the commissioning of Jonas Parker a captain in the 7th Regiment.

---

* Crane's regiment.

Feb. 14, 1776, David Parker was 2nd major in company from Salem and Lynn, 1st Essex.

Capt. Eli Parker was captain of a company in 4th Hampshire, April 1, 1776.

William Parker was 2nd lieutenant in 7th Company, 2nd Essex, April 29, 1776.

Joseph Parker was captain of 2nd Company, 4th Plymouth, May 9, 1776. He commanded a company of 56 men in the Rhode Island services, in Col. John Cushing's regiment.

John Parker was 2nd lieutenant of 15th Company, 4th Regiment of Essex, 1776.

Andrew Parker was 1st lieutenant of 1st Company, 7th Regiment Worcester, June 7, 1776.

Freeman Parker was adjutant in 1st Barnstable Regiment, as archives attest bearing date May 8, 1776.

James Parker was 1st lieutenant of 7th Company, in 4th Suffolk, April 24, 1776.

The officers in Col. Dike's regiment who engaged "to tarry on Dorchester Heights to ye 1st of March, 1777, 2nd Lt. Isaac Parker, Ensign Aaron Parker."

"Officers of the regiment raised in Bristol and Cumberland:" Avery Parker, 2nd Lt., March 13, 1776.

March 15, 1776. Officers of armed vessels. Daniel Parker surgeon of the sloop "Freedom," Sept. 19, 1776.

In the list of officers commissioned in the two regiments raised for the defense of the New England States, commanded by Colonels Jacobs and Wade, are Capt. Joshua Parker, dated March 14, 1778; Ensign Abel Parker, dated March 14, 1778.

Capt. Gideon Parker, in 1776, commanded a company of 55 men in Col. Moses Little's regiment. Of these he had eight who deserted and six who died.

Lt. Levi and Capt. Jonas Parker are recorded on the muster rolls subsequent to 1780. (File No. 1.)

Capt. Joshua Parker's company, in Col. Robinson's regiment, contained John Parker and Isaac Parker.

Capt. Eli Parker was an Amherst man. He encouraged to his best ability interest in the Continental service, and among the archives we find

"AMHERST, May ye 15, A. D. 1778.

"A return of the men procured by Capt Eli Parker to Serve in the Continental Army." They came from six different towns, as the record proves.

"AMHERST, May ye 18, 1778.

"Then Capt. Eli Parker personally appeared & made oath to the truth of the above account of the above named Persons inlisting for the town of Amherst.

"Before MOSES DICKINSON, Justice of ye Peace."

He marched May 8, 1777, for Ticonderoga commanding a company of 61 men, and was in the service two months and nine days.

Capt. Joshua Parker of Westford served nine months and ten days in 1778 in Rhode Island, for which his account for pay is preserved in the State archives, amounting to £168—12 *s.*—0 *d.*

Capt. Enos Parker commanded a Berkshire County company in Col. Benj. Symonds' regiment of militia to re-enforce the Continental Army at Bennington. Their service on that occasion was short. Among the company was Anerca Parker. It seems that again he raised a company and it was out 27 days, and among these names we find Ezra Parker.

Capt. Enos Parker at another time raised a company and marched to the assistance of the Continental Army at Ticonderoga and served one month, and his followers included Giles Parker, Natheel Parker, Phillip Parker, Peter Parker.

Capt. Jordan Parker commanded a company of 55 men in Col. Samuel M. Cobb's regiment. The roll of men is dated Dec. 1, 1781.

Among the archives we find: "Please pay Wm. Clark the Bearer the contents of the pay rolls due to me from the State.

"East Hoosick, Jan. 20, 1779. CAPT. ENOS PARKER."

Benjamin Parker was a Capt. in Col. Wade's regiment.

ADDITIONS.

Page 72. II. The child of David and Abigail (Smith) Tuttle was Abigail Tuttle, who m. Jonathan S. Parker, pp. 271 and 272.

Page 75. IV. John Munroe m. Lydia Macy of Nantucket.

Page 78. After "Cambridge and Lexington Streets" add, at corner of Parker Street where cellar hole remains.

Page 96. Between Susannah Parker and Lucinda Parker insert Lucy Parker, b. probably 1791; m. John Jacobs, and probably removed West.

Under Lucinda Parker substitute Elmer Baker of Princeton for John Jacobs. On the Princeton records we find the entry of the intention of marriage of Lucinda Parker of Sterling and Elmer Baker of Princeton bearing date of Oct. 23, 1813. She d. soon, however, Feb. 12, 1815, aged 21, and left one child, probably Lucinda, perhaps Warren, which one, however, is not plain. Warren Baker lived in Chester, Vt., and while there his half sister Lucinda visited him.

Page 101, *under No.* 29. Sally Baker, dau. of Esq. Joseph Baker, was b. Feb. 22, 1762.

Page 123. IV. Substitute Elmira Amelia Smith for Elinor Smith. She m. Jacob Batchelder.

Sarah Smith m. Daniel French.

Page 165. Sally Bigelow d. March 27, 1864.

Page 140. Achsah A. Lockwood never married. She d. Aug. 29, 1843. Bathsheba B. Lockwood m. Sylvester Ellison and resides in North Springfield, Vt. Their daughter, Achsah A. Ellison, m. Jan. 1, 1866, Orville N. Fullam and had Clinton O. Fullam, b. Feb. 22, 1870.

Azro D. Ellison, son of Sylvester and Bathsheba Ellison, m. Jan. 1, 1879, Ida Eaton. Their son, Leon S. Ellison, b. Feb. 1, 1881.

Page 147. Ann Isabella Lawrence d. Oct. 26, 1890.

Leonard Frederick Lawrence, d. Oct. 1, 1891. By wife Edith G. he had son Leonard Lawrence, b. July 12, 1877.

Ellen Sophia Lawrence m. William H. Sherman.

Henderson Greene Lawrence d. Aug. 15, 1881.

Nancy J. Lawrence d. Feb. 9, 1851.

Page 155. The issue of David and Ruth (Parker) Bent:

1. ASAPH BENT, b. Aug. 25, 1788.

2. RUFUS BENT, b. July 5, 1793; m. Dec. 29, 1818, Ann Starratt, and d. Nov. 19, 1854. His children were:

1. Sarah Ann Bent, b. Jan. 1, 1820; m. Jan. 18, 1852, James More. She d. Aug. 7, 1867.
2. George Starratt Bent, b. Nov. 1, 1822; m. Jan. 18, 1855, Mary Ann Inglis. He d. March 30, 1884. Their children were:
   - i. Annie Elizabeth Bent, b. Feb. 1, 1856.
   - ii. Frank Fenwick Bent, b. Sept. 26, 1858; m. Dec. 30, 1891, Amelia Goodwin.
   - iii. Amanda Starratt Bent, b. Sept. 8, 1861; m. Dec. 31, 1890, Albert Goodwin, and have:
     1. Wilder Clifford Goodwin, b. June 19, 1892.
   - iv. Laura Jean Bent, b. April 20, 1864; m. Dec. 18, 1889, Lemuel Elliott, and have:
     1. Minnie Estella Elliott, b. Feb. 11, 1890.
     2. George Ansley Elliott, b. Jan. 26, 1893.
   - v. Minnie DeWolf Bent, b. April 27, 1867; m. July 12, 1892, Frederick Bent.
   - vi. Clara Belle Bent, b. Feb. 2, 1870.
   - vii. Archie Clifford Bent, b. June 16, 1873.
3. David Parker Bent, b. Sept. 23, 1824; d. May 29, 1879.
4. Zenas Edwin Bent, b. June 28, 1827; d. Dec. 14, 1835.
5. Elizabeth Caroline Bent, b. May 7, 1829; m. Oct. 20, 1858, Simeon Freeman. She d. Nov. 14, 1878. Their children were:
   - i. Bertha Freeman, b. April 12, 1860.
   - ii. George Rufus Freeman, b. Feb. 18, 1862; d. July 20, 1887.
   - iii. Mary Arabella Freeman, b. April 28, 1863.
6. Mary Amelia Bent, b. Oct. 12, 1833, She resides in Belleisle, N. S.
7. Edwin Bent. He is deceased.
8. Caroline Bent; m. Eli Boehner. They reside in Somerset, Kings Co., N. S. Children:
   - i. Bessie Boehner.
   - ii. Eugene Boehner.
9. Elizabeth Bent. She resides in Somerset, N. S.

3. ARATHUSA BENT, b. Oct. 29, 1789; m. Charles Barteaux. She d. Aug. 17, 1867.

4. ISAAC BENT, b. Oct. 13, 1791.

5. RUFUS BENT, b. July, 1793.

6. ABIGAIL BENT, b. May 14, 1795; d. Jan. 19, 1829. She m. Simon Starratt. She page 156.

7. DAVID BENT, b. May 17, 1798.

8. REBECCA BENT, b. Sept. 29, 1800; d. May 15, 1846. She m. Joseph Starratt. See page 156.

9. Ruth Bent, b. March 5, 1803; d. Jan. 1, 1884.
10. Miriam Bent, b. May 14, 1804; d. June 21, 1869.

Page 161. Joseph Parker d. in Weston, June 21, 1816, aged 49. His widow, who survived him many years, spent her last years with her son, Isaac Parker of Waltham.

Page 162. Elisha Parker and Jerusha Wentworth were m. Aug. 18, 1800.

Jerusha Wentworth was b. Oct. 22, 1782. While in Maine they lived in the town of Lincolnville. Mrs. Jerusha Parker d. June 1, 1834, and Elisha Parker m. (2) Susan Ryder. Elisha Parker d. in Stoughton, Mass., Oct. 5, 1846.

In the list of children make the following changes:

Chloe Parker, b. in Weston, March 7, 1801.
Isaac Parker, b. in Weston, April 23, 1803.
Samuel Austin Whitney Parker, b. June 25, 1810.
Hannah Parker, b. Jan. 5, 1813.
Jonathan Capin Parker, } b. April 23, 1820.
David Manley Parker, }

Page 167. John B. Messenger was b. in Sherborn. He and family reside in Natick.

Horatio Morse resides in Lafayette, Ind., and has a family.

John Chamberlain Bixby was b. Nov. 10, 1800; d. in Lowell, Jan. 26, 1883.

Page 168. Mrs. Ruth Eaton Haven Bixby d. in W. Newton, Nov. 26, 1884. Children:

John Haven Bixby, b. March, 1834; d. Dec. 21, 1892, leaving six children, who reside in Canton, N. Y.

Henry Lyman Bixby, b. July 26, 1842. He is superintendent of the Fire Department, West Newton, Mass.

Page 175. *No.* 177. Sarah S. Parker and Alvin W. Davis were m. April 5, 1868.

Page 177. Sophia B. and Dorastus Wright had dau. Amanda Wright.

Page 178. Rhuhamah Parker d. June 19, 1885, and was buried at Stanstead, P. Q.

Dana Robinson Parker d. May 22, 1863. His wife d. May 13, 1877.

Page 179. Lucy Robinson Parker m. Asa S. Hodge, May 8, 1845. He was son of Levi and Tappath (Towne) Hodge. She d. Feb. 4, 1874. All their children d. in infancy.

Amory Parker and Lydia Parker were m. Dec. 8, 1805. Lucy Robinson Parker, their dau., d. in Lowell, Jan. 10, 1870.

Page 189. Mrs. Lydia B. Paige d. in Milford, Del., 1890.

Page 190. Reed Paige lives in Bakersfield, Vt.

Louisa M. Smart lives in Milford, Del.

Marion Green lives in Middletown Springs, Vt.

Gardner W. Paige lives in Amesbury, Mass.

Harris Lee Paige lives in Milford, Del.

Maria Horigan lives in Bakersfield, Vt.

Page 193. *No.* 97. III. Substitute lived for resides.

Page 209. Col. Amos Andrew Parker died in Fitzwilliam, N. H., May 12, 1893, aged 101 years, 7 months, 4 days. He met with an accident a few days previous and he gradually lost his strength, but retained his faculties to the very last, and died peacefully.

Page 211. *No.* 250. Edward Nelson Parker m. Louisa Moore Lackland. He d. April 28, 1881.

Page 214. *Under* 5. III. Children of George W. and Lizzie I. (Hammond) Gould:

Susie Jennie Gould, b. in Cambridgeport, Jan. 14, 1865; m. Charles W. Hanscom of Portsmouth, N. H., and they have children.

Carrie Gibson Gould, b. in Fort Warren, B. H., Jan. 9, 1869.

Annie Maria Gould, b. in Charlestown, March 24, 1872.

Lizzie Louise Gould, b. in Mattapan, May 22, 1875.

Sadie Hamblin Gould, b. in Dedham, Oct. 3, 1879.

George Washington Gould, b. in Chelsea, Sept. 7, 1882.

Willie James Gould, b. in Boston, Sept. 11, 1885.

Page 215. Mary Elizabeth Dodd, b. Dec. 18, 1837; m. Feb. 28, 1866, Pierre LeB. Coombs. Children:

Theodore Sedgwick Coombs, b. March 13, 1867.

Caroline Elliot Coombs, b. Jan. 24, 1869; m. April 9, 1890, John Russell of Plymouth, Mass.

Henry Ware Dodd, b. Oct. 18, 1849; m. April 9, 1881, Mary Dillingham of Bangor, Me. He is a banker in Boston. Children:

Ethel Dodd, b. Feb. 20, 1882.

Mary Dodd, b. March 14, 1884.

Page 228. Nathan Parker d. in Woburn.

Page 230. Mrs. John Thomas Parker d. Feb. 3, 1892. John Thomas Parker d. June 12, 1892.

Harriet Emeline Parker m. Lorenzo Dow Miles.

Doratha Caroline Parker m. Henry Wiggers.

Page 234. *No.* 122. II. Sarah Ellen Wyer m. Orlando Brooks of Woburn.

Page 237. Marietta Neville d. in Woburn, Jan. 18, 1892.

Josephine Smith Hinckley m. John R. Carter of Woburn.

Page 280. Mrs. Isaac Parker of Waltham d. in Waltham, Feb. 20, 1893, aged 85 years, 11 months.

Page 283. *No.* 317. James Parker to James H. Parker.

Mary B. Parker to Mary Benjamin Parker.

Page 295. Dea. John Parker d. in Malden, March 27, 1893, aged 94 years, 9 months, 11 days.

Page 307. William Parker Thompson m. Mary Ellen Dumphy, b. in Cavendish, Vt., Aug. 30, 1858. Their children are:

George Horace Thompson, b. April 28, 1880.

Maud Leone Thompson, b. Aug. 25, 1882.

Alva T. Pierce was b. in Londonderry, Vt., Feb. 15, 1859.

Mrs. Sarah S. (Parker) Davis resides in Galva, Ida Co., Iowa, and has two sons.

Page 308. Grace Olive Smith was b. in Chester, Vt., Oct. 13, 1860; m. E. D. Hulett. They reside in Keene, N. H., and have children: Frank Walter Hulett. Clara Belle Hulett.

Forrest Calvin Bates was b. May 11, 1857; m. Luella Whitcomb, and reside in Langdon, N. H. Children: Fanny Pearl Bates. Leon James Bates. Lina Bates.

Cora Fanny Bates, b. Oct. 13, 1859; m. G. B. Perrin. They reside in Springfield, Vt., and have children: Lewis Leroy Perrin. Hazel Perrin.

Page 318. Change Josephine Williams to Ellen Josephine Williams, b. in Boston, Oct. 15, 1856, dau. of James A. and Sarah M. (Searles) Williams.

Page 319. James Leonard Hunting, b. in Baldwinsville, July 7, 1883.

George Milton Hunting, b. in Baldwinsville, April 20, 1887.

Herbert Eugene Hunting, b. in Baldwinsville, Jan. 25, 1891.

v. Eli Adelbert Hunting m. July 9, 1887, Minnie Merritt, b. in Templeton, Jan. 6, 1868.

Page 320. Mrs. Sarah D. (Parker) Hale d. in Hubbardston, May 3, 1891.

Page 325. Amos Andrew Parker d. in Reading, Vt., Feb. 6, 1892, aged 77 years, 3 months, 9 days.

Page 327. Henry Clinton Fay m. Dec. 14, 1858, in Richmond, Me., Caroline Elizabeth Tallman, b. in Woolwich, Me., July 2, 1832, dau. of Benjamin Franklin Tallman, b. in Bath, Me., April 30, 1800, and Alice McKown, b. in Woolwich, Me., Sept. 30, 1800. Mr.

Fay fitted himself for the ministry from 1847 to 1857, at Leicester Academy, Amherst College and Bangor Theological Seminary. He has preached since 1858, and is now pastor of the North Reading Presbyterian Church. Children:

Franklin Fay, b. in Northwood, N. H., Jan. 15, 1860; d. in Richmond, Me., Nov. 29, 1873.

Alice Parker Fay, b. in Northwood, Aug. 9, 1861.

Hattie Therese Fay, b. in Northwood, March 4, 1864.

Henry Clinton Fay, b. in Norton, Mass., June 27, 1866.

Lucy Maria Fay, b. in Norton, Feb. 12, 1868; d. in Hubbardston, April 17, 1870.

Page 348. The middle names and dates of birth of the children of Silas and Cho Augusta (Parker) Hall, all b. in Pendleton, N. Y., were:

Herman Deforest Hall, b. Dec. 18, 1836.

Addison Parker Hall, b. Oct. 8, 1839.

Caroline Augusta Hall, b. Dec. 2, 1841.

Cornelia Amanda Hall, b. Nov. 26, 1845.

Charles William Hall, b. Dec. 25, 1848.

Henry Clinton Hall, b. May 18, 1852.

Alice Mary Hall, b. July 6, 1854.

Infant daughter, b. Feb. 21, 1857.

Cornelia Frances Marvin was b. in Hall's Station, N. Y., Nov. 16, 1864; m. Dec. 31, 1885, Albert J. McDonald, son of Leslie and Mary (Wilson) McDonald. Their children were:

Cho Augusta McDonald, b. in Lockport, N. Y., Feb. 2, 1888.

Erdman Glover McDonald, b. in Lockport, Aug. 15, 1891.

Edward Payson Marvin, Jr., was b. in Lockport, N. Y., Jan. 14, 1868; m. Dec. 10, 1891, and resides in Tonawanda, N. Y.

Silas Hall Marvin, b. in Lockport, N. Y., July 4, 1869.

Walter Clark Marvin was b. in Lockport, N. Y., Feb. 25, 1871; m. Jan. 18, 1893, Marian F. Ross, and resides in Tonawanda, N. Y.

William Roy Marvin was b. in Lockport, N. Y., Feb. 25, 1879.

Page 393. *No.* 302. 2. Floyd W. Brooks was b. in Sherburne, N. Y., May 4, 1841, son of Thomas and Melissa R. Brooks. Their children were:

May M. Brooks, b. in Sherburne, Sept. 14, 1869.

Chancellar D. Brooks, b. in Sherburne, Sept. 18, 1871.

Florence A. Brooks, b. in Smyrna, N. Y., Sept. 29, 1873.

Edith F. Brooks, b. in Smyrna, N. Y., April 12, 1880.

Page 397. *No.* 308. Mrs. Georgianna (Parker) Converse d. in Woburn, Dec. 24, 1892.

Page 398. Albert Parker d. in Potsdam, N. Y., Dec. 14, 1890.

ERRATA.

Page 47, under No. 15, Marrett Munroe instead of Monroe.

Pages 68 to 77, also 117, all Monroes to Munroe.

Page 70, v., read Abigail (Ingolsby) Smith in place of Lucy (Stone) Smith.

Page 72, II., after David Tuttle read, they both lived and died in Lexington.

Page 73, 7th line from bottom, substitute L. A. Saville for John Hudson.

Page 75, VI., 2, I, read Julia Elizabeth Johnson.

Page 96, under Lucinda Parker, substitute Elmer Baker of Princeton for John Jacobs.

Page 101, under Silas Parker, change d. 1836 to Jan. 19, 1835.

Page 102, change date of decease of Mrs. Sally (Baker) Parker, Jan. 7, 1838, to Jan. 17, 1838.

Page 122, strike out "or 12 as Princeton Records have it" in third and fourth line from bottom.

Page 123, for III., 4, substitute Leander Smith for Thomas Smith.

Page 123, for IV., change Elinor Smith to Elmira Amelia Smith.

Page 123, 4, change May 27 to May 23.

Page 124, 7, change Aug. 3 to Aug. 4.

Page 125, 9, change Dec. 29, 1791, to Dec. 29, 1802.

Page 140, VII., after "1823" strike out to VIII., and add same to VIII.

Page 155, strike out 1, David Bent. Add to 3, David Bent, m. Suzan Stronach, and resides in Forest Glen, Annapolis Co., N. S.

Page 162, in 3rd line from top, change Dinsmore to Dunsmore. Fourth line from top change Cythia to Cynthia.

Page 167, change 7 to 3, 8 to 6, 9 to 7.

Page 168, change Millitiah Eames to Meletiah Eames.

Page 174, under No. 175, substitute of Chester for in Chester.

Page 175, under No. 71, Ellen (Johnson) Parker d. Feb. 14, instead of Feb. 11, 1865.

Page 177, under Sophia B. Parker, strike out "They left no issue." Read They left dau. Amanda.

Page 179, No. 202, strike out Lysander Batchelder and add Henry Burr Howells.

Page 185, No. 227, 2d word in 2d line from bottom change Margaret to Margary.

Page 190, III., change Etta P. Rice to Editha P. Rice.

Page 193, VI., change Allison D. to Allison H. Foster.

Page 215, bottom line, read Henry for Harry.

Page 230, under Dorothy C. Parker, read Wiggers for Wegors.

Page 231, 1, change Elizabeth Johnson to Julia Elizabeth Johnson.

Page 239, 13th line from bottom, change "page 229" to page 231.

Page 274, 2d line from bottom, change Squares to Squire.

Page 290, 8, 1, change Vermont to North Monroe, N. H. V. Change Lisbon, N. H., to Landoff, N. H. VIII. Charles Strain to Charles H. Strain. XI. Harry Strain to Harry J. Strain. XII. Eva C. Strain to Eva M. Strain.

Page 307, No 176, 2, 3d line, change daughters to children.

Page 316, strike out 2. After Vt., 8th line from top, read Their son was:

Page 330, strike out Joshua Parker.

Page 393, for Chauncy D. Brooks read Chancellar D. Brooks.

INDEX OF PARKER NAMES.

N

O

P

Q

R

S

NAMES OTHER THAN PARKER.

C

N

O

P

Q

R

T

Y

Family Record.

Marriages.

Births.

Deaths.